FORTEAN TIMES 42-46

IF PIGS COULD FLY

The true portraiture of a Roman youth.whoſe ſtrang birth & life
cannot ſufficiently be admired hee was borne houlding 3 little
ſtones in one hand.and in the other 2.& being hold to his Mothers
breſt he refuſed it with other ſuſtenance.whereby his Father being
Phiſitian conjectured.that nature had given him theſe Stones for
foode.& by trial finding it ſo.fed him always with ſtones & read-
wine.which in 6 days ſpace comes from him converted into ſand.
thus hee hath lived the ſpace of 17 years.

Pubd. by Caulfield and Co Novr. 2d 1794.

Francis Battalia, the Stone Eater,
engraved by Wenzel Hollar in 1641. See FT45:38

FORTEAN TIMES 42–46

IF PIGS COULD FLY

JOHN BROWN PUBLISHING
LONDON 1994

This edition was prepared by Fortean Times (PO Box 2409, London NW5 4NP)
and was published in September 1994 by John Brown Publishing Ltd.

Fortean Times is now published every two months
by John Brown Publishing Ltd.
It is also available on subscription - inquiries to:
Fortean Times, 20 Paul Street, Frome, Somerset BA11 1DX, UK.
☎ 0373 451777.

British Library Cataloguing-in-Publication data available.

Fortean Times 42-46: If Pigs Could Fly.

ISBN 1 - 870870 - 476

Printed in Great Britain by

Redwood Books, Trowbridge, Wilts.

PREFACE

The five issues of *Fortean Times* in this book are reproduced facsimile, except for new running heads. Our thanks again go to Steve Moore for compiling the contents lists. As before, these have been made as detailed as possible as compensation for the lack of a full index. However, readers will be pleased to know that a Grand Index of all issues is under way, beginning with last year's issues, in our annual *Fortean Studies*.

FT42 saw the introduction of our worldwide weird news round-up called 'Strange Days' (inspired by the John Lennon song). The previous system of collating data under themes meant that the publication of many stories was unduly delayed while enough material gathered to flesh out what became small features under one of Hunt Emerson's surreal cartoon headings. With 'Strange Days' we could give a better indication of the range of Forteana constantly happening all around us.

I took the editorial chair for issues 43 to 45 to give Bob Rickard a much needed break. He and his wife Sam were exhausted from the constant nursing of their two boys who had suffered from severe eczema from birth. During this sabbatical, on 10 March 1985, one of them, Frederick, died from complications that followed an infection of his eczema. He was just two-and-a-half years old.

After issue 46 we divided the time and effort to create our little 'sporadical'. American press coverage began to take off after a feature by Barry Newman on the front page of the *Wall Street Journal* (30 September 1985), abstracted in *Reader's Digest* the following March. Newman visited Bob's home: "The study has one chair and no room for another. Books jam the shelves, floor to ceiling [..] folders spill from file cabinets and litter the floor with the accumulated evidence of anomalous events: mysterious oozings, freak plagues, invisible barriers, odd clouds, unusual darknesses, phantom smells." Matters have got a lot worse in the ensuing nine years, as we strive to file the data that pours in torrentially every day.

Contributors to this volume include Wilford R. Anderson, David Barritt, Janet Bord, Peter Christie, William R. Corliss, Hilary Evans, David M. Frost, Richard Gwynn, Ulrich Magin, Kevin McClure, Michel Meurger, John Michell, Roger Musson, John Prytz, Jenny Randles, Leslie Shepard, Doc Shiels, Dennis Stacy, Nigel Watson, Ron Westrum, Dwight Whalen and Mr X.

Our title comes from a story about an enigmatic porcine deposit found repeatedly on the first floor balcony of a house in Huntingdon Beach, California, in 1982 - see ***FT45:36***.

Paul Sieveking
August 1994

PREFACE

FORTEAN TIMES 42-46 (1984-1986)

CONTENTS

FORTEAN TIMES 42 - Autumn 1984

FORTEAN TIMES 43 - Spring 1985

FORTEAN TIMES 44 - Summer 1985

FORTEAN TIMES 45 - Winter 1985

FORTEAN TIMES 46 - Spring 1986

FORTEAN TIMES DISPATCH DATES

FT42: ? October 1984 ◆ FT43: 18 March 1985 ◆ FT44: 15 August 1985

FT45: 23 December 1985 ◆ FT46: 19 May 1986.

Fortean Times

ISSUE NO.42 — The Journal of Strange Phenomena. — PRICE £1.50 $3.00

(Please note our new address. Valid til February, 1985)

Fortean Book Club & Mail Order
Old Barn. Hescott Farm.
Hartland. Nr. Bideford.
North Devon. England. UK.

(Below are a selection of our specials. F.T. subscribers please deduct **10%**)

'The Evidence for UFOs' by H. Evans..........................**£UK3.50/$US7.00**
'The Evidence for Visions of the Virgin Mary' by K. McClure....**£UK3.50/$US7.00**
'The Evidence for Alien Abductions' by J. Rimmer..............**£UK3.50/$US7.00**
'The Evidence for Bigfoot (et al) by J. & C. Bord.............**£UK3.50/$US7.00**
(The above titles are the first in **'The Evidence'** series, edited by Hilary Evans and published by Aquarian Press, UK. As we think they are all worth having; take the four and we'll discount it further.) The four.**£UK12.00/$24.00**
'Phenomena' by J. Michell & R. Rickard (Thames & Hudson UK.)...**£UK4.00/$US8.00**
'Morgawr' Monster of Falmouth Bay by A. Mawnan-Peller..........**£UK1.10/$US2.20**
'Complete Works of Charles Fort' (Dover NY. USA) Europe only..........**£UK18.00**
'House of Lords UFO Debate' notes by J. Michell...............**£UK3.50/$US7.00**
'Ancient Science of Geomancy' by N. Pennick (Thames & Hudson).**£UK5.50/$US11.00**
'Visions:Apparitions:Alien Visitors' by H. Evans (Thorsons)..**£UK11.50/$US23.00**
(All the above prices include P&P. Please allow up to 6 weeks delivery for orders outside Europe. If you haven't yet got a catalogue send a S.A.E. to us at the above address. New catalogue is in preparation.)

FORTEAN BOOK CLUB

We would like to know which **Fortean Times** readers want to join the book club. The Fortean Book Club is not like a normal book club where they send you cheaper editions of mass produced works. Books from the Fortean Book Club are straightforward publishers editions, carefully selected by us for the contents and presentation, offered at less then publishers prices. We ask only that you take 3 books from the 100 or so you will be offered throughout the year. To become a member, simply send your name and address and select one of the titles below for your first selection;

'Phenomena' by Robert Rickard & John Michell..................**£UK3.50/$US7.00**
'Any one of The Evidence series................................**£UK3.00/$US6.00**
'Searching for Hidden Animals' by Dr. Roy Mackel.............**£UK9.00/$US18.00**
'Hypnosis for the Seriously Curious' by Dr. K. Bowers.........**£UK10.00/$USask**
'Shaman: The wounded healer' by J. Halifax....................**£UK5.25/$US9.80**
'Photographs of the Unknown' by R. Rickard & R. Kelly........**£UK6.25/$US12.50**

All the above Book Club selections include post & package so there are no hidden extra costs. Two or more books entitles you to a **10%** discount on the listed price. Please send your remittance along with your selection as we keep prices down by not having accounts. If for any reason you are not happy just return the book within 10 days of receipt for full, no problem, discount.

Fortean Times

Cover art:
See p62.

The Journal of Strange Phenomena.

Autumn 1984
ISSN 0308.5899

FEATURES

FORUM

FROM OUR FILES

STRANGE DAYS, INDEED

COMIX

USUAL STUFF

Fortean Times

96 Mansfield Road,
London NW3 2HX, UK

GANG OF FORT
Editor Robert J M Rickard
Mike Dash
Steve Moore
Paul R A de G Sieveking
Art Dir. Richard Adams
Comix Ed. Hunt Emerson

SPECIAL CORRESPONDENTS
Australia Greg Axford (Vic.)
Paul Cropper (N.S.W.)
Rex Gilroy (N.S.W.)
Tony Healy (A.C.T.)
Richard King (Vic.)
Belgium Henri Premont
Canda Dwight Whalen (Ont.)
Mister X (Ont.)
England Richard Cotton
Peter Chrsitie
Peter Hope Evans
Alan Gardiner
Chris Hall
Valerie Martin
John Michell
Higel Pennick
Paul Screeton
Bob Skinner
Anthony Smith
David Sutton
Paul R Thomas
Finland Tuuri Heporauta
France Jean-Louis Brodu
Dr Bernard Heuvelmans
Phil Ledger
Greece Anastasios D Panos
Ireland Doc Shiels
Robert Anton Wilson
Japan Jun-Ichi Takanashi
Malaysia Ahmed Jamaludin
Roving Ion A Will
Scotland Roland Watson
Jake Williams
South Africa Chris J Holtzhausen
Sweden Ake Franzen
Anders Liljegren
Sven Rosen
USA George Andrews (MO.)
Larry E Arnold (PA.)
Tom Adams (TX.)
Loren Coleman (MA.)
Richard T Corwe (IL.)
Ron Dobbins (AZ.)
David R. Fideler (PA.)
Mark A Hall (MN.)
Steve Hicks (KS.)
Michael Hoffman (NY.)
Kurt Lothmann (TX.)
Gary S Mangiacopra (CN.)
Joseph Swatck (NB.)
Paul Willis (MD.)
Joseph W Zarzynski (NY.)
USSR Vladimir V Rubtsov
Wales Janet & Colin Bord
Yugoslavia Milos Krmelj

Typesetting Susan Morgan
Mayhew Typesetting
91 Chesterfield Rd
Bristol BS6 5DS
Photosetting Words Illustrated
1 Thorpe Close
London W10
Print Agent Dick Gwynn

THIS ISSUE

After the longest delay yet, here we are back with a bit of a facelift. I offer my regular, but nonetheless sincere apologies and hope you'll agree the wait was worth it. Those who wish an explanation of the circumstances should read the enclosed editorial letter.

For some time now I've been aware that our treatment of Fortean news has been less than satisfactory. By the time we come out many items are 'cold' and our old subject heading format was not suitable for what, in news terms, would be many categories of one item. So we are changing to a more experimental, and I hope flexible, format. Starting this issue the bulk of our Fortean reports will be treated in a tabloid-type layout, called STRANGE DAYS. "Nobody told me there'd be days like this. Strange days, indeed!" sang John Lennon. Where longer treatments are needed, or back-up data from our archive, we will use our much-loved heading illustrations, by Hunt Emerson, in a supplementary section called FROM OUR FILES.

We will continue to carry articles, of course, though our columns will be under review. Of two new planned features, one begins this issue (SCIENCE FRONTIERS, science news items with Fortean implications selected from William Corliss' newsletter of the same title), and the other (DIARY OF A MAD PLANET, a chronology of recent world-wide weather and seismic disasters compiled for us by Albert Thomas) has to be postponed until next issue.

PRICE RISE

From this issue we have to raise our UK price to **£1.50**. Because the pound has shrivelled compared to the dollar, our US prices will remain unchanged. We've held off this regrettable move as long as we could, but it has become necessary due to the continuing increases in the costs of materials, services, labour charges and postage.

NEW EDITOR FOR FT

For the new year FT will be edited by my able colleague Paul Sieveking. The circumstances of my holiday from the editorial desk are explained fully in the accompanying letter to subscribers. I will still be contributing to each issue, and look forward to resuming my duties when I have revitalized.

A FORTEAN INSTITUTE

Our plans (incomplete though

Cont on p **61**

BIRTH IMAGERY IN UFO ABDUCTIONS

I have long enjoyed my sporadic contacts with FT, and am appreciative of your journal's objective presentation of my ideas in Hilary Evans' essay in FT41 (Winter 1983). However, I have several objections to the Bords' article in the same issue. With regard to their references to my work, I would like to respond at length to their rather muddled representation of my ideas, their old and groundless objections to the imaginary abduction study's methodology, and their implication (following Budd Hopkins) that our conclusions were motivated by a need for a "safe" CE-III theory in the face of unearthly horrors. I would like to, I say, but I do not have the time.

Instead I want to point out that the Bords ignore completely the fact that the birth trauma hypothesis (BTH) was proposed as a scientifically testable – ie. falsifiable – idea – a rarity in UFO research and especially so among abduction investigations. None of their comments are relevant because the only appropriate response to the BTH is to conduct a test of it.

As I have indicated elsewhere, the test could involve three approaches: First, since human birth imagery is unrelated to presumed alien visitors, its presence in CE-III narratives is a criterion which distinguishes BT fantasies from "real" abductions. Thus the BTH can be "falsified" by the discovery of any abduction report which *lacks* birth imagery. (I emphasize that of the hundred or so published cases, not one lacks perinatal imagery; indeed, most are dominated by it.) Second, an abductee's narrative can be scrutinized for echoes of his/her own birth history. We have found that subjects who were born breech, with forceps, etc., tend to reflect such events in their abduction reports. For example, one frank breech imaginary abductee emerged from her UFO by first sitting on a trap-door and then falling through. A test of this part of the BTH would result earlier in replication or a failure to find such parallels. Third, if any abductees who report late-stage birth sensations such as extreme head pressure with sudden relief are cesarean-born, and so lacking in such natal experiences, the BTH would be proved false. If there are *no* such cesarean abductees, it would be confirmed.

I find it ironic that the Bords admonish other ufologists for a dearth of scientific rigor when they fail even to acknowledge the testable nature of the BTH, let alone withhold judgement pending a clinical test of the hypothesis. Or do they feel that a test is unnecessary – ie. "it cannot be, therefore it is not" . . . ? With regard to the Bords' charge that the BTH has been accepted "uncritically," no one who was present at the 1981 Chicago CUFOS conference when the BTH paper was first presented, or who has followed the impassioned post-conference rhetoric in various publications would hold such a preposterous view. In the past three years there have been less than five favorable published critiques of the BTH, worldwide. Regrettably, there have been no attempts at replication (ditto the 1977 imaginary abductee study), and therefore no serious assessments of it.

I wish to go on record here as I have before with a disclaimer: I am not wedded to the BTH; if it is disproved tomorrow, I will return to square #1 – though perhaps with a sorrowful wince or two. But if ufology's critics continue their vague and irrelevant grumblings about the BTH and no one else tests it, it is hard to see how abduction research can ever get beyond square #2.

Alvin H. Lawson
5861 Huntley Ave.,
Garden Grove, CA 92645,
USA.

FACES: REAL OR ILLUSION?

I've read Jerome Clark's 'Confessions of a Fortean' now several times – in the *Zetetic Scholar* and in FT41. He seems to be punishing himself for having been conned into believing the Cottlingly Fairy photos, and

Cont on p75

RARE ANIMALS SEEN

A good beginning to 1984 came with the news that a thylacine, the rare marsupial wolf-like carnivore known popularly as the Tasmanian tiger, had been sighted by a Wildlife ranger on the island. The sighting was actually made 15–18 months previously (reports vary) and kept secret to protect the creature which has not been reliably sighted in years, and which has officially been feared extinct since the last one died in captivity in 1935 and a survey in the early 1940s failed to find any physical evidence of surviving groups in the wild. *Standard* 19 Jan; R/*The Scotsman*, R/*Guardian*, R/*D. Telegraph*, AP*Times* 20 Jan 1984. Mike Goss has sent us a long article on thylacine sightings on mainland Australia, and we shall print this at the earliest opportunity.

That same week came news of another rare Australian by the name of *Rheobatrachus silus*, a curious frog once common in the hilly rainforest northwest of Brisbane and which vanished *en masse* in 1979 (some reports say 1981). The curator of the Queensland museum, Glen Ingram, said: "Scientists are enthralled by the unique biology of this frog." It incubates its eggs in the female's stomach; the eggs and tadpoles clearly producing a subsance which inhibits the actions of hydrochloric acid and digestive enzymes. The mother frog can carry up to 25 young and can spit them out up to two feet when they are ready to face the world. But Mr Ingram is being generous: he was one of the authors of the paper which first described this curiosity 10 years ago, shortly after its discovery in 1972, and which was widely thought to be a hoax. Now specimens of a related, but larger, species of gastric brooding frog have been discovered 1200 km north of the last known habitat. *New Scientist* 26 Jan; UPI/Plattsburgh (NY) *Press Republican* 30 Jan; *Guardian* 4 Feb 1984.

Nearer home: a foot-long, coal-black fish, netted off Polperro, Cornwall, in July 1983, has been identified as an "extremely rare" Cornish Blackfish. Cornwall's chief fishery officer said: "Only one such fish has previously been taken in British waters, again off Polperro, in 1859." *West Briton* 29 Sept 1983.

TOMB IT MAY CONCERN

In an interview, published in Egypt on 17th March, Egyptian archaeologist, Ahmed Osman, claimed that a mummy at the Cairo Museum was actually that of Joseph, the son of Jacob whom, as the Bible has it, brought the Israelites out of Egypt. Osman says Joseph described himself as a "father to Pharaoh" and in all of Egyptian history this description is unique and applies to U-ya, a minister at the court of Amenophis III. In Osman's eyes Joseph *is* U-ya, whose mummy was recently found at Luxor.

The claim was immediately dismissed as "nonsense" by fellow archaeologist, Ali Hassan, who says the title "father to Pharaoh" had been conferred on other ancient Egyptian officials. And Bishop Gregorios, of the Coptic Orthodox Church, said the Bible clearly states that Joseph was buried *outside* Egypt. There are the makings of a fine academic feud here . . . Albany (NY) *Times Union* 18 March 1984.

THE EARTH MOVES

The 3.3 Richter tremor that rocked central and southern Wales, just after 10pm on the 15th April surprised many folks who thought tremors, of any sort, happened only in foreign countries. But Britain has a respectable history of tremors, from the earliest records to the last one of this magnitude, in roughly the same area, in 1974 [see FT (*The News*) 5 July 1974].

Throughout late March and April the whole earth trembled – Italy, Austria, Japan, Russia had major quakes, Mount St Helens fumed, tidal waves sloshed Japanese beaches, avalanches slid in Swiss Alps. Among other things in this period, a cricketball-sized meteorite fell into a Wolverhampton park (*D. Telegraph* 26 April 1983), and sand showered southern England and Wales [see DUSTING DOWN on p8.]. This is the sort of correlation that we hope will show up in our new feature, DIARY OF A MAD PLANET.

Since the 15th April there have been a series of sizeable tremors affecting west and central England:

★ 30 May – at 3.59pm; 2.7 Richter; felt in adjacent parts of Leicestershire, Nottinghamshire and Lincolnshire.
★ 19 July – at 7.57am; 5.5 Richter; felt throughout Wales and west of England, the east coast of Ireland, and as far north as Glasgow.
★ 27 July – just before 2pm; 4 Richter; North Wales.
★ 29 July (some papers say 30th!) – 10.26pm; North Wales and Irish coast.
★ 4 Aug – early morning; 3.2 Richter; North Wales.
★ 6 Aug – 6.20am; 3.6 Richter; North Wales.

Three of our colleagues (Paul Devereux and the Bords) made interesting observations of aerial lights during the tremor of 15th April; and Jenny Randles told us her experience, and that of her co-author Peter Warrington, during the tremor of 19 July. We hope to distil these into a feature for *next* issue.

LUCK RUNS OUT FOR HUMAN LIGHTNING ROD

Remember Roy Cleveland Sullivan? – the retired forest ranger of Waynesboro, Virginia, who is listed in the *Guinness Book of Records* because he survived being struck by lightning *seven* times. At 3am, on 28 Sept 1983, aged 71, he succeeded by his own hand where Jupiter's bolts had failed. He shot himself, and was finally earthed.

During his 36 years as a ranger in Shenandoah National Park he became a celebrity for, but never understood, his singular affinity for the electrical fluid. In 1942, he lost a big toenail to lightning. In 1969, his eyebrows were blown off. His left shoulder was seared in 1970; and his hair set on fire in 1972, after which he always carried a few gallons of water in a can in his car. On 7 Aug 1973 he was out driving when "a bolt came out of a small, low-lying cloud, hit him on the head through his hat, set his hair on fire again, knocked him 10 feet out of his car, went through both legs and knocked his left shoe off." He once made the remarkable statement that he could see the lightning travelling towards him. PA/*Standard* 30 Sept; *D. Express* 1 Oct; AP/Houston (TX) *Chronicle* 4 Oct 1983.

Ranger Sullivan pictured shortly after being struck by lightning for the fifth time. He had two more 'hits' to come. [© *Guinness Book of Records*.]

THEY COME!

A Ministry of Argiculture official warned of a new breed of 'super rat' which is spreading across Hampshire at about three miles a year. It is immune to conventional poisons, like Warfarin, and breeds fast: one pair can produce 200 young a year. The first mutant rat was noted in the north of the county in 1970. *Sun, Scotsman* 7 Feb 1984.

On 5th March a frighteningly huge swarm of bees invaded the Mission District of San Francisco. The dark cloud of 10,000 (estimated) bees hovered for several hours during the afternoon before heading for a building where they had a giant nest. UPI/ Plattsburgh (NY) 7 March 1984.

Dorset coastal waters have been invaded by octopuses, some of them a reasonable size, whatever we mean by reasonable. One fisherman caught eight in one go, while another battled his for 20 minutes. *D. Telegraph* 12 March 1984.

A GOOD TRIP

Dick Roberts, 37, blind since he was attacked by thugs in 1981, has good reason to be grateful to his Pekinese dog called Freeway. He was in his kitchen trying to make a cup of tea when he turned around and tripped over the dog. His head crashed into a cupboard door and the next thing he knew was his wife wiping his forehead, after she had come back from shopping to find him lying on the floor. He didn't say anything at first, but noticed that the vision was clearing in his right eye. "I kept it to myself for two hours, then I told Mary. It's wonderful . . . I've never been so happy to see my mother-in-law. The doctor says I'll need glasses, but I can see." *D. Telegraph* 18 April 1984.

MORE BLEEDING STATUES

□ Thousands of Christians flocked to Rmaich – a Christian village in southern Lebanon and just over the border with Israel – to see a small statue of the Virgin Mary said to be seeping blood. The flow was first noticed by the village *mukhtar*, or headman, in whose house the statue stood, on 18th November 1983, and it was moved to the church so more could see it. Melchite Archbishop Maximos Salloum said that he had been to the church and saw the figure, which has changed colour from red to gray, ooze that appeared to be blood and olive oil. "It is hard to say this is a miracle, but it is extraordinary," he said, "and could reflect the deep pain of the Virgin over the bloodshed of Her beloved sons in Lebanon." UPI/Plattsburgh (NY) *Press Republican* 28 Dec 1983.

□ A similar sensation centers on a 10ft high statue of the Virgin, built in 1979, near the Baguio City Airport, Philippines, and the legend runs thus: sometime in early February 1983 a group of 20 worshippers were drawn "by an unknown urge" to a small unfinished hillside chapel, where, in the light of early morning they saw a bright red stream pour from the image of an exposed heart on the statue's breast (*see photo*). The flow was so copious that it splashed and soaked a white sheet placed under the image. Two women, Lourdes Paredes and Myrna Apsum, claimed visions in which they were given a mandate to heal. Lo! the crippled and the infirm swarmed there and many cures have been reported; muteness, lameness, high blood pressure, intestinal ailments, etc. – in fact, the usual pantheon of complaints which could also have psychosomatic origin. But cures of heart disease and even cancer are claimed, one of the latter successes being the sculptor of the statue himself. One of the cured, Joy Ruff, also became a medium. Early corroboration of the alleged miracle was given by Supreme Court Justice, Juvenal K. Guerrero, whose own wife was claiming messages from the BVM. The judge went to see for himself, and wrote to a newspaper that the red liquid flowed down [the statue's] blue-spotted dress, splattering the flowers and plants offered at her feet." AP/*Guardian* 14 Feb 1983; *Globe* 24 Jan 1984.

For more BVMs, see VISIONS on p26.

Blood flowing down the statue near Baguio City Airport. [Photo: *Globe* 24 Jan 1984.]

SIMULTANEOUS DEATHS OF TWINS

The so-called 'Cot Death Syndrome' is still one of today's persistent medical mysteries, and the spectre of it must loom in the minds of all parents of new-born children. The only good to come out of such tragedies are the sparse clues to the condition leading to its eventual detection and treatment, but that is little comfort to Arthur and Linda Connolly, whose twins Samantha and Gabrielle died of CDS in the early morning of 8 Oct 1983.

The identical twins were just four-months old, and had been put to sleep in different rooms of their parents' guesthouse in Rhyl, North Wales. Mrs Connolly found Gabrielle dead first, in her cot on the first floor. Horrified, she and her husband dashed up to the second floor where Samantha was sleeping. Mr Connolly said: "It was hard to describe the horror. When we found one child dead we thought, 'Oh God. No – the other can't be dead too.' But she was." What compounds the mystery is that Home Office pathologist, Dr Donald Wayte, who carried out the post-mortems, said he believed the twins had died at exactly the same time.

The Connolly twins are not the first such case. Twin boys, aged seven months, also died in separate cots, in Bacup, Lancs, earlier that same year, 1983. *S. Express, S. Times, S. People, Observer, News of the World* 9 Oct; *D. Express, D. Star, D. Telegraph, D. Mail* 10 Oct; *Guardian, Scottish D. Express* 11 Oct; *Scottish D. Express* 13 Oct 1983.

Tragically, it happened again recently. Three-month-old twins, Kevin and Louise Croucher, died together in the cot they shared, in Denton, Manchester, in the night of 9/10 May. *Sun* 11 May 1984.

MORE NAME GAMES

• Three people who scooped nearly £50,000 each on Littlewoods pools are John Gamble, Mr Riches and Janet Luck. *Standard* 14 March; *Sun* 15 March 1984.

• A man who stole three Jack Russell puppies from a farm near Truro, Cornwall, is being hunted by PC Jack Russell. *Sun* 19 April 1984.

• Similarly . . . when a large African tree frog leaped from a crate of bananas in a supermarket in Newton Abbot, Devon, it was handed over to PC Ralph Hopper. *D. Telegraph* 23 April 1984.

• And lastly, our winner this issue is . . . the examining attorney in the extradition hearing in New York of Joseph Doherty, who escaped from the Crumlin Road prison, Belfast, is Ms Ira H. Bloch. *Guardian* 6 April 1984.

SWEDISH MYSTERY SUBS

We shall have to tighten up our watch on Swedish fjords. From time to time we've snipped the odd sightings of 'unidentified subs' and they'e not to hand right now, but the phenomenon has been going on a long time. John Keel told us his file on this goes back at least to the 1920s. It is very easy to dismiss these events as secret Soviet submarine skulduggery, but, again, as Keel has pointed out, the Soviets too have been pursuing the damned things at times! Undoubtedly espionage goes on – in 1981 a Soviet sub ran aground near the Swedish naval base at Karlskrona, and since 1980 the Swedish government has protested repeatedly about Soviet subs in its territorial waters. Nevertheless there are some very odd aspects of many of these sightings which make us wonder if they are indeed conventional subs at all. As alternatives we suggest the USOs (unidentified submarine objects) to which Keel, Vincent Gaddis and Ivan Sanderson first drew attention in their early books; and the ancient tradition of 'sea serpents' in Scandinavian waters.

The latest alert began in July 1983, when the Swedish navy blockaded the deepwater harbour at Tore, near Kalix, nor far from the border with Finland. Log rafts, anti-submarine nets, and a publicized willingness to use depth-charges, failed to flush out any sign of a mysery sub. Looking at the first reports, we see that the alert was sparked off by "strange movements in the water" around mid-July, followed, on 21st, by "an unspecified military sighting of what may have been a foreign submarine." Hardly unequivocal proof of a nuts-and-bolt sub! The intruder, if such it was, eluded boat patrols, shorebased continuous observations and sub-detecting helicopters. At the same time, we learn, there were two other

Mystery Subs →

→ MYSTERY SUBS. alerts: near the Karlskrona base, and in Sundsvall Bay, where 20 people saw a peculiar "backwash" which they thought might be from a periscope. Nothing was found in either case. Further sightings of something kept the hunt at Karlskrona going into early September. The first half of September also brought two known sightings of a "submarine-like object" which had the Norwegian navy on a wild goose chase in the area of Skaaneviksfjord, south of Bergen. *Guardian* 25 July, 5 + 13 Sept 1983.

In January this year, the Swedish defence staff issued a communique which told of the first sighting of unidentified frogmen, seen near a remote control mine-station, part of the country's anti-submarine defenses. The frogmen – who could well have been in black (FIBs?) – were observed coming out of the water, but "disappeared after a few minutes." Said defense staff spokesman Bertil Lagerewall: "We have never had a report like this one." UPI/ Schenectady (NY) *Gazette* 30 Jan 1984. For an Australian mystery sub, see I SPY on p57.

BRAINS — WHO NEEDS THEM?

- A 20yr-old French housewife discovered that the cause of her severe headaches was a .22 bullet her husband fired at her as she slept. Evelyne Muxart, of Saint-Etienne, near Lyons, work up one night in May 1983 to find a little blood in her hair. She washed her hair then went back to bed with her husband. But when her headaches continued for 10 days she went to hospital, where x-rays showed the bullet in her skull. It was removed, and her husband charged with attempted murder. *Guardian* 18 June 1983.
- A scenario for *Eraserhead 2* was played out in a Columbus, Ohio, police station, in what police believe was a bizarre attempt to evade a court appearance on a drunk-driving charge. On the day he was to be tried Dale Elder, 22, walked into the police station, where Officer Dan Canada was manning the information desk. In response to Canada's query, Elder said: "Yeah, I need an x-ray. I want to make sure I have a brain. They took me brain." Then Elder reached up to his forehead and began tugging at a thin wire protruding from it. "Blood started to trickle down his forehead," Canada said. "At first I thought he was pulling his hair. Then I realized that it was a wire, and I yelled, 'Hey, sergeant!' " Elder had pulled about three inches of wire out before the officers handcuffed him. They took Elder to Grant Hospital where he was stable after doctors removed the remainder of the wire. Elder said he had drilled a hole in his head and slid the wire inside to check if he had a brain. He felt no pain throughout the adventure, and whatever you might think of the cranial consequences we suspect that his marbles were lost before he picked up that drill! Columbus (OH) *Citizen-Journal* 27 Oct 1983.
- The China News Agency revealed that a 32yr-old man, in Kunming, had lived fairly normally after the right hemisphere of his brain was removed to prevent severe epileptic seizures 17 years ago. Doctors say he has a slight paralysis on his left side, mainly manifesting in a slight limp, but is otherwise leading a normal life. He is said to be looking for a wife saying: "I don't think I can live forever with my mother." *Weekly World News* 13 March 1984.

THE VULNERABLE GIANTS

Scientists who study giant squids have to be pretty Fortean – their subject matter is elusive and mysterious, and opportunities to study confined to the infrequent and unpredictable discovery of a rotting corpse on a remote beach. Now, a Norwegian biologist, Ole Brix, of the University of Bergen, sheds some light on the problem, following his luck in finding a 30ft specimen of *Architeuthis monachus* which was still alive when landed by fishermen at Bergen. Brix managed to take blood samples before the unfortunate creature expired, and found that when heated from 6°C to 15°C the blood carried four times less oxygen. The squids have haemocyanin, which is less efficient than haemoglobin for carrying oxygen, suggesting these fearsome creatures are slow movers and cannot tolerate changes in their environment. Brix and others had noticed that strandings of giant squid on the other side of the Atlantic, particularly Newfoundland, coincided with the inflow of warm water to the coast. The conclusion is that Brix's squid had drifted across the Atlantic, slowly suffocating in the warm water of the Gulf Stream. *Nature* v303p422, 2 June, *Times* 3 June, *N Sci* 16 June 1983.

DUSTING DOWN

A large area of southwest England and southern Wales was powdered with a sandy-coloured dust from the sky, on 22nd April, just seven days after the Welsh quake (see THE EARTH MOVES on p4.) FT Correspondent, PR Thomas, said that in Bristol his and neighbour's cars were lightly coated with a reddish dust. It must have been blown from North Africa, opined the weathermen, as they always do. *D. Telegraph* 23 April 1984.

For other falls, begin reading ICE COLD IN PORTSMOUTH on p18.

APRIL FUEL

A Taiwanese man, Chin Hsiang-peng, has been arrested for fraud in Taipei. He persuaded four friends to invest in a process which, he claimed, could turn water into petrol. When the demonstration failed, the four beat him up and shopped him. Reuter/*Guardian* 24 April 1984.

MANGYAN MAYHEM

. . . or what's going on in the Central Philippines?

- A 15yr-old boy, member of the Mangyan tribal settlement in the Mindoro Oriental province about 100 miles south of Manilla, was swallowed whole by a python he disturbed while searching a cave, local police said on 27 Nov last year. Other tribesmen managed to kill the snake and cut it open, but the boy was dead when found. *Guardian, Yorkshire Post, D. Telegraph* 28 Nov 1983.
- *D. Telegraph* 4 Feb 1984 cites a Manila paper, *Tempo*, which reported that Mangyan tribesmen had hogtied and speared to death a suspected cattle rustler. Then they roasted and ate him!
- Sometime about the middle of February a Mangyan woman was raped and chopped in half, and those fiery tribesmen went out for bloody revenge again. Two men were caught, castrated and beheaded at the scene of the crime. A week later three other suspects were roasted alive and tossed into a well full of cobras. Reuter/*Standard* 23 Feb 1984.
- Five Mangyan women jumped to their deaths from a 700ft cliff, a local paper reported on 21st March, rather than go through with marriages arranged for them to men of a different tribe. Reuter/*Standard* 22 March 1984.

SHAW SIMULACRUM

The profile of George Bernard Shaw (*right*) was recognized in the outline of the southern tip of the Iles Radisson (*left*), an island in Ungava Bay, Quebec, and because of the remarkable likeness has been officially named Pointe Bernard Shaw by the Canadian Permanent Committee on Geographical Names, and by the Commission de Toponymie du Quebec. *Niagara Falls Review* 5 July; AP/Schenectady (NY) *Gazette* 6 July 1983.

NEW MONKEY GIRL

A wild girl, aged between seven and eight years, has been discovered by an Italian missionary in Sierra Leone, and given the name 'Baby Hospital'. Doctors say she is more animal than human, seemingly brought up by apes or monkeys. She is not able to stand upright, preferring to walk on all fours. She dips her head down to her foodbowl instead of using her hands. Her arms and hands are "amazingly" strong, but her leg muscles are undeveloped. She chatters and shouts like an ape or monkey. She has resisted attempts to 'civilize' her, and spends most of her time crying and looking longingly towards the jungle.

Our French source suggests the girl is black, but the *WWN* offers a quite different identity, suggesting that the girl might be Sara Jurgenson who was five years old when the jeep, in which she was touring Sierra Leone with her parents on holiday from New Zealand, crashed in 1969. Her parents were found dead in the wreckage, but of Sara, it seems, no trace could be found. *D. Star* 26 Jan; *Weekly World News* 13 March; Montpellier *Midi Libre* 3 April 1984.

POLTERGEIST PHOTOGRAPHED!

On 5th March, a Columbus, Ohio, family – identified at first only as "Joan and John and their six children" but later reports gave the family name as Resch – moved out of their home. "I don't believe in ghosts," said Joan, "but the stereo would blast, and radios and TVs would turn on without electricity." Objects would move or fly through the air, lights would flash, a clock's hands turned faster, and a shower turned itself on. The disturbances began on Saturday, 3rd March, when all the lights came on simultaneously, and after two frightening nights and days, the family had had enough and checked into a motel. The events seemed to center upon the 14yr-old daughter, Tina, who had been struck by a brass candlestick, a clock and a wall-hanging, all of which had flung themselves at her.

On Sunday evening, the family summoned three Mormon elders to pray with the girl. They stayed for 25 minutes and said there was a "calmness" in the house. But as they left they "saw some things happening." Likewise, appeals to the police and an electrician brought no peace from the pesky polt's pesterings. The electrician, Bruce Claggett, said: "I was up there three hours, and the lights were just turning themselves on all over the place. I tried taping over the switches, but as fast as I would tape them in the down position they'd come back on!"

At this point, Mike Harden enters the story. A reporter for the *Columbus Dispatch*, he had met the "rock-solid type" family before and was interested enough to write the story for the paper's 6th March edition. As he stood in the home that Monday morning, Harden himself saw a telephone leap into the air and a coffee mug flip off a table onto Tina's lap before flying up to smash itself into the fireplace. He called Fred Shannon, a *Dispatch* photographer. Twice, when the parents alone visited the house, nothing happened – the movements of objects only seemed to occur when Tina was present.

Shannon also saw the phone move several times. "It seemed to want to attack her [Tina]. It hit her a couple of times and she yelled." Shannon said that the phone refused to budge whenever he looked at it directly, so he tried to "outfox the ghost." Having set his camera, he looked away slightly, keeping the phone in view "at the rim of my glasses . . and then the thing was starting to blur out. It was the phone streaking towards her. She screamed at the same time, and I hit the trigger of my camera. I'm not saying I believe in poltergeists or demons, but after seeing this, it made a believer out of me on psychokinetic energy."

Inevitably the news attracted vocal skeptics. For example, one Leslie Blatt, head of the physics department at Ohio State University, said, when asked for his reaction to the notion that agitated teenagers can externalize emotions like anger, "Nobody has ever been able to measure any energy projected from people that would do this sort of thing." He's right, of course, but might simply mean that we haven't been looking in the right way.

Matters were not helped when the girl was actually caught moving something. Television news footage appeared to show a lamp fly off a table near Tina, but in slow motion Tina could be seen shoving the lamp. She later confessed readily, saying she did it because she was tired of the intensive media attention. Students of contemporary poltergeist cases will know this is a common scenario – genuine phenomena to begin with, then becoming adulterated for a variety of reasons. There is some suggestion of this in the Enfield case [see FT33p4,5,11]. In the inevitable accusations of hoaxing which followed the editor of the *Dispatch* publicly endorsed the honesty of Harden and Shannon, the latter of whom had been with local newspapers for more than 30 years.

Significantly, for theorists who believe that polt energies originate in "projected repressions", and in clinical tradition, we learn that Tina had been adopted into the family but "recently came into contact with her biological family in the city [Columbus], and she has a lot of ambivalent feelings in her life right now," said Bill Roll, director of the Psychical Research Foundation, Durham, N. Carolina, who is investigating. Harden confirms this, saying: "Tina's adoptive mother acknowledges that there is a lot of tension in the 14yr-old."

For what it's worth, our correspondent Joseph Trainor noticed that President Reagan visited Columbus, the day the polt manifested, to address a congregation of evangelicals, we guess that's enough to disturb anybody!

We have many sources giving the AP and UPI versions, but our thanks go to Larry Arnold, of ParaScience International, who has provided copies of all the original Columbus (OH) *Dispatch* reports which we briefly chronicle here . . . • 6 March: Mike Harden's first report. • 7 March: the Resch family feel better for spending two quiet nights at a model. • 8 March: the family sheds anonymity and holds a press conference in face of mounting interest from national and international news and TV media. Tina tells of her awareness of being abandoned when only 10 mths old and says she loves her biological mother. And yet she has periods of deep inexpressible anger for which, she thinks, the strange occurrences are a punishment because they only seem to happen "when

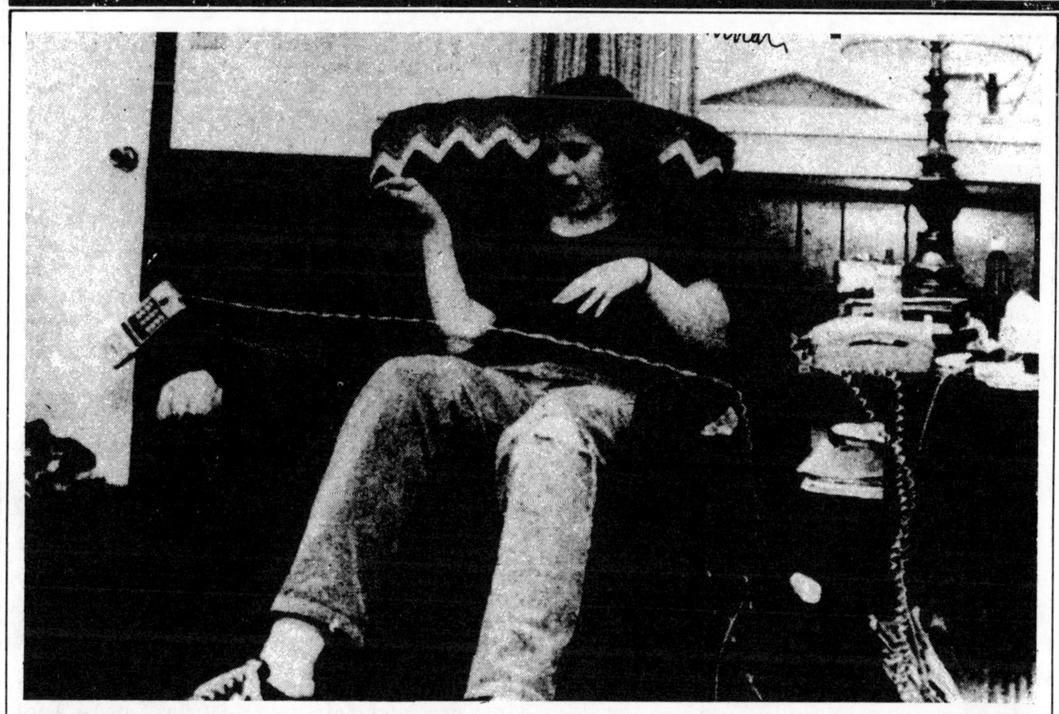

Fred Shannon's photo of the moment the telephone flew in front of Tina Resch. Later, CSICOP astronomer, Steven Shore, endorsed it, saying: "It shows a kink in the cord that is not consistent with a continuous trajectory. That violates the laws of physics." [© Columbus (OH) *Dispatch*.]

I'm really mad." ● 9 March: reports on the press conference. The family naively thought this would satisfy the media curiosity, indeed Tina only agreed to it because she thought reporters would be gone by 2 pm; but they were still coming at 9.30 pm. They even lurked outside the bathroom when Tina went in. We also learn of the WTVN-TV film of the lamp-pulling episode. According to Tina it was not an attempt to hoax an incident, but an impulsive action because she was getting angry and resentful of the media intrusion. She had told her mother, and the TV reporter, and readily admitted the incident to Mike Harden. What the AP and UPI reports don't say is that the TV reporter, Drew Hadwal, far from being discouraged, acknowledged that he had seen other incidents – e.g., chairs moving in the kitchen – when Tina was nowhere near them. ● 10 March: enter those intrepid 'skeptics' Paul Kurtz, the Amazing Randi and two CSICOP heavies (astronomers!), who while boasting of open minds seem to be publicly salivating at the prospect of catching the girl red-handed when they come to visit the following week. ● 11 March: *Dispatch* editor Luke Feck endorses the honesty and professionalism of Harden and photographer Shannon against attacks on their credibility. News also that the Reschs' had filed a claim for damage by an unknown "force" under the "malicious Mischief" section of their insurance with Midwestern Indemnity of Cincinatti. ● 12 March: Bill Roll and assistant, Kelly Powers, settle into the Resch home amicably. But Mrs Resch expresses doubts about the CSICOP team: "If it's scientists or astronomers who are interested, fine. But that magician is not going to visit." She said she was worried by the "sensationalism" surrounding Randi. We also learn that life outside the Resch's house in Blue Ash Road has lost its tranquility: hot on the heels of the media have come the sightseers, pranksters, children aiming snowballs, hot-rodding teenagers. ● 14 March: Mrs Resch is offended by Randi's offer of $10,000 for proof of an authentic incident: she let the other members of the CSICOP team inside, but the caped Randi had to wait outside. ● 15 March: Tina agrees to accompany Roll back to his Psychical Research Foundation labs, in Chapel Hill, NC, for further study. Roll said that during his stay "there were incidents that I was not able to account for in normal ways." These included a picture falling; a taperecorder flying through the air; a pair of pliers sliding over the floor; all while Tina was "under complete observation". ● 19 March: the change of scene

Polt →

→ RESCH POLT.

was doing Tina good, says Roll; but her 'force' seemed to be taking a holiday too, with no further incidents reported. • 18 March: no progress on insurance claim. • ? March: Mike Harden reminisces about Tina. • ? March: another column from Harden on the spectacle of psychic research. He also reveals that Tina had seen the film *Poltergeist* six times, and was profoundly influenced by a book, *If There be Thorns* by V.C. Andrews, in which a 9 yr-old boy fantasizes about a parent he never knew, and who was very clumsy, "Tables fell, lamps toppled . . . " Tina said the boy's search made her think of herself. • 13 April: at a news conference at Chapel Hill, Roll said he was unable to offer conclusive evidence, but told of several incidents, in his home, that Tina could move objects by "mental energy". He told of a candle and an ashtray moving, but declined to describe other incidents. A Chapel Hill psychologist, Dr Rebecca Zinn, said Tina was once struck from behind by a telephone receiver which had flown from a desk 6–8 ft away. Roll says he will tell all at the Foundation's conference in October.

EGGS-TRAORDINARY!

With suspect timing, or as some believe, with miraculous timing, an egg made for Easter celebrations and decorated with the thorn-crowned head of Jesus, wept tears from its right eye.

It was made by a Salvation Army girl, Anne Schutterlin, 26, who gave it to Naomi Drury, 11, whose family also belong to the group, and Naomi took it to her school, Doncaster Junior School, in Mexborough, Yorks. Her teacher, Trevor Whitehead, who first noticed the stream, said he is not a religious person, but found it "an unnerving experience". Headmaster Gordon Garrity said: "I've been a headmaster for 27 years and I don't have illusions about anything. But I find what happened quite disturbing . . . Naomi's was the only egg [out of 160 brought to the school] to weep. It only wept from one place – the eye – and as soon as we wiped the tear away, it reappeared." He did this at least a dozen times. "There must be some natural or scientific reason . . . all I know is that there was certainly no jiggery pokery," said Whitehead. Anne Schutterlin said she felt sure there was no moisture or water in the egg – "I boiled it for over 10 minutes. It was rock hard." – had a different view. "What happened is divine intervention." *D. Mirror, Sun* 14 April 1984.

GRAVE MISGIVINGS

In Berlin, "recently", the funeral service of an 81yr-old man was interrupted when mourners heard him clearing his throat in the coffin. He was rescued and revived successfully. The incident drew a lot of public discussion – perhaps some of our German readers have clippings? – in which the public could hardly have been reassured by the statement from an eminent forensic scientist, Prof. H-J Mallach of Tübingen, that at least 20 persons a year are wrongly certified dead and buried alive, in West Germany alone. Following on the statement by Dr Peron-Autret, in his book [see FT39p61], that about 200 people a year suffer the same fate in the USA following a supposedly fatal coronary, we are surprised at the lack of attention in world media to this sensational if not horrifying phenomenon. Helsinki *Helsingen Sanomat* 27 Oct 1983.

CALIFORNIAN SEA SERPENT

Five members of a repair gang working on Highway 1 on a hillside in Marin County, near the community of Stinson Beach, California, claim they saw a 100ft long sea serpent, about a quarter of a mile away and 100yds offshore.

Just before 2pm, on 31 October 1983, a flagman named Gary noticed the creature swimming towards a cliff. He called Matt Ratto on his walkie-talkie, who fetched his binoculars. Ratto saw three black humps and a long neck (*see his drawing*) as the creature looked around, submerged and headed out to sea again. A credible detail is that he noticed many birds and sea lions in the monster's wake. Truck driver Steve Bjora said he saw only two humps, and exhausted his eloquence by adding: "That sucker was going 45 to 50 miles an hour. It was clipping. It was boogeying. It looked like a long eel."

Ratto told reporters: "I'm not psycho. I'm a regular guy. If I was going to make up something, I'd make up a 12ft Mickey Mouse with five arms." He has a point; and another convincing detail – in the opinion of the reviewer of the reportage of the sighting, in the International Society of Cryptozoology *Newsletter* v2n4 (Winter 1983) – is the admission that the road-crew kept binoculars handy for spying on nude sunbathers. Other reports – cited in the *ISC Newsletter* – found further witnesses and even more sightings. One, Mrs Marlene Martin, a Transportation Department supervisor, saw four humps, but was "not available" for comment. For Roland Curry, 19, who saw it from the beach, it was the second sighting in less than a week, or so he claimed. More dubious is the *post facto* claim of a group of surfers who said they saw a sea serpent "just the way it was described", mid-afternoon on 2nd November, very close to the Santa Ana River jetty, near Costa Mesa. It was like "a long black eel," said Young Hutchinson, after it surfaced 10ft from his surfboard. "At first I thought it was a whale . . . but it didn't look the same. The skin texture wasn't the same . . . I didn't see the head or tail."

The Stinson Beach sea serpent, drawn by Matt Ratto.

Additional sources: AP/Ashland (KY) *Daily Independent*, San Francisco (CA) *Chronicle* 3 Nov; *Weekly World News* 13 Dec 1984.

PYRAMID GAS PANIC

Egyptian police banned visits to the famous site of the pyramids near Cairo, on 16 April, after fears that a mysterious gas is "leaking" into the chambers of the tomb of King Khafra and his family. The alert was sparked off by collapsing Spanish tourists who said they felt suffocated and developed eye inflammations. The AP reports speculated wildly, suggesting, in order, gases seeping in the tomb chambers through undiscovered cracks in the bedrock from undiscovered underground lakes of water or sewage, a stinkbomb left by a childish tourist, and a can of Mace fallen from a tourist's handbag (when no can could be found a curious "sponge wrapped in a handkerchief" was blamed, though how anyone could carry around with them a sponge soaked in tear-gas solution beats me!). Nassef Mohammed Hassan, Inspector of Antiquities for the Cairo area told reporters on the 17th that "the effects of the gas are decreasing" which is officialese for the difficulty in finding anything to analyse. "There will be nothing in two or three days, and we can open the pyramid to the public." Perhaps, there was no gas in the first place; to our jaded eye it looks more like a case of 'mass hysteria', more familiar to us in busy work environments or schools etc – see MALAY MALAISE on p16. *Standard, Shropshire Star* 17 April; Reuter/*D. Telegraph, Times* 18 April; AP/Houston *Chronicle* 18, 19 & 22 April 1984.

WEATHER PROPHET HONOURED

Andrei Dyakov, who lives in the Siberian Altai Mountains, has successfully forecasted the weather since the 1950s, using theories about the influence of the sun which he developed after graduating from university in the 1930s. So accurate are his predictions, particularly of such disasters as droughts, that he has been given an official appointment by the regional Soviet authorities, reports the newspaper *Sovietskaya Culture*, and an observatory is being built for him at his mountain home. However, despite the honour, he predicted a rainy summer followed by another drought in western Siberia. *Standard* 1 March 1984.

WW2 SHELL FALLS IN LOS ANGELES BACKYARD

A dud nine-inch shell, of World War II vintage crashed from a sunny sky into the backyard of Fred Simons, 79, in Lakewood, 20 miles southeast of Los Angeles.

The incident happened at about 4pm, on 1st January 1984, and could have been the Cosmic Joker's attempt to get the New Year off with a bang! Instead – or anyway – the rusty 22lb missile merely left an oblong crater four feet deep in old Fred's patio. Sheriff's Deputy Wes Slider said neighbours remembered hearing a whistling sound before the shell hit. A bomb squad from the Los Angeles County Sheriff's Department found the shell was just that – no explosives inside. Ben Harris, of the FAA could only suggest "an aerial prankster" was responsible for the puzzling event – yet Slider found that no-one reported seeing or hearing a plane.

Could this curious displacement of over 30 years and thousands of miles be the result of teleportation? For more falling mysteries see ICE COLD IN PORTSMOUTH on p18. DUSTING DOWN on p8. and FALLING OBJECT HITS PLANE on p23. AP/Durham (NC) *Morning Herald*, AP/Schenectady (NY) *Gazette*, AP/Houston (TX) *Chronicle* 3 Jan 1984.

SMURFS ON RAMPAGE

A curious rumour spread rapidly through a number of junior-high schools in the Houston, Texas, area last year, reaching its peak in March, that a vicious gang of Smurfs was terrorizing pupils and slaughtering headmasters in schools across the city. Various versions held that the normally cute blue cartoon characters were wearing blue body paint or black jackets and carrying knives or machine guns. Some kids believed that pupils wearing sky blue clothes were in danger; others that this colour would ward off attack. In the Aldine school district, the Smurfs were thought to be lurking in toilets, and severe disruption was wrought when youngsters feared going to the bathrooms. Attendance in some schools dropped, and frantic parents complained to school administrators and police. One family was said to have moved their child from Fondren Middle School back to Philadelphia because she was so frightened.

It seems the rumours started back in January (1983) after a Houston TV station reported that several juveniles, members of a gang believed to be called 'the Smurfs' had been arrested for a series of petty crimes. After that, fact seemed to have got mixed up with fantasy. Franklin Turner, principal of Johnston Middle School, who was widely rumoured to have been murdered by Smurfs, said that children "desperately wanted to believe that the Smurfs were there – they wanted some excitement." At the Welch Middle School, principal Bill Morgan fought fire with fire, announcing over the school's public address system that Garfield the Cat and the Greatest American Hero were on their way to deal with the menace. Houston police said they had arrested about 40 youngsters and seven adults, during the general panic, for "Smurf-related goings-on", mostly burglary and petty theft – but added, somewhat wearily, that the original 'Smurf' gang had never invaded any Houston schools. *Newsweek* 4 April 1983.

NEW ANIMALS FROM OLD

The *Guardian* 16 Feb 1984 said Cambridge scientists had genetically engineered eight hybrid animals, half-goat and half-sheep. The paper cited a report in *Nature* by Dr Carole Fehilly and colleagues at the Institute of Animal Physiology, which brings nearer the day of artificially created animals, called 'chimaeras'. In this case they took fertilized embryos from female goats and sheep at the eight-cell stage, treated and merged them in different combinations to produce hybrids with a variety of coat and other characteristics. They say: "The animal behaves like a male goat but has proved infertile in natural matings with female goats. Almost all the spermatozoa have a characteristic tail defect."

Meanwhile Mother Nature had proved no slouch, but then she's been at it longer! *D. Telegraph* 5 July 1983: the products of a gander and an Aylesbury duck have caused ornithological interest on Patrick Heagerty's farm at Streat, Sussex. The four 'gucks' or 'doslings' have long legs and necks and a goose-type beak. Heagerty says he hopes to start a new breed. We wonder how far he's got.

At the Biobehavioural Science department of the University of Connecticut, a strange half-beagle half-coyote hybrid was bred from three generations of animals taking six years. One night, it was stolen from the department building and found in the back of a truck about a mile away. It had been beaten to death. The detective in charge of finding the mutant-murderers – himself a part of the great Name Game – is Lt Michael Pander of the campus police. Houston (TX) *Chronicle* 9 Oct 1983.

Hybrids →

→ HYBRIDS.

An experiment in surrogate motherhood at the Louisville Zoo, Kentucky, ended successfuly when a horse, implanted with an embryo from a zebra, gave birth to a stripey little colt. *Sun* 19 May 1984.

But what on earth is this one? The *Guardian* 7 Feb 1983, citing a Canton newspaper, said that a new animal had been found by peasants in central China. It has the head of an ox with the tail and feet of a goat. It was female, weighed more than 660 lbs and ate bamboo.

The plant equivalent of these stories involves some 400 yr-old plums found on Henry VIII's flagship *Mary Rose*, raised from the south-coast seabed last year. Scientists – the *Sun* 5 March 1984 does not say where – are going to culture them in a bid to recreate some 15th century plum trees.

UNCOMMON BAD LUCK!

☐ Heart transplant patient, Norman Meredith, 33, was knocked down by a car on his first shopping trip since coming home. He was dragged across the street, in Pontypridd, South Wales, and then the driver got out threatening to punch him. *D. Mirror* 9 Sept 1983.

☐ On a hot, sticky night in Palmero, Sicily, Salvatore Rosella opened the windows of his apartment, but the noise from his neighbour's children was driving him and his wife mad. Countless times he had told them to keep quiet to no effect, so he grabbed his pistol intending to frighten them into silence. When he banged on the neighbour's door an argument developed. Antonella Rosella leaned out of the window to tell her neighbour to shut up. Salvatore lost control and threatened to shoot the neighbours and fired the gun into the air. You guessed it. He shot his wife! He was charged with man's laughter. *S. Express* 18 Sept 1983.

☐ In the *British Medical Journal* for Nov 1983, is the story of a motor mechanic who made medical history. While operating an electrical grinding machine he spat on a live terminal. A blue flash jumped from the machine, into his mouth and down his throat, punctured his windpipe inside the left lung, collapsing both lungs, and generally making his eyes water. The *BMJ* intones that it was "a pattern of injury not, to our knowledge, noted before." Some comfort! *D. Telegraph* 7 Nov 1983.

For more tales of tangled karma and all round black humour, see Paul Sieveking's column on p36.

TALE OF A TAIL

Police in Newport, Isle of Wight, are looking for a South American lizard which can grow to 5 ft long, after a council workman found a tail, nearly 3 ft long (see photo), while cutting hedges in the Whitehouse Rd/Vittlefields area of Porchfield, near Newport. An expert said that it belonged to a fringeback iguana, a species which can shed both its skin and its tail. The puzzle is how it came to be on the island, and the usual irresponsible or careless owner is supposed. The identity of the workman, too, is a mystery, for he left quickly after leaving the grizzly trophy at the house of RSPCA Inspector Ray Burrows (pictured). Our own silly idea, for what its worth, is that there is something significant, or not, in the fact that this were-reptile is the IOW 'puma/lynx/etc' transmoggyfie d for it appears during the winter hiatus of this foxy feline. Portsmouth *News* 21 + 22 Feb; *D. Star, D. Mirror, D. Telegraph* 22 Feb 1984.

For news of another OOP lizard, the Isle of Wight 'puma', the 'Beast of Exmoor' and our continuing catalogue of contentious cattery, see OUT OF PLACE on p40.

POWER SURGE?

There was terror in the little Suffolk village of Honey Tye, in mid-December last year. Residents fled their homes as light bulbs exploded, electrical appliances switched themselves on and burnt themselves out. "It was really weird. We had no idea what was happening," said Mrs Jackie Pearce of the Red Lion pub. If it had happened in just a single house the story would have been written up as a poltergeist. Meanwhile the Eastern Electricity Board – who had repairmen working in the area at the time. [Well, where there's a traffic cop there's a holdup, right?] – explained that it was a mystery power surge of another kind. *S. Mirror* 18 Dec 1983.

MALAY MALAISE

When 55 students, mainly girls, were "struck by mass hysteria" (no details!) at a 500-pupil school in Kota Kinabalu, Sabah (part of what used to be Borneo, but is now East Malaysia), the school principal, Jaibin Sindan, closed all classes and called in two *bomohs* (Malay shamans). The two men, Samijan Saradi and Wasli Matsih, conducted an overnight exorcism, in which they declared the place possessed by *hantu* (tormented ghosts). Saradi said the spirits were angry at being "rudely awakened" from "slumber" by the noise of children's sports and play. I know the feeling! Saradi added that the hantu wanted a girl to jump to her death from the school building before the attacks on children would stop. "I told them to go to hell," he added, "and they went." *Le Populaire du Centre* (France) 4 April; *Djakarta Post* 5 April 1984.

SCIENTIST SAYS YELLOW RAIN IS A LOT OF CRAP

Accounts of and references to 'yellow rains' occupy many pages in the early chapters of Fort's *Book of the Damned*, but he doesn't have much to say about the idea that they are caused by the excreta of bees. In Fort's day the going theory was that falls of yellow rain and yellow dust were composed of prodigious quantities of pollen – so Fort responded with incidents which were out of season or which showed, on examination, they were not pollen. Perhaps the idea wasn't so advanced in Fort's day, but recently the notion of bee dung received some high-powered military and political attention.

The United States has made allegations that Soviet-made chemical weapons – said to be fungal toxins called trichothecenes which are yellow – had caused at least 10,000 deaths in Laos, Cambodia and Afghanistan. Refugees in these regions have spoken of a 'yellow rain' which causes sickness and death, and several labs have found evidence of such toxins on yellow-spotted leaves collected from Southeast Asia. But Prof Matthew Meselson, a Harvard University biologist, says "It is a mistake to identify yellow rain as an agent of chemical warfare. It is in fact the faeces of bees."

In a joint statement with Thomas Seeley, a honeybee specialist from Yale University, he said: "We have discovered that wild colonies of Southeast Asian honeybees perform massive defecation flights which can cover a swath thousands of square meters in area with 100 or more spots of yellowish faeces per square meter." They say they found 10 such swaths of bee droppings and at one point were actually caught in one of these yellow showers. "It lasted about five minutes," said Meselson. "There were three of us in our team [in Thailand], and we each had about a dozen spots on ourselves. There were about 200 per square meter on the hood of the Land-Rover." Meselson concludes that trichothecenes are produced naturally by fungi, which in turn would be spread as the bees eat fungus-contaminated food; or the toxins could be produced by fungi growing on the bee droppings.

Spokesmen from the US State Department have been highly critical of Meselson's rather inconclusive theory, saying that it does not dispose of the evidence of chemical warfare, eg toxins on a Soviet gas mask retrieved from Afghanistan. Such warfare is banned by international treaties and the charges are denied by the Soviets. For our part, we can accept that there have been rains of artificial toxins, rains of bee dung and other yellow substances, rains of artificial toxins deviously disguized as bee dung, etc. But what really taxes us is the thought of millions of bees straining in unison. And how does that help us explain one of Fort's cases from 1870 in which hundreds of thousands of tons of yellow organic pollen-like matter which was not pollen fell for three successive days on parts of France and Spain? [*Books* p. 26f.]

Nevertheless, a recent TV documentary on the subject [I forgot to make a note of it, but I think it was 'Horizon' – blushing Ed] filmed near the Thai-Cambodian border gave testimony from villagers to the reality of defecating swarms of bees, which have a distinctive flight, going back and forth over the same large area. The same programme gave the opinions of an American anthropologist in the area who has proposed an altogether more sane hypothesis. He said he had

Yellowrain →

→ **YELLOWRAIN.**
heard stories from *both* sides of things falling out of clearly marked planes (of the opposing side) following which the local people suffer nausea, stinging eyes, diarrhoea, internal bleeding and even birth defects, but he put this down to the usual folklore of wartimes because there were obvious elements of mythologizing in the stories as well as blatant inconsistencies. These spread as rumours and are soon grafted onto the almost legendary rains of bee dung. It only needs a swarm to dump on some fearful or unsuspecting villagers for a new account of dastardly 'yellow rain' to be on its way.

AP/*D. Telegraph* 29 March; AP/*Arab News* 30 March; *Weekly World News* 5 June 1984.

STELLER'S SEA COW

The skeleton of a huge sea mammal, identified as the remains of a Steller's sea cow, has been found on the beach of a Soviet Pacific island, reported Tass. It would be interesting to know just how recent this relic, said to be the first such find this century is, for although officially believed extinct since the 1760s, when these gentle vegetarian giants were last hunted, there have been rumours of sightings. *Guardian* 19 Dec 1983.

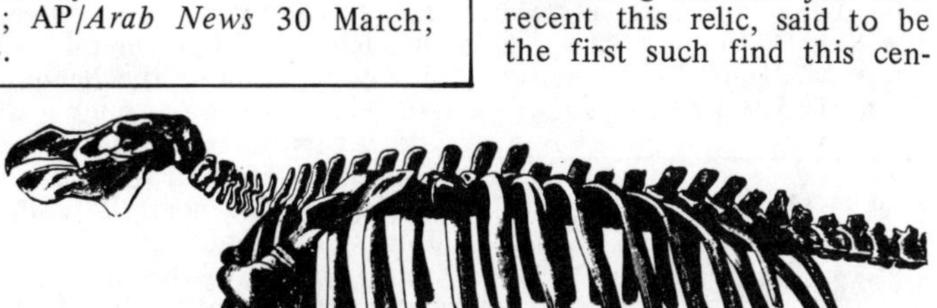

A skeleton of *Rhytina stelleri*, from *The Voyage of the Vega* [in C. Gould's *Mythical Monsters*, 1888.]

WOTSIT?

Reports of a half-man half-ape animal, three metres tall, roaming the rain forest in West Kalimantan, have spurred Indonesian wildlife officials to mount an investigation. While generally "human-like" the creature is said to have eyes towards the sides of its head "like a goat." NZPA/Auckland (NZ) *Star* 25 Aug 1983.

CHICAGO'S YOUNGEST MOTHER

An unnamed girl became the youngest mother, at the age of 10 yrs and 8 mths, to give birth naturally in Chicago, and the second youngest in the United States, when she was delivered of a 6lb 4oz girl on 5th April, at the city's famous Cook County Hospital. The record holder was four months younger who had a Caesarian section in 1964. UPI/Harrisburg (PA) *Evening News* 6 April; *D. Telegraph* 7 April 1984.

The above reports mention that the all-time youngest mother title is held by a Peruvian girl in 1939, Lina Medina, who at 5 yrs 7 mths gave birth to a boy of about 6lbs, but the reports get several things wrong: one says Lina was six and a half, and both say her baby was stillborn. In the *Examiner* (?) for 20 Dec 1983, we read that Lina became her doctor's secretary, and her son, named Gerado after the doctor, was a brilliant scholar and became a successful accountant. More of Lina's story is told in Paul Sieveking's *Man Bites Man* (p. 35) where we learn the views of her parents, Inca-Spanish peasants. Lina's mother believed the girl had been bitten by a magic snake which holds power over women who sleep in the open air, as Lina often did; while her father supposed that the girl was the victim of a mountain pool with legendary fertility properties in which women bathed who wished to be pregnant. Lina frequently swum there.

Coincidentally, Lina was brought to doctors in Chicago in 1940, home of the latest young mother; but where the father of Lina's baby was never discovered, the man responsible for the latest Chicago prodigy was being sought by police. The girl had been raped and the two suspects were her uncle and a babysitter's husband.

Curiously, in this issue, we can tell of a much younger 'pregnancy', see BROTHER'S KEEPER on p22.

LONG MARCHES

- A Friesian cow, parted from her calf at the market at Hatherleigh, Devon, jumped a farm gate and trudged six miles along country lanes and across fields to be reunited with her offspring. *Shropshire Star* 2 Dec 1983.
- Bill Shillaw, of Wentwork, South Yorks, thought his prize pidgeon called Cut Throat was dead. He had taken the bird nearly two miles from home and released him in woodlands, then heard the gunshot which downed CT. Two days later the plucky pidgeon walked up Bill's garden path trailing a wing shattered by shotgun pellets, after staggering, presumably, across the intervening fields, woods and main road. *Sun* 19 March 1984.

A GREEN DOG

In nothern Italy a farmer's gundog has given birth to six puppies, and one of them has green hair. With all the appearance of saying something the report quotes unnamed "scientists" speculating that it is "probably a spontaneous mutation." And an equally unnamed vet told the *Sun* he thought it was a "type of dandruff." *Standard* 17 April; *Sun* 19 April 1984.

LADY OBLOMOV

At the age of 14, Hilda Matthews contracted tonsilitis and was sent to bed to rest. Having had just four days at work, she decided she had had enough and refused to get up. She spent the remaining 50 years of her life in bed, in her flat in Norton Green, Stoke-on-Trent. The main features of her bedroom existence were wearing make-up, eating chocolate, drug overdoses and attempts at self-injury, the North Staffordshire inquest was told. Deputy coroner, John Wain, recording death by misadventure, said the woman was an "attention-seeking hypochondriac" who thought friends and neighbours had nothing better to do than dance attendance on her. *D. Mirror, D. Telegraph* 28 March 1984.

GOOSE COOKED

As a Republic Airlines plane landed in South Dakota a large goose smashed through the cockpit window. The pilot was injured, but the copilot managed to land the plane safely. The pay-off of this particular synchronistic gag is that the company symbol, with which the plane is emblazoned, is a flying goose! *NY Post* 8 Nov 1983.

BALL LIGHTNING IN RUSSIAN PLANE

On the 9th or 10th January, a Soviet Ilyushin-18 passenger jet flew close to a thunderstorm shortly after take-off from Sochi, on the Black Sea. What happened next, according to TASS, the Soviet news agency, astonished the witnesses. "At a height of 1,200 yards a fireball about 10cm (four inches) in diameter appeared on the fuselage in front of the crew's cockpit. It disappeared with a deafening noise, but re-emerged several seconds later in the passengers' lounge, after piercing in an uncanny way through the airtight metal wall," said TASS. Then "The fireball slowly flew about the heads of the stunned passengers. In the tail section of the airliner it divided into two glowing crescents which then joined together again and left the plane noiselessly." The plane returned to Sochi where two holes were found in the fuselage – one near the cockpit and one in the tail section – presumably made by the lightning entering and leaving. In a brief mention of the incident – in which a wrong date is given – the *New Scientist* 26 Jan 1984 comments: "In electrostatics, Gauss's Law shows that the interior of hollow metal conductors is unaffected by external electic fields. This is confusing, Why, then, should ball lightning have formed inside the plane? And how did the lightning apparently penetrate metal?" All we can add is that it's not the first such case; several others are on record. *Standard* 13 Jan; AP/Dallas (TX) *Times Herald*, AP/ *The Scotsman, D. Star, D. Telegraph, Shropshire Star*, 14 Jan 1984.

ICE COLD IN PORTSMOUTH

Mrs Joan Powell and her husband Ronald are glad they were not in the garden of their home at The Crossway, Portchester, Portsmouth, Hampshire, at lunchtime on 23rd March 1984. That was the time a guestimated cubic foot of ice weighing about 5lbs, demolished their daffodils. Mrs Powell said they had returned from a trip out when they noticed the damage. "There it was, sitting in the garden. I couldn't believe it. It had spread flowers and stones all over the place where it had dug in so deep." The police and Civil Aviation Authority made all the usual meaningless noises. Somehow two local ambulancemen, Keith Lloyd and David Broscoe, heard of the incident and rushed there in time to retrieve the ice and thoughtfully photographed it. Portsmouth *News* 24 March 1984.

Other recent falls of ice:

★ **Coulsdon, Surrey** – the report gives no date, but we guess it happened sometime between Christmas Day 1983 and 7th Jan 1984. Eric and Peggy Bitten were spending a quiet evening when a tremendous crash brought them running outside to investigate. On the paving by their back door and against the garage wall were large chunks of splintered ice. They collected the pieces and stored them in their freezer. They then contacted the police but were passed first to Heathrow airport (only 20 miles from Coulsdon) and then to the Safety Data Unit of the Civil Aviation Authority. They were given the usual 'illegal toilet-dumping' and 'it's impossible to identify the culprit' routine.

About three or four days after the first event there was another explosion of noise outside the Bitten home. Again they rushed outside, and again they found large chunks of

→ **ICEFALLS.**
ice, this time on the conservatory roof and all around. Mrs Bitten then noticed *leaves* frozen into the ice. Even though she saw a plane overhead at the time, she suspected that perhaps the ice did not fall from a plane at all. It was not long before a "full confession" was extracted from the neighbour's children and their friends who had just gone inside from playing in the garden. Yes, said 10yr-old Richard Franke, they had been playing with ice from a pond, hurling it over the fence into the Bitten's garden.

As connoisseurs of explanations this leaves us cold. Even if you accept that young children can lob ice chunks onto conservatory roofs, we are led to believe that the explanation applied only to the second incident, leaving the first incident a genuine mystery which the boys were copying. But somehow, the Bittens began to doubt the first incident also, and to minimise their embarassment cancelled the visit of a CAA man who intended to examine the first lot of ice. It's a real pity he didn't. *S. Express* 8 Jan 1984.

★ At **Mauzar, Haute-Garonne**, France. At 5.30pm, 13th May 1984, the Brugnerotto family were terrified when a mass of ice "many hundreds of grammes" smashed into the earth uncomfortably close to them. An unusual feature of the case is that the ice was chestnut-coloured (*marron*). One of the explanations offered by the French meteorological service is also novel to us: that the mass solidified in a cold, wet cloud around grains of Sahara sand – but there is no evidence in the story to suggest that sand was found in the ice. *La Depeche du Midi* 16 May 1984. The idea is not beyond improbability; aerial sand gets around – see DUSTING DOWN on p8.

For more falling mysteries see PLANE HIT BY FALLING OBJECT on p23. , and WW2 SHELL FALLS IN BACK YARD on p14.

Ambulanceman Keith Lloyd on the scene with part of the ice block. [© David Briscoe.]

BIGBIRD IS BACK

A paramedic who works for the Harlingen, Texas, Emergency Medical Service, James Thompson, has claimed the latest sighting of the mysterious giant bird, sporadically seen in the Rio Grande Valley since 1975. He said that on 14th Sept 1983 he was driving his ambulance some four miles east of Los Fresnos returning from South Padre Island, when the creature glided through the air in front of him. He describes it as "pterodactyl-like". It had a Brahma-bull type of hump on the back, something like a pelican's pouch at its throat, and a 5–6ft wingspan. It was not covered in feathers. "I'm quite sure it was a hide-type covering, with a black or grayish rough texture . . . (It had) almost no neck at all," and its tail, which first caught his attention, was thin and more like a fin. It was not until the creature flapped its wings that Thompson realised it was not a model plane. All the UPI reports of 16 Sept paraphrase the original report in the Harlingen (TX) *Valley Morning Star* 15 Sept 1983.

BALDNESS CURE

Farmer John Coombs, of Compton Chamberlayne, Wilts, reckons he has found the cure for baldness. After carrying sacks of cattle food he found the dust would settle on his head and shoulders and was soon licked off by a cow when he bent down. A few weeks later hair was growing on top where he'd been bald for years. He said anyone was welcome to try the cure, but warned that a cow's tongue was very rough, and was as likely to pull new growth out as it was to encourage it. *Sun, D. Telegraph* 7 March 1984.

WHAT'S GOING ON IN CHILE?

Following the controversial visions of the Virgin Mary at Villa Alemana [see MIRACLES on p44] there has been an interesting clutch of omens in the southern agricultural area of Chile. In late December 1983, the region was afflicted by a plague of Black widow spiders, and nearly 400 people have been treated for bites. No one has yet died, but when men are bitten, the poison of the *Lactrodectus mactans* causes a permanent and painful erection requiring treatment with powerful analgesics and at least 24hrs hospitalization –hence the Chilean colloquial expression for local gigolos: "Stung by a spider."

The swarming of millions of the spiders is blamed on a drought which began in September – at the height of the Villa Alemana visions – said to be the worst in the area for 40 years. Applications were being made by farmers for emergency funds, after the wheat harvests were down by half. Cloud-seeding with silver iodide produced only a useless light drizzle.

The spreading despondency was not helped when, in the first week of January this year, almost like a Biblical judgement, millions of locusts appeared "suddenly" on the shores of Lake Calafquen, south of the regional capital of Temuco. Curiously they were all dead. While locusts are regular visitors at this time of year, they usually disappear after a few days, their deaths, and in such numbers, have been unheard of in the area. Perhaps it had something to do with the 80 temors reported from the nearby volcano, Mount Villarica, that and the previous week. The volcano has an established cycle of 12 years – in 1972 it erupted leaving 30 dead and extensive damage – and is right on schedule. *Guardian* 10 Jan 1984.

DOUBLE BIRTH

• A double birth of a different kind, also involving a Karen, occurred at the Greenbank Maternity Hospital, Darlington, Co. Durham, on 7th March this year, when Karen Smith gave birth to two healthy boys within minutes of each other by Caesarian section. The remarkable thing is that they are *not* twins. They were conceived at different times and grew in different wombs. Consultant gynaecologist Edwin McKenzie said he could only find records of 10 similar cases, and has asked WHO, Geneva, for any case histories. *D. Mirror* 20 March 1984.

WHERE THERE'S SMOKE ...

A Dutch airliner, *en route* to Alaska, 9th April, reported passing through a huge "suspicious-looking cloud" shortly after leaving Tokyo. So curious was it that the pilots, thinking there had been a nuclear explosion, requested checks for radioactivity. A similar experience was reported by a Japanese cargo plane. *D. Telegraph* 10 April 1984.

Our clipping sort threw up a datum which might be related, or might not. It seems that a vast fire has burned unchecked and largely undetected for *five months* in the rain forest of East Kalimatan, Borneo. The area has never had a census, so the toll of human lives will never be known, but an aerial survey of the devastation suggests that the economic and ecological effects will be felt for at least the next 70 years. A team from the International Union for the Conservation of Nature flew there immediately news of the disaster reached their Geneva HQ, and they are calling it "the greatest ecological disaster of our time." Well, until the next one, anyway. *S. Express* 22 April 1984.

TWO HEADS

Dr Tony Matticola, of the Marine Biology Association, holds up a curious two-headed spurdog fish. Its mother aborted it when her catch was landed on the deck of the fishing vessel *Ella*, out of Plymouth. For other representatives of the epidemic of supernumary heads and limbs, see FREAKS on p38. *The Researcher* n1, Feb 1984.

THE HUMAN FLAME-THROWER

During the trial of Carole Compton, the Scottish nanny accused of setting fires in Italy, allegedly by paranormal powers [see FIRES on p46.], mention was made of the concurrrent native sensation Benedetto Supino, a 10yr-old boy who can demonstrably set objects ablaze by gazing at them.

Benedetto is the son of a carpenter, and lives in the resort of Formia, not far from Rome. A fairly shy and studious boy, he is slightly embarrassed at all the attention he is getting for purely involuntary incidents. It began, so we are told, in 1982, when a comic he was reading, in a dentist's sitting room, caught fire. One morning he awoke to find his bedclothes on fire – he was painfully burned. He does not smoke and the incident mystified and frightened him and his family. "I don't want things to catch fire. But what can I do," he shrugs.

A plastic object held by his Uncle Erasmo burst into flames as Benedetto stared at it. Everywhere he went furniture, fittings and objects smouldered. Pages of books were scorched where he touched them. Along with the fiery phenomena came the peculiar electromagnetic effects which were a familiar feature of the famous Rosenheim poltergeist case and others. Electrical objects in the house would function erratically, and the power supply actually failed several times. When he visited his father's workshop machinery would stop or not start, and the firm spent over £3000 on repairs before they made the surprising connection. Witnesses have seen his hands glow at such times.

His distraught parents began taking him to doctors, and so prominent was the boy's unwanted gift that he soon came to the attention of top scientists. Dr Giovanni Ballesio, Dean of Physical Medicine at Rome University said: "It is wrong to call him an 'Electric Boy' because he really doesn't possess any more electricity than anybody else." Prof Mario Scuncio of the Tivoli Social Medical Centre said the boy was "perfectly normal." We wonder what abnormal or paranormal means to this professor? Dr Massimo Inardi, a celebrated TV doctor, thought the boy was "clearly capable of projecting his aggressive powers on outside objects in an extraordinary manner." Though the family got no comfort from these statements, they were undoubtedly relieved when, after an examination, Archbishop Vincenzo Fagiolo pronounced the phenomenon "not malign," and warned, "Neither must his extraordinary powers be considered miracles." Meanwhile, a noted parapsychologist, Dr Demetrio Croce, has taken Benedetto under his wing, hoping to channel his "extrasensory powers of considerable force" into healing and research by teaching the boy how to control the phenomenon. *S. Mirror* 21 Aug; *Weekend* ? Nov 1983.

Benedetto Supino, holding one of his sheets which had burned through. [Photo: *Weekend* ? Nov 1983.]

NEW LIFE

A relatively newly discovered form of life – marine tube worms that live around the sulphur-ridden vents of submarine volcanoes – has turned out to be more ancient than expected. Colonies of the worms were first found in 1977, but last year impressions of the tubes that surround these mouthless worms were found off the coast of Oman, and have since been dated 95 million years old. Binghampton (NY) *Evening Press* 23 March 1984.

HIS BROTHER'S KEEPER

In a bizarre reprieve from the spectre of a tumour in his chest, Andrew Donker learned that for 21 years he had been carrying his unborn twin in his own chest cavity. The discovery was made during a medical examination for Army enlistment, and x-rays showed a huge shadow beside Andrew's heart and lungs. His application was rejected but further tests, at Liverpool's Broad Green Hospital, showed the tumour, which was nearly as big as a lung, contained human hair and embryonic characteristics. It was removed in a three-hour operation, but there was no obvious clue to its sex. A doctor said it was "a very rare thing", caused when one twin fails to develop and is absorbed by the other. *Sunday People* 11 Dec 1983.

A similar biological mishap in the case of Trina Bazlava was detected much earlier, in fact just two days after her birth, giving rise to the inevitable headline from the *Weekly World News* of 20 Dec 1983: 'BABY BORN PREGNANT!' Trina's parents are farmhands in the remote village of Bregiova, in the Rhodope Mountains of southern Bulgaria. She was 11 lbs 13 ozs, and 32 days late, when she was delivered by a farmer's wife who also serves as local midwife. The midwife said the birth was without any complications except that she noticed the bloated appearance of baby Trina's tummy. On pressing, she felt something hard in the baby's abdomen and called another "birthing woman" from the next village for another opinion. Agreeing that it was unusual, the ladies convinced the mother to let them take the baby to a hospital in Plovdiv, where xrays revealed a solid dark mass. Dr Torgev Zalav operated and removed the dead foetus of a girl. In his opinion it had been alive during the birth and had died since. Had it not been removed, he said, baby Trina might have died from septicemia. For other stories of precocious motherhood, see YOUNGEST MOTHER on p17.

MAGICAL MURDERS

- Last year the Indian government and police decided to act tougher on the "epidemic" of wife burnings. Michael Hamlyn, who sent a report to the *Times*, 9 June 1983, said that in the previous week nine young women in Delhi had died horribly at the hands of their in-laws, mainly because of dissatisfaction over dowries. The figure for 1982 was 260 burnings. "The figures are known here," writes Hamlyn, "because someone in the police department keeps count – no one in the rest of India bothers to do so much."
- A 16yr-old boy was stabbed to death by a tribal priest, near Bombay, and his blood sprinkled over paddy fields to increase the rice yield. The priest was paid by a rich farmer to kidnap the boy from a school hostel. Local social worker, Prakash Amte, said six such cases had been investigated in the last two years, but no one has been convicted because of the difficulty in securing evidence. Right out of *The Golden Bough* this one. *D. Express* 9 Jan 1984.
- At Molethlane, South Africa, on 5th Jan this year, police arrested 18 villagers in connection with the deaths of a man and woman who had been burned alive. In the following four weeks seven more people were burned at the stake and two were hanged, in the remote Lebowa region, all accused of witchcraft, specifically bringing down lightning. Eighteen witchdoctors were being held for the murders. At this time of year, every year, northern South Africa is swept daily by thunderstorms, and tribesfolk ask village elders, called *inyangas*, to "sniff out" those who have directed lightning bolts at people and property. One South African paper, the *Star*, cited by our *Sunday Express*, interviewed a mother of five children who was condemned to the stake by her village elders. She said she could not run away, as two others had done, because then another member of her family would suffer. She hoped that after her death the tribal laws would be revised, because she was innocent of any witchcraft. By mid-February the sacrificial toll had risen to 12; the latest being a man and two women who were set alight while tied to a lorry, in Zebediela. AP/*Guardian* 6 Jan; *Shropshire Star* 12 Jan; *S. Express* 15 Jan; *News at One* (ITN) 23 Jan; Reuter/*Guardian* 7 Feb; AP/*D. Telegraph, D. Express* 21 Feb 1984.
- Kuala Lumpur, Malaya, a 16yr-old boy was beheaded by a Chinese medium, as a sacrifice for a lucky lottery number. No one won the prize that week! *Standard* 20 Nov; *D. Mirror* 21 March 1984.
- In the Philippines, a tribesman killed two women with a spear because he thought they were witches. The report said he had recently been converted to Christianity! For other Manila-flavoured madness, see MANGYAN MAYHEM on p9. and BLEEDING STATUES on p6. *Sun* 7 April 1984.
- In Kenya, a 10yr-old girl narrowly escaped crucifixion thanks to a tip-off which allowed police to ambush the celebrants at midnight on Good Friday. Three people were arrested, including the girl's parents. UPI/D *D. Telegraph* 24 April 1984.

ECHOING IMAGE

From time to time we've commented on the way our existence seems to reflect back to us some of the themes of an FT shortly after publication; well here's an interesting variation, noticed by Dave Fideler. Compare this cover to the Shambhala spring 1984 catalogue with Pokkettz' marvellous illustration of a quote from Fort on p18 of last issue (*inset*).

WILD MAN

Chinese scientists are so convinced of the existence of ape-like wild men in the Shennongjia region, in Hubei Province, that a portion of the national park has been designated a special reserve for them, reported the *Workers' Daily* paper, cited in *International Herald Tribune* 25–26 Feb 1984.

This commendable action is no doubt a welcome response to the report, to the Science and Technology Institute of Guangxi Association, at the conclusion of 35 months of field research by Liu Mingzhuang of the Chinese Wildman Research Association. Since 1976, Lui and a 'Wild Man Investigation Corps' conducted five expeditions to remote parts of Hubei, Sichuan and Hunan provinces, and other reputed wildman haunts, and have recorded over 1000 footprints, 31 of them being 19 inches long, samples of glossy golden or red hairs which have both ape and human characteristics, and other material evidence. Liu said the evidence indicated that the creature, which seems active in 13 of China's 29 provinces, when full grown, is more than eight feet tall weighing about 550-lbs. Three members of the team had even seen one, in the Shennongjia Mountains the previous year (1982).
UPI/New York *Post* 19 Dec 1983.

FALLING OBJECT HITS PLANE

Thanks to the skill of its crew, a Chinese military plane landed safely after a mystery "falling object" lopped off a major portion of its tailplane. Our source cites a Canton newspaper story in which Cpt Sun Ejun and his crew were officially commended following the incident on 2nd November 1983, at 36,000 feet over Northern China.

No further details were given, and the Chinese Embassy in London has not responded to our queries – not surprising considering a military vehicle was involved. Could it have been one of those pesky ice chunks? like the one that fell on Wuxi, eastern China in April last year [see FT40p32]. If so, the idea of cometary origin would look more valid. *Lloyds List* 14 Dec 1983.

HOMING VALUABLES

In 1972 Ricky Shipman went swimming with friends near Sunset Beach, North Carolina. His wallet slipped out of his swimsuit pocket and was lost in the waters of the Atlantic. But 11 yrs later his driving licence was returned to him by N.C. Gause, who owns a restaurant at Little River. A friend of Gause had been fishing near Sunset Beach, in August 1983, and caught a fairly large Spanish mackerel. Upon slicing it open he found the licence, and on it Shipman's details. Shipman – who said the photo of himself is still "crystal clear" thinks the licence, encased in plastic, was snapped up when the wallet eventually disintegrated. AP/St Catherines, Canada, *Standard* 10 Sept 1983.

John Bembers, now a retired fisherman of Sioux Falls, South Dakota, lost his watch while fishing in Lake Michigan in 1976. The watch was eventually discovered in the stomach of a 42lb salmon, caught by Thomas Kresnak, of Grand Rapids, Michigan, in 1979. Kresnak said it took him a few years to trace Bembers, because acids in the fish's stomach had eroded the inscription. UPI/Schenectady (NY) *Gazette* 16 Feb 1984.

OLD JOKE

Our fossil chuckle for this issue comes, tantalizingly from the *Sun* for 14 May 1984. An international symposium of 500 paleontologists, called in Granada, Spain, to look at the newly discovered skull of a "prehistoric man", had to be hurriedly called off, on the 13th, because the skull was identified as that of a donkey, albeit a million year-old one.

LOYAL DOGS

• When Dorothy Ashworth, 71, lay freezing to death on a beach at Barton on Sea, Hants, a young dog kept an all-night vigil beside her, licking her face and tugging at her coat, until a search party found them in the morning. Despite the dog's attention the old lady died of hypothermia in hospital. The remarkable thing is that the dog, Smartie, a mere 6mths old, belongs, not to the old lady, but to the hotel where she was staying. *Sun* 7 Dec 1983.

• A more bizarre tale involves a spaniel who belongs to an unidentified man in Butte, Montana, who so loved his master he just couldn't get enough of him. The man was working on a house when a power saw severed all five fingers of his right hand. Before his horrified colleagues' eyes they fell to the floor and the thumb was gobbled up by the dog. Happily the thumb was retrieved 20 minutes later, after the dog was made to vomit. Four lengthy operations by microsurgeon, Tristan Stronger, restored three fingers and the wandering thumb to their rightful places. Talk about biting the hand that feeds! *Weekly World News* 13 March 1984.

MISSING SHIPPING

• Firstly, do we have a Bay of Biscay Triangle myth developing? It is not a frivolous issue amongst Italian sailors, who are said to be "stiff with fear" after a second Italian ship has vanished in a region 200 miles southwest of the French port of Brest. The last message from the *Tito Campenella*, at 10.47 am on 22 Dec 1983, read: "All's well; no problems." Since then there has been no sign of the sheet-metal carrying ship, the captain and his wife, and the 23-man crew, bound for her home port of Savona, near Genoa. Ships and planes searched the area for days finding no sign of wreckage, and the weather at the time of the last message, although choppy, was not dangerous. Gianurria Carta, the Italian Minister of Shipping, said: "It is a baffling case." And what makes it more puzzling is the almost identical disappearance of the *Marina di Equa*, almost exactly two days previously, in the same area, also involving an "all's well" message. *S. Express* 29 Jan 1984.

• On the other side of the world, a listing American oil-drilling ship, *Glomar Java Sea*, vanished last October off Haiwan island in the South China Sea. Its last radio message was calm and clear, an American board of inquiry was told, but was suddenly cut off. The sunken wreck of the ship was later found, but there were no bodies and the two lifeboats were missing. One member of the board said: "This is not a normal accident and there is no precedent." Some relatives believe the crew might have drifted 90 miles to Vietnam, where they might be still alive. *D. Telegraph* 31 Jan 1984.

• Finally, an echo of the *Mary Celeste* . . . A Dutch freighter, *Pergo*, steamed across the North Sea, engines running, lights blazing, and not a soul on board. Its five-man crew abandoned it when it got into "difficulties" in the Norwegian sector, and it kept going for 200 miles before running aground on the Scottish coast near Dunbar. *D. Telegraph* 17 Jan 1984.

FT ON TV

Behind the scenes more and more media men are beginning to realise the uniqueness of our archive. Just as we helped Yorkshire TV's *Arthur C. Clarke's Mysterious World* off to a good start a couple of years back, so too we proved useful to Orbis' *The Unexplained*, which is being spun off like mad (see book review of *Incredible Phenomena*, this issue) as the TU staff have expressed to us on several occasions. FT is also being used as a source for 'File of the Fantastic', in TV-am's *Datarun* on Saturday mornings.

We recently learned from Yorks TV that a new Arthur C. Clarke series is being filmed for showing next year, on the 'World of Strange Powers', but so far we have not had anything to do with it. However publicity for us has come in quite a different form, a play called *Unfair Exchanges*, written by Ken Campbell, to be shown on BBC1 or BBC2 later this year. Directed by Gavin Millar, and produced by Kenith Trodd, it stars Ken, David *Time Bandits* Rappoport and Oscar-nominee Julie Walters in a story of a housewife who stumbles on the fact that the international telephone and computer networks have become a living entity. Ken tells us that a magazine called *Fortean Times* is featured in the plot and various of our issues are waved prominently at the camera. We can hardly wait to see it!

Finally, we have just learned that BBC TV are to show Dickens' vast novel, *Bleak House*, this coming Autumn. The eight one-hour episodes are produced by Jonathan Powell and star the very excellent Michael Hordern. Among his prolific interests Dickens found time to investigate falls of fishes and frogs, and the spontaneous combustion of human beings, and *Bleak House*, as most Forteans know by now, features a scene in which the character Crook is incinerated by SHC. After critics reacted with disbelief to the incident, Dickens carried out an extensive and literate defense of SHC, claiming he had examined the historical authorities and cases "as a Judge might have done." We'll see just how well, in these days of astounding video special effects, the BBC dramatizes the incident.

HOLE IN ONE!

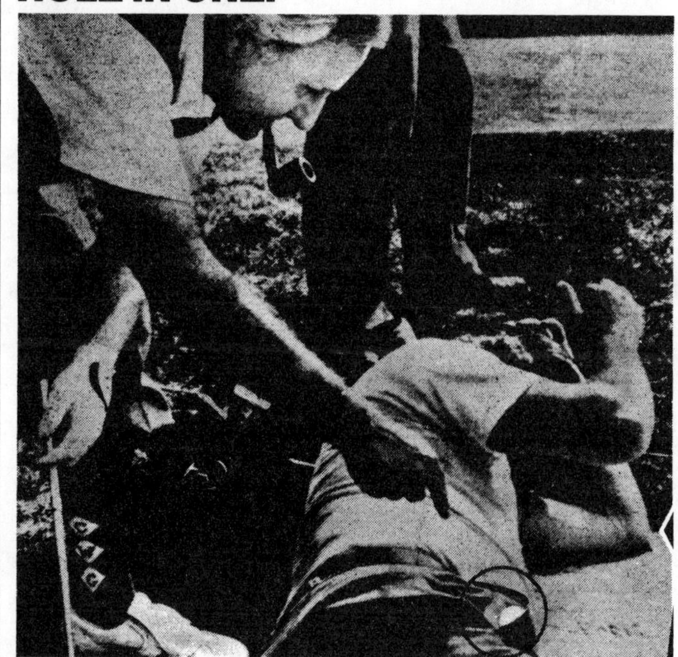

The camera records the extraordinary scene during a Pebble Beach, California, golf tournament, when a ball landed in the pocket of spectator A.L. Baker. He had to lie perfectly still while contestant Clive Greavers (*piped and pointing*) figured out what to do next. *Weekly World News* 13 March 1984.

CRIMES OF FASHION

We know Life is a spectacle, but even we have to boggle at the latest manifestation of human idiocy. It seems that police in Philadelphia and New York are concerned enough about a craze for an expensive brand of West German spectacle frames to have issued a public warning. The glasses, made by Creations Cazal, are in such demand that a growing number of people have been mugged and at least four people have been murdered for their Cazals. *D. Telegraph* 2 April 1984.

Bearing in mind this intelligence comes so close to Fool's Day, we might be tempted to think it a publicity stunt, in poor taste, on behalf of the importing company Ultra/Palm Optical – but the report convincingly gives details of those who died for their style. But jest or not, we know enough not to be too surprised if it should be true.

CROCS IN THE SEWERS

Municipal workers in the ancient sewers below Paris, on 8th March 1984, found a young crocodile wandering aimlessly through the dark, dank tunnels, which are now a tourist attraction and home to partying gangs of punques. Ten firemen called to the scene overpowered the 2ft 7ins reptile, thought to be about four years old, and carried it, bound and gagged, to the Jardin des Plantes, where it now sports itself in a vivarium. AFP/*Times*, AP/*Guardian, Sun, D. Mirror*, Paris *Liberation* 9 March; Reuter/*Arab News* 11 March 1984.

Perhaps our folklore is catching up with us, for these stories of sewer-dwelling crocs are popping out at us all over the place. The incident of most note prior to the Parisian saurian (above) happened almost a year previously, to 19-yr-old Barry Robertson, who was minding his own business, trucking down a sidewalk in Cairns, Queensland, when a 1.20 metre crocodile lunged at him from a gutter drainhole. Only Barry's cowboy boots saved him from a nasty leg injury. A passing taxi-driver helped him chase the animal. *Sun* 14 May; Paris *Presse-Ocean* 15 May 1983.

BVM VISIONS

The visions in Yugoslavia are continuing. We last mentioned the sightings at Citluk, in FT38p20–22. Our correspondent in Yugoslavia, Milos Krmelj, sent us a long report, but this did not add substantially to our summary. However, we have heard from him that there is another outbreak of BVM sightings elsewhere, and hope to have a further report from him before long.

In the meantime, we note that a Belgrade Catholic newspaper, cited by the *Guardian* (9 Dec 1983) reports the sentence of a schoolgirl to 15 days in jail for claiming to have had a vision of the Virgin Mary, but whether this is related to the series of Citluk, or something else entirely, is not stated.

For other BVMs see p44.

MISTAKEN IDENTITY

□ When police announced on February 19th, 1983, that the body of a young climber had been found in the Cairngorms, Scotland, Angus and Ethel Clunas thought the description fitted that of their son, Stephen, and rushed to the morgue. Stephen's brother-in-law, Fraser Ross, who accompanied them, declared the dead man's resemblance to Stephen was "quite remarkable". Moreover, the man was wearing the same design of sweater, Parka anorak, underwear and gold watch as the missing Clunas. But 24yr-old Stephen, who had gone bird-watching, had spent the weekend at a hotel. He did not read the reports of his 'death', and the mistake only came to light when one of his friends, who had just had tea with him, heard of his supposed demise on the local radio. His shocked parents were reunited with Stephen on the day set for the wrong body's funeral. The identity of the dead man, who was barefoot, remains a mystery.

□ This case has strong parallels with the famous story of Albert Steer [FT33p19], an itinerant gardener who vanished in May 1907. Shortly afterwards, a man was found drowned, and was identified as Steer by his son and daughter. Both Steer and the body were one-eyed, had a crushed toe and a dent over one eyebrow. Two months after the dead man was buried Steer turned up.

□ Almost as curious is the note in the *Guardian* 27 March 1984 of a West German, wrongly imprisoned for bank robbery simply because he had a long nose and had been in the wrong place at the wrong time. Klaus-Peter Zimmer's six year sentence was based on the evidence of a mistaken eyewitness and a photograph of the real bandit who looked similar and who also had a prominent nose, said a "court-appointed nose expert". Zimmer was released, having served two years.

THE PLAGUE HAMSTERS

Like a real-life paraphrase of *The Plague Dogs* comes the story that three hamsters, whose brains were injected with a virus, were declared "missing for a fortnight" from a laboratory at Yale University, New Haven, Connecticut. The virus was one which affects the human nervous system with invariably fatal results, but people in the environs were assured there was no cause for alarm. We wonder what *does* constitute 'cause for alarm'? But what really caught our eye was the temporary nature of the poor creatures' escape. It was said that the labs were in sealed rooms from which escape was "practically impossible", and which were no doubt thoroughly searched, and yet the animals were presumably found in these rooms or back in their cages two weeks later. One hamster might be elusive, but three of them? We like to think that they sought relief by teleportation, and the notion of three neuro-virus-ridden teleporting hamsters on the loose we hand to any of you writers at a loss for an idea. *D. Telegraph* 18 Oct 1983.

DINOSAUR HUNT

In December 1981, Herman Regusters, a Pasadena space scientist and his wife Kia VanDusen, a chiropractor and psychologist, returned from Africa to tell a packed news conference about the dinosaur they had seen on a Congolese lake. They had no photos, no footprints, no convincing evidence. It was a debacle, the likes of which the world hadn't seen since Professor Challenger was laughed out of a London Zoological Institute meeting. But the Regusters were not dismayed. They are convinced enough to have arranged a second expedition, with permission of the Congolese government. The creature they saw and heard on Lake Tele was brontosaurus-like, but smaller, about the length of two hippos. It had a long neck, small head, and gray, shiny skin. The natives call the creature *Mokele Mbembe*.

Since then, they have had sound recordings analyzed which do not match any known large animal in the region, and droppings, believed to be from the creature, were still being studied. The first trip was quite an ordeal and Regusters suffered the effects of malnutrition, exhaustion and tsetse fly bites for months afterwards. They say they will be better prepared this time, when their team leaves in December. Some encouragement has come from the People's Republic of the Congo's own expedition to the shallow equatorial lake, surrounded by swampy forest. Led by biologist Marcellin Agnagna, the team claimed to have seen the creature (see drawing) but describe it differently (ie. brown head and shiny black body). They were able to watch it at a distance for quite a long time, but the photographic evidence proved almost useless. Fuller reports of the Agnagna's expedition are in *Cryptozoology* v2 p103f, and (an interview) *ISC Newsletter* v3 n2 p7f (summer 1984).

The Regusters have formed a non-profit outfit – the Unicorne Research Foundation – to raise money for their search, and this time hope to include more conventional observations too. Last time they found gorillas where none were known to exist before; this time they hope to spot the pygmies reported by natives to live in the area but which haven't been seem for 40 years. We wish them success, and hope the Mokele Mbembe proves less fabulous than their totemic unicorn. Philadelphia (PA) *Enquirer*, 4 March 1984.

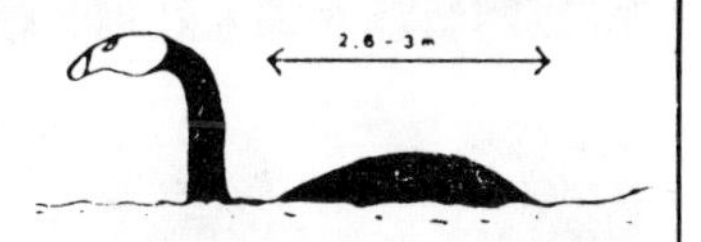

Marcelin Agnagna's drawing of the large unidentified animal seen on Lake Tele.

SLEEP-DRIVER

In an incident curiously reminiscent of the classic cases of somnambulism investigated by pioneering French psychologists towards the end of the last century, a 15 yr-old Hampshire boy drove a car miles in his sleep.

The unnamed boy woke up at 3.30 am on 6th Dec last year, in his father's car, in the middle of Southampton, 27 miles from his home in Portsmouth. The father, who thought the boy was in bed, was woken by a phone call from the lad, who found himself in the car wearing pyjamas and dressing gown, unable to get home. The father called the police, who said the boy was "very confused" and waiting by the car. Even more curious than the fact that the boy had driven the car so far without any mishap is his protestation, confirmed by his father, that he didn't know how to drive and had never driven before! A Dr Jacob Empson, of Hull University's Psychology Department, said the incident was "quite extraordinary. I have never heard of anything like this. People who sleepwalk usually do things they would normally do."

A police spokesman said there would be no charges because although the story "sounds incredible, we have no reason to disbelieve it." Instead they recommended the boy, who had some history of sleepwalking, seek treatment. Portsmouth *News, Sun, D. Express, D. Star, D. Telegraph* all 7 Dec 1983.

THE OLD AND THE HAIRY

☐ As a result of a recent national census, China has discovered it has 3,765 centenarians, two-thirds of them women. The oldest is a man named Kuerban-yosheng, at 130 yrs-old, of Xinjiang, Central Asia. In commenting on this, Hugh Davies, Peking correspondent of the *Daily Telegraph* (13 Feb 1984), remembered that foreign correspondents being shown around that city last year were told that a 136 yr-old man lived in a vineyard in nearby Turfan. On asking to interview him, they were told he's just been killed in a motorbike accident.

☐ Li Xiaomo is one of China's extraordinary number of hairy people. Her name means 'Little Hairy', because she was born with thick glossy black hair all over, except for her palms and soles. But she also had another unwanted claim to fame: two enormous extra breasts, weighing nearly 22lbs each, which were amputated in 1980. According to the *Workers' Daily* Li had just given birth to a normal child. Reuter/*Standard* 2 March 1984.

FISHES FALL IN EAST LONDON

Ron Langton shows the two remaining flounders. [© Newham *Recorder* 7 June 1984.]

At the end of May, your Editor was alerted to a possible fall of fishes in the London borough of Newham, where, as fate would have it, I am currently residing. "Oh dear!," I thought with all the enthusiasm of a ufologist who finds himself abducted, "There goes my credibility!" The call had come from FT's mole (or is it carp) in the Natural History Museum's Fish Dept, Jim Chambers, who had been contacted by the *Newham Recorder* for comment.

I phoned the *Recorder* to learn that their story came from one Ronald Langton, who lives at the end of Central Park Road, where West Ham have their football ground at Upton Park. I trudged there, cursing because my knee hurt and I'd started at the wrong end of this long road. Near the house was a fish and chip shop, whose owner I cynically elevated to suspicious godhood alongside the notorious Fishmonger of Worcester. Ron Langton, a large man and typical East London character, greeted me affably and quickly got down to the matter of the fish.

The fish had been discovered on Monday morning, 28th May, by builder Edward Rodmell and his son, who were altering and decorating the property for Mr Langton. They found four fish: two flat ones (see photo), which he thought were like dabs, were found in the narrow yard; a longer one "rather like a whiting" which had since been accidentally thrown out with some rubble; and another could be seen from an upstairs window still on the red tile roof. Mr Rodmell kindly went up a ladder to retrieve this for me, and spotted a head and body of a similar fish in the rain gutter. Whether these belonged to the same fish or were the remains of two was hard to tell. My visit was on the 5th June, by which time they had been alternatively drenched and dried out at least once in nine days, and been pecked by birds. Ron was certain the fish that was thrown away was different from the two long thin ones we had recovered.

That made four specimens in hand and two lost. I began to ponder on the familiar characteristic of the extreme localization of the fall – there had been none in the neighbouring gardens, nor any other in the area that Ron had heard of. Ron's cat gave me a smug, sleepy look that suggested the feline population of Upton Park might have beaten me to any other evidence. Ron's wife said that while walking up Green Street on the day of the fall, she had seen another fish, like the long ones, in the gutter of the road near Upton Park underground station, about half a mile from their house. That made six.

The two flat fish had been kept in tapwater for three days, frozen for several days and thawed for several days by the time I saw – make that smelled – them. The long fishes were well dried out and stiff. At arm's length I goaded the tangible five into a food flask, and the next day (6th June) uncorked them under Jim Chambers' nose. His colleague, Oliver Crimmen, quickly identified the flat fish as flounders (*Platichthys flesus*) and the long ones as smelts (*Osmerus eperlanus*). I left them at the BM (Nat. Hist.) – the first specimens of fallen fish they'd actually examined – as the foundation of the FT collection.

The *Newham Recorder* put the story on the front page of the 7 June 1984 edition, and included my phone number. That evening, a man called, saying he found about 30 fishes in his garden. He lived in Canning Town, about one and a half miles east of Ron's house. It was not a convenient time to call so he promised to ring later – he never did! But I think he told the truth, because a little later a caller from another area of Canning Town, about a mile and a quarter south of Ron's house, said he had four fish. His description of them was ambiguous: he said they were flat, "like the ones in the photo", but also said they were silver. The flounders were flat and dark with a pale underside – only the smelts could be called silver, and they weren't flat! Perhaps they were like the one that Ron's builder threw away. Domestic circumstances prevented any opportunity to see the fish, and the man did not leave his phone number or respond to my letter. A check with street vendors of newspapers, and the Newham refuse collection department brought no recall of fishes being found on streets. So, there we have four known locations – all roughly on the perimeter of a mile and a half diameter circle. So much for localization!

Another fact: no one saw the fish fall. In each case the fish were found, on the morning of 28th May, under conditions suggesting they fell from above. We can't even tell if the fish were alive when they landed! The night of Sunday/Monday, at the tail end of a Bank Holiday, had rained heavily and thunderously. Ron Langton supposed the fish had come down in the night with the rain. Ron remembers the heavy thunder preceding the curious slapping sounds which came with the rain as he watched TV on the night of the 27th May. Others I spoke to accepted the water-

Fishfall →

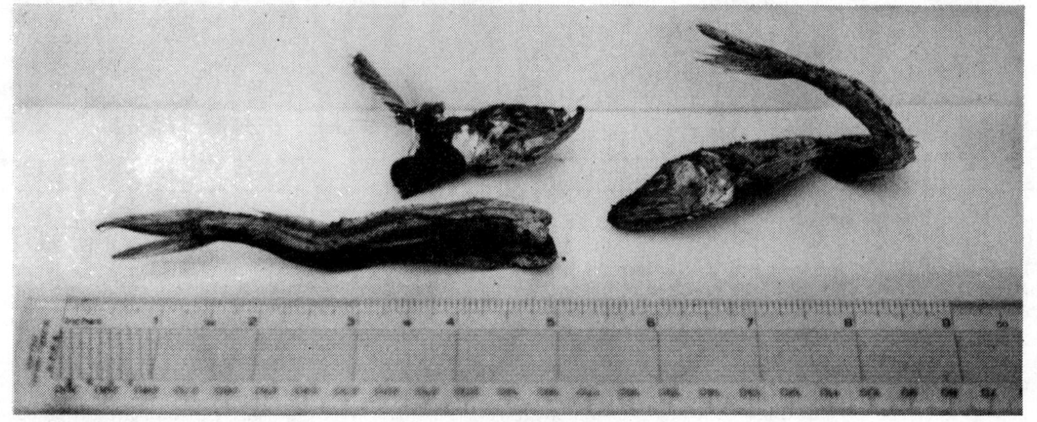

The smelts retrieved from Ron Langton's roof nine days after the East Ham fish fall. [© Fortean Picture Library.]

→ **FISHFALL**

spout idea as reasonable. One man rang me with his notion that a flight of herons, from a heronry at Barking, had been attacked by blackbirds and disgorged their breakfast. He had seen such attacks before – though not disgorgings – and it was clear he didn't know of the other reports of fallen fish.

The most obvious hypothesis was the old faithful; a waterspout. The storm and the proximity of the Thames (not more than two miles away from the furthest report location– made this a strong possibility. Indeed, the head of the BMNH Fish Dept (whose name eludes me) said that flounders and smelts were "just what you'd expect in the Thames below Newham." But lest you think that wraps it up, I found no evidence of waterspouts in the Thames that night, nor (according to the area coastguards, who said they'd certainly remember if one had been reported) in the Thames estuary. A brief check with the London Weather Centre confirmed that the dense rain-clouds and gusting winds were not conducive, in their opinion, to waterspouts developing on the Thames.

So where does that leave us? Your guess is as good as mine! There was some coverage of the story in the nationals, and area TV news, on 8 June 1984, but mainly derived from the *Recorder* write-up, and getting an appalling number of things wrong. We have forwarded a more concise and technical report to our esteemed colleagues at the *Journal of Meteorology*.

HAIR BANDIT STRIKES AGAIN

Lynn Quay, 20, (*pictured*), thought the man who pushed up against her as she browsed in the Westland shopping mall, in Columbus, Ohio, was a "lunatic" after her purse. Then she noticed the dark-haired, bearded man was holding a 10-inch long lock of her own waist-length hair and a razor blade. The dis-tressed Lynn, who had let her hair grow for 14 years, yelled and gave chase as the man fled, but she lost him in the parking lot.

Security chief at the mall, Cal Potter, said this incident, on 12th Dec 1983, was similar to another the previous week, in which the unfortunate girl did not know a portion of her hair was missing until her husband noticed it when she got home. "Whoever did it has a long hair fetish," he said.

Ummm . . . this is our third Columbus item so far this issue! AP/Boston *Herald*, AP/Indianapolis *News*, AP/Attleboro (MA) *Sun-Chronicle* 16 Dec; AP/Beaumont (TX) *Enterprise* 17 Dec AP/*Grand Rapids Press* (MI)19 Dec 1983.

CLIPPING CREDITS

Our thanks to the following contributors to this issue: Tom Adams, James Alexander, Larry Arnold/PSI, Alice Ashton, BM Barter, Lionel Beer, P A Belding, Janet & Colin Bord, Jean-Louis Brodu, P Burch, Peter Christie, Loren Coleman, R Collyns, Mike Crowley, Jim Darroch, Mike Dash, A J Dixon, Dr F Dokter, Martin Eads, Philip Hope Evans, David Fideler, John Fullerton, Alan Gardiner, G M Garner, Ron Gauntlett, D Geall, Bob Girard, Mike Goss, P Gunkel, Brian Hain, Chris Hall, Mark A Hall, John Halliday, Tony Healy, Tuuri Heporauta, Michael Hoffman, Susan Kavanaugh, Mark Kindt, D Laird, J Lang, Bill Leet, J Lewis, John Macmillan, Nick Malloret, Valerie Martin, Liz Massey, John Michell, Mark Moravec, Angie Murphy, Ian Murray, Roger Musson, Ray Nelke, Steve Ogden, Steve Parker, Dennis Prater, Nigel Pennick, Michel Raynal, David Rees, Rickard Pere, Andy Roberts, Paul Screeton, Dick Seary, Fiorella Severi, Doc Shiels, Bob Skinner, Anthony Smith, M G Smith, Philip E Smith, P L Stiles, Albert Thomas, P R Thomas, J Tierney, Andy Townsend, Joseph Trainor, UFO Newsclipping Service, Dwight Whalen, V White, Jake Williams, Steve Wrathall, Joe Zarzynski.

PHENOMENOMIX
HUNT EMERSON
GULLY BULL, ACE REPORTER FOR FORTEAN TIMES, IS SHARING AN ESSPRESSO WITH BEBOP SAX PLAYER MAX ZILLION...
I BEEN READING THIS GREAT BOOK, MAX, ABOUT STATUES THAT BLEED AND WEEP!
Y'DON'T SAY! WEED AN' BLEEP?...
YES - USUALLY STATUES OF RELIGIOUS PERSONS!
WELL, THAT'S INTERESTING!
COZ I ONCE HAD A STATUE OF A RELIGIOUS FIGURE THAT KINDA BLED!
'ZAT SO?
YEAH.... 1943 IT WAS...
WHIPS OUT REPORTERS NOTEBOOK AND STARTS SCRIBBLING
I FOUND THIS COOL LITTLE PORCY-LANE FIGURE OF LESTER YOUNG IN A THRIFT SHOP OFF 52ND STREET....
1¢
25
LESTER
15¢
WELL, ONE DAY, MAN, THAT STATOOETTE COMMENCE GIVIN' FORTH WIT' THIS BLOOD-TYPE LIQUID!
SPLOR
SCIENTIFIC TESTS REVEALED THAT IT WASN'T ACTUALLY BLOOD....
shlp shlp HEY! EL VINO!
WOW! I EXPECT YOU TREASURED EACH RARE DROP!
NO NEED TO, MAN... THERE WUZ GALLEONS OF THE STUFF!
SCRIBBLE SCRIBBLE
LIKE, FAUCETSVILLE! CATS CAME FROM MILES AROUND, AND WE JUST HANDED OUT BEAKERS OF IT TO EVERYONE!
slurp
yum
OBOY ANOTHER GALLEON FULL
ALL THE CATS WUZ AGREED IT WUZ A SOLID-GONE A-1 FRONT-LINE MIRACLE!
Hip to sip
Cool to drool
Flash to Splash
ALL THAT SUMMER OF '43 WE HAD A BALL! ME'N 'BIRD'N'MONK'N'DIZZY'N'KENNY..... Hot Damn!
'Sh'av Sh'more! el vino!
Righteous Juice! Sets me loose!
Where's ma horn! I wanna blow some jazz!
Oh Man Gimme Some mo' dat miracle!
Well all reet!
.......AND ON THE WAY WE INVENTED BEBOP!
God, I'm too drunk to be doin' this!!
....Dunno what I'm playin!
....I can hardly see my hands...
....Blarg.... Too pissed for this....
Hey-dis is kinda good. OK!
FASCINATING! SO IT'S TRUE THAT BEBOP WAS COSMICALLY INSPIRED!!
WELL, MAN.... $30 WOULD SAY IT WAS TRUE!
A FEW DAYS LATER, GULLY IS TELLING BEBOP DRUMMER NOISY LABONGO ABOUT HIS REPORT ON THE PARANORMAL ORIGINS OF MODERN JAZZ....
....ZILLION TOLD YOU THAT? YOU GOT THIRTY BUCKS? OK-LEMME TELL YA WHAT REALLY OCCURRED! SEE, ONE NIGHT I SEE DIS FLYIN' SAUCER..... MUSTA BEEN 1942.....
Wow! More Truth!
HOW MUCH TRUTH CAN YOU AFFORD??

Science Horizons

Compiled by William R Corliss

Hot Plants

You've heard of hot potatoes, but they aren't naturally hot. However, in the early spring skunk cabbages are and so are some philodendrons during their flowering periods. In fact, some philodendrons burn fat to generate their heat, just like animals. Metabolism based on fats allows some philodendrons to reach temperatures of 124°F. In terms of their rates of metabolism, they rival those of the humming birds. Furthermore, philodendrons can regulate their chemical fires, whereas skunk cabbages, which burn only starch, consume all their stored energy like a rocket in one snow-melting crescendo. Why do plants generate heat? Apparently to attract pollinating insects. A hot skunk cabbage poking through the snow is the only food in sight for early spring insects, while the philodendrons may attract pollinating insects who like to bask or mate in warm places. (Blakeslee, Sandra; New York *Times*, August 9, 1983, p. C4. Cr. P. Gunkel) *Are plants really "lower" forms of life?*

Incredible Phosphorescent Display on the China Sea

On April 29, 1982, the m.v. *Siam* encountered – or perhaps *caused* – a most baffling display of marine phosphoresence lasting some 2½ hours. The complete report is 6 pages long, with 8 diagrams, so only the highlights can be reported here. As is often the case, this display began with parallel phosphorescent bands (2 sets) rushing toward the ship at about 40 mph. They were 50–100 cm *above* the sea surface. The bands then changed into two rotating wheels; then a third wheel formed. All three rotated counterclockwise, with their hubs 300, 300, and 150 meters from the ship. The spokes stretched to the horizon. The display ceased for about 20 minutes and recommenced with four systems of onrushing parallel bands, which soon metamorphosed into four rotating wheels. Radar, visible light (from and Aldis lamp), and engine revolution appeared to have no effect on the spectacle. Next, evenly distributed, circular, flashing patches of brilliant blue-white light appeared all around the ship out to a distance of about 150 meters. This system of patches flashed away simultaneously with the wheel display. The patches varied from 15–60 cm in diameter, and flashed 114 times per minute. When an Aldis lamp was played steadily on the patches, nothing happened. When the lamp was flashed, the whole array of flashing patches *disappeared*, only to reappear in about 2 minutes. Each patch seemed to consist of worm-like segments 2½ cm long, 2½ cm apart. The worms were all aligned perpendicular to a vector from the ship. In contrast to the bands and wheels, the worms were located about 5 cm *below* the surface of the water. Water samples revealed no luminous organisms – only a few animals a few millimeters long. The sea was calm, visibility excellent, although atmosphere electrical activity could be seen all around. (Kuzmanov, Zoran; "Phosphorescence in the China Sea," *Marine Observer*, 53:85, 1983.) *The luminous "worms" resemble the spinning crescents sometimes associated with radar.*

Horsing Around with Evolution

In the Borrego Badlands of California, Barbara Quinan has stumbled upon the fossilized skull of a modern horse, E. equus. The skull was found in situ, partly mineralized, a process usually requiring hundreds of thousands of years. Mammoth bones punctuate the strata immediately above and below those containing the horse fossil. The paleontological anomaly is that modern horses were supposed to have evolved in Asia and not brought to the New World until the Spanish explorers landed. The only way to evade rewriting horse history is to: (1) Cast doubt on the dating of the strata, or (2) Insist that the fossil is not really a horse at all but a similar animal, such as the long-headed zebra. (Smith, Gordon; "E. Equus: Immigrant or Emigrant?" *Science 84*, 5:76, April 1984)

The Oklo Phenomenon and Evolution

A decade ago, French scientists discovered the remains of a natural nuclear reactor at Oklo, Gabon, in Africa. Somehow nature had concentrated enough uranium-235 in one place to start a chain reaction, with the attendant production of heat and radiation. Now U-235 is radioactive, and there is now much less around than in past geological eras. This has led some scientists to speculate that many more Oklo phenomena may have flamed momentarily in earlier times, especially Precambrian days. The mutagenic radiation from such natural reactors could have been a major driving force in evolution. ("Natural Reactors Helped Evolution," *New Scientist*, 100:737, 1983.)

An Ordovician Hammer?

This article begins with a startling photograph of an obvious hammer partly embedded in rock. Data: "1. The hammer was discovered on the Liano uplift, south west of the Paluxy River, Texas, U.S.A. The Llano uplift is a granite intrusion covered by Ordovician sandstone. 2. The hammer was discovered within a concretion of shell-bearing sandstone. (Initial reports incorrectly labelled it as limestone.) 3. The hammer handle is probably of spruce wood. 4. The interior of the handle is partly coalified. 5. The handle contains pockets of fluid. 6. The wood in the handle was hard and fibrously intact when discovered. 7. When the stone surface was first removed the iron (alloy?) head was shiny and began to corrode only several months later. 8. The concretion contained fossil shells which can just be seen at the top left of the picture. (Nacula Pelecypods). 9. When the concretion was first broken open there was a significant space around the hammer." ("Ordovician Hammer Report," *Ex Nihilo*, 6:16, no. 3, 1984). *If the hammer was really deposited with the sandstone, it would be about 400 million years old, according to present geological dating. This item was taken from a creationist publication, which has an obvious stake in undermining the prevailing scheme of geological dating. Nowhere does the report say the concretion was found in situ in the Ordovician sandstone. It may have been loose on the surface. Furthermore, concretions often contain peculiar things, as described in UNKNOWN EARTH. And finally, the discovery was made near the Paluxy River, where one also finds intermingled dinosaur and human-like tracks! The whole business is at once fascinating and suspicious.*

Rubberneckia

The long-standing belief that unlimited rotary motion is impossible in animals has been shattered. It was, after all, a very reasonable assumption, because necks and other appendages turn only so far before bones and muscles begin to snap. Well, it seems that inside termite guts there resides a single-celled animal with a head that rotates constantly 30 times a minute. Since none of its membranes shear during rotation, we must infer that membranes are basically fluid structures rather than solids as supposed. This animal, called Rubberneckia, has a shaft running the full length of its body plus a motor of undetermined character. To make Rubberneckia even more bizarre, thousands of tiny, rod-like bacteria occupy long grooves on the cell's surface. Like galley slaves, the bacteria row with their flagella row to keep Rubberneckia moving – a curious symbiotic relationship. (Cooke, Robert; "A Tale to Make Your Head Spin," Boston *Globe*, March 20, 1984, p. 1.)

A Mysterious Object

Winnipeg, Manitoba. "On January 14, 1983, I observed a perfectly round black orb crossing the sun. It started at 17h54m23s Universal Time and ended at 17h-54m26s Universal Time and lasted three seconds. On a projected solar disk with a diameter of 18 centimetres, the object had a diameter of one-half centimetre." (Lohvinenko, Todd; "A Mysterious Object," *Royal Astronomical Society of Canada, National Newsletter*, 77: L19, 1983). *The object travelled too fast to be an intramercurial planet; too slowly for a meteor.*

Hushing up the Guadeloupe Skeleton

Just offshore of Guadeloupe, in the West Indies, lies a kilometer-long formation of extremely hard limestone dated as Miocene, or about 25-million years old. Nothing surprising so far! However, history records that in the late 1700s, many human skeletons – all indistinguishable from modern man – were excavated from this limestone. One of the quarried specimens, ensconced in a 2-ton slab, was shipped to the British Museum. It arrived in 1812 and was placed on public display. With the ascendance of Darwinism, the fossil skeleton was quietly spirited away to the basement. The discovery of these human remains has been well-documented in the scientific literature. Here is another pertinent geological fact: the limestone formation in question is situated 2–3 meters below a 1-million-year-old coral reef. If the limestone is truly 25 million years old, the human evolutionary timetable is grossly in error. Even if this is not the case, and the bones are merely 1 million years old or so, as required by the coral reef, fully developed men lived in the New World long before the Bering Land Bridge went into service. The only way a serious geological or archeological anomaly can be avoided is to predicate that the limestone formation was laid down in the last 10–20,000 years – something that doesn't seem too likely. (Cooper, Bill; "Human Fossils from Noah's Flood," *Ex Nihilo*, 1:6, no. 3, 1983.) *This sort of dating puzzle is manna to the scientific creationists. It is thus not surprising to discover that* Ex Nihilio *is published by the Creation Science Foundation of Australia. Nevertheless, the Guadeloupe skeletons truly exist – it's just that the creationists seem to be the only ones talking about them.*

A Delusion of Doubles

R.J. Berson has reviewed 33 cases of a curious delusion called Capgras' Syndrome. People displaying this syndrome believe that important people in their lives (family members, etc.) have been replaced by exact doubles. No hallucinations or illusions are involved; rather it is a *belief*. Those afflicted with Capgras' Syndrome may even believe that they themselves are represented somewhere by a double they never see. Not all persons with close emotional ties are believed to be doubled; and these unreplaced persons are always identified accurately. People with these beliefs usually possess normal perceptions and memories but are (obviously) disturbed emotionally with paranoid tendencies. (Berson, Robert J.; "Capgras' Syndrome," *American Journal of Psychiatry*, 140: 969, 1983.) *This strange mental state is apparently not related to autoscopy, where one hallucinates one's self. See UNFATHOMED MIND.*

Science Frontiers *is extracted from William Corliss' bimonthly collection of digests from current literature, which is sent free to regular customers of his publications. For more details write to* **The Sourcebook Project, Box 107, Glen Arm, MD 21057, USA.**

Do mermaids exist? It's an ancient topic, but one recently brought alive by a discovery in Papua New Guinea, and its unsavory consequence.

OF MERMAIDS AND MEN

While the world has been enchanted by the charms of Daryl Hannah playing a voluptuous mermaid in the film *Splash!*, an alleged race of genuine mermaids has been the subject of a right old ding dong in cryptozoological circles.

It all started in late 1982 when the International Society of Cryptozoology (ICS) published a report by Roy Wagner in the newly founded society's journal ('The Ri: Unidentified aquatic animals of New Ireland', *Cryptozoology* v1p33–39, 1982). In it, Dr Wagner, an anthropologist from the University of Virginia, says the Ri resemble the traditional mermaid – it is an air-breathing human-sized mammal with a human-like head and armless torso, breasts and genitalia, the lower half legless and ending in a pair of fins. Whatever it is, says Wagner, who did the fieldwork in the New Ireland province of Papua New Guinea in 1979–80, the natives know it well and distinguish it from dugongs and porpoises. Ri are "frequently sighted by fishermen, occasionally netted or found dead on the beaches, and sometimes eaten." Males, females and juveniles have been reported.

This is sensational news by any standards, but despite this endorsement from the (deliberately) serious and authoritative ICS, it took nearly a year for the Press to notice it (AP 12 Aug: *Weekly World News* 13 Sept 1983.) And more: Wagner not only claimed to have seen such a creature with his own eyes, he photographed one! From mid-June to mid-July 1983, Wagner, ICS secretary J. Richard Greenwell, and two other ICS members made an expedition to Ramat Bay, on New Ireland, to gather more data, the results of which are in the second ICS annual (*Crytozoology* v2p113–125, 1983.) They interviewed more witnesses, and one of their number observed what he thought was a Ri for 20 minutes in Nokon Bay. The photographs he took, for various reasons, show little more than a blurred blob. Lacking adequate funds, equipment and time to obtain more precise descriptions, remains or even a specimen, the team resolved to return another time better equipped.

News of Wagner's sighting and report reached Jon Erik Beckjord an active Bigfoot investigator, in Seattle, Washington. Beckjord flew to Papua New Guinea at the first opportunity – he was there for two weeks in June 1983, just before the ICS team arrived. When he returned, Beckjord sent letters all over the place claiming he found no evidence of mermaids. In an open letter to *Fate Magazine* dated 10 Sept 1983 (I don't know if it was ever published) Beckjord claims he interviewed most of the people mentioned by Wagner and some others, and found: "no trace of Mermaids at high tide at Ramat Bay, despite ten days and nights of observation with a night vision device"; witnesses, including Wagner's, "identified from photos that it was dugongs that they had killed, butchered and eaten, not mermaids"; and that "different villages have different meanings for the term 'Ri'. To some it means mermaid, others use it for *dugong*."

What has rankled with cryptozoologists is not that Beckjord has dared to challenge an ICS report, but the obvious relish with which he thinks he has trounced them. The letter to *Fate* warns them that they have been "had" because they published a version of Wagner's first report ('The Ri', *Fate* Aug 1983 p43–49). He goes on: "Merely because a man is an anthropologist, a report he publishes in a new and untried journal need not be necessarily accurate." This is obvious sophistry: new and untried *Cryptozoology* may be, but ignorant, careless and inexperienced its editorial panel are not. One would have more confidence in Beckjord's criticism if he were more rigorous himself: eg in one part of his letter he says he "found no trace of mermaids" after interviewing "perhaps 100 natives and officials", and later that "I did, however, encounter ten stories of mermaids seen at a distance."

Beckjord's points are largely answered by information in the second *Cryptozoology* article. The ICS team found that the 1970s incident involving the killing and eating of a Ri was the subject of an extensive village dispute, most villagers deploring the act. One of Wagner's witnesses to the incident insisted it was a dugong, not a Ri, yet a relative and others stated he was being contradictory "for his own reasons." Given that the Ri were a sensitive issue, and the villagers were showing the reticence of villagers everywhere to uninvited, unauthorized strangers, too inquisitive about unmentionable matters (and Beckjord is not reknowned for his tact), it's no wonder to us that they closed ranks and denied any knowledge of the Ri. They may have opened up more to the ICS team partly because they had the blessing of the province's premier. We also learn that sightings were few in Ramat Bay, compared with daily appearances at Nokon Bay, 50 miles to the south. At Nokon, the Susurunga people call the same creature *Ilkai,* because they are in a different language group (the Ramat villagers are Barok), but maintain the clear distinction from dugongs. As an experiment Greenwell pointed to two "easily identifiable dolphins" and shouted, "Ilkai! Ilkai!," to see if the villagers would agree simply to please a westerner. They were not tricked, and calmly pointed out that the objects in the bay were dolphins.

Why has Beckjord used the 'mermaid' research to attack the ICS? Only Beckjord knows for sure, but the hostilities underlying this dispute go back many years. Beckjord's erratic genius takes second place to his monumental ego, and his boorish behaviour has antagonized almost every major cryptozoologist, not only in Bigfoot research. Many of his disputes with other researchers have arisen out of his ability to see paranormal faces and creatures in photographs where others see only patterns of shadow – see his letter on page p3. He has loudly claimed that the ICS refused him membership because he has proposed paranormal origins of mysery animals (including the Papuan mermaids), but if this were a criteria for exclusion one has to ask why many other prominent exponents of these ideas remain happy in their membership. In retaliation, Beckjord created his own National Cryptozoological Society. His antics have so exasperated the ICS that Greenwell was recently obliged to circularize an open rebuttal. In it he states flatly that Beckjord was refused admission because of his "known behaviour". Greenwell adds that the natives of Ramat Bay expressed their reservations about Beckjord to the ICS team when they got there.

In indirectly accusing the ICS team of perpetrating, or rather perpetuating, a fraud Beckjord is on extremely thin, even libellous, ground. In March this year a Superior Court in Seattle ordered Beckjord to repay the $85,000 he had borrowed from an ex-girlfriend for a film about Bigfoot which he never completed, the court upholding the woman's claim that the film was a "fraudulent and hopeless venture". *Seattle Times* 16 March 1984. This time last year, Beckjord annoyed many investigators at Loch Ness by claiming to news agencies and papers that he had images of Nessie on his continuous surveillance video camera system. While the claim was widely reported by newspapers, a number of TV news and video who *did* view his film were unimpressed, even in this silliest of seasons. Some LNM investigators said he had filmed ducks in the distance, others, more charitably, said the objects were tiny featureless dots.

The 'Feegee Mermaid' as it appeared in the New York *Sunday Herald* 17 July 1842,

But back to the Ri. Wagner told the *Weekly World News* that "the closest thing I've seen to the merpeople I saw at New Ireland" is "a woodcut of a mermaid in the Smithsonian magazine". This illustration is of the infamous 'Feejee Mermaid' brought to England first in 1818, which astonished English society again in 1822, and which was bought by the great showman Barnum in 1842. Barnum had several woodcuts made, but when three NY papers found Barnum had sold them all the same 'exclusive', the papers denounced the object a "scaly trick" – for more see Peter Dance's *Animal Fakes & Frauds* (Samson Low, 1976). In fact the Feejee Mermaid was a fairly obvious amalgum of orangutan and fish, and an unfortunate reference to make in the circumstances. The ICS team say the identity of the Ri or Ilkai has eluded all the marine mammalogists they have consulted so far, and that they believe it is not a part of the known inventory of zoology. There will be more expeditions to New Ireland, and we'll follow them closely.

●

Bob Rickard

THEY GOT IT WRONG . . .

Novelist Arnold Bennett died of typhoid in Paris after drinking a glass of water to prove the water was perfectly safe. (*D. Mirror* 7 Aug 1978.)

♦

Francis Schklowsky, a French freelance photographer taking pictures for a magazine article on how safe New York City parks are for children, was stabbed in the stomach in Central Park by a man trying to steal his camera. (*Int. Herald Tribune, Toronto Sun* 30 May 1980.)

. . . BUT THEY DIDN'T

In August 1980 Mrs Isobella Lazic of Delmore, near Inverness in Scotland, who had been complaining about the dangers of manually operated barriers at level crossings, was killed when her car was struck by a train on an unmanned level crossing in Delmore, and carried 230 yards along the track. She had called the crossing a "death trap". (*Guardian* 7 Aug 1980.)

And in October, Herber Foster, a chemist in Auckland, New Zealand, who had been campaigning to have a dangerous pedestrian crossing outside his shop re-sited, and who the previous week had said someone would die on the crossing, was struck by a car on the crossing and died later in hospital. (*Canberra Times* 20 Oct 1980.)

♦

Five mountain rescue police helping to make a film about the dangers of avalanches were swept away and killed by an avalanche in the French Alps. TV cameramen looked on in horror. (*D. Mirror* 29 Dec 1980.)

♦

Mike Stewart, 31, president of the Auto Convoy Company, Dallas, was filming a movie on the traffic dangers of low-level bridges when the truck he was standing on passed under a suburban bridge and killed him. (*Northwest Arkansas Times* 7 April 1983.)

♦

Walter Hallas, 26, a market stall assistant in Leeds, was so afraid of dentists that he asked a workmate to cure his toothache with a punch on the jaw. He fell, hitting his head, and died later from a fractured skull. (*Guardian* 18 Dec 1979.)

♦

An 83-year-old man in Tiberias, Israel, allowed police to destroy a suspicious ticking package, only to learn it contained a gold watch, his reward for banking 40 years at the National Bank of Israel. (*Times* 18 July 1983.)

♦

Mrs Carson of Lake Kushaugua, NY, was laid out in her coffin, presumed dead from heart disease. As mourners gathered round, she sat up and gazed wonderingly around. Her daughter dropped dead from fright. (*Niagara Falls Journal* 8 July 1983.)

♦

Brian Sandford spent ten years perfecting his three-foot model of the Titanic. The final authentic touch came when he launched it on a pond in Wimbledon; it sank. (*D. Star* 30 July 1980.)

♦

BAPTISMAL BUMMERS

A 62-year-old Pentecostal preacher was about to baptise a boy in front of a congregation of 200 in Stockholm. Pentecostal baptism is by total immersion and Swedish fonts are electrically heated. The preacher, standing in water up to his waist, was handed a microphone and was electricuted. (*D. Telegraph* 11 March 1980.)

The Rev. James Gaxele, 43, a Baptist minister, was about to baptise four new members of the church in the Silver Park River, Transvaal. He stepped into the water praying, and as he uttered the words "Holy Spirit" he sank into the mud and drowned. (*D. Telegraph* 17 June 1981.)

Bachelor John Blue, 47, was drowned in a baptismal ceremony in Lake Cochituate, MA, when he lost his footing. Said the pastor – like Blue, a non-swimmer – "Maybe God wanted him." (London *Standard* 7 Sept; *Weekly World News* 13 Sept 1983.)

♦

80,000 followers of the "Kepercayaan" (an animist organisation) gathered on the slopes of Wilis Mountain, 6,000 feet, 500 miles east of Jakarta in Java, preparing to bathe in the Sedudo waterfall at Nganjuk. They believed that total immersion in the waterfall under a full moon brings eternal youth. Panic swept the crowd (why, we are not told), and 26 fell 400 feet to their death. (Waukegan (IL) *News-Sun* 24 Nov; *D. Telegraph* 25 Nov 1980.)

♦

TOUGH LUCK

A man arranged to go to Haydock races in Surrey on 7th July 1979, and dreamed for several nights beforehand of the number 7. He thought his guardian angel might be trying to tell him something, so when the 7th race came round he put all he could afford on horse number 7, Haywire, to win. It came 7th. (*D. Telegraph* 12 July 1979.)

♦

The law making the wearing of seat-belts compulsory was so effective that it was causing a shortage of kidneys available for transplants, according to the transplant coordinate at St Mary's hospital, Portsmouth. (*D. Telegraph* 8 Mar 1983.)

♦

A fierce gust of wind blew Vittoria Luise's bubble car into the river Sele near Naples. Vittoria, 45, managed to break a window, climb out and swim to shore, where a tree blew down and killed him. (*S. Express* 13 Feb 1983.)

♦

Private Robert Wade, 22, survived one of the fiercest Falklands battles and escaped a bomb blast in Northern Ireland, only to be killed on his first night of home leave when he was run down by a drunken motorist. (*D. Telegraph* 16 Sep 1983.)

♦

Abel Ruiz, 22, in despair after being jilted, hurled himself in front of the Gerona–Madrid express. He fell between the rails and sustained only minor injuries. After first aid at Gerona hospital he leapt in front of a lorry, but was again only slightly hurt. Back in hospital, he promised doctors he wouldn't try again. An hour later he was wheeled back on a stretcher. He had been trampled by a runaway horse – a complete accident. This time the injuries were serious, but he pulled through and said he was "glad to be alive." (*S. Express* 18 June 1978.)

♦

George Schwartz, 54, was working late alone in the office of his factory in Providence, Rhode Island, when a huge explosion virtually flattened the building and sent flames racing through the wreckage. Only one wall was left standing. The blast swept him clear of falling masonry and flames, and dumped him on the front steps. After treatment for minor injuries and shock, he returned to the factory to try and salvage business files. The last remaining wall collapsed and killed him. (*S. Express* 11 Dec 1983.)

♦

A "Good Samaritan" who gave mouth-to-mouth resuscitation to a woman knocked down by a vehicle in Park Lane, Mayfair, was being sought by police because the woman (a drug addict) had infectious hepatitis. (*D. Telegraph* 27 Aug 1983.)

♦

Depressed because he couldn't find a job, Romolo Ribolla, 42, sat in his kitchen near Pisa, gun in hand, threatening to kill himself. For nearly an hour his wife Emilia pleaded with him not to. Finally he burst into tears and threw the gun to the floor. It went off and killed his wife. (*S. Express* 5 April 1981.)

♦

A Florida man was rushed to hospital after a snake bit him on the finger. Doctors removed the poison, saved the finger, and told him to stick it in an ice-pack. Two weeks later the finger had to be amputated because of frostbite. (*D. Telegraph* 24 April 1981.)

♦

A young German tourist in a fur sleeping bag was shot dead on the island of Elba by a man who mistook him for a wild boar. (*D. Express* 4 June 1982.)

♦

A farmer, aged 54, using the stairs because the lift was out of service, collapsed and died after climbing five flights for a heart checkup in Messina, Sicily. (*Guardian* 21 Aug 1982.)

♦

TRUTH TRICKED OUT

On Friday, May 13th 1983 a man excavating peat in Lindow Moss, a peat bog in Cheshire, found a skull with hairs adhering to it, and an eyeball still intact. Initial tests indicated that it belonged to a European woman aged between 30 and 50, which had been buried for between 5 and 50 years.

300 yards away was a cottage where, 23 years earlier, former airline officer Peter Reyn-Bardt (now 57) had been living when his wife Malika disappeared. Reyn-Bardt, a homosexual, had married her in 1959 to gain respectability with the airline, but they separated before the end of that year. One day in June 1961 she turned up and demand cash, threatening to expose his homosexuality to his employers.

When interviewed by police in January 1983 (why they had waited over 20 years is not revealed) he said he had given her £15 after which she had left. In June they confronted him with the skull. He confessed that he had strangled her, cut her up and buried the pieces near his cottage.

The skull was then sent to the research laboratory for archaeology at Oxford, where tests were completed on 12th October. It was declared to be of a European woman who died in the year 410 AD (how can they be so accurate?), just as the Roman legions were leaving the area.

Reyn-Bardt pleaded innocent at his trial in Chester in December, but was found guilty and sentenced to life. No trace of his wife has been found. (*D. Telegraph* 13, 14, 15, Dec; *D. Mirror* 13 Dec, *NY Post* 14 Dec 1983.)

●

Paul Sieveking

It has been quite a time for teratological tricks, so here is a little side show of recent animals who've been Nature's sports.

LOOK EAR
In 1982 a one-eared rabbit (*below left*) was bred by James Lister, of Berry Avenue, Trimdon Grange, Co Durham. In 35 years of breeding rabbits he'd never heard or seen the like. Curiously, he adds: "I was told that millions of years ago rabbits had only one ear." (Is this. rabbit-breeder's folk-lore?) Hartlepool *Mail* 29 Sept 1982.

Curiously, this rare occurrence was repeated last year (1983) when four rabbits, born at an animal sanctuary in Surrey, were found to have only one ear each. Our source note says *T+P* 29 Feb 1983, but we've forgotten what the initials mean!

HORNS APLENTY
An unusual lamb with three pairs of horns was born at Birchen Close Farm, West Tytherly, Hampshire, *D. Mail* 23 April 1983. Its owner, Lee Raymond, thinks it is unique. It may well have been, but only for a few months because we know of another, born later in the Chinese province of Xinjiang. His father sported the usual two horns, but his mother had four. AP/*Grand Rapids Press* (MI) 8 Nov 1983.

MORE DOUBLE-HEADERS
Elanore Fletcher, known at Juno Beach, Florida, as 'the turtle lady' found a small two-headed Green Sea turtle. A photo appears in AP/St Louis (MO) *Globe-Democrat* 10 Nov 1983.

A two-headed water snake (*below right*) has become a major attraction at the Miami Serpentarium. It is about 3ft long and both heads are active. Both can eat and see, but get confused about which way to go. Serpentarium director Bill Haast said: "You can see a kind of vibration being set up, as if there's a tug of war going on." Haast has aptly named it/them 'Hatfield and McCoy' after the notorious feuding clans of West Virginia. AP/St Catherine's (CAN) *Standard* 13 Sept; *Weekly News* 24 Sept 1983; *Awake* 22 Feb 1984.

[© Hartlepool *Mail*/John Pollard.]

[Photo: AP 13 Sept 1983.]

[Photo: *National Enquirer* 11 Oct 1983.]

A two-faced kitten (*above*) was born in an otherwise normal litter to a cat owned by Dan Lizza, of Latrobe, Pennsylvania. Lizza named it Gemini, but we don't know if Gemini survived. *National Enquirer* 11 Oct 1983.

LEGS OF LAMB

A five-legged lamb (*right*) and its normal twin were born to a Border Leicester Cross ewe, on 15 March 1982, at Cwm Farm, Forden, owned by Mr G.O. Evans near Welshpool, in Powys, Wales. Janet & Colin Bord, who live nearby, investigated for us, and learned from the vet who removed the leg that it was in fact two legs, as evidenced by the double foot, joined together. It/they were not connected to the animal's pelvis, merely attached to its lower abdomen by flexible tissue.

Finally, an eight-legged lamb, again with a normal twin, were born to a Chios sheep, at a livestock project farm at Hamala, in Bahrain. It survived for only 15 minutes. *Gulf Mirror* 1 Feb 1984.

•

Bob Rickard

[© Fortean Picture Library.]

We have not given much data on out of place animals for some time, and so append here a few notes on recent zoological aliens, prefixed by another Big Cat round-up.

THE EXMOOR BEAST, CONTINUED

The last we heard [FT40p52-61] the Beast was lurking around the Simonsbath/Dulverton area, at the beginning of August 1983, possibly heading out of Devon and into Avon and Somerset. Like all Fortean shows which have been running too long, a pollution, adulteration or degradation sets in. For instance: a lamb with its throat torn out at Old Bury Farm, Dulverton, on 4th August was declared "not consistent" with prior killings. *D. Telegraph* 5 Aug 1983. There may have been other killings but they're no longer newsworthy; the next that was noted was on 12 August. Then, out of the silence, on 16th September, a man calling himself 'Bob' phoned a Devon radio station saying he shot the 'Beast' three weeks ago (ie last week in August). He said he was a gamekeeper, and worst of all he said the creature he had killed on the lonely Molland Common was a *black bear*! *D. Star* 17 Sept; *Mail on Sunday* 18 Sept 1983. Naturally the police proclaimed, almost smirkingly, that this was a hoax – *D. Star, D. Mail, Scottish D. Express* 19 Sept 1983 – but we can't help feeling they might be too hasty here. Granted that an almost anonymous caller saying he'd seen the animal not supposed to be there is not the most convincing of proofs, but we've come upon claims of bears [eg the Hackney Bear, FT37p44-46] often enough not to be dismissive – for a recent case see OUT OF PLACE ANIMALS on p44. If the claim is true – and no one even bothered to locate the alleged carcase – we wonder why it should turn up in the middle of the mystery of the Exmoor Beast, because, despite the dead bear Beast-type killings and sightings have continued.

Nearly a month after the bear 'hoax' there were two sightings not far from Drewstone Farm, where Eric Ley bore the brunt of the early depredations. The first (no date) was by retired Major Paget King-Fretts, who lives in an isolated cottage at Whitechapel Green between South Molton and Twitchem. In a dense wood near his home he saw, 70 yards away, an unusual animal, "jet black, and grey around the jowls." The second was by Mrs Mary Rawle who was on horseback at Longstone Wells, near Heasley Mill, where she has a smallholding. Looking down the hill she saw a deer run in front of her chased by a "large black cat with a white flash and thick coat." When the animal saw her it vanished into undergrowth. "I have never seen anything like it in the area before." *N. Devon Journal-Herald* 6 Oct; *Western Morning News* 7 Oct 1983.

The animal seen by farmer Eric Colwill and his wife on their land at Lower Culleigh, Frithelstock, near the end of October was "smaller than the Best of Exmoor" (which one?) Colwill said it was dark, striped, cat-like and "about half the size of a puma." (Oh! that one.) Later the same day they learn that a lamb on an adjacent farm, owned by David Allin, had had its throat torn out. We also learn that a cat-like animal, about the size of a small lioness, had been seen in the Parkham and Littleham areas, around the end of September. *North Devon Journal-Herald* 27 Oct 1983.

A ewe killed at Simonsbath, Somerset, is said to be the victim of the 'Beast of Exmoor'. Hull *Daily Mail, D. Telegraph* 19 Nov 1983. Lorry driver Ray Chilcott believes he saw the 'Beast' early in the morning of 17 November, while driving between South Molton and Brayford. The black cat-like animal came out of a field to the left, onto the road, into the headlight beam about 50 yds ahead. "It was much bigger than a labrador dog, in fact its tail was about half the length of its body." It ran into a wood. *North Devon Journal-Herald* 24 Nov 1983. "It was certainly in good condition and looked well fed." Bideford *Gazette* 2 Dec 1983.

An isolated, perhaps unconnected killing, of a calf at Elworthy, Somerset. But in this continuous multiverse mere suspicion might be connection enough. Though the 'Beast' of last year's rampage specialized in sheep-ripping, this calf's death is blamed on the 'Beast'. *D. Mirror* 7 Jan 1984. And that was the last of it until March this year and a sudden burst of action. After three sightings south of Dartmoor, itself 30 miles south of Exmoor, a police helicopter joined an organized search for a "mystery black animal". Gardener Jane Derbyshire was one of those who had seen it in a field near Modbury. "It was jet black, four times the size of a fox and moved like a cat." *D. Mirror* 8 March 1984. Further north, the news of sightings has farmer Eric Ley nervous. By early April last year (1983) he had lost many lambs, but so far this year all is quiet around his farm. Local farmers are said to be convinced it is not dead. *S. Express* 22 April 1984. Has the 'Beast' gone from Exmoor? Are the sightings around Dartmoor of the same animal? Do the sightings near Dartmoor precede more sheep killings on Exmoor, as they did in 1983? If there is a flesh and blood puma, how much longer can it evade capture? Where did the bear and other animals reported come from, and why? Stay tuned for the next episode of . . . 'The Beast of Exmoor!'

●

OTHER BIG CAT NEWS

● The Earlston 'Puma' continued [FT40p61]. We've since discovered that Earlston (not Earlsdon, as we had it) is near Melrose in Berwickshire. For additional reports, see Scottish *Daily Record* 29 July, 1 Aug; Scottish *S. Mail* 31 July 1983. Where the "large cat-like animal resembling a puma" had killed two sheep and a prize ram, there was something else, more dog-like, killing chickens. Scottish *D. Record* 2 Aug 1983. No further sightings we know of.

● The Surrey 'Puma' continued [FT40p61]. A large brown cat-like animal, "with tufts on its ears, big furry legs and a cat-like face" was seen by train driver George Christy, wandering along the track, as he pulled out of Cobham station towards Guildford, on 10 Sept. "I saw it was a puma." *Guildford Times* 17 Sept 1983.

● The Chiltern 'Puma' continued [FT40p50f]. Mrs Jean Sellars, of The Vale, Chalfont St Peters, Bucks, was calling her cat in for the night, and heard a cat fight. Investigating, she saw a huge puma-like black cat ("wearing a studded collar"!) jump into the air and pounce on her kitty. Since then she has seen it several times, but a police search found nothing. *Buckinghamshire Advertiser* 10 Aug 1983.

● Inverness-shire. Three sightings in several weeks of a large cat-like animal likened to a black panther, in the Balmachree, Balloch and Smithton Park areas, all not too far from Cannich where the puma was trapped two years ago. *Inverness Weekly Focus* ? April 1983.

● The Welsh 'Puma' continued [FT40p53]. Three sightings of a "puma-like creature" in two weeks near Llanfrecha, Gwent. *Western Mail* 30 May 1983. An orange-red coated Chow, lost by a Birmingham man, is hunted by armed Powys farmers in Rhayader area after it is blamed for attacks on lambs at five farms. *Western Mail* 8 June 1983. Sheepdog found savaged to death in Dyfed's Brechfa Forest is blamed on a "big wild cat" haunting the area. Local vet talks of bite marks and crushing blows to ribs and back by "something out of the ordinary". Prior sightings. The legend of the 'Beast of Brechfa' is born. Manchester *Eve News, Western Mail* 11 Aug 1983. Report says it looks like a "large ginger cat, four feet long, short fur, thick legs, long tail." *D. Mirror* 15 Aug 1983. A Wolverhampton pensioner says that just a few days before news of the Brechfa killing, he saw a "big wild cat" in a garden at Bryncoedifor, North Wales. It was 3ft tall, cat-like head on elongated neck, pure white with two black patches on hind quarters. Wolverhampton *Express & Star* 17 Aug 1983. "A very large animal" killed a calf at Ffes-y-Gasey, Abergorlech, Carmarthen, by tearing away one entire hind quarter. Tracking the killer failed when Forestry Commission refused permission for armed men to enter plantations. Description, possibly of the Brechfa Beast: "a golden cat about 2ft 6in high and 3ft long." *Farming News* 9 Sept 1983. A party on foot, following the Spitre hounds, had just shot two foxes in woods on Trebwl Farm, Llanpumpsaint, Carmarthen, when they noticed a large animal running across an adjacent field, "with the bounding action of a tiger" and the hounds in pursuit. Cyril Evans, of Spitre Farm, said it was orange coloured, about the size of a sheep and the movements of a cat, tallying with descriptions he'd heard about the Brechfa Beast. *Western Mail* 4 Nov 1983. More killings of sheep and cattle. Police at Llandeilo say they have 18 sightings since the first dog killing, and want to coordinate information on the Brechfa Beast. Among them is one of a puma with a collar around its neck (another one?) *Western Mail* 3 Dec 1983. No further developments known to us.

● We will pay more attention to overseas sightings of out-of-place big cats in future, but for now we note the appearance of a puma-like animal in the Hannover area, West Germany. Tracks found are being investigated by zoologists. *Soester Anzeiger* 4 July 1983.

● The Cuffley 'lion'. [FT-40p53]. A report, by Michael Lewis, appears in Andy Collins' *EarthQuest News* no8-p4–8 (for address see next item).

● The Essex 'panther'. There

were three sightings of a large ferocious black cat between Bulphan and Hordon-on-the-Hill, in the Thurrock area. All sightings were on the same day, 4th November 1983. About the same time a goat was found slaughtered at Langdon Hills. One witness said: "I would take it to be a panther." A police search found no tracks. *Thurrock Gazette* 11 Nov 1983. Omnipresent researcher Andy Collins has produced a privately circulated illustrated two-part study of this outbreak based on his own theories of the paranormal (Andy Collins: 19 St Davids Way, Wickford, Essex SS11 8EX.)

• The Isle of Wight 'puma'. This mystery animal has been sighted many times since our first note, that a holidaying couple, Mr & Mrs Goodwin, spotted a 2ft 6in high, 3ft 6 in long, sandy coloured animal they believed was a leopard, in a country lane near Apse Heath. It was only 60yrds away and they watched it for about 5 minutes. After looking in a reference book Alan Goodwin said: "I think it would have been a young adult puma." A similar animal was also seen in a field by the disused Ashey railway station. Police searches found nothing. Portsmouth *News* 20 Aug 1983. Ref. to another five sightings since previous report. Portsmouth *News* 12 Sept 1983. On the 14th a day-old calf was found disembowelled and its back legs stripped to the bone on East Upton Manor Farm, outside Ryde (see photo). The killing method and amount eaten was proclaimed consistent with puma behaviour. Portsmouth *News* 15 Sept 1983. A teenager, Colin Rea, sees a large grey cat-like creature on Newbarn Road, East Cowes; the second sighting in the area in a fortnight. We also learn that one of the investigating policemen, Sgt Joy Pritchard, had, four years previously, sighted a lion at Wooton, and the capture of an escaped lion at Havant on the mainland. Portsmouth *News* 13 Oct; IOW *Weekly Post* 14 Oct 1983. A late-night sighting at Seaclose, Newport. Portsmouth *News* 20 Oct 1983. Enter Eddie McGee, the SAS man who successfully stalked triple-killer Barry Prudom, on special safari funded by *The News*, partly to raise money for charity (!) We learn of "23 sightings since May". Colours range between black, gray, sandy, silver, and latest, "reddish". Hunt closing in on Firestone Copse, near Wooton. As usual after such publicized hunts, there's a discreet silence. Portsmouth *News* 16+18+19 Nov 1983. Then a winter hiatus until a "mottled tan or sandy" big cat, with "tufted ears, and flat pug-like face" surprised two men in a parked car on the Briddlesford Rd, near the Lynnbottom tip, Newport, "just after midnight" (no date). Portsmouth *News* 15 March 1984. Our last note to hand: *S. Express* 29 April 1984 gives three sightings but says there have been "five in last two weeks". Currently, a lynx is favoured. We note a Name Game curio: one of the witnesses is leader of IOW County Council Mr Maurice Barton, only one letter away from Maurice Burton, the distinguished explainer away of Nessie and the Surrey Puma!

Isle of Wight police view one of the slaughtered calfs, thought to be a victim of the island's phantom feline. [© Portsmouth *News*.]

OUT OF PLACE ANIMALS REPTILES, etc

• The annual influx of accidental immigrants from the Caribbean, usually attributed to drifting up the Gulf Stream, begins . . . 25th Jan: leathery turtle, weighing over 1000lbs, caught off the west of Lewis, Scotland. *Scotsman* 26 Jan 1984. Two West Indian loggerhead turtles washed up on beaches at Perranporth and Hayle, in Cornwall. Bristol *Eve. Post, Scotsman, D. Telegraph* 2 Feb; *D. Express* 3 Feb 1984. Five turtles seen in the Thames at Oxford are believed to be Marine turtles "from America", and if so, they may perish in our cold (fresh) waters. But how did they get so far up the Thames without prior sightings, if they swam in a clump of five? *D. Mail* 7 Feb 1984.

• A two-foot long lizard (no details) mistaken for a young croc was found at a health centre in Norbury, South London, (when?). Curiously it was "identical" to a lizard found by local police two months previously. *Sun* 27 Sept 1983.

• 40 residents of the Middle Touches area of Chard, Somerset, have signed a petition protesting against the mail-order business of Melvyn Spry, run from his home and specializing in exotic animals, reptiles and insects. His 71yr-old next-door neighbour, investigating a disgusting smell from a cupboard, found the decomposing body of a 4ft South American rat snake wedged in a central heating flue. The neighbour on the opposite side found a large lizard in her son's bedroom. The reason why this item is here is that Mr Spry insists that the snake the old man found "was not one of mine." *D. Telegraph* 25 Nov 1983.

• A teenager kills a mystery in Ohio, by pumping six bullets into an African lizard, nearly 6ft long, lurking in a Findly, Hancock County pond. Very brave of him; this Nile monitor was probably already dying. How it got there, nobody knows. Columbus (OH) *Dispatch* 26 Feb 1984.

• For two out-of-place crocodiles see CROCS IN THE SEWERS on p26.

•

INSECTS, etc

• Police constable Keith Hartley, found a strange five-inch-long insect, with a thorny body, in the garden of his Cadbury Heath, Bristol, home (no date). He thought it was a praying mantis, but Charles Copp, curator of the Natural History dept at Bristol Museum and in whose charge the insect now resides, identified it as an Australian spiny stick insect. No one knows how it came to be in the garden. Bristol *Eve. Post* 1+2 Aug 1983.

• Jennifer Cobb found a live scorpion while she was vacuuming the living-room carpet in her Banbury Park, Torquay, home (no date). She offers an origin novel to us: the luggage of foreign students. *Sun* 27 June 1983.

•

BIRDS

• A rare Western Reef heron was first sighted on Nantucket island, Massachusetts, on 26 April 1983, and has since drawn many thousands of birdwatchers to its new home on Quaise Marsh. One man even made the trip from England to see it. The duck-sized bird, usually a resident of the tropical coast of west Africa, had never been sighted further west than the Azores before. Bangor (ME) *D. News* 29 Aug 1983.

• Two unusual arrivals in the Isles of Scilly; the North American Baltimore Oriole, of which there are only 20 European sightings on record; and the Bobolink. *D. Telegraph* 27 Sept 1983.

• Another Scilly Isles sighting – in fact a British first – is the North American cliff swallow (it has a square-ended tail) which should have been engaged in its annual migration to Argentina. *S. Express* 23 Oct 1983.

• An exhausted Arctic skua, presumed "blown off course", was so tired when it came down on the roof of the police station at Lewes, Sussex, that it fell off. It was treated at the sick bird pen at Bentley and later released at Newhaven beach. Brighton *Eve. Argus* 1+3 Nov 1983.

• A phenomenal irony – the Scandinavian wryneck, thought to be extinct in Britain. Onc has been found in a garden at Bradmore, Notts – killed by a cat. *D. Telegraph* 11 Nov 1983.

• A red-breasted goose, a rare visitor from Russia, is being watched near Stiffkey, Norfolk. *Sun* 16 Nov 1983.

• The first known sighting of another Russian invader – this time in the USA. The slaty-backed gull, which normally migrates through Siberia to Japan, has set up a winter home in Missouri. UPI/Providence (RI) *Journal* 5 Jan 1984.

• A rustic bunting – which normally breeds in Siberia and migrates to Japan, like the slaty-backed gull was spotted at Stone Lagoon State Park, outside Eureka, California, 90 miles south of the Oregon border, by a park ranger and a biologist. This, the first ever sighting of the bird in "the lower 48 states", and the West Coast appearance of the other East Asian avians (above) has made the "unusual" winter a remarkable one for US birdwatchers. AP/14 Jan; *S. Express* 29 Jan 1984.

• Another red-breasted goose, far from its normal wintering grounds in Bulgaria and Rumania; seen at Sir Peter Scott's Wildfowl Trust, Slimbridge, Glos. *D. Telegraph* 20 Jan 1983.

• Rustic buntings – which normally breed in Siberia and migrate to Japan, like the sla~~ty-bkaced~~ gu~~ll —~~ have appeared on the west coast of America (no details where). *S. Express* 29 Jan 1984.

• An olive-backed pipit, another Siberian who flunked his navigation, has turned up in the back garden of a house in Bracknell, Bucks, attracting flocks of bird-watchers. *D. Mail* 25+27 Feb 1984.

• 22 April is the first recorded sighting of a stilt sandpiper in Britain since 1976. This wader from America was being watched in Frodsham, Cheshire. *D. Telegraph* 23 April 1984.

FISH

• Stanley Clarke and his son, Alan, were swimming in the River Leven, at Ulverston, Cumbria, when an enormous silver-blue fish leapt out of the water, twisting in mid-air, several hundred yards ahead of them. Investigating from the safety of the riverbank, they noticed the fish leap again and again, but more astonishing was its huge swordfish-like spike. Eventually, it hurled itself onto rocks, and the Clarkes saw that it was badly gashed about the gills and dying. They killed it quickly. It was identified (from a photograph) by the British Museum of Natural History, as a white marlin, an ocean fish common off the coasts from Africa to Portugal and never before recorded further north than Brittany. The Clarke's had witnessed its death-throes in fresh water – but just how and why did this 58lb, six foot denizen of more tropical waters find its way a couple of miles inland in a relatively shallow (4ft) lakeland river? One fish expert thought the marlin might have come, not from North Africa, but from the North Carolina coast, where they teem in August, via the good old Gulf Stream. *S. Express* 18 Sept 1983.

•

OTHER ANIMALS

• A bear scare in Kent? Mark Russell, 11, and his brother Peter, 9, saw what they thought was a young bear fall out of a tree in a neighbour's garden, in Slip Mill Lane, Hawkhurst, about 7.30am on 15 August. Police were called and they took away samples of fur from the tree. The boys said it was bigger than their 60lb dog, two feet tall, rounded with brown fur, "shaggy, with big black claws and a long nose." It ran off when the boys began to chase it from Henrietta Waters' garden, bordering Bedgebury Forest. Large scratches were found on the tree bark. The boys resisted suggestions that it was a large cat or even a monkey (!) No further information. *Kent Messenger, Kent & Sussex Courier* 19 August 1983.

• To the list of ocean-going animals given by Michell & Rickard in *Living Wonders* (1982, p103f) we can add a racehorse. The £3000 Irish mare 'Russell's Touch' had unseated its trainer, David Kiely, while training on the shore at Dungarvan, Co Waterford, before dashing into the foam and heading out to sea. Kiely spent the next two hours finding a phone and trying to raise a rescue boat. Eventually the horse was spotted by a returning trawler – the *Rosgall* skippered by Don Hayes – four miles out in the Atlantic. A rope was passed through the horse's stirrups and the noble but daft beast ignominously towed ashore. It recovered in a few days. *D. Express* ? Feb 1984.

• A commotion in the chicken coop had Mrs Mair James investigating at 2 in the morning, on her Snowdonian farm at Gellilydan, Maentwrog, near Portmadoc, Wales. In the torchlight she saw a strange creature and rushed back to wake her husband and call the RSPCA. It was a North American racoon. No zoo escapes, etc. *Sun* 25 Oct; *Cambrian News* 28 Oct; *S. Express* 30 Oct 1983.

• Two badger-sized coatimundi, relatives of the racoon, were found wild in a nature reserve near Redhill, Surrey, run by the Surrey Trust for Nature Conservation. None have been reported missing from zoos, and no one knows how they got there. *D. Telgraph* 30 Sept; Brighton *Eve. Argus* 4 Nov 1983.

•

Bob Rickard

Religious phenomena abounds as never before. Here are a few on-going vision centres.

THE PRIEST AND THE PROSTITUTE

Regular visions of the Blessed Virgin Mary (BVM) to Maria de Jesus, a 16yr-old reformed prostitute,are at the center of another breakaway traditionalist Catholic cult, this time in the Mexican state of Michoacan. The movement began on 13th June 1983, when an ecstatic peasant woman, called Mama Salome, allegedly "found" an image of the BVM "engraved" on cloth, rather like the Shroud of Turin. On the site of the first of many apparitions to Mama Salome now stands a full sized copy of the engraving, which is worshipped by the peasants as the "fixed abode on earth" of the BVM. To the sceptical the original 'engraving' is little more than a crude painting, but to the villagers it is the most sacred of relics.

Mama Salome found a champion in Padre Nabor Cardenas, now 55 and excommunicated. Together they proselytized the messages given to Mama Salome in her trances, and found an eager reception among the poor and largely ignorant peasants. Their village – called New Jerusalem – is about 300 miles west of Mexico City, and too tiny to be on the map. In 1981, Mama Salome died, and the cult was saved from extinction by the (timely!) discovery of the fallen girl, Maria de Jesus, who is said to bear a miraculous (suspicious?) resemblance to the sacred portrait. Her appointment outraged a large section of the cult, culminating in a skirmish in October 1982, in which Nabor's followers, armed with machetes and clubs, drove out about 2000 protestants from the village.

Maria fills the role of village seer well. Her daily vision sessions are attended by most of the 8000 loyal villagers and bus-loads of pilgrims from miles around. Unheard by the crowd the BVM talks to Maria, who relays the messages to them over a microphone as is the growing fashion on the ecstatic scene. Maria's tone of voice and facial expressions take their cue from the content of the messages, by turns stern with warnings of the immanent end of the world ("before the year 2000") and pleading for more prayers and piety. As high priest Nabor's sermons are also fairly conventional: he scorns Rome for corrupting the true faith; he uses the banned Tridentine Mass; and believes that Pope Paul VI did not die in 1978 but is alive and imprisoned in the Vatican; and that the Anti-Christ is on earth and already in control of the twin evils of inflation and nuclear power. This vivid doom-mongering has even attracted more articulate and educated Americans, who form the core of an elite 'caste' of about 900 monks and nuns, distinctively dressed in ankle-length tunics and heavy colourful rosaries. Our notes are from a report by John Carlin in the *Times* 26 Nov 1982.

MEANWHILE IN CHILE . . .
Between July and November 1983 more than 100,000 people trekked to a hilltop shrine near Villa Alemena, 68 miles northwest of Chile's capital, Santiago. They came – and presumably are still coming – to see a ruddy, casually dressed, orphaned youth, Miguel Angel Poblete, aged about 16, who regularly holds conversations with an invisible Virgin Mary. The boy periodically falls to the ground in trances and gets up to wander through the crowds with a glazed look in his eyes. Sounds like someone we know, but Miguel is followed around by a group of anonymous men who, when asked, will only identify themselves as "lay Catholics for humanity". These assistants carry a microphone and loudhailer with which they relay the boy's rather one-sided conversations to the crowds, and lead prayers and singing.

The whole proceedings and the contents of the alleged messages – men should stop dressing like women; Russia should come closer to God; couples should not have sex outside marriage, etc. – are very similar to those of Bayside, New York [see FT28p3–5], and like the circus at Bayside have been roundly condemned by at least two archbishops. Archbishop Juan Francisco Fresno of Santiago publicly advised Catholics against going to the meetings at Villa Alemena, calling them "highly harmful to the true image of the Church." Nevertheless, more than 5000 attended one session. And the pilgrims, from humble farmers to middle-class matrons, keep on coming.

Irrespective of whether or not Miguel's trances are genuine – as yet there has been no official investigation – the bishops think the credulous mass of ordinary people are being manipulated for political reasons. Archbishop Francisco de Borja Valenzuela of Valparaiso, who has jurisdiction over the area, has publicly stated that the organizers of these radical traditional revivals – and presumably he means the boy's secretive 'assistants' – "receive support from outside the Church that is not only inappropriate but suspect."

One example gives the hysterical and patriotic flavour of the meetings. At one point the boy pointed skyward, saying: "Yes, ma'am, I see you. I hear you." Then he tells the assembly to wave their handkerchiefs to welcome Mary, and take snapshots of the sun. Amid the fluttering and clicking, several people gasp, saying they see Mary in a long gown among the cloud formations. "Mary is here," booms the prayer leader from the loudhailer. Miguel sings *Ave Maria*. One woman shouts. She says she has seen the Virgin sitting between the flags of Chile and Argentina, which she later interprets as a divine call for peace between the two countries in the dispute over ownership of three islands in the Beagle Channel. "What's that you say?" Miguel asks, staring at the sky. "God is willing to help Russia?" A man nearby explains confidently: "This is a sign, because Chile is the only country in the world to have controlled communism." And almost as one, the people thrust their crucifixes and rosaries skyward.

One last snippet: we are told that the BVM first contacted Miguel, earlier this year (1983), as he was about to sniff glue with his friends in the town.

AP/Houston (TX) *Chronicle* 25 Nov 1983.

VIRGIN MARY AGAIN

Palestine – on 1 Sept 1983, Associated Press gave the world the news that the Virgin Mary was back on home ground, a small, predominantly Greek Orthodox, village called Beit Sahour, just southeast of Bethlehem, on the Occupied West Bank. One of the first witnesses was Mrs Amalia Ahanouneh, who is quoted referring to her first sighting as "on Monday, the day after the Feast of the Virgin." This feastday is on 15 August, which in 1983 *was* a Monday. It seems that just outside the village, below a road on a hillside there is a man-made grotto with an ancient well, called in Arabic *Bir Sayida* (the Lady's Well). Local legend holds that the Virgin Mary stopped off here for a drink, with Joseph and baby Jesus, during their flight to Egypt. In the grotto is a shrine called the Church of the Well of Mary, and it was here that the first witnesses were worshipping when they saw something highly unusual. Mrs Ahanouneh: "Then I saw her. There was a light, a shining white light about one meter high [presumably, off the ground]. All of a sudden it became a mist, and it was the Lady, our Mary, Mother of Jesus." She then goes on to say that a series of chalky white marks appeared on the wall of the grotto, which they believe is an image of the BVM.

As the news spread, more and more people came to look. At first the reports spread by mouth, but then an East Jerusalem Arabic-language newspaper, *Al Fajir*, began covering the story. By the end of August the crowds swelled to thousands every day, fighting and queuing for hours to file down the narrow stairway into the grotto, which only holds about 60 people to stare at the white marks for a few minutes. Inevitably, more claims followed of seeing the Virgin Mary, or rather the image on the wall leave the wall and drift across the water of the pool.

Even one of the directors of *Al Fajir*, Michael Bahbah, saw something which he described in the paper as "one foot tall, with the shape of the robe the Virgin Mary usually wears. She was turning around and walking back and forth." On Thursday, 25 August, a second figure appeared on the wall – "a sketch in charcoal-coloured lines resembling a man in long robes with his left arm outstretched . . . about 18 inches tall." It is popularly believed to represent Joseph. One priest, who declined giving his name, thought the phenomenon was a sign to his troubled flock. "Our people are suffering from the high inflation, and from the [Israeli] occupation, so they turn to God," he explained. Reports of the apparition were still being made at the time of the AP news, about two and a half weeks after the feast of Mary.

We'd like to know much more about these events, which seem to have more in common with stories of holy images weeping [see MORE BLEEDING STATUES on p6.] or moving than with the traditional 'vision' stories. A ball of light seen at a sacred site (holy well) is nothing new, nor is the use of an altered state of consciousness (the vision, or ecstasy) to interpret random patterns (perhaps cracks in the rock wall?); nor is it unheard of for people who have stared intently at something to see movements in the afterimage. But is this the case here? And can we rule out fraud (however piously motivated) in the appearance of the second image, if not that of the first one? Kansas City (MO) *Times*, Houston (TX) *Chronicle. Miami News* 1 Sept; Little Rock (AR) *Arkansas Democrat*, Schenectady (NY) *Gazette*, 2 Sept; Houston (TX) *Chronicle* 3 Sept 1983.

•

Bob Rickard

Over several issues we have followed the story of the fire-prone nanny, and we offer here a summary of her eventual trial and release. Plus news of yet another fire-prone girl.

FIRE-PRONE NANNY FREED

While we were diverted by the material of our last two issues, the story of Carole Compton, the 21yr-old Scottish girl imprisoned in Italy, came to a head. Carole, if you remember [see FT39p28-30], was accused of arson and attempted murder because she was the only common link in a series of otherwise inexplicable fires. She was arrested and locked up at the beginning of August 1982, after the second family for which she nannied in Italy (the Cecchinis) believed she was responsible for the plague of odd fires; old Granny Cecchini even going so far as to say that Carole was a witch. Many cantankerous old ladies must have thought, at some time or another, that the young girls in their households were proper little witches – but what made this more sinister was the superstitious fear spread by this particular old lady. Every international report of the case raised the spectre of a witch-hunt, in every sense of the phrase. Carole languished in Bolzano prison until she was formerly charged in January 1983, and then had to wait until December before her trial began. The whole proceedings were widely reported, so we will omit tedious references here – but all the clippings will be in the file.

The trial was convened at Livorno, on 12th December, in a mixture of farce, drama and what several papers called "three-ring circus". As Carole was led into a cage, built for a terrorist trial years before, more than 70 press, TV and radio reporters surged forward, climbing over each other or scrambling up towers of tables and chairs to point their cameras and microphones at the startled girl. It was more than two hours before the "incredible scenes" died down, and the furious chief judge, Mr Guido Galligani, ordered most of them out of the room before he would come back himself. Then there was an adjournment while inquiries were made about missing witnesses. When the judges returned there was another delay as a lone cameraman was spotted and his film seized. Carole was then allowed to sit outside her cage after a plea by her advocate, Mr Sergio Minervini. Carole denied all the charges. Further confusion and protests arose out of the "atrocious" translations, into Italian, of gum-chewing Carole's Scottish useage (eg. 30 minutes were taking up deciding what she meant by "making the tea"). And so on . . .

Carole talks to her mother through the bars of her courtroom cage. [Photo: *D. Mail* 17 Dec 1983.]

The second day got off to a good start too as Carole's entrance to the dock was greeted by kisses from her mother and several large bouquets of flowers. The prosecutor rowed with the judge and slammed his books down; the media complained that the bad acoustics of the converted convent chapel venue had them guessing most of the time about what was being said; the interpreter burst into tears, shouting that everyone was picking on her; Mrs Ricci, Carole's first employer, complained loudly to everyone about the inconvenience of waiting and the expense of travelling from Rome; and Carole wrestled with a witness for the microphone in front of the judge's bench. The fight occurred as Carole listened to the accusations of another maid, Nicole Annasawury; Carole snatched the mike from her, shouting that she was lying, and Nicole grabbed it back. Not surprisingly the judge quit early, deciding he'd had enough for one day.

Somewhere in there was the testimony of Prof Vipolo Nicolo of Pisa University about the fire in two matresses next to the Cecchini's child's cot, the basis of the attempted murder charge. Calling it "phenomenal", he said: "In my 45 years I have never seen a fire like it." Although the two matresses were made of quite different materials (wool, and horsehair) they each burned in the same peculiar way. "They were only burned on the outside, not on the inside," and had burned downwards instead of upwards. "They seem more like fires caused by a heat source, like an overheated iron, than by a flame." Mrs Ricci told of Carole's obvious unhappiness both in her work and in her love-affair with an Italian conscript. Then Mrs Ricci told how her superstitious Sicilian maid, Rosa, feared Carole. Rosa complained of madonnas falling off walls, an electric meter spinning when Carole neared it, and of vases smashing off tables. Surprisingly the judge allowed this second-hand accusation of paranormal agency, saying there was no need to call Rosa! Mrs Ricci added that her 2yr-old son was also frightened of Carole. He used to cry out that she was burning him whenever she touched him.

The third day must have

been the high point for the media circus with an episode headlined 'Enter the Exorcist'. Like a scene from a Hammer horror classic, the incident began with an increasingly noticeable muttering from an old lady, dressed all in black, in the public gallery. Before the court's collective astonishment, Ciara Lobina – whom the press quickly dubbed 'The Black Nun' – shuffled towards Carole muttering incantations and holding high a large wooden crucifix. She was evicted in tears by police. Carole's attorney, Mr Minnervini, dramatically jabbed his temple, shouting "Bats. Bats." seemingly delighted to demonstrate his grasp of English to the gawping journalists. Outside, the Black Nun, who is well known as a healer and clairvoyant, did not disappoint the panting pressmen. She said that the Devil came to her in a dream the previous night and told her that Carole and her mother were possessed by the spirit of a young 18th century witch, who had "given them the power of fire." Then she said an odd (to us) thing: "The Devil entrusted me to touch both of them to cleanse them of the demon." Who is working for whom? Why should the Devil be concerned to revoke a possession? Typically, this is the sort of confusion-mongering we've come to expect from 'entities' from our studies of, for example, poltergeists and Contact Ufology. One reporter (Diana Hutchinson in *D. Mail* 17 Dec 1983) said the old lady got so far as to yank Carole's head back by the hair and throw Holy Water over her mother before she was restrained.

Apart from that the rest of the day was comparatively orderly, as the *Telegraph* said, taken up "with mere psychic phenomena and xenophobia." This last refers to Granny Cecchini who readily confessed to the court that she had blamed Carole because she was "the only stranger in the house." The nanny prior to Carole spoke of the old lady leaving smouldering cigarette ends all over the house, as well as faulty or overloaded power sockets. This girl, Theresa Hunter, was in no doubt: "If I had stayed, I would probably have been accused of the crime Carole is charged with today."

On the fourth day the public prosecutor summed up. In pressing for a sentence of seven years, the prosecutor reiterated that "This trial is not about witchcraft. We are here to talk about facts, not fantasies." And yet very little could be established, for no witnesses saw Carole set the fires, nor was she in their immediate vicinity when they started, and the forensic experts agreed that there was no evidence linking Carole to the fires. So he could only accuse Carole of lying and cunning and not above pretending to be a witch to torment a household she did not like, so that her employment would be terminated allowing her to get back to Rome and her boyfriend. Two psychiatrists seemed very unsure about the prosecution's desire to label Carole an "abnormal personality", psychotic enough to set fires "for amusement" etc, though they weakly conceded this. Carole was unable to understand the ways of these Italian middle-class families. The defense said it was absurd to talk of Carole terrorizing two such families, and that it was *she* who was confused, frightened and not a little anxious. Carole was described as a bit "backward", highly introverted and understanding no Italian. It is doubtful that such a girl could fox two families with such success, and have the knowledge to set fires by means which baffled the forensic experts and which behaved like no fire they were aware of. Her other advocate told the panel: "You run the risk of convicting a young girl of things for which there is no scientific explanation."

The prosecution played on another curious detail, which they thought created a "uniformity" in Carole's behaviour. More than once, it was said, Carole was found looking out of a window, staring, or looking around "as though to make sure no-one was approaching" when she was found or looked for, after the fires were noticed. While we can see how this might seem suspicious, it does have a striking similarity to the shock or trance-like state which so many scholars have noticed in the people at the center of a paranormal happening – especially poltergeist type phenomena – and which Fort noticed about the girl in the Binbrook Farm case [*Books* p663f]. She was found sweeping the floor, quite oblivious to the fact that the dress on her back was on fire. She too was a servant girl. Like many of these phenomenal 'agents' Carole came from a broken home, and apparently had not had much contact with her mother as a child – very like the polt-girl Tina Resch, see POLTERGEIST PHOTOGRAPHED on p10.

On the fifth day there were more "incredible scenes" as Carole was found guilty of arson and attempted murder, but cleared of the remaining charges, including attempted murder. She was said to have laughed and cried, as well she might, these being the emotions the case inspired most. The judge read through the verdict so rapidly – as though he had an urgent engagement elsewhere – that even the lawyers were unsure what was happening, Carole was sentenced to two and a half years in jail, but released immediately because she had already spent 16 months in the company of prostitutes, lesbians and drug offenders. As more than 100 journalists surged forward, joined by 80 spectators, Carole was hustled away in the "pandemonium" to collect her belongings from the prison. Outside the court women were hissing and shouting "Strega" (witch). These protestors may have been from the more superstitious south, Sicily and Sardinia, where the Cecchinis came from; the people of Livorno, in the sophisticated north, frequently told reporters they thought the accusations of witchcraft were utter nonsense, and that the modern connotations of the word merely implied secret meetings for sex at best and rather silly white magic at worst. Understandably, the Comptons were back in Aberdeen by the following day.

Despite procedures which would never be acceptable in a British court – lacking proof the case would surely have been dropped? – the verdict was inevitably (and wisely) expedient; one welcomed by the Italian media. *La Nazione* said the verdict condemned Carole but also allowed her to go home. The people of Livorno did not want the taint of medievalism in being seen to condemn a "witch". On the other hand, to be found not guilty on all counts would have denied the inescapable fact that Carole was the only common denominator to the series of unlikely fires in two different households. In that case, it would have been a verdict in support of the idea that extraordinary coincidence (of the kind Jung meant by 'synchronicity') was at work; or worse, that Carole could actually start fires, however, unwillingly, by paranormal means.

The 'Black Nun', Ciara Lobina, warding off photographers (unsuccessfully) outside the courtroom. [Photo: *D. Star* 15 Dec 1983.]

Lord knows what would have resulted if the defendant had not been a foreigner! Well, perhaps we do – see THE HUMAN FLAME-THROWER on p21. for the story of Benedetto Supino, to which a passing comparative reference was made during Carole's trial. He is from Formia, between Rome and Naples – not too far south – and yet the only supernaturalism in his case is that a Church investigation found no evidence of demonic origin in the fires he can cause, seemingly at will. He is now being cultivated by parapsychologists.

AND ANOTHER FIRE GIRL

While Carole Compton was in prison, we received news of yet another fire-prone youth – 12yr-old Nadine Calojine, of St Pierre on the Indian Ocean island of Reunion.

On 16th February 1983 a neighbour's flat in their seafront apartment building was devastated by an unexplained fire while the owners were out. Two days later another mystery fire gutted the same flat completely. A few days later the fire brigade was called to a blaze in the Calojine flat which destroyed a mattress. By now locals were muttering about "mysterious forces". Over that weekend (19–20 Feb) and on the Monday (21st Feb) Nadine's clothes were said to have "caught fire repeatedly". Fires were found in two matresses, and some linen in a cupboard. Nadine, believing herself bewitched by spells from the grimoire known as 'Little Albert' (how she came to this conclusion is not revealed), is said to have taken to wearing a Mauritian charm of salt, pepper and a nail in a handkerchief. Local police say it is most likely the result of children playing with matches. *Independent Catalan* 27 Feb 1983.

•

Bob Rickard

Earthquakes and Space-Time Transient Events

An Interview with Dr Michael A Persinger

Michael Persinger is one of the few full-time scientists who are equally active in Fortean research. His influential articles relating aerial lights and sounds, among other anomalous phenomena, to regions and times of seismic stress have helped fuel exciting debates, like that currently in session about the geophysical origin of some UFOs. To give us some extra insight into the man and his ideas, we are pleased to present this interview with him, conducted by **Dennis Stacy**, Director of Publications for the Mutual UFO Network, and contributor to journals of ufology and the paranormal in the USA, England, Belgium, Germany and Japan.

Michael Persinger [© Dennis Stacy/Fortean Picture Library.]

Dr. Michael A. Persinger is a full professor of psychology and head of the Neuroscience Laboratory at Laurentian University, Sudbury, Ontario, Canada. He is the author of *ELF and VLF Electromagnetic Field Effects* (1974), *The Weather Matrix and Human Behavior* (1980), and co–author with Gyslaine F. Lafreniere of *Space-Time Transients and Unusual Events* (1977), a computerized study of anomalous phenomena such as earthquake lights and other luminous displays, and the fall of such objects as fish and frogs out of the sky. Dr. Persinger was one of the first scientists to draw widespread attention to the possibility that tectonic strain several weeks to months before earthquakes could be a possible explanation of some UFO events, including the experience of physical abduction. The most well known application of the theory includes the piezoelectric effect.

Persinger has published more than 50 technical articles in the fields of neurobiology, psychology, biometeorology, and pharmacology. His research is concerned mainly with the cellular aspects of brain function and the analyses of multivariate problems, like that of weather, on human behavior.

Recently, Persinger delivered the Keynote Address to the International Symposium on the Biological Effects of Electromagnetic Radiation, sponsored by the Learned Societies Conference held at the University of Ottawa. His most recent book, co-authored with research assistant, Lynn Henry, is *TM and Cultmania*, a critical look at the belief systems surrounding Transcendental Meditation.

•

☐ **QUESTION**: How does a research psychologist become interested in space-time transients, or what might be called anomalous phenomena?

☐ **PERSINGER**: First of all, I am a behavioral scientist and not just a psychologist. It may seem like an artificial contrivance, but it's not. In behavioral science you deal with behavioral principles, patterns that are retestable and from which predictions can be made.

For example, if you wanted to know when you would become satiated with a particular person, especially one of the opposite sex, or when you would habituate or get tired of going to school, we could predict that for you fairly accurately on the basis of a number of variables, such as response duration and the time between responses. So we deal with very clear behavioral principles, whereas psychology has more of an aura of artsy, opiniated interpretation. That still occurs, by the way, but it's not very useful, because you can't generate any predictions from it.

One of the interesting aspects of behavior is that you find the dynamics by looking at changes over time. In the case of humans, one of the ways we measure change over time is by history. And one kind of behavior that has changed over time, of course, is that of science itself. I mean, humans do engage in scientific behavior every so often. While I was at the University of Wisconsin between 1964 and 1967, I had several courses in the history of science and I realized that there were periods of time when the popularity of a particular idea or philosophy or observation came and went.

About the same time I read a book which I can never forget by R. DeWitt Miller [*Impossible. Yet it Happened* (Ace, 1947) – Ed.] saying that there had been a dark day in May of 1780. I went to the historical archives there, looked up the date in question, and sure enough, there were all the original newspapers telling me the same thing. There *had* been a day of darkness and it was reported by every newspaper in the vicinity of Connecticut, Massachusetts and New York. About midday it suddenly turned dark, there was the smell of burning sulphur, and everyone was running toward the churches, thinking it was the end of the world.

So here indeed was a space-time transient event that was fully documented and that was the beginning of the study. Next I began to look at the mass of data accumulated by Charles Fort and quickly realised that there was just too much of it for one human to handle. and that was when Lafreniere and I began to put it on the computer in the summer of 1974. We loaded the information on an IBM 360-40 and let it sort it according to the inductive technique to see if the reports were based on patterns that could be predicted or could be useful in demonstrating scientific principles. One idea underlying the study was that by looking at the exception, very often, you can find the principle.

☐ **QUESTION**: You refer to anomalous events or phenomena as space-time transients. Charles Fort called them "the Damned" in his book of the same name, because they were damned by orthodox science. Exactly what kind of events or phenomena are we talking about here?

☐ **PERSINGER**: We had several major categories and between ten and fifteen subcategories in each. They included things like unusual falls of objects, such as rocks, or slag, or ice, unusual sonic phenomena such as screeches or the odd series of booms off the East Coast four or five years ago. Another category was UFOs, widespread visions, or illusions of forests in the sky, unusual human events, such as telekinesis or phantom sniper reports, geographical and astronomical anomalies and so on.

☐ **QUESTION**: How did you draw the line between these types of events and, say, for example, natural disasters, or people suddenly going beserk and attacking their fellow humans?

☐ **PERSINGER:** In the beginning we did stop or draw the line, but now we don't. In fact, something very contemporary we're working on right now is called the Catastrophe File. It is made up of events that have occurred since 1970 and includes airplane crashes, people running amok, revolutions, *et cetera*. Again, though, this is a sampling procedure and because these reports usually appear in the press, you have to take certain precautions to account for the momentary popularity of press reports. But we do look at these now, particularly peculiarities in electronic instrumentation.

Since computer access became available to the average individual in the mid-1970s you'd be surprized what you can do with a normal computer and above average software, especially if you're in any way competent with numbers. You don't have to be brilliant, but you have to have common sense analyses and the ability to think in numerical terms. You'd be surprized at the patterns that are there waiting to be discovered.

☐ **QUESTION:** But say you do find an immediate correlation or pattern between event A and event B. Is there a tendency to stop there and not look for correlations with event C or D or Y?

☐ **PERSINGER:** I think what you're asking here is really two questions, the first having to do with a prediction model and the second with an explanation model.

If you have a relationship between two things and one precedes the other systematically, say, by six months, then you can still use the first event to predict the subsequent. That's a prediction model of the type frequently used in economics.

A mechanism, or explanation, model is a different problem because there you have to start talking mechanics: the specific thing that should be changing, the principle or process involved. The two are useful and they certainly complement one another, but you don't have to have an explanation before you predict.

A classical example might be the way bats avoid solid objects in flight. One does not necessarily have to know about ultrasonic theory, or even know that ultrasound is emitted, to study, or to predict bat avoidance of solid objects. You can measure the stimulus, a wall, and the response, avoidance by the bat, without knowing ultrasonics ahead of time. Another way to put it: once you've got a systematic phenomenon that's measurable, and you've isolated the stimulus/response aspects of it, *then* you can start talking about mechanics and mechanisms.

Mechanism is always a pretty arbitrary thing, although most people think it's fairly routine. Compare, for example, a series of sudden deaths, and then at a distance, a series of apparition reports, with another series of people placing their hands on a red hot stove and suddenly withdrawing them. Most people would probably think there is a great difference in these two pairs of events, but there really isn't *operationally*. Hundreds of people dropping dead and hundreds of people seeing strange apparitions is still a stimulus-response relationship, and it's just as robust, if replicated, as hundreds of people putting their hands on a red hot stove and removing them. The only difference between these events is that one, *a priori*, has a very evident mechanism – the nervous system. But that doesn't mean you can't study the other event as well.

We may think the response to a hot stove is pretty simple because of the proximity of the human observer, but in reality it's a pretty sophisticated process, involving the transfer of an electric signal along the spinal column to the brain and the generation of the appropriate muscular response. In fact, if you really want to examine it closely, at the ion or electro-physical level, it's almost as ambiguous in places as the mechanism between those hundreds of people dropping dead in one place and those hundreds of others seeing an apparation in another.

☐ **QUESTION:** So we get into cause and effect. Is there some reason orthodox science has simply overlooked space-time transient events such as you've mentioned, because the cause has not been readily apparent or obvious?

☐ **PERSINGER:** Well, we rarely use cause and effect in the technical sense, anyway. We deal with correlations. Cause and effect is a semantic, or word, equivalent of truth and no truth. Words only have two options: they're either there, or they're not there. By semantic criterion you're either dead or alive. You're not 65% alive and 35% dead. Semantically, cause and effect considerations may be very helpful; mechanistically, however, they're no help at all. You have to have all those infinite possibilities between yes and no, 0 and 1, and that's where the correlations model comes in.

Even if you stike a match a hundred times and it bursts into flames every time, and you say the flame is caused by the striking of the match, it's still an assumption you're making. The two events are highly correlated, true, but it doesn't *always* happen that way, and if you really want to get down to it, there are perhaps millions of events taking place between that striking and that flame that you are unaware of. So where do you draw the line between cause and effect?

What we do instead is talk about probability which irritates laymen and legal people alike because they want to talk about yes, no, definitely. Yet there are few scientific questions which are absolute yes and no.

□ **QUESTION**: Let's take as an example two seemingly unrelated events which have a correlation only in time: the eruption of Mount St. Helens on May 18, 1980, in the Pacific Northwest, and race riots which broke out the same day in Miami, Florida, diagonally opposite the United States. One is an eruption in geology, the other in sociology. Is there anyway of establishing a strong correlation between these two events? Moreover, is there a scientific discipline even interested in asking the question?

□ **PERSINGER**: Historically, there was a school of German physiological philosophers around the turn of the century who were quite interested in geo-psychology, the effects of geology, geography, topology, the distribution of trees and so forth, on human behavior, but that tradition has basically died out.

To evaluate something like a volcano eruption in one corner of the country and a race riot in the opposite, you need to look at systematic changes. It's very difficult to isolate the controlling variables for an infrequent, or one time, event like this example or the Tunguska explosion in Siberia, in 1908. There may be a lot of good documentation, but you need to see it changing. If it's only happened once, you can't do very much with it. You can't analyze the correlative variables or determine the time-varying patterns. Optimally, you like to have some key variable so that predictions can be made.

This particular instance, however, in a general way, is predictable from my theory. The data indicate, for example, that immediately before and after optimal earth strain, there are no luminous displays. So what takes place? Apparently there are three phases with some correlational data to back them up. In the first phase there are crude electromagnetic-like effects, which are associated with power failures, stimulation of human beings, sickness, malaise, increase of flu-like symptoms, likelihood of reporting phosphenes (blinking lights at night), agitation, fugues, amnesia, and sudden disappearances.

If the strain continues, what seems to happen, and this is inferred from data, is that luminosities become more evident in very close proximity to the strain. When the strain level increases very quickly, there is a flurry of UFO activity. When the strain level increases more slowly, the UFO reports may dribble along over several months.

In the third stage, if there is no quake yet and the strain obviously increases to a higher stage, the luminosities disappear and the very unusual things begin to occur. This is where you start to get PK, or psychokinetic events, phantom snipers and mutilation displays, where you have actual, very, very localized damage. In fact, I just published an article looking at the correlation between UFO reports and these types of events, and what you find is that in the six month period *before* an increase in UFO sightings, there are clusters of mundane electromagnetic-like interference on equipment, such as power failures and plane crashes, where electronic instruments might be involved. Then come the luminosities, a marked enhancement of the more bizarre events, and finally the earthquake, or the release of strain. The earthquake can be either volcanic or tectonic in nature, although geophysicists would distinguish certain characteristics between the two. In the tectonic earthquake, you have the build and release of plastic deformation strain involved, whereas the volcanic earthquake may be more explosive and include the flow of magma. So there are certain seismographic features which differ.

□ **QUESTION**: How did earthquakes enter the data base for correlation in the first place?

□ **PERSINGER**: You mean as opposed to volcanoes? For one thing earthquakes are very discrete events. They happen within a very specific time-frame and that's that. Volcanoes tend to be more periodic and drawn out over time. There is also the further problem that there has been no systematic, global study of volcanoes until just very recently when the Smithsonian's Center for Short-Lived Phenomena began keeping records. Before that it was a rather haphazard and piecemeal process, a pilot might report one here, another one there, and so on. Unfortunately, from what I understand, now even the center itself is mostly moribund because of a lack of funds.

□ **QUESTION**: But why look to the earth, to geology, for correlations with UFO phenomena in the first place?

□ **PERSINGER**: Well, we didn't necessarily look to earthquakes to begin with, but we did have to make some basic assumptions. In dealing with unusual, energetic phenomena, for example, the energy had to be significant. Where would it be localized? It could be thunderstorms, they're pretty energetic, or solar impact from massive flares, or tectonic strain, which is very energetic. The theoretical transformation of plastic, or deformation, energy into mechanical or electromagnetic energy is absolutely stupendous. So we began by looking for obvious sources of energy and the correlation was there.

As a matter of fact, I might add that we were getting reports of luminous displays and other

Fortean (anomalous) phenomena from the Mount St Helens area *before* the eruption. A top notch field investigator, Lynn Henry, my co-author for *TM and Cultmania*, was there to collect the data. After the event there is always the problem of memory to be corrected for, the classic example being 'did you notice any odd animal behaviour?' and the witness saying, 'hmmm, well, now that you mention it, yes'. The Japanese in particular have tried to attenuate this problem by sending out an animal anomaly questionnaire on a daily or weekly basis. Then if an earthquake does occur in a given area, you have some control for the effects of memory modification.

☐ **QUESTION**: Do you see your own approach as perhaps leading to a wider, more encompassing awareness of the planet earth as a gestalt system in itself, the same way astronauts, for example, seeing the world without any international boundaries, apparently have their perspectives changed?

☐ **PERSINGER**: Well, I don't think there's any doubt that the more we look at the world from, say, a reconnaissance level, the more organized it appears to be. In fact, there should be some patterns that *only* show up at a larger level. For example, you would not predict, or even detect, the presence of a large air mass, or even an isobar, by looking at the records of a single weather station. You need the records of hundreds of stations hundreds of kilometers apart before the lines of the isobar appear.

☐ **QUESTION**: It seems like we have this problem of a limited perspective which is being expanded, almost in spite of ourselves. Yesterday it was that of the city, today perhaps it's that of a planet, but tomorrow perhaps it will be that of a solar system or an entire galaxy.

☐ **PERSINGER**: We always will have that problem as long as humans depend on language for their proof of an event, because words in themselves tend to produce psychological closure. Language is yes and no, all or nothing, and that's how all the intermediate data gets left out. Language is the limit.

You see, scientists don't talk in numbers or equations, even though they sometimes say they do. They talk in words. The human being is a verbal animal. He uses verbal equivalents for the numbers and equations and this runs over, even into the laboratory. If there is a discrepancy or something that doesn't fit, then you forget about it. You can say it's a methodological error or a graduate student that didn't know what he was doing. Usually it's not very serious because the contemporary paradigm of how we see things is based upon a massive inertia of repeated patterns. But very often robust, bona fide phenomena get swept under the carpet for that very reason.

☐ **QUESTION**: Is that what happened to most space-time transient events?

☐ **PERSINGER**: Oh yes, very definitely. Classically, what happens is that once you have a label for it, in the case of ball lightning or some ice falls, for example, scientists come along and say, yes, of course, we knew about it all along, so what? As I pointed out in *Space-Time Transients*, science itself is also social behavior and once you get two reputable scientists going in a certain direction, you very often get a cascading effect.

This happens in very orthodox areas of research, such as cancer, where very clear procedures are ignored simply because they don't fit contemporary ideas of funding. Sooner or later all the decisions are made by humans, and just because they're high up in the hierarchy does not mean they are immune to the effects of language.

To continue the example, there is one model of cancer which suggests that cancer –aberrant mitosis – is spontaneous in everybody. It's simply the nature of mitosis, or cell division. And since we have more than 100 trillion cells in the body and a good number of them divide, it's only a statistical necessity to have aberrant mitosis. Under normal conditions, however, the body's immune system takes care of most cases. But what if the person is psychologically depressed or under a massive physiological stress and the immune system cannot handle the aberrant mitosis? It continues, of course, until it's beyond the capability of the immune system to handle it, say 20 or 30 cell divisions until a tumor is evident.

This is a very viable cancer model that has been around for awhile, but it's not compatible with the contemporary viewpoint that cancer is a disease and that therefore there must be a magic bullet, or whatever, with which it can be eliminated. As a result, any data which seems to support the natural model is immediately suppressed or the research simply isn't granted any further funding.

In a way, though, this should be expected by any knowledgable behavioral scientist, because it's *human* behavior, not science behavior.

•

Dennis Stacy

Screening the Paranormal:

The First International Festival of Films of the Paranormal, at Lille, 14-15 April 1984
by Hilary Evans

Most English-speaking people were unaware of the *Festival International du Film sur les Phénomènos Paranormaux*; for many this was probably just as well, for all the films had a voice-over commentary in French which drowned the original soundtrack, so there was I struggling to understand a French version of what Matthew Manning could be seen but not heard saying in English. Which was all very good for my French, but frustrating for my film-going.

However, quelle opportunité splendide to judge the films as *pure cinema*, as your true cinéaste would surely wish us to do. Unfortunately, the films are hardly chefs-d'oeuvres of the cinematic art. No, these were films made for a purpose, let the plastic values of the lighting fall where they may. And that purpose was to demonstrate what the cinema can contribute to research into the paranormal.

In the film, *Le monde du paranormal*, a "sorceror from the border between Togo and Ghana" is seen to rise from a circle of fires.

If a picture is worth 1000 words, then a moving picture must rate considerably more. To watch, say, Kulagina deploying her psychokinetic powers to move small objects across a table-top is not as exciting as watching Truffaut watch Spielberg's IFO making contact with Planet Earth, nor is it even solid evidence for man's superconscious powers; but at least it shows us that something happened, one afternoon in Russia, and under what conditions.

What we all hope to see, of course, is an authentic film record of ghosts walking, of poltergeists at play, of fish falling from the sky and the Virgin Mary manifesting to her fans. Alas, the camera-shyness of these anomalies, coupled with the improbability of a witness happening to have a loaded ciné-camera on him at the time, to say nothing of the appropriate conditions for filming, means that the film record of spontaneous happenings is non-existent. Such records as exist are of contrived happenings and experimental set-ups at best: more often, they are of people telling us what happened.

As evidence, therefore, films of the paranormal have yet to realise their potential, though high-tech lightweight cameras and infra-red film and such like developments hold promise of better things to come. Meanwhile, what has a festival of films of the paranormal to show us in 1984? We saw healers at work, and practitioners of biofeedback, and exorcists, and a psychic artist. We had 47 minutes of static interview in black and white with Hans Bender, whose wit and charm could not stand up to the tedium of French made-for-TV documentary at its least imaginative.

Light relief came from a professional exorcist from Antibes, with a blonde girlfriend and a motor-bike, a wardrobe full of lovely robes and a splendid line in Crowleyesque mumbo-jumbo which would have any sensitive demon in fits. Less amusing was a German TV spectacular made up of filmed-on-location incidents chosen for their blood-and-death content, notably related to voodoo in Brazil and psychic surgery in the East. The fixation on nastiness brought boos from the audience, proving that spice *can* be tasteless.

Nevertheless it was this film which contained the festival's most dramatic sequence, an apparent levitation by a native priest somewhere, unnamed ('to protect the priest from tourists'), in darkest Africa. Superb camerawork showed us the priest rising from the ground clearly and unequivocally – though admittedly it was after dark, and he was surrounded by a circle of flickering flames, and he rose vertically in a straight line, and there were tall if bendy trees behind him . . . Had the film as a whole earned our belief, we might have been more impressed.

The film which most impressed the jury, and ultimately won the prize, was paradoxically the most ineptly-made of the festival, a Dutch-made record of the visit of the Dutch clairvoyant Croiset to Tokyo, to help find a missing girl. Most of the 30 minutes were taken up with studio chat in Japanese; the actual film, all hand-held stuff, occupied only a few minutes, and much of them were taken up with Croiset actually landing at Tokyo airport in an actual aeroplane, to show how actual it all was. Then he was whisked to a studio where he immediately indicated where the girl's body would be found, pointing out buildings and other landmarks. Off we rush in a flurry of cars to see if he's right – and would you believe it, there, in a place already searched, the girl's body is just surfacing in time to be filmed by our camera in the dawn's early light . . .

Well, yes, you can see why the jury gave this film the prize; here was no post-hoc compilation, but your actual *cinema verité*. Except, how veritable was it? Even if I hadn't read Piet Hobens' exposé of Croiset in *The Zetetic Scholar*, I'd have been skeptical of an incident in which everything panned out so pat. Suppose the body *hadn't* surfaced then and there, suppose Croiset had boobed, would we have been shown the film of him boobing? Indeed, have films ever been made in which he is seen boobing?

And so even the prize-winning film was unsatisfying – yet how could it be otherwise, in a field where nothing ever satisfies? Nor does it in any way reflect on the enterprise and dedication of the organisers, Vladimir Verovacki and Jean-Rémi Deléage, whose courage in creating the event, and whose skill in organising it so efficiently, made this truly a landmark in anomaly research. The intention is that it will be a biennial if not an annual event; the next need is to make some provision for English-speaking audiences, so that it can justify its title of 'international'.

•

Hilary Evans

Enigma Variations

by Nigel Watson

DOOMED!

The consequences of belief in the existence of extramundane forces who visit us in flying saucers can have a far-reaching influence on all of our lives, whether we subscribe to such beliefs or not.

In the case histories of alleged encounters with 'space people' which have been published by MUFOB/Magonia (e.g. 'A Stranger in the City' MUFOB Ns 14) I have tended to interpret these experiences as projections of individual mental conflict. On a wider scale UFO experiences and beliefs can be seen as a reflection of the many worries which concern humanity as a whole. So within the chaos of world events and internal mental events a kind of order can be established by belief in cosmic saviours from the beyond.

These thoughts were given more substance when in November 1983, I met a woman who claimed to have mental contacts with 'space people'. One communication told her that she should visit the Greenham Common women, during the equinox. After consulting her dictionary she found that this is when day and night are of equal length all over the earth. So on the vernal equinox, which occurs on the 21st March, she visited the women who are protesting about the stationing of cruise missiles at the Greenham Common, USAF base. Her message to them was that they should leave tombstones with their names carved on them outside the base as a permanent reminder of their protest. According to her, the Government would be unable to move the tombstones since their existence would mean that the ground on which they are placed would become consecrated. I am very doubtful about this argument, but she did give this information to the women at the camp. Apparently they were not convinced enough to carry out these intructions, especially since she told them that they should all go home once they had erected their tombstones.

As another line of attack she telephoned Monsignor Bruce Kent, the general secretary of the Campaign for Nuclear Disarmament (CND), to see if he could get the Greenham women to carry out the instructions. In reply, he said that he had no official connection with the Greenham women and he wondered if her message might have come from the devil rather than from good forces.

This woman, whom I shall call Mrs P.L., like many people who claim contact with alien forces, is convinced that the end of the world will come about very soon. She believes that there will be 5 years of upset followed by a final revelation. Only those who maintain certain moral standards and work for good rather than evil will come to see the final revelation. This she thinks will be the return of God in a flying saucer. His craft will destroy many as it lands but others will finally discover what our existence is all about. The onset of the 5 years of upset will probably be caused by our own nuclear weapons. To avoid the dangers caused by nuclear war she wants, with like-minded individuals, to obtain enough money to buy a submarine. Apparently, only a submarine will offer the best form of protection as land based shelters are 'useless'.

This is not very different from the experience of John Keel who took to the hills with gallons of water when he was told that some calamity would occur. It is, however, unfortunate that as a result of his research John Keel thinks that we can never make any sense of 'The Phenomenon' [FT40p70]. In the same way it is unfortunate that Mrs P.L. and others like her have a fatalistic acceptance that 'the end of the world is nigh'. Indeed, today the UFO is seen increasingly as a symbol of that change to a completely different way of life rather than as a shining example of the kind of technological hardware we might one day create.

It is a sad indictment of our society that people should seek salvation on hilltops or in submarines rather than contemplate more positive 'mundane' alternatives. Equally, we can see the seeking after encounters with the unknown as a form of escape (e.g. 'Anatomy of a Percipient' in MUFOB Ns 11 and 12). Only recently a person who has had all manner of bizarre experiences noted that:

My dream world adventure, or rather actual experiences on planes other than the earth during sleep, are many times more vivid, colourful and solid than so called dull 'reality'.

Another person, in a letter to Jenny Randles, wrote: *Satan wants to obliterate everything. Man must pit himself against the forces of evil destruction and disease. The downfall of man on earth is imminent.*

It might be cruel to speculate that this person was suffering from the after-effects of reading one of Jenny's books, but it is obvious that many people are discontented with themselves and society. UFOs and space people are seen as an answer to their prayers.

•

Nigel Watson

I Spy with my Little Eye, Something beginning with 'S'

by John Prytz

While working on an unrelated project, I recently came across a news item from late 1976 which, to some, has a quasi-relevance to ufology. The story involved the sightings of a USO – unidentified submarine object. While such sightings have been frequently reported overseas, in particular in Scandinavian regions, [see latest reports on p7 – Ed.] they are rare in Australian regions – which may be a function of our long coastline and low population density. Anyway, although I am fair ly sure that this particular USO was in fact a terresterial submarine, there is room for doubt and debate. It makes for interesting reading.

On Tuesday, 28 December 1976, a party of about 20 Aboriginals saw a "submarine" surface about 200 metres off Coomlieyna Beach, near Ceduna, in the far west of South Australia. The Aboriginals, from the Yalata Lutheran Mission, had gone to the beach for an afternoon's fishing, when, about 3 p.m., "this thing popped out of the water", according to the Mission manager, B.R. Lindner, and "scared the living daylights out of them". The party "ran from the beach to the sandhills". Press reports then differ as to whether the object stayed on the surface and sailed out to sea, or immediately submerged, then reappeared far out to sea before submerging again. The length of the sighting was not stated, but apparently all but one witness agreed the object was about 90 feet long. So far there is nothing overly mysterious about the report. However . . .

All the witnesses agreed that whatever the object was, it had a white conning tower, with a ladder going from the tower to the deck, a black centre line and a red stripe/bottom at the water-line. Alas, the reported markings and description did not match the colours of any submarine in any of the world's navies. According to a Royal Australian Navy (RAN) spokesman, the sighting was being treated seriously, even though there were some official doubts that the object was a submarine. "Submarines tend to be black or a dark blue in colour so they can hide in deep water and not be seen from the air" according to the RAN official. "A white conning tower would stick out a mile."

Further, there were no known submarines, or underwater exploratory craft – from the RAN or from other nations – operating in waters off the S.A. west coast. Thus, commercial aircraft, the Royal Australian Air Force (RAAF), shipping, and even local police patrols were alerted to be on the lookout for the mystery vessel in the Great Australian Bight. However, over a day had elapsed between the original sighting and official notification to the Defence Department in Canberra, so it perhaps should not be surprising to learn that nothing was ever seen of the strange submarine again.

Although the Defence Department did not

speculate on the nature of the object sighted by the Yalata Aborigines, others weren't as reserved. The "obvious" solution was that it was Russian or from some other foreign, and one would presume unfriendly, nation, and on a spying mission. However, for the submarine to have been in that close to shore, near reefs, and caught-in-the-act as it was broad daylight, suggested to the RAN spokesman that "the sub was in trouble, or it's got a lousy captain". If the submarine had been from the RAN, the captain would have faced a court martial according to the Navy's spokesman, operating that close to reefs. Further, the remote west of S.A. doesn't smack as being a likely espionage-targeted region. Thus . . .

A spokesman for the Marine Operations Centre, in Canberra, suggested a theory that the object was an overturned vessel, possibly a large yacht. However, there were no reports of any vessels missing or overdue in the Bight area.

•

John Prytz

Literary Assistance of a Curious Kind

by Jenny Randles

For quite a few years I have admired the writings of psychologist Dr Stan Gooch, and I have also been interested in synchronicity. For ASSAP I have operated an 'Incidence of Coincidence' research project, but I never expected these two things to blur together in a very strange series of events. They are almost so mind-boggling I am going to have to ask for your acceptance that they are all true – honestly! For a time I thought the 'Cosmic Joker' was really having fun.

It began in Spring 1983 when I found one of Gooch's rarer books at the library and avidly read his ideas about the right brain and the left brain. He believed that the cerebrum and cerebellum controlled different functions, and whilst the latter appeared physically smaller and insignificant, it actually governed psychic and creative functions. Coincidences were relevant to it.

The night after reading the book I had a dream, which I entered into my "dream diary" (the device which long ago proved to me the reality of precognition). I noted how I had been in a house with two rooms. One room looked small compared with the adjacent space, but when you got inside the difference was less marked. The smaller room looked bigger. The main room was the living room, the smaller one was mostly free space. But it had a phone in it. I noticed the number and realised (in the dream) that it was close to, but not the same as, Peter Warrington's phone number. I said to myself "what a strange coincidence".

Naturally, I regarded this as a nice expression of the Gooch ideas by my mind. The dream symbolism has been marvellously apt. So I decided to write to Stan Gooch, care of his publishers, and tell him my dream. I also wanted to complain, because in his book he had dismissed UFOs as unimportant. I obviously disputed that! But more importantly, I wanted to tell him how I had found UFO study full of synchronistic items (as I had occasionally written about – eg. in my *The Pennine UFO Mystery*, Granada).

I received a speedy reply from Stan Gooch and we both saw the first coincidence immediately. Indeed Stan said in his letter he could not believe my address – 9 Crosfield Road, Wallasey. He could not believe it, because his address was 11 Crossfield Road, London. We lived metaphorically in two addresses next to each other (ie. my dream of two adjacent rooms!)

Stan apologised for his comments about UFOs and told me about his new book, now published, but then still being written (*Creatures from Inner Space*). *Creatures* was about a subject dear to me, bedroom visitors, and UFOs would feature. He asked me to let him know of any good cases of incubi, or succubi, I found.

The week his letter arrived I had got a note from a woman who had read the UFO article in *New Scientist*, written by Peter Warrington and myself. This woman was a medical journalist and she had undergone an interesting and seemingly unexplained UAP event. I recalled the address, got it out and checked her letter, because it came from the same district of London as Stan Gooch lived in. The woman had insisted in her letter that she was going to get a street map and send it to me, a very unusual thing for a witness to propose. Even as I waited the couple of days for it to arrive, I knew what it was going to show. Sure enough, the woman lived just a few hundred yards from Stan Gooch – and she had been looking towards his house when she saw the UAP!

All I had to do now was write to Stan, suggest he take a two minute stroll out his door, and he could find out first-hand that he was wrong to dismiss UFOs so quickly!

Stan's letter about his book had lead to me working out a radio programme on bedroom visitors. I was at the time doing a weekly show with Radio City, the commercial station serving one million people in north west England and north Wales. So I thought I might be sent some useful material for Stan. I received just one that was exactly what he needed, a prime incubus case. The woman lived in Wallasey – and the address sounded familiar. So I got out the street map, and sure enough – it was a couple of hundred yards from *my* front door. A two minute stroll enabled me to find out first hand that Stan's incubi theories were justified.

In this we had each helped out one another in a way that chance leaves standing. It was certainly intriguing. But there is more to come.

Wallasey is a big town, and the proximity of the witness to me was much stranger than it might seem. The part of London where Stan Gooch lives is large too, and so the proximity of the UFO witness to him is also odd. I will call that district – Wimbledon, although this is not the real area. I have changed it to protect Stan's address in print. But accepting that for Wimbledon you should read the true London district, I discovered, only when I got out the street map to find the address of the incubus witness, that she lived in Wimbledon Road Wallasey! Yet another amazing coincidence was added to the chain.

I got out the phone book to call the witness and arrange to speak to her. I noticed that her phone number began 051-630, just as my own did. This in itself is no real coincidence. All Wallasey numbers begin 051-63x. So the odds were small. But the last four numbers were also exactly the same as mine, just slightly re-arranged. This compounded the odds to several hundred to one against.

No sooner had I smiled at this last coincidence than I recalled the dream which had prompted me to write to Stan Gooch in the first place. I had come round full circle so that the phone number coincidence, prompted in a dream by reading about Stan Gooch, had lead to me contacting Stan Gooch and producing a phone number coincidence.

If anybody has any idea what all of this means I would love to know!

•

Jenny Randles
21 Whittlewood Close, Gorse Covert,
Warrington, Cheshire WA3 6TU.

End Times Bulletin

by Kevin McClure

THE LAST WORD.

There haven't been many successful prophets of world events in the past thousand years. Actually, there haven't been any. But that hasn't deterred numerous writers from pretending otherwise, particularly with regard to that undoubtedly wise old Frenchman, Michel Nostradamus. And of his work you will hear a great deal in the next sixteen years.

As source material, suitable for free interpretation, the prophecies of Nostradamus have clear advantages. There are many of them: they run, I believe to 4,772 lines, grouped into four-line 'quatrains'. Supposedly for the protection of their author from charges of witchcraft or something, they were written in obscure codes, with bastardised words from assorted languages used to represent significant names and places. They were also, it seems, intentionally muddled, put out of temporal sequence. Often, lines grouped within the same quatrain appear to have no link with each other.

There is no limit to the variety of interpretations made of the quatrains. They were used by Hitler to damn the British, by the British to confuse the Germans, and by Gary Harlow, British ufology's resident alien, to prove that he is not only the Antichrist, but a good many other things besides. And while earlier prominent translations, such as those by James Laver and Erika Cheetham, retained sufficient of the original's obscurity to protect their speculations from serious criticism, the rising 'end times' mood has produced two much more vivid attempts to relate the quatrains directly – and as coherent units – to the events of the rest of this century.

The first of the two to be published in English was marginally the more reasonable – this was Rene Noorbergen's *Invitation to a Holocaust* (NEL 1981). This selected 265 of the quatrains, and used them to delineate the onset and consequences of a Third World War. By Quatrain 165 England has already sunk into the sea, Scotland is an island and the government, troubled by Scottish rebels (and presumably by the sea as well) has moved to North America. The *real* enemy appear to be the Chinese and the Arabs. There is a great deal of speculative detail none of which, three years on, shows any sign of being proved correct.

The more famous recent book based on the prophecies is *Nostradamus: Countdown to Apocalypse* by Jean-Charles de Fontbrune (Pan, 1983). It first appeared in France in 1980, and caused a considerable stir. Here most, though not all, of the quatrains are used. About half of the book is devoted to interpretations involving past events, an exercise not unlike playing Scrabble with a million pieces. You can make up every word you ever wanted. My French is barely adequate, I will admit, but many of the interpretations appear to have nothing at all to do with the original French source.

The rest of the book – some 170 pages – is devoted to the future. Well, maybe not *the* future, but some future or other. It seems to last for about 40 years. It is markedly Franco – centric, with the King of France leading many a battle against the wicked Russians, and eventually being crowned by the Pope and becoming a world leader. There is a 27-year War of the Antichrist (1999–2026), a nuclear holocaust, a Soviet invasion of Britain, Christians are persecuted, Rome is burned, and the Moslems prove to be a lot less than helpful as well. A miserable time is had by one and all, and there isn't even a happy ending. Anyone interested in modern apocalyptic writing really shouldn't miss this book.

Anyone, however, who is tempted to take *any* advance interpretation of Nostradamus seriously, should bear two points in mind. Firstly, the interpretations are so loose that the prophecies are much more Fontbrune's than they are those of Nostradamus. Fontbrune frequently crosses the line from the abstruse to the absurd. And secondly, extensive research on my part has failed to find one single interpretation of Nostradamus made *before* the events that displayed even the vaguest inkling that either the First or Second World Wars were to occur. Despite his overwhelming concern with France he failed to communicate two wars of unprecedented devastation and suffering for his own country. Obscurity is one thing, but my own judgement is that Nostradamus can only be seen as a parochial, political prophet, who had scarcely a clue as to what was to happen to the world at large. He certainly isn't worth worrying about, though that isn't going to worry Fontbrune. If he's wrong, we're grateful; if he's right, we'll be well past caring.

•

Kevin McClure

Book Alert!

by Janet Bord

During 1984 the number of books published which will be of interest to Forteans is less than in the heady years of the seventies, but the quality is generally much higher. Fortean books are getting serious!

In the first part of the year came Paul Dong's **The Four Major Mysteries of Mainland China** (Prentice-Hall, $16.95 & $8.95), the mysteries being UFOs, psychic phenomena, Qi Gong, and the wild man. Harry Oldfield and Bruce Durie's **New Discoveries in Kirlian Photography** came from Element Books (£9.95), and **Is There Life After Death?** by American clinical psychologist Robert Kastenbaum came from Rider (£4.95), who also published Stan Gooch's **Creatures from Inner Space** (£8.95), an intriguing investigation into the power of the unconscious mind to generate paranormal entities, which should be read along with Hilary Evans' latest book, **Visions * Apparitions * Alien Visitors: A Comparative Study of the Entity Enigma** (Aquarian Press, price unknown, c.£9), the first published attempt to make some sense of the vast range of entity reports, and essential reading for all Forteans.

Also relevant to any research into the genesis of UFOs and entities are: **Cartographers of Consciousness** by Judith Hooper and Dick Teresi, which examines the relationship between the brain and the mind (Rider, £7.95 & £4.95); **Eyewitness Testimony**, edited by L. Wells and E. Loftus, which 'offers an overview of what is currently known about eyewitness testimony and illustrates how accurate or distorted such accounts can be' (Cambridge University Press, £20); **Ghosts in the Mind's Machine: How we Create and Use Pictures in our Brains** by Stephen M. Kosslyn (W.W. Norton & Co., £15.85/$23.95).

Fans of John Michell's books should not miss his new one, which is well up to standard: **Eccentric Lives and Peculiar Notions** (Thames & Hudson, £9.50), a survey of extraordinary characters; and his earlier **Megalithomania** has now been issued in paperback (Thames & Hudson, £3.95).

UFO books have been thin on the ground during 1984, but these two will keep the subject controversial: **Sky Crash: A Cosmic Cover-Up** by Brenda Butler, Dot Street and Jenny Randles (Neville Spearman), which offers an account of events during and after the Rendlesham Forest UFO sightings; and **Clear Intent** (Prentice-Hall, $14.95 & $8.95) by Larry Fawcett and Barry Greenwood, about the supposed U.S. government cover-up. In Australia, Space-Time Press of Sydney published **Aliens Over Antipodes** by Murray Scott ($8.95 August), covering all aspects of the UFO phenomenon in Australia and New Zealand.

The summer also saw the publication of Joseph W. Zarzynski's study of the monster in Lake Champlain: **Champ – Beyond the Legend** (Bannister Publications, $16.95 & $8.95), and Charles Berlitz's **Atlantis: The Eighth Continent** (Putnam, U.S.A., $16.95; UK publisher Macmillan).

Two new titles in the growing 'Evidence' series from the Aquarian Press were scheduled for autumn publication: **The Evidence for Phantom Hitch-Hikers** by Michael Goss, and **The Evidence for the Bermuda Triangle** by David Group (both £2.95). 'The latest theories on forty great enigmas' were promised in **Great Unsolved Mysteries**, edited by John Canning (Arthur Barker, £10.95), Michael Gauquelin's **The Truth About Astrology** was due in a paperback edition from Hutchinson (£3.95), and Paul Davies offers us **Superforce: The Search for a Grand Unified Theory of Nature** (William Heinemann, £9.95). A follow-up to the amazingly successful **Arthur C. Clarke's Mysterious World**, by the same authors John Fairley and Simon Welfare, was scheduled for September: **Arthur C. Clarke's World of Strange Powers** (Collins, £10.95), but I feel that this is unlikely to achieve the bestseller status of the first book. Also due in September was **Strange Gifts: A Guide to Charismatic Renewal** edited by David Martin and Peter Mullen (Basil Blackwell, c.£15.00 & c.£4.95).

The most intriguing book of the autumn slipped out almost unnoticed, a slim paperback entitled **Mary Queen of Peace** which gives accounts of the regular appearances of the Virgin Mary at Medjugorje in Yugoslavia. The authors are Sister Lucy Rooney and Father Robert Faricy, who have visited the village, as recently as late June 1984 when Sister Rooney was one of many to witness the sun spinning. (Published by Fowler Wright Books, Leominster, Herefordshire, price £2.95)

1985 already offers some good and varied reading, beginning with **Dreamtime: About the Boundary between Wilderness and Civilization** by Hans Peter Duerr (Basil Blackwell, January, c.£17.50). This book on witchcraft and primitivist cults provoked a storm of controversy when published in Germany, and sold more than 100,000 copies. The same publishers have **Science and the UFOs** by Jenny Randles and Peter Warrington (February, c.£12.50), a study of ufology's relationship with science, what has been done and what should be done.

Scheduled for March are **The Violent Earth** by Frank Lane (Croom Helm, c.£13.95), a photographic representation of natural phenomena, from tidal waves to meteorites; and **Multiple Man** by Adam Crabtree (introduction by Colin Wilson) (William Collins, Canada, $22.95), a survey of the subject of multiple personality, its history and interpretation.

Aquarian Press (Thorsons) has **The Occult Roots of Nazism: Secret Racist Sects in Austria and Germany 1890-1935** by Nicholas Goodrick-Clarke (£12.95) coming in April, while another Thorsons imprint, Turnstone Press, has a new book by Paul Devereux, co-author Nigel Pennick, due in May: **Earth Mysteries: A World-wide Compendium** (£12.95) – 'UFOs, the mysteries of the ancient sites, occult organisations, the ancient understanding of nature's geometry, the links between mind, body and our planet are all considered.'

The months of publication for 1985 titles given above can only be approximate, and it is likely that many of these books will be delayed, since publishers rarely seem to be able to keep to their initial publication schedules. Constable have wisely not offered a date for their **Relics** by James Bentley: 'Extraordianry stories about religious and secular relics scattered all over Europe, ranging from splinters of the Cross to John the Baptist's finger.'

To conclude on a high note (at least from this author's point of view!): June 1985 will see the publication of the first hardback edition of **Sacred Waters: Holy Wells and Water Lore in Britain and Ireland** and also a paperback edition (revised and updated) of **Alien Animals** (both from Granada). Granada will also publish a new edition of **The Dark Gods**, the provocative book on conspiratorial theology from Tony Roberts and Geoff Gilberston, previously by Rider.

•

Janet Bord

EDITORIAL

cont from p2.

they are) to incorporate our academic pretentions are set out in the accompanying letter. I hope you will read it and decide to support us.

★TRUSS FUND★

We record our thanks to the following for their kind donations: *Mahmood Alliho, Lionel Beer, Tim Dinsdale, E.G., Alan Gardiner, Ronald Gauntlett, Mia Gerhardt, CW Murray, Roger Musson, Anthony Smith, Douglass St Clair, TA Taylor, Valerie Thomas, Terry Tiplady, Ken Toth, Mike & Linda Ward.*

FORTEAN BOOK CLUB

This side of our activities had to be split off in order to keep it viable and to save it from the admin delays that plague FT.

However, Dick Gwynn Seary, FBC supremo (who is dropping the Seary), has asked us to make several announcements. Firstly, please note the FBC address change (see the ad on inside front cover). Secondly, if you wish to make a donation to the IFS (see above) in the following way, he is willing to provide the services free by selling any unwanted books and forwarding the proceeds. And thirdly, he wishes to start a postal library for those who can't find or afford to buy expensive or rare Fortean books.

SMALL ADS & HELP!

Due to chaotic circumstances, we regret that small ads, and the HELP! column, have to be postponed until next issue. We apologise for any inconvenience to the advertisers and the desperate.

•

Bob Rickard, Editor.

COVER: A coloured drawing by Doc Shiels shows an undiscovered form of giant squid sporting itself in a manner which might explain his famous photo of Nessie [ANS2, taken on 21 May 1977, © FPL.] Cover artwork by ADCO.

Mother Nature's Jumbo Jet

by Doc Shiels

The Picts carved many naturalistic images of animals on their stone monuments, but only one enigmaticly stylized design (*inset*) known as the Pictish beast or 'swimming elephant', like this one at Meigle, Aberdeenshire.

It is not very often that a challenging new idea comes along in cryptozoology so we are privileged to be party to this brave new guess at the identity of Nessie and other lake monsters. At one time the existence of giant squid was ridiculed, but by 1884 they were well known enough for at least one naturalist, Henry Lee, to explain all sea-serpent sightings by them. **Doc Shiels** told us that while many different kinds of monsters may exist at sea, he could not 'accept a pinniped, newt or a pleisosaur as Nessie. Only some kind of huge weirdly adapted mollusc, or a bizarre paraphysical entity would fit the bill.'' And despite his standing with the paraphysical school, Doc here explains the zoological possibility of a giant squid he names *Dinoteuthis probscideus*.

On August 2nd, 1979, *New Scientist* published an interesting photograph. Taken by Admiral R. Kadirgama, it showed an elephant swimming off the coast of Sri Lanka, and the magazine jokingly suggested that sightings of 'long-necked' sea serpents and lake monsters could be misidentifications of swimming elephants. A little later, in the pages of *Fortean Times*, Mike Crowley compared the Admiral's elephant with a mysterious animal-image, found on ancient stones carved by Pictish artists and known as the 'Beast' or 'Swimming Elephant' [FT30 p28–29]. In 1982, *Living Wonders* [1] appeared and, on page 105, authors Michell and Rickard proposed a possible link between swimming elephants, the Pictish 'Beast', and the Loch Ness Monster. To a Fortean, such 'relations of things' are a source of inspiration.

The Loch Ness Monster has often been described in elephantine terms (leaving aside, for the moment, the 'pink elephant' aspects of the case). Mr and Mrs George Spicer saw 'an abomination' with a long undulating appendage like 'an elephant's trunk', crossing the road between Dores and Foyers in the summer of 1933. When Miss Margaret Munro encountered Nessie, in 1934, she said 'the skin was like an elephants's'. In 1960, 'Torquil MacLeod' watched the monster through binoculars and likened its 'head and neck' to 'an elephant's trunk which kept moving from side to side and up and down'. *Science Now* (Vol.3. Part 36. p.978) suggested that my own 1977 photograph of Nessie (ANS.1.) looked 'like an elephant's trunk sticking out of the water'. . . I agree. There are many descriptions along these lines, not just of Nessie but of various lake and sea monsters throughout the world. When the 'Mary. F.' pictures of Morgawr were first published in the *Falmouth Packet* (March 5th, 1976), one of the newspaper's photographers almost convinced me that they showed an ocean-going elephant. It's certainly true that Morgawr looks remarkably similar to Admiral Kadirgama's paddling pachyderm, and this similarity could be significant.

The Pictish 'Beast', at first glance, looks like a piece of artistic invention and not at all like a swimming elephant, in spite of its archeological name. The Picts who carved these stones, some time in the sixth century, were skilled artists. They depicted various 'normal' animals, such as bulls, horses, salmon, deer, eagles and wolves, in a naturalistic manner. Their 'elephant' appeared on the same stones, in the company of these creatures, drawn in exactly the same straightforward style, and the symbol has mystified generations of Celtic scholars. It's a puzzling monster, with a 'beaked' dolphin-like head; legs which curl spirally like the tentacles of an octopus; and a 'trunk' sprouting from the forehead and curving over its long arched back. It is always portrayed at an angle, as if rising through water. I looked long and hard at photographs of this enigmatic 'elephant', eventually deciding that, if it represented a *real* aquatic animal, then the trunk and back of the original 'life model' would be the parts likely to have been observed most often, above the waterline, by Pictish sculptors. In which case the creature began to seem very much like a swimming elephant. Perhaps the Picts had never actually seen the underwater section of the beast, and based their representation on intelligent speculation? After all, maybe the thing behaved rather like a dolphin, so they gave it a dolphin's 'beak'. . .but those spiralling legs worried me.

I mulled over the bizarre notion of a genuinely aquatic elephant. Was it possible? Well, dead elephants have, from time to time, been washed up by the ocean. Once upon a time, a specimen turned up in Cornwall on a beach near Bude; and in 1982, the crew of a fishing boat encountered an expired elephant in the North Sea off the coast of Aberdeenshire. Charles Fort was interested in beached sea monsters with 'trunks', and noted several examples. In *Living Wonders*, Michell and Rickard describe and illustrate a strange elephant-like carcass washed ashore at Margate, Natal, in 1922. Then I read *The Aquatic Ape* [2] (and *that's* another story!) by Elaine Morgan, and became very excited by the ideas she expressed. In Appendix.3., she lists eleven very good reasons why she considered the modern terrestrial elephant to be a perfect example of an ex-aquatic animal. Her reasoning was so logical that I instantly grabbed at the possibility of a surviving branch of the family. Very soon it became apparant that, although a relict species of marine elephant could explain many sea monster sightings, it wouldn't do for

George Spicer's drawing of the long neck and large body which crossed the 12ft wide road, from left to right, in front of him at Loch Ness. Interestingly, for our discussion of elephants and molluscs, he said it was: "a terrible, dark elephant grey, of a loathsome texture, reminiscent of a snail." The dark patch where the 'trunk' meets the blob, which the Spicers thought might be the end of a tail curved behind and over its 'shoulder', might well be a parapod of some kind.

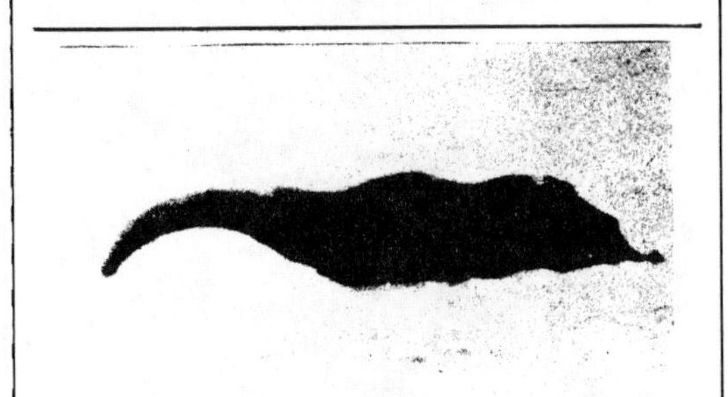

One of 'Mary F's two photos of the 15ft long creature, dubbed Morgawr, she saw in the waters of Falmouth Bay in 1976. [© FPL.]

An artist's impression of the monstrous 'polar bear' with a 'trunk' which was beached at Margate, Natal, in 1922. For the full story, see *Living Wonders* [1] p28. [© Penny Miller/ T.V. Bulpin Publications Ltd.]

Nessie and Co. Elephants, like their cousins the dugongs and manatees, are perfectly herbivorous. They comsume vast amounts of vegetation and simply couldn't exist in the inky, plantless waters of Loch Ness.

I continued worrying about the Pictish 'Beast' with its weird beaked head and spiralling legs, until one day I saw a marvelous underwater colour photograph of a common squid, *Loligo*, cruising along, under jet propulsion, with the short tentacles held, grouped tightly, in front of its eyes. . .looking for all the world like a beak! In fact, the head and tentacles formed an image remarkably like the beaked head of the Pictish 'elephant'. Could our mystery animal be a mollusc, a cephalopod, a weird type of squid?

Years ago, 'Ted' Holiday expounded his theory of a monster invertebrate, basing much of his speculation on the 'Tully Monster' [3], or *Tullimonstrum gregarium*, a small fossil creature, about 280 million years old (I think this beastie has an even older cousin, a fossil found in the Burgess Shale deposit, British Columbia. It's known as *Opabinia*). Dr E.S. Richardson, Curator of Fossil Invertebrates at the Field Museum of Natural History, Chigago, described the Tully Monster as 'a most curious prodigy' with a 'dirigible-like body', a 'long thin proboscis', and a 'spade-shaped' tail. The creature was so strange that expert paleontologists failed to classify it in any known group, though Holiday saw it as a worm. I've never seen a worm with a tail like Tullimonstrum's, but squids have tails like that. The Tully Monster has what appears to be a series of ridges along its back, rather like the ridges on the chambered shells of ammonites. According to *The Invertabrata* [4] by Borradaile and Potts: 'The fact that in the most primitive cephalopod now existing there is a kind of segmentation of the body cavity and mantle organs has been taken to support the origin of the cephalopods from a metamerically segmented ancestor'. Tullimonstrum also has a pair of rounded lateral organs which could be eyes (Dr Richardson thought he detected retinas) but which Holiday thought were parapodia. The eyes of some cephalopods are mounted on stalks. I suggest that Tullimonstrum may be related to Nessie but, if it is, then it's more likely to be a mollusc than a worm.

A model of a reconstructed *Tullimonstrum* in the Field Museum of Natural History, Chicago. [from Holiday's *The Great Orm of Loch Ness*.]

Annelid worms simply cannot reach the proportions of a Loch Ness Monster. They may, in theory, attain an impressive length, but they are banjaxed when it comes to diameter. Nessie is a bulky hump-backed beast and, as Professor R.J. Pumphrey of Liverpool University wrote to Holiday: 'I think of no physical mechanism which would lift a hump of this size out of the water *except filling it with gas*.' (my italics). . . Collapse of stout annelid! Cephalopods have gas operated buoyancy mechanisms.

Cephalopods come in many shapes and sizes, from the diminutive cuttlefish, *Idiosepius*, just 15mm long, to the giant squid, *Architeuthis*, which can reach a length of well over 100 feet. They are the most highly evolved molluscs, with sophisticated sensory and nervous systems, and are equipped with a directional jet propulsion tube called a hyponome. According to Professor J.E. Morton, [5] some early cephalopods may have had a trunk-like 'suctorial proboscis, breaking down food externally as do many modern decapods by salivary enzymes.' Architeuthis is one of these modern decapods and the larval form, once known as *Rhynchoteuthis*, has two long tentacles joined together as a flexible spout or proboscis. Cephalopods can be brilliant shape-shifters and masters of camouflage. They are intelligent predators and, in the Mesozoic oceans, competed with large marine reptiles, such as the plesiosaurs.

So. . . I begin to form a picture of a hypothetical water monster, combining elements of the Pictish 'Beast', aquatic elephant, Tullimonstrum, and Architeuthis. Let's call it the 'Elephant Squid' and consider its possibilities.

Our speculative beastie is a huge humpbacked coleoid cephalopod. Its humps are quite elastic and inflatable, shaped by the workings of the animal's buoyancy mechanism: a flexible chain of gas-filled cavities, the cartilaginous remnants of internal shell chambers, joined by a siphuncle, a tube which controls the ratio of gas to fluid within the flotation cavities. Along its broad back there is a mid-dorsal ridge, an aid to stability. Its tail is muscular, with a pair of horizontal lobes, creating a spade or leaf shape, useful as a stabilizer and for swimming. In the centre of the creature's head is a prehensile eversible probiscis, used for catching prey. When withdrawn, the proboscis brings food straight to the mouth, which is surrounded by a group of six short arms or tentacles. These hold the food as it is bitten by two overlapping jaws, shaped like a parrot's beak. At the base of the elephantine 'trunk' there are two lateral organs, eyes, or light-sensitive palps, which are directionally independent. Immediately below the mouth area is the hyponome or jet propulsion funnel which can be pointed in various directions. It is especially useful for high speed backward swimming. On each side of the group of short arms is a large muscular tentacle, used for crawling or for holding particularly lively items of food. These 'crawling arms', equipped with suckers, are joined to an undulating membranous fringe or fin on each side of the creature's great body, reaching to the base of the tail. That, then, is my basic 'elephant squid'; purely speculative, something of a surrealist *cadavre exquis*, slightly bending but certainly not breaking any of the rules of cephalopod morphology. Could it possibly be a candidate for the role of Nessie?

The primary objection to my hypothesis would, I imagine, be based on the freshwater problem. Cephalopods, we are told, are exclusively marine animals. All molloscs (like all living things on this planet) were originally marine, but nature came up with some amazing methods of adaption to estuarine, freshwater, and terrestrial life. All members of a phylum have a basically common structure and, although the Phylum Mollusca is noted for its morphological variety, a very few elements are involved. To quote Dr. G Alen Solem (Curator of Invertebrates at the Department of Zoology, Field Museum of Natural History, Chicago)[6]: 'They are altered and combined

THE EVOLUTION OF A MONSTROUS IDEA

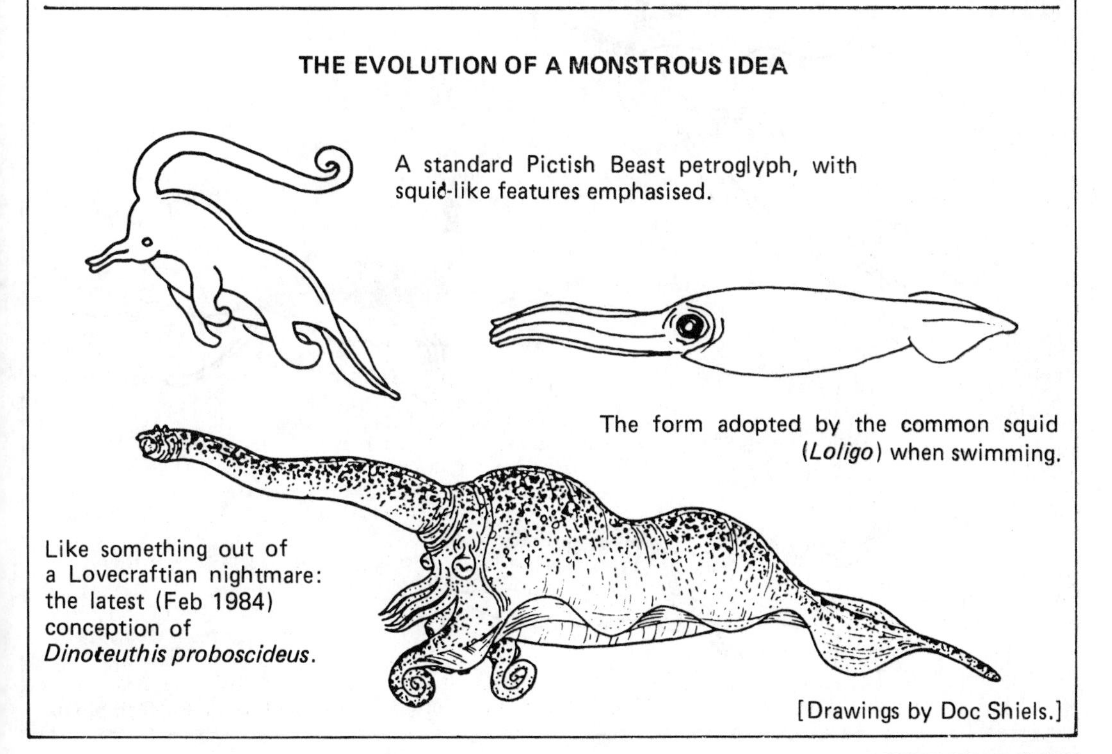

A standard Pictish Beast petroglyph, with squid-like features emphasised.

The form adopted by the common squid (*Loligo*) when swimming.

Like something out of a Lovecraftian nightmare: the latest (Feb 1984) conception of *Dinoteuthis proboscideus*.

[Drawings by Doc Shiels.]

in the various ways that form the confusingly different patterns of the major molluscan groups.' In order to adapt to a freshwater environment, our 'elephant squid' would have to regulate its body fluids. Freshwater, flowing into its body through the gills or skin, would tend to dilute these fluids and upset the salt balance unless the animal found a method of excreting large quantities of salt-free water. I suggest that the 'elephant squid', like so many other adaptive molluscs, has found such a method. In fact, I would go further and propose that the creature can pass freely from salt to freshwater by adjustment of the gill mechanisms: the chloride cells of the gills working either as salt-secreting or salt-absorbing devices. These changes may occur as part of a seasonal reproductive process. The blood pigment of molluscs is haemocyanin, a blue copper-containing respiratory pigment that functions rather like haemoglobin. In cephalopods, the pigment is several times more concentrated than in other molluscs, and an animal such as our elephant squid would need a highly concentrated form in order to increase the oxygen capacity of its dark blue blood. Circulation would be boosted, as in other cephalopods, by auxiliary hearts and contractile veins; and the kidneys would develop, in this active predator, increasing their nitrogen-excretion efficiency.

On rare occasions, the 'elephant squid' has even been seen ashore. This means that it must have a lung surface, in addition to gills, for aerial respiration. Blood may be employed to hydrostatically extend the proboscis which could, perhaps, be used as a prepulmonary organ. The animal's terrestrial excursions are probably limited in distance and duration, and I'm assuming that its 'gas balloon' buoyancy mechanism is important to this kind of activitity. Mr G. Spicer's drawing of the monster on land may be a very accurate picture. As well as reminding him of an elephant, he said the creature 'looked like a huge snail with a long neck.'

You see, I'm attempting to describe something which would relate to the *widest* range of Loch Ness Monster evidence, and which would override the limiting objections raised to such previous candidates as giant worms,

DINOTEUTHIS AT WORK AND PLAY

[Drawing by Doc Shiels.]

plesiosaurs, amphibians, pinnipeds, and vegetable mats. Nessie has been reported and described by many hundreds of witnesses over the years, with such variations in size, shape, colour, skin-texture, and behaviour that only something like the 'elephant squid' could provide the 'flesh and blood' answer to such a confusing and seemingly contradictory enigma.

This does not mean that I am now ignoring the paranormal aspects of the monster, far from it; there are a lot of awkard questions remaining which cannot be properly answered in zoological terms. At the same time, just because a creature is very large, can alter its shape and colour, and has bizarre behaviour patterns, we must not deny the possibility of its physical existance. Coleoid cephalopods can achieve quite staggering proportions, and I am not suggesting that the 'elephant squid' is even half the size of a full grown Architeuthis. Many species can expand and contract in a variety of ways, and are equipped with colour-changing pigment cells and light-producing organs known as chromatophores and photophores. Professor J.Z. Young, of London University [7], a world authority on cephalopod behaviour, has said that the octopus is 'more like a cat or a dog than a primitive sea-creature'; and Professor J.E. Morton has written: 'The coleoids have become adapted to swim, leap, walk, bury themselves, migrate up and down, even to fly. Ommastrephid squids in fact perform the only rocket or jet-propelled flight other than man.' All very weird, but natural rather than supernatural.

'The evolution of a new species can occur comparitively rapidly, perhaps in a space of two or three thousand years.' (Gordon Rattray Taylor. *The Great Evolution Mystery* [8])

In October 1673, during a great storm a monstrous cephalopod was driven ashore at Dingle, Co Kerry, Ireland. Nineteen feet long, its broad body was fringed with an undulating fin, similar to that of a cuttlefish. 'It swoom by the lappits of the mantle', according to showman, James Steward, who exhibited parts of the creature [9]. He claimed that it had two heads, one large and one small: 'the little head could dart forth a yard from the great, and draw it in again at pleasure'. . . rather like the proboscis of my speculative coleoid. The eminent Irish zoologist, A.G. More [10], recognising the 'little head' as something else entirely, was apparently much impressed by this feature of the Kerry Kraken because he named it *Dinoteuthis proboscideus*. . . undoubtably a fearsome first cousin to the 'elephant squid'.

•

The strange giant squid found at Dingle, Co Kerry, in 1673. "It swoom by the lappits of the mantle." [From a plate in Bernard Heuvelmans' *In the Wake of the Sea-serpents* (Rupert Hart-Davis 1968.)]

• 1.*Living Wonders* by John Michell and Robert J. M. Rickard. (Thames & Hudson, London, 1982.)
• 2.*The Aquatic Ape: A Theory of Human Evolution* by Elaine Morgan. (Souvenir Press, London, 1982.)
• 3.*The Great Orm of Loch Ness* by F.W. Holiday. (Faber & Faber, London, 1968.)
• 4.*The Invertebrata* by Borradail and Potts. 4th edition, revised by G.A. Kerkut.(Cambridge University Press, London, 1961.)
• 5.*Molluscs* by J.E. Morton. (Hutchinson, London, 1979.)
• 6.*The Shell Makers* by G. Alan Solem. (Wiley-Interscience, New York, 1974.)
• 7.'Octopus Learning' by J.Z. Young. *Biological Review* 36. (London, 1961.)
• 8.*The Great Evolution Mystery* by Gordon Rattray Taylor. (Secker & Warburg, London. 1983.)
• 9.Handbill describing the monster of Dingle-I-Cosh by James Steward, 1673. (National Library of Ireland, Leinster House, Dublin.)
• 10.'Notice of a gigantic Cephalopod which was stranded at Dingle in Kerry' by A.G. More. *Zoologist*, 2nd series, no.118. (London, 1875.)

•

Doc Shiels 1984

FACTS YOU MIGHT FORGET

THE CLASPROOT PAPERS

ERM... WHILE I STEP OUT FOR A SECOND, YOU MIGHT CARE TO CONSIDER THE PROPHECIES OF GEORGHEAN MACGOHOUIL THE 12th CENTURY SEER...

MACGOHOUIL WORKED AT THE POTCHEEN-SPRINGS OF OLD IRELAND, DISTILLING AN ELIXIR HE CALLED HIS "INSTANT CALMER"...

FATHER EAMONN O'ENSIS RECORDED MANY OF THE SAGE'S SAWS. HE WAS WELL QUALIFIED, AS THE WRITER OF THE VERY FIRST SHORTHAND BIBLE...

IN 1147, HE COMPILED THE "WAGGE'S GAGGES — A CORPUS OF CELTICK CRACKS"

...NEVER HESITATE TO PISS ON A DROWNING MAN — HE WILL GET NO WETTER, AND HE CANNOT CHASE YOU!

BUT IN 1154 CAME THE VOLUME OF ARCANE PHILOSOPHY SOMEWHAT TENTATIVELY ENTITLED THE "MAGNUS DELUDI"

TO BE CONTINUED...

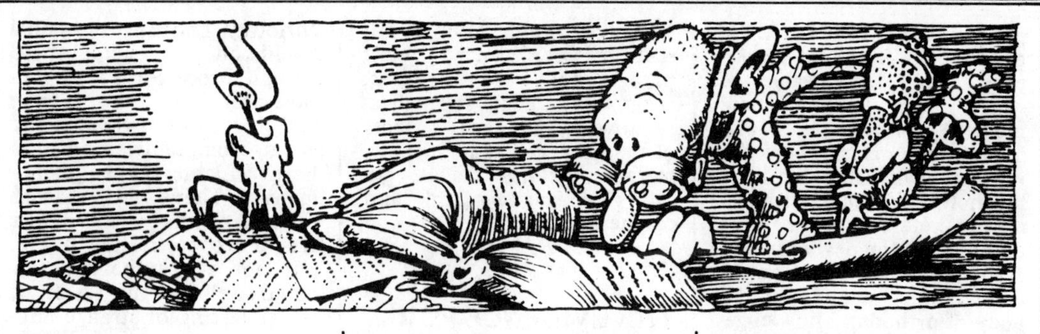

WILDMEN:

Yeti, Sasquatch and the Neanderthal Enigma
by Myra Shackley.
Thames & Hudson, London; 1983, £7.50 hb, pp192, index, notes, plates.

Myra Shackley, lecturer in Archaeological Science at Leicester University, has received wide media coverage for this book (with an article in the *Sunday Times* magazine, and an appearance on breakfast television). Her theories were initially published in *Antiquity*, a notably sober journal which has little time for wild notions – even less for wildman notions. All of this hopefully indicates a growing appreciation of the astonishing fact that Neaderthal Man has survived.

This is a well produced volume, well up to the usually high standards of the publishers, with a lavish ration of 60 illustrations, well chosen for the most part.

Readers of FT will want to know if this is something more than a prettily produced piece of media hype. The actual text runs to 170 pages and in that quite short space covers Wildmen in prehistory, Bigfoot, the Yeti, and the Chinese Yeti, the Mongolian Almas as well as reports from the Caucusus, the Pamirs and Siberia. Shackley believes there are two distinct types involved in these reports: the smaller Almas are in fact surviving Neanderthalers, while the larger Yeti and the Bigfoot are evolved forms of Gigantopithecus.

This conclusion is reasonable enough, and as an introduction to the whole problem this is an excellent book. But her selection and treatment of evidence is often lacking in detail, and this can be misleading. A good example of this is her treatment of the creature found by Ivan Sanderson and Bernard Heuvelmans – the misnamed Minnesota Ice-Man – which is quite unfair, and does little justice to the case which Heuvelmans makes out in his own book, written with the Russian Boris Porshnev, *L'Homme Neanderthal Est Toujours Vivant*. A surprising amount of Shackley's material derives from that book, though of course she has added a very great deal of material which has come to light since it was published in 1974.

I am mystified as to why she uses Sanderson's very poor sketch of this creature on p16, when Heuvelmans own measured drawings and photographs were readily available. (See *The Unexplained* No. 98, where Heuvelman's version of the story is recounted.)

She concludes her book with a hope that one of these elusive creatures might be tracked down. It is a great disappointment that she cannot bring herself to deal fairly with the one case where a body was found. So while it gives an air of open-mindedness, Myra Shackley's book has not quite managed to throw off the chains of her academic caution.

Aside from this the book does cover the ground, and bring events up to date, and along with John Napier's *Bigfoot*, would make a fine starting point. It is far from being the last word.

However, credit where credit is due, and I think she could have given the living pioneer Bernard Heuvelmans as much praise as she gives the late Boris Porschnev. Perhaps the interest aroused by this book may encourage some enterprising publisher to bring out a translation of the Heuvelmans/Porschnev book. Meanwhile it will open up the discussion.

But does it suggest an academic takeover of the crypto zoological field?

Peter Costello

EARTHQUAKES, TIDES, UNIDENTIFIED SOUNDS and Related Phenomena. *(1983, pp214.)*

RARE HALOS, MIRAGES, ANOMALOUS RAINBOWS and Related Electromagnetic Phenomena.

(1984, pp238.)
Compiled by William R. Corliss. The Sourcebook Project: Box 107, Glen Arm, MD 21057, USA.

The latest two hardbound volumes in Corliss' ambitious 25-volume 'Catalog of Anomalies'. As with his previous publications, these are indexed, illustrated, reference works, the value of which goes beyond mere money. Historical and modern reports are here salvaged and catalogued in a hierarchy of topics with examples, references and (most usefully for the new inquirer) evaluations of the anomaly and evidence relative to the body of orthodox knowledge, and some suggested explanations. It is impossible to do justice to the scope of these volumes, or to comprehend the amount of dedication and work which went into them, so, with an awe-struck boggle peruse the following summary of their contents.

EARTHQUAKES: Unusual phenomena of water surfaces; geysers & wells; strange tides; odd turbulence and circulation in oceans; giant waves & anomalous wave forms. Animal responses before and after quakes; quake 'hairs' & objects thrown upward; magnetic phenomena during quakes; quake periodicities (lunar, solar, meteors, polar wobble, 42-minute cycle, planetary, etc); vibrations & weather effects. Aerial bangs and seaboard detonations (Barisal Guns type); anomalous echoes, hissings and rushing sounds; natural musical sounds; quake & meteor created barometric waves.

HALOS: Rainbows etc (multiple, intersecting, white, lunar, red, moving, offset, fogbows, dewbows, cloudbows, purple, parallel to horizon, perturbed by thunder, with radial streaks, with dark centers, distorted, with odour, that divided the sky colours, with prismatic pillars, etc etc); unusual halos, coronas and other displays; Brockens and 'glories' (some with spokes); low-sun phenomena (the Green Flash, colour effects in sky, sunsets, shadow bands, abnormal refractions on horizon, diverging rays, Alpine glow, landscape flourescence, etc); mirages and Fata Morganas; radio and radar anomalies; shadow phenomena; effects of moon, eclipses, planets, meteors, gravity waves, etc on geomagnetic field and magnetic storms).

RJMR

THE EVIDENCE FOR ...

In late 1983 the Association for the Scientific Study of Anomalous Phenomena (ASSAP) launched possibly its best idea yet; a series of paperbound books which present the evidence for and against a topic of general interest, published by Aquarian Press (*Denington Estate, Wellingborough, Northants NN8 2RQ.*) These simple but pleasantly produced books aim quite high, attempting an unbiased summary of present argument and knowledge while at the same time serving as the most balanced introduction to the complexities of the chosen topic for beginners and others.

★ **THE EVIDENCE FOR UFOs** by Hiliary Evans (*1983; £2.50 pb, pp160, index, bib, illus.*) An eminently rational digest of the UFO enigma, long needed and now readily available. Evans is a competent and affable guide, admirably wise about the whole weird maze of truth and untruth that is ufology. He summarizes 71 cases as he takes us on a tour of the numerous theories and schools of UFO origin, the witnesses and their reliability, the reports and their distortions, the photographic and physical evidence, the researchers and their techniques, the research and its implications. Evans adds a 'Personal Assessment' postscript in which he affirms his belief in the reality of the UFO problem. He gives the following four possible sources of UFO reports, curiously omitting the equal likelihood of unidentified natural processes (eg responsible for the more bizarre ball lightnings, which itself is far from understood, and Earth Lights type phenomena). There are reasons to believe that many UFOs *are* of extraterrestrial origin, but not all of them; a few could well be the result of secret testing of strange military weapons, and others might well be "natural biological objects which manifest as balls of light". A significant percentage, including many contactee cases, must be psychological in origin, but far from being a reason for dismissal, these cases demonstrate "a phenomenon of the utmost significance, promising us a dramatic new insight into the human mind." And this last is the general tack of his latest book *Visions*Apparitions* Alien Visitors* (see review below).

★ **THE EVIDENCE FOR VISIONS OF THE VIRGIN MARY** by Kevin McClure. (*1983, £2.50 pb, pp158, index, bib, photos.*) There are possibly hundreds of books on the celebrated apparitions of the BVM written by Catholics for Catholics, and they are typified by inadequate or absent referencing, because, one presumes, they were for the faithful who need no proof, with the notable exception of the writings of Father Herbert Thurston. McClure's book is the first about the subject of such Catholic visions, to my knowledge, which (again with the exception of Thurston's work) attempts some sort of rigorous assessment, but unlike Thurston's this is intended for general consumption. McClure confesses, in the 'Personal Verdict' chapter, that years of research into the two dozen or so visions discussed, have disappointed him by failing to provide any evidence of the objective existence of an entity known as the Virgin Mary; most of the investigations were hardly impartial, often muddled, filled with leading questions, and the witnesses (who often gave their testimony *years* later) equally confused, often barely able to express themselves, and frequently contradicted each other on important details. However, of the reality of the subjective experience, however it originated, McClure is convinced. But the glimpses of that psychological experience, before it is claimed by Catholics and imprinted with the Marian cult imagery, are scant indeed, and McClure has room only to mention it rather than discuss it. A bold, and on the whole skeptical book, but that's not a bad thing about a phenomenon too many people accept uncritically.

★ **THE EVIDENCE FOR BIGFOOT AND OTHER MAN-BEASTS** by Janet & Colin Bord. (*1984, £2.50 pb, pp160, index, bib, notes, photos.*) The Bigfoot scene in the USA has degenerated sadly into a far from gentlemanly scuffle between different individuals and groups each with allegiance to different theories or techniques. This must be partly due to the pressures created by the paradoxical state of Bigfoot research: everyone agrees that the enigma of manlike creatures in North America is extensive, as sightings are reported regularly from almost every state and province; on the other hand there is the remarkable paucity of convincing evidence to back up the notion of an undiscovered humanoid race cohabiting the same continent as the most technologically advanced nation on this earth. But man-beasts, or rumours of them, exist on every continent, and the Bords have boiled a mountain of literature into a concise and excellent summary of the hunters and conservationists, the theories and reports. There is also a chapter devoted to the more paradoxical evidence involving phantom-like creatures, UFOs and psychic experiences of the witnesses.

RJMR

VISIONS ★ APPARITIONS ★ ALIEN VISITORS:

A Comparative Study of The Entity Enigma
by Hilary Evans.
Thorsons/Aquarian Press, Wellingborough, Northants; 1984, £9.95 hb, pp320, index, bib, plates.

Since Jacques Vallee's pioneering *Passport to Magonia* (1970) first pointed out the similarities between contemporary contactee cases and the dealings between mortals and fairies recorded within almost every culture, a number of researchers, independently, have seen further analogies between reports of abduction by aliens and strikingly similar phenomena in the fields of shamanism, demonology, near-death experiences, out-of-the-body experiences, visions of the Virgin Mary and some kinds of phantoms, and even drug induced hallucinations. In 1975, Ronald Siegel demonstrated the similarities between the imagery of drug experiences and those of mystical or visionary experiences; work which Stanislav Grof extended to include experiences of 'past lives', 'astral projection' and the reliving of the birth trauma. In 1977, at the first International UFO Congress, in Chicago, Rev. Gordon Melton suggested that: "a fruitful field of research would be the comparison of contactee experiences with the entire range of other religious experiences . . ."; and in 1982 we saw the publication of David Hufford's model study, *The Terror which comes by Night,* in which the New England 'Hag' traditions were compared to the Dark Age entities known as succubi and incubi, and to the close (even sexual) encounters of ufology. Running through all this has been the continual flow of papers from Alvin Lawson exploring hypnotically induced abductions which mimic the 'real' abductions so closely that he has sought a common and fundamental origin for the imagery in memories of the birth trauma itself.

It was inevitable, then, that someone would begin the work of correlating these ideas on the assumption that it is the imagery which creates the diversity of expressions, beneath which these seemingly different kinds of experience share a fundamentally similar structure. Hilary Evans has addressed himself to this task, and the result is a trail-blazing book which tries to find some unity among the different schools, which to some extent have been prevented, by their allegiance to a particular dogma or theory, from seeing beyond their narrow subject. Just as Paul Devereux did with his *Earth Lights* (a synthesis of ufology, earth mysteries and geophysics), Evans initializes a whole new field of study, in which the UFO contactee is but the latest form of an ancient and universal psychological and spiritual experience.

In a comparative study of this complexity the new ground has to be established, and Evans cites a great number of cases from the literature on all these subjects. The work is in three parts. The first deals with twelve kinds of experiences, or states of consciousness, in which entities, benign, malevolent or indifferent, can be encountered. Compared with this body of "spontaneous" experience are what Evans calls the experimentally created entities; that is deliberately invoked, and often repeatedly, by techniques ranging from so-called black magic and the spiritualists' seance to the artificial inductions of Lawson's hypnotic experiments. The third and concluding part of the book is the most important, for having analysed his cases at every step – and there are frequent helpful summaries of his findings – Evans discusses eight possible directions from which possible explanations of the phenomena may be derived: the collective unconscious; the idea of collective and individual reservoirs of expressive images; the hypothesis of psi-substance; the possibility of induced dreaming; the phenomena of dissociated personalities; pathological and other kinds of hallucinations; the discovery that many of the descriptions by witnesses of UFOs and associated entities are paralleled in early (and obscure) science fiction; and the subtle 'grafting' process by which unexpected images (eg UFO with portholes and aliens) are seen by witnesses superimposed on (or instead of) an optical object (eg the moon or a plane). Before Evans launches into a final assessment, he briefly discusses the degree of motivation which predisposes the witnesses to see what they report they see, and devotes a whole chapter to the implications of Hufford's important work, which underlines the fact that the primary experience, shorn of its witness- and culture- specific imagery, crosses all the categories and hypotheses.

The concluding chapter is a masterpiece of summation, brief and to the point. While in principle opting for a psychological theory (a creative part of our brain/mind he calls, for convenience, the 'producer' has control over the means and the material), Evans accepts the need for a psi component (the producer usually shows great telepathic, precognitive, clairvoyant and synchronistic skill and precision in its choice of imagery and occasion). Naturally in a bridge-building work of this magnitude – it is a substantial book set in smaller than usual type – there are matters which could only be touched upon all too briefly; eg both Evans and Hufford acknowledge the problem of exteriorized phenomena (like poltergeist movements of furniture, or marks left on people and objects) and the way is left open for future exploration and experimentation. Now that Evans has laid the foundations for a new area of interdisciplinary study, we all look forward to further studies along these lines.

Evans is to be congratulated for his worthwhile labour in producing what his peers immediately recognize as a seminal work. It deserves to be mandatory reading for anyone interested in the bizarre and paranormal extremes of human experience, and especially so for those who have not thought beyond the blinkered confines of sectarian ufology. Heartily recommended.

RJMR

MYSTERIOUS AMERICA

by Loren Coleman.
Faber & Faber, Boston, Mass., & London; 1984, $9.95/£6.95 pb, pp301, bib.

Loren Coleman was first attracted to the Fortean mysteries in the late 1950s, and has since become one of the world's leading researchers in cryptozoology and Forteana through his writing in almost every Fortean publication, including his column in FT. Built around a selection of his articles is a guide to American Forteana which rambles, in an enchanting way, through a variety of familiar topics. I suspect that the introductory tone is mainly the publisher's intention, to reach the widest public in the States, but once Loren gets his steam up he draws upon his own unique files of historical material and extensive fieldwork. The five appendices list locations relative to spook lights, erratic crocodiles, phantom ships, bedevilled names, and lake and river monsters, encouraging the inquisitive traveller to go and see for himself.

Among the expected chapters on lake monsters, bigfoot, the Jersey Devil, giant snakes and pre-Columbian sites are subjects which Loren has almost made his own: alligators in city sewers; devil names and Fortean places; mystery panthers and lions; the strange little 'demon' of Dover; the North American ape; epidemics of kangaroo sightings; possible teleportations of animals; and the strange name coincidences of people and places involved in Fortean events. We are also treated to the Coleman version of such famous phenomena as 'The Mad Gasser of Matoon' (an Illinois relative of Springheel Jack); the seige, in 1955, of a Kentucky farming family by little men/"goblins", that became a part of the canon of ufological entity contacts; phantom clowns; and the contemporary belief in the three "wandering Nephites", a peculiar Mormon combination of the Wandering Jew/Flying Dutchman type of myth.

Being an old hand, Loren knows there are no easy answers to the myriad questions raised by these excursions into the unexplained.

This is a hoary point which many newcomers to the Fortean world cannot or will not grasp. Instead, the concluding chapter tries to tie these subjects together by demonstrating the philosophy of open-minded curiosity which allows Forteans to accommodate such diversity regardless of whether it is understandable. What makes *Mysterious America* different from most other Fortean books is its personal touch; Loren's humour, knowledge, experience and curiosity – not to forget his admirable energy in driving all over the USA in pursuit of mysteries – come across without pretension. It is a book all Forteans (ie any child with imagination and curiosity) should read.

RJMR

UFO CONTACT AT PASCAGOULA

by Charles Hickson & William Mendez.
Wendelle Stevens, 3224 S. Winona Circle, Tucson, AZ 85730, USA; 1983, $14.95 + $1.25 p&p hb, pp274, index, photos.

On 11 October 1973 Charles Hickson and Calvin Parker had an experience they will never forget. While fishing at Pascagoula, Mississippi, they were abducted into a UFO. This book presents full details of the event, mainly via Charlie's written account and transcripts of the hypnotic regression sessions; also by comparison with a secret tape recording made at the Sheriff's office within a few hours, an interview conducted less than 24 hours later at Keesler Air Force Base, and William Mendez's taped interviews. There appear to be very few inconsistencies, and there is no obvious reason for disbelieving the men's story. Particularly convincing is a secret tape made of their conversation when alone together soon after the abduction: this gives no hint of a hoax but shows two genuinely frightened and bewildered men.

In an attempt to decide what happened to them, Mendez discusses all the possible explanations: hoax perpetrated by Hickson and Parker; them as victims of a hoax; shared hallucination; some experience 'beyond science'; experimental terrestrial craft; abduction by extraterrestrial creatures in a spacecraft. Mendez strongly favours the last possibility, and his assumption that the abductors must have been extraterrestrial is a weak point in the book. His and others' belief in an extraterrestrial origin for UFOs is not based on logic and fact. If we face the truth, we must admit that we do not as yet have any reasonable explanation for the experiences of Hickson and Parker and others.

Mendez has done a thorough job of collecting and presenting the facts relating to this abduction, and Charlie's later UFO experiences which are described in his own words, and the main value of the book is as a source of information. However Mendez is not quite critical enough: when discussing hypnotic recall, he is too enthusiastic about its value, and gives no hint of its well-publicised shortcomings. Hence one wonders if he has possibly been too kind in his evaluations of Hickson and Parker – though he does present independent psychological reports on them in the appendix. The book is enhanced by frequent photographs – of Hickson and Parker at various locations, Hickson's family, the site of the abduction, drawings of the entities and craft, and other people involved in the case. This is a valuable record of a puzzling case, but marred by the author's conviction that UFOs are extraterrestrial.

Janet Bord

ALSO RECEIVED

Because there were no reviews last issue we have quite a log-jam to clear. We'll have more space next issue.

★ **THE SPHINX AND THE RAINBOW** by David Loye. An absorbing and at times heavy discussion of the latest ideas about the growth and function of the brain and its two hemispheres, consciousness, our perceptions of space and time, concepts of reality, and the emerging theories of the holographic aspect of 'reality' compared to the holographic behaviour of the brain. PSI is touched upon, but only precognition gone into at length. A good reference to have. *RKP/Shambala, Henley-on-Thames, London & Boulder (CO); 1983, £7.95 pb, pp236, index, refs, notes, diags.*

★ **THE SELF AND ITS BRAIN** by Karl Popper & John Eccles. Basically a review of the mind/body problem, in two sections, with Popper arguing from historical and philosophical standpoints and Eccles arguing from contemporary knowledge of neurology and biochemistry. The third part is adapted from recorded debates between these two eminent scientists. *RKP, London & Henley, Oxon; 1984, £7.95 pb, pp597, index, bib, diags.*

★ **THE COSMIC CODE: Quantum Physics as the Language of Nature** by Heinz Pagels. A tour through the development, discoveries, and mysteries revealed by the alien world of quantum physics, with chapters devoted to all the famous paradoxes and problems. Weird stuff! *Michael Joseph, London; 1983, £10.95 hb,* *pp370, index, bib, drgs.*

★ **THE SECRET TRADITION IN ARTHURIAN LEGEND** by Gareth Knight. An analysis of the Arthurian cycle based on qabalistic and other Western mystical traditions. *Thorsons/Aquarian Books, Wellingborough, Northants; 1983, £5.95 pb, pp302, indexes, diags.*

★ **THE GODS AND THEIR GRAND DESIGN** by Erich von Daniken, EvD's notion that an ET 'Commander' took some inhabitants of Jerusalem to South America to build a replica of the Temple of Solomon. EvD claims to have found this replica at Buritaca, in Columbia, and most of the book is an interesting (if you can ignore his annoying style) account of his exploration of these ruins, in which he inevitably sees evidence of his beloved Ancient Spacemen. He describes a curious disk seemingly designed with a re lief illustrating the conception and growth of a fetus. *Souvenir Press, London; 1984, £9.95 hb, pp218, index, bib, photos (36 in colour).*

★ **THE HOLY GREYHOUND** by Jean-Claude Schmitt. In our *Living Wonders*, John Michell and I devote a chapter to the martyred baby-sitter; the myth of the animal, usually a dog, who defends a human baby against attack by a wild beast, and who is wrongly killed when the returning parents assume the worst upon discovering much blood and the baby missing. One of our main sources was this, the only full-length study of this surprisingly universal theme that we know of, then only available in French. This translation (by Martin Thom), in the Cambridge Studies in Oral and Literate Culture series, gives its full and complex history, unravelled by Schmitt from the mysteries surrounding the suppressed cult of St Guinefort, healer of children, as the dog-saint was personified in 13th century France. Excellent detective work, with fascinating data on the sites associated with the cult. *Cambridge University Press, London & NY; 1983, $34.50/£20 hb, pp215, index, bib, notes, illus.*

★ **MARY QUEEN OF PEACE** by Lucy Rooney & Robert Faricy. A brief history of the BVM visions, which began at Medjugorje, Yugoslavia, in June 1981, and the six young visionaries, and which are continuing today. The Catholic authors went there, interviewed the seers and witnesses, and were present themselves during a BVM appearance. *Fowler Wright Books, Leominster, Herefordshire; 1984, £2.95 pb, pp80, illus.*

★ **LORD OF THE UNDERWORLD** by Colin Wilson. In my opinion this interpretation of Carl Jung's life and work is probably Wilson's best recent work. Wilson's insatiable curiosity about the origins of the sexual impulse and its influences upon thought and deed, is turned upon Jung, with his mystical visions, his vivid dreams and inner voices, his experience of occult phenomena, his own strange psychological problems, his techniques of 'active imagination', and the development of his archetypal psychology. A fascinating book, full of gems and insight, and one which will undoubtedly provoke controversy among Jung-worshippers. *Thorsons/Aquarian Press, Wellingborough, Northants; 1984, £7.95 hb, pp160, index.*

BOOKLETS

★ **SACRED GLASTONBURY: A Defence of Myth Defiled** by Anthony Roberts. In *The Ley Hunter* (Aug 1983), an article by Cara Trimarco interpreted the features of ancient Glastonbury and environs, and the myths attached to them, in the light of current feminist enthusiasm for claiming any antiquity as its own. So, in her view, the landscape becomes a panorama of breasts and vaginas, etc, dedicated to Goddess worship, 'raped' by patriarchal Christianity. This so incensed Tony, who lives in the town, that he has published this broadside, showing how shallow, ill-conceived, fundamentally wrong and frought with silly Freudian slips is Ms Trimarco's view of probably the greatest of Britain's sacred sites. Not that Tony defends Christianity; far from it. His is a condemnation of anything less than a holistic harmony of opposites. "At Glastonbury there is the marriage of Heaven and Earth" writes Tony, something the militant feminists have overlooked in their haste to expunge the sign or symbol of the masculine. This is the first in a projected series of 'Anti-Feminist Papers'. And you thought the Earth Mysteries scene had no politics. *Zodiac House Publications, 29 Main Rd, Westhay, Glastonbury, Somerset BS6 9TN; 1984, no price, pp14, drgs.*

★ **EARLY TUBE RAILWAYS OF LONDON** by Nigel Pennick. An account of the development of tunnelling under London, from Brunel's Thames tunnel in 1818 to the beginnings of the present underground system. *Electric Traction Publications, 142 Pheasant Rise, Bar Hill, Cambridge CB3 8SD; 1983, £1.25, pp32, illus.*

★ **THE AQUARIUS GUIDE**. Names & addresses of groups & magazines world wide. *UFON, 39 Birkbeck Rd, London NW7; 1984, £1.25.*

★ **COMPTE RENDU**. Proceedings of the May 1983 congress of the Federation Francaise d'Ufologie, at Lyon. *Jean-Pierre Troadec, FFU, 45 rue du Bon Pasteur, 69001 Lyon, France.*

LETTERS
Cont from p3.
the expose of these by Robert Scheaffer and the computers of Ground Saucer Watch as being simply cut-outs suspended by an almost invisible thread seems to have been almost more than he could bear. I say, Take Heart, Jerome, all is not lost. The problem with the Cottingly Fairy photos was that they were too sharp. If and when we get photos of Santa Claus, God, Rama, the Tooth Fairy, a local leprechaun, Bigfoot, Nessie or a Phantom Panther (such as roams England these days), the photo will not be sharp or too terribly clear. There will be just enough to show the image of something vaguely recognizable, but there will be slight distortions, misty edges, blurred motion, and in many cases, a suspicious amount of graininess.

Ted Serios' photos are a good case in point. The buildings in most of his photos were just a bit off from the real buildings. A door would be in the wrong spot, or a window would be just a slightly different shape, as if the image was formed (in Serios' case) by a memory of that particular building, seen by either Serios in astral projection, a visiting spirit that liked buildings, or some other paranormal phenomenon. In my own case, I have found that photos I have taken of the woods in the Sierra mountains, as discussed in ZS no. 6, were not actually of a physical Bigfoot, as I once had thought. Perhaps one was, for this creature, squatting, had a whole body, but all the dozens of other strange animal-like faces in the main photo were without bodies, although several had shoulders and torsos. These images were intertwined with rocks and tree branches, and used a grainy background as a sort of "screen" upon which to focus themselves, or attach themselves.

I've found other such faces – in other photos by other people. Often they occur in 110 color negative photos, taken by pocket cameras. One nice one shows an ape/human head in a cloud of mist over the head of my girlfriend•, in a picture of her with myself and her child. We are not sure if this was due to the photographer, another woman, or due to Cindy, or myself, the child, or all three. I tend to suspect Cindy, since she has some psychic ability in contacting relatives wordlessly. She can think about her father, and in two days, he will arrive out of the blue. Another photo, recently examined and validated by Dr. Bruce Maccabbee, the UFO photo expert as being "not tampered with in the negative" ★, was taken by a truck driver in a graveyard in Chico, California in 1982. This one, the "Purple Sweater Photo" (*see this page*) shows his girlfriend in the foreground, and dozens and dozens of both human and animal faces in the background, on the ground, in trees, and over bushes. One might, using imagination only, force a face or so out of some photos, but this one is overpowering in its sheer numbers of face. In only one instance is there a full body.

I have dozens of others, taken by various ordinary and not so ordinary people. But as one can see in these, and in Bob Rickard's book, *Photographs of the Unknown*, none are too terribly sharp and distinct. So Jerry Clark, chin up – all is not lost. Spirits of animals and humans seem to want recognition, and somehow or another, they are manifesting on camera film, but just don't expect to see every wrinkle and pore.

Erik Beckjord
National Cryptozoological Society.
Box 31990, Seattle, WA 98103, USA.

[• *Not the girlfriend who sued Beckjord successfully for the return of thousands of dollars loaned for a Bigfoot film he never finished.*
★ *Beckjord's quote makes it seem as though Dr Maccabee endorses his view of the paranormal origin of the 'faces' he sees. But because Beckjord appended a copy of*

Dozens of faces? The 'Purple Sweater' photo [© Ron Hoffas.]

Maccabee's letter, we were able to read, as the quote continues: "I further believe that the 'faces' are chance arrangements of shaded and illuminated areas of the background caused largely by the effects of the sun shining through the trees." Over many years Beckjord has claimed to see such faces and figures in many Fortean photos, from the famous Patterson Bigfoot frames to the Rines' 1975 shots of an underwater Nessie.

A summary, by Janet Bord, of the recent intensive analysis of the Cottingly fairy photos, by Geoffrey Crawley, editor of the British Journal of Photography, *will appear in FT next issue – ED.*]

Phillip Nolan's Buck Rogers was on the cover. I used to have the first 25 years complete until I took a foolish interest in things like rent and food.

Dennis Stacy
Box 12434,
San Antonio, TX 78212,
USA.

INVISIBLE INK

What happened to Jenny Randles' article in FT41? Was she billed as a contributor for the invisible text produced in the margins? We need an explanation!

Nigel Watson
Westfield Cottage,
Crowle Bank Rd, Althorpe,
South Humberside
DN17 3HZ.

[*Yes, and Jenny deserves an apology. As last issue was finalized, it became clear that at over 76 pages it would be the biggest yet. We had to limit it to 76 pages because that was a handy number of 4-pages to a plate, and the maximum thickness on our printer's folding and stapling machine. The difficult choice on what article to drop, to meet that specification, unfortunately fell upon Jenny's article simply because it alone was the right number of pages we needed to lose. The paragraph on p75 describing Jenny as a contributor was there because I forgot to take it out. Sorry Jenny – we'll make it up to you some other time – Ed.*]

FIRST SAUCER CORRECTION

Just received the 10th Anniverary Issue of FT and can't congratulate you enough, so I won't even try. But I do have two cavils. In the reprinted article by Robert Barbour Johnson, "Charles Fort and a Man Named Thayer," the author incorrectly sites Kenneth Arnold's saucer sighting as "over Denver". John Keel, in the following article, corrects, or rather mentions correctly, that the Arnold incident took place near Mt. Ranier, in the Cascade Range of Washington State. The earlier mention should have been footnoted or corrected in parentheses, as such things have a way of creeping back into the literature. Understood, of course, that one cannot be expected to catch everything, else why a letter column?

Unfortunately, Keel makes at least one mistake of his own (p. 52) when he writes *Amazing Stories* was "created in 1929 by the inestimable Hugo Gernsbeck." The first issue was dated April, 1926, and if memory serves me well

FT Backissues.

ALL AT SINGLE ISSUE PRICE

31

32

33

34

35

36

37

38

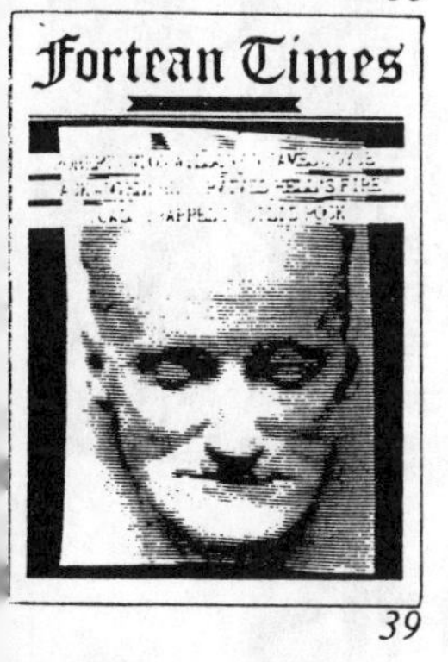

39

40

41

Sub-scribe Here.

- **SUB RATES** - £6.00/$12.00 for approximately four issues a year.
- **SINGLE COPIES** - (UK) £1.50; (Airmail) $ $ 3.00. We can send a recent issue and our literature to a friend.
- **PAYMENT** - payable to *FORTEAN TIMES* . Dollar cheques acceptable; for other currencies we prefer a sterling cheque drawn on a bank with a London office. *PLEASE no Euro cheques or Irish Postal Orders.* European readers may prefer to remit through GIRO services to our National Giro account - **No 50 782 4008 (Fortean Times)** - but if you do so **please** also send this form to us anyway, so that we know what you intend the money for, or state it on your giro cheque.

96 MANSFIELD RD, LONDON NW3 2HX, UK.

Fortean Book Club & Mail Order

MAIL ORDER

(Below are a selection of our specials. FT subscribers please deduct 10%)
All prices in pounds sterling and US dollars.

'The Evidence for UFOs' by H.Evans . . . . £3.50/$7.00
'The Evidence for Visions of the Virgin Mary' by K.McClure . . . . £3.50/$7.00
'The Evidence for Alien Abductions' by J.Rimmer . . . . £3.50/$7.00
'The Evidence for Bigfoot (et al) by J. & C. Bord . . . . £3.50/$7.00
(The above titles are the first in 'The Evidence' series, edited by Hilary Evans and published by *Aquarian Press, UK.* As we think they are all worth having; take the four and we'll discount it further.) The four . . . . £12.00/$24.00
'Phenomena' by J.Michell and R.Rickard (*Thames & Hudson) UK*) . . . . . . £4.00/$8.00
'Morgawr' Monster of Falmouth Bay by A.Mawnan-Peller . . . . £1.10/$2.20
'Complete Works of Charles Fort' (*Dover NY. USA*) *Europe only* £18.00
'House of Lords UFO Debate' notes by J.Michell . . . . £3.50/$7.00
'Ancient Science of Geomancy' by N.Pennick (*Thames & Hudson)* . . . . . £5.50/$11.00
'Visions:Apparitions:Alien Visitors' by H.Evans (*Thorsons*) . . . . £11.50/$23.00
(All the above prices include P&P. Please allow up to 6 weeks delivery for orders outside Europe. If you haven't yet got a catalogue send an SAE to us at the address below. New catalogue is in preparation.)

FORTEAN BOOK CLUB

We would like to know which *Fortean Times* readers want to join the Fortean Book Club. Books from the Club are straightforward publishers editions, offered at less than publishers prices. We ask only that you take 3 books from the 100 or so you will be offered throughout the year. To become a member, simply send your name and address and select one of the titles below for your first selection:
'Phenomena' by Robert Rickard and John Michell . . . . £3.50/$7.00
Any one of **'The Evidence'** series . . . . £3.00/$6.00
'Searching for Hidden Animals' by Dr. Roy Mackel . . . . £9.00/$18.00
'Hypnosis for the Seriously Curious' by Dr. K.Bowers . . . . £10.00/$ ask
'Shaman: The Wounded Healer' by J.Halifax . . . . £5.25/$9.80
'Photographs of the Unknown' by R.Rickard and R.Kelly . . . . £6.25/$12.50

All the above Book Club selections include post & packing so there are no hidden extra costs. Two or more books entitles you to a 10% discount on the listed price. Please send your remittance along with your selection as we keep prices down by not having accounts. If for any reason you are not happy just return the book within 10 days of receipt for full, no problem, discount.

FORTEAN BOOK CLUB & MAIL ORDER. Address until May 1985:
Old Barn, Hescott Farm, Hartland, Nr.Bideford, North Devon, UK.

Fortean Times

ISSUE NO. 43 | The Foremost Journal of Strange Phenomena | PRICE £1.50/$3.00

Fortean Times

Cover art by
Mikki Rain

The Journal of Strange Phenomena.

Spring 1985
ISSN 0308.5899

Contents

FEATURES

FROM OUR FILES

STRANGE DAYS

COMIX

USUAL STUFF

Fortean Times

96 Mansfield Road, London NW3 2HX, UK

Typesetting	Cecilia Boggis, 11 Ashburnham Road, Bedford, MK40 1DX
Photosetting	Words Illustrated, 1 Thorpe Close, London W10.
Print Agent	Dick Gwynn.
Overseas Mailing	Overseas Postal Services Ltd. 2-8 Hornsey Street, London N7 8HF.
Sub & Label Computing	Anagram, 316A Richmond Road, Tickenham, TW1 2PD.

Hello readers from Alabama to Zimbabwe, fourteen hundred of you thirsting for data on the outer edges ! I feel I can be this familiar, as I know so many of you by name from handling the subscriptions. It is an honour to sit in the editorial chair of a journal which Bob Rickard has constructed over eleven years as one of the most respected in its field. I hope I can live up to its high and wry standard, and complete my term undisturbed by Men-In-Black, or other sinister aspects of the phenomenal.

Back in 1978 when Bob put out FT direct from his typewriter, the Forteans used to meet every Tuesday afternoon above a sci-fi bookshop in Soho, open the post and chortle over the latest japes of fate. Every now and then there would be the ontological challenge of the Fort Sort, when the data would react to our attempts to categorise it, and the result would be a deceptive truce... until the next time. I was enthused right away, and thereafter 'processed' the mail, which affords endless entertainment and instruction, well worth the long hours with the paperknife.

■ Flicking through Clarie's *Occult/Paranormal Bibliography* (Scarecrow Press 1984) I found a note under Rickard and Kelly's *Photographs of the Unknown* that Jerome Clark in *Fate* magazine found "a number of dubious photographs" in the book and was surprised to find these "lapses into carelessness or credulity" by "experienced Forteans". Peter Rogerson in *Magonia* was on the same tack: "Whole sections seem to consist of fake photographs... This book...seriously detracts from Bob Rickard's valuable work in Forteana."

It's true that a daft blurb had been put on the book by the publisher, claiming that the photographs were 'proof' of ghosts, UFOs, levitation, etc. Bob clarified the issue in *Magonia* 8: The objective "was to give some of the photographs, bandied about in various areas of the anomalous, a quality printing." "To encourage a premeditated skepticism," he continued, "spoils the fun as well as the evidence... We acknowledge a world of difference between evidence and proof." The point is that *not one* of these photographs is beyond dispute: they all fall somewhere in the spectrum of dubiousness.

I revive this controversy here because a fundamental

Cont. on p.72

Letters

BRITISH FRINGE WILDLIFE

Wouldn't it be marvellous if the two coatamundis found out Redhill way [FT42p44] were somehow related to the solitary specimen reported lost by Hackney petshop owner Doreen Pemberton in October 1983? (*News of the World* 20 Oct 1983.) Having parted company with "Ginger", the lady wailed pitifully that the replacement coatamundi obtained from a Northampton dealer just wasn't the same. Just how many of these coatamundi things *are* there on sale over here and how many escape/ vanish/get stolen? From the viewpoint of a Latin American racoon-like mammal, is Redhill an improvement on Hackney or not?

The Out-of-Place column mentioned many unusual bird sightings. Various wildlife journals have remarked that 1984 was a bumper year for "twitcjers" (bird-spotters) and of course a white-tailed sea eagle sighting somewhere in the south made the nine o' clock news. At the same time, the number of introduced or exotic species seems to be on the rise; *BBC Wildlife* recently announced that the aesculapian snake is on the verge of being accepted as a bona fide breeding (naturalized) species. The incredible upswing in phantom panther accounts must have some relevance; it's as if the phenomenon provided the best and most contemporary expression of some underlying emotion/tension/whatever.

On this score, a policeman commenting on the recent Lancs panther made an interesting comment. People were describing the animal as a mountain lion or puma, he observed: how many of them really knew what a puma looked like at all? In fact, *if* the felines actually *are* phantasmal, how come the percipients are fixated by pumas as opposed to some other kind of cat? What is there special or stimulating about the puma, which has never been native to this country – in other words, why should it become a vehicle of expression, if such it is? Are these cats real (perhaps escapees)...and if they are, how come they aren't caught? Are they urban legends, perhaps updates of black dog stories or an anti-anthropomorphic trend away from humanoid entity stories? Above all, how come when I went to Exmoor last summer all I saw was a funny-looking goat in a field?

Michael Goss.
57 Belmont Road.
Grays Thurrock,
Essex RM17 5YJ.

BECKJORD REPLIES

With reference to the alleged 'Ri' or mermaid-like creatures of New Ireland, Papua New Guinea, that one investigator claimed the natives had been capturing and eating [FT42p34], the bottom line was this: I found no physical evidence that this had ever happened; and members of the expedition that immediately followed mine also found no physical evidence to back up this claim. One might wonder why, if such proof exists there, no new expedition has gone to New Ireland since Summer 1983? Perhaps some future expedition will prove me wrong, and if so, I shall be delighted indeed.

On a second more personal matter, mentioned twice in FT42, I wish to reply with my side of the lawsuit report against me. The woman who

Cont. on p.70

COMPUTER QUIRKS

That ultramodern symbol of technology, the computer, is attracting its own share of cosmic daftness....

■ In a well-known short story, Arthur C. Clarke once wrote about a computer being used by a Tibetan monastery to calculate the 'Nine Million Names of God'. It was inevitable that we would hear, sooner or later, of real-life applications, and *Personal Computer World* (Oct 1984) tells us that many of the larger Buddhist temples in Japan now have their own computer departments. One firm, Denkei Computer Systems, is even writing special software for temples, including a programme for keeping records of ancestors' posthumous sacred names.

■ Also from Japan is the news that the third most common cause of computer failure in that country is *rats*. It seems that the critters are attracted to the power supply hums (around 24kHz) and end up gnawing cables and urinating over the remaining wiring. And rats popping out of various holes in the computer case has made many an unwary operator prematurely grey. So serious is the problem that the Trade and Industry Ministry has commissioned a member of the ancient and honourable profession of rat-catchers, who invented a suitably technological rat-trap. It consists of an ultrasound generator (duplicating the power supply hum) and an automatic vacuum device to suck the inquisitive rodent into a lethal carbon dioxide chamber. However, there's a but in this solution too; literally. The trap's own sound generator is attracting snakes and spiders. This story, in all seriousness, came from the sober *Computer Fraud & Security Bulletin*, cited in *Computing* magazine 11 Oct 1984.

TWO PECULIAR BULGARS

Georgi Ivanov, an 80-year-old Bulgarian electrician with a natural immunity to electricity, has been found by Dr Georgi Tomasov. Ivanov never bothered to switch off the mains when doing domestic electrical repairs; it meant too much walking to and fro from the fuse box. He had never had a shock, only a tingling sensation. Household voltage of between 200 and 240 can be enough to kill an ordinary human. Dr Tomasov took Ivanov to a Sofia hospital where specialists ran a series of tests. They found he could take up to 380 volts without feeling any real shock.

The results were published in the *Bulgarian Medical Journal*. (Ivanov's body appears to be eight times as resistant to electricity as that of a normal person. According to the International Electro-Technical Commission in Geneva, just 50 volts can give dangerous shocks, and in cases of high humidity can be fatal. *S.Express* 20 May 1984.

■ Dr Stefan Marinov is taking the refusal of his articles by the magazine *Nature* very badly. The articles by the Bulgarian physicist, who lives in the West, are on the design of a perpetual motion machine, an attack on Einstein's special theory of relativity and a 'manifesto'. On 8 August he arrived outside the British Consulate in Genoa and said he was going to kill himself. He fled when Consulate staff threatented to report him to the police for being in Italy illegally. The following month he announced he was going to set fire to himself outside the British Embassy in Vienna, but changed his mind when police arrived. *D.Telegraph* 4 Oct 1984.

TERRORS FROM THE DEEP

They are hitting back, of course, driven mad by the endless pollution of their world. Whatever the reason, there have been a few remarkable attacks on men in boats by denizens of the deep.

● According to Dr Peter Barss, medical superintendent of the Provincial Hospital in Papua New Guinea, there have been at least 25 cases of fishermen impaled on the long bony snouts of needlefish in the last 10 years, 12 of them fatal. The larger species of needlefish can grow between five and six foot long and can leap out of the water at speeds of about 20mpg, spearing anything in their path. The main target seems to be night fishermen, who use lights to attract fish. *Nat. Enquirer* 24 July 1984.

● The *Weekly World News* is our favourite reading for over-the-top "journalism", and their exuberance was in full flight over the story of a "20-ton" stingray (or devil-fish), "200 feet long" from the nose to the tail-tip. If they are not exaggerating – they give no references, as usual – this terrifying monster has been responsible for sinking at least 22 boats and killing 150 people between the Philippines and the Marshall Islands, where one overloaded ferryboat carrying 53 islanders was sunk with no survivors. A fisherman who survived the attack, is quoted. He said the creature's first leap missed his boat by a few yards. "Its body was so huge it blocked out the sun!" The waves from its impact with the water overturned the boat, and then, as the man, his wife and her brother clung to its hull, the creature flew out of the water and landed on top of the boat, killing his brother-in-law. According to the *WWN,* the Philippine government has ordered three of its largest gunboats to hunt the monster with sonar and mines – and another gunboat, dispatched earlier to investigate the fears of the islanders, is missing, presumed lost. *Weekly World News* 28 Aug 1984.

● Two unlucky fishermen, spearfishing in a lagoon on the island of Taraua, part of the Pacific island nation of Kiribati, were killed when they were dragged out of their boats and held under water by several giant octopuses. Our sources agree in basing the story on a statement in "a New Zealand newspaper" (of 10 Sept 1984) by the Kiribati National Resources Minister, Mr Babera Kirata (although one calls him Barbara!). The exact number of octopuses is nowhere mentioned – though I would have thought that news of two or more acting in concert would have had the world of marine biology sitting up with interest. Perhaps the communiqué merely meant that such creatures are not unusual in Kiribati waters and one of them got the men? The giants are described as "9-12ft long", but does that apply to the tentacle-length or the total span? It's all so vague! The *Weekly World News* of 23 Oct 1984, which insists on referring to "writhing, bloodsucking tentacles of the sea's most loathsome killers" etc., goes on to quote Mr Kirata to the effect that it is a Kiribati tradition for a diver to let an octopus – they normally hunt 3-6 footers for food – cling to them and surface with it before killing it – by biting the nerve behind its eyes. Perhaps the killers thought it was a game and joined in, albeit heavy-tentacledly. (AP) Additional sources: *Guardian, D.Express, D.Mirror,* Frederick (MD) *Post,* 11 Sept; *Sun* 12 Sept 1984. (For more about Taraua, see MORE MISSING SHIPPING p.30).

By kind permission of the Mary Evans Picture Library

On the day our editor-in-absentia Bob Rickard clipped his own clipping of the above story, he received in the post *ASSAP News* No 14, and was pleasantly surprised to see, on p3 thereof, a brief item by Michael Raynal on giant octopuses. Raynal draws attention to an octopus attack near Sedmouth, Cornwall, in the 1890s, in which a number of people were killed by the "monsters". Can anyone help us establish the reality of this astonishing-if-true incident? A narrative of it by a 'Mr Fison' appears in an old French magazine, *Yachting Gazette* for 16 Dec 1899, and, says Raynal, undoubtedly formed the basis for H.G. Wells' fictional *The Sea Raiders* (1897). Thank heavens the octopus-invasion of Dorset earlier last year [see FT42p5] involved only small ones! Blame Doc Shiels if you think there are more octopus items around than usual. It must be a phenomenal backlash from his article last issue!

● Finally – on 30 Sept 1984 thousands of jellyfish shut down two nuclear reators at St Lucia, on Hutchinson Island, Florida. Huge swarms of the little wobbly critters are not unknown in these waters and this is not the first time they had clogged the plants' cooling systems' water filters. Eight months previously, another large swarm did similar damage to the 40 rotating screens. Well, it COULD have been an attack, couldn't it? Duluth (MN) *Herald & News-Tribune* 1 Sept; *D.Telegraph* 3 Sept 1984.

NEW WORLD LAKE MONSTERS

LAKE TAHOE MONSTER

A spurt of reports came from Lake Tahoe, on the California-Nevada border, in July 1984. They described a 17-20 foot long hump observed twice on the 1,600 feet deep lake in June.

On the 19th of that month, Patsy McKay and Diane Stavarakis of Tahoe City saw an object on the lake while hiking. McKay told the press, "I grabbed Diane and said, 'Look, that boat's sinking!' Then it just kind of emerged like a submarine. It went in a circle and then submerged briefly and came back up again. It was definitely alive."

Two or three days later Roxane Brodnick of Kings Beach was out rowing on the lake when she saw something she at first took to be a rock or a shoal of fish, but on further inspection decided was an animal 17-20 feet long. Again, no useful description was reported. Taho City (Calif.) *World* 5 July 1984; UPI/Belleville (Ill.) *News Democrat* 12 Jul 1984. These reports were *preceded* by press coverage speculating about the possible existence of the monster. (UPI) Albuquerque (NM) *Journal* 3 Apr 1984.

And in a fine example of tabloid reporting, the *Sun*, a weekly US news magazine, followed up the June sightings with a story about a monster 100 feet long with 'foot wide jaws' which 'lives between 1,000 and 1,600 feet below the surface', and leaves webbed tracks on shore.

A honeymooning couple, Ramon and Amanda Cummings, "were driving around outside of town one day in early April when they spotted an enormous creature which looked like a dinosaur.

"It stood on its rear legs and its tail must have been 50 feet long," recalls Amanda Cummings. "It was black in colour, and it had scales like a snake. It must have been as tall as a ten storey building, but I can't say for sure." *Sun* 17 Jul 1984.

STAFFORD LAKE MONSTERS – MYSTERY SOLVED

One in the eye for all those

SYMPATHETIC DEATHS

Michael Scott, 16, was watching TV at a friend's home when he became agitated. He started changing channels, went into a trance and collapsed. He was taken to Thomson Hospital, Canandaigua, NY, and pronounced dead of an unknown cause at 11.55pm. His mother, Carol Scott, went to the hospital and left her 11-year-old son Christopher at home. When she returned she was crying.

"The boy must have sensed his brother was dead", said police chief Pat McCarthy. He stiffened, his eyes rolled, and he went into a trance, dying shortly afterwards, less than 95 minutes after his brother. Neither boy had been known to touch drink or drugs.

"This case is interesting", said Ontario County Coronor Dr Charles Bathrick, "because the family also had a nephew who collapsed and died suddenly in the same way (about seven years ago) but no one knows why." Albany, NY, *Times Union*, 27 July; *D.Express* 28 July; *S.Express* 2 Sept 1984.

■ Florence and Salvatore Graziano met at a dance in Chicago in 1932, married a year later and from then on were never apart. When Salvatore, 77, had a series of heart attacks in July 1984, he was taken to Chicago's Illinois Masonic Hospital where Florence visited him daily.

On 22 July she complained of chest pains and was put in a room near her husband's. Everyone expected her to be released soon. On 30 July at 9am she was wheeled into her husband's room. Minutes later she was back in her room, Salvatore died and Forence suffered a cardiac arrest. She was pronounced dead an hour later. Her heart stopped at the exact moment her husband was pronounced dead – 9.09am. **St Louis** *Post Dispatch* 3 Aug; *S.Express* 7 Oct 1984.

RAMPAGING ELEPHANTS

A herd of wild elephants led by a large white bull elephant has destroyed large areas of rice and banana crops and damaged 14 villages since early November 1984 in Syamtalira Bayu, Sumatra.

A villager, identified only as Hussein, tried to defend his crops by grabbing hold of the trunk of the charging bull and slashing out with a knife. Witnesses said the elephant hurled him 10 feet in the air with his trunk. When he landed, the whole herd of 36 elephants trampled him to death. The Government planned to recruit trainers in Thailand and Burma to help control the elephants. *Jakarta Post* 24 Nov 1984.

● An elephant in Karlsruhe Zoo in Germany reached through to the hippo enclosure, and turned on the hot water tap. As the hippo pool filled with scalding water, 28-year -old Purzel hurled his two tons against the pen. But it was Sunday night, 15 July, and no-one was there to hear. By morning, Purzel, his mate and one-year-old baby had suffocated. *D.Mirror* 17 July 1984.

who hum and haw about draining Loch Ness to find out once and for all what's there.

For years tales had circulated of a giant fish in Stafford Lake, near Novato in California. And when the lake was drained to allow repairs to be made on a dam, a 50-70 year old sturgeon weighing 150lb and measuring 7 feet was found in a pool on the lake bottom. The fish was taken to a San Fransico aquarium.. **(UPI)** Montreal *Gazette* 24 Aug 1984; London *Sunday Express* 9 Sept 1984.

CANADIAN LAKE MONSTERS

Maned lake monsters have been reported from Saddle Lake and Christina Lake in Alberta, Canada.

At Saddle Lake, 60 miles NE of Edmonton, local fisheries biologist Ray Makowecki planned a helicopter search after fishermen complained of large holes in their nets, and he received "numerous reports of a hairy monster with Bo Derek-style braided hair."

Christina Lake, a further 400 miles to the north, is said to house a creature described as being 10-13 metres in length with a 1 metre long hairy neck, horse-like head and eyes as big as saucers. It was seen by a fisherman in June 1984, and he sent Makowecki a list of 16 other witnesses – whether to this or other incidents isn't clear.

The description closely matches that of Bernard Heuvelmans' hypothetical 'Mer-horse'. In his seminal *In the Wake of the Sea Serpent* (pp.562-7), Heuvelmans describes the animal as being perhaps 30-60 feet in length, with a long mane, a head resembling that of a horse or camel, and enormous eyes. UPC/Toronto, Ontario *Sunday Sun* 2 Sept 1984.

At Lake Shuswap, British Columbia, which has a monster tradition, the Griffiths – a family of five – reported sighting seven humps at 100 metres range while out sailing on the lake. Mrs Griffiths commented, "I could see seven dark greyish humps out of the water. It looked like a snake but it moved in a straight line. It was about 20-25 feet long and was moving quite fast." They watched for two minutes before the object dived. Vancouver, BC, *Province*, June 8 1984.

FORTEAN FEAST

Bob Rickard enjoys a pint and the Fortean cabaret. Also pictured are Roger Morgan, John Rimmer, Mikki Rain and Steve Moore. (Photo: John Walsh.) Right: The Charles Fort cake by Denise Adams. (Photo: Nigel Coke / ADCO.)

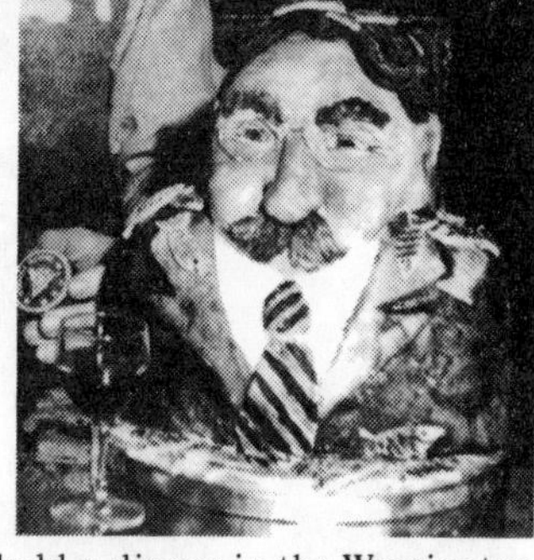

The Friends of Fortean Times held a dinner in the Warrington Hotel, Maida Vale, London, on 15 December 1984. About seventy guests attended to celebrate the eleventh anniversary of the magazine, and to honour its founder/editor, Bob Rickard, who is taking a year's rest from the editorial chair. Hunt Emerson presented Bob with his painting of Charles Fort which was reproduced on the cover of FT29, and Denise Adams made a magnificent cake in the shape of Fort's head and shoulders. Bob was also given a picture of falling fish and a bundle of banknotes. Paul Sieveking, John Michell and Ken Campbell made short speeches and an impromtu fortean cabaret was laid on by James Tavere and Mark Lockyer. The evening afforded a good opportunity to match faces with names, and to forge links generally. Quite a few people thought it should become an annual event.

BVM VISIONS IN POLAND

Now it can be told. When discussing cover ideas for our 'Photos of the Gods' issue [FT36 – Winter 1982] Richard Adams, of ADCO, suggested creating photographically an image of the BVM appearing outside the gates of the Gdansk shipyards, then in the news because of strikes by the Solidarity Union. Gary Woods and David Larcher engineered various manifestations of the apparition, and we reproduce here the version for the FT cover that never was. It would have been interesting to see how far such a fictitious apparition would have travelled, and how it would have been accepted in Poland itself at such an anxious time and with such strong links between Solidarity and Poland's Catholic Church. But commonsense prevailed – we felt that if FT perpetrated and promoted such an insensitive hoax, we would lose all credibility. And rightly so, for this world we live in offers mysteries more strange and more plentiful than any we mortals can devise.

It came as no surprise, then, to learn that according to popular belief, in Gdansk, just after martial law was declared, a wooden cross was oozing blood, and in a village near Lublin a crucifix was weeping salt tears. (For other bleeding and weeping images see STRANGE DAYS last issue, and LAUGHING GUNMAN on p.19.) There were also rumours of several occasions when the Virgin Mary (BVM) appeared "in such solid form that she can be touched and rubbed." Admittedly, this intelligence comes to us over two years late – in Roger Boyes' 'Letter from Warsaw', *Times* 22 June 1984 – but we are always glad to hear of such things.

But the public need for miracles did not end there for many reasons, the interest snowballed, and, writes Boyes: "This week (ie early June 1984) there are two miracles running concurrently, both of them centred on a vision of Mary." Even General Jaruzelski commented publicly on the "thousands of naive people" who rushed to the vision-centre at Olawa, in Silesia, which started up in Autumn 1983. At that time, a pensioner named Kazimierz Komanski had gone to his garden shed for string to tie up his tomato plants and saw the BVM standing on his bench, wearing a crown and a beige robe tied at the waist with a rosary. As he knelt to pray, Komanski said the vision told him to get up. "I healed you in hospital. Now you go and do likewise." Since then Komanski claims to have other visitations, and attempts to heal, sometimes successfully, the thousands who trek to his allotment. (For other allotment-apparitions see FT38p22 and FT40 p.3)

The other vision-site is a grove of poplar trees outside the normally quiet farming village of Pulawy, near Karczew. The initial impetus here seems more slender than than at Olawa: a boy, told that his mother was dying, went to the park, where a voice from the trees told him, correctly, that she would recover. After the boy told nurses in his mothers' hospital of the ethereal prophecy, many rushed to the site and some discerned the figure of the Virgin in the white bark of the trees – see photo. Since then many people claim to have seen apparitions of the BVM – most favoured time is 9pm, after dark – among the trees, which according to customs older than Christianity, are now festooned with beads, badges, pictures, bits of cloth, and tokens from the sick and the healed (eg spectacles, crutches, etc). For a further report see *Guardian* 29 Sept 1984.

In referring to the deep-seated faith awakened and focussed by these events, Boyes observes that "no institution, not even the church, can control the unleashed energy." And Jaruzelski's attempt at rebuke – "We still have large areas of backwardness and are even witnessing a return of superstition." – neither convinces nor reassures. He need not feel alone in his shame at such widespread backsliding; for the Yugoslavian visions, see FT38p20, FT42p26, and NIGHTRIDERS on p.21.

This photo of what is claimed to be the image of the Virgin Mary, in a tree at Pulawy, was given by Henryk Kowalski, to ASSAP News, *who have kindly allowed us to reproduce it. A more detailed report on the current apparition and UFO phenomena of Poland, by Kowalski and Caroline Wise, will appear in ASSAP's new journal of record, Anomaly (expected late January 1985).*

STUNNING PROOF

British naturalist Dick Watling's year-long search in Fiji for Macgillivray's Petrel, thought to be extinct, ended when it crashed on his head.

The one and only record of this small black-and-brown bird before May 1984 was in 1855, when a survey ship caught one on the island of Gau, midway between Fiji's two main islands. It was stuffed and is now in a London museum.

Mr Watling, who is sponsored by the International Council for Bird Preservation in Cambridge, lured the bird in from the sea at night, using torches and amplified recordings. It crashed on his head and after examining the dazed bird he let it go. "I can't take a specimen until I know how many there are", he told *Reuters. Standard* (10 May 1984).

THE MYSTERIES OF BOURNEMOUTH

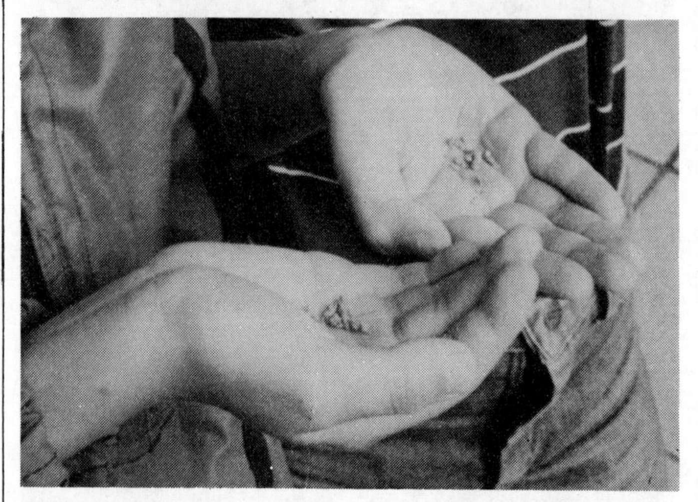

Some of the mystery sand balls. Photo: courtesy of Bournmouth Evening Echo.

Sand continues to fall over parts of Britain and Europe, just as various 'experts' continue to assert positively (upon no discoverable evidence) that it has come from the Sahara. Fort argued, just as convincingly, that it was being blown from the beaches of stationary islands in the sky! For example: On the 19th June 1984 a rain, coloured yellow by fine particles of "sand", fell on Spain's south-eastern coast. *D.Telegraph* 20 June 1984. And a reddish-brown rain, blamed on Saharan sand, fell on parts of south-eastern England on 9th Nov. *D.Telegraph* 10 Nov 1984.

■ On 31 Aug 1984, the *Sun* carried a small item about a strange fall of little balls of damp sand over the Tuckton area of Bournemouth. It's said they came from the Sahara too. The Bournemouth *Evening Echo* of the same date reveals the situation is more complicated. Mrs Hilary Samson, of Tuckton Road, said: "They've been coming down for a few weeks. It's just peculiar. These things appear from nowhere. They are about the size of a large pin-head. [See photo.] They have landed on me. Some of them retain their shape but if they break up they turn into sandy dust. We broke one up yesterday and it appeared to be damp." To his credit, a spokesman for the Met Office actually resisted the Sahara explanation, no doubt aided by the fact that "the winds are not from that direction at the moment", as he had to admit. So where is this sand coming from? By what meteorological (or any other) process has it formed into small balls? And how do we explain a seemingly stationary appearing point over Tuckton? *S.People* 16 Sept 1984: John Morley, who lives opposite the Samsons, claims he was responsible, after he practised his Iroquois rain dance during the hot weather. He might be right, for all we know.

■ Even a well-meaning raindancer can claim no credit for an even more mysterious downpour in Bournemouth. It seems that after a severe thunderstorm on 5th June 1983 pieces of coke fell into the garden of a man who informed the area Meteorological Registrar, Peter Rogers. Mr Rogers then told of this astonishing event on the local radio and was contacted by more people from different parts of Bournemouth, Poole and Christchurch, telling of coke found on lawns, paths and roads after the storm on the 5th, some of them two-and-a-quarter inches wide! In a letter to *J.Meteorology* (v9n91 Sept 1984), he writes: "At one lady's house I picked up 92 pieces of coke and there were still many pieces left." Another woman showed Rogers some small stone chippings which, she claimed, had been left by melting hailstones. The incident is being investigated by Dr G.T. Meaden, and we hope to have a full report in the near future.

■ Bournemouth isn't the only place on England's south coast to be pelted from on high. See LIVE FALLS on p.10. to learn of a fishfall in Kent earlier in 1984, and, most intriguingly, of the crab which fell at Brighton on the very same day that the coke hit Bournemouth, 5 June 1983. There's something strange going on in those Channel skies.

LIVE FALLS

FISH

● Terry Deadman, of Woodside, Wigmore, Kent, found a fish – looks like a small flounder from the photo – on his lawn after the "howling gales of the last few nights". Maybe it was dropped by a bird and maybe it wasn't. If it was a prank, it was pointless. *Medway Eve. Post* 17 Jan 1984.

● C.J. Ann, a Korean attending school in Buffalo, NY, was sightseeing at the base of the Niagara Falls when "something black came by." It was a 15lb Chinook salmon which shot over the falls, hit the Hurricane Deck, and ricocheted off his leg. AP. Schenectady (NY) *Gazette* 19 Sept; Winona (MN) *D.News* 20 Sept 1984.

● A.D.Ellmers and his wife Neva were standing in the drive-way of their home in the Bonita suburb of San Diego, California, on the evening of 20 August 1984, when tiny fish began falling all around them. There were no planes or pranksters in sight. After a widely reported erroneous identification, the two-inch fishes were later found to be thread-finned shad, a population of which exists in the Sweetwater Reservoir about two miles away. Is a local waterspout the culprit? The last report blames feuding pelicans disgorging over the Ellmers' house – you take your pick and I'll take mine. AP. Boston (MA) *Globe* 24 Aug; *Die Welt* 25 Aug; Portland (ME) *Press Herald* 31 Aug 1984.

CRABS

● On 5 June 1983, a large spider crab dropped out of dark stormy clouds a few feet from Julian Cowan outside his home in Baer Rd, Brighton. The crab was dead (with parts missing) and had a legspan of nearly 10 inches. Almost immediately wind-driven hail, about the size of marbles, came down. *J.Meteorology* v9n86 Feb 1984.

● Barry Clifton was called by his colleagues at the tourist office on Bridlington's promenade, North Humberside. They were looking out the window at his car. Rushing outside he found the windscreen smashed, and crawling about among the splinters on the back seat was a hermit crab complete with shell. By way of explanation, he believes that a seagull with a habit of dropping crabs to crack their shellsdropped the 12oz crustacean on his car by mistake. Barry returned the crab to the seashore and drove off to face an £80 repair bill. *D.Express, D.Mirror* 4 Feb; and a letter from Mr Clifton in *Weekly News* 25 Feb 1984.

WINKLES

● We haven't had a good winkle-fall in Britain since the great Worcester shower of 1881, which canonized Fort's explanatory diety, The Fishmonger. Now, at last, we can tell that on the morning of 18 June 1984, Neill Baldwin went to open the petrol station he owns just outside Thirsk, Yorkshire. He was astonished to see the forecourt covered with what he first took to be gravel. "Then we spotted the starfish." Neill and his mechanic Andrew Wallis swept them all up, and later they found many more shells on top of the forecourt pump canopy. They concluded the winkles must have come down with the previous night's torrential rain. Neill's wife, Anne, tasted them – they were salty, which convinced her at least that they originally came from the sea, at least 30 miles away, possibly in a waterspout. "Well, no one goes spreading those things about in the middle of the night," she protested. Ah, but that's exactly what the Fishmonger was accused of doing in 1881! Darlington *Northern Echo* 19 June; *Sun, D.Star, D.Mirror* 20 June 1984. *J.Meteorology* v9n93 Nov 1984.

MONKEY BUSINESS

The last half of 1984 saw no less than four separate outbreaks of monkey sightings.

In early July, two rare Indonesian silver leaf monkeys escaped from an animal sanctuary in Combe Martin, Devon, into extensive woods. An RSPCA inspector said the monkeys would have a good time of it during the heat wave, but once leaves start to fall in the autumn they could begin to go hungry. We have no further news of sightings. *Sun* 5 July; *S.People* 8 July 1984.

On 1st August, a male rhesus monkey was first spotted on the outskirts of Frome, Somerset, bounding across a road. The next day, the 18-inch-high monkey was seen at Westbury, in Wiltshire, just north of Warminster. Attempts to catch it proved futile, and on the 3rd it was hit by a car at the onimous Black Dog crossroads, near Devizes. It was so badly hurt it had to be put down. The police of the two counties were unable to trace an owner – and the keepers at Longleat Safari Park said it wasn't one of theirs. Bristol *Eve.Post* 2 & 3 Aug; *Sun* 3 Aug; *D.Mirror, Shropshire Star* 4 Aug 1984.

About a week before the rhesus monkey's freedom bid (above) a similar-sized Capuchin monkey escaped from the Vale Garden Centre, in Castleton, between Cardiff and Newport, South Wales. He had better luck, and at the time of our report he was still free after more than three weeks, having eluded the police, the RSPCA and his owner, Jon Maffey. He was seen most in the Coryton area, near the M4 motorway. *Western Mail* 14 Aug 1984.

Finally, on 19 Oct, three chimps decided to have some fun at the expense of the police, their keepers at Colchester Zoo, and the visitors. After fleeing from their cage and leading all a merry dance, one was caught, one was tranquilized, and the other just walked back to his cage. *Sun* 20 Oct 1984.

MARTIAN PANICS

In September 1984, the American magazine *Discover* ran an article about the history of theories concerning the planet Mars, from the Chaldeans via Gauss, Tesla, Schiaparelli's *canali* and Lowell to the American panic caused by Orson Welles' radio dramatisation of H.G. Wells' *War of the Worlds* on 30 October 1938.

▲ Exactly 46 years later, anxious listeners, including someone from the American Embassy, jammed the switchboard of London's Capital Radio, which had re-broadcast the play. Will they never learn? Something seemed to be brewing, and indeed it was.

▲ On 17 November, the Animal Liberation Front announced that it had injected Mars Bars (a popular British chocolate snack) with rat poison in five cities, as a protest against alleged Mars funding of a project at Guy's Hospital, London, studying tooth decay by force-feeding monkeys a sugar-rich diet.

▲ The following day, the message on the *Daily Mirror's* answering service for children, Telefun, was: "Kids, guard your health. Don't smoke, have a Mars Bar instead."

▲ The day after that, a long article by Adrian Berry appeared in the *Daily Telegraph*, about the supposed 'face' on Mars photographed by NASA in 1976 (and published in FT19, December 1976). Recent image-enhacement has revealed further 'facial' details – a left eye socket, a pupil, an eyeball and a continuation of 'hair' around the forehead. On the same day, it was revealed that the Mars Bar poisoning had been a hoax.

▲ A leading article in the next day's *Telegraph* warned of the danger of the proposed manned expedition to Mars by the Russians. Apparently, they might get hold of some useful information left by the advanced and extinct Martian civilization and use it to "conquer the Solar System and dominate their rivals on Earth" (Berry). Was the *Torygraph* turning into a crank UFO magazine? Only time would tell. *Sun* 31 Oct; *Guardian* 31 Oct, 20+21 Nov; *News of the World* 18 Oct; *Telegraph* 19+20 Nov; *D.Mail + D.Express* 20 Nov 1984.

INCONCLUSIVE ILLNESS

The Blue Angels Jazz Band attended a donkey derby on 9th June 1984. and had marched about a mile and a half from Rawcliffe Green to Rawcliffe Bridge near Goole when one of the girls fell ill. The band leader, Mrs Iris Betts, called an ambulance: within minutes other girls were affected. The nine girls, aged between 9 and 20, were detained in hospital overnight suffering from shortage of breath, fainting, headaches, chest and stomach paints, unconsciousness and diarrhoea. The symptoms were consistant with fungicide or insecticide poisoning, and the Ministry of Agriculture was called in. Whether their findings were positive or not, I don't know; there is no follow-up report to hand. We are reminded of the jazz band mass faintings in Nottinghamshire in July 1980 (see FT33p22) which were thought to be an example of mass hysteria. *Yorkshire Post* 11 June 1984.

● Over the weekend of 20-21 October 1984, more than 200 postmen and sorting office staff were struck down by a "mystery stomach ailment" at Eastern Central district sorting office in the City of London. Half were not well enough to return to work on the Monday. *D.Mail,Standard* 23 Oct 1984.

BIG CATS' BIG DAY

On 18 October 1984, five lions escaped in Wexford, southern Ireland, and five tigers were let loose near Canterbury.

The lions escaped from Chipperfield's Circus, and three were quickly caught. The other two were rounded up after four hours. One had been hit by a car and the other was cornered in a farmyard. The tigers were deliberately freed from Howlett's Zoo which belongs to John Aspinall. Two adult Indian tigers, Gelam and Putra, and three of their offspring, were seen wandering about by a postman. Four were caught, but a three-year-old female headed across fields towards Littlebourne. Mrs Maureen Taylor saw it stalking her goat. Keepers arrived and shot the tigress dead after 45 minutes of freedom.

Four years before, two keepers at the zoo were mauled to death by a Siberian tigress, one after she lept a 10 foot fence. A bull elephant at Port Lympne zoo park, also run by Mr Aspinall, killed a 22-year-old keeper in April 1984. *Shropshire Star + Standard* 10 Oct; *Scotsman, Telegraph + Sun* 19 Oct 1984.

ALIEN ANIMALS

We continue our regular rodeo of runaway and out-of-place animals. We normally include big cat sightings in this cat-egory but this issue is crammed enough as it is, so we'll round them up next issue. For now, we'll just say that these elusive felines have been reported from the Isle of Wight, Lancashire,

The Papuan spiny stick insect found in an English field. D.Mail, *23 July 1984.*

Wales, Surrey, Dartmoor and Exmoor in Devon, and several parts of Scotland. For other out-of-place animals who have arrived seemingly by known or conventional means, see STRANGE VISITORS on p.24.

● A badly injured parrot was found 500ft down the Celynen North mine, in South Wales. *Sun* 2 May 1984.

● A spiny stick insect from Papua New Guinea, *Eurycantha cararata*, (see picture above) was found in a field near Surbiton, Surrey. *D.Mail* + *Express and Star* 23 July; *Sun* 24 July; *St Louis Post-Dispatch* 12 Aug 1984.

● A Florida King snake, nearly five feet long, was captured on a Birmingham carpark by a policeman armed with a tablecloth. There was no clue as to how it got there, but it eventually ended up at Dudley Zoo. *S.Mercury* 5 Aug 1984.

● A racoon has been seen wandering along the tracks of the Boston, Massachusetts, underground, at Park Street station. From the evidence it has been down there some time, and the MBTA have decided against hunting it. Boston (MA) *Globe* 22 Aug 1984.

● A caterpillar of a South African death's head hawk moth was found in a market garden at Claverham, near Bristol. The five-inch, green caterpillar was taken to the Cheddar Tropical House in the city. Bristol *Eve. Post* 14 Sept 1984.

● A six-legged insect with a scorpion-like tail was found at Preston in Lancashire. Experts were trying to identify it. *Sun* 20 Sept 1984.

● A giant fruit-bat from New Guinea with a three foot wingspan was found clinging to a car radiator in the middle of Exeter in Devon. Taken to the RSPCA kennels, it tucked into bananas and apples. Origin 'a total mystery'. *ITN News, D.Mirror* and *Shropshire Star* 3 Oct 1984.

● We recall two other critter-on-vehicle items. Mr T.B. Bryan drove 110 miles down the M1 motorway and pulled into a layby. He found a small grass snake curled up on the front bumper, which wasn't there when he left home. *S.Express* 24 June 1981.

● A train from Denver arrived in Chicago on 7 June 1937 with its headlight broken. Inside the shattered lamp lay a dead trout. It was thought that the train had struck an eagle with a trout in its beak, but no eagle had been seen, and no feathers or blood were mentioned. *The Fortean Society Magazine* No.2, Oct 1937. (For another eagle-with-fish item, see FRENCH NEWS, p.47)

● An enormous Japanese hornet was terrorizing staff at a Nissan garage in Nottingham. It had arrived, it was thought, in a crate of spares. (AP) *Scotsman* 19 Oct 1984.

● According to the *Sunday Express* (25 Nov 1984) "at least half a dozen [wallabies] are on the loose in the countryside surrounding Henley in Oxfordshire." Our first inkling of this potential rival to the famous feral wallabies of Derbyshire came in the *Sun* a week earlier (17 Nov 1984): that a wallaby was seen in a Henley street, on 16th Nov, hopping off after it was scared by a dog. Others have been seen on roads and in fields, and have been reported to police. In this case their origin is known, even if their comings and goings are more mysterious. Their owner is William McAlpine, senior member of the Zoological Society, son of the millionaire builder and brother to Lord McAlpine, the treasurer of the Conservative Party. He adopted 12 wallabies from Whipsnade Zoo, when they ran out of space [when?] and put them in a 70-acre park enclosed by a six-foot-high fence. But six of them tunnelled out [again, when?].

● For a curious cluster of monkey sightings, see MONKEY BUSINESS on p.11.

PHANTOM FRIENDS

The *Sun* of 21 Sept 1984 devoted a double page spread to a boy prodigy they called the 'Baby Mastermind'. Anthony McQuone, of Weybridge, Surrey, is only two years old but he has a very large vocabulary, recites Shakespeare that his father reads to him, identifies architectural styles and about 200 makes of cars, and has definite views on music, diet, sport and politics. At 12 months, said his father (also called Anthony), the boy threw away his fairy tale book, calling it "silly". He particularly disliked the rhyme 'Tom,Tom the Piper's Son' because, he said, the line 'The pig was eat" was ungrammatical. Anthony frequently corrects the bad grammar he hears around him.

Expressing his dislike for miners' leader Arthur Scargill, Anthony said he preferred Mrs Thatcher: "She is bonum." His puzzled dad looked up the unusual word, and found it was Latin for 'good'. Anthony knows more Latin, and it comes out when he goes for country walks with his father. He accurately names the varieties of trees and gives their Latin names. This is perhaps the most puzzling of his precocious talents, for his father does not know Latin and ha no books in the house with Latin tree-names until he bought an encyclopedia to check up (the boy was right). Besides, although Anthony knows his alphabet he cannot yet read. In other respects Anthony is reassuringly childish – when asked what he would like to do when grown up, he says gravely: "I want to go shopping for cakes and things on my own." His father separated from Anthony's mother when he was five months old, since when he has brought up the boy single-handed. He insists: "I have never tried to cram his little mind with facts...", and stresses that he doesn't want the boy branded a child prodigy.

Now the whole point of this story is that Antony is in no doubt where his extraordinary knowledge comes from. He says he has an invisible tutor called Adam, who is with him always,

TOO RICH TO EAT

George Veriopoulos, an Orthodox priest, was preparing to tuck into a dish of *kefalaki,* to the Greeks a delicacy but boiled sheep's head to you and me. He did a doubletake as he noticed that the bottom half of the sheep's teeth were made of gold. He scraped away more flesh and saw gold along the jawbone as well. He was given the young sheep by his sister and her husband to celebrate the birth of their first child. The feast was forgotten as Father George put the head into a bag and rushed off to see a jeweller. Sure enough the gold was 14-karat and had an estimated value of about £3000. He phoned his brother-in-law, Nicos Kotsovos, who said: "I rushed out to check the rest of my sheep, but there was not a trace of gold among the whole flock of 400." A local vet was stumped as to how the gold could have been deposited in such quantities in coin-sized areas of the teeth and bones. Other farmers have suggested the sheep chewed grass covered with gold dust from a nearby small gold mine – but no other cases have been heard of, and besides no one would quietly "lose" gold of this value and purity. The Greek Ministry of Agriculture investigated and found the story of the gold-bearing teeth true, and unique, and also inexplicable. Their chief vet, Andreas Anastasovitis, rejected the farmers' theory on another count: such a deposition of gold would take years, and this sheep was only eight months old. "There is also gold in the jawbone. How do you explain that? I can't. I'm completely baffled." Meanwhile, back in the Patission suburb of Athens, where this drama took place, farmers have adopted a new ritual; regularly peering into the mouths of their flocks while their wives actually pan the sheep's milk for that golden sparkle. *S.Express.* 10 June; *Globe* 21 Aug 1984.

◆ Sometimes I think we are marvels at really obscure knowledge, because after all we can tell of something like this, but it happened so long ago – in 1595 to be exact – that it is perfectly irrelevant, but here it is anyway. It seems that a boy of seven, in Silesia, was found to have a solid gold molar, which was doubtless untimely plucked, because no less than four learned treatises were written about it before a goldsmith discovered it was an artifact of skilfully applied gold-leaf! The full story, for what it's worth, can be found in Fontenelle's *Histoire des Oracles,* instructing him about the world and correcting his manners. Anthony described Adam to the interviewer. Adam was tall with black hair, brown eyes, and wore a white toga and caliga. "That's Latin for sandals," said the boy. As an afterthought he added: "Adam has a Van Dyke beard too." His father said: "I've never heard him mention Van Dyke before... Sometimes I can hardly believe the little guy. He confounds me but he has taught me a lot."

The reporters added several testimonials to the child's talents. Frank Sherwood, director of the National Association for Gifted Children, said: "Such children do, of course have to be taught. They cannot acquire knowledge without some aid." And what if that aid was an imaginary friend called Adam? "This is something new to me," said Sherwood. That answer surprised us, because we thought the phenomenon of 'imaginary playmates' was fairly well known, even if not well understood. This has been the most striking instance of it for many years of our own interest in the subject. But as to whether Adam is an etheral entity from the past, a previous incarnation, a secondary personality or a creation of Anthony's mind, we cannot say. His father wisely says: "I have an open mind about Adam. I keep asking myself where else can he get all this information from? Perhaps a child's mind can perceive things we cannot." Also, *Sun* 22 Sept 1984.

FIREBALL

A witch's crystal ball, in the window of the Games and Giggles shop in Ipswich, Suffolk, concentrated the sun's rays and started a fire. *Telegraph* 2 Oct 1984.

MYSTERY MILITARY PLANES

A four-engine, olive-drab cargo plane was seen by many people flying very low over Clinton, Iowa, about 7pm on 31 May 1984. It looked like an Air Force C-130 Hercules. The police received several calls, with some reporting that it nearly 'took the top off' the Wilson Building, and others reporting it flying at treetop level.

The local Air Force base at Belleville, Illinois, had no record of such a flight. The Air Force spokesman added that all military aircraft filed flight plans. Inquiries at all other Air Force bases and airports in neighbouring states drew a blank. Our correspondent Warren Smith talked to two witnesses who said that the plane made no engine sound.

A week earlier, on 24 May, an aircraft with the same description was seen flying at 500 to 1,000 feet over Clinton, Fulton and the Mississippi river. *Clinton Daily Herard* 1 June 1984.

In early October, a military style transport plane few in low over the Selly Oak region of Birmingham, England. Both RAF and American bases in the Midlands denied having any aircraft in the area.

"There have been training flights in the region of Birmingham airport", said a RAF spokesman, "but there could be nothing over any densely-populated areas. We don't do that." *Sunday Mercury* 7 Oct 1984.

FALL OF GLASS

On Sunday 23rd Sept 1984, one of the strangest of the many falls we've chronicled occurred in Norfolk St, Swansea. The ragged fragments of black glassy material, each about 4mm in diameter, were found by physics teacher Paul Carter on a 50yd stretch of road outside his house (the first source says: "for 50yds *around* his home".) After reading about the story in the *Western Mail*, Prof. Derek Ager of the University College. Swansea's geology department, contacted Carter, and offered to analyse the material. Initially, he said he could not rule out the suggestion that the "glass rain" originated in the recent eruptions of the Philippine volcano, Mt Mayon (see p.24). While we welcome the academician's investigative spirit, we are curious as to just how he was prepared to explain how hundreds of glass beads could be kept in the air long enough to travel the considerable distance from the Philippines. And how did they keep together in any hypothetical strong wind? And why was the fall confined to so small an area, as we have noticed time and again? To give Prof. Ager due credit, he did voice some doubt, observing that the glass beads were somewhat larger than the usual sizes of airborne dirt and dust particles.

The geochemistry department was called in and they soon pronounced the material "some kind of industrial refractory material, possibly iron mullite." It seems the glass was made of uniform grains of silicon, aluminium and iron with traces of calcium, magnesium and chronium – in other words, manmade. Southern Wales has a great number of furnaces which use refractory linings, and it seems likely that the glass is some by-product of some kind of industrial smelting; but the mystery of how it came to fall in Norfolk St remains; *Western Mail* 27+29 Sept 1984. For the equally peculiar but classically Fortean datum of a fall of coke, see BOURNEMOUTH on p.10.

RECENT POLTERGEISTS

● For eight years Mrs Maureen West, her daughter Jenny and son-in-law Paul Roos lived happily in an old house, under large trees in Sunnyside Lane, Pinetown, Natal. Then, on Christmas Eve 1983, they were visited by a very un-Dickens-like Christmas ghost. During the night Paul Roos heard a loud scraping sound "as if a big piece of steel sheeting was being dragged along the roof". Then came a crash from the kitchen "as though someone had fallen and dragged pots and pans down with him, " said Paul. He went outside to investigate and saw nothing, and in the kitchen all was as it should be. The roof noises woke the family again that night, and then all was quiet until New Year's Day. Jenny's daughter, Wendy, aged 14, heard a terrible noise: "I though the house was caving in. It sounded as if a large boulder had crashed onto the roof." Again, nothing could be found. Several days later came the sounds of beds being moved; Paul rushed from the toilet and Jenny from the kitchen, but again there was no sign of the expected chaos. Everything was in place. Jenny's brother's friend spent a night on the couch, a few days later, and was woken by several slaps on his face. As he woke-up he says he saw an old man standing in front of him. South Africa *Sunday Times*,? Jan 1984.

● In Devon a polt is getting the better of Mrs Thatcher – not the one currently haunting Downing Street, but Mrs Sharon Thatcher, her husband Tony, and their four young children, who live in a three-bedroomed council house at Mill Meadow, Ivybridge. The disturbances began at the end of the first week in November 1984, with a creaking on the stairs which went on all night. Then followed non-stop tappings on the walls of the bedrooms and "strange musty smells". The last straw came with the sound of a child screaming, which did not come from the sleeping children; since then the whole family eats and sleeps downstairs. After a week of this disruption, the family called in the Vicar of Ivybirdge, Rev Douglos Obee, who conducted a blessing of the house. But the noises continued. If anything, adds Sharon, "The spirit's power is now stronger than before." The sound of pacing in the upstairs rooms and "vague forms like a smoke haze" have been seen. The family believe they are troubled by the ghost of a previous tenant, an old bachelor, who committed suicide after his dog died – but according to the report he had killed himself, not at the house,but at the mill where he worked. Nevertheless, the South Hams District Council are impressed with the family's terrified state enough to consider rehousing them. *Western Morning News* 22 Nov 1984.

● More dramatic were the incidents in a house in Santa Fe, Argentina. In March 1984, neighbours complained to police about the horrific screams and "other eerie noises" coming from the house. Police Chief Angel Juan Villareal, thinking vandals were at work, began an investigation. Two of his officers "witnessed a number of rocks and stones coming down from the sky near the house...and told me of their own terror" at hearing the screams, rattling-chain-noises, and seeing locked doors mysteriously open. Fearing a panic, he asked Judge Gabriel Lanteri for permission to make the house secure. "We even roped off three city blocks to guarantee that no stranger or undesirable could enter the premises." Then three different parapsychology research groups conducted experiments. The phenomena continued. The screams and other noises were successfully recorded, along with a female voice calling "Mother, mother," and the sounds of objects falling onto the roof. Objects, whose positions were carefully marked, were later found some distance away. The judge was convinced of the reality of the 'haunting', as was the Chief, who added: "I personally did not believe in the supernatural until this evidence forced me to change my mind." *National Enquirer* 4 Sept 1984.

PIONEER MULE

Krause, a mule on Bill and Oneta Sylvester's farm in Champion, Nebraska, escaped, and is thought to have mated with a horse; anyway, she has since become a mother. "It is the first documented case ever of mule fertility" said Dr Oliver Ryder, a geneticist at the Center for the Reproduction of Endangered Species in San Diego, California. *Guardian* and *Sun* 2 Aug; *S.Express* 14 Oct 1984.

WELL, STONE MY ARMPITS!

Police discovered 38.8 pounds of heroin being sold as talcum powder at a shop in Split, Yugoslavia, according to the Tanjug news agency. The shop obtained the 'talc' at a customs post auction on the Yugoslav-Austrian border, after it had been confiscated from a foreigner. *Guardian* 2 July 1983.

MAN CUTS THROAT WITH CHAINSAW AND LIVES

■ Forthman Murff is a 74yr-old lumberjack (see photo), and with a name like that he deserves to be immortal. He was cutting timber not far from his home in Gattman, Mississippi, when a big branch fell from a tree and knocked him backwards into a ditch and on top of the chainsaw he was still holding. It sliced across his neck, severing his windpipe, most of the neck muscles, two external jugular veins and an internal one – as doctors later discovered – leaving only his spine and the vital carotid artery intact. Such is the fortitude of this hardy old timer that he crawled to his truck, despite the additional injuries of a broken left leg and crushed foot. "I can't explain to anyone about the pain in my throat and the blood going down into my lungs. I knew I had to get that blood out of my lungs so I could breathe", recalls Mr Murff. "I just used the principles of gravity, like pouring water out of a bucket. So, I held my head way over and let the blood run out of my lungs. I did it first while I was still on the ground. Then I had to do it again on the way to the truck. I did it again when I got back to the truck, because I knew I would have to be sitting up and that I had to breathe. My foot was really hurting, but you can't let something like that stop you. I made that thing walk." Murff then drove several miles to a neighbour's house. He got out of his own truck and into his neighbour's, and did his head-down routine as the man drove him immediately to a hospital in Tupelo, about an hour away. Dr Roger Lowery, one of the physicians who attended Murff said: "It's a miracle he's alive. I've seen this kind of injury before, but never in one who survived. Just think about walking with your head cut halfway off." No thanks! Murff's last comments: "I wasn't worried about dying. I know where I'm going when I leave here. The Lord left me here for a reason...and I can tell you that it wasn't to chase widow women." *Globe* 28 Aug 1984.

■ Not so lucky was Russell Minckler, of Chateaugay, NY, whose chainsaw kicked back while he was notching logs and chewed out his throat. Coincidentally, just 20 minutes later and 10 miles away, at Churubsco, there was another chainsaw accident – but in this one, Morton Cole survived with only a cut over one eye. Plattsburgh (NY) *Press Republican* 21 May 1984.

■ Another elderly victim with luck is Arthur Cross, 70, a farmer from near St Louis, Missouri. He was recovering from six days of surgery after being thrown from his tractor into the vehicles's power-saw. He was sliced across his abdomen, from his left rib-cage, across his liver, bowels and genitals, before his son pulled him out. He was still conscious when a helicopter brought him to a hospital in St Louis. *Sun* 10 Dec 1984.

Forthman Murff shows his scars. Photo: Globe *28 Aug 1984.*

THE END IS NIGH!

The small coral island of Maziwi has disappeared. Situated off the Tanzanian coast, and famed as one of the last breeding places of an endangered species of green turtle, it is though to have been dynamited by fishermen and finally demolished by a monsoon. Local legend is that the disappearance heralds the end of the world. Wonder if we'll have time to put out this issue? *Observer* 2 Sept 1984.

PRIESTLY PROBLEMS

● The "high priest" of a sect called New Jerusalem, Moses Miche, 44, has been arrested in a part of Peru in which he claims to have created paradise. While decreeing that members should be celibate, Miche had 25 "wives" Two disgruntled members reported him to the police, accusing him of corruption. *D.Express* 1 Nov 1984.

● The Rev. John Vile lived down to his name...by sexually assaulting young boys, aged between 11-17, after drinking parties. He would invite them to stay for the night, showed them sex magazines, and interfered with them as they slept. He was jailed for 12 offences, at Swansea Crown Court. *D.Mirror* 17 July 1984.

● Rita Milla, 22, has been given permission by a judge to sue the Catholic archdiocese of Los Angeles, alleging that seven RC priests had sex with her, and that one is the father of her daughter. She is accusing the Church of "abusing its power and exploiting its relationship" with her, claiming damages of $21 million. *Guardian* 22 Aug 1984.

● A defrocked RC priest, Gilbert Gauthe, is to face 34 charges of sexually molesting altar boys at his church in Abbeville, Louisiana. He was barred from duties after the complaints, going back seven years, came to light. Gauthe had told the boys that the sexual acts "were part of secret Roman Catholic rituals." Let the conspiracy-buffs have this one to ponder. *Sun* 20 Oct 1984.

LOCUSTS ON THE MOVE

In December 1984, South Eastern Australia faced the worst locust plague since 1955. The invasion started in western New South Wales in late November and crossed into Northern Victoria, stripping everything in its path, including green paint. Attempts to control the outbreak by aerial spraying in October had failed. The last plague was in 1979, but there were far fewer locusts then. *Daily Express* 11 Dec 1984.

WEST COAST METEORS?

A puff of brown smoke and a brilliant silver glow lit up the sky for less than ten seconds over 400 miles of northern California and southern Oregon at 2.50 pm, Friday, 20 July 1984. John Melvin, a Prairie Creek State Park ranger, said the object (? a meteor) could have been 50 miles from him and 5000 feet high. Dozens of people called authorities and radio stations from as far away as Medfield, Oregon, 90 miles northeast of Prairie Creek, and San Francisco, 330 miles to the south.

Gilbert Sena, a coastguard helicopter pilot flying at about 1,500 feet near Eureka, 270 miles north of San Francisco, also saw the object, which appeared to be 7,000 feet above sea level, and going *up*! (AP) Duluth, MN, *News-Tribune and Herald*, 22 July 1984.

On the following Friday, a strange spark-tailed white and orange something splashed down a thousand yards south of Lummi Island in the Puget Sound, off Washington State. The event was reported to the Coast Guard at 3.45 am, 27 July, by the *Steeva Ten*, a 42 foot fishing vessel. The object made two "U" turns before splashdown and sent up a plume of water a hundred feet high. A flash in the sky was noted at the same time by a tugboat at Anacortes about five miles to the south.

The Coast Guard investigated, but found no debris. Checks with other authorities turned up no reports of missing planes or space junk crashing in the area. The object sank in water 270 feet deep in Rosario Strait, an area of intense currents which made it difficult to do a survey, according to Rich Rogala, the chief of the Coast Guard station at Bellingham, WA, which sent a boat to the scene. At 5.05 am the Coast Guard vessel reported a large lighted object in the sky going east, which quickly passed out of view.

So what was it that plummeted into Rosario Strait? The time of year is known for above-average meteor activity, particularly the Perseid shower which peaks around 12 August. But does a meteor ever make "U" turns ? (AP) St Louis *Post-Dispatch*, 28 July; *Just Cause* New Series No.1, Sept 1984. (This is a mag. about UFO–Government cover-ups. PO Box 218, Coventry, CT 06238.)

WELSH MUTILATIONS

In September, the savagely mutilated bodies of 100 animals and birds were found on the mid-Glamorgan refuse tip at Maesycwmmer. The grisly collection in plastic bags included goat hooves, fox heads, canaries, budgies, badgers, moles, hares and stoats. There were no vivisection laboratories in the area, and an official said that they would not experiment with protected species like badgers anyway. *Daily Express* 21 Sept 1984.

About the 13th of September, the latest sheep massacre was discovered in the hills behind Tywyn Cwyned, North Wales. In all, nearly 70 sheep on four farms had been injured. Farmer Richard Lewis discovered two of his lambs dead, two dying and many bleating pitifully. Altogether he lost 12 lambs as a result of that night's carnage. All the injuries consisted of smallish entry wounds with larger ones on the other side of their bodies. Vets speculate that they were made by a powerful cross-bow fitted with a bolt. *Sunday Express* 23 Sept 1984.

LAUGHING GUNMAN SHOOTS WEEPING MADONNA

On 25 July 1984, as 20-30 people were kneeling in silent prayer before a 39-inch wooden statue of the Virgin Mary in the Catholic church of St John of God in Chicago's southwest side, a gunman burst in and fired three shots at it. Two slugs hit the wall, but the third struck the statue in the left knee, and no 'real' person was hurt. Then comes the strangely stirring line: "The gunman escaped, laughing loudly as he fled."

The statue had arrived from Italy on 12 May after being specially blessed in a shrine at Montichiari. About a hundred people claim they saw the statue shed tears from both eyes on 29, 30 and 31 May. In the following two weeks, about 15,000 people, some from as far away as India, came to see the statue.

"They were regular tears, flowing down the nose, on the chin, in the folds of her cloak", said the Rev Raymond J. Jasinski, the pastor of the church. Cardinal Joseph Bernardin appointed a deputy bishop and two pastors to investigate. No tears had been collected, but the church's custodian, Sigmund Urbanski, 57, said he had tasted them, and that they were salty, like human tears. He claimed that the Madonna's features changed as she wept. "She has a puffiness in her face. Her cheeks are more rosy when she cries." Some visitors said she was getting ready to cry again about the evil in the world.

On 3 August, police arrested Ronald O'Neil, 23, and charged him with the shooting. He had a history of mental problems and was under treatment. He had caused disturbances at two other churches, St Stephen's in Chicago and St Bernadette's in nearby Evergreen Park, Illinois, where a policeman took his photograph. *Clinton Herald* 1 June; Belleville (IL) *News-Democrat* 10 June + 6 Aug; *Globe 14* Aug; *Our Sunday Visitor* (USA) 26 Aug 1984.

The Chicago weeping madonna.

● Another near-4ft-high BVM statue – of 'Our Lady of Fatima', in the Mater Ecclesiae RC church in Thornton, near Sacramento, California, – cries and moves on its own, claim the church's staff. The movements are detected on the 13th of most months (coinciding with the favoured dates of the BVM apparitions at Fatima, Portugal in 1917). Cleaners have found the 60lb statue on the floor, instead of on its pedastal, and even at the altar. After the first movement the six people with keys to the church suspected each other. So the church was again locked and the statue bolted to a stand: a few days later it was found 20ft from its secured position. No one has yet seen the movements: a local TV crew even kept a 24hr vigil unsuccessfully. A good number have found "tears" forming on the right eye, or running down the cheek to drop into the figure's folded hands. Photos of the tearful face are said to be prominently displayed in the church, which has not unexpectedly enjoyed a swelling of its usually small congregation. Bishop Roger Mahoney has appointed a panel of priests to judge the phenomena, and they are in no rush to make statements. AP: Clinton (IL) *Herald* 1 June; (? USA) *Star* 7 June; UPI: Belleville (IL) *News Democrat* 10 June 1983.

● Finally, a Polish professor of biology, said to be a genius, was arrested during a visit to Rome and charged with damaging several statues by hacking off their noses. As he was being restrained the police found a bag containing 86 stone noses (a nose-bag?). The professor didn't help his case by claiming to be a Martian working under orders from the Red Planet. As luck would have it, our clipping of this important datum has been torn in half, with all the corroborating details in the missing portion. Does anyone have any more on this story? For other interplanetary madness see MARTIAN PANICS on p.12.

PUZZLING FIND

A 300yr-old mummified head, with hair and teeth intact, has been found – on its own – in a phone box in Islington, London. Strange tattooings suggest it once belonged to a Maori chief.

Some absent-minded collector of curiosities could have mislaid it, of course; but in all probability it was swiped from a medical school museum. In either case, we'd like to know more. *Sun* 21 Jan 1984.

ICE FALLS

★ A bumper crop of 12 ice falls – and these are only the ones that have come our way since our listing last issue!

★ **Spring Valley, Wisconsin** – Ron LaGran and his family were gathered for a photograph outside their residence, just west of Spring Valley, when the "dark blue ice" fell. He said: "We were in the yard, taking pictures and getting ready to go to graduation when it seemed like it was the fourth of July. We heard a whistle and a bang and whatever it was hit the ditch breaking into pieces." LaGran put some in his freezer and gave some to the local Sheriff's Dept. He doubts the plane-toilet theory. "Whatever it was, it came down fast and made an indentation in the ground. If it had hit somebody it would have killed them," he added. Ellsworth (WI) *Pierce Co. Herald* 23 May 1984.

★ **Skipton, Yorkshire** – Broughton Copy Farm owner, John Taylor, was strolling around his 300 acres when he heard a curious noise above him, like a rushing wind. As the noise grew louder, he stopped, and then heard something crash to earth behind him. He was astonished to find it was a mass of jagged ice, about the size and shape of a beach ball, partly embedded in the soft ground. Tentatively he prodded the "dark blue" ice with his boot and layers of crystals fell away. Bending lower he recoiled at the smell of "chemicals". Police investigated it, but it had melted beyond salvation. *S.Express* 27 May 1984.

★ **West Chester, Pennsylvania** – a 2ft-wide chunk fell through the roof of Shirley Cialini's house, as the family held a backyard Memorial Day picnic. *USA Today* (Arlington, VA) 29 May 1984.

★ **Woking, Surrey** – Fred Shears, aged 75, was cycling home with his morning paper when "I suddenly heard this whooshing sound, like a wartime bomb dropping. There was a big splatter of green ice just in front of me." *Guardian* 29 May 1984.

Elsie Down stares at the massive ice block wedged in the ceiling of her Exmouth home. Could it really have formed on a plane? [Photo © Exeter Express & Echo.*]*

★ **Exmouth, Devon** – As they settled down to watch 'Crossroads' (which starts at 6.35) on 19th June, Fred and Elsie Down, both aged 80, were startled by a crash which rocked their terrace home in Halsdon Road. It was one of the biggest ice-bombs we've seen evidence of in recent times (see photo). The report gave no estimated size or weight, but the hole in the ceiling is over 2ft by 1ft. Fred said: "When we opened the bedroom door I could not believe my eyes. There was a terrible mess. You could see the sky through the roof. It smashed clean through the slates and broke a rafter. There were also lumps of ice the size of two men's fists lying on the bed." Exeter *Express & Echo* 20 June; *Transport 2000, Devon Group Newsletter* Summer 1984.

★ **Calumet City, Illlinois** – A frozen mass, more than a foot across in parts, demolished the roof of Maria Jiminez' house. UPI: Belleville (IL) *News-Democrat* 1 June 1984.

★ **Poiçon-les-Fayl, Haute-Marne, France** – A large ice block fell through the roof of a house in the week of 4-10 July. *L'Yonne Republicain* 11 July 1984.

★ **St Julien-les-Villas, near Troyes, Aube, France** – An ice block weighing about ten kilos fell from a clear sky on 8 July, making a hole 5 foot 7 inches by 3 foot 11 inches in the roof of a house belonging to pensioners Mr and Mrs Payen. Analysis showed that it was 20% urine, and it was established that four planes were passing overhead at the time, so this one looks as if it conforms to the standard explanation. *L'Yonne Republicain, Republicain Lorrain + Die Welt* 11 July; Auckland (NZ) *Star* 12 July 1984.

★ **Easton, Maryland** – At about 3pm on the 8th Sept, Thomas I. Andrews, a retired poultry company manager, was sitting with others on the porch of his home in the Swann Haven Trailer Park. "I heard this whoosh noise and by the time I looked up there was this green ice all over the yard," he said. He estimated its size was that of a basketball, and collected fragments. He called in various authorities, including a "part-time investigator of bizarre phenomena from UFOs to spontaneous human combustion" who took samples for analysis at the University of Maryland. Meanwhile, a jar of melted ice – now a dirty green liquid with "quite an odor" – resides on the desk of Cpl Thursby Cooper of the State Police. Washington (DC) *Post* ? Sept; *D.Mail* 14 Sept 1984.

★ **Leominster, Massachusetts** – For the second time in just over two weeks big chunks of blue ice fell onto Leominster. On 23rd Sept, an apartment building roof at 100 Central St. was holed. And on 9th Oct Mrs Wanda McManus was in the basement of her home at 14 Woodside Ave. at about 5pm, when she heard a loud bang and felt the house shake. Going outside, she found her lawn littered with shards of blue ice. UPI. Providence (RI) *Journal* 12 Oct 1984.

★ **Kazan, USSR** – Anatoly Kozhukhov was strolling along the sands at a holiday resort near Kazan, on the River Volga, when he heard a whizzing noise in the air. Out of a clear sky, a large block of ice narrowly missed him, thudding into the sand near his feet. He took the block home and stored it in his freezer until excited Moscow scientists came to see it. They have proclaimed it part of an ice meteorite. Tass. Aukland, NZ, *Star* 14 Aug; *Soviet Weekly* 6 Oct 1984.

★ **Leicester** – Beatrice Dixon, 78, did not get up at 6am on 23rd Oct, deciding instead to stay in bed. Just as well, because a huge block of ice smashed through the roof of her Thomson Close bungalow leaving a 10ft hole and wrecking her kitchen below. *D.Mail, Sun, Star, D.Mirror* 24 Oct 1984.

★ In every case above – except for the Russian one – the falling ice is blamed upon a hypothetical leak from a hypothetical plane's toilet. We also notice another correlation: that, in the majority of these cases, the near-victim is elderly or retired. This age-group also figures significantly as poltergeist and spontaneous combustion victims! Eventually, this is the sort of clue we would be able to explore with the IFS database (known to us as TOAD). For other falls see LIVE FALLS on p.10, SAND FALLS on p.10, and FALL OF GLASS on p.15.

THE WINNING GOLFBALL

Scott Palmer, 26, Californian author and golfer, hit a hole-in-one 18 times between June 1983 and the following January. Besides that, his drives have hit the pin on 50 other occasions. Since such a statement is met with incredulity, Palmer has collected affidavits from 65 witnesses. *Golf Digest* says it's a clear record – the previous one was 11 in a year, set by a Californian doctor in 1962 – and that the chances of hitting a hole from the tee are 33,616 to 1.

Four of Palmer's holes-in-one came on consecutive days in October, seven have been on par-4 holes and the average length of all 18 is 209 yards.

He started lessons half way though his streak. Now instead of hooking holes-in-one he gets them in straight. He has hit all but one of his aces with the same ball: a Spalding Top Flite XL No.2 with a hide so tough that after nine months of almost daily use he has been unable to put a frown on it. £7,000 has been offered for the ball, but he has turned it down. At the instant of his charmed strokes, he gets the mental image of a faceless woman pouring a glass of milk. *D.Mail* 9 Feb 1984. (For an odd hole-in-one picture, see FT42, p.25.)

NIGHT RIDERS

We have tried to keep in touch with the BVM apparition reports from Yugoslavia. Last issue [FT42p74] we told of the first English book on the phenomenon, and lately we learned, thanks to Michael Hoffman's vigilance, of an American paperback called: *The Apparitions of Our Lady at Medjugorje, 1981-1983: An Historical Account with Interviews* which we are obtaining for review.

Against this background of rising charismatic Catholic feeling, an even more remarkable snip of information came our way, via the *Guardian* of 4 Aug 1984. Yugoslavian police raided a cemetary, at midnight it seems, in an unnamed village. They found "entranced naked women riding imaginary horses" while a farmworker "played recordings of religious music". If this had happened in Britain or the USA, the vent would have been written off as a silly manifestation of the popular interest in 'revived' witchcraft. But the pragmatic communist police were obviously more concerned about fraud than superstition, saying the farmworker was charging villagers up to £50 for curing their problems by organizing such ceremonies. We think a third view is possible, and that among country fold everywhere, less touched by the disenchanting influences of modern 'progress', very ancient beliefs and practices have survived centuries of attempted suppression by Church and State. The roots of such rites are part of a universally spontaneous shamanism. For example: Malay shamans ride phantom tigers and horses in their trances; and the graveyard vigil features in the initiation rites of the more shamanic lamas of Tibet.

ARTEFACTS OF CONFUSION

According to Sergei Yeger, writing in the Soviet journal *Kommunist*, Soviet airship experts are framing plans to build 'flying saucers' to open up the remote areas of Siberia. It is believed that disc-shaped airships would be best suited to the high-wind conditions. They would be 150 meters in diameter, able to lift up to three hundred tons, with a cruising speed of 150 kilometers per hour, and a flight range of 4,000 kilometers. Fuel consumption would be a fifth to a quarter that of a conventional airoplane, which has to expend about half its energy to privide lift. *Soviet Weekly* 1 Sept 1984.

● Scientists at the Washington Air and Space Museum are designing a robot pterodactyl (Quetzalcoatlus northropi) with a 36-foot wingspan, based on the impressive fossil found in Texas in 1971. (See FT42, p.19 for reports of recent 'pterodactyl' sightings.)

"Big Q' will cost about £170,000 and be ready for a test flight over Washington in 1986. No-one knows how well it will fly – aerodynamic theory suggests that it won't. The original critter weighed about 12 stone, and flew with the aid of two membranes stretched between its body and a grossly elongated forelimb. It had no tail with which to steer. The idea for the radio-controlled reconstruction came from Paul MacCready, who built the first human-powered flying machine in 1977.

After Washington, it is planned to fly Big Q in Bradford, England. This is because the special film on the history of flying featuring the monster will be made for a special camera projection, IMAX, which throws vast, clear-cut images onto 50 foot by 60 foot screens. The only IMAX cinema in Britain is in Bradford's National Museum of Photography. *D.Mail* 18 Oct; *Observer* 11 Nov; *Telegraph* 21 Nov; *S.Times* 2 Dec 1984.

BRITISH TWISTERS

We kick off with a strange story from the vicinity of Cheddar in Somerset. Mrs Neila Taylor checked her washing on the rotary clothes line and went into the house. The weather was mild and there was hardly any wind. A few seconds later she went outside again and saw her washing strewn all over the garden. It had obviously been ripped with considerable force from the steel dryer. The remaining washing was tightly wound to the pole which was slightly askew. One of the quarter-inch-thick struts had been strongly bent *downwards*. Strawberry plants stacked in neat heaps were also strewn everywhere. All this happened in less than a minute and without a sound. A whirlwind would probably have bent the metal *upwards*, and anyway it would have made a loud noise. *S.Express* 8 July 1984.

● On 4 July, there were mini-tornadoes in several parts of Shropshire. At Minsterley, one of them messed up a freshly-cut hayfield. Margaret Downes heard a whirling noise and saw large clumps of hay ascending. "It was a large spiral column going hundreds of feet into the sky." *Shropshire Star* 5 July 1984.

● On 20 July, it was raining straw at Bishop's Tachbrook in Warwickshire. Pub landlord Frank Hextall said "it was coming down in clumps about 8 inches wide by 2 feet long. It was very high in the sky and just floating down and breaking up as it touched the ground. It was very odd." Four large boxes-full were collected. Stratford-on-Avon *Evening Telegraph* 21 July 1984.

● Gotham in Nottinghamshire was devastated by a 100 mph tornado on 2 August. It caused £200,000 worth of damage in 30 seconds. There was a mighty roar like an express train (compare with the silent event in Somerset, above). One report talks of "the spiralling ball approaching". 50 houses were damaged and three families made homeless. A garden shed was left hanging on power lines, and Mr Harry Lander watched from an upstairs window as his garage flew across the road and landed in an allotment. *Express and Star* 3 Aug; *Mirror, Telegraph* 4 Aug 1984.

● Shortly before 7pm on 22 September, a waterspout 200 yards across and 300 feet high swept into Barmouth, mid Wales, from Cardigan Bay. Five boats, including a

20-foot cabin cruiser, were sucked up 15 feet into the centre of the spout, and were sunk. Then the spout moved up the Mawddach estuary and gradually petered out. The coastguard said he had never seen anything like it in 45 years. "We didn't realise what it was at first. It looked like a hovercraft until we saw it reached into the sky."

Local fishermen stayed in port the next day. One explained that "old superstitions warn fishermen not to go out after a whirlwind." On the evening of the 24th their fears were justified when another spout 250 feet high swept into the harbour. *Shropshire Star, Guardian, Express* etc. 24 Sept; *Telegraph + Express* 25 Sept 1984.

● On 3 October, a whirlwind swept through Hampton Park, Hereford. Walls, windows and doors were damaged, and hundreds of roof tiles were ripped off. Rachel Kennet, 11, was swept seven feet in the air and hurled in front of an oncoming car. At the same moment, a giant oak crashed down on the spot where she had been standing. She escaped with a few cuts and bruises. *Shropshire Star, Express & Star* 4 Oct; *Guardian, Express, Sun, Star, Mirror* 5 Oct 1984.

● On 18 October, a mini-tornado damaged 6o houses in Tuffley, near Gloucester, and flattened trees in a two-mile radius. Bill Finch, 68, had to dig his wife out from under a pile of rubble which buried her as she lay in bed. She escaped with shock and bruises. *Guardian* 19 Oct 1984.

INEPT CRIMES

The last round up of these entertaining buffoons was in FT34p35. Here are a few recent cases.

Two 78-year-old burglars were caught red-handed in a house in São Paulo, Brazil, on 8th March 1984 when the occupants of the house returned unexpectedly. The one inside was too deaf to hear the warning of his friend outside, said police, and the look-out man was not fit enough to escape. (AP) *Guardian* 10 Mar 1984.

Anthony Brown, 42, broke into a £70,000 house in Fulham, London, to steal copper pipes. He cracked open a gas main, blundered around in the dark, lit a match and blew the place up. Amazingly, he survived and carried on as flames roared around him. The house was completely wrecked. The next day, he returned for more and met police investigating the blast. He was jailed for four and a half years. *Sun* 27 Mar 1984.

A mugger who snatched what looked like cash from Mrs Lebuvu in Krugersdorp, South Africa, got away with ten bottles of urine. The woman worked for a doctor and was en route to a laboratory to have the samples analysed. The headline in the *Telegraph* (11 Oct 1984) was *Taking the Urine.*

Thieves who stole 15 homing pigeons from bird fancier Peter Ball of Langley, Berkshire, tried them out....and they flew straight back to his loft. *Daily Mail* 15 Oct 1984.

Tony Wallcott, 19, was burgling a flat in Fulham, London, and took off his shirt because of the heat. He fled in panic when he was disturbed, leaving his shirt behind. In the pocket was his *Sun* bingo card with his name, address, phone number and his occupation, which he wrote as 'a layabout'. Police soon nabbed him, and he admitted to two other crimes. He got 18 months youth custody. *Sun* 28 Nov 1984.

TROPICAL HACKNEY

A rare species of tropical grass, *Paspalum pasalodes*, never before recorded in Britain, was found flourishing beside the Regents Canal at Kingsland Basin in Hackney, north London. It was discovered by botanist Tony Hare. "It has flowers which suggest two fingers sticking up in the air, and I was so surprised when I saw it that I fell in the water" he said. It is normally found in the tropics in South America, Africa and around the Mediterranean. *Standard, D.Mail, Telegraph, Bristol Evening Post* 29 Oct 1984.

■ Ten days earlier, it was reported that botanist Ron Davies had found a rare and poisonous aphrodisiac Indian plant (unspecified) somewhere in the west Midlands, he wasn't saying where. *Sun* 19 Oct 1984.

VANISHING GOO

Some time between the 12th and 18th of December, the west end of North Reading in Massachusetts was bombarded with blobs of jelly-like goo, greyish-white and oily-smelling. The first blob – two feet in diameter – was found by Thomas Grinley in his driveway. He thought something was leaking from his car until he found similar blobs on Main Street and on the gas station pumps.

State officials denied that the blobs were dropped by a plane. They were soon absorbed into the pavement, but a little goo was saved and was being studied at the state's Department of Environmental Quality Engineering. Preliminary results showed they were not toxic. Arlington, VA, *USA Today* 22 Dec 1983.

SIGNS AND WONDERS IN THE PHILIPPINES

President Marcos of the Philippines became 'President fo the World Government of the Age of Enlightenment' on 13th September 1984. He said it was his honour "to offer my people in the Philippines, and through them the whole population of the world, the scientifically tested and proven technology of the Unified Field". He was the only national leader in the world to accept the title from the Maharishi Mahesh Yogi. Two months later, it was evident that the 67-year-old Marcos was seriously ill, if not dead. Officially, he had 'flu, but it was commonly believed that he was suffering from systemic lupus erythematosis. The symptoms of this include skin rashes, fever, swelling of the joints and, eventually, in about half the victims, dementia or psychosis.

The First Lady, Imelda Marcos, received the 'Crown of Consciousness of the Royal Order of the Age of Enlightenment'. Like her husband, she consults her astrologer and soothsayer before taking important decisions. She confided to the cabinet that "There is a hole in outer space through which cosmic rays bear down upon our islands". At the beginning of October, K.H. Snell, the president of the Hollow Earth Society based in Sydney, announced in Manila, "We are investigating reports that an underground cave system, which we have so far penetrated 19 miles down, leads to another civilization". *Standard* 3 Oct; *Observer* 7 & 14 Oct; *Guardian* 20 & 26 Nov; *Telegraph* 23, 26+28 Nov 1984.

More than 1,200 disciples of the Maharishi's Transcendental Meditation 'technology' had arrived in the Philippines by mid-October. Their literature explains how practice of the theory by the square root of one per cent of any community produces a coherence in society of truly incredible physical, social and political properties. They claim that their experiments have pushed stock markets up, crime rates down, and produced lulls even in such conflict-torn countries as Lebanon. In the Philippines, only 750 mediators would be needed to produce these problem-solving effects. The organisation was pouring money into the country and attempting to gain control of three universities, including the University of the East, the biggest in the country. *Guardian* 19 Oct 1984.

Some miracle is certainly needed in the Philippines, where 1984 has been marked by violent conflict, political tension, economic decline and spectacular natural disasters. Last issue we reported the wave of violence in central Philippines (p.9) and a bleeding statue near Baguio City airport (p.6) At the end of August, the government announced that tropical storm June had killed at least 53, left more than 30,000 homeless and demolished two major bridges. On 2nd September, Typhoon Ike lashed the Philippines with winds reaching 130mph. The death toll was expected to exceed the 500 killed in a similar storm in 1970.

On 9th September, the 8,000 foot Mount Mayon volcano, 250 miles south-west of Manila, began to erupt after six years' inactivity. Hot black mud cut through four villages making 26,000 homeless. (Three days later, 16,000 fled from the erupting volcano of Karangetan on the Indonesian island of Siau.) Mayon erupted again with a huge column of fire on 24th September. 150 were saved from the scalding mud and lava. An ash-cloud six miles high hung over the entire province. All the next day, Mayon spewed out boulders as big as cars as flashes of lightning repeatedly hit the cone of the volcano: 50,000 people fled from their homes. The Mayon eruption in 1814 killed 1,200. *Telegraph* 1, 3, 13, 18, 24, 25, 26 Sept; *Daily Express* & *Daily Star* 25 Sept 1984.

On 5th November, Typhoon Agnes tore into the Philippines at 128mph, causing at least 140 deaths and making thousands homeless: it was the 18th major storm and third typhoon to hit the island in 1984. *Telegraph* 6 & 7 Nov 1984.

On 20 November, an earthquake measuring 7.1 on the Richter scale occurred in the vicinity of Southern Mindanao. *Standard* 20 Nov 1984.

STRANGE VISITORS

☐ A lesser spotted heron – only a few are recorded in Britain each year – was watched for several days by eager bird-watchers at a sanctuary at Bigwaters, near Wide Open, Newcastle-upon-Tyne. Alas for them it was some time before someone spotted the bird was dead, stuffed and still on its wooden mounting board. Who placed the specimen among the lakeside trees, or where it came from, is not known; but so convinced were the punters that many left donations to the Northumbria Wildlife Trust, which runs the sanctuary – and (this is one for those of you interested in freaks of suggestibility) according to an official: "Some people actually claimed to have seen it making movements." *Shropshire Star* 9 July 1984.

☐ Two young Swedish fishermen – Marcus Lenngren and Magnus Hilpden, both 10yrs-old – were nearly in tears when their parents didn't listen to their fishy story, for the very odd fish they caught in the bay of Braviken, outside Norrkoping, was later identified as a cuttlefish (*loligo vulgaris*). This cuttle is fairly common in the North Sea, but unheard of on the shores of the Baltic Sea. One expert said the cuttlefish could not have navigated the Kattegatt – the channel between Denmark and Sweden – on its own, but must have been washed out of a ship's ballast tanks into the Braviken, the ship having taken on the ballast elsewhere. There's al ways a first time, we suppose, but there are few facts here which can replace mere conjecture. *Sydsvenska Dagbladet Snällposten* 15, 17 & 23 Aug 1984.

☐ A "rare" tropical trigger fish, weighing nearly two and a half pounds, was caught on 1st Sept near Bournemouth, by a member of the Boscome Sea Fishing Club. There is no record of any prior catch of this species along the South Coast. *D.Telegraph* 3 Sept 1984.

☐ A large white spoonbill – which rarely reaches these shores in its autumn migration – was sighted at the Wildfowl Trust, Slimbridge, Glos. *D.Telegraph* 12 Sept 1984.

☐ An Arctic penguin crash-landed in London's Sloane Square, in September 1984, after "being blown hundreds of miles off course." It was believed to be the first such visitor to London under such conditions on record. Named Marianne, the young bird was looked after by an RSPCA inspector, who released her at Portland Bill, Dorset, on 10 Oct, after nursing her back to health. London *Eve.Standard* 11 Oct 1984.

☐ An 8ft 3ins long swordfish – see photo – normally found in warm, clear waters, was washed up, dead or dying, on the beach at Clevedon, near Bristol, on the Bristol Channel. Bristol *Eve.Post* 31 Oct 1984.

☐ A North American bobolink was spotted on Lundy Island, in the Bristol Channel. The seven-inch, brown and yellow songbird has only been seen in Britain "about a dozen times". *Guardian* 3 Nov 1984.

☐ For recent out-of-place animal sightings, see ALIEN ANIMALS on p.12.

Nigel Evans, Ken Hewlett and Alex Coles, assistant curator of Woodspring museum, Weston-super-Mare, with the Bristol Channel swordfish. Photo: Bristol Evening Post, *31 Oct 1984.*

MYSTERY CREATURE IN ICELANDIC LAKE

Two Icelandic bird-hunters claim they saw a pair of unidentified animals, "bigger than horses", playing on a beach on the shore of Lake Kleifarvvatn, 20 miles south of Reykjavik, during the first week of November 1984. Julius Asgeirsson and Olafur Olafsson watched from a few hundred yards as the creatures emerged from the lake to play and return to the waters.

Asgeirsson said: "We have never seen anything like this before and at first we were reluctant to tell anyone. They were larger than horses, they moved about like dogs but swam like seals. At first we thought they were rocks but as they started to move we had the surprise of our lives. The footprints were larger than those of horsehoofs and split like those of a cloven-footed animal, but with three cloves instead of two."

If this sighting is verified it should prove one of the most exciting cryptozoological discoveries in recent years, because no new large land animal – as these undoubtedly were if the cleft foot description is accurate as far as it goes – has been scientifically described since the finding of the South American peccary, *Catagonus wagneri,* in 1972. But many questions have yet to be answered: eg how does a hoofed animal swim like a seal? and how does a breeding colony of animals "larger than horses" remain undiscovered not 20 miles from a modern city like Reykjavik? UPI. *Helsingin Sanomat* (Helsinki) 14 Oct; New Haven (NY) *Register,* 15 Nov 1984. (For more Icelandic news see p.45.)

THE MIRACLE THAT NEVER WAS

When British doctor Jan Lavric stepped out of his wheelchair, seconds after being blessed by the Pope, cries of "It's a miracle!" rang out. Perhaps to some it was – but the GP from Clayton, near Doncaster, helping to run the trip for disabled people to see John-Paul 2 in the Vatican, said he felt tired so he sat down in an empty wheelchair for a rest. Suddenly a nun whisked him away, and before he could protest he was being presented to the Pope. *Shropshire Star* 2 May 1984.

IT'S FOR YOO-HOO!

Ken Campbell's long awaited Fortean play, 'Unfair Exchanges', had its national airing on BBC2's *Screen Two* slot (10.0pm) on 20th January this year. In it, the heroine, played by Oscar-nominee Julie Walters, is led be a series of seemingly accidental situations, familiar to many chaotic households, to the conclusions that the telephone networks have become a living powerful force controlling human lives. Among the phenomena woven into the plot are other ideas that Ken has developed from the inspired notions of Ion Will: phone conversations as the network's 'education', perfect imitation of any voice that has used the system, a modern *I Ching* divination by ramdon dialling, and phone-induced spontaneous combustion. Much of this is made to look incidental, like the splendid fictional interview with the victims of the 'Talking Toilet' poltergeist [see FT38p24] on the TV in the background of one scene.

Ken also appears in the play, as Tim Ricketts, an editor of *Fortean Times* who provides words for a featured song, called, suggestively, 'I ring, therefore I am.' It is to the character of Ricketts that the heroine turns for the explanation of all the phone-linked mischief in her life, and after slapping a copy of FT on the table, and filling her head full of the phone-system conspiracy, she has to ask him if he believes all this. "Of course not," he replies in the punchline to a grand Fortean joke, "I'm a Fortean."

But as science-fiction it was rather banal and old hat, and instead of filling this reviewer with a sense of wonder, simply made me wonder about the sense of it all. The conspiracy of inanimate objects is an ancient bugbear of mankind – especially of the clumsy and the paranoid – and these days we tend to take for granted the crossed-lines, the wrong numbers, the strange noises, echoes and silences we suffer from our phones. Here, these are portrayed as eerie, and were therefore difficult to take seriously. Just why the network was pursuing the quite unthreatening heroine was unclear, when there seemed to be other characters at liberty who knew a lot more about the insidious and lethal system. The exchanges shown (perhaps more for visual interest) were the old mechanical variety – not a hint of 'System X' or the new solid-state exchanges, nor of the growing and more sinister use of the phone network by computers.

But then, perhaps it was only a fable after all, showing the ways the pestiferous speaking tube can intrude into our private lives? As Fort says, somewhere: "The telephone is a marvellous invention – and then it rings!" As if to demonstrate that real life goes way beyond fictional constraints, we have to observe that the authors and producers omitted the system's most diabolical weapon, one which can devastate without recourse to difficult-to-engineer phenomena – the phone bill.

Nevertheless it was an enjoyable piece of propaganda for FT on TV screens nationwide (and on BBC too). Thanks Ken!

RJMR

Clipping Credits

Our thanks to the following for data used in this issue:
Larry Arnold/PSI, Bob Barter, Chester L.Behnke, Cecilia Boggis, Janet & Colin Bord, Jean Louis Brodu, John Chalke, Peter Christie, Alan Cleaver, Loren Coleman, R.Collyns, A.J.Dixon, Peter Hope Evans, Geoffrey Featherston, Alan Gardiner, Robert Gillham, Richard Goulding, Dick Gwynn, Brian Hain, Chris Hall, Mark A.Hall, Joan Halliday, Richard Heiden, John Hitchens, Chris J.Holtzhausen, Walter J.Langbein, Alexis Lykiard, Nick Maloret, Gary S.Mangiacopra, Valerie Martin, John Michell, Steve Moore, Ian Murray, Roger Musson, Ray Nelke, Cory Panshin, Nigel Pennick, Paul Pinn, B.Pittman, Clive Potter, Rickard *pere*, Sue Rose, Sven Rosen, Ronald Rosenblatt, R.Schiller, Paul Screeton, Bob Skinner, Anthony Smith, Warren Smith, Paul Swan, Joe Swatek, A.L.Thomas, Paul Thomas, Joseph Trainor, UFO Newsclipping Service, Nigel Watson, Dwight Whalen, Ion Will, Jake Williams, Joe Zarzinski.

PHENOMENOMIX

Science Frontiers

Compiled by William R. Corliss

The Guadaloupe Skeleton Revisited

In FT42,p33, an article in *Ex Nihilo*, an Australian creationalist publication, was reviewed. This article described the discovery of the famous Guadeloupe skeleton in limestone that seemed very ancient indeed from all indications. The article also stated that the British Museum suppressed discussion of this paradigm-shifting discovery by hiding it away somewhere.

It seems that the skeleton was never hidden and, in fact, was on public display between 1882 and 1967. The claimed Miocene dating of the skeleton has also been challenged, although no one seems to agree on just how old the bones may really be. The geological facts mentioned in FT42 are not discussed at all in the present article. A post Columbian date was suggested on the basis that implements and a dog skeleton were also found with the Guadeloupe skeleton. The whole business has split the ranks of British scientific creationists. (Howgate, Michael, and Lewis, Alan; "The Case of Miocene Man", *New Scientist*, p44, March 29, 1984) *The facts presented in the* New Scientist *and* Ex Nihilo *are so discordant that we await further developments with great interest and some amusement. Beach rock forms quite rapidly in some areas; and the skeleton* could *be very recent. However, the 'facts' presented in* Ex Nihilo *speak for great antiquity!*

A Russian Paluxy

"This spring, an expedition from the Institute of Geology of the Turkmen SSR Academy of Sciences found over 1,500 tracks left by dinosaurs in the mountains in the south-east of the Republic. Impressions resembling in shape a human footprint were discovered next to the tracks of the prehistoric animals." Professor Kurban Amanniyazov, leader of the expedition elaborated, "We've discovered imprints resembling human footprints, but to date have failed to determine, with any scientific veracity, whom they belong to, after all. Of course, if we could prove that they do belong to a humanoid, then it would create a revolution in the science of man. Humanity would 'grow older' thirty-fold and its history would be at least 150 million years long." ("Tracking Dinosaurs," Moscow *News*, no 24, p10, 1983. Cr. V.Rubtsov) *Strata along the Paluxy River, Texas, contain a similar mixture of dinosaur and human-like tracks.*

What Makes a Calculating Prodigy?

The above title is also that of a new book by Steven Smith. Naturally, the book is full of anecdotes about the phenomenal accomplishments of calculating prodigies, both unlettered children and such famous scientists and mathematicians as Euler, Gauss, and A.C.Aitken. The latter ". . .had the uncanny power of mentally computing, to a long string of decimals, the values of e and $e^{\pi\sqrt{163}}$. When asked (by his children) to multiply 987...1 by 123...9, he remarked afterwards: "I saw in a flash that 987...1 multiplied by 81 equals 80 000 000 001, and so I multiplied 123...9 by this, a simple matter, and divided the answer by 81." But what, asks Smith, led Aitken to 81? To this question, which is the heart of the mystery, he commendably admits he has no reply. And the same deep mystery confronts us even after all has been said about the *surface*, as distinct from the *underlying*, structure of the processing. At the unlettered end of the spectrum of mental calculators is the "....ignorant vagabond, Henri Mondeux, who at the age of 14 years, before the French Academy of Sciences, was able promptly to state two squares differing by 133." *Of course,* some *mental feats of calculation can be done* consciously, *employing various shortcuts and mathematical tricks. The really fantastic performances, however, are accomplished* unconsciously. *No one knows how, even the calculators themselves. (Cohen, John; "What Makes a Calculating Prodigy?"* New Scientist, *100:819, 1983.)*

Wanted: Disasters With A 26-Million Year Period

John Sepkoski and David Raup, two researchers at the Universtiy of Chicago, have drawn up graphs showing the numbers of families of marine organisms that have vanished from the fossil record over the eons. From this overview of manifest mass extinction emerged a puzzling and potentially profound pattern. Roughly every 26 million years over the last 250 million years, the number of extinctions jumped well above the background level. Some cyclic phenomenon seems to have been killing off life forms on a systematic basis. But no natural 26-million-year cycles are known. Although meteors and comets are favoured causes of mass extinctions these days, they display no such cyclic period. (Simon, C.; "Pattern in Mass Extinctions," *Science News*, 124: 212, 1983.) *Instead of looking outward to astonomical catastrophism, perhaps we should look inward. The earth itself may undergo cyclic paroxysms; or life might undergo intrinsic phases of decline and rejuvenation.*

Mystery Cloud of AD536

Abstract. "Dry fogs appear in the atmosphere when large volcanic eruptions inject massive quantities of fine silicate ash and aerosol-forming sulphur gases into the troposphere and stratosphere. Although the ash gravitationally settles out within weeks, the aerosols spread around the globe and can remain suspended in the stratosphere for years. Because solar radiation is easily absorbed, and backscattered by the volcanic particles, a haziness in the sky and a dimming of the Sun and Moon are produced. Very dense and widespread dry fogs occur, on the average, once every few centuries. The sizes and intensitities of some of the largest of them before the modern scientific era have been estimated by several indirect methods. The densest and most persistent dry fog on record was observed in Europe and the Middle East during AD536 and 537. Despite the earliness of the date, there is sufficient detailed information to estimate the optical depth and mass of this remarkable stratospheric dust cloud. The importance of this cloud resides in the fact that its mass and its climatic consequences appear to exceed those of any other volcanic cloud observed during the past three millenia. Although the volcano responsible remains a mystery, a tropical location (perhaps the volcano Rabaul on the island of New Britain, Papua New Guinea) can be tentatively inferred." (Stothers, R.B., "Mystery Cloud of AD536", *Nature*, 307:344, 1984) *Some of the "dry fogs" were accompanied by luminous nights, as in 1821 and 1831. See the* Catalog of Anomalies.

Grand Canyon Shamed Again

Exploration and mapping of submarine canyons cut into the continental shelves of Alaska and Siberia emphasize once again the colossal scale of these crustal gashes;

"Erosion of some of the largest known submarine canyons has removed more than 20,000 km^3 of former subduction margin between the Aleutian Islands and Cape Navarin, USSR. The canyons are incised as deeply as 2,400m into Tertiary sedimentary and igneous rocks that make up the margin and attendant deep sedimentary basins along the outer Bering shelf. Cutting of the seven major canyons probably occurred during low stands of sea level when the Bering Shelf was exposed to a depth of about -135m, which allowed the ancestral Anadyr, Yukon, and Kuskokwim Rivers to carry large volumes of sediment to the outer shelf. Although their positions appear to be structurally influenced, the canyons apparently were cut by combinations of massive slumping and sliding of sediment deposited near the shelf edge and of scouring action of the resulting turbidity currents that carried debris to the sea floor, where deep-sea fans have formed." (Carlson, Paul R., and Karl, Herman A.; "Ancient and Modern Processes in Gigantic Submarine Canyons, Bering Sea," *Eos*, 64:1052, 1983.) *The authors believe that submarine slumping and turbidity currents were sufficient to have eroded these huge canyons. Other geologists doubt this. The other possibility is that sea level was once a mile or more below present levels and that the canyons were cut by rushing water spilling over the continental shelves.*

Does String Hold the Universe Together?

Cosmological speculation is getting more and more bizarre. Astronomers are now postulating a kind of cosmic 'string' that is very, very thin (10^{-30}cm), enormously massive (10^{22} grams per centimeter), and very taut (10^{42} dynes tension). This string exists only in closed loops or infinite strands. Such string in loop form could have seeded galaxies and even black holes of solar mass. But these are not the major reasons why astonomers like the string hypothesis. It turns out that this bizarre string can tie the universe together gravitationally; that is, provide the long-sought 'missing mass'.

The so-called 'missing-mass problem' is two-fold: (1) Astronomers cannot see, with eye and instrument, enough mass to keep the universe from expanding indefinitely. If the kinetic energy of cosmic expansion is to be balanced by gravitational potential energy (an apparent philosophical imperative), we have so far identified only 15% of the required mass. (2) On a smaller scale, galaxies in large galactic clusters are moving too fast. They should have flown apart long ago, but some unseen 'stuff' holds them together. Is it cosmic string? (Waldrop, M. Mitchell; "New Light on Dark Matter?" *Science*, 224:971, 1984) *Since cosmic string weighs about 2×10^{15} tons per inch, the whole business is beginning to sound a bit silly. Actually, all action-at-a distance forces, which we readily accept as real, are only artificial constructs of the human mind. Gluons, coloured 'particles', top quarks, cosmic string; where will it all end?*

Earth's Magnetic Field Jerks

"It now seems almost certain that around 1969 a spectacular change took place in the geomagnetic field. The change was almost synchronous over the whole of the Earth's surface, took place in less than two years, and is now known to have consisted of a 'jerk': a step change in secular acceleration of the magnetic field that has its origin inside the Earth." (Whaler, K.A.; "Geomagnetic Impulses and Deep Mantle Conductivity," *Nature*, 306:117, 1983.) *No-one really knows just how a 'jerk' in the magnetic field is initiated; in fact, the origin of the geomagnetic field as a whole is not well-understood.*

Spores Still Viable After 7,000 Years

Bacterial spores embedded in muds lining Minnesota's Elk Lake – the muds were carbon-dated at 7518 years (!) – grew vigorously when placed in a nutrient-rich solution. ("Spores Still Viable After 7,000 Years", *Science News* 124:280, 1983.) *Such long periods of suspended animation support the panspermia concept, which states that life can be transported through outer space on meteorites and other debris.*

Science Frontiers ***is extracted from William Corliss' bimonthly collection of digests from current literature, which is sent free to regular customers of his publications. For more details write to*** **The Sourcebook Project, Box 107, Glen Arm, MD 21057, USA.**

ANOTHER STOMACH-TURNER [See FT40,p17]

Doreen Luckett, 11, went for a swim near her home in Darrow in the Mississippi delta and swallowed a lot of water. For the next fortnight she complained of stomach ache, and an x-ray showed a foreign body there. Doctors in the general hospital in Baton Rouge, Louisiana, opened her up and found a harmless Garter snake, about a quarter of an inch in diameter and nine inches long. It was still alive. *Sunday Express* 14 Oct 1984.

■ Mark Parker brought home a pound-and-a-half black bass he'd caught in a lake in Minden, Louisiana, in the first week of April 1984. He threw it in the sink to clean it, stuck his finger in its mouth and was bitten by a foot-long water moccasin that the fish evidently had swallowed prior to getting hooked. Parker, hospitalised for snakebite treatment, said he intended to mount both fish and snake. *Miami Herald* 6 April 1984.

TWO-HEADED TURTLE [See FT42, p20,28]

A two-headed baby loggerhead sea turtle was found on Hutchinson Island, Florida, in early August 1984. Though lethargic, it was moving both its heads to breathe, all four eyes seemed alert, and it was quite possible that it would survive. Three to four per cent of all sea turtles are deformed at birth, but the two-headed variety is extremely rare. St Louis *Post Dispatch* 12 Aug 1984.

MORE MISSING SHIPPING [See FT42, p24]

Some kind of 'triangle' or marine black hole seems to have opened up in the central Pacific. According to the *8 O'clock* (Auckland, New Zealand, 7 July 1984), more than 48 craft have gone missing around the island of Taraua in the previous ten months. The island was a major battle ground in World War II, and some locals believe the spirits of dead Japanese and Allied soldiers are luring local fishermen to their graves.

But 'some scientists' think it is a subterranean effect, similar to that which causes underwater volcanoes to appear and disappear suddenly in the waters around Tonga. Only a few of the lost craft have ever been traced. In 1983 the Kiribati government spent 50,000 dollars vainly searching for them, "And it looks as if we could top that this year," said local Marine Superintendent Beiaiti Highland.

■ On 9 June 1984 the motor fishing boat *Carmela Madre* (60 tons, 100 feet long and 18 feet wide) left Torre del Greco, near Naples for Vibo Valentia in southern Italy to repair nets. As she passed between Capri and Iscia in the Bay of Naples, the crew swapped news with Guiseppe Scognamiglio in another fishing boat. The weather was fine and the sea calm. Suddenly, the man in the *Carmela* cut in:

"Christ, I can't say any more!" he exclaimed. "There's a big light." Then there was silence. About a week later three of the crew were found drowned – Ciro de Rosa, 19, near Capri; Antonio de Rosa, his father, 20 miles away; and Raimondo Granato, 63, 20 miles from the other two. No wreckage was found.

The Tyrrhenian Sea between Sardinia, Rome and Sicily where the boat went down is supposedly known by fishermen and pilots as the 'Triangle of the Damned'. In 1980 an Alitalia DC9 entered the area and the controls went haywire, radio contact was lost and there was an explosion. The 81 passengers died. Shortly before that a Cessna plane had vanished. No trace of passengers or craft was ever found.

Over the last few years, dozens of small ships have been lost, the bodies of their crews picked from the sea weeks later. Empty fishing boats have been found drifting, and captains have reported strange objects in the waters. *S.Express* 21 Oct 1984.

■ On 28 August 1984, a Dutch vessel, the *Pacific Violet*, reported sighting trimaran wreckage bearing the name of *Beefeater* about 350 miles south of the Azores. Ten days earlier, the British yachtman Chay Blyth left Dartmouth for New York with his wife and daugher in *Beefeater II*. The last reported position was on the 26th, 500 miles NNE of the Azores, and many people were concerned for his safety.

Doubts were dispelled when he made radio contact on the afternoon of the 29th. He planned to try and beat the sailing record from New York to San Francisco via Cape Horn, held since 1851 by the American clipper *Flying Cloud*.

My Blyth's original *Beefeater* trimaran was due to be delivered to him in New York, but had to be abandoned in heavy seas 800 miles short of its destination in October 1983. This was the wreckage spotted by the *Pacific Violet*...... probably. *Sun, Telegraph* 30 Aug 1984.

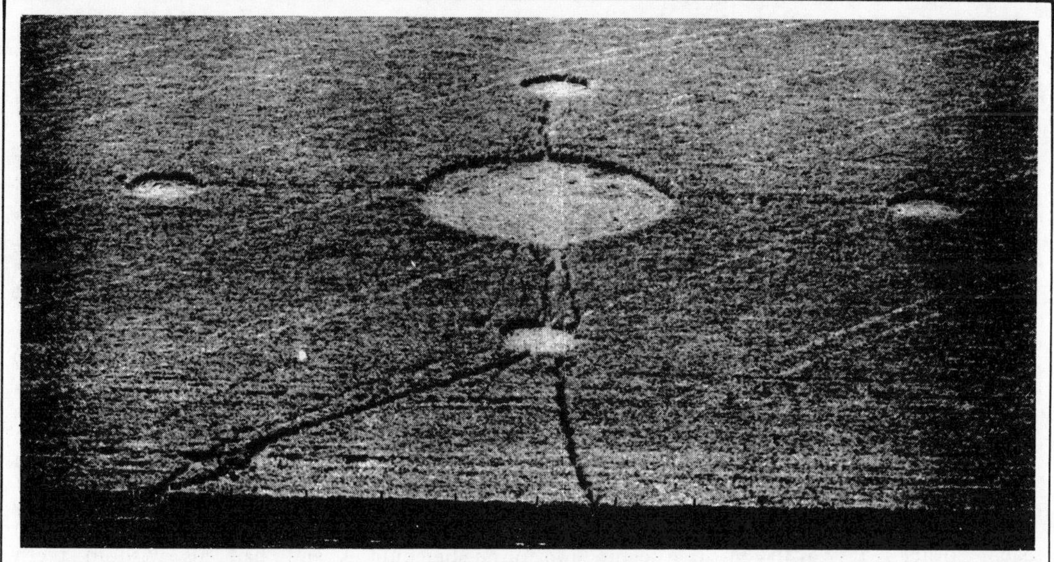

MORE CIRCLES

The summer of 1984 brought a new crop of circles in the corn [see ALIEN CORN in FT40p27] in July, some were spotted in Hampshire, and one at Cleyhill Heights in Wiltshire. Another collection was spotted in a field at High and Over in East Sussex. One 20-foot diameter circle was surrounded by four evenly-spaced outer circles about five feet across. There were no scorch marks or footprints to be seen. Express *23 July;* Evening Argus *31 July & 1 Aug 1984.*

A slightly larger version (central disc 30 feet, outer circles 12 feet in diameter) appeared a few days later beside the home of Shadow Foreign Secretary Denis Healey in Alfriston, Sussex. He took this picture. Mail *4 Aug 1984.*

THE BRITISH BOG MAN

Last issue, I described how Peter Reyn-Bardt had been tricked into confessing his wife's murder after a Roman skull was found in a Cheshire peat bog in May 1983 [TRUTH TRICKED OUT, FT42,p37]

On the 4th (or 5th) August 1984, a well-preserved body was dug out of Lindow Moss near Wilmslow in Cheshire, near where the Roman skull had been found. 'Pete Marsh', as he was nicknamed, turned out to be a 5 foot 6 inches tall Iron Age Briton in his twenties or thirties who had been garrotted, had his skull crushed with an axe, and his naked body dumped in a shallow pool between 900 and 500BC. Judging from his perfectly manicured fingernails, it appeared he did little manual work, and so

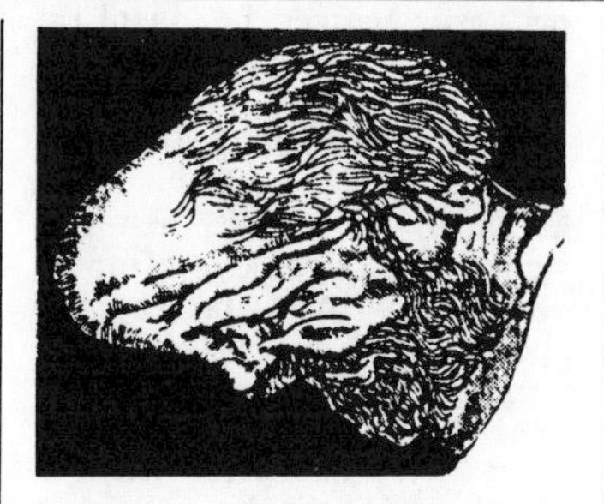

probably belonged to the 'ruling elite'. He was the first 'bogman' discovery in mainland Britain, and the most informative prehistoric find in Europe since Tolland Man was discovered in Denmark in 1952. This chap had also been garrotted. From Tacitus we know that 'barbarians' placed the bodies of those who had committed heinous crimes such as murder, adultery or sodomy in bogs. Alternatively, Pete Marsh may have been a sacrifice to Mother Earth. *Guardian* 11 Aug, 5 Oct + 13 Nov; *New Scientist* 13 Sept; *Mail on Sunday* 30 Sept; *Standard* 4+8 Oct; *Observer* 7 Oct; *S.Times* 16 Sept, 7+14 Oct; *Mirror, Express, Telegraph* & *Mail* 5 Oct; *Bristol Evening Post* & *Telegraph* 27 Nov 1984.

HOT CURES FOR BALDNESS

A cow's tongue is not the only cure for baldness [FT42, p19] Burning the scalp also seems to work. 54-year-old Jim Naso was badly burned over 50 percent of his body when his yacht blew up off the New Jersey coast on 1 July 1979. Having been bald for 30 years, he soon started to grow a full head of hair. Thirty years of baldness also came to an end for 75-year-old Danny Winter in August of that year. He went for a walk in Hastings, Kent, and had his bald pate sprayed with hot tar from a road surfacing machine. (The references for these items are unfortunately mislaid at the moment. Ed.)

MORE TWINCHRONICITY [FT30,p18]

We have accumulated hundreds of twinchronicity items on file since I last wrote them up. Here are three new ones.

■ Pauline and Pat Collister, 26 years old, are believed to be Britain's only identical twins married to identical twins, Peter and John 27. On 11th August, Pauline and Pat gave birth within an hour of each other at Scarsdale Hospital, Chesterfield, Derbyshire. *Aberdeen Press and Journal* 13 Aug 1984.

■ Identical twins Lynn Hughes and Kay Press, 33, gave birth to their first babies on the same day at Southmead Hospital in Bristol. Lynn had an 8lb 12oz girl, and six hours later Kay had a son weighing 7lb 15oz. *Telegraph* 28 September 1984.

■ Twins Roberto and Marco Ferrieri made a 3,000 foot parachute pump near Milan airport, and Marco broke his right leg. Driving home later, Roberto crashed....and broke his right leg. *Sunday Express* 25 Nov 1984.

HEAD BANGING MIRACLES [FT42,p.5]

The head-banging which restored Dick Robert's sight is not an isolated case. The Swede Henry Wahlberg was blinded when a fish hook stuck in his eye as a child. In 1981, a tree branch went into his bad eye and restored his sight.

■ Edwin Robinson, 62, blinded nine years previously, regained his sight after being struck by lightning in Falmouth, Maine, on 6 June 1980. He could also hear without his hearing aid. (Source references for these have been mislaid – sorry!)

■ Joe Sardler, 32, of Mount Airy, North Carolina, blind for six years after a childhood injury which claimed his sight bit by bit, tripped over his dog's dinner dish and fell down the basement steps. "At first I was dazed. Then suddenly, I realised I could see again." *Globe,* 7 April 1981.

■ In May 1981, Calatina del Toro-Lopez, a Spanish mother who had been dumb for the previous six and a half years through paralysis of the vocal chords, let out a scream in the middle of the night at her home in Mula near Alicante, and found she could talk again. A picture of the Virgin Mary, hanging above her bed, had fallen on her head while she slept. Even doctors cried "miracle"!

■ Yvonne Brown, 18, lost her sight through eye disease at the age of eleven. Her boyfriend walked out because he couldn't cope with her blindness, she banged her head on the wall in despair, and her sight returned. They were married in Hereford. *Houston Chronicle* 7 Nov 1983.

■ Kevin Willis, 28, lost the sight in his right eye after an accident with a dart at the age of three. In 1982 a nerve complaint blinded the other eye. A 'playful' clout on the head by his wife with a plastic bucket in his garden at Ash Road, Newark, Nottinghamshire, restored the sight in his left eye the following day. *Shropshire Star + Mirror* 20 Aug 1983.

■ After three years of deafness, 12-year-old Claire Booth's hearing returned when she banged her head on the wall during an argument with her mother at their home in Harvey Road, Congleton, Cheshire. *Sun + Telegraph* 17 Nov 1983.

■ A different type of cure happened to Gun Thoresson, 43, who had been blind since she was 20. She went to her dentist in Burea, northern Sweden, where her sight was restored after three heavily-filled molars were extracted. The explanation may lie in 'oral galvanism' – a small electric current set up in the mouth between two dissimilar metals. British dentists were, however, skeptical that its effects could spread to the brain, causing blindness. *New Scientist* 27 July; *Mail on Sunday* 13 Nov 1983.

■ Ian Kirby, 20, from Hindhead, Surrey, had been told he would never see again after gradually going blind at the age of 15. In December 1984 he went into hospital and had his wisdom teeth removed, after which he could see again, although he still could not distinguish colours. But his sight was improving every day. *D.Mail* 2 Jan; *D.Telegraph* 3 Jan 1985.

WELSH QUAKE NOTES [FT42p4]

An earthquake was felt over 400 square miles of Powys on 15 April 1984, its epicentre being near Felindre, 7 miles SE of Newton. Explosions were heard, for example at Abermule, Newtown, Kerry and Knighton. Janet and Colin Bord were driving home to Montgomery from the Midlands, and at 12.10am, two hours after the quake, near Churchstoke, 9 miles NE of Felindre, Janet noticed what looked like a star of average brightness, a little below and to the left of the moon, where it was obscured by a small cloud which had drifted from the right. The cloud moved on in the same direction, but the'star' had vanished, leaving a completely clear area of sky. The whole incident lasted about a minute. "I should add," writes Janet, "that although I was definitely awake at the time, I had awoken from a short nap only half a mile before the sighting began." (Letter, 18 April 1984.)

At the time of the 19 July quake (7.57am), Terry Wogan was playing the Beach Boys "Good Vibrations" on the radio. (*D.Mail* 20 July 1984.) That evening, the BBC repeated the *Horizon* special on earthquakes – which had obviously been scheduled in advance. Jenny Randles was staying with her parents in Birchwood, near Risley Moss nature reserve, and the evening before the quake, dozens of birds sat motionless for a long time on the rooftops opposite the house. The family cat began a fearful mewing a few minutes before the quake. The following morning, the house was invaded by earwigs.

Jenny's colleague in Ufology, Peter Warrington, was in his bathroom when the quake struck, and the lightbulb shattered, the only damage in the house. Since he is skeptical of the connection between unidentified lights and geolgoical fault lines, Jenny thinks that this was a Sign for him not to be so hasty. (Letter, 20 July 1984.)

Foaflore

The following reported stories have that indefineable strand of improbability about them suggesting the making of a myth.

THE BODY IN THE BACK

The following story belongs firmly in the 'Granny on the roof-rack' genre. A thief who stole an estate car from outside a Social Security office in Warrington, Lancs, abandoned it just half a mile away, when he discovered to his surprise a body in a coffin in the back. The car was being used by a local undertaker. *D. Telegraph* 30 Sept 1983.

DOUBLE CAR TROUBLE

AA Sergeant Howard Jenkins's radio crackled a bit, but he thought he'd got the message: pub landlady Mrs Beatrice Edmonds had abandoned her Wolseley Six in a pub carpark in Great Barr, near Birmingham, because the drive shaft to the near-side front wheel had broken. Without much trouble Jenkins found the Old Horns pub and the Wolseley, and sure enough, the keys were in the ignition as promised and part of the drive shaft on the rear seat. He towed it to Mrs Edmonds' pub, in Stourbridge, Worcs, but to both their astonishment it was not the right car. My Wolseley is brown, said Mrs Edmonds, looking at the maroon one Jenkins had brought. He went back to the carpark in Great Barr and, sure enough (again) found the brown Wolseley, keys and drive shaft. It was a memorable coincidence: two cars the same make, in colours which looked alike in the dark, with similar registration numbers, left in the same carpark, with the same broken part inside! The other had been stolen from people in Bartley Green, West Midlands, it turned out. *S. Express* 18 March 1984.

ROSY'S LAST RIDE

Rosy Sutton went through life with a laugh and a smile, said her friends when she died, aged 72. But the biggest laugh of all, and the one everyone in her hometown of Doncaster, Yorks, will remember, is her funeral. For as the procession of cars made their way to the municipal crematorium, the streets were lined with thousands of people cheering and waving flags, saluting police and flashing cameras. The crowds mistook the cortege of Rolls-Royces for the cars of Prince Charles and Princess Diana, who were visiting the city that day. Son Richard said: "Mum always liked a laugh and she had a right royal funeral. People keep saying what a good send-off she had." Who says that isn't any good news anymore? *Sun* 26 March 1984.

IN THE ROAD

Ambulance men sped through the night, down the main road from Sutherland to Golspie, in Scotland. They had been called out by a motorist who saw two bodies and a fallen motorbike on the side of the road. He was on urgent business, he said, and couldn't stop to help them, so he decided to get help from the nearest town. When the ambulance men investigated the scene of the supposed accident they could hardly believe their eyes. The partially clad motorcyclist (still wearing his helmet!) and (presumably) his girlfriend were making passionate love. Before quickly resuming their journey, the man explained to his unexpected audience that they were overtaken by irresistible urges and simply stopped the bike and let impulse have its way. *Sun* 22 March 1984.

☐ The only comparable item in our files is a tantalizingly brief note in the *D. Mirror* 8 Nov 1983: that following a complaint from a startled motorist, who stumbled upon the scene while crossing Dartmoor, police were trying to trace a nude couple making love in the road urged on by a group of men and women, near Hexworthy, Devon.

THE SKY CHILDREN

In July 1983, Pakistani authorities were checking on a mysterious report that two children who had fallen from a plane 29,000 feet above the Persian Gulf were alive and well.

On 22 December 1980 a Saudi Arabian Airways Tri-Star took off from Dharhan in Saudi Arabia bound for Karachi. On board were Ziauddin Khatoon, a hospital technician going home on leave, his wife Anna, their daughter Samina, 10, and their 6-year-old son Ahmed. About 11.30pm a damaged tyre burst on one of the landing wheels, retracted into the plane's belly, and the massive blast tore a hole about two feet six inches wide in the underside of the passenger compartment. The sudden decompression in the cabin sucked the children out into the night.

The plane made an emergency landing in Qatar, and an immediate search was made for the children, without success. There was no news until nearly three years later.

In Karachi a foreign ministry spokesman said that a Pakistani was visiting a small port in Abu Dhabi, saw the two children, and the little girl told the story of how they had been found by an Arab fisherman floating in the water, and how, thinking they had dropped from heaven, he took them home and raised them as his own.

The presence of the children was reported to the Abu Dhabi authorities, but by the time a check was made the fisherman had sailed on. If and when he is found, said the foreign ministry spokesman, he will be given an honour by the government of Pakistan.

At Burbank in California, James Ragsdale, spokesman for Lockheed who make the TriStar planes said: "Stranger things have happened. In the 1960's when a plane broke up in a thunderstorm while flying over the jungles of Peru, a little girl still strapped in her seat fell about 15,000 feet, landed in a treetop and walked away virtually uninjured." *S.Express* 17 July 1983.

SIAMESE TWINS FACE FIRING SQUAD (!)

One afternoon sometime in 1983, Anna Lopez drove her donkey wagon to the local market near her shack in Villarrica, Paraguay. With her were her 19-year-old sons Jose and Alfredo, who are Siamese twins joined at the side. The twins waited in the waggon while their mother shopped for corn and tea.

"We were just sitting there in the fresh air, singing a song, when the woman drove up in her big car and started honking and cursing at us," recalled Jose. Louisa Rodriguez, wife of Judge Higinio Rodriguez, accused the twins of blocking the parking spot she wanted. "She was very nasty. She yelled at us to move the cart and we tried to tell her we couldn't...then she came over and started shaking the cart and we almost toppled out. I was afraid, so I picked up mother's rifle and shot her."

Jose was convicted of murder in a 30 minute trial by Judge Juan Flores. A doctor told the court the boys couldn't be separated because they shared several vital organs. But the judge sentenced Jose to the firing squad, and the ill-fated brothers have been on death row since January. "This is outrageous – how can they do this to me?" wailed Alfredo, according to Joe Berger's account in the *Weekly World News* (15 May 1984). I haven't seen any confirmation of this tale, but couldn't resist passing it on.

ONCE MORE WITH FEELING

One moonlit night in April 1984, Jorge Reba, 32, was seine fishing in the Amazon delta a few miles north-west of the Brazilian port of Macapá, when he netted a mermaid. The upper half was a beautiful woman, the lower a porpoise, pink and leathery. They gazed at each other, she sang a haunting melody, told him her name was Sirena (a dead giveaway, that) and invited him to kiss her and come and live with her for ever beneath the sea. All night she talked, Reba resisted her advances with great difficulty, and at daybreak she leapt overboard and was gone.

This story is presented as a factual account in our old favourite, the *Weekly World News* (8 May 1984). The haunting myth of the siren's song luring mariners to their doom is at least as old as Homer. According to *Monsters of the Deep* (Anon; pub. Nelson & Sons 1876), history's most famous John Smith, the adventurer and reputed founder of European colonisation in North America, was off the coast of the new continent in 1614

"The siren of America". From Monsters of the Deep *(1876).*

when he saw, "gracefully swimming, a woman whose eyes were large, beautiful and expressive, though slightly round; her nose and ears sufficiently well made, and her tresses green and long. The captain felt he was falling in love with this beautious and faery creature, and manning his boat, rowed away in pursuit; but, unfortunately, she made a somersault and discovered to her admirer a fish's tail."

According to folklore, the treasure-rich lake of El Dorado, somewhere in the fastnesses of South America, is guarded by a siren named *mai das aguas*. The man known as Columbus (see p 58) is said to have encountered three sirens dancing in the waves near San Domingo. They didn't sing, and he thought them 'ill-featured'. Later, these waters were seen to host manatees (in Spanish *peje muger* – woman-fish), whose fingers, pendulous breasts and short bristled snouts might well be described as "ill-featured' in anthropomorphic terms.

DOLLS FROM HELL

The craze for Cabbage Patch dolls, those hideous toys which caused riots in American stores over Christmas 1983, has turned into paranoia after an article in the tabloid *National Enquirer,* according to Britain's *Daily Mirror.*

Veteran psychic researcher Ed Warren, said the report, had been called in to exorcise at least three of the little horrors. "We face a plague of devil infestations and possessions because women are treating these dolls as real children", he said.

He cited the case of one childless woman in her early thirties who transferred all her love to the toy. She'd put the doll in a crib and later find it in another room. Then there were the strange odours – pleasant, or of burning sulphur. One night she and her husband heard a crash and found several prized china tea cups fallen from their shelf. As they tidied up, they heard a low growling snarl coming from the doll's room. The wife went in and saw the doll sitting up in its crib. It looked menacing with reddish piercing eyes, ruddy complexion and a pointed chin. A deep voice from its head said: "You didn't cover me. You didn't tuck me in! That's why I broke the cups. You and I are going to be together for ever. I'm not just a doll – I'm the Lord of Hell."

The couple saught Warren's help, and he saw the doll floating about eight inches above the crib." I quickly made the sign of the cross and held out my crucifix, and the doll flopped into the crib." They buried it in the garden and sprinkled holy water on the grave. Since when – no bother.

In another case, Warren was called in to help a woman who said she was nearly strangled by a demon with the face of a baby. Later she found her Cabbage Patch doll in her room – still clutching a button that had been yanked off her nightgown. Warren again buried the doll with the usual precautions.

"One woman was literally forced out of her house because of the hallucinations she was having following her purchase of a Cabbage Patch doll and heaping affection on it", he said. "A simple exorcism solved that case as well." *D.Mirror* 29 Aug; *National Enquirer* 4 Sept. 1984. Big quotation marks round this item. Up to you to find the lines between showbiz, mass hysteria and anomalistics, that is if you are fond of lines. Measuring the circle takes you on the boundless line, however. Time for tea, and feed the Thing...

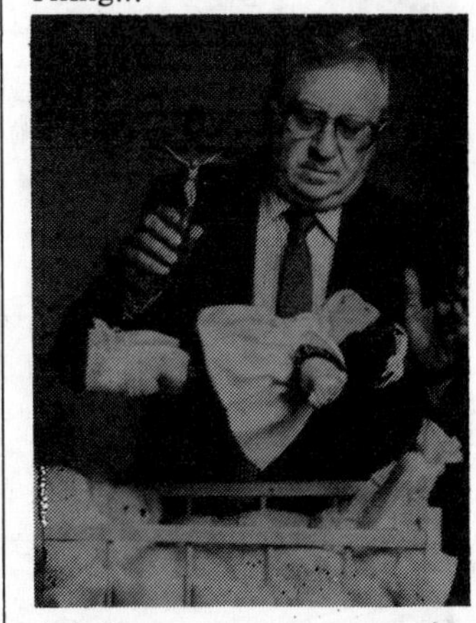

Ed Warren reenacts confro -ntation with possessed Cabbage Patch doll. Photo: National Enquirer, *4 Sept 1984.*

Human Horns

"But my horn shalt thou exalt like the horn of an unicorn: I shall be anointed with fresh oil."
Psalms, xcii, 10.

Since the earliest human cultures, horns have been symbolic of wisdom and power. The sacred kings and shamans wore a head-dress of antlers like that found in New Grange in Ireland. Fertility cults, involving a horned god, phallic rituals and ecstatic dances, were spread all over Europe in palaeolithic times. The satyrs, Dionysus, Pan and the Gaullish god Cernunnos all had horns. Pan worship was still going strong in England in the seventh century, when archbishop Theodore devoted a whole chapter of his *Book of Penitances* to anathemising the old rites. Indeed, horned-god worship was the most serious threat to emergent Christianity, which was unable to incorporate it as a harmless feature in its mythological Weltanschauung: it had to be given a totally negative aspect. The attributes of Pan, including his horns, were transferred to the Christian Satan.

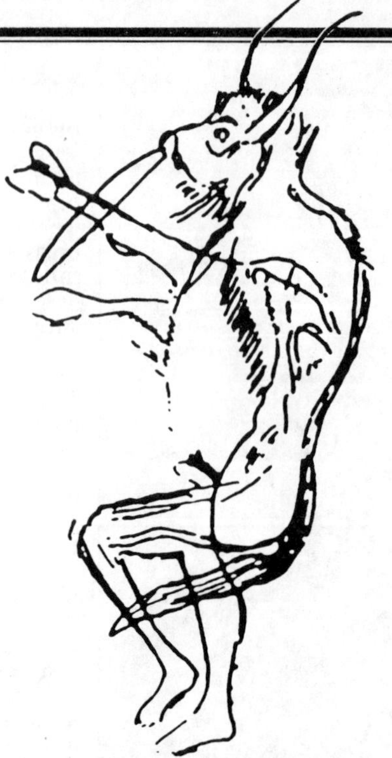

A horned man playing a musical bow. Palaeolithic engraving in the Sanctuary cave, Les Trois Frères, Ariège, southern France.

Horns in fashion: a woodcut by Albrecht Dürer, printed by Bergmann von Olpe, 1494.

Alexander the Great is depicted with horns on his coinage. According to Josephus, the High Priest in Jerusalem showed Alexander the prophecy in the Book of Daniel which promised him dominion of the East. The prophecy referred to Alexander as the 'two-horned king'. He appears in the Koran as *Dhul Karnain*, 'the two-horned'. Moses was also 'two-horned'[1], and in Arabian legend, 'El Hidr, the ever-young prophet' befriended both Moses and Alexander 'at the meeting place of the two seas'. St Jerome and the early Church Fathers made a poetic identification of Alexander's horns with those of Moses. Michelangelo's famous sculpture of Moses sports a pair of horns.

Strangely enough, even while the horned Satan was still a potent figure of dread, the wearing of artificial horns became a feature of high fashion. It was introduced into England in the reign of Henry V, and from the effigy of Beatrice, Countess of Arundel, at Arundel church, who is represented with two horns outspread to a great extent, we may infer that the length of the head-horn, like the length of the shoe-point in the reign of Henry VI, etc., marked the degree of rank. To 'cut off' such horns would be to degrade, while to extend them would be to add honour and dignity. Conversely, the wearing of horns symbolises the cuckold. This probably derives from the antlers of stags, who win and maintain their harem by duels with rivals.

Rhodius[2] observed a Benedictine monk who had a pair of horns and was addicted to rumination. Human horns are far more frequent than is generally supposed, and nearly all the earlier medical writers cite examples[3].

François Trouille was born in France in the seventeenth century, and lived almost always in the woods[4]. Here he was found, aged about thirty-five and dressed in a wolf's skin, by M. Laverdin while he was out hunting. As Trouille would not remove his hat, it was pulled off, and the horn projecting from the right side of his forehead astonished the onlookers. He was sent to the king in Paris[5]. He was exhibited there for two months in 1598, and then in Orleans, where he died soon after. Fabricius describes him in his *Chirurgical Observations:*

He was of middle stature, a full body, bald, except in the hinder parts of his head, which had a few hairs upon it; his temper was morose, and his demeanour altogether rustic: he was born in a little village called Mezieres, and bred up in the woods amongst the charcoal men. About the seventh year of his age, he began to have a swelling in his forehead; so that about the seventeenth year of his age, he had a horn there as big as a man's finger end, which afterwards did admit of that growth and increase, that when he came to be thirty-five years old, this horn had both the bigness and resemblance of a ram's horn. It grew upon the midst of his forehead, and then bended backward as far as the coronal suture, where the other end of it did sometimes so stick in the skin, that, to avoid much pain, he was constrained to cut off some part of the end of it; whether this horn had its roots in the skin or forehead, I know not; but probably being of that weight and bigness, it grew from the skull itself: nor am I certain whether this man had any of those teeth which we call grinders. It was during this man's public exposure at Paris, (saith Urstitious) in 1598, that I, in company with Dr. Jacobus Faeschius, the public Professor of Basil, and Mr Joannes Eckenstenius, did see and handle this horn.

A silver coin, showing Alexander the Great with horns. Issued postumously by Lysimachus, circa 300 BC.

François Trouille (or Trouillu or Trovillou) shows his horn. Left: engraving by Granire. Right: engraved by Kirby from an earlier print.

Published in Caulfield (6).

According to the portrait of Mary Davis, she was born in Saughall near Chester about 1594; while a tract of 1679 says she was born in Shotwick, within four miles of Chester, around 1603. She was a midwife by profession, and married Henry Davis who died about 1644. In her youth she noticed a soreness where later horns were to grow, occasioned, it was thought, "by wearing a straight hat". This soreness continued 20 years and ripened into a wen the size of a large hen's egg, which after another 5 years changed into a horn, which grew long, "but slender as an oaten straw." After about 4 years she shed this horn and grew a thicker one which was also shed after a simlilar period. These first two horns were preserved by a Mr Hewson, the vicar of Shotwick.

The third time she grew two horns together, solid and wrinkled like those of a ram. These were broken off by a fall backwards. One of these was nine inches long and two in circumference. The small one was obtained by an English lord, who supposedly presented it to Louis XIV. Gould and Pyle[3] mentioned an old woman in France in 1696 who constantly shed long horns from her forehead, one of which was presented to the king. If these are two separate cases, it appears that Louis was a human horn collector. Sir Willoughby Aston had yet another horn from the midwife's prodigious head. At the time of the 1679 pamphlet she was growing a further pair which promised to outgrow all the others. She could be seen at the Swan tavern in the Strand, near Charing Cross[6].

Probably the most remarkable case was that reported in the *New York Medical Repository*, in 1820. Paul Rodrigues, a Mexican porter, had a horn fourteen inches in circumference dividing into three shafts, which sprouted from the upper and lateral part of his head, and which he kept hidden under a specially shaped red cap. There is also a case of an old woman with a horn branching into three. The greater frequency among females is mentioned by most authors, and old age is a predisposing cause. One horn was on a 97-year-old.

James Caulfield[6] mentions some further horns. One from the head of a man was said to be in the possession of Astley Cooper, the celebrated surgeon. Mr Ward, peruke maker in the Strand around 1800, had one several inches long which he used as a snuff box. This he claimed came from a woman then alive who

The horned nature god Pan (Greek for 'the all') as the force unifying the protean shapes of nature in heaven and earth. By Athanasius Kircher in his Oedipus Aegyptiacus, *Rome, 1652.*

had grown several others. The university library in Edinburgh had a horn cut from the head of Elizabeth Love, a woman of fifty. It grew three inches above her ear, for seven years. A Mrs Allen was to be seen in Coventry Street, Haymarket, in 1790, who had a horn of some years' growth, cut from above the ear. She settled in Leicestershire in 1792.

On 7 April 1812, a Mrs Bumby of Ekring in Hampshire died in her eightieth year. In her youth she had been a schoolmistress, and married when she was fifty. After leaving the church on her wedding day, a mental derangement took place, from which she never wholly recovered. A horn sprang in her later years from one side of her forehead, and grew in a crooked form to the length of nearly six inches: another also appeared but was stunted, owing, it was supposed, to her frequently rubbing it. *Hampshire Telegraph*, 13 April 1812.

Kirby[4] mentioned the case of Elizabeth Westly, about seventy years old in 1805, living in Macroom in County Cork, who suffered from about 1798 onwards a considerable degree of pain at one side of her head, from which a horn, resembling in form and substance that of a ram, grew to nine inches. From a similar sensation on the opposite side of her forehead, she was led to expect another horn on that side.

Thomas Bartholinus (17th cent.) mentions a horn twelve inches long, which is in the running for the longest recorded. Contenders include one of eleven inches long and two and a half inches in circumference in a London museum, and one of ten inches from the forehead of a woman of eighty-two, recorded in the *American Journal of Medical Science* in 1857.

The following account from New South Wales, probably embellished by some journalist, is given in Ballantyne's *Teratologia*: The child, five weeks old, was born with hair two inches long all over the body; his features were fiendish and his eyes shone like beads beneath his shaggy brows. He had a tail 18 inches long, horns from the skull, a full set of teeth, and claw-like hands; he snapped like a dog and crawled on all fours, and refused the

A peg-legged devil accosts an itinerant monk. Drawing by Urs Graf, German, 1512, Basel.

MARGARET VERGH GRYIFFITH.
Aged 60 — 1588.
Exhibited with a Horn in her forehead, 4 inches long
Pub^d Augt 6. 1813 by R.S.Kirby. 11 London House Yard

She was the wife of David Owyn of Llahan Gaduain in Montgomery, and was to be seen in London. Caulfield (6) writing in 1813 comments: "Like several married women in Scotland at the present time, [she] went by her father's sirname in preference to that of her husband's." The picture is copied by Kirby (4) from the frontispiece of a rare tract printed in London by Thomas Orwin in 1588.

natural sustenance of a normal child. The mother almost became an imbecile after the birth of the monster. The country people about Bomballa considered this devil-child a punishment for a rebuff that the mother gave to a Jewish peddler selling Crucifixion-pictures. Vexed by his persistence, she said she would sooner have a devil in her house than his picture.

In recent years, the cases of horned humans in the Fortean Archives come from the Far East. Some of them were written up in 1980 (FT33, p.41), including Zhao Lishi – 'Madam Chow' (see picture). A further example is My Decai , 92, of Fushan City in north-east China, known as the 'Goat Man'. The two-and-a-half inch horn from the back of his head began to grow in 1980 when he was 87. Doctors removed it in 1981, but it began to grow again. The local people consider his horn to be magical or lucky and beg him to let them touch it as a good luck charm. Doctors have offered to remove the new horn, but he is quite happy to keep it, says the *Weekly World News* (25 Sept. 1984).

•

Paul Sieveking

NOTES

1. Moses' horns result from a mistranslation, according to Brewer in his *Dictionary of Phrase and Fable* (1870). The Hebrew *karan* means "to shoot out beams of light", but has been erroneously rendered in some versions as "to wear horns". "Moses wist not that the skin of his face shone." (Exodus xxxiv, 29.)
2. Joannes Rhodius: *Mantissa anatomica* (1654).
3. See Gould and Pyle; *Anomalies and Curiosities of Medicine* (1896) pp.222-226.
4. R.S. Kirby: *Wonderful and Scientific Museum* (1803-20).
5. *Aldrovandi Monstrorum Historia* p.126.
6. James Caulfield: *Portraits, Memoirs and Characters of Remarkable Persons from the Reign of Edward III to the Revolution* (1813).

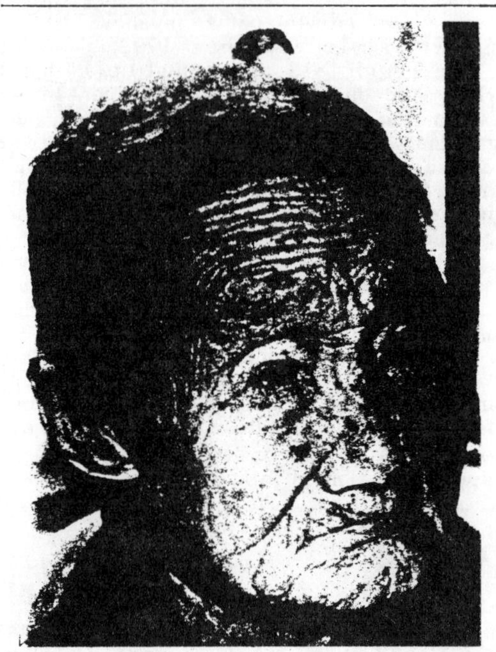

Zhao Lishi, of Hebei Province in China, with her two horns, the larger a quarter inch long, which took six months to grow. Xinhua News Agency.

One of Schedel's 21 marvels of India from his Nuremberg Chronicle, *1493.*

The widow Dimanche of Paris who became known as 'Mother Horn', and My Decai, the 'Goat Man' of Fushan City, China.

INTRODUCED BY **DR. TAD RICHELIEU**
(LECTURER IN INTERSTICIAL EPISTEMOLOGY AT THE UNIVERSITY OF AKRON)

LET ME ASK YOU THIS... WHAT, EXACTLY, DO WE THINK WE'RE DOING? OR RATHER, DO WE DO WHAT WE THINK WE'RE DOING OR THINK WE'RE DOING WHAT WE'RE THINKING? UH... AND WHAT DID MACGOHOUIL THINK HE WAS DOING WHEN HE DICTATED THE **"MAGNUS DELUDI"**?

TAKE, FOR EXAMPLE, THE REMARKABLE ACCURACY OF THE OBSERVATION IN BOOK 4 (viii(C3)29 et seq)

Its dripping barb staineth
ITS DRIPPING BARB STAINETH
the breast of them that
THE BREAST OF THEM THAT
take it for a quill
TAKE IT FOR A QUILL

THE BALL-POINT PEN, OF COURSE

AND WHAT DO WE MAKE OF THE REFERENCES TO "THE HOOTING-GLASS" — OR TELEVISION-SET AS WE KNOW IT.

"A THREE-FINGER'D MAN LAUGHS [IN] THE FACE OF DISASTER.... HAUNTED BY AN ENGEON OF AVARYSE" (2xi(D2)43)

TED ROGERS HOSTS 3-2-1

AND FROM BOOK 2 (iii(D2)362) "BEARE-BLOATED [AND] TABBACA -WREATH'D/AGAIN HE SITS BEFORE THE VISION OF CONSUELA IN THE DARK." IF WE READ **"CONSUELA"** AS **"SUE ELLEN"** THEN MACGOHOUIL PREDICTS THE INVENTION OF VIDEO RECORDING!

Trees

BLEEDING TREES

On 19 June 1984 a tree-feller in Madagascar tried to cut down a eucalyptus tree, but with the first axe blow, what looked like blood spurted out wildly. Since that date, villagers of Ambohibao, nine miles from the capital Antananarivo, have worshipped the tree, according to the newspaper *Midi-Madagascar* on 5 July.

The story is true, according to Professor Albert Rakoto-Ratsimamanga, the Madagascan ambassador in Paris and a member of the Academy of Sciences; but an analysis of the liquid showed no red cells. The red pigment was probably an anthocyanin (water-soluble flavonoid). The only trouble is that the tree stands in a place called 'Ampasampamosavy' – literally, 'the tomb of the sorcerers'. *l'Yonne Republicaine, South Africa Star,* and *Guardian,* 7 July 1984.

● Another bleeding tree is the yew growing in the 6th century churchyard of St Brynach at Nevern, Near Newport, Pembrokeshire, in Wales. From a natural gash seven feet from the ground, the yew, estimated to be 700 years old, constantly exudes a blood-like liquid, and has been so doing for decades. When it began is unknown. Although other trees like the elm, cherry and pine are known to exude resin and gum, it is very rare for a yew to do so. 1979 saw 16,000 visitors.

There is a convenient legend that a mediaeval monk was hanged in the churchyard protesting his innocence of some crime, and prophesying the trees would bleed for him. Derek Patch from the Forestry Commission provided the mundane explanation: rainwater gets trapped in a hollow causing a reddish decay of the wood which gradually oozes out. *S.Express* 7 Oct 1979.

CURSE OF THE BEECH

A beech tree by the churchyard in Walsham le Willow in Suffolk was found to have, high up its trunk, a death's head carving with some mysterious inscription. A lot of the villagers said the tree was cursed, but farmer Ronnie Rayson, father of two, laughed at them. He cut the tree down.

Village butcher David Rolfe said Rayson "was very fit – never a day's illness – but he cut his hand very badly on his chain saw, then trod on a nail and his foot turned sceptic. After that he got jaundice and was rushed to hospital where he died. It may all be a coincidence, but some people think it is a bit spine-chilling." Rolfe was displaying the carving in his shop window. Let's hope nothing sinister happened to *him* since. *Sun* 26 May 1983.

SPEAKING TREES?

In July 1982, people in Daveyton on the East Rand in South Africa gathered round a huge Tipuana tree every day for weeks, following claims that it spoke. The tree was one of 12 Tipuanas planted in the town ship by the East Rand Administration Board's Parks Department in 1970. The huge tree was shedding 'tears' from its leaves and branches every year between September and February – sometimes so heavily that a pool of water formed at its base.

"I first noticed this unusual phenomenon in 1980 when I was checking on the growth of all our trees", said William Masondo, a Parks Department clerk. "It was a sunny day when I felt drops of water falling on me, and then I noticed that the drops were actually coming from the leaves and branches of the tree. I also checked on the other trees but found they don't have the same characteristics." *Rand Daily Mail* 30 July 1982.

● Next to a small house in Farmingam, Mass., owned by 83-year-old great-grandmother Elaine Roida, stands a special elm tree. Mrs Toida's son Ollie attempted to trim it, but each time he brought the saw near a branch, the elm emitted a low, moaning sound.

"Ollie thought he was hearing things", said Mrs Roida, "but then I rememberd the time my two grandchildren were carving their names on the trunk of the tree. We heard strange sounds and the kids were scared to death. They haven't gone near the tree again." She asked the reporter from *Astrology & Psychic News* to place her arms around the tree and hug it. A very soft, quiet 'sigh' came from the base of the tree.

Scientists have asked to perform experiments on the tree, but Mrs Roida has refused. "No one is going to touch that tree but me. He or she is my friend and I wouldn't let anyone experiment with my friend."

Astrology & Psychic News Vol. LXVI, No.3, Feb 1984. (For other noisy trees, see FT35, p.38 & FT39, p.25.)

ANDRICUS AND THE OAKS

In the Autumn of 1983, nature lovers were very worried about the future of the English oak, having noticed that 90% of the English acorn crop had been 'galled' by a parasitical French wasp, the female *Andricus quercuscalicis*, which lays up to 1,000 eggs in the emerging bud. More wasps than ever before should have emerged in the Spring of 1984 to gall more acorns than ever before. It didn't happen.

Michael Crawley, who has been studying the problem for four years at Imperial College, London, says it was a 'genuine mystery'. One suggestion was that February's huge emerging generation of females got their timetable wrong....

Andricus crossed the Channel in 1960 and thrived, especially in 1983. The oak types in danger are the English (common) oak and the non-native and rarer turkey oak. The sessile is less vulnerable. Andricus has a half year life cycle. One birth wave happens in late February, and the other in late Spring, the first galling the turkey oak, the second the English oak. The surprise was that a mere one tenth of the turkey oak crop was spoiled. A big drop in English oak galling was expected. But another shock – 30% of the Autumn's crop was zapped. Said Crowley: "It is rare for an insect that attacks plants to become so abundant." *S.Times* 7 Oct 1984.

D.Telegraph (9 Nov 1984), however, reported a record crop of acorns, especially in the New Forest and Hertfordshire. Two million acorns had already been gathered to meet the needs of the Forestry Commission and the private forestry sector, and it was hoped that part of the crop could be exported. Yields in other parts of Europe were said to have been poor. So has the dastardly Andricus been thwarted? Tree-lovers please keep us informed.

A vigilant tree on the island of Lejima off the coast of Okinawa, Japan. Photo from the Pretoria News, *27 Feb 1980.*

AN UNKNOWN TRIBE

An Unknown tribe has been discovered by government officials in an isolated mountain region of Papua New Guinea during a helicopter survey. Two hundred were spotted, but it is believed hundreds more may be living in the area. They were naked, had bones through their noses and were thought to be cannibals. The officials found they were fascinated by mirrors and radios and formed the impression that they had never encountered outsiders before. However, they grew their own tobacco. I can't decide if this is odd or not. Livingstone found the use of tobacco already well-established in the heart of Africa; but the extremely rugged Papuan terrain isolates one valley from the next. Meneses discovered the western end of the island in 1526, and today tobacco is among the chief crops. Maybe the tribe in question obtained tobacco by trade; or was it a seed-fall or a cargo cult that worked? *The News* and *D.Star* 4 Oct 1984.

Drunken Animals

Alcoholism seems to be a problem among the animal population of Romania where two cases have recently come to court. One concerned a carthorse which had become "completely addicted to beer". The horse was given buckets of low-quality beer which only animals would drink and now indulges in constant loud neighing, kicking and biting. "Its owner tied it to a tree outside the flats where he lived," reports the *Guardian* (October 14 1982). "Because it terrorised the neighbourhood he moved it into the hall of the building where it terrorised the inhabitants still more. So he moved it inside his own flat, only to discover that it was impossible to cohabit with a drunken horse." The other Romanian case concerns a cow fed bread soaked in wine by a party of amateur thieves out to milk it of all it had.

● A drunken squirrel nicknamed Scrumpy kept its owner barricaded in his bedroom for two hours after consuming cider. Steve Wroot was finally forced to jump from his bedroom window. He said later, "I'm a biggish fit bloke who was terrified out of his mind by a tiny squirrel." Unable to cope, he passed the animal on to the RSPCA, who were reported to be 'rehabilitating' it. *D.Mirror* 21 Jan 1983.

● Meanwhile in Zimbabwe.... drunken cattle ran amok after a brewery delivery truck overturned near Marondera, spilling about 100 litres of beer. "Several passers-by were chased by furious drunken cattle but there were no casualties," reports the *Spotlight on Zimbabwe* (5 Dec 1982) and more inebriated cows turned up in Gloucestershire after eating sugar beet which had fermented during

the slow digestion process. *D.Mail* 28 Jan 1983. Two pigeons were rendered incapable by whisky left for them by Canon Kevin Byrne of St Lawrence's church in Birkenhead. He was hoping the pigeons would go into a peaceful stupour and stop bothering the congregation. Instead, in behaviour reminiscent of many an animal attack reported in FT, they began dive bombing the assembled worshippers before flapping uncertainly into the sunset. *D.Express* 18 June 1983.

Birds drunk on fermented berries have also been reported. Two currawong birds which had eaten fermented hawthorn berries were found insensible north of Melbourne, while in Sweden hundreds of waxwings indulging in fermented rowan berries became a hazard to motorists. *Straits Times* (Singapore) 20 May 1982 + *D.Mail* 28 Jan 1983.

● A one-year-old Hereford cross Fresian bullock discovered the intemperate delights of windfall apples while grazing the orchard next to his owner's cottage in Mansell Gamage, Hereford and Worcester, in October 1984. He ate so many that they turned to alcohol after fermenting in his stomach.

He was found lying on his back with what his owner Maureen Russell described as 'a happy leer'. A vet estimated it would take him four days to sober up. The six-hundredweight beast was nicknamed Brewster after the incident. "When we tried to get Brewster up," said Mrs Russell, "his legs kept buckling and his eyes were bloodshot, just like a drunken man". *Standard* and *Shropshire Star* 17 Oct; *D.Mail* 18 Oct 1984.

● This item prompted a letter from Stanley Edwards, who had encountered the following scene while on patrol in Rhodesia with the British South African Police: "As we followed a path through the bush my horse shied and I saw in the grass a big dog baboon lying face down in the grass. It was feebly beating the ground with its paws and, thinking it sick, I dismounted to dispatch it when my African constable drew my attention to another casualty, standing with his chest to a tree, his arms clasping the trunk for support, this accompanied by much grunting and shaking of the head.

Our arrival had disturbed the rest of the troop which we now saw making for their rocky kopje. Baboons, being very destructive of growing crops, are hunted by the tribesmen and consequently make off at high speed upon the approach of humans. The slow retirement of this troop was clear when we saw two females supporting one another and others having difficulty in finding their way home.

A pungent alcoholic scent on the wind solved the mystery – a fermenting windfall of the apple-like fruit from a huge 'marula' tree (sclerocarya caffra), on which, the locals told me, even the elephants got sozzled.

Our guides from the nearby kraal were all for getting the enemy while they had the chance, but I ordered the patrol on its way." *Telegraph* 29 Oct 1984.

Nordic News

ICELANDIC FAIRIES

The Icelandic Road Department trying to build a new road at Akureyri, a town in the north of Iceland, has run into a lot of unexpected difficulties and mishaps for which fairies are blamed. At least the natives of Akureyri believe that the obstacles are caused by fairies and Helgi Hallgrimsson, manager of the Museum of Natural History at Akureyri, is inclined to agree.

"There are many things in Nature that Science cannot yet explain," Hallgrimsson says. He has for many years been collecting eye-witness accounts of fairies and ladies of the woods. "Those who tell me these stories are honest people", Hallgrimsson says, "and many of them did not believe in such creatures until they saw them themselves."

Residents of Akureyri say that the new road is planned to run through the outskirts of an area densely populated by fairies. Excavators fail without technical faults, and road-labourers are inexplicably taken ill. Local people say that fairies cause it. They can see nothing wrong with this explanation since they know that it has happened before: there was, for example, a similar incident about 20 years ago.

In 1962, when the new harbour of Akureyri was constructed, it became necessary to blast some rocks. But no matter what the workers did, they never managed to carry out the blastings: there was nothing wrong with the equipment, except that at the critical moment it never worked. Progress was also halted because labourers constantly got injured or were unexpectedly taken ill.

A young man called Olafur Baldursson went to the authorities and told them that the cause of the troubles was fairies inhabiting the spot they intended to blast. He offered his services as a mediator between the magistrates of Akureyri and the fairy people, which the magistrates accepted. Finally an agreement was made, and the harbour was completed without any further problems. This is no fairytale – the above story was fully confirmed by the magistrates of Akureyri.

The fairies of Iceland only inhabit certain districts. They hardly show themselves to people, except in damp weather, and not everyone has the ability to see them. Most of the reports collected by Hallgrimsson of encounters with fairies come from the district surrounding the bay of Eyjafjördur where Akureyri is situated. On the rocky shores outside Akureyri many residents claim to have seen the town where the fairies live, the fairy houses, and so on: some also claim to have witnessed fairy ships put in at the harbour of the fairy town.

Hallgrimsson does not exclude the possibility that it is only because of the fairies that this is one of the most fertile agricultural districts and almost the only woodland of Iceland. "Fairies do have green fingers, you know," he says.

Many times fairies have presented people of their liking with rare and expensive gifts. The cloth named "The fairy woman's cloth of Burstafjäll," is probably the most well-known of these items. According to legend, the wife of the district police superintendent and public prosecutor at the farm of Burstafjäll in Vopnafjördur in the east of Iceland, received this cloth as payment from a fairy woman whom she had midwifed. The cloth is now in the National Museum in Rekjavik.

Thor Magnusson, who is the president's Custodian of Antiquities, says: "Certainly it's a unique cloth, but it often happened in the old days that if people did not remember, or could not explain, the true origin of a rare item, they claimed that fairies had made it."

Magnusson does not believe in fairies and ladies of the woods. "Personally I think that those who see fairies and little people should have their eyes examined," he says. *Sydsvenska Dagbladet Snällposten* 5 Aug. 1984.

PAGAN PRANKS

One Sunday afternoon in November 1982, a 28-year-old woman visited a public bar in the centre of Reykjavik, Iceland, and was joined by a 40-year-old sailor. Several hours of merry-making followed. Also present were a gode (high priest) of the heathen Aesir cult who had drunk three quarters of a bottle of Icelandic 'Black Death' (60 degrees proof).

In the heat of the moment, someone suggested that the young woman and the sailor should get married in a truly Viking manner, and the party staggered out to the main square where the blotto gode, who just happened to have all the necessary official forms in his pocket, performed the ceremony at the feet of the statue of patriot Jon Sigurdsson in front of the parliament building. The marriage was witnessed and attested by several other merrymakers and the newly-weds signed the fateful document "in memory of a Sunday afternoon full of fun", and returned to the bar.

The two never met again until each was shocked by an official letter from the Ministry of Justice enclosing their marriage certificate, made out on the basis of the document the gode had dropped in a local letterbox. "Now it looks as though we're going to have to go through an official divorce with all the legal problems that involves", said the woman. *Sydsvenska Dagbladet Snällposten* Sweden, 13 May; *Telegraph* 16 May 1983.

A block of stone bearing the image of Thor's hammer, Mjöllnir, found on the pagan holy hill at Menez-Bré in Brittany. Credit: Nigel Pennick.

Public idol worship had been prohibited in Iceland in the year 1,000 AD. Þorgeirr Ljósvetningagode (the 'chairman' of parliament and himself a heathen) stated that private worship was not affected by this ban. All heathen MPs were however, persuaded to be baptised. The most stubborn among them agreed for the sake of peace, but only on condition that the dip would take place in the hot springs of Reykjalang on their way home, and not in the cold water of Þingvellir (the 'parliament place'). The fanatic missionaries had to agree (see the *Kristni Saga*).

The ancient prohibition on public heathen worship was declared void in the constitution of 1874, and the Aesir cult, which, according to the Reykjavik correspondent of the *Daily Telegraph*, "includes the offering of supermarket-packed legs of lamb to Thor", was fully legalised – given the full privileges of a church – in 1972. Today, Thor's hammer pendants can be purchased at Reykjavik airport.

● Iceland is not the only seat of Thorism. The year before the above-mentioned incident, a ball of light appeared above the ancient chapel on the Menez-Bré pagan holy hill in Brittany. Shortly afterwards, writes Nigel Pennick (*The Symbol* No.2), "It was suggested that the god Thor had manifested there, and blocks of stone bearing the image of Thor's Hammer, Mjöllnir, were found near the summit (see photo).

In 1984 it emerged that the stones were placed there by the Odinist Church of Brittany, which issued a press release concerning the history of the Iron Hammer, a relic of the pagan temple of Uppsala, which is now in Brittany. The statement is reproduced in *The Symbol*. It ends: "Today, in the north of Brittany, on the Menez-Bré mount, holy site of the Odinist church of Brittany, the Sons of Thule perpetuate the Hyperborean traditions of their ancestors." (*The Symbol* is available from Nigel Pennick, 142 Pheasant Rise, Bar Hill, Cambridge, CB3 8SD, UK).

BALTIC SEAL MUTILATIONS

Up to a tenth of the entire population of seals (*Phoca vitulina)* in the Baltic died in the summer of 1984. About 50 were living on the Måkläppen banks near Falsterbo in the south coast of Sweden, and a third of these were presumed dead. 16 corpses had been recovered, and all but one were headless.

The bodies were taken to the National Museum for examination. It was thought that pollution could have been the cause of death, but that doesn't explain the missing heads. Jan-Ake Hillarp, president of the nature sanctuary of Falsterbo, was mystified. Birds or other creatures could have eaten them, but only the heads? No previous observations confirmed such a selective diet. *Sydsvenska Dagbladet Snällposten* 25+26 Aug 1984.

French News

On the 13 February 1983, a young blond woman of about 20, smartly dressed and pleasant looking, was arrested after trying to attack a petrol pump attendant in the Avenue Mozart in Paris. Interviewed by police and magistrates, she never uttered a word. Doctors concluded that she was deaf, dumb and illiterate; and she didn't understand the deaf and dumb language. By the time of the report in *Le Courrier de l'Ouest* (1 April 1983) no-one had come forward to identify her, and she was not on the list of missing persons. She was a complete mystery.

◆ At the beginning of June 1984, a primary school at Orzi was plagued by bad smells, which seemed to emanate from the head-mistresses office. The headmistress herself was poisoned and the parents and teachers went on strike. Surveys could discover no pollutants or other cause, and the deputy mayor, M. Jean Istace, decided to have the place demolished and a stone-by-stone survey carried out. The 470 pupils were having part-time lessons in prefabs next to the school, which was not used until the physical causes of the smell were determined, "If they are physical...." concludes the report in *Libèration* (9/10 July 1984).

◆ On the evening of Friday, 22 June, Mme Francis Fêtique, née Michele Ruby, 27, was working in her garden in Berthelming. She drew a glass of water from the tap in the corner of the terrace, lit a cigarette, and was transformed into a human torch. Everything burnt within a range of 15 metres – vegetables and trees were reduced to cinders. Neighbours rushed to her help, and she received first aid at Sarrebourg hospital before going to the burns unit at Freyming-Merlebach, where it was hoped she could be saved. Specialists from Metz were trying to determine what had happened. *Le Rèpublicain Lorrain* 24 June 1984.

◆ A young pregnant woman, Mme Lucienne Messaoudi, was overcome by gas fumes in the lift of her apartment building at 1 Amsterdam Street, Belfort, near the Swiss border, at 12.30 on 27 June. At first it was thought that chloropicrine, used in the kiling of foxes, was to blame, but vets quickly ruled this out. The next day the 'gas' had gone, without being identified. *L'Est Rèpublicain* 28 June 1984.

◆ Meanwhile, the motors in the fishing trawlers of Grande-Roi, near Nîmes, were smoking and refusing to turn over at full throttle. At first, fishing bosses blamed 'bloody-minded machinery'. But 30 trawlers broke down at practically the same time. Investigations showed that 'the oil was ill'.

Cleaning the petrol tanks led to several tons of waste, apparently deposited by bacteria which were new to science. The result was a bill of three and a half million francs for damages. Experts in the oil business were beginning to wonder whether this menace could spread to petrol tanks in cars.... *Le Rêpublicain Lorrain* 7 July 1984.

◆ For 48 hours the inhabitants of the residential area of Valescure, near Saint Raphaël in Var, have been wondering what has become of the feline seen bounding through the undergrowth near houses by two trustworthy witnesses. It is thought to be a puma, an animal apparently not dangerous to man. In spite of denials by zoo officials of nearby Fréjus, many people think it is an escaped wild animal. The 'beat' organized yesterday afternoon with the help of four army dog-handlers, seven gendarmes and eight policemen, failed to uncover the 'beast of Estérel'. *Le Parisien Libre* 17 Feb 1983.

◆ A fisher-eagle, a very rate migratory bird which disappeared from France about 40 years ago, blacked out the whole area round Rambervillers in the Vosges mountains in April 1983. When electricity board workers came to remove the electricuted bird from the 20,000 volt power line, they discovered it was holding a complete carp between its claws! The fisher-eagle is protected globally and is usually found in Africa. *Le Courier de l'Ouest* 8 April 1983.

Cottingley Unmasked

by Janet Bord.

It is now 66 years since the story began, and during those 66 years argument has raged, with varying degrees of intensity, over whether or not Elsie and Frances really did photograph fairies in the glen at Cottingley in Yorkshire. Now the truth is at last revealed, thanks to the patient detective work of a man with the photographic knowledge necessary to elucidate all the technical mysteries – Geoffrey Crawley, Hon FRPS, DGPh, MBKSTS, Editor of the weekly 'British Journal of Photography'. In ten episodes in the Journal, he has revealed the full story of the Cottingley affair, and I will now summarise his findings for the benefit of those who do not have access to the *BJ*.

PART ONE (24 DECEMBER 1982)

GC retells the well-known story – how the girls (Frances 10 and Elsie 15) played together in the glen and said they saw fairies there, borrowed Elsie's father's camera in order to photograph them to convince the adults they were telling the truth, and produced the first of the now-famous photographs – Frances with four fairies dancing on the grass in front of her (**photograph A**). This was in July 1917, and two months later they borrowed the camera again and took the photograph of Elsie with a gnome (**photograph B**). At this point the photographs might have sunk into oblivion, had not Elsie's mother, Polly Wright, mentioned them at a folklore lecture in Bradford in January 1920. The pictures thus found their way to Theosophist Edward L. Gardner, who was amazed by them and used them to illustrate a lecture, whence their fame spread to Sir Arthur Conan Doyle. When the pictures were shown to photographic 'experts', the verdicts varied from 'genuine' to 'fake', though those who believed them to be hoaxes were unable to say how two young girls without photographic experience could have produced such impressive photographs. This, as GC remarks, 'has proved the stumbling block to an elucidation of the curious affair'.

Gardner went to Yorkshire to meet the girls, and as a result remained convinced of the photographs' genuineness until his death in 1969 aged 100. As a result of Conan Doyle's *Strand* magazine article published in December 1920, the fame of the photographs spread, and the girls began their skilfully worded interviews with the media which were to occur periodically for 63 years. It was revealed that more photographs had been taken in August 1920, at the instigation of Gardner: Frances with a leaping fairy (**photograph C**), fairy offering flowers to Elsie (**photograph D**), and transparent fairies in the grass (**photograph E**). In 1922 Conan Doyle's book *The Coming of the Fairies* was published, in which he expressed his opinion that the fairies were thoughtforms created by the 'associated aura of the two girls'.

Elsie was by now fed up with the fairies and longed to get away from all the publicity. She escaped to Maine, USA, where she married Frank Hill and moved with him to India. Frances was also able to travel. Conan Doyle died in 1930, and in the 50 years since then, the subject of the Cottingley fairies has remained submerged, occasionally surfacing and creating puzzlement to later generations. The Society for Psychical Research remained silent on the matter until Gardner published *The Evidence of Fairies* in 1945, when it published a dismissive review in its Journal. The Folklore Society also remained silent, until Stewart Sanderson gave a reappraisal of the evidence at his presidential address at the 1973 AGM. Only in the 1970s with the increasing interest in all things occult, did the photographs achieve widespread publicity again, and GC as editor of the *BJ* decided that the time was right to expose them once and for all. He comments that it is obvious at a glance that the photographs are fabricated, but that the photographic experts should acquaint the photographically inexperienced with the reasons for this certainty.

PART TWO (31 DECEMBER 1982)

The Midg camera used to take photographs A and B is described in great detail. It is a box magazine plate camera. The actual camera Elsie used was loaned to GC by its present owner, who bought it in 1972 at Sotheby's. It became clear to GC that the glass plate negative

A. *'Fairies' with Frances Griffiths, photographed by Elsie Wright at Cottingley Glen, West Yorkshire, in July 1917.*

deposited by Gardner's son Leslie in the Brotherton Collection at Leeds University and labelled as the original negative of photograph A could not have been taken by the Wrights' Midg camera. This puzzling statement heralds the existence of an exceedingly complex chain of events, the gist of which is that the photograph everyone has always understood to be the original photograph A is in fact a much retouched version of the actual original. The latter is reproduced by GC, and the blurred photograph shows a girl's head below which are are vaguely fairy-like white forms. By comparison the oft-published photograph A is clear-cut and detailed. This result was achieved by expert hand retouching followed by rephotography to produce the negative labelled by Gardner as the 'original'. Did Conan Doyle know what was going on? asks GC. The Wright family were certainly not a party to the manipulations, which seem to have been instigated by Gardner, probably in a genuine attempt to clarify the fairy image rather than to deceive.

PART THREE (7 JANUARY 1983)

Examination also shows that the so-called 'original' negative of photograph B (Elsie with gnome) is not the original exposed in the Midg camera. By comparing prints from the actual original and the so-called original, it became clear that considerable work has been done to 'improve' the photographic image.

There has been much discussion as to the source of the fairies copied by Elsie for photograph A, and the most likely source seemed to be *Princess Mary's Gift Book* (1915) which contains very similar images to those in the photograph. GC presents a visual comparison.

Between 1917 and 1920, when photographs C, D and E were taken, Elsie had considerable practice at using a camera, and so when a Cameo camera and plates were delivered for the new experiment, Elsie soon mastered the new equipment. GC was able to examine the Cameo, and gives a detailed description of it. The original plates of photographs C, D and E are those deposited at the University of Leeds, and GC discusses various problems: how many plates were delivered to the girls, was it 24 or 72? The plate used for photograph C is a different size from the others, and GC discusses why this is so. After taking C, D and E, the girls claimed that the fairies were slowly fading away – obviously the pair were tired of the whole business. In 1921 they were presented with a stereoscopic camera and a cine camera, but no pictures were taken. It must have been obvious to the girls that producing convincing stereoscopic photographs, or on cine film, was beyond their capabilities.

GC draws attention to a 'secret mark' which is visible on photographs C, D and E, the plates having been marked by knife point before being delivered to the girls. This mark shows that the three later photographs have not been retouched. GC has also traced another photograph showing the mark, a Wright family snapshot which was obviously made on one of the same batch of plates, of which GC believes there were 72.

Photographs C and D were, believes GC, superimpositions (intentional double exposures), the fairy image being photographed first, indoors, its position being marked on the focusing screen so that when the plate was exposed a second time out of doors, the complete picture of girl with fairy could be convincingly composed. The camera would need to be supported on a tripod to allow for the necessary manoeuvres to be accomplished without moving the camera's position. The subject would need to pose for 20 seconds or so. Photographs C and D have been carefully focused, which is clear evidence of the use of a tripod. The slight blur of Frances' head shows that she has not jerked her head back, away from the fairy, as often stated, but was in fact turning her head to the right during the exposure. All the care obviously taken to produce the photographs shows that these were not snapshots grabbed quickly when the fairies appeared, but were carefully posed. The best camera for quick use would have been a rollfilm camera, not a plate camera, but it would be well-nigh impossible to produce fairy photographs of the kinds the two girls did produce, if they had used a rollfilm camera.

PART FOUR (21 JANUARY 1983)

At this point, GC was able to report that Elsie and Frances had admitted, in an article by Joseph Cooper published in 'The Unexplained' (issue 117), that the photographs were fakes (though Frances still maintained that photograph E shows real fairies). Photograph A and B were said to be cut-out artwork, as GC had already determined, but Frances also said that C and D were cut-out artwork attached to the foliage. GC disputes this, still believing them to be superimpositions. He continues his report with a description of the probable method used to prepare photographs C and D by means of superimposition. He presents evidence supporting his belief that C and D were superimpositions rather than cut-out artwork, including the fact that neither Frances nor Elsie is looking directly at the fairies. Obviously they were looking towards empty air, not a cut-out, and it is impossible to focus one's eyes on nothing. GC illustrates this clearly by moving the fairies' positions in the photographs.

There would have been no difficulty, GC, believes, in Elsie finding out about and learning the technique of superimposition. He presents an account of the events of 1920 based on contemporary documents, rather than on Gardner's account in his 1945 book which reveals numerous discrepancies. An interesting point is that there were several unsuccessful attempts to photograph the fairies, and these plates were thrown away. As GC rightly comments: 'If the photographs were actually of paranormal beings, how could they possibly have been thrown away? Of course they were thrown away because they were failed hoaxes, and would betray their fabrication. GC pinpoints this as the main giveaway that the photographs were fabrications.

Photograph E (fairies in the grass) is an accidental double exposure of cut-outs, says GC, and he has found evidence for this on the original negative.

PART FIVE (28 JANUARY 1983)

GC assesses the involvement of Sir Arthur Conan Doyle in the affair, and notes that ACD 'was the one who really set up the financial framework'. He, Gardner, and Snelling made money from the sale of prints after publication of the *Strand* article, but the girls received practically nothing as Elsie's father objected to their benefiting financially from the photographs. However, money was no one's prime objective, and ACD's intention in promoting the Cottingley photographs was presumably thereby to help the cause of spiritualism, to which he had devoted himself since 1916. GC describes ACD's life and philosophy. He points out that it was the mere fact of ACD's involvement that caused the photographs to achieve worldwide publicity, but if read carefully, ACD's statement in his *Strand* article of December 1920 is seen to be non-committal, and GC suspects that ACD was well aware that the photographs could be fakes, but as a skilful photographer himself (a fact he did not reveal) he had also assured himself that any hoaxing could not easily be proved. GC stresses that ACD's motivation was not money but that, in ACD's words, 'The recognitionof their (the fairies') existence will jolt the material 20th century mind out of its heavy ruts in the mud, and will make it admit that there is a glamour and a mystery to life.'

PART SIX (4 FEBRUARY 1983)

More information on Sir Arthur Conan Doyle's involvement includes the extent of his photo-

B. *'Gnome' photographed by Frances Griffiths at Cottingley Glen, West Yorkshire, September 1917.*

C. *'Fairy' with Frances Griffiths, photographed by Elsie Wright at Cottingley Glen, in August 1920.*

D. *'Fairy' with Elsie Wright, photographed by Frances Griffiths at Cottingley Glen, in August 1920.*

E. *'Fairies' photographed by Frances Griffiths and Elsie Wright at Cottingley Glen, in August 1920.*

graphic knowledge, which makes it difficult to believe that he did not suspect the true nature of the photographs. ACD may have been fascinated by the idea of fairies: his uncle, Richard Doyle, was an eminent artist specialising in paintings of the little people, and his father, Charles Doyle, was also obsessed by them, keeping a diary illustrated with fairy paintings and drawings during his last years in mental institutions.

Theosophist Edward Lewis Gardner's involvement was total: owing to a bereavement he was in a susceptible state when he learnt of the Cottingley photographs.

PART SEVEN (11 FEBRUARY 1983)

More information on E.L. Gardner and Theosophy, followed by a close scrutiny of H. Snelling's role. He was a studio and darkroom technician of high skill, especially at retouching, and although there is no documentary proof of the nature of his work on the Cottingley photographs, by careful examination of the surviving prints GC believes that Snelling produced an exhibition quality picture from Elsie's poor original (photograph A) using internegative, re-photography and local reduction processes. Ironically when the results were examined by Kodak and Ilford experts, they said that the photographs were 'studio work' – because of a double lighting effect which was introduced during Snelling's manipulations. Had they seen Elsie's original effort, they would most likely have recognised it for what it was: cut-out figures in an outdoor scene. GC points out that when he undertook the work Snelling probably assumed he was only improving the picture for showing to Theosophists as a lantern slide. He could not have anticipated the publicity to come, and was only doing his job as a skilled retoucher as requested by his client , Gardner. GC analyses Snelling's testimonial in the light of our present knowledge and insight.

GC comments that Arthur Wright, Elsie's father, 'emerges as the total sceptic over the Cottingley fairy photographs', with his reaction to Photograph A that 'These look like sandwich papers!' GC discusses AW's attitude to the photographs, and wonders who conspired with whom to fool whom.

PART EIGHT (18 FEBRUARY 1983)

Mrs Polly Wright's correspondence shows her to be aware and intelligent, and she was in a dilemma: if the photographs were genuinely of paranormal beings, then the implications were worrying; if they were faked, then the children were liars, an even worse possibility. The Cottingley affair was obviously troubling to both Mr and Mrs Wright.

Leslie Gardner, E.L.Gardner's son, was also concerned in the affair. When his father died in 1969 he took over ownership of the documents and letters, which he deposited with the University of Leeds (300 items). Like his father he would not allow a re-examination of the negatives because they felt 'that photographic experts all started from the assumption that the photographs were fakes and therefore could contribute nothing to an understanding of them.' GC feels that Elsie and Frances may have felt more able to reveal the truth once LG had died, which happened in 1981.

PART NINE (1 APRIL 1983)

A detailed biography of Elsie Hill (née Wright) reveals that she is a skilled artist who had the ability to produce cut-outs or models. GC reproduces a facsimile of a letter he received in February 1983 from Elsie after he had sent her copies of his articles so far published in this series. In her letter Elsie confirms that the so-called 'Cottingley fairy photographs' taken in 1917 and 1920 were a 'practical joke' which 'fell flat on its face'. The girls felt they could not reveal the truth once Sir Arthur Conan Doyle was involved, so they decided to wait until ACD and Gardner were dead. She also said that the article in 'The Unexplained' was unauthorised, and that no one, not even her husband, has been told exactly how the photographs were taken. She will reveal the truth in a book she is writing.

One amazing fact which came to light is that in 1972 Elsie sent the two cameras together with prints and letters to Sotheby's for sale, and she included with them a letter revealing that the photographs were a practical joke. Sotheby's failed to understand what they were handling and returned the letter to her, saying they only dealt with antique documents! Elsie decided as a result to write her autobiography with a full disclosure of her photographic methods.

GC comments: 'If you take as the criterion of success coverage in the national media in column inches and television time quite apart from articles, books, and having a street named to commemorate your efforts, then Elsie is by far the most successful photographer in the craft's history.' He goes on to illustrate how the girls became 'locked into the chain of events' which kept their practical joke going for 65 years. Frances has confirmed Elsie's revelations and added more details of her own.

PART TEN (8 APRIL 1983)

GC summarises the affair, noting a few loose ends. He cites some fairy lore, and shows by scathing reference to Ted Serios and Uri Geller that the possibility of there being any 'real' paranormal phenomena need not be entertained. He wonders if Conan Doyle was

Elsie Wright and Frances Griffiths with Geoffrey Hodson at Cottingley Glen, c.1921. [© Brotherton Collection, University of Leeds. Leeds LS2 9JT.]

justified in supporting the photographs, bearing in mind his probable suspicion of their origin. Finally GC acknowledges all those who have helped in his marathon investigation and adds some reference notes.

•

Each part of this series is accompanied by relevant photographs, some of them rarely if ever seen before, e.g. Arthur Wright's 1921 shot of Frances and Elsie with Cameo cameras sitting beside the beck, with Geoffrey Hodson also visible; and Elsie photographed by Gardner in 1920 at the bank shown in photograph A.

It has been impossible in this brief summary to do justice to GC's long and diligent examination of a 20th-century mystery, and I have had to omit many of the finer points of detail. Anyone wishing to purchase the relevant back numbers of the 'British Journal of Photography' should write to their office (28 Great James Street, London WC1N 3HL) asking the price of the complete set and quoting the issue dates given above. The total cost will be around £3.50 for the ten issues.

When the *BJ* series was completed, BBC TV's Nationwide programme ran an item on the Cottingley fairy photographs in which Elsie was interviewed. She came over as an intelligent, artistic, well balanced old lady with a grand sense of humour. One cannot feel at all annoyed with her for having deceived the world for so long; on the contrary she has unwittingly provided us with many lessons in Fortean awareness!

God's Mysterious Way?

Or did he spell it out at York Minster?

by John Michell.

At 2.30 in the morning on 9 July 1984 York Minster was found to be on fire. By the time its fire-detection apparatus (installed in 1969 and only recently inspected) gave the alarm, the roof of the south transept was firmly ablaze, and the first firemen on the scene saw 30-foot flames shooting up from it. As fire brigades arrived from all areas around York, the chief in charge of operations ordered them to flood the roof with thousands of gallons of water, causing it to collapse. It was three hours before the fire, described as intensely hot, was brought under control; morning light showed the floor of the transept (the traverse part of the cruciform Minster) piled with the wreckage of 15th-century timbers and melted lead.

Reports of the catastrophe, in the national press the following day, spoke of certain school-children, about three of them staying in a nearby hostel, as being the first to have raised the alarm. The *Sun* said they were "three young Scots tourists" peering from a hotel window. But whoever they were and whatever it was exactly they saw (variously said to have been a lightning storm, a "faint ruddy glow" and "huge orange flashes coming straight down to the ground – *D.Telegraph*) they soon faded from attention. Inquiry began as to the cause of the fire. How had it started?....and why?

The first, obvious theory was that lightning had struck York Minster. Several local residents said that earlier on the night of the fire they had seen lightning flickering along the transept roof. The Minster is protected by modern lightning conductors, but these had somehow failed to do their duty. So it was first assumed. However, on BBC television, weatherman Michael Fish said that on the night of the fire no thunderstorms had been reported over York, and though a few minor ones had occurred in the district, their centres had been at least ten miles from the Minster.

Arson, of course, was suggested, but it was unlikely that anyone had climbed up to the roof to set light to it, and there was no evidence of this having happened. The *Times* (17 July) light-heartedly blamed the fire on the ghost of mad Jonathan Martin, religious-fanatic brother of the apocalyptic painter John Martin, who in 1829 fulfilled what he supposed to be God's purpose by setting ablaze the Minster, ceremonially clad in its ecclesiastical hangings.

On a previous occasion Martin had interrupted the confirmation of the Bishop of Durham by threatening the assembled prelates with a pistol and screaming accusations of blasphemy against them. Thus was set up the first leg of a series of coincidences linking together a Bishop of Durham, York Minster and cries of blasphemy.

York Minster, February 2, 1829

Three days before the latest fire, on 6 July, a pompous ceremony had taken place in York Minster, somewhat marred by rowdiness. On that day the Rt Rev David Jenkins, former Professor of Theology at Leeds University, was installed as the new Bishop of Durham. Academic theologians, being more cloistered than most of us from the unpredictable vicissitudes of normal, everyday life, are by no means inclined to be Forteans. In their world of college lectures and dining-rooms their familiars are other professors, the priests of rationalism and science. Not willing to be odd-men-out in the pervading consensus of scientism, the theologians reject those old religious stand-bys, marvels and miracles, explaining the Biblical examples as being types of spiritual allegories. The fact that all Jesus's miracles have been – and continue to be – reproduced in non-Christian traditions, by shamans, holy men and – dare one say it? – seance mediums, is scarcely recognized by your average academic theologian; he does not normally subscribe to Fortean literature. His world-view is reconciled to that of his scientific colleagues, and he goes out into the world (if go he must) with prayers in his heart to Newton, Darwin, Freud, Marx and the secular prophets of contemporary academic fashion.

Three months before he became Bishop, the Rt Rev Jenkins appeared on the London Weekend 'Credo' programme and startled those whose profession it is to be startled by such things by saying that he was no supernaturalist and found it unnecessary to believe in the literal occurrences of Jesus's virgin birth and bodily resurrection. So much was clear, but just what Jenkins believed instead was less easy to grasp. The BVM was apparently to be called simply the BM, and as to the Resurrection, the story arose mysteriously from "a series of experiences". Not many people saw 'Credo' or read what Jenkins had actually said, but the popular impression fostered by almost the entire Press was that the new Bishop of Durham was a denyer of Scripture, a heretic, a blasphemer, a subverter of Christian doctrine. Protestant fundamentalists, the natural enemies of the academic theologians, raised loud their voices. From Parliament and pulpit the sternly orthodox demanded recantation. If David Jenkins believed or disbelieved in whatever he was said to believe or not believe in, he should either resign or be ousted from his episcopal appointment. Against this storm the hierarchy held firm, and on 6 July Dr John Hapgood, Archibishop of York, began the service to consecrate David Jenkins as Bishop of Durham.

It was marked by two separate disturbances. As the new Bishop was about to be introduced to the congregation in the Minster, a shabbily

An aerial view of York Minster shows the wrecked south transept. D.Star 10 July 1984.

dressed man called Barry ("The rest of my name is known to the Lord" he told reporters) began to orate loudly against Jenkins's supposed beliefs. A few moments later he was grabbed by a posse of clerics and led away, still shouting. He was succeeded by a latter-day Jonathan Martin, a leading anti-Jenkins campaigner, the Rev John Mowll, vicar of Buglawton, Cheshire. Before the service he and his followers had been distributing tracts outside the Minster. Inside, during the reading of the Royal Warrant, he stole up to the lectern and read out some paragraphs of his tract, upholding Protestant Truth and proclaiming Jenkins's deviations from it. Minster stewards and a plain-clothes policemen appeared behind him and began tugging at his coat, but he continued his reading. The incident ended as told in the *D.Telegraph* headline (7 July): "Protesting Vicar Frogmarched from Cathedral".

Three days later the fire struck. AN ACT OF GOD? asked the *Daily Star*; THE WRATH OF GOD? loudly queried the *Sun*. According to the *Star*, "a thunderbolt from the heavens was blamed by some churchmen yesterday for the £2 million York Minster blaze. They claim it showed God's fury over the ordination there of the new Bishop of Durham." Said the Rev Mowll to the *Sun*, "I'm not surprised people are talking about divine intervention." Asked by the *Telegraph* if he himself attributed the fire to divine agency, he replied cautiously (but surely with a knowing look), "Who can say?"

Mid all the uncertainty about God's part in the affair, two men were quite certain, the two Archbishops. "Ridiculous explanation," growled Dr Hapgood of York. "Responsible Christian people do not go on like that." Likewise the Archbishop of Canterbury, Dr Runcie. The day of the fire he was in York to inspect the ruins. There was, he said, absolutely no connection bewtween the conflagration and the installation of Bishop Jenkins. He allowed the possibility of divine intervention, not in the destruction of the Minster but in that "God was on the side of the fire-fighters". It was, he claimed, a miracle that the damage had been limited to the south transept. By thus allowing that the salvation of the Minster was a miraculous event the Archbishop rather weakened his case against a divine cause for its smiting. An interesting point, raised during the newspaper correspondence which followed, was that, in denying the fire to have been an Act of God, Dr Runcie may have prejudiced claims made under that head to the insurance company. It turned out, however, that the Minster was covered by the Church's own insurance office which, oddly enough, no longer referred to Acts of God in its policies.

The strangest argument against a divine attack on York Minster was in a *Times* leader which said that God moves in a mysterious way (which is not a statement from Scripture but from a Protestant hymn), and the zapping of the Minster so soon after Bishop Jenkins had been consecrated therein was too obvious a coincidence to have been His handiwork. On the other side, Philip Preston in a letter to the *Guardian* (4 Aug.) remarked that the timing of the fire, following a General Synod debate on 'the care of church buildings', was nicely ironic. "However", he went on, "it is also clear that the ordination is still likely to be the primary cause, the lapse of some days giving a chance for reflection, but not breaking any chain of causality." As a possible contributary reason he pointed out that the Minster is now run more as a museum and tourist attraction than as a House of God; also that Jesus had condemned those who could not "read the signs of the times".

UFOs, St Elmo's fire and a bolt from the blue

If it were not arson, and since no thunder storms were reported over York that night, the means by which God or nature smote the Minster remained a mystery. The flickering lights observed playing over the roof previous to the fire were explained by some (e.g. the *Telegraph*, 1 Aug.) as an example of St Elmo's Fire, "an electrically charged bell of shaped cloud"(!). Against this a writer to the same paper (8 Aug.) said that St Elmo's Fire ("a discharge of static electricity during a period of intense electrical activity...generally seen as a ball of blue light on ships' masts or aircraft fuselages during severe thunderstorms") actually protects wherever it appears from lightning strikes. A few days after the disaster two witnesses stepped forward with dramatic testimonies. Bill Whitehead, a taxi driver, and van driver Eddie Acaster both claimed to have seen a glowing, cigar-shaped UFO hovering over the Minster on the night in question (*Daily Mirror*, 14 July). In a fuller report (*Daily Star*, 19 July) Whitehead said that he saw the UFO sending down orange-coloured rays onto the roof, while Acaster said that the object glowed bright orange and left a white vapour trail. The two sightings and the statements about them were said to have been made independently, and both men were respectable and middle-aged (44 and 55), but their evidence was ignored in every official report and Church officials made merry at their expense. "Have these chaps seen opticians lately?" quipped Canon Bowering of York Minster.

The official explanation, when finally it began to take shape, featured a meteorological phenomenon as strange as any of the unofficial speculations. Newspapers on 31 July and 1 August carried extracts from a Fire Brigade report to the Home Office. Satellite photographs taken over York on the night of the fire apparently showed a certain "cloud formation known to produce lightning bolts", also referred to as "an isolated weather cell". The *New Scientist* (8 Nov.) called it "a small fast-moving rainfall cell", quoting the Met. Office Research Lab's comment that it was "surprising" for it to have apparently produced such devastating lightning. Here was one of those explanations which, as Fort said, need themselves to be explained. The general impression was that the Minster had been hit by a "freak bolt of lightning" (*D.Mirror*, 1 Aug.) but neither the mysterious errant cloud nor the freak bolt which supposedly descended from it had a very convincing scientific ring about them. To believers in divine intervention they offered comfort, for in the Bible God's favourite conveyance is said (e.g. in Exodus 24, 16 and 34, 5) to be a small cloud, from which He occasionally casts thunderbolts. Nor were doubts cleared up by the report published in the September issue of the firefighters' trade journal, *Fire*. The cause of the fire was there said to be still unknown, but the balance of probabilities was that 'side flash' – the discharge of lightning from one conductor to another – set alight to the transept's roof timbers. However, the investigators were unable to rule out other possible causes, including arson.

For the rest of 1984 Bishop Jenkins continued swimming in the tide of publicity. He infuriated the Government by apparently siding with Marxist firebrand Arthur Scargill and his striking miners while, as some thought, insulting the head of the Coal Board, a Mr MacGregor, as an "elderly imported American". Later he returned to the subject of the Resurrection which, according to the *Express* and other papers he described as a "conjuring trick with bones". This, he explained obscurely later, was the very opposite of what he had ment to say. Declaredly he has every intention of continuing his campaign against literalism in religion. If God is indeed a fundamentalist we may expect further meteorological phenomena.

Lightning and churches

The great Victorian man of science, Francis Galton, remarked that if clergyman really believed what they preached they would not think it necessary to protect their churches with lightning conductors. In fact, until the arch-infidel Benjamin Franklin invented the lightning rod, churches were quite commonly struck. Figures quoted in Barbara Walker's *Woman's Encyclopaedia of Myths and Secrets* tell of 400 church towers damaged and 120 bell-ringers killed by lightning in Germany in 33 years up to 1783. The blame in these cases was cast upon the Devil who, as Lucifer, has associations with lightning. In the case of York Minster the only recorded attributionof the disaster to the Devil came from no less a source than Mrs Bishop Jenkins. In the *D.Telegraph,* 19 Dec., she repeated the view of her daughter that the incident was part of the "machinations of the Evil One", vainly and belatedly trying to prevent her father's installation.

The Devil in Nailsea

A minority view in the York Minster affair was that the thunderbolt was a sign directed against Billy Graham's evangelical tour of Britain which took place the same year. According to its organizers, even before it began it was dogged by satanic spoiling tactics. A clipping from *FT* back files (*Sunday Times,* 12 June '83) tells how three Graham campaign officials were involved in separate car crashes in the course of one weekend. "I believed it was enemy action at the time", said Nailsea (near Bristol) lay-preacher Anthony Bush, regional head of the Grahamites' Mission England. His suspicions were greatly strengthened when, a month later, his own house was partly destroyed by a thunderbolt. He and colleagues had just concluded a meeting to plan details of Graham's itinerary. "This", he said, "is no coincidence". The *Sunday Times* comment was that thunderbolts are generally considered to be the work of God. "There is evidence of their use in the past against Philistines and Egyptians, but this is believed to be the first time they have been used against a lay-preacher in Nailsea."

JONATHAN MARTIN IN PRISON

Another dissenting voice at York was that of well-known architect Cedric Price. Ten years previously he had suggested that the old Minster should be pulled to the ground as an inspiration and challenge to young members of his profession. In the *Sunday Times* (12 Aug. '84) he pointed out that the C of E Synod and the installation of Bishop Jenkins were not the only events taking place at York near the time of the fire. The Royal Institute of British Architects was also meeting there. The destructive thunderbolt might therefore have been a sign of God's displeasure at the state of British architecture.

•

John Michell

CREDITS

Sid Birchby for his useful summary of events; Ion Will and Paul Sieveking for sorting and finding clippings, and the many *FT* readers who contributed them.

The Curious Columbus Confusion

by William R Anderson.

"Christopher Columbus" never lived. The name is a fabrication combining the careers of two men:

(1) Cristoforo Colombo, born in the latter half of 1451 to Dominick and Susana Colombo in Genoa (Italian "Genova") in the Liguria section of Italy;

(2) Cristobal Colon, born in mid-1460 to Prince Carlos (Charles IV) of Viana, and Margarita Colon in the Jewish ghetto of Majorca, near the village of Genova which is now a district of Palma, the principal city.

The missing pieces of the jigsaw puzzle have only recently been disclosed, but the obvious contradictions in widely-disseminated "history" should have been noted by *someone*. The Columbus opus includes:

Admiral of the Ocean Sea, Samuel Eliot Morison (Little, Brown – 1942), Pulitzer prize winner, Book-Of-The-Month Club author, admiral in the U.S. Navy, Harvard professor. As some sage once noted, if you can't trust a Harvard professor, *whom* can you trust?

Sails of Hope, Simon Wiesenthal (Macmillan, 1973). Famed researcher who sent hundreds of Nazi World War II criminals to their just des erts. Unfortunately, the culprits under study died centuries too soon;

Encyclopaedia Brittanica, 1973 edition, volume 6. Or other comparable reference work;

Universal Jewish Encyclopedia, 1969 edition, volume 3.

These are some of the basic characteristics and achievements of our hero:

Place and date of birth

Morison: "There is no mystery about the birth, family and race of Christopher Columbus. He was born in the ancient city of Genoa sometime between August 25 and the end of October, 1451."[1]

Wiesenthal: "He is one of history's most controversial and shadowy figures, with mystery surrounding his birth, his character, his career and his achievement."[2]

U.J.E.: "His place and date of birth, generally described as Genoa, in 1446 or 1451, are sharply disputed...Local Genoese records referring to the Colombo family *are assumed to be identical with the family of the later Spanish admiral.*" (Emphasis supplied).[3]

Patriotism

Morison: "There is no more reason to doubt that Christopher Columbus was a Genoese-born Catholic Christian, steadfast in his faith and proud of his native city, than to doubt that George Washington was a Virginian-born Anglican of English race, proud of his being an American."[4]

E.B.: "The fact that in the battle (i.e. of August 13, 1476) he fought on the Portugese side, against Genoa, shows him to be no Genoese patriot... One explanation...is that Columbus came from a Spanish-Jewish family settled in Genoa."[5]

Parentage

Morison: "Domenico Colombo was not a journeyman weaver dependent on wages, but a master clothier (to use the old English term), who owned one or more looms."[6]

Wiesenthal: "His father, Domenico Colombo, is supposed to have been a tower sentinel in Genoa and later a weaver in Savona. The family just managed to sustain itself by manual labor."[7]

Education

Morison: "One thing is certain, he had little if any schooling."[8]

Wiesenthal: "(He) had an excellent command of Latin and Spanish...was well informed in history, geography, geometry, religion, and religious writings...Columbus's whole bearing as a mature man belies the notion that he came from people of small means and had no more than an elementary education behind him."[9]

The references cited provide other contradictions but do not suggest the obvious answer: there *must* have been two men. For that we go to two obscure publications of Brother Nectario Maria of the Venezuelan Embassy in Madrid: *Juan Colon the Spaniard* published by the Chedney Press of New York (now defunct) in 1971, and *Cristobal Colon Era Espanol y Judio,* privately printed in Madrid in 1978. Morison was aware of the alleged duality but "those who insist that Colon the discoverer was a different person from Colombo the

"Christopher Columbus" by the Venetian artist Lorenzo Lotto, reputedly the best portrait.

Genoese" were rejected along with "others with even wilder theories."[10]

Nectario presents evidence that Colon was the illegitimate son of Prince Carlos (Charles IV) of Viana, Spain, and Margarita Colon, of a prominent Jewish family in the ghetto of Majorca.[11] The author found a letter from the prince to the governor of Majorca, dated October 28, 1459, describing the meeting with Margarita [12], from which can be deduced the birth of Cristobal in the summer of 1460.

This premise provides logical answers to "mysteries" concerning his education and marriage, and reconciles with generally-accepted facts:

1472-73 – He was in the crew of the pirate René d'Anjou on the Mediterranean Sea.[13] It would not be unusual for a boy to run away to sea at 12, especially from a fatherless home. Carlos died in 1461 under suspicious circumstances; some scholars believe he was poisoned on orders from his step-mother.

1473-74 – He sailed to the Greek island of Chios. The Brittanica asserts: "Columbus must be believed when he says he began to navigate at 14." [14] A capable boy of that age with two years of experience would likely be given an occasional turn at the wheel.

1476 – He fought with Casenove-Coullon (possibly a relative) against Genoese ships. When his ship caught fire, he swam to the southwest tip of Portugal, near the seamanship academy of Prince Henry, the Navigator[15] who is believed by some historians to have reached America around 1395.[16]

1477 – He sailed to England, Ireland and Iceland.[17]

1478 – Married in Portugal to Filipa Moniz Perestrello of a prominent Portuguese family.

1478-83 – He and his wife lived with her brother, Bartholomew Perestrello II, who had inherited the captaincy of the island of Porto Santo in the Madeiras. From this base, Colon made several voyages to the Gold Coast of Africa.[18] He acquired the papers of Bartholomew I as well as documents from another visitor to the island, Alonso Sanchez de Huelva[19], who will be discussed later. Colon gained much of his navigational skill during this time, as well as broadening his self-education – the earliest notation in his voluminous library is dated 1481. Morison concedes that "Columbus's exact movements during the eight or nine years that he spent under the Portugese flag can never be cleared up."[20] Records of Colon are sketchy; records of Colombo end abruptly with his death in 1480.

1484 – Colon went to Portugal, where his petition was rejected by the king, probably because there is evidence of a voyage to America in 1472 by the Portugese mariner Jaoa Vaz Cortereal (known also as Telles) who had a Norse pilot, Pothorst (Jan Skolp).[21] Colon's wife had died during this period, so he left his young son Diego at the monastery at La Rabinda, near Palos, Spain, and went to live with Luis de la Cerda, Count of Medina Celi, at Puerto Santa Maria, for the next two years.[22]

1486 – Met Ferdinand and Isabella, with the help of the Jewish bishop and professor of theology at Salamanca, Diego de Deza.[23] At about this time he became involved with Beatriz Enriquez, to whom was born their son Fernando on August 15, 1488.

1488 – Colon wrote to their majesties on July 7, 1503: "I came to serve you at the age of 28."[24] The U.J.E. gives the date as 1487.[25]

1489 – He was granted the privileges of being lodged and fed at public expense.[26] The next two years are "conjectural" according to Morison. They may have been spent with Beatriz, with his son Diego at La Rabida, or with the Count of Medina Celi.

1491 – He appears at Cordoba, where his petition to Ferdinand and Isabella is successful, largely through the efforts of Luis de Santangel, financial minister to the king.[27]

Some of the records of the Italian Colombo are in direct conflict with those of Colon as shown above; other records show the probability that the two men met in Portugal or in Porto Santo – or both. Of the "fifteen or twenty notarial records and municipal records" found by Morison, these are a few:

October 31,1470 – Genoa, a wine purchase is recorded by Domenico Colombo and his son Cristoforo, "over age 19".

March 20, 1472 – Colombo witnessed a will in Savona

August 26, 1472 – He purchased wool in Savona

August 7, 1473 – Sale of a house in Genoa

1474 – Lease of land in Savona, occupation of lessee shown as "wool buyer".[28]

"After that, no trace of the family for nine years," according to Morison.

But Nectario was able to find records of several wool-buying trips to Portugal by Colombo, during the years 1475-78.[29] In 1479 he went to the Madeiras to buy sugar (which was also noted by Morison).[30] Nearest to Portugal in the Madeiras is the island of Porto Santo, where Colon was living at the time. Colombo would certainly have reported to the captain of the island, Bartholomew Perestrello, Colon's brother-in-law. Nectario reports that Manuel Lopez Flores records the death of Colombo at sea the following year, 1480. There is no evidence that Colombo was pushed overboard by Colon.

Acceptance of this origin of Colon provides logical answers to two major mysteries that have puzzled historians for centuries:

(1) How had he managed to marry a woman of such prominence? Difficult for a penniless Italian weaver and wool merchant, it would have been no problem for the son of a Spanish prince, legitimate or not;

(2) Where did he obtain funds for his broad education, then available only to the wealthy who employed tutors? Such funds would have come from the royal treasury – actually, there are records of such payments from 1487 to 1489, as previously noted.

A woodcut from a Basel pamphlet of 1494, describing "the islands lately discovered in the Indian sea." It depicts Columbus landing on Hispaniola.

A Spanish-Jewish origin is supported by several well-known facts. He invariably wrote in Spanish, and in some letters he referred to Spanish as his "mother tongue." He spoke fluent Spanish, apparently without foreign accent. He was able to meet and obtain vital aid from several prominent Jews: Diego de Deza, who arranged for his introduction to their Spanish majesties; Abraham Senior and Isaac Abravanel, who had considerable influence at the court; Gabriel Sanchez, royal treasurer; Juan Cabrero, royal chamberlain; and Luis de Santangel, mentioned above.

Several crew members were Jewish, including Bernal, the ship's doctor, and Marco, the surgeon. Abraham Zacuto provided astronomical tables which saved the lives of Colon and his crew on the fourth voyage. By the use of the tables, he was able to predict an eclipse of the moon on February 29, 1504, which so awed their Indian captors that they released Colon and his men unharmed. Aboard also on the first voyage was a Hebrew interpreter, Luis de Torres, who was probably the first man ashore, and who initially reported the use of tobacco by the Indians.[31]

Colon signed his name with the Spanish

form "Cristobal Colon" and in his will insisted that his descendants not vary the signature. He often employed the cryptic form:

S
SAS
XMY
Xpo ferens

This was interpreted by Maurice David, in *Who Was Columbus?* as Hebrew for "The Lord, full of compassion, forgiving iniquity, transgression and sin." In letters to his son Diego, in the upper left corner, regularly appear the Hebrew letters *beth he,* for "be'ezrath hashem" (with the help of God) which pious Jews employ to this day.[32]

Colon assigned Spanish names to islands he found, such as San Salvador, Punta Lazada and Punta de la Galera: there is no record of his assigning Italian names to any islands. He is known to have been an accomplished map-maker, primarily a Jewish talent where the activity was centred in Majorca..

Three men of limited fame played critical roles in Colon's voyage and its historical account:

ALONSO SANCHEZ de HUELVA

Nectario found a letter to the Spanish rulers indicating that Alonso Sanchez left the port of Huelva on May 15, 1481, in the ship "Atlante" with a crew of sixteen. It stated that the vessel reached the island of Santo Domingo (called "Quisqueya" by its inhabitants) and on its return stopped at Porto Santo in the Madeiras, where its captain lived for a time. On his sudden death the ship's papers were given to Colon, who was helping in the business of his brother-in-law, captain of the island. It is difficult to believe that such a sensational document is authentic and has been kept a secret for 500 years. It would, however, provide an important clue – it states that Alonso Sanchez's first mate was

MARTIN ALONZO PINZON.

A wealthy shipowner of Palos, Pinzon was responsible for Colon's acquisition of the Nina and the Pinta, and for hiring the crew for the expedition. Garcia Fernandez, steward of the Pinta, stated that "Martin Alonzo...knows that without his giving the two ships to the Admiral he would not have been where he was, nor would he have found people, because nobody knew the said Admiral, and that by reason of the said Martin Alonzo and through his said ships the said Admiral made the said voyage." [33] Some historians suggest that Pinzon was the actual leader of the expedition to the New World and that Colon was merely a "front" because of his favour with the Spanish monarchs. As later captain of the Pinta, Pinzon was second in command to Colon.

The steward's letter reconciles with accepted facts:

(1) Pinzon's descendants tried for half a century to obtain some of the honors and wealth which had gone to Colon. In the series of lawsuits recorded it was disclosed that Colon had access to the Vatican Archives, which contained records of Viking voyages over a period of several centuries, probably including the original of the famed "Vinland Map" of which Yale University has a 20th century copy. It also indicated that Pinzon had obtained from Rome information about lands to the west of the Atlantic.[34]

(2) Pinzon was able to get Colon to alter his course on October 6th.[35] What better reason would the Admiral have had for accepting the urging of a subordinate than the fact that Pinzon had been there before?

PETER MARTYR

Also known as Father de Angliera (or Angheria) Martyr wrote the first biography of Colon and is credited with coining the term "New World". Born in 1457 near Lake Maggiore in northwestern Italy, 100 miles north of Genoa, he interviewed Colon extensively after the first voyage.[36] He would have quickly determined that Colon was *not* a native of northern Italy, but would naturally be reluctant to deprive an alleged countryman of his honors by publicizing the fact. He did, however, reveal it in a letter to a close friend, Count Giovanni de Borromeo, who in 1494 left the deposition found in the binding of a book purchased a few years ago from a street vendor in Milan. (A copy is said to be in the library of Barcelona University – the original is held by the family of the count.) The letter reads in part:

> I, Giovanni de Borromeo, being forbidden to tell the truth that I have learned as a secret from Señor Pedro de Angheria, Treasurer of the Catholic King of Spain, must preserve for history the fact that Christobal Colon was a native of Majorca and not of Liguria... He had been advised to pretend, for political and religious reasons, in order to request the help of ships from the King of Spain. Colon, after all, is the equivalent of Colombo, and there has been found living in Genoa one such Cristoforo Colombo Canajosa, son of Domingo and Susana Fontanarossa, who should not be confused with the West Indies navigator.[37]

There is, of course, a possibility that the letter was forged. However, until a battery of experts has submitted it to the necessary scientific tests, the letter fits neatly into the jigsaw puzzle that has baffled historians for centuries.

Studies by the Norse author Kåre Prytz and by such American scholars as James

Enterline and Paul Chapman indicate that Colon had access to a number of maps reflecting trans-Atlantic voyages over a period of several centuries [38]. The existence of the American continents was known throughout Europe, certainly as early as 1070, from the writings of historian Adam of Bremen. Commerce continued with Norway and Iceland, and with Bristol in England, and America. By the end of the 15th century, Europe was ready to develop the lands that lay beyond the Atlantic. If Colon and his almost-namesake, Colombo, had never been born, the final rediscovery, and the development, of the New World would have been postponed only a few years.

EPILOGUE

Incredible though it may appear at first glance, that is the true story of "Columbus", Last Rediscoverer of America. An obvious question is "Why has the truth been concealed for almost 500 years?" The effective deception has been traced to Colon himself – in the biography of his famed father, Fernando Colon explained that "As God gave him all the personal qualities for so great an undertaking, he wanted to have his country and origin more hid and obscure." The logical reason: Colon feared for his life.

Carlos was the first son of John II, king of Navarre and later Aragon by marriage to Princess Blanche. A bitter emnity arose between John and Carlos, intensified by the birth of Ferdinand to John's second wife. John was forced to admit that Carlos was his rightful heir, but on several occasions had him imprisoned or banished from Spain – the last time in 1459 to Majorca, where Carlos arrived on August 20, 1459. Ferdinand succeeded to the Spanish throne only after the death of Carlos.

Undoubtedly informed of the situation by his mother, Colon took her name and, conveniently, the identity of the dead Colombo, in his last-resort quest for support by his ruthless uncle Ferdinand, who certainly would have had Colon extermiated had he known the truth.

●

W.R. Anderson

adapted from his *Viking Explorers and the Columbus Fraud.*

(Valhalla Press, Box 301, Chicago, Il 60690, USA.)

FOOTNOTES

[1] Morison, p 7. [2] Wiesenthal, p93. [3] U.J.E., p 306. [4] Morison, p7. [5] Brittanica, p111. [6] Morison, p11. [7] Wiesenthal, p102. [8] Morison, p104. [9] Wiesenthal, p104. [10] Morison, p 55. [11] Nectario Maria, *Cristobal Colon Era Espanol* (1978), p14. [12] ibid p16. [13] Brittanica, p111. [14] ibid. [15] ibid. [16] Pohl, *Atlantic Crossings Before Columbus* (Norton, 1961) p 227 et seq. [17] Brittanica, p111. [18] ibid. [19] Nectario, p21 seq. [20] Morison, p 35. [21] Boland, *They All Discovered America* (Doubleday, 1961) p381 et seq. [22] Brittanica p111. [23] U.J.E., p310. [24] Morison, p644. [25] U.J.E., p310. [26] Brittanica, p111. [27] U.J.E., p310. [28] Morison p13 seq. [29] Nectario, p8. [30] Morison, p37. [31] & [32] U.J.E., p306 seq. [33] Morison, p136. [34] Morison, p137. [35] ibid, p212. [36] ibid, p52. [37] Nectario, p13, Wiesenthal, p113. [38] Prytz, *Lykkelig Vinland* (Ashehoug, Oslo, 1975); Enterline, *Viking America* (Doubleday, 1972); Chapman, *Norse Discovery of America* (One Candle Press, 1981).

I would like to thank those of you
(Paul S. has given me a list)
who so kindly sent their good wishes for my temporary retirement,
and who so generously sent gifts of money,
presented to me at a memorable Fortean Feast.
Thanks too to those who organized and conducted it.
It has all been deeply appreciated and quite unexpected.
I shall not be idle
– a change is as good as a rest, it's said –
and the results should show up in FT and the IFS in years to come
Nor will I be far away, but helping Paul all I can.
Paul will discover that editing FT is a solitary job,
but not a lonely or thankless one as you have well demonstrated.
I have every confidence in Paul, and hope that you
– readers, contributors and colleagues –
will afford him the same degree of trust and cooperation
you have given me over the last eleven years.
Thanks again, to one and all.

Bob Rickard

Reviews

MARCOS:

Wild Child of the Sierra Morena.
by Gabriel Janer Manila.
Condor/Souvenir Press, London; 1982, £8.95 hb, pp167, notes, plates.

The author, a well-known Catalan novelist, won his doctorate at the University of Barcelona on the subject of wild children, and his thesis was based upon the facts in this book. Marcos was about seven years old when an old goatherd he had been sold to died, leaving him alone in the desolate mountains of Sierra Morena in southwest Spain. For twelve years he survived in the wild, until, in 1965, he was caught, barefoot and dressed in skins, by the Guardia Civil. Today Marcos lives and works in Palma de Mallorca, but still can't shake off the memories and habits of his life in the wilderness.

Dr Manila met Marcos in 1975 and uses his story to shed some new light on the stories of the Aveyron wild-boy and the pathetic wolf-children of India among others. Unlike them, Marcos was abandoned *after* he acquired speech, and so for the first time we are privileged to hear the story of a wild-child in his own words. There is much humour, wonder, delight, fear and sadness in his amazing relationship with a family of wolves, and the other animals with whom he shared his mysterious and dangerous world. A fascinating and thought-provoking book.

RJMR

MYSTERIES:

Encounters with the Unexplained
by John Blashford-Snell.
Bodley Head, London; 1983, £8.95 hb, pp251, plates.

By now the whole world must know of Blashers; that archetypal and English Colonel who leads expeditions into the forgotten corners of this earth. With disarming honesty, he says he is not motivated by the desire for personal aggrandisement, but some satisfaction in striving to seek and to find. He writes: "If we believe that an enigma is a fact that cannot be explained in any usual manner, then perhaps a new approach is needed to unraval it. This does not necessarily call for a person of high intelligence, but quite simply for one with an inquiring mind and determination – someone who is driven by insatiable curiosity." The Colonel embodies these attributes perfectly; he is a throwback to that great Victorian hero, the fearless explorer who has seen places and done things. He has had his share of trouble on the way (attacks by tribesmen, etc), but as Fort (who applied these qualities to library research) said: "Oh, the finds."

Mysteries is a collection of reminiscences of unexpected and strange discoveries made during Blashford-Snell's numerous expeditions: the sunken great gun of the legendary port of Paphos; the negative evidence for 'Atlantis' at Bimini; the 'Fountain of Youth' at Bimini; the searches for the lost Scots colony of Caledonia Bay in Panama, and the legendary white walled city in Honduras; the remains of long-lost planes and their crews found crashed in the Libyan desert; parts of the Blue Nile where no white man had ever been; an undiscovered tribe in Papua New Guinea; monster-hunting at Loch Ness from the Goodyear blimp; meeting "Oliver" the strange ape from Zaire; hunting giant (15ft!) lizards in West Irian; yeti; and the amazing discovery of a cave where elephants mined salt, at Mt Elgon, Uganda; plus a few ghostly experiences.

Whether he knows it or not, Blashford-Snell has the Fortean spirit. May he have many more adventures like these, and note them for our pleasure and interest.

RJMR

WHEN THE SNAKES AWAKE:

Animals and Earthquake Prediction.
by Helmut Tributsch.
MIT Press, Cambridge, Mass./ London; 1982, £18.00 hb, pp248, refs.

It is a standard folk-belief, in most quake-prone countries, that animal behaviour changes unusually prior to a quake, and there are proverbs and traditions based on this change which anticipate or predict a coming quake. For example: two days prior to a severe quake at Helice, Greece, in 373 BC, according to Diodorus Siculus, all the weasels, millipedes, worms, rats and snakes left the city. Granted that man, of old, has regarded the anomalies of nature, and animal behaviour in particular, as omens of disaster and change, there has, nevertheless, been a growing trend towards acknowledging that, as in many other areas of rehabilitated folklore, there might well be something to it.

The author, now a professor of physical chemistry at Berlin University, was made aware of the phenomenon of animal precognition of quakes when his family and friends lost their homes in the devastation at Friuli in May 1976. Many of the peasants told him, when he visited the area, that the animals behaved strangely just before the tremor. This book grew out of the thoughts set in motion when one old lady said to him: "If we had only understood them." The result is a marvellously Fortean book which explores the interconnectedness of the animal kingdom and the planet they live on.

Tributsch first reviews the historical evidence of omens of quakes in a fascinating chapter, followed by a search for likely signs of the seismic stresses which precede a quake (which is mainly the release of the stress). There are no less than 282 geophysical changes preceding a quake, including changes in watertable levels, gases bubbling up in lakes or ponds, changes in the colour of pond or well water, release of radioactive radon gas. But most of these are unreliable indicators of coming quakes, especially in the important period of a few days to a few minutes immediately prior to the timespan in which bizarre animal behaviour, strange underground noises and mysterious aerial lights occur. Now most readers will be familiar with the work of Persinger (see his interview in FT42, and article in FT41) in correlating mysterious aerial lights and seismic stress zones. Indeed, Paul Devereux has built upon it (in his book *Earthlights*) a plausible and testable theory of the origin of some forms of UFO phenomena.

It will come as no surprise to learn that successful quake predictions were being made from 1855 in China, based on such warning lights, sounds and animal behaviour, and that written data on these had been kept for at least 1,500 years. The sensitivity of animals to vibrations, changes in electrical and geomagnetic fields are discussed, and the latter two largely discounted as the main precognitory mechanism because there are records of even effectively screened animals acting strangely, and the author then settles on the little explored area of charged particles in the air. In the middle of this thesis (p113) is the fascinating datum of a powerful magnet losing its power two hours prior to a quake and regaining it afterwards, and one can't help wondering if this is a clue to the electromagnetic interference and vehicle/motor stoppages reported during some UFO incidents, especially those falling within the zonal reach of (non-quake intensity) seismic stress. Our author then launches into the whole piezoelectric effect as a source of electrostatic changes in the ground and air above it, especially the weather (eg. fogs associated with quakes). Here too is the source, he argues, of the almost universal feelings of nausea, depression and other exaggerated nervous disorders felt by humans during quakes.

Tributsch admits that irrefutable proof of the electrostatic connection between quakes and animal behaviour is not forthcoming but his great triumph (apart from a delightfully informative book) is to pioneer the context in which confirming or refuting experiments might be made. Nonetheless, the general reaction of the scientific establishment was antipathy, including the rejection of his papers from scientific journals. After his hypothesis was finally published in *Nature* in 1978, he was contacted by a scientist (S.A. Hoenig) who had detected emissions of charged particles from experimentally crushed rock, at the University of Arizona, which both agreed was "the first experimental proof of electrostatic earthquake precursors" (p214), which Tributsch had deduced from popular traditions about quakes. The book is an open-minded interdisciplinary detective story; in an eminently readable translation (by Paul Langner), and thoroughly recommended.

RJMR

SEARCHING FOR HIDDEN ANIMALS:

An enquiry into Zoological Mysteries

by Roy P. Mackal.

Cadogan Books, 15 Pont St, London SW1X 9EH; 1983, £8.95 hb, pp320, index, bib, illus.

This is a new edition of the book printed in 1980 by Doubleday, but Cadogan Press have made some commendable improvements: a well designed cover, quality paper, and a much better printing of the illustrations and photographs.

The nod given in the title is not all this book owes to Bernard Heuvelmans classic *On the Track of Unknown Animals.* It is a worthy successor, scientific in the true sense of the word, and in most cases Mackal avoids any duplicates of material. He has wisely chosen to present a series of essays discussing topics in which he has a personal interest or experience; the result is a book of great diversity and one which, unlike his previous *Monsters of Loch Ness,* proves to be readable.

Much of the book is given over to aquatic cryptozoology and Mackal follows his earlier work with a series of excellent and interconnected essays dealing with lake monsters of Canada and the USA, and the sea serpents of the northern Pacific, accompanied by a pioneering discussion of salps as an explanation for some sea serpent reports. The field of water monsters is the author's speciality and his ideas are exciting. Perhaps the most interesting is that the seemingly transitory presence of many American lake monsters may be explained by the migration of animals from the sea and along interconnected river systems. Certainly many lakes with monster traditions are connected but whether such migrations are possible today, when many rivers are bridged, blocked or polluted, is not discussed.

Mackal also deals with reports of giant octopuses (drawing heavily on the work of Gary Mangiacopra) and with the mystery of 'Steller's Sea Ape'. Moving onto land there are brief discussions of the 'Maybe Animals of South America', including giant sloths, snakes and otters, and an essay on the possible survival of the flightless giant birds of the Southern Hemisphere. There is a most welcome re-appraisal of the case of the Himalayan Buru, a lizard-like creature said once to frequent remote valleys in Assam, and two useful excursions into esoterica to debate the chances of trilobite survival and the existence of the man-eating trees of Madagascar. The author adds a cautious essay on another of his favourite topics, dinosaur survival in central Africa.

Though a confessed romantic, Mackal does his best to be scientific. ("The narrative of this adventure is utterly delightful, but our concern at this time is page 157 only.") Yet a careful approach to the evidence is marred by his conclusions, often quite definite and masked only by the most token of modifiers. Many are quite believable, but there are glimpses of a tendency to draw conclusions from selected material, perhaps even a single case. While specific identification from a solitary report may be possible if the observer is a naturalist of the stature of Steller, it is a risky business. As an old Loch Ness hand Mackal should know that if two or more reports are received of what might be supposed to be the same phenomenon they may differ substantially; indeed it has recently been suggested that the discrepancies in such reports may be their most significant factor.

Searching for Hidden Animals is a solid, well illustrated and beautifully produced book with an excellent index. It marks a useful advance in analytical cryptozoology, and though Mackal does not display Heuvelmans' mastery of the primary sources, he has produced a volume which complements and adds to the earlier work.

Mike Dash

THE SPIRITUALISTS:
The Passion for the Occult in the 19th and 20th Centuries
by Ruth Brandon.
Weidenfeld & Nicolson, London; 1983, £12.50 hb, pp308, index, bib, notes, photos.

MEDIUMSHIP AND SURVIVAL: A Century of Investigations
by Alan Gauld.
Paladin/Granada, London; 1983, £2.50 pb, pp288, index, bib, photos.

Ever since the Fox sisters first produced mysterious raps in 1848 and started a craze which still lingers on nearly 150 years later, believers and sceptics have continued to argue about the nature of the phenomena produced under the banner of 'spiritualism' – the activities of the seance room such as movement of objects, materialisations, voices, levitation. Ruth Brandon's contribution to the debate is a practical one, and her approach is so eminently sensible that it is hard not to accept her findings. Surveying the whole spiritualist scene and its most famous mediums, she reports their confessions, their exposure as frauds, and the work of magicians who have shown how it is possible to duplicate the mediums' seance-room effects. She also shows how magicians are much more able to detect trickery than are scientists, and she ponders the question why eminent people such as Sir Arthur Conan Doyle and Sir William Crookes came under the spell of spiritualism. Despite Houdini's denials, Conan Doyle continued to believe that the magician was able to dematerialise and walk through a brick wall. There are many other equally fascinating tales in this clearly written book, which should be compulsory reading for anyone interested in spiritualism. The long appendix, 'The Machine in the Ghost', is an appropriate climax, being a catalogue of mediums' techniques.

Having cleared away the 'dead wood' of physical mediums' trickery, we come to Alan Gauld's story of another aspect of spiritualism. The greater part of his book deals with the major mental mediums and the messages which they obtained, ostensibly from dead communicators. There is also discussion of other related phenomena: reincarnation, out-of-body experiences, and apparitions, and some very complex thoughts on 'memory and the brain'. Dr Gauld's intention, having surveyed the evidence, was to decide whether there is any genuine evidence for survival, but despite his efforts the verdict must remain 'open'. That this is so is no criticism of Dr Gauld's work, but a realistic assessment of the situation, which he shows to be far more complex than is generally realised. An investigation of this kind highlights the limitations of our knowledge and the fact that we have really progressed nowhere in this aspect of psychical research during the last hundred years. This challenging book is highly recommended, as are the other titles in this Society for Psychical Research series, all available as Paladin paperbacks: *Beyond the Body*, *Hauntings and Apparations*, and *Through the Time Barrier*.

Janet Bord

ECCENTRIC LIVES AND PECULIAR NOTIONS

By John Michell.
Thames and Hudson, London; 1984. £9.50hb, pp240, index, bibliography, photos.

A few months ago, I was researching eccentric lives in the British Library Reading Room, where I encountered John Michell, who was doing the same thing. While his work has resulted in this immensely entertaining and urbane book, mine still languishes in files of unwieldy notes. The fact that our work doesn't overlap is some indication of the enormous breadth of the field.

The emphasis in John's book is on those characters whose eccentricity has manifested in outlandish theories. As Paul Screeton says in *The Shaman* No.8: "It is admirable that there is no preface or introduction, for to attempt a blanket explanation of people holding bizarre, absurd, or revolutionary notions would be to attempt an assessment which would only appear pseudish or apologetic." Miles Kington says much the same in the *Sunday Times*: "There is scarcely any rhyme or reason behind the selection, and it's probably all the better for that, as nobody wants to know what's round the next corner." By contrast, Ion Trewin in the *Hampstead and Highgate Gazette*, is way off beam when he writes: "The sadness of John Michell's researches is that he fails to advance any theories or come to any conclusions."

The book contains scores of fascinating characters, and I'll list a few here to give the reader some idea of the treats in store: John Rutter Carden, who spent his life and money pursuing a girl who didn't love him; Colonel Sibthorp, the most diehard reactionary ever to sit in Parliament; Edward Leedskalnin, the Latvian who built and carved in coral by an unknown technique; Geoffrey Pyke, inventor of ice battleships; Comyns Beaumont, who thought Edinburgh was Jerusalem; William Price, the Welsh shaman and pioneer of modern Druidism who succeeded in having cremation legalised; and classic crackpots like Monboddo, Rokeby, Galton, Donnelly and Nesta Webster. The book also teems with Baconian and other Shakespeare heretics, trepanners, ufologists, bibliomaniacs and British Israelites.

Here is the first comprehensive account of the Flat Earthers and the inconclusive experiments at the Bedford Level. Stranger still, and one of my favourites, is the chapter on Cyrus Teed ("Koresh") and his followers, whose elaborate 1897 experiment with the Rectilineator, projecting an 'air-line' over several miles along the coast of Florida, seemed to confirm their belief that the earth curved upwards, and that the centre of the earth was above our heads. As John muses, "Perhaps the answer lies in the malleable, obliging nature of the universe, which reflects every image projected upon it and gives every experiment a tendency to gratify the experimenter."

The Koreshan community, which numbered around 200 at its zenith, seemed to be happy and prosperous, and survives to this day at the site of New Jerusalem at Estero in Florida. "It may be", writes John, 'that the more outrageous and exclusive are the beliefs which a group holds in common, the more effective they are in holding that group together in defiance of the outside world."

ALSO RECEIVED

★ PIG OVERBOARD! ...and other strange but true letters to The Field.

Compiled and illustrated by Merry Harpur.
Robson Books Ltd., Bolsover House, 5-6 Clipstone St, London W1P 7EB; 1984 £6.95 hb, pp143.

A fascinating collection of closely observed oddities from the animal world, with some charming drawings by the compiler. Racoons abounding in Kent, a crow's funeral, whistling trout, telephathic dogs, animal ghosts, hypnotising scorpions, the pond that devours tons of rubbish, a fish in a loofah... Hours of fun. A pity the letters weren't dated.

★ THE GREAT SEA SERPENT CONTROVERSY – A CULTURAL STUDY

By Paul Lester.
Protean Publications, Flat 4, 34 Summerfield Crescent, Edgbaston, Birmingham, B16 0ER; 1984, 60p + postage, pp24.

An elegantly written pamphlet on the sea serpent in history, culminating in the nineteenth century when it became the symbol of the Great Unknown, putting a check on the arrogant scientism then prevalent. Well footnoted, though the miniscule print is a bit of a strain on the eyes.

★ **JOHN BUNYAN** by John Nicholson. New life of this famous English visionary and reformer. First in a series of 'Essays into England'. *Bozo Publications, BM-Bozo, London WC1N 3XX; 1983, £2.40, pp114.*

★ **THE ENLARGED DEVIL'S DICTIONARY** by Ambrose Bierce. This famous satirical work is a classic of acid wit, and its definitions and descriptions are prevented from being merely sarcastic by being simultaneously erudite, funny and thought-provoking. Bierce – a famous mystery himself (he vanished in 1913, after setting off for Mexico) – has an iconoclastic style not dissimilar from Fort's, which is only one of several reasons why Forteans should read Bierce. The original *Dictionary* of 1911 had about a thousand entries – this is a new edition, edited by Prof EJ Hopkins, who has restored 851 'lost' entries. *(Penguin 1984, £3.95 pb pp324.)*

★ **THE GREEN STONE** by Graham Phillips & Martin Keatman. A story of demons, psychic forces, ancient and ritual magic, psi, synchronicity, influences across time, dreams and legends leading to a discovery of a short sword and a green stone. Constructed like a contemporary thriller exploiting UFOs, earth mysteries, psychic research and folklore studies, there is no doubt it is a ripping yarn. The narrative "may sound fantastic and unbelievable", write the authors, but is it as "true" as they insist? Unfortunately the critical reader is given nothing tangible or convincing in the way of proof that this has not been a bizarre form of collective hallucination or a clever hoax. The authors are at their most unconvincing when they claim they "stand to lose much" by making public their adventure, as though this implies they are telling 'the truth'. The central members of the Parasearch team, as they called themselves, have become celebrities of the burgeoning overlap between UFO, ley, folklore and psychic research, and they should at least be honest enough to admit their apparent enjoyment of the notoriety. Still, there should be enough avid believers in all this to make the book a success, ensuring that any losses will be of the tax variety. *(Panther/Granada, 1984, £2.50 pb, pp256, index, notes, photos.)*

★ **MIND IN SCIENCE** by Richard Gregory. Professor Gregory, one of our leading perceptual scientists, authored the influential *Eye and Brain*, and now gives us the benefit of his considerable learning in this seemingly vast subject. He reviews ancient ideas of the mind, and how over the centuries these have been inextricable from the unfolding philosophies of science and the concepts of form, motion, energy, time and space, etc. Memory, intelligence, the mind/body problem, knowledge and consciousness are dealt with in detail (including commentary on the ideas of Eccles & Popper, see previous title). Excellent reference material. *Penguin Books, London; 1984, £7.95 pb, pp641, index, bib, notes, illus.*

★ **FENG-SHUI** by Ernest J Eitel. The third modern edition (1984) of this classic work on balancing topographical forces. This one is better printed and illustrated than the others and carries a forword and afterword by John Michell, who, of course, was instrumental in introducing this old Chinese science to today's ley-hunters. (*No price details – inquiries to publisher: Synergetic Press, 24 Old Gloucester Street, London WC1.)*

★ **STRANGE TO RELATE** by Allan Barham. Barham is a Church of England clergyman who has spent many years in the service of the SPR and the Churches' Fellowship for Psychical & Spiritual Studies, which has allowed him to witness and investigate many varieties of psychic phenomena and many famous mediums. This is a book of his reflections upon those experiences. There are very interesting chapters on hypnosis in psychic research; direct voice phenomenon; PK experiments; non-medical healing; out-of-the-body experiences; the Shroud of Turin; and even UFOs (his interest goes back thirty years). A balanced and very reasonable book. *(Collin Smythe, Gerrards Cross, Bucks, 1984; £6.75 hb, pp128, index, bib, illus.)*

★ **THE WORLD'S STRANGEST STORIES** – a further selection of articles from *Fate Magazine* by its editors – grouped under the following headings: Things from out of this world; Things from out of the sky; Glimpses of other realities; Intruders; Things that weren't there; Strangest UFOs; Unnatural nature; Legends into life; and Out of time – ranging from Harold Wilkins' 'History of the Talking Mongoose' to our own Sven Rosen's 'Dragons of Sweden'. *(1983, price unknown – inquiries to publisher: Clark Publishing Co, 500 Hyacinth Place, Highland Park, IL 60035, USA.)*

★ **THE MEGALITHIC ODYSSEY** by Christian O'Brien. A detective story, searching for the identity of the builders of the stone circles on Bodmin Moor, with an analysis of their design and purpose as astronomical instruments. *Turnstone Press, Wellingborough, Northants; 1983, £4.95 pb, pp176, index, bib, foldout map, illus.*

Classified Exchanges

FT welcomes an exchange of publications with those of mutual interest. This listing represents exchange publications received since last issue. Symbols: # = issue number; Pay = to whom cheques should be made if different from title, O = overseas rate; E = European rate; all rates inland or surface unless indicated; NFC = no Foreign cheques, many offer airmail rates, so inquire. Please mention FT when writing to listings.

FORTEAN

• **ASSAP News** – [*n9, Oct 1983 – n13, June 1984*] Newsletter of the Association for the Scientific Study of Anomalous Phenomena. 6/yr. Free to members. Enquiries to: *Caroline Wise, ASSAP Membership Secretary, 56 Telemann Sq, Kidbrook, London SE3.*

• **Bulletin of the Tychonian Society** – [*March 1984*] Dedicated to a geocentric cosmology. This is the last issue from veteran editor Walter van der Kamp (age 75yrs) who has plugged away for 16 years. Dr G.D. Bouw will be the new editor. No sub price: free to any who request it, but donations appreciated. *BTTS: 14813 Harris Rd, RR 1, Pitt Meadows, BC VOM IPO, Canada.*

• **Clypeus** – [*n81, Oct/Dec 1983 – n82, June 1984*] Fortean journal in Italian from the group Clypeus. Enquiries to: *Clypeus: Box 604, I-10100 Torino, Italy.*

• **Common Ground** – [*n8*] Statistical evidence for leys; the transitions of Stainton Moses; astrology anomaly; entity warnings; etc., [*n9*] Alien body tales; earthlights debate; psychic research; ASSAP philosophy. The last two issues in the 'old' format and marks the point that CG breaks away from ASSAP, being no longer ASSAP's journal. Editor Kevin McClure wants to develop new approaches, and promises that CG10 will deal with the question of why UFO phenomena (as we know them) should begin with 1947? Apx 3/yr. £3.60. E:£5. O:$10. NFC. *CG: 11 Asquith Boulevard, Leicester.*

• **Fortean Tape Recorded Information Service** – [*n1*] Not strictly a magazine list, but Dennis Pilichis runs this very laudable self-funding project to preserve Fortean information from lectures, TV and radio shows, investigations and interviews etc. Send for his lists covering Forteana, UFOs and cryptozoology. He sometimes has lists of books and magazines for sale too. *FTRIS: Box 5012, Rome, OH 44085, USA.*

• **INFO Journal** – [*n42, Sept/Oct 1983 – n44, May/June 1984*] Getting better each issue with an interesting variety of Fortean material. Essential reading for Forteans. $10/yr. *International Fortean Organization: Box 367, Arlington, VA 22210, USA.*

• **Journal of Meteorology** – [*v8 n8, Sept 1983 – v9 n90, July/Aug 1984*] Frequently has items of Fortean meteorology. 12/yr. Has a variety of sub rates from £15.50. *J. Met: 54 Frome Rd, Bradford-on-Avon, Wilts BA15 1LD.*

• **Nuove Realta'** – [*n3, Aug 1983*] News & reviews in Italian, mainly UFOs & parapsychology but some Forteana. Enquiries to: *Lorenzo Massai: via Filippo Strozzi 56, I-50047 Prato, Italy.*

• **Pursuit** – [*v16n1, 1983*] Features a 'lost' article by Ivan Sanderson on Arctic traditions of a race of pygmy humans; Friedman on 'AntiUfology'; aerial archeology in the Sahara; Persinger on UFO reports; a first-hand fire-walk; and much more. [*v16 n2, 1983*] Andrew Thomas on the mystery vaults of Egypt; an official interpretation of the 'ET Law'; ancient aquanauts; Dwight Whalen on Niagara's fish falls; Sue Blackmore on hallucinations; and much more. This is the journal of the Society for the Investigation of the Unexplained, and essential reading for informed Forteans. 4/yr. Memb:$12. O.rates on application. *SITU: Box 265, Little Silver, NJ 07739, USA.*

• **The Searcher** – [*v6 n1&2, Jan/April 1984*] Journal of the Society for the Research and Investigation of Phenomena, of Malta, edited by Ivan Sant. 6/yr. Inquiries to: *SRIP: Box 318, Valetta, Malta.*

• **The Shaman** – Editor Paul Screeton consistently puts out a lively and informative review of books and mags in the subject areas listed in this exchange section. Essential, if you want to keep up to date. [*n3, Hallowe'en 1983*] A long profile of the shamanic life of Doc Shiels' family. [*n4, ? 1984*] A new book, critical of ley hunting, is pistol-whipped at length. [*n6, May 1984*] Special tribute to John Michell issue, with profile, essay (by JM) and bibliography. 4/yr. £2. O:$6 (surf), $13 (air). Pay: *Paul Screeton: 5 Egton Drive, Seaton Carew, Hartlepool, Cleveland TS25 2AT.*

• **Zetetic Scholar** – [*n11, Aug 1983*] The size and scope of editor Marcello Truzzi's ZS are truly impressive, containing ongoing bibliographies, and ding-dong debates between top pioneering scholars in their fields and their critics, and further replies, all in the same issue. You are not informed until you've read it. ZS11 features more arguments about the infamous 'Mars effect affair' (also called the sTAR BABY debacle) in which those spoilsports at CSICOP were caught fudging the results of research into birthsign-related phenomena. Other topics debated at length (196pp!) are UFOs, crypto-science and parapsychology; also has original of Jerry Clark's article, seen in FT41. Apx 2/yr. US:$12. O:$18. NFC. *ZS: Dept. of Sociology, Eastern Michigan University, Ypsilanti, MI 48197, USA.*

CRYPTOZOOLOGY

• **Champ Channels** – [*v1 n2, Aug 1983 – v2 n2, ? 1984*] News, reports and discussion of Champ and other US lake monsters, from Joseph Zarzynski's Lake Champlain Phenomena Investigation. 4/yr. US:$8. NFC. *LCPI: Box 2134, Wilton, NY 12866, USA.*

• **Cryptozoology** – [*v2, Winter 1983*] articles on Almas, China's wildman, a South Atlantic sea serpent, sea serpent movement, Sasquatch footprints, and wildman folklore. Field reports on the Lake Tele, and New Ireland mermaid expeditions. 1/yr. Apply to *International Society of Cryptozoology: Box 43070, Tucson, AZ 85733, USA.*

• **ISC Newsletter** – [*v2 n3, Fall 1983*] Interview with Roy Mackal. [*v3 n2, Summer 1984*] Interview with Marcellin Agnagna about whether he really did leave his lens cap on when he spotted Mokele Mbembe! and a report on the Paris ISC conference. 4/yr. *International Society of Cryptozoology: Box 43070, Tucson, AZ 85733, USA.*

• **Nessletter** – [*n59, Aug 1983 – n64, June 1984*] The latest news of sightings, expeditions and controversies about Nessie and her cousins from the Ness Information Service. 12/yr. £2.50. O:$9. *NIS: Rip Hepple: Huntshieldford, St Johns Chapel, Bishop Aukland, Co Durham DL13 1RQ.*

PSI

• **International Journal of Paraphysics** – [*v18 n1&2, 1984*] Contains important papers on dermo-optics, the detection of radiation from the hands of healers and its role in healing wounds; skin-perception; and gravitational waves. Enquiries to *B. Herbert, Paraphysical Laboratory, Downton, Wilts.*

• **Journal of the Society for Psychical Research** – [*v52 n796, Feb 1984*] Surveys of OBEs, and premonitions; PSI-field testing; interesting comparison between sex research and psychic research. [*v52 n797, June 1984*] Profile of psychic (Mrs M); quantum measurements; ESP in children. Memb:£13/$34. *SPR: 1 Adam & Eve Mews, London W8 6UG.*

• **New Frontiers Center Newsletter** – [*n7/8, Fall/Winter 1983*] News and views from Walter Uphoff and friends, pioneers of psychokinetic research in the States. ?/yr. $25. *NFC: Fellowship Farm, Rt 1, Oregon, WI 53575, USA.*

UFO

• **APRO Bulletin** – [*v31 n9 – v31 n12*] Essential reading for current US investigations from the venerable Aerial Phenomena Research Organization. 12/yr. Memb:$15. O:$18. *APRO: 3610 E. Kleindale Rd, Tucson, AZ 85712, USA.*

• **BUFORA Bulletin** – [*n11, Nov 1983 – n13, June 1984*] Magazine of the British UFO Research Association; lately more informative and better produced. 4/yr. Memb:£12.50. *BUFORA Membership Sec: Pam Kennedy, 30 Vermont Rd, London SE19 3SR.*

• **Centre Update** – [*n3, June 1983*] Newsletter & reviews from the Resources Centre of the Organisation for Scientific Evaluation of Aerial Phenomena. 3/yr. Enquiries to: *OSEAP: 170 Henry St, Crewe, Cheshire CW1 4BQ.*

• **Inforespace** – [*n65, March 1984*] Journal of the Belgian UFO society SOBEPS. 4/yr. Enquiries: *SOBEPS: 74 Ave Paul Janson, 1070 Bruxelles, Belgium.*

• **Journal of Transient Aerial Phenomena** – [*v2 n5, Aug 1983*] The Dumfries UFO; investigation network; BL update; analysis of Shirley McIver's survey of 'What kind of people join a UFO group?' 2/yr. Free to BUFORA members, and for exchange. See 'BUFORA Bulletin' above.

• **Magonia** – [*n13, 1983*] Claude Mauge on UFO 'reality'; Roger Sandell on conspiracies; more Earthlights debate. [*n15, April 1984*] Report on the Anglo-French conference at Brighton; UFOs in China; the impact of psycho-social ufo theory on French ufology. Essential reading. 4/yr. £2. US:$5. O:£2.50. Pay: *John Rimmer: 64 Alric Ave, New Malden, Surrey KT3 4JW.*

• **Northern UFO News** – [*n102, May/June 1983 – n107, May/June 1984*] Vital news & investigations from the north of England, including the thoughts of Jenny Randles. 6/yr. £4.50. New Address. *NUFON: 21 Whittlewood Close, Gorse Covert, Warrington, Cheshire WA3 6TU.*

• **Quest** – [*v2 n6, Jan/Feb 1984*] Journal of the large and active Yorkshire UFO Society, full of investigations, news and reports from this large and seemingly UFO/IFO/UAP active region. ?/yr. Memb: £5. *YUFOS Membership Sec: 67 Lovell Park Towers, Leeds LS7 1DR.*

• **Senzatitolo** – [*v8 n1, Jan/Feb 1984*] Mainly UFOs but other subjects included. Enquiries to: *Alberto Lazzaro: 91 via Torino, I-33100 Udine, Italy.*

• **UFO Newsclipping Service** – Clippings from all over the world, with several pages of Forteana too. 12/yr. Apply for rates. *UFONS: Route 1, Box 200, Plumerville, AK 72127, USA.*

• **UFO News Flash** – [*n9, Jan 1984*] Italian news and sightings in English. ?/yr. Details from: *Massimo Greco: Box 29, I-25121 Brescia, Italy.*

• **UFO Phenomena** – [*v4 n1*] 'We are not alone'; computer analysis of photos; New Zealand UFO film analysis; UFO's dark side; UFO witnesses; reviews. Indexed. A serious review and paper journal for scientific ufology. Enquiries to *UPIAR: Box 11221, I-201110 Milano, Italy.*

• **UFO Research Australia Newsletter** – Well-written and produced news, reports and discussions of what's up down under. Essential reading for the fully informed ufologist. 6/yr. $Aust 15. O: $Aust 18. $Aust only NFC. *UFORAN: Box 229, Prospect, SA 5082, Australia.*

• **UPIAR Research in Progress** – [*v1 n1*] Changing times; computer evaluation of photos; time distributions of Spanish flap; Austrian witnesses. Both this and the preceding publication are an attempt to create a serious forum for European research papers. Enquiries to UPIAR address, see 'UFO Phenomena'.

EARTH MYSTERIES

• **Archaeoastronomy** – [*v5 n3, July/Sept 1982 – v5 n4, Oct/Dec 1982*] The bulletin of the Center for Archaeoastronomy. Academic studies of cultural and historical evidence of 'native' systems of astronomy. 4/yr. $15. US:$12. *CA: University of Maryland, College Park, MD 20742, USA.*

• **Caerdroia** – [*n13, Oct 1983 – n15, July 1984*] This well-illustrated and enthusiastically produced journal, pioneering research into and cataloguing the world's mazes and labyrinths, shows what you can do with scant resources. Apx 4/yr. £3.50. E:£4.50. O:$10. *The Caerdroia Project: 53 Thundersley Grove, Thundersley, Benfleet, Essex SS7 3EB.*

• **Earth Giant** – [*n3, Winter 1983 – n4, Spring 1984*] Formerly 'Picwinnard', records Wessex antiquities and mysteries, including some good historical Forteana admirably collated by its editor Jeremy Harte. 4/yr. £3. *EG: 35A West St, Abbotsbury, Nr Weymouth, Dorset.*

• **Earthlines** – [*n1, Summer 1983 – n3, ? 1984*] Looks like the old TLH format, but deals with Welsh Border earth mysteries, with snippets of historical regional Forteana. 4/yr. £4. O:$10. *Earthlines: 7 Brookfield, Stirchley, Telford, Shrops TF3 1EB.*

• **Earthquest News** – [*n7, Summer 1983*] The old stones of Essex; The Wandering Bishops (not a new wave pop group but rogue apostolic succession); Bligh Bond; rescues of ghosts & polts; and more. [*n9/10, Spring 1984*] Editor Andy Collins investigates the black panther sightings at Horndon, Essex; activities of the Markstone Liberation Front. 4/yr. £3. E:£4. O:$8. *Earthquest: 19 St Davids Way, Wickford, Essex SS11 8EX.*

• **The Ley Hunter** – [*n95, Winter/Spring 1983*] Articles on stone circles as Medicine Wheels; mind and megaliths; and the Feminist interpretation of the Glastonbury mysteries, to which Anthony Roberts has so passionately reacted (see booklet reviews). [*n96, Summer 1984*] Back after nearly a year's absence. Almost entire issue written by ed. Paul Devereux, summarizing state of art ley/energy research and reactions to criticism of the 'Earthlights' hypothesis. New A4 format, and a 3 issue + separately edited supplement planned. £4. E:£6. O:$20 (air) $15 (surf). *TLH: Box 13, Welshpool, Powys, Wales.*

• **Quicksilver Messenger** – [*n9*] pt2 of the interview with RA Wilson; wakes; more. 4/yr. £4. E:£5. O: $16. NFC. *QsM: Garden Flat; 46 Vere Rd, Brighton.*

• **Stonehenge Viewpoint** – [*n54, July/Aug 1983 – n59, May/June 1984*] Each issue is filled with informative and imaginative explorations of every aspect of megalithic culture. 6/yr. £5. US:$8. Can:$10. *SV: 2821 De La Vina St, Santa Barbara, CA 93105, USA.*

• **Touchstone** – [*n2, July 1983*] Includes a mystery cat sighting at Folly Hill, near Farnham. [*n3, Feb 1984*] Newsletter for Surrey Earth Mysteries, edited by Jimmy Goddard. Enquiries to: *Touchstone: 25 Albert Rd, Addlestone, Weybridge, Surrey.*

OTHERS

• **American Forum for the Opinionated** – [*Mar 1984 – April 1984*] Letters and ads. ?/yr. US:$5. *AF: Box 261, Staten Island, NY 10302, USA.*

• **Conspiracy Chronicle** – [*v1 n5*] Sent out by Frater Biffo. No address, but 40p "from occult bookshops" – very Discordian.

• **The Conspiracy Tracker** – [*n1, Sept 1983*] Explores the occult and extraterrestrial/extradimensional clues in the Illuminati/Great White Brotherhood conspiracy theories. This is a trial issue, so no sub rates yet. Only 10 pages, but well written and produced. US:$2. Elsewhere:$3. Pay: *Dennis Passero: 150 Putnam St, Paterson, NJ 07524, USA.*

• **Creative Mind** – [*n10, ? 1984*] Alternative values. ?/yr. £3.10. E:£4.80. *CM: Lark Lane Community Centre, 80 Lark Lane, Liverpool L17 8UU.*

• **Formaos** – [*v1 n1, Winter 1983*] Well-put-together mag from editor/illustrator Paul Ryan. 4/yr. £5. Pay: *Paul Ryan: Glebe Farm, England's Lane, Great Witchingham, Norfolk NR9 5PE.*

• **Golden Rays** – [*July 1983*] New Age/health/mysticism mag attempting to introduce an incomprehensible new 'Universal' language and script. Enquiries to: *Universal Foundation for Education and Advancement: 525 East Gurley St, Suite 111, Prescott, AZ 86301, USA.*

• **Insight** – [*n28*] Occultism, paganism & magick. ?/yr. £3.60. O:$7. *Insight: 25 Calmore Close, Stourvale Meadows, Bournemouth, Dorset.*

• **Maggie's Farm** – [*n27, Summer/Autumn 1984*] Australia's alternative network magazine; with some coverage of occultism & PSI research, and Abo resistence to the erosion of their beliefs and sacred sites. Inquiries to: *MF: Box 29, Bellingen, NSW 2454, Australia.*

• **The Stark Fist of Removal** – [*n40 v17*] Indescribable lunacy from the cult of hi-jinks and zero gravity. Send whatever you like to: *The Church of the SubGenius: Box 140306, Dallas, TX 75214, USA.*

• **The Symbol** – [*n1, Winter 1983 – n2, Spring 1984*] a magazine about red, ritual and traditional signs, sigils and symbols, including architectural and geomantic geometry. 4/yr. £3.50. Pay: *Nigel Pennick: 142 Pheasant Rise, Bar Hill, Cambridge CB3 8SD.*

•

Small independent magazines are labours of love and need your support. Please mention **Fortean Times** *when you respond to these listings.*

LETTERS

Cont from p3.

sued me was a business associate who wanted to become associated in a personal way, which I did not desire. The lawsuit was instituted for this reason. Readers who care to check the court record in Seattle (some have already) will note that the film contract calls for a completion date of 1986. Since the suit was started in 1983, this should tell readers something. The film is in progress, and will be completed in 1986, despite the delay caused by this harrassment lawsuit. There was a stipulated settlement out of court in November 1984.

John Erik Beckjord
Box 1412, Topanga Canyon, CA 90290, USA.

[Bob Rickard ***comments:*** *As the author of the mermaid report in FT42, I made a serious error in confusing an already complex story with what amounted to a personal attack on Erik Beckjord, something I've not done before in FT. By dragging in the matter of the lawsuit against him I wrongfully implied that he was little more than a thief and a liar, and I apologise to him for this. Although the matter is of legitimate interest in itself, it had no bearing on the ISC/mermaid issue, and I foolishly let it colour my supposed impartiality in the difficult mermaid issue, which lacks positive proof for claim and counter-claim – and for that lapse I apologise to our readers.*

In a welter of letters to me, Beckjord continues to complain about his treatment at the hands of International Society of Cryptozoology (ISC) secretary **J.** *Richard Greenwell, who also edits ISC publications. Beckjord claims that Greenwell consistently refuses to print his letters criticizing the Wagner's original Ri report and the subsequent ISC expedition. In the end he elicited the help of ISC board-member Dr George Zug, a curator at the Smithsonian, who recommended Greenwell to publish the comments, after Beckjord* *agreed to rewrite passages that Zug though were 'discourteous".*

Behind this dispute is yet another – Greenwell refuses to grant Beckjord membership of the ISC. Beckjord claims this "has no validity, other than some personal bias on the part of Grover Krantz". Prof. Krantz, an anthropologist at Washington State University and ISC board-member, had a prior bitter dispute with Beckjord. Beckjord's angry reaction entrenched the ISC decision and no doubt Greenwell then felt justified. But if it is true that membership has been decided so subjectively, it rather goes against the founding idea of the society as a "neutral" ground for scientists and laymen of all persuasions. Beckjord was refused a copy of the by-laws, so he cannot judge the legality of his rejection, or any right of appeal. Again he sought help from a board-member, and Leigh Van Valen, a biology professor at the Universtiy of Chicago, has sponsored Beckjord's fourth application, but with the extraordinary recommendation that Beckjord does not associate his activities with the ISC. Beckjord wrote to me: "If they have me inside rather than storming the gates, all this conflict shall cease. I would not disgrace a society that I would be a member of. I would also have no need for an alternate society with a similar name. All I've asked for is a fair hearing and equal treatment. I won't rest until I get it."]

FORT AND ZEN

There are many aspects of Fortean philosophy that greatly interest me and I believe your magazine conveys well the interconnectivity between the various disciplines.

My own personal interest is in Zen Buddhism (I am in fact a Buddhist layman) and there is much in the writing of various (non-buddhist) authors that interests me. In particular I feel that there may be similarities in the style and content of Charles Forts' works and the apparently nonsensical and illogical aspect of traditional Zen writings and stories. They are both designed, perhaps, to stun the intellect and point the way to a more direct and intuitive understanding of a basic truth, or, at least, some kind of appreciation of a less duellistic conception of reality.

We are taught that Zen is simply inaccessible to the purely literary or scholarly approach, and it is said that Zen training merely *does* 'point the way'. My own feeling is that this could also partly be said of Charles Fort's writings; that his "bewildering, intoxicating, impenetrable" style 'points the way' to a deeper...experience of some aspect of reality.

However, I could be totally wrong about this!

Jon Felix
West Hoathly, Sussex.

THAYER AGAIN!

A brief footnote to the articles in FT41 by John Keel and Robert Barbour Johnson.

The much abused Martin Gardner, in his *Fads and Fallacies in the Name of Science* (New York: Dover Books, 1957), which was originally published in 1952, gives due weight to the Shaver stories (p61f).

He also discloses that Tiffany Thayer "is one of the country's top-flight advertising copy-writers, working six months of each year for a Manhattan agency where he turns out radio jingles for Pall Mall cigarettes." So he was not living off *Doubt*, but *Doubt* was living off him.

In 1956 he published the first volume of a 21-volume series of novels *Mona Lisa*. By the end of the volume the heroine is not even born! "But plenty of things have been going on in the streets and bedrooms of Thayer's Renaissance Italy."

He sounds like a curious character. Perhaps we could hear more about him someday.

Peter Costello
15 Wellington Place,
Dublin 4, Ireland.

[*More can be learned about Thayer in Damon Knight's biography* Charles Fort: Prophet of the Unexplained *(Doubleday, and Gollancz, 1970). But if any of our older readers, some of whom were members of the old Fortean Society, have any recollections of Thayer we'd be pleased to read and perhaps even publish them – Ed.*]

EDITORIAL Cont. from p.2

point is at issue. Fort says in the first chapter of *The Book of the Damned*: "When I say that there is nothing to prove, I mean that to those who accept Continuity, or the merging away of all phenomena into other phenomena, without positive demarkations one from another, there is, in a positive sense, no one thing. There is nothing to prove[....] We substitute acceptance for belief."

The true scientific spirit is one of conditional acceptance, never one of certainty. The task of *Fortean Times* is not to offer *proof* of anything, or to encourage readers to believe anything in particular; it is to present the range of evidence for all manner of phenomena which our inscrutible universe presents to us. It is up to FT readers to pick and choose and interpret as they see fit. FT readers are not sheep. As Tiffany Thayer said years ago: "The Fortean Society is the Red Cross of the human mind. Its business is to provide antitoxin against all forms of mental paralysis and intellectual stagnation."

Paul Sieveking

Truss Fund

We record our thanks to the following for their kind donations:

Mahmood Alliho, Lionel Beer, Tim Dinsdale, Alan Gardiner, Ronald Gauntlett, Mia Gerhardt, Kurt Lothmann, C.W. Murray, Roger Musson, Thomas Pender, Rupert Sheldrake, Anthony Smith, Douglass St Clair Smith, Michael Taylor, T.A. Taylor, Terry Tiplady, Valerie Thomas, Dave Tomlin, Ken Toth, and Mike & Linda Ward.

Help!

○ Researcher seeks help from anyone interested in their **dreams** – examples, views, ideas, comments. **Brenda Mallon: 270 Dickenson Rd, Manchester 13.**

○ I would like reports of **treasure animals** – animals that stumbled upon buried treasure or were somehow instrumental in the discovery of unsuspected wealth. Will exchange Fortean clippings. **Dwight Whalen: 5319 Victoria Ave, Niagara Falls, Ontario L2E 4E6, Canada.**

○ Would anybody, perfectly at home with bibliographical research, and having access to the most important British libraries, accept to supply the president of the *International Society of Cryptozoology* with photocopies of articles or portions of books on an equal exchange base of xeroxed information on all cryptozoological subjects? Reply to: **Dr Bernard Heuvelmans, Centre de Cryptozoologie, Verlhiac, Saint-Chamassy, 24260 Le Bugue, France.**

○ I am interested in meeting people who share my interest in telekinesis, fasting & raw diet, and physical immortality. Reply to: **Charles R.Kaelin, 89-44-217 St, Queens Village, NY 11427, USA.**

○ I have developed a number of theories, ranging from a new concept involving Ether (as an atmosphere of photons) which explains E-M radiation; permanent magnetic fields and how a direct current creates them; gravitation; red shift in a static universe; the missing mass; black holes; and a method of possibly generating out-of-body experiences. The Ether concept leads directly to a concept of the 'Astral Plane'. These theories are at present, non-mathematical; therefore I could use some help from readers in this area. Reply to: **R.J. Cameron, 584 Campbell St, Winnipeg, Manitoba R3N 1C1, Canada.**

○ I am interested in 'Voice Phenomena'. Can anyone give me some up-to-date information on this very significant manifestation? Reply to: **L.Goodge, 44 Hillside Road, Southminster, Essex CM0 7AL.**

Small Ads

Stop Press.

POSSIBLE SPONTANEOUS HUMAN COMBUSTION BEING INVESTIGATED OFFICIALLY. COOKERY STUDENT JACQUELINE FITZSIMONS, 17, WAS STANDING IN A CORRIDOR IN HALTON COLLEGE, WIDNES, CHESHIRE, WHEN SHE COMPLAINED OF BURNING ON HER BACK. FRIENDS PULLED OFF HER APRON AND FOUND HER JUMPER ALIGHT. SHE WAS ENGULFED IN FLAMES AND WAS HOSPITALISED WITH 18% BURNS. SHE DIED TWO WEEKS LATER ON 25 FEBRUARY.

(S.MAIL 24 FEB, D.TELEGRAPH 25 FEB 1985.)

The end of the world was nigh

DAILY MIRROR, Thursday, March 11, 1982

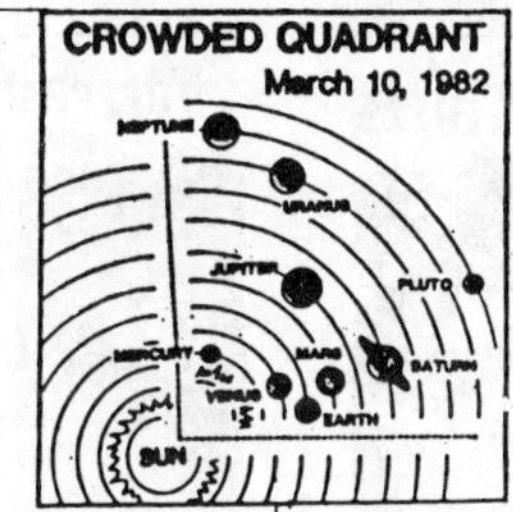

CR: NM.

D.TELEGRAPH 9 OCT 1982.

3 HANDICAPPED MONKEYS MUG MOUNTAIN MEN

By GRAHAM EARNSHAW in Peking

Police are scouring the slopes of one of China's holiest mountains for three mugger monkeys who have been robbing tourists and pilgrims, the CHINA DAILY reported yesterday.

"Each of the three old monkeys has a physical defect. One is hare-lipped, another is one-eyed and the third has only three fingers on its right hand," the paper said.

Thy have been attacking visitors to Omei mountain in central China and stealing watches and bags. Tourists are advised to bring food which will distract the simian sneak-thieves long enough to facilitate escape.

HOUSTON CHRONICLE AUG 82 CR S.P.

Double amputee denied new trial in beating death of his dwarf wife

D. STAR 26 JAN 83. CR: AG.

Elephant tries to eat man

STOWAWAY FLEA GROUNDS JET

Thieves at risk from parrots

GN. 14 JUL '82. CR IAW.

JELLYFISH SHUT ATOM PLANT

By Our New Delhi Correspondent

D.TG. 7 NOV 83

DAILY STAR, Shelby, NC – Sept. 16, 1983 CR: T. Beckley

The day the yucko stuff fell to the earth

KHALEEJ TIMES (U.A.E.) OCT 82. CR. P.B.

Attends funeral of own leg

Snake stops trains

8 MAR 82.

FT resumes publication

Man says 'devil' made him fake report of rat on cafeteria's plate

GUARD DOG STOLEN

EX-NOVICE NUN USED MACHETE TO ROB GARAGE

4 NOV 82. CR: IAW INT. HER. TRIB.

Philippine Army Tests A Coconut Oil Bomb

JAIL 'IF COFFEE IS REFUSED'

WIFE DROWNED SAVING GOLDFISH

While apparently taking the advice of a radio programme to save the life of ... a woman di... mental pon...

MERMAN STABLE AFTER SURGERY

18. Columbus Citizen-Journal ★★★★ Thurs., Oct. 27, 1983

CR: MK.

Man drills hole in head to check for his brain

TELEGRAPH 12 FEB 1981

Detective looks in his mirror, discovers bullet wound in head

CR: KL. HOUSTON CHRONICLE 15 OCT 81

'EXCITEMENT OF SUICIDE' KILLED MAN

A 24-year-old man became so excited after possibly deciding to kill himself that his heart stopped beating, an inquest at Northampton was told yesterday. The emotional state of his heart, coupled with a rush of adrenalin could have caused Mr Stephen Butler to die of natural causes.

The legless lady hops it

A WOMAN went home well and truly legless after a night out at the local.

She hopped it — leaving a false leg behind in the loo.

Landlord P... said: "...

Ex-pop st... keepin...

PRAdeGS MAR 84

CR: GEORGE IVES

AN "AIR FORCE" OF WASPS FOR CANADA

WAR ON THE CATERPILLAR

FROM OUR CORRESPONDENT

BUDAPEST, Sept. 2 1936.

TELEGRAPH 16 MAY 83.

POLICE GET STUCK INTO A SAFE JOB

THE irresistible police force has met an immovable object.

Police at Halesowen station were told by telephone that a safe had been abandoned by the roadside.

The nearest panda car went to the scene, and an officer stood guard for an hour until detectives arrived to dust it for fingerprints.

Traffic division sent a Land-Rover with towing gear, and uniform branch sent beat constables, who heaved and strained while the Land-Rover pulled.

A spokesman said yesterday: "That was when we realised it was a Midlands Electricity Board junction box, which was cemented into the ground.

"We turned our coat collars up and crept away."

Cr: SP Houston Chronicle Friday, December 2, 1983

'Death march' by 200 turtles leaves wildlife workers mystified

DTG. 22 MAR 83.

Ex-BISHOP, 92, DIES IN SEPTIC TANK

10 APR 83

Whales once walked in Himalayas

'ICE BROKEN' IN PEACE SEARCH SAYS STONE

FT Backissues.

ALL AT SINGLE ISSUE PRICE

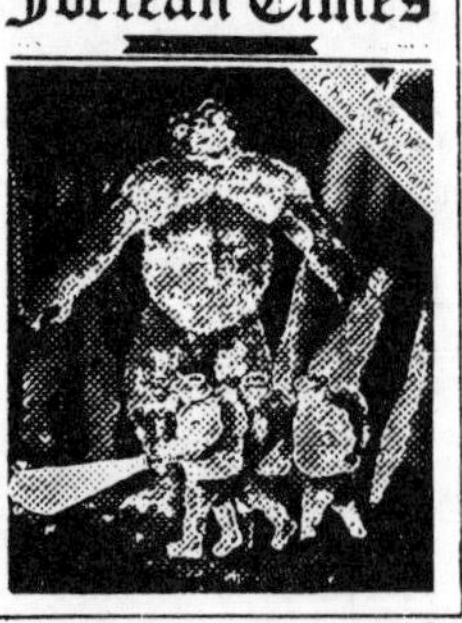

31

32

33

34

35

36

37

38

39

40

41

42

SUBSCRIPTION RATES – UK:£6; Overseas: $12 (US) or equivalent. This is for 4 issues, which we try to get out in one year. FT is a 'sporadical'.

SINGLE COPIES – UK: £1.50; Overseas $3 (US) or equivalent. We can send a recent issue and our flyer to a friend. (Overseas mail is sent by accelerated surface post, which ought to arrive within six weeks.)

PAYMENT – Payable to FORTEAN TIMES. Dollar cheques acceptable; for other currencies we prefer a sterling cheque drawn on a bank with a London office. PLEASE no Euro cheques or Irish Postal Orders. European readers may prefer to remit through GIRO services to our National Giro account – **No 50 782 4008 (Fortean Times)** – but if you do so please notify us directly, so that we know what you intend the money for.

96 MANSFIELD RD, LONDON NW3 2HX, UK.

Fortean Times

ISSUE NO. 44

The Foremost Journal of Strange Phenomena

PRICE: £1.50/$3.00

Fortean Times

Cover art by ADCO

The Journal of Strange Phenomena.

Summer 1985
ISSN 0308.5899

FEATURES

FORUM

FROM OUR FILES

STRANGE DAYS

Stars, *not falling down, raining down in Showers.*

A.D.	
761	All March, great
764	March, very great
1095	They fell thick at Noon, and on St. Ambrofe's Night
99	Fell very thick
1106	Great Falling
21	They rained down
1243	June 26. rained Stars all Night

A list from Thomas Short's History of the Air, 1749. See page 50.

COMIX

USUAL STUFF

Subscription and back issue info — see back cover.

Fortean Times

The Journal of Strange Phenomena

96 Mansfield Road, London NW3 2HX, UK

Typesetting Cecilia Boggis, 11 Ashburnham Road, Bedford, MK40 1DX.
Photosetting Words Illustrated, 1 Thorpe Close, London W10.
Print Agent Dick Gwynn.
Overseas Mailing Overseas Postal Services Ltd. 2-8 Hornsey Street, London N7 8HF.
Sub & Label Computing Anagram, 316A Richmond Road, Tickenham, TW1 2PD.

Well, we had a lot of post since last time, some of it relayed to you in the letter section. Falling stuff is the subject of Messrs Moore, Musson and Barritt; Hilary Evans and Nigel Watson comment on current UFO theories, Dick Gwynn on the goings-on in England's wild west, Leslie Shephard and Doc Shiels on those Yorkshire fairies; and we report some exceptional enigmas, like the Washington state earth divot. Bob Rickard brings us up to date on the nation-wide big cat flap.

Congratulations to Peter Christie for becoming the first fortean mayor (for Bideford in Devon), and also the first mayor from the Green Party. Some more of his gleanings from *The Gentleman's Magazine* appear next time. A couple of names got misspelt in the last issue: Wilford R. Anderson wrote the Columbus article [p58], and *Pig Overboard* [p66] is the work of Merrily Harpur. Sorry! I would like to appeal for any information leading to the discovery of Gang-of-Fort member Mike Dash, who seems to have vanished...

As there's so much to cram in (as usual), I won't ramble on, but leave you with a disruptive semiological statement from our mentor, Mr Fort: "Everything that ever has meant anything has just as truly meant something else."

Truss Fund

We record our thanks to the following for their kind donations:

Peter Binsse, Janet & Colin Bord, A.S. Evans, Ron Gauntlett, H.O. Hendricks, Harry Lane, A.R.G. Owen, David Rose and Autumn Swan.

The giant New Guinea fruit bat found in Exeter – see FT 43, p13. D.Express, *3 Oct 1984.*

Letters

FAIRIES

The massive plug for Crawley's articles [COTTINGLEY UNMASKED, FT43 p48] does not even mention the fact that the reason for the hoax was that the girls saw fairies, or the fact that one of them has continued to maintain that the 'bower' picture was genuine. Crawley's ability to ignore evidence for psychic photography should rule him out as a serious critic, as he simply brushes aside the evidence of, say, Eisenbud. [*See* THE FAIRIES WERE REAL p61 and ELSIE AND THE LIDDELL PEOPLE p60.] Then there is that preposterous review of Ruth Brandon's book [FT43 p65] clearly written by somebody who knows nothing of the subject. I am all for a sceptical approach, but these are too much!

Brian Inglis
London NW3

ANOTHER BOG MAN

You say, presumably quoting someone else, that Pete Marsh was the first bogman discovery in mainland Britain [FT43 p31] However, in 1850 the well-preserved body of a Romano-British man was found in a peat bog on Grewelthorpe Moor, North Yorkshire. He was wearing a green cloak, a scarlet garment, yellow stockings and leather sandals. Quite a dandy!

Janet Bord
Powys, Wales.

CULT INSULT

Why, when referring to Odinism in Iceland, was it termed a "cult"? It would perhaps be understandable if you were describing some new Pagan or Christian group which had just formed in Croydon, but where you are applying it to the elder religion of much of northern Europe, and where in that country it has an unbroken tradition and is a state recognised religion, it seems nonsensical and may give offence.

D.R. Wardell
Peterborough.
Cambridgeshire.

ONE MYSTERY CLEARED UP

With reference to the story of mutilated animals found on a Maesycwmmer, Mid Glamorgan tip [FT43 p18]. The police discovered that the carcasses were dumped by a local taxidermist due to the failure of his deep-freeze cabinet.

Alan Price-Talbot
South Glamorgan, Wales.

OF BIRDS, BEARS AND ELK DUNG

There are some bloody strange animals in FORTEAN TIMES 43. Like the "Arctic penguin that crash-landed in Sloane Square" (p25). Presumably it was trying to get back to its Antarctic homeland and forgot that penguins are flightless birds... And the "lesser spotted heron" (p24) is pretty amazing too. Alive or stuffed, it's a creature hitherto unknown to science. Perhaps you can twist the arm of a passing zoologist to do a bit of subediting on FT, before it goes to print?

Anyway, thanks for recent issues. The new layout looks good. I meant to write some time ago with a brief comment on The Exmoor Beast update in FT42.

You'll recall that in a Devonair phone-in, a man called 'Bob' claimed to have shot the Beast – and that it was a bear. Bob Rickard, in a rare attack of editorial omniscience, states that "no one even bothered to locate the alleged carcase".

Not true. A journalist and photographer from the Torbay News Agency travelled north in search of 'Bob' and a good story – and had him pointed out to them in a local pub. At first, he refused to admit to anything. But after being easily swayed by a free pint, he took them aside and said, confidentially, that it was all true, but that pressure from local farmers had forced him to keep quiet.

Why? Well apparently one extra-vigilant sheep farmer had discovered that his flocks were only insured against attacks by dogs. Bears definitely excluded. The neighbouring farmers had checked their fine print, and also discovered "dogs-only" clauses. Hence the swift cover-up and the denial of any bears or non-canine beasts ever having been sighted within a million miles of Exmoor. Just had to be dogs.

Could be true. Take it or leave it. But that's what the journalists were told. Myself, I think another couple of pints might have done the trick.

What else? Well, there's an article in Vol 18 Part 1 of the *Bulletin of the British Mycological Society* called "Fossil Dung: Modern Fungi" which gives an account of the discovery of an unidentifiable mould found growing on native British elk dung uncovered whilst digging a drainage ditch in Norfolk peat. The elk dung is estimated to be some 3000 years old. The unidentified fungus could be a modern contamination – or, much more interestingly, new growth from a "perennating propagule" which I take to mean a 3000 year-old dormant bit of fungus. This in turn suggests that there may be a native British

cont. on page 68.

THE DEATH OF A WOLF BOY

According to the United News of India (UNI), a wolf boy called Ramu died in Prem Nivas, Mother Theresa's Home for the Destitute and Dying in Lucknow on 18 (or 20?) February 1985. He had developed cramps two weeks earlier and did not respond to treatment. The report said that he had been captured in a forest in 1976, aged about 10, in the company of three wolf cubs. He was on all fours, had matted hair, nails like claws, and his palms, elbows and knees were calloused like the pads of a wolf's paws. He ate raw meat, and after his capture he would sneak out and attack chickens. He learned to wash and wear clothes, but never to speak. (AP) Houston (TX) *Chronicle*, 23+27 Feb; *Shropshire Star, The News* (Portsmouth), *Express & Star*, 23 Feb; *Seattle Times, Le Republicain Lorrain, Observer, Sunday Mail, Cincinnati Enquirer*, 24 Feb; Belleville (IL) *News-Democrat*, 26 Feb 1985.

I got a sense of dejà vu reading these reports, and looking through my files, found this Reuters report for 20 April 1968: "Ramu the Wolf Boy, found naked in a third-class waiting room at Lucknow station 14 years ago, died today in Lucknow hospital. . ." *Washington Post, S. Express*, 21 April 1968. When found in 1954 he was about 10 years old, had deformed limbs, uttered animal cries, and ate raw meat by snatching at it with his teeth. He spent the next 14 years at the hospital and probably died of a chronic respiratory infection. There are photo-features on this child in the *Illustrated London News* (27 Feb 1954) and the *Sunday* magazine (Calcutta) (4 Mar 1979).

The "Ramu" who died this year is probably the child found in May 1972, aged about 4, in the forest of Musafirkhana, about 20 miles from Sultanpur in Uttar Pradesh. Narsingh Bahadur Singh, a *thakur* (landowner) from the village of Narayanpur, found him playing with four or five wolf cubs, with no she-wolf in sight. Narsingh caught him and was bitten, so he trussed him up with a cotton towel, lashed him to his bicycle and rode home. The boy had very dark skin, luminous clear eyes like fireflies, long hooked fingernails, uneven sharp teeth, matted hair and callouses on his palms, elbows and knees. Some of the villagers said he had been reared by a she-bear and named him Bhaloo (like Baloo the bear in Kipling's *Jungle Book*), but Narsingh called him Shamdeo.

It was said around Narayanpur that Narsingh was no samaritan really, that he was only picking up free labour for his 30 *bighas* of land. In 1961 he had rescued an infant, practically a foetus, from a drain, and taken him home. Naming him Ramdeo, he brought him up, but although he was physically sturdy, he was a congenital idiot and an epileptic. Still, he had a few uses about the house.

Shamdeo cowered from people, played with dogs, and at night he had to be prevented from following the jackals that howled round the village. At first, Narsingh took him with him every day to work – he ran a tea stall in a railway depot. Large crowds frequently gathered to see the boy, who obliged them with occasional outbursts of jungle behaviour. He once pounced on a chicken, disembowelled it with his teeth, and ate it, entrails and all. Narsingh was later to deny indignantly that he charged money to see the boy. Some claimed him as their own. One such was Pallar, a washerman from a neighbouring village, whose child had been kidnapped in infancy. He changed his mind when he saw the growling, spitting creature on all fours. Shamdeo's limbs began straightening out with regular mustard oil massages, and after five months he began to stand. Two years later he was doing useful jobs like taking straw to the cows. He was weaned off raw meat, and took to eating earth for a while, but eventually came to terms with rice, dal and chappatis. He never talked, but learned some sign language, like crossing his thumbs and flapping his palms – his symbol for 'chicken' or 'food'.

In 1978 he was discovered by nuns, Sisters of the Little Flower of Bethlehem from the Stella Maris Convent in Sultanpur. Sisters Clarice and Lyta were in Narayanpur to visit two of their pupils, and, hearing about Shamdeo, went to see him. They told their superior, Father Joseph de Souza, who had him brought to the convent on Good Friday. The following day he was taken to Prem Nivas, Mother Theresa's Home for the Destitute and Dying in Lucknow, where the nuns renamed him Pascal. He soon made friends with a dog, but one day took its ear in his mouth and bit it. At first he ripped off his clothes, but within a week he began to settle down. He learned the Indian salutation of palms pressed together, the *namaste*. He had to be watched with other children. Sometimes, without warning, he would flick his fingers into their eyes. He liked to travel round the garden sitting upright in the back of a bicycle rickshaw.

Most of these details come from the report by C.Y. Gopinath in *Sunday* magazine, Calcutta (4 Mar 1979), which I assume to be the most reliable: as with many Indian news reports, the

Shamdeo the wolf boy [Photo © Bruce Chatwin, Sunday Times Magazine, *30 July 1978.]*

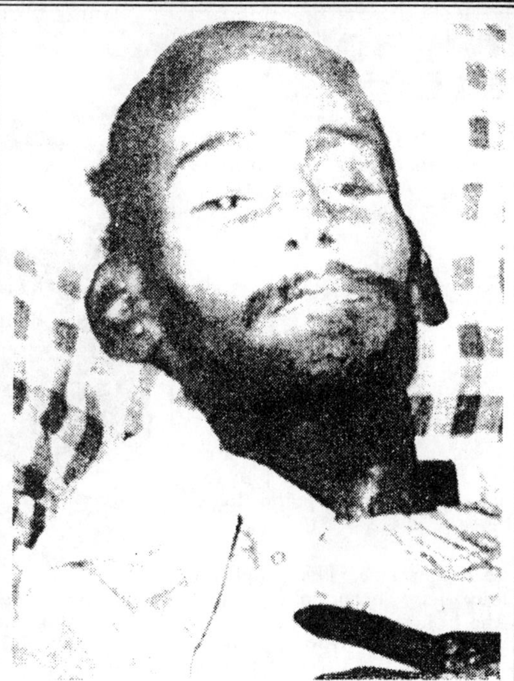

"Ramu" the wolf boy on his death bed in February 1985. [AP Photo]

details vary. For instance, Bruce Chatwin in the *Sunday Times Magazine* (30 July 1978) said that the boy was "slightly wall-eyed" and was called Sham*dev* by his guardian, *Narsing* Bahadur Singh, *headman* of the village of *Narangpur*. And the Sisters of the Little Flowers of Bethlehem heard about him in Easter Week from a Muslim woman who had seen him roaming around the western part of Sultanpur, scavenging for scraps. The Sisters found him on Good Friday, filthy and abandoned, crouching in a wall niche. The neighbours said a laundry*woman* had come to claim him a few days before, but changed her mind when she saw him. He was named *Baloo*, said this report, because during his second week at Lucknow he became excited by a performing bear with a troupe of Rajasthani entertainers. In Chatwin's account published in the *Chicago Tribune* (22 Oct 1978) we have the extra detail that, in addition to his two sons, Singh had reared four boys he had found abandoned in the wild.

Other papers stated quite baldly that he had been brought up by bears (*D. Express*, 18 April, the *Austrlian Herald*, 19 April 1978). The *News of the World* (14 May) elaborated: "A hunter in the Indian jungle followed the tracks of a bear to a cave. Suddenly he saw a little boy scamper out on all fours." According to the Catholic *Universe* (28 April), "the villagers who brought him to the mission said the boy had been kept in a cage for a year by the jungle people, who had been beating him for stealing chickens – which he ate raw."

The *Indian Express* (28 July 1979) said that "the bear boy Bhaloo" was not expected to live long, as he had a remittant fever which had not been diagnosed positively. As can be seen from the photographs, Shamdeo/Shamdev/Bhaloo/Baloo/Pascal seems to be the same boy as "Ramu" who died this year.

He showed several similarities to the famous wolf girls Kamala and Amala, allegedly dug out of a wolf den in Orissa in 1920: sharpened teeth, craving for blood, earth-eating, chicken-hunting, love of darkness and friendship with dogs and jackals. (See *The Wolf Children* by Charles Maclean: Allen Lane 1977.) Five of the six cases of wolf children in Sleeman's *A Journey Through the Kingdom of Oudh* (1849-50) came from the region of Sultanpur.

Next time, I'll review the other cases of feral children and wildmen. For earlier reports and discussion of this fascinating theme, see: FT1,pp14-15; FT3,p4; FT4,p14; FT7,p14; FT24,pp23-4; FT25, pp8-10; FT26,pp5-6; FT32,p40; FT33,p18; FT36, pp13-16; FT42,p9; and FT43,p63.

Paul Sieveking

THE HOLE STORY

On 18th October 1984, Rick and Pete Timm were rounding up cows on their father's wheat farm, near Grand Coulee, Washington, when they found an irregularly-shaped hole, about 10ft by 7ft and about 2ft deep on land adjacent to a wheatfield. The Timms had harvested the area in mid-September, and the hole had certainly not been there then. To their greater astonishment a large plug of earth, the same size and shape as the hole, rested on the ground 75 feet from it (see diagram). The plug had obviously been taken from the hole because between the two were "dribblings" of stones and earth which had dropped to the ground as plug travelled through the air. But there was no sign upon the hole or plug, or on the surrounding ground, that it had been mechanically made, or somehow rolled or dragged.

Deeply puzzled, the Timms called in Don Aubertin, director of mining for the Colville Indians, whose reservation is near the site. Aubertin speculated initially about a meteoric impact, but changed his mind after visiting the site with Bill Utterbach, a geologist retained by the Colvilles. Aubertin said: "The hole was not a crater. It had vertical walls and a fairly flat bottom. It was almost as though it had been cut out with a gigantic cookie cutter." But this image, and the suggestion that the hole was made by a helicopter-borne grab, are disproved, if disproof were needed, by the fact that roots dangled intact from the vertical sides of both the hole and the displaced slab. Digging underneath the displaced block showed

Geologists near Grand Coulee, WA, examine the chunk of earth from the hole in the foreground. [Photo ©Paulette Andrejcik, US Bureau of Reclamation.]

undisturbed vegetation, and plants on top of the plug showed it had been set down the right way up. Although a whirlwind might have the vertical suction needed, can it account for the general neatness of the action?

It was clear that some force had torn – not cut – the three-ton plug from the hole, transported the mass through the air without breaking it up (some say because the plug had a dense root mass), and set it down (gently?) at a slight angle relative to the hole; but what force, how and why? When contacted, a spokesman for the Smithsonian's Scientific Event Alert Network said they knew of no similar phenomenon. Alas, in the weeks that followed the site has been trampled by cows, and the evidence – particularly the plug – rapidly disintegrated beyond further scientific value.

However, some light can be shed on this enigma from other directions. A geologist with the Bureau of Reclamation at Grand Coulee Dam. Greg W. Behrens, eulogized, in some reports, the "interesting" geology of the area. The hole sits in a depression in a plateau at 2,360 feet above sea level, probably scraped out by an ice-sheet many thousands of years ago. The wheat field is dotted with "huge" boulders left behind when the ice-sheet retreated, and known locally as "haystack rocks" though some are larger than haystacks. Near the mystery site is what Behrens calls a "kettle", a geologist's term for a place where an underground mass of ice has melted

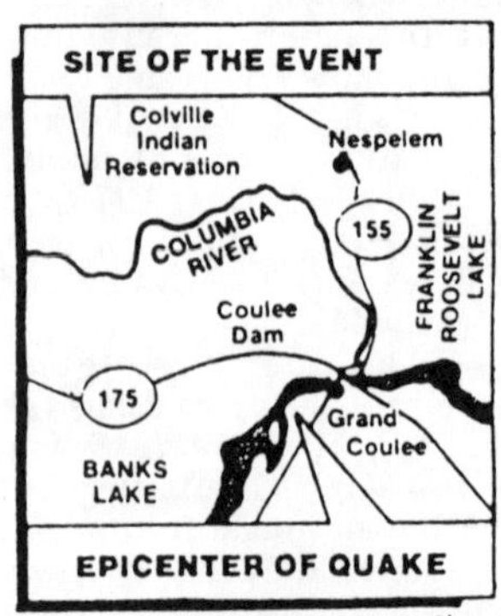

Robert Massa / Seattle Times

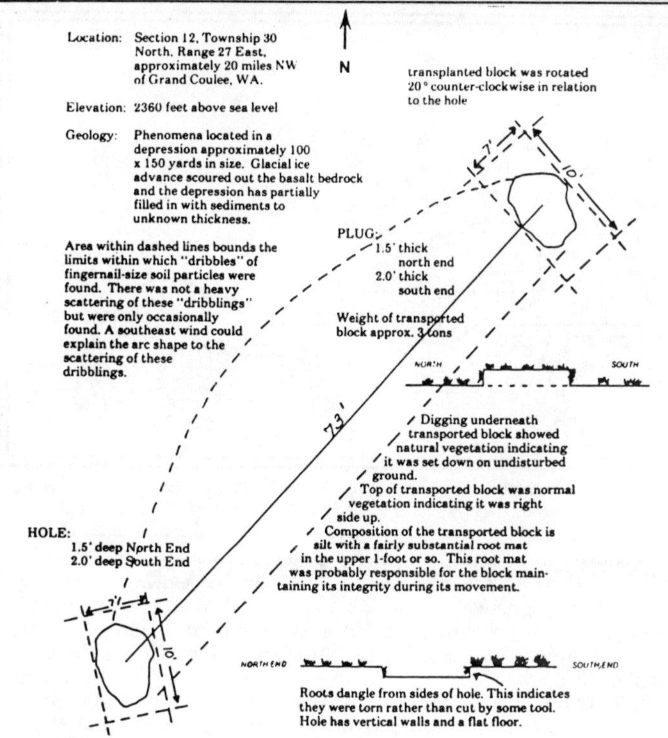

Diagram made by geologist Greg Behrens – as printed in the APRO Bulletin, 32:10.

causing the ground overhead to collapse. The mystery hole was quite different from a 'kettle'. More interesting, says Behrens, is the fact that a small quake (3.0 Richter) occurred about 20 miles southwest of the mystery site (see map) at 8.24pm on 9th October, just nine days prior to the discovery by the Timms boys. While Behrens was prepared to consider the possibility of converging shock-waves which might have popped the divot out of its hole whip-crack fashion, another geologist, Stephen D. Malone of the University of Washington, was quoted as saying this was "very, very unlikely". It must be said that although the tremor was felt in towns in the area, it was not noticed at the Timms farmhouse a few miles from the mystery site.

And yet...perhaps I can do a little better than the Smithsonian, cracking the whip of a query and seeing what data pops out of dusty concealment. Apart from the reports listed below, the only discussion of the case I've seen has been in the *APRO Bulletin* 32:10 (Feb 1985) where the anonymous writer mentions three possibly similar cases...

- 1) Following a 3.5 Richter quake in the Little Malad River Valley in northern Utah, a strange cruciform hole was found, about 14ft in diameter, with clods of topsoil hurled some 14ft beyond the limits of the feature, landing overturned. The Utah Geological & Mineral Survey report describes the mark as "mysterious". (UGMS *Survey Notes* Feb 1979.)
- 2) The case of 'The Impossible Hole', given in Aimé Michel's *Flying Saucers and the Straight Line Mystery* (1957) p132. Following the sighting of a glowing object in a field in front of her house at 8pm on 4 Oct 1954, Mme Yvette Fourneret, of Poncey-sur-l'Ignon, France, investigated an egg-shaped hole about 3ft 6ins on the main axis, and halfway down the hole was wider than at ground level. On the fresh earth in the hole white worms wriggled, and scattered all around were clods 10-12ins across. Similar clods dangled on the sides of the hole attached by roots. In the center of the hole lay a plant with a very long root, the end of which was still *in situ* in the soil at the bottom, and all its exposed roots were quite undamaged. Michel says that it looked as if the mass of earth had been sucked out by a gigantic vacuum. No explanation was found.
- 3) Following observations of a shape – and colour – changing UFO, which also seemed like a searchlight beam, at Rosmead, Middleburg, South Africa, on 11 Nov 1972, chunks of tar were found ripped out of a tennis court belonging to one of the principal witnesses. Although no damage was done to the surrounding high fence, chunks of tar were found caught in the fencing, and later on a nearby hillside. A subterranean gas explosion was postulated to account for the upward and outward projection of tar chunks, but this was inconsistent with other facts. A whirlwind was similarly disposed of as the culprit. Interestingly, guards on a nearby petrol dump told police they had seen small red lights circling in the tennis court area just before a "strange incandescent light" lit up the whole area. (*APRO Bulletin* Jan-Feb 1973.)

At this point I can only comment that the connection of localized aerial lights and strange geological disturbances, as characterized by these cases, might provide some grist to the Earth Lights debate, though, of course, the projectile mechanism in these cases remains vague indeed.

Perhaps I can add more. From Fort's *Books*: (p247) reference to Humbolt's account of the Riobamba quake (no date) in which the vertical motion was so strong a graveyard was demolished and "bodies were tossed several hundred feet in the air." Curiously, thousands of fishes appeared on the ground at the same time; Humbolt thought they came from subterranean sources.

On the same page, in one of his rare unreferenced allusions, Fort mentions that during a quake in Calabria "paving stones shot far in the air."

Lastly, I have a good story, which I commend to the curiosity of the Dorset forteans, from the records of the Tudor annalist, Stowe. I do not yet have the original chapter and verse, but use the quote given by Harold Wilkins (*Mysteries Solved and Unsolved* 1958). The quote goes...: "a piece of earth suddenly quitted its place of former time, and was transferred and transported forty yards to another paddock, in which there were alders and willows. It stopped the high road leading to the little town of Cerne. Yet the same hedges which surrounded it still enclose it today, and trees that were there are still standing. The place this bit of land occupied is now a great Hole." Stowe says this event took place on Sunday, 3 January 1582, at The Hermitage 'in the valley of the Cerf Blanc", in Dorset.

[Sources for the Grand Coulee hole story: Seattle (WA) *Times* 23 Nov; lots of AP reports of 25th Nov 1984.]

•

Bob Rickard

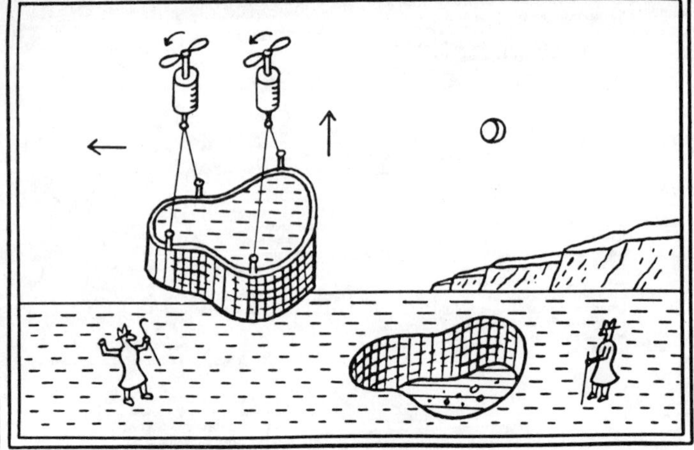

How the earth divot was moved. [Drawing © Maris Bishofs, Atlantic *magazine, April 1985.]*

PREPOSTEROUS PREPUCE

The prized possession of the parish of Calcata, a mediaeval village in the province of Viterbo, north of Rome, was the Holy Prepuce, deemed to be the foreskin of Christ, severed when Jesus was circumcised in the Temple. It was stolen in 1983 from the wardrobe of the parish priest, Don Dario Magnoni, where he had put it "for safety's sake". The priest feared it was not the relic itself that tempted the thieves, but the recepticle in which it was kept. This was a 300-year-old silver box in the shape of two angels, holding aloft a vase crowned with jewels. "La carne vera santa" (real holy flesh), as they call it, meant a great deal to the village. "It had worked so many blessings", said Guiseppina, one of the older generation.

The *Gospel of the Infancy of Jesus Christ,* which dates from no later than the second century, states that when Jesus was circumcised, his foreskin was kept by an old woman who preserved it in an alabaster box used for oil of spikenard. And "this is the alabaster box which Mary the sinner procured and poured forth the ointment out of it upon the head and feet of our lord Jesus Christ" (Chapter 2, verse 4.)

The relic had been an embarrassment to the Vatican for a long time. A decree from the Holy Office on 3 August 1900 threatened anyone "writing or speaking" of the Prepuce of Calcata with excommunication. Not only are there similar claimants with a local following in Spain and Switzerland, thus encouraging skeptical thoughts, but the very existence of such relics stimulates "irreverent curiosity."

Villagers suspected the church authorities of the theft, and a number stayed away from the village's annual procession on New Year's Day, the Feast of the Circumcision, refusing to don their traditional white robes or carry the ritual wooden crosses.

According to legend, the Prepuce was brought to Calcata in 1527 by a fugitive soldier after the sack of Rome. Over 700 years before that, Pope Leo III had been given the relic by Charlemagne, who had in turn received it from an angel. Said the local bishop after the theft: "The church would actually prefer it not to be discussed." *S.Times*, 15 Jan 1984.

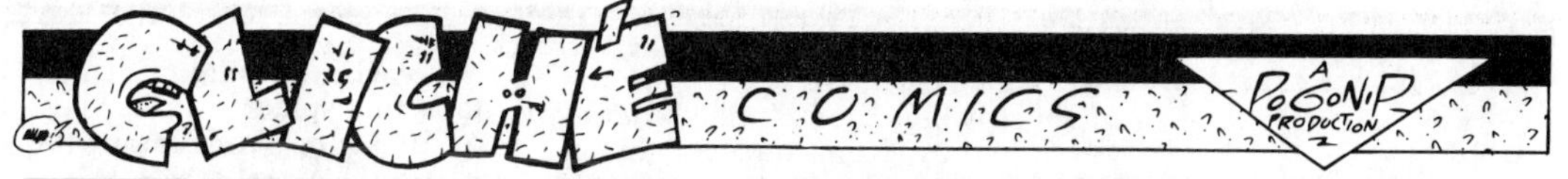

LE GOD + ROZBUD

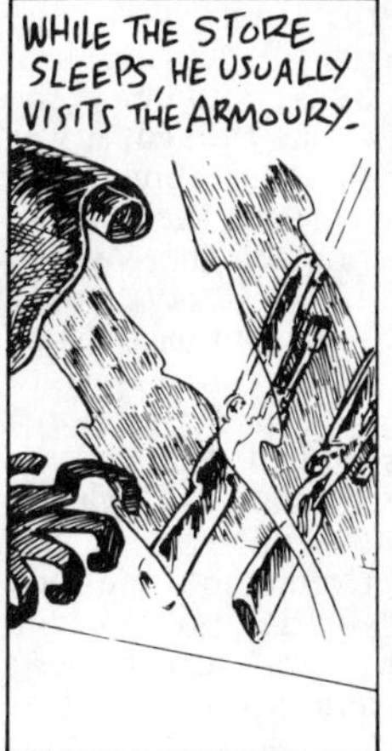

MORE FOAFLORE

The following stories seem to fit in established categories of foaflore, [See FT43 p33] such as "Granny On The Roof-rack" or "Let's Do It In The Road". The American magazine *Whole Earth Review* (No. 46, May 1985) published a selection of bad-luck stories from recent issues of FT, rounded off with some musings from the publisher Stewart Brand: "How many are journalism, how many are classic urban legends disguised as journalism?...the surest test is when the identical story turns up elsewhere with different details." Of course, this might equally demonstrate a recurring manifestation of a genuine social or natural pattern; or perhaps the story happened once for real, and then turned into foaflore through repetition or alteration...

☐ Distraught relatives were about to attend a funeral in Valencia when the hearse containing the body was driven off at speed. The driver, a young drug addict, was arrested at a road block. *D.Telegraph*, 30 Jan 1985.

☐ Robert McQuade, 30, of Salisbury, South Australia, put his five-month-old step-son in a microwave oven and turned it on. The child had to have three toes amputated, then McQuade was charged with assault. *Standard*, 30 Jan, *Sun*, 31 Jan 1985.

☐ A group of elderly people were holding a séance in a darkened town hall meeting room in Wadebridge, north Cornwall, when they heard moans and groans – but they were not coming from beyond the grave. Two teenagers were making love in a corridor outside, watched by a group of cheering friends. They fled on discovery. *Sun, D.Mirror*, 15 Feb 1985.

☐ Dutch tourist Peter Levy, 33, stripped off for a wash and shave in his moving caravan. His wife in the towing car pulled away jerkily from traffic lights in a busy Barcelona street, and Peter hurtled through the door, landing at the feet of office girls going to work. His unsuspecting wife drove on, while grinning Spaniards clapped and cheered. One gave him a handful of cabbage leaves from a market lorry, and he cowered in a doorway until a police car rescued him and chased after the caravan. When he stepped out with his cabbage leaves, his wife fell about laughing. *D.Mail*, 15 June 1984.

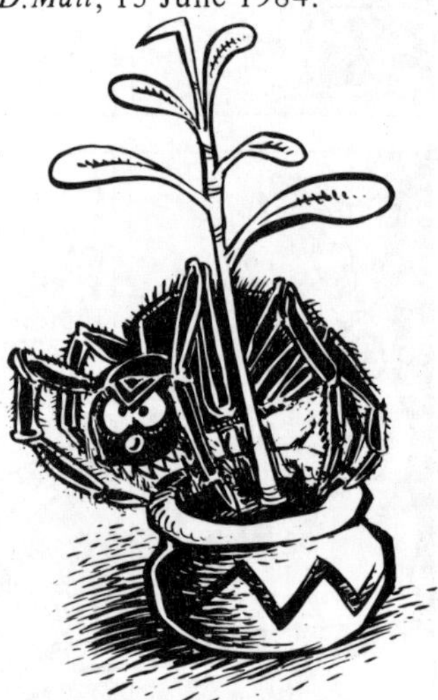

☐ Mrs Suzanne Zingler of Cologne bought a potted palm for the living room. During the first week the plant made squeaking and hissing noises when she watered it. She thought it was simply the air escaping from the dried earth in the pot. Six days later, when she watered it again, it not only squeaked,but the earth around the roots began to heave. She called the florist where she had bought the palm and demanded that he come and take it back. The florist arrived, took one look and called the police, who called the local zoo. Experts arrived and took the tree away. At the zoo staff removed a large female tarantula spider, and her nest of 50 young, from among the roots. They said the spider must have been in the pot when the plant was imported from southern Europe. *S.Express*, 24 Mar 1985.

Our correspondent Alan Cleaver had been told a similar story in his office: it had happened to a foaf (friend-of-a-friend) of the narrator. This time it was a yucca plant from Marks and Spencer's, and was taken to Kew Gardens. That evening, he recounted the tale to a meeting of a local folklore group he had started, and two women had heard it from a foaf of theirs. This time it was a banana plant.

John Passmore (*D.Mail*, 20 April 1985) reported that the story had spread across the country, the most popular version being the yucca plant from Marks and Spencer. In the plant deparment of Marks and Spencer's in Oxford Circus, the manager Tony Kelly said: "It's getting beyond a joke. Now we've got an official complaint from the Irish Ministry of Agriculture because someone in Dublin claims one of our people offered a woman £100 to keep it quiet!" Marks and Spencer's stores around the country have been bombarded with complaints and demands for action, says the *Guardian* (19 April 1985). M&S head office claim that the story is "virtually imposible" since the yuccas are imported from Africa via Holland where they are re-planted and potted.

Jim Keesing, the plant inspector in Kew Gardens, said: "One of our gardeners said it had happened to a friend of his son's. He asked me if it was possible. I told him it was – but a bit unlikely." Our correspondent Brian Hain heard the story from different informants in the Bristol area.

HELP US CATCH A DINOSAUR (ON FILM)!

Surely the most exciting cryptozoological mystery challenging us today is the possibility that dinosaurs may still be living in the remote jungle of the Congolese Republic's Likouala province. Two joint American/Congolese expeditions to Lake Tele have taken place so far, and both were curtailed by the heat, the terrain, the pests and simply running out of time. Although no tangible proof of dinosaurs was brought back, there were enough clues, tantalizing glimpses and sounds, and native stories to convince the expedition members, regardless, that there was indeed a mystery reptile-like creature in the region which the natives called *mokele mbembe.* In fact the Congolese zoologist Dr Marcellin Agnagna actually observed an unidentified "sauropod" for 20 minutes; disappointingly he only learned later that his camera had been wrongly focussed – see 'Dinosaur Hunt', FT42,p27.

The mokele mbembe of the Congo, by Gérard Deshayes. From Les Survivants de l'ombre *by Jean-Jacques Barloy.*

OPERATION CONGO

Now a third expedition – called Operation Congo – is being organized by Bill Gibbons (a long-time Fortean) and Mark Rothermel, for a November departure. Bill told us that all four team-members are under 30 yrs of age and have proved themselves on survival courses or previous expeditions, supplementing the various medical, navigation and photographic skills they will need. Bill himself taught survival techniques while in the British Army in Belize; and Mark has gathered scientific specimens up the Amazon (twice) and the Luangwa valley in Africa. They are joined by Jonathan Peacock, an accomplished underwater photographer, and Jonathan Walls, a linguist and experienced in the field. They are hoping that a small team of fit, field-experienced young men will be able to accomplish more than the earlier expeditions of comparatively elderly academics. Once in the Congo they will be joined by an official Congolese team of four scientists and two soldiers, led by Dr Agnagna.

The emphasis, Bill told FT, will be on two well-equipped and highly mobile three-man teams making daily sallies from a base camp on the shore of Lake Tele. The initial concentration will be on lobes 8 and 9 of the lake, which are feared most by the natives as the feeding ground of *mokele mbembe.* The group will employ a wide range of camera and surveillance techniques, and no attempt will be made to capture or kill a monster. To maximise their time, rare and interesting specimens of plants, fishes and insects will also be sought, and, if possible, study will be made of the rare forest gorilla now known to inhabit the region.

In view of the importance of visual evidence, a key part in the plan is the co-operation of the BBC Natural History Unit, who will be lending them sophisticated cameras to record the expedition (and hopefully its discoveries) and transmitters to provide a daily radio report for national broadcasting. In a letter to Bill, Dr Bernard Heuvelmans, the world's foremost cryptozoologist, pointed out the almost universal preconception that the *mokele mbembe* is reptilian, whereas another very likely possibility is that the creature could be a mammal which looks like a dinosaur through convergent evolution. The consequences for all branches of zoology of a successfully filmed encounter would be far-reaching.

HOW YOU CAN HELP

At this very minute Bill is busy raising funds, making arrangements and planning their transport and field schedules. But to the shame of our nation the response from the great institutions which usually help expeditions has been shortsightedly negative. However, there is still time, and Bill is very persistent.

We feel Bill and his colleagues should have the support of the Fortean fraternity at least, and we've thought of two practical ways to show our encouragement. Firstly we are setting up a special fund to receive donations from readers. Bill says every penny will help. Contributions will be recorded and open to inspection. In return Bill promises to keep us informed of progress before and during the operation, and we'll have access to the photographic evidence of any discoveries for a special report if the venture is successful.

The second way fits in with our own plans for raising funds by selling special FT-shirts. One of the designs will have an 'Operation Congo' theme, the profits of which will go to the expedition. This will be advertised in more detail next issue.

Meanwhile, your donations are solicited. Please send what you can afford, large or small, to us at Fortean Times in the usual way. **FT: 96 Mansfield Rd, London NW3 2HX, UK.**

RELIGIOUS DECAPITATION

At 6.30am on the morning of 2 March 1985, police were called to a quiet residential area of Miami. There they encountered a naked Alberto Mesa, 23, holding the freshly-severed head of a woman which he had carried from his flat four blocks away. "Then the incident gets a little bizarre" (!) said police spokesman Mike Stewart. Mesa began screaming "I killed her, she's the devil!" The rest of the body was found in Mesa's flat, and it was discovered that during the previous weeks Mesa had been taking a great interest in religion. (AP) Beaumont (TX) *Enterprise*, Cincinnati *Enquirer*, St Louis *Post-Dispatch*, Belleville (IL) *News-Democrat*, 3 Mar 1985.

WOOD FLATTENED

Martin Laakso and George Kind examining the trees bent and broken by a mysterious force near River Falls, Wisconsin. [Photos ©Pat Petricka, River Falls Journal.]

The close of 1984 has produced some A1 Fortean enigmas; the mystery Grand Coulee hole is one – see THE HOLE STORY on p6 – and here is another phenomenon found by chance some time after it happened in a remote area.

In mid-September George Kind was walking through the Foster tree farm, near River Falls, Wisconsin, to get to his adjoining tree farm. He came upon an area, approximately 90ft in diameter, in which all the trees were bent nearly to the ground, and in some cases snapped a few feet from the ground (see photos). Most of the trees were bent in an easterly direction and some were down towards the east and south. About 75 trees were involved, perhaps a quarter of them broken and dying – the bent ones remained green. The trees around the circle had branches broken off and scattered in the area. It seems that whatever happened, happened in the previous six to twelve months.

Kind alerted city forester Martin Laakso, a retired University of Wisconsin at River Falls professor, who said that a check amongst his books and colleagues revealed no similar event that they could recall. Kind said: It appears as if some thing came straight down on them in the middle of the wood." Laakso said that he could only guess at the "mystery phenomenon", supposing that a "big downdrift" came straight down, twisted a little and then went straight up again. "How else could the surrounding trees escape damage?" he asks. An airplane flight over the two tree farms, covering 80 acres, revealed no other damage. *River Falls Journal* (WI) 27 Sept 1984.

WILDMAN RUMOUR

On 23 October 1984, a small hairy man-like creature attacked two young women with sand and stones in southern Hunan's rugged Chengbu county in China. The women, one of them called Deng Yucui, 30, wearing a red jacket, fled home, and the following day 32 peasants from Shuitou village with 11 hunting dogs tracked down and netted the creature in neighbouring Xining county, which is honeycombed with caves. It clawed the ear off one human captor and was knocked unconscious with a pole.

After a few days the "mao gong" or "hairy male" became used to his captors and started eating fruit and nuts. The peasants sold him to local traders for about £12, and he was exhibited in several cities, netting about £30 a day, and attracting the attention of scientists. He was confiscated by a county magistrate and handed over to the Wildman Research Institute, who put him up in a nice warm flat in Wuhan, capital of Hubei province.

The story broke in the outside world after a report in the *Shenzhen Special Economic Zone Daily* in early February, which claimed that the 53 pound, 3 foot 8 inches tall creature was a yeti or wildman. Li Guangyu of the Wildman Institute described the beast as "having brown hair all over his body, wih a big beard covering a face similar to a man's." He said the creature could eat and drink like a human and produced human-like sounds.

The initial excitement at FTHQ was tempered by the short stature of the beast, and an article in the *Yangcheng Evening News* (9 Feb) finally put the dampers on. The front-page story quoted Li Jian, 62, deputy secretary of the Wildman Institute, as saying that the beast was a short-tailed rhesus monkey, though twice the usual weight, and with a tail 1½ inches long, half the usual length. He was middle-aged, about 15 years old. "He doesn't move around much. He's pretty silent," said Li. "But when some girls walk in front of him he likes to get near them. He makes goo-goo eyes at them and says ah, ah, ah."

Meanwhile, the Institute continues the search for the Wildman and offers 10,000 yuan (about £2,800) for any live specimen.(AP, UPI) *D.Express,* 8, 11, 15, Feb; *Western Mail, The News* (Portsmouth), *D.Mirror, N.Y.Post,* 8 Feb; The Burlington (VT) *Free Press, Times,* 9 Feb; *S.Express, Mail on Sunday,* St Louis *Post-Despatch,* 10 Feb; *Times,* Duluth (MN) *News-Tribune & Herald*, Belleville (IL) *News-Democrat*, 11 Feb 1985.

BABES WITH TAILS

On 3 September 1984, a little girl was born to a 24-year-old mother in Hangzhou, Zhejiang province in China. She weighed 6 pounds and 4 ounces, and had a one-inch tail, smooth and flesh-coloured, one-third of an inch in diameter. It was planned to have it surgically removed. She is the second Chinese girl to be born with a tail in 1984, according to the Xinhua news agency. Duluth *Herald and News-Tribune + D.Mirror* 10 Sept 1984.

THE GREAT WALL GROWS

A survey of the Great Wall of China, began in 1979 to trace remains of the structure in remote areas, revealed that the 2,400-year-old wall's meandering route covered about 6,200 miles, instead of the 3,700 miles referred to in history books. *D.Telegraph* 7 Mar 1985.

SEEDS OF TIME

In 1983, several carbonised objects that appeared to be fruit and nuts turned up in a 2,000-year-old Han dynasty tomb in Chengdu, Sichuan Province, China. These objects were covered with boiled and sterilised blankets, and a month later, according to the English language *China Daily* (27 Feb 1985), the remains had germinated, producing about 40 green buds. The plants continued to grow and bear fruit, which looked at first like dates, but then turned red and were identified as tomatoes. It had previously been supposed that tomatoes were introduced to China in the nineteenth century. AP. *The Saratogian*, 27 Feb; *Guardian, Telegraph,* Portsmouth *News*, 28 Feb 1985.

HOLY LAND IN ARABIA?

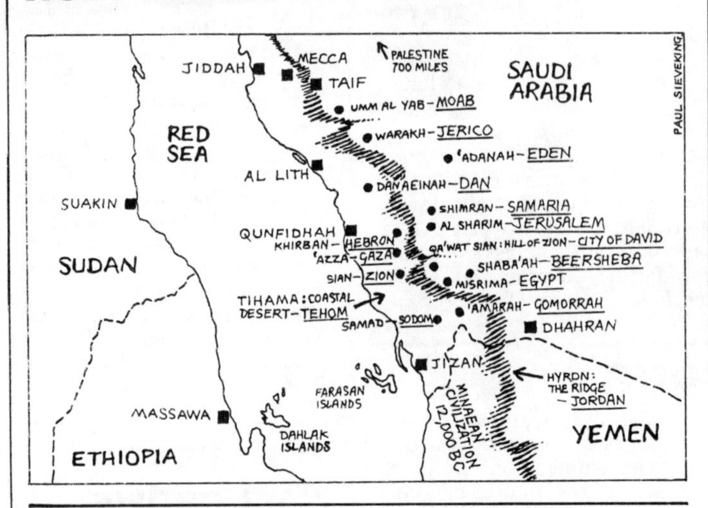

According to *The Bible came from Arabia* by Professor Kamal Salibi, a highly-regarded Lebanese Christian scholar, the events in the Bible took place, not in Palestine, but in the coastal provinces of Asir and the southern Hejaz, south of Mecca in Saudi Arabia. It is here that David and Solomon established their kingdoms.

He tells us that he stumbled on the theory by accident while studying the pre-Arabic place names in the region, made possible by the first comprehensive Saudi gazateer of place names published in Riyadh in 1977. Nearly all the biblical place names are concentrated in an area roughly 350 by 150 miles. All the coordinates of the places involved, as described in the Bible, are also traceable there – which is more than can be said of Palestine.

Salibi compared the pre-Arabic names with the original unvowelled Hebrew texts which scholars had often unwittingly misconstrued. A case in point is the word translated as "Egypt" – *msrym* in the original unvocalised script. He believes that, in some contexts, it clearly does mean Egypt, but that in other crucial passages, it refers to the area around the southern Asir villages of Misrima and Al-Misr. The captivity of the Israelites was in this area, whence Moses led them on a wandering route before Joshua finally conducted them across *hyrdn* (the Ridge), translated in the Bible as Jordan, into the Promised Land. Tehom, usually translated as "the deep", really refers to the Tihama, the coastal desert that runs along the Red Sea shore.

The four ancient Biblical place names still found in Israel were carried there by nostalgic migrants from west Arabia, when the focus of Jewish history switched to Palestine around 500 BC. Archaeological findings like the Maobite stone, the Lachish ostracha and the Gezer calendar prove no more than that the Jews were among the inhabitants of the Palestine area before this time. The issue can be decided when the Saudis agree to excavations in the Asir, which is rich in uninvestigated ancient sites. Even if Salibi's theory is incorrect, he has certainly uncovered a wonderful simulacrum! *Sunday Times*, 12, 19, 26 Aug; *Telegraph* 13 Aug; Belleville *News-Democrat*, 1 Sept 1984.

ANTICS ON ARARAT

In August 1984, one of the longest-running and dottiest mysteries was in the news again when the Turkish government seized some Noah's Ark 'samples' from an American fundamentalist. "I accept", wrote Fort, "that anybody who is convinced that there are relics upon Mt. Ararat, has only to climb up Mt. Ararat, and he must find something that can be said to be part of Noah's Ark, petrified perhaps."

Evidence is very obliging, especially to the convinced. There are over a hundred flood legends from every continent on the earth, at least twenty of which involve escape to a mountain in a vessel. The location of the 'Mount Ararat' in Genesis is not established, the present mountain of that name being named after it around the fourth century AD. Perhaps the earliest report of the stranded boat comes from a Babylonian historian in 275 BC, who stated that the ark of Xisuthros was still to be seen in the Kurdish mountains of Armenia, and the remains have been turning up ever since. (See Rickard and Michell's *Phenomena*.)

Mount Ararat, now Mount Agri (16,945 feet) stands on the borders of Turkey, Iran and Soviet Armenia. The arkeology bonanza was stopped in 1972 when the Turks closed it to foreigners after Soviet complaints that expeditions had included cover for spying missions.

James Irwin, an astronaut with the Apollo 15 lunar mission in 1971 and a born-again Christian, requested permission for an Ark search on the mountain in 1977, which was refused. Gradually winning the confidence of President Evren over several visits, he was allowed up in

August 1982. Fifty-three years old with two heart attacks behind him, Irwin fell and lay unconscious for several hours on his first attempt. He tried again a month later, but found nothing.

In August 1984, quite a few fundamentalists were clambering over the mountain looking for the 450 foot boat of gopher wood which had been stranded for 4,333 years. On the north face were Professor John Morris, Don Barber and Hali Husrevoglu of the US Institute of Creation Research. On the south face were James Irwin of the High Flight Foundation of Colarado Springs (on his third attempt), accompanied by John Christianson and Dick Bright. Tagging along were Ron Wyatt, a nurse-anesthetist and member of the Loud Cry of Nashville Tennessee; and the team from US International Expeditions led by Marvin Steffens, 54, of Monroe, Louisiana (on his fourth attempt), his wife Marjorie and daughter Marianne, along with Louis McCollum, Tim Brentley, and Bulent Atalay of Turkey.

On 22 August Irwin showed Steffens and Wyatt a rock simulacrum shaped like a boat 5,200 feet up the south-west face which had originally been photographed by Turkish journalist Ara Guler in 1959, following a tip from Turkish military cartographers. It was the necessary 300 cubits (roughly 450 feet) long, and Guler's photograph had appeared in numerous publications including *Life* magazine. "Definitely not Noah's Ark" said Professor Morris.

Irwin went off to explore the northern side of the mountain near the peak, while Wyatt and Steffens took samples from the 'boat'. On the 25 August Steffens held a press conference in Ankara, brandishing his plastic bags of clay and two pieces of 'soft wood': after which he disappeared, and Turkish border guards were alerted to prevent him taking his booty out of the country.

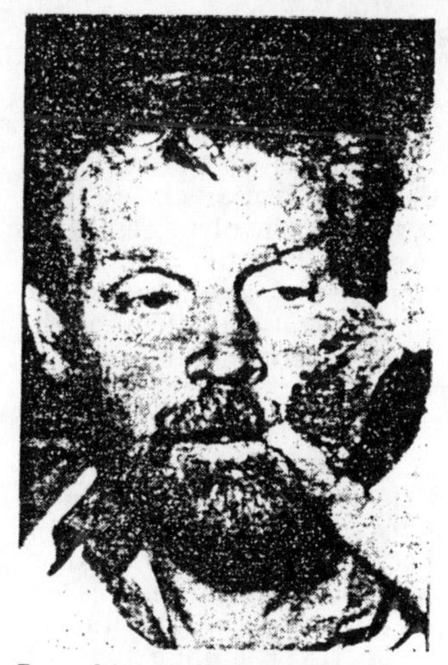

Ron Wyatt holds up one of his "Ark fragments" in a New York press conference, August 1984. [AP Photo]

Two days later, Wyatt turned up in New York with *his* samples, which were to be analysed at Galbraith Laboratories in Knoxville, Tennessee. Steffens was not so lucky. On 29 August he was detained three hours with his family at Istanbul airport and his 8.6 pounds of samples seized. Mukerrem Tascioglu, the Turkish minister of culture and tourism, announced that they were only rocks and soil, not wood, and of no historical value.

"... and here I have one already completed!"

The same day, the *Daily Mail* in London reported that London opthalmologist Barry Burbrett, 38, who makes annual trips to Mount Ararat, had been shot and robbed by shepherds and crawled naked for three days before being found by a villager and flown home. No connection was drawn with Biblical research. Irwin, Wyatt and Steffens all announced that they intend to go looking again later.

Meanwhile, a creationist museum is being built near the Paluxy River, west of Glen Rose, Texas, to the shape and dimensions of Noah's Ark. The organizer, Carl E. Baugh, president of International Baptist College, gained attention in 1982 when he claimed to have found human footprints among fossilized dinosaur tracks near the Paluxy River. The money for the new Ark is coming largely from born-again Fort Worth millionaire T. Cullen Davis. St. Louis *Globe-Democrat* 27 Jan, (R) 29 + (UPI) 30 Aug; St. Louis *Post-Dispatch* (AP) 26+30 Aug; Boston *Sunday Globe* (R) + *S.Express* 26 Aug; Dallas *Morning News* (AP) 26+28 Aug; Belleville *News-Democrat* (UPI) and Lewiston, Maine, *Daily Sun* (AP) 28 Aug; *D.Telegraph* (R) 28+30 Aug; *D.Mail* 29 Aug; *Scotsman* (AP) 30 Aug; Houston, TX, *Chronicle* 9 Sept; *New Scientist* 22 Nov 1984. And *Arkansas Gazette* (AP) 31 Dec 1983.

In 1985, 73 foreigners, 68 of them American, have sought permission to go Ark-hunting on Ararat. Among them is Ron Wyatt, who claims that analysis of his samples showed that they were decayed wood between 5,500 and 5,900 years old. The Huntsville (AL) *Times*, 18 April 1965.

VISIONS: FIND THE LADY

BVM fever, of a sort, broke out in the tiny French market town of Montpinchon (Manche), when the inhabitants were caught up in a "paroxysme" of excitement over a surpise visit by the Virgin Mary, or at least something that was mistaken for her, encountered down the spooky village lanes.

As far as we can decipher, the panic had a very dubious beginning, involving as it did two youths from a travelling circus, and a quite unsatisfactory end. But then, as the village postman admitted to a reporter a few days later, the region has a strong tradition of folklore and rustic 'healers', and the villagers were superstitious and ready to believe in the slightest wonder. Anyway, on the evening of Friday, 14th Sept 1984, the two boys, Yvanof Gayet, 16, and his cousin, claimed to have seen brilliant streaks of white light which coalesced into the shining form of the Virgin Mary "with blonde hair and without legs". The boys said the figure's hands moved and pointed, and the light was so bright the features of the face could not be made out. One of their companions, a 16yr-old trapeze-girl called Marion Beautour, said she threw a stone at the figure but the stone was deflected away from it.

The next day – 15th Sept – news of this wonder spread through the 528-strong community. Large crowds gathered at the scene, and nearby the only bar in town did a roaring trade. Soon the apparition wasn't the only thing haunting the lonely lanes. And so they waited each evening for four days, roaming the village streets and the surrounding countryside in expectation. At about 10.30pm on Tuesday, 18th Sept, a group of six women and young girls decided to wander down a particularly eerie lane, lined with thickets and trees, close to a cemetery. As they were returning they found their way barred by a shining "white lady". Josiane Halbout, a mother of nine children, fainted, and, with the cries of alarm from the others, the apparition disappeared. One of the girls, named only as 14yr-old Fabienne, said the figure was dressed in "a long white robe" and flapped its arms around.

Fabienne's mother wasn't the only one who thought it sounded like someone trying to scare the daylights [an odd

BITS AND PIECES

According to Dr Martin Kurtz, of the New York Health Dept, bites from humans are on the increase, and now considered second only to dog bites in seriousness. Human bites become infected quickly, and are usually in seriously disfiguring places. NY is the only city that requires doctors to record human bites, and for the last year they noted 1,581 – an increase of 77% over six years – and probably as many again are never reported. Just last year in the city an angry soccer player bit a chunk out of a referee's nose, and two men lost their sex organs and two women parts of breasts in biting incidents. Here are a few recent cases from our own files... *D.Mail* 5 Oct; *Weekly World News* 13 Nov 1984.

★ Jilted husband Jimmy Brown bit the nose off his wife's boyfriend, chewed it and then swallowed it. "I wanted to scar him for life," he told police. Chelmsford Crown Court jailed him for three years. *Sun, D.Mirror* 31 May 1984.

★ Pensioner Francis Proctor, 73, said he was merely kissing Darcia McKenzie, 43, goodbye, but her boyfriend, George Weeks, 47, thought there was too much life in the old dog and bit off his ear during a fight. He told Southwark Crown Court that he remembered biting something but had no idea it was an ear. He said the ear must have come off "accidentally" as Proctor struggled to run away. He picked it up to "give it back" but Proctor had gone, so he tossed it into the dustbin. Proctor himself had no idea his ear was missing – until several days later when his wife, a nurse, pointed out the fact. *Shropshire Star* 15 June 1984.

★ Police in Stockton, Cleveland, are seeking a small blond-haired Teddy Boy, who went berserk in a pub. The youth suddenly jumped upon Harry Welsh, 37, for no apparent reason, sank his teeth into Harry's nose, and then bit him all over his body. The Ted then ran off before stunned onlookers could seize him. Mr Welsh is in hospital for surgery and skin grafts. *D.Mirror* 14 Aug 1984.

★ Dewi Hitchcock, an army lieutenant and student at Pembroke College, Cambridge, appeared before the city magistrates charged with biting off Paul Wells' ear. *Telegraph* 30 Oct 1984.

★ Lawrence Mark Cullen, 24, of Swansea, was jailed for two years for biting off William Powell's nose outside a pub. He had been jailed in 1981 for a similar nose-biting offence. *Telegraph* 19 Dec 1984.

★ 21 young women in Sumatra complained to police that a man had bitten their necks to draw blood. Ah, but we'll have to leave more vampire stories to another time! *Western Mail, Guardian* 14 Jan 1984.

★ There were other incidents in the mid-six-months of 1984 that we all omitted to clip. Shame on us!

term that] out of the foolish. She said she would believe it if she saw it herself; that's not a proven criterion for judgement of reality, but we know what she meant, and many shared her suspicion of the 'phantom' episode. Others extended their scepticism to the entire affair. Without much concern for its dubious origins many villagers used the excitement as an excuse for a bit of a carnival, drinking and laughing and talking over other strange stories. Mrs Halbout was dissuaded by her doctor from wandering down dark lanes again.

There were no more sightings – too many people and too much noise, said the wise ones. By the 20th, the gendarmes decided to investigate, starting by tracing those who thought they witnessed something. "It is the first time we have done anything like this and it leaves me perplexed," admitted one policeman. The religious authorities kept a very low profile, and made no official comment. Our French correspondent, Jean-Louis Brodu, told us of his suspicions that the story might have been started as part of a 'circulation war' between rival provincial newspapers. Even if that were true, he pointed out, this kind of social hysteria falls justifiably into our sphere of interest. *Courier de l'Ouest* 21 Sept; *France Soir* 22 Sept 1984.

JOURNEY TO THE INTERIOR

Hilda Austin veered off a mountain road between Melbourne and Sydney and thought she was driving through a very long tunnel. She followed the twisting passages for six hours until she ran out of petrol. Fortunately, she had been spotted, and was rescued by police from the opencast coalmine. *Weekend*, 23-29 Jan 1985.

TEXAS WORM TURNS

For about an hour in the afternoon of Friday, 13th July 1984, a 20-foot-long, 2-foot-high bulge stretched the surface of a street in Fort Worth, Texas. The bulge "looked like a giant earthworm was trying to come up from under the road. It stayed up for a while, and it swayed back and forth. It seemed almost alive" said Charlie McCafferty from the fire department. "What spooked me was there wasn't even a crack in the road."

Street crews used jackhammers to break through the street's two inches of asphalt and four inches of concrete. They found silt layers intact, and no evidence of a gas build-up that might have caused the bulge. Firemen who arrived after the bulge had gone thought their colleagues were either drunk or crazy. Schenectady, NY, *Gazette*, 16 July 1984.

This report was re-cycled six months later by one Frank Kendal in the *National Examiner* (12 Feb 1985), and extended into a lurid fortean yarn: 20 FOOT EARTHWORM TERRORIZES CITY. . .SWALLOWS DOGS ran the headline. Shortly after the above event, we are told, a strange disturbance in the ground was spotted on a homestead on the outskirts of Fort Worth. Called to the spot by his three children, Calvin Lang prodded the bulge with a rake, and the spreading mound disappeared. Looking round he noticed buildings had been mysteriously ripped apart, fences torn down and shrubs and trees uprooted.

Later, Jeremy Boiter reported spotting what appeared to be a giant tentacle erupting from the ground about two miles away. "Suddenly this terrible thing sprang from the ground in a shower of gravel and dirt" he reported. "Then it seized a cat and her litter of kittens and devoured them in seconds. I wanted to be sick, to run away. Two snapping and growling dogs then approached the monster. And – and I couldn't believe my eyes [nor we our ears] – it engulfed the dogs in its slick and dripping mouth and swallowed them whole." Boiter screamed and ran three miles to the home of his friend Phil Dewar. When they returned to the site, they found scraps of birds, rabbits and other wild animals among the rubble of a destroyed hut.

A VANISHING PILOT?

At 1 am on Tuesday, 26 February 1985, Richard Michael Brownell, 27, and his fiancée Sandra O'Grady, 25, left a Newport Beach, California, bar with another man after they had told friends that they had paid him £90 to fly them to Vegas for a spot of gambling. An hour later, a single-engine Cessna 152 two-seater plane plummeted into the Pacific off Newport Beach. The bodies of Brownell and O'Grady, neither of whom could fly a plane, were found strapped to the seats. No engine faults could be found that might account for the crash, and three separate ocean searches failed to find a third body. A post mortem revealed traces of alcohol and cocaine in both bodies.

A car belonging to the plane's owner was found near the plane's tie-down spot at John Wayne Airport. Authorities had been unable to trace him, and refused to divulge his name. Detectives theorised that Brownell and O'Grady had been victims of an elaborate airborne mugging. "We discovered that the dead people were carrying something like 3,000 dollars in cash when they set out" said Lieutenant Richard Olsen of Orange County sheriffs deparment. "But they had no money on them when we fished them out of the ocean – just some change." Although the plane was a two-seater, there was a small space behind the seats where a third person could ride "if all three passengers were of light build and the one behind the seats was in the foetal position."

If the mugging theory is correct, where was the third person when the plane crashed, and how did he/she escape? The plane does not normally carry parachutes, and with a third person on board there would have been very little room for one. Olsen admitted total bafflement. Joseph Trainor, who sent us the original clipping on this, comments: "I wonder if the mysterious pilot is some sort of variant, a particularly deadly one, of the 'phantom hitchhiker'. A fellow hires a pilot for the day. Off they go in a Cessna. As soon as they hit 20,000 feet, the figure at the yoke vanishes!" Duluth, MN, *News-Tribune & Herald*, 1 Mar; *S.Express*, 28 April 1985.

CHESHIRE CATSEYES

In September 1984, 250 catseyes disappeared from roadworks near Grantham in Lincolnshire. A month later, 114 catseyes marking the Suffolk-Norfolk border at Bungay disappeared. A month after that, 120 went from the side of the road near Tilshead, Wiltshire, where they had been left for cleaning. Is some specialist mania being acted out...or a secret highway being constructed? Or, perhaps, somewhere, a fall of catseyes goes unrecorded. Any further into to the editor please. *D.Mirror*, 26 Sept, 30 Oct & 30 Nov 1984.

GNOME GNASTIES

Andy Johnson has gone into production in his dead-gnome factory, in Merthyr Tydfil, South Wales. Varieties include gnomes with spears through their bodies, hatchets in their heads, beheaded and hanged gnomes. They are prone, with faces twisted in agony, 18 to 24 inches tall and made of cast concrete.

"Many people dislike gnomes that stand up in gardens" he said. "Why should they be standing up all day doing nothing, when they could be dying and entertaining people?" *Western Mail*, 23 Nov 1984.

NAME GAMES

A delightfully named stationers and printers in Belfast. [Photo D.Telegraph, *26 Feb 1985.]*

The Phantom Lexilinker was having fun in November 1984. Smash and grab raiders escaped with gems worth £20,000 from a jeweller in Cheap Street, Newbury. Mrs Careless left her cheque card after buying theatre tickets in Reading, Berkshire. A tanker carrying heating oil overturned and began leaking its load onto Freezing Hill Lane, Wick, near Bristol. And *Autocar* magazine reported that the sales director of Sabaru UK, Richard Friend, had left the company 'on amicable terms'. *Mail* 17+20 Nov; *Bristol Evening Post* 22 Nov; *Telegraph* 23 Nov 1984.

★

A former mental patient from Georgetown County, South Carolina, was jailed for hitchhiking and resisting arrest. The next day he killed himself in his jail cell by stuffing his jogging shorts down his throat. He was Franklin Lee Funnye, 28. *Weekly World News*, 25 Sept 1984.

★

Judge Hilary Gosling got in a flap during a robbery trial after two pigeons flew into Stafford Crown Court and perched on his bench. He moved the trial to an empty room next door only to find a sparrow holding court. Portsmouth *News*, 29 Mar 1985.

This bus was photographed in Victoria, British Columbia. There was one passenger aboard, but he decided not to go along in case he couldn't find the right way back. D.Telegraph, *7 Sep 1982.*

A pig was killed on 17 February 1985 when it fell from a lorry on the M5 near Exeter and landed on the car bonnet of a 34-year-old secretary called Linda Hogg. *Sun, D.Express, D.Telegraph* etc, 18 Feb 1985.

★

Two babies born at around the same time on the same day to mothers called Anne Shaw in the same ward of Torbay Hospital, Devon, were both called Christopher. *D.Mail*, 17 Dec 1984.

SANDY SKIES

Red, brown or pinkish rains are not as rare as you might think over southern England. Other European countries, such as France (our colleague Jean-Louis Brodu has contributed a number of clippings on this to our files), seem to have at least as many instances as we do, perhaps more. The colouring agent, whether dust, grit or powder, is usually said to have been blown here from the Sahara desert.

Last year, 1984, there were at least four instances – two were mentioned last issue [FT43p10] – the last being a "reddish brown rain" containing sand particles which splattered south-eastern England on 9th November (*D.Telegraph* 10 Nov; *Sun* 12 Nov 1984). We have also commented from time to time that the declaration of the Sahara as the point of origin seems to be a reflex with meteorologists – but now we have some positive proof that this actually happens. The whole idea of Saharan dust storms over England was discussed in an article of that title by Dennis Wheeler, in *New Scientist* 14 February 1985, who refers to records of seven such occurrences in the last 80 years. (That seems too few to us.)

The key to these falls, says Wheeler, is the persistence of a pressure system and associated air-currents. Sandstorms were recorded in the western Sahara on 7th November. Meterological records, and satellite infra-red photography of western Europe, show that a low-pressure system, stationary over the Bay of Biscay from 4-8 November, allowed a southerly air-flow to persist for several days (see chart). In that period the winds, at altitudes above 5000 metres, were between 45-60 knots, needing only 2-3 days to transport material from North Africa to England, resulting in the November 9th dustfall.

It was difficult to estimate the quantity of fallen dust. In northeast England, where the fall was less intense, the deposition rate was estimated to be over 400 kilos per square kilometre. The mineralogy of the dust was typically Saharan – if the grains had not been flushed out of the clouds by rain, Wheeler muses, "the natural turbulence of the air could have kept such fine material in suspension indefinitely. This is the first instance, says

The weather chart for Western Europe on 8 Nov 1984 shows the stationary low in the Bay of Biscay, and the probable route (dashed line) of the sand-transporting winds. [Chart © New Scientist, *14 Feb 1985.]*

Wheeler, in which all the conditions necessary for a dustfall have been documented.

Meanwhile, according to AP reports dated 6&7 December 1984, meterologists in eastern America have noticed an increase in reddish dust deposits in their rainguages. A suitably (Shakespearean) named University of Miami professor, Joseph Prospero, suggests the increase corresponds with the spread of the drought in east Africa. Prospero's studies of "red mud rains" collected in Florida and Barbados shows that the dust is definitely African and the summer airborne concentrations are normally 10-100 more than in winter, but recent increases correspond with African droughts.

If windborne dust from Africa can reach northern Europe and the American Atlantic seaboard so regularly, two different routes must be involved. It is astonishing to think of jet-streams of dust travelling some 4000 miles from Africa to Florida, and it would surely be stretching things to explain dustfalls on the USA's west coast by the same mechanism. So when a large quantity of "sticky white powder" fell over 7000 square miles of southern California in mid-February this year, it was reassuring to find it explained locally. Thousands of people were alarmed when the "soupy rain", as thick as snow in some areas, covered cars and houses from Lancaster to Barstow, pitting the cars, and reducing visibility in the atmosphere to the consternation of pilots. A spokesman for the South Coast Air Quality Management District said the muddy rain was a combination of alkaline dust from the dry bed of Owens Lake, desert sand, and dirt blown into rain clouds by the 'Santa Ana' winds. One wonders how they could pinpoint the lake so precisely! *Seattle Times* 21 & 22 Feb 1985.

Sandy deposits left by rain in Bristol on 22 April 1984. One of four sand rains that year. [Photo © Western Mail, *23 April 1984.]*

FRUIT & NUT FALLS

Some of the strange "pink" beans which fell in Mrs Gibsons' garden at Topsham, Devon, in March 1983. [Photo © Exeter Express & Echo.*]*

Sometimes during the first week of March 1983, Mrs Rita Gibson, of Topsham, near Exeter, found a "scattering" of strange pink beans in her back garden. "They could not have been thrown," she says, "because our house is surrounded by three walls around a courtyard." But if they fell, where did they come from? The nearest Mrs Gibson could come to identifying the beans, which were larger than rice grains and smaller than orange pips – see photo – is that they looked a bit like iris seeds; but iris seeds are orange, not pink. Another oddity is that the seeds/beans are quite out of season. Mrs Gibson adds: "They do not look like last year's because they are fresh, not dried out." Exeter *Express & Echo* 12 March 1983.

◆ During the night of 8/9th November 1984 the residents of East Crescent, Accrinton, in Lancashire, were bombarded with apples – best quality Bramleys and Coxes. Derek and Adrienne Haythornwhite found at least 300 on their back lawn, on the path and in their hedges, and more were found in neighbours' gardens. The couple were woken up during the night "by thundering noises on the roof." Derek said: "When I looked out, I thought they were giant hailstones. Then I rubbed my eyes and saw they were apples." Adrienne thought they might be falling from a plane, and went outside to check. Most of the obvious explanations for this phenomenon founder on a single observation. Adrienne said: "They kept on falling for an hour or longer." *D.Mail* 10 Nov 1984.

TWO FIERY FATES

Last winter there were two remarkable reports of women bursting into flames, which sound very like scenarios of the classical but still hypothetical notion of spontenous human combustion (SHC). By 'hypothetical notion' I mean that the term SHC is purely descriptive of what happens, and that however indisputable the facts of the phenomenon there is still a lack of any testable theory to account for them.

So...our first story is almost Dickensian in its timing and simplicity. Late on Christmas Eve 1984, Mrs Christine Middlehurst, 36, ran screaming from her house in Drake Road, Newton Abbot, Devon. A neighbour, who lives opposite, saw she was smouldering and helped her back into the house, up to the bathroom, and put her into a bath of water. As she did so, Mrs Middlehurst's skin "floated off". Another neighbour, Mrs Elaine Fox, told the *Western Morning News* (27 Dec 1984): "It was the most terrible thing I'd ever seen." As far as she knew of the evening's events Mrs Middlehurst and her common-law husband, Martin Folan, had friends in for drinks, and after the friends left Mr Folan went upstairs, where the couple's two children, aged 11 and 16, were asleep. "Christine was sitting in the lounge when whatever happened happened," said Mrs Fox. "Even Martin doesn't know what happened. He came downstairs and she was in the sitting room, near the corner unit, on fire. He threw water over her and shouted for help." Mr Folan was burned about his hands, arms and body as he tried to beat out the flames, which is some indication of the intensity of the fire.

Det. Insp. Dave Westlake, of Newton Abbot CID, said: "What happened is a complete mystery. We won't know until we can talk to Mrs Middlehurst." She was rushed to Torbay Hospital suffering 50% burns, and later transferred to a hospital in Plymouth, where a few days later she was said to be "improving" and the police were waiting to question her – but we 've not heard the outcome of that interview. DI Westlake also revealed that the mystery blaze which turned her into a human torch left the house "virtually untouched". Additional sources: Exeter *Express & Star, D.Star* 27 Dec 1984.

● The fiery affliction proved fatal in our second case, which, as far as we can discover, began on 28th January this year. Jacqueline Fitzsimons, a 17yr-old cookery student at Halton Technical College, Widnes, Cheshire, left the kitchens on her break and was talking to friends in a corridor when she complained of a burning on her back. One of the friends, Karen Glenholmes (quoted unreliably in the *Globe* 19 March 1985), said: "We were chatting when...suddenly, Jacqueline said she did not feel well. There was a smell of smouldering and we saw her skirt burning. She screamed to us for help and said she was burning all over. In a moment even her hair was on fire." At this stage we have no authoritative version of what went on, but certainly she was not then "burned to a cinder" as the *Globe* went on to say.

According to snatches of testimony that filtered through to the papers from the inquest, held at Whiston, Merseyside, on 22 February, immediately after the girl complained of the burning sensation on her back, the friends around her pulled off her cooking apron and found her knitted jumper alight. Staff and students joined in trying to stifle the flames as the girl screamed in pain and fear. The injuries were severe – 18% skin loss – and Jacqueline died on 12 February after 15 days in intensive care at Whiston Hospital. One curious element in the inquest was the attitude of Cheshire fire prevention officer Bert Gilles, who admitted that investigating officers were stumped enough to look into the SHC hypothesis. Mr Gilles said: "I have interviewed seven eyewitnesses. So far there is no clear explanation of the fire ...We must look for other causes like spontaneous combustion." Giving us an interesting insight into the official view of SHC, he added, "Spontaneous combustion is a theory most of us have previously treated highly skeptically, but it should be examined."

What puzzled forensic investigators was the "complete mystery" of the origin of the fire. At first it was thought the fire might have lingered in her clothing after she had accidentally leaned over a cooker, but this line of reasoning seems to have been quickly abandoned because of an inescapable fact. Jacqueline had been wearing a protective apron when she collapsed in flames, but it was the clothing *underneath* the apron which ignited first. To SHC-buffs this suggests the fire came from within or on her, not from outside. Because of the "other possibilities" raised by Mr Gilles, the coroner adjourned the inquest the same day, ordering an investigation into the tragedy involving the police, fire chiefs and the Government's Health and Safety Executive.

The inquest resumed four months later with an astonishing admonition from the coroner, Gordon Glasgow, to the jury. He warned them specifically to ignore any speculation or suggestion that Jackie's death was due to SHC. Detective Sergeant Geoffrey Able who interviewed Jackie in hospital said she told him: "I must have been standing too near the cooker. I was right next to it. I may have been leaning on it. We had left the gas rings on to the warm the classroom." Home Office pathologist Philip Jones flatly ruled out SHC. He told the court that "the necessary chemical reactions required were not evident", whatever he means by that. On the other hand, he said, tests showed that Jackie's clothing could smoulder for "a few minutes" after catching fire.

In view of the coroner's warning, it was inevitable that the jury gave a verdict of 'Misadventure'. But we feel quite disatisfied; the whole proceedings seem to have been designed to reassure officials who prefer tidy processes and endings. We know, to the contrary, that there is an unruly side to our existence which many find too frightening to contemplate. How do the "experts" equate clothing which merely smouldered with the fact of Jackie in flames severe enough to cause fatal burns? By all accounts Jackie had been wearing a heavy protective apron, how then did the fire start underneath it? We are not told. Instead we are asked to take, as an undeniable and accurate explanation, the *suppositions* of a shocked girl on her deathbed (and for all we know, in answer to leading questions) that she *might* have leaned on a burning stove. We'd like to know a lot more before we can accept that, or SHC. *Mail on Sunday* 24 Feb; *Western Mail, D.Express, The Scotsman, Shropshire Star, D.Telegraph* 25 Feb; *Sun* + "local paper" (?), 29 June 1985.

AMERICAN ALLIGATOR WAVE

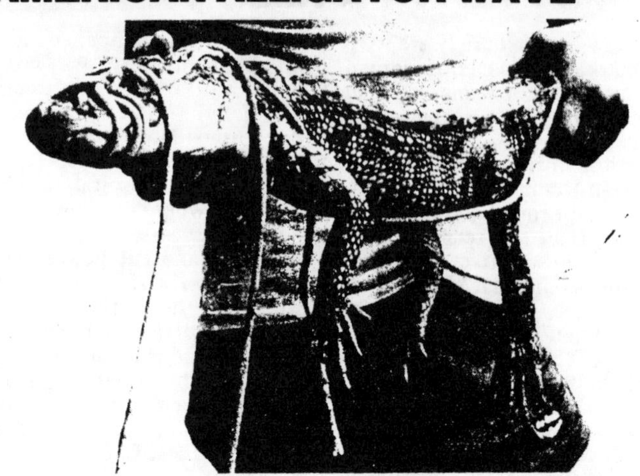

One of the three alligators from Massapequa. [Photo © Don Norkett, Newsday, *28 Dec 1984.]*

A four-foot long, thirty-pound, American alligator was spotted in Grand Lagoon, south of the Massapequa Preserve on Long Island, about 25 miles east of downtown Manhatten. It was caught with ropes by Nassau County police around 11am, 19 July 1984, and sent to the Bronx zoo. Cathy Caivano, a local resident, said: "We heard rumours that someone had thrown it in the water on Friday the 13th, but this is the first I've seen of it."

On 1st August, two more alligators were seen in Carroon Lake, across Merrick Road in the Massapequa Preserve. These ones eluded immediate capture. Police reported another sighting on the morning of 3rd August. Local children claimed to have seen as many as five of them, while an anonymous caller to the Long Island newspaper, *Newsday*, said he had put seven in the lake, and would continue to put one in each day until something was done about the high taxes in Nassau County.

Early in the morning the next day, a Federal game warden trapped two alligators in the lake. One was four feet, the other two feet, long. It was generally assumed that they had been brought from the south as babies and released in the lake. (AP) *Newsday*, NY, 20 July, 2+4 Aug; Duluth, MN, *News-Tribune and Herald* 20 July; Portland, Maine, *Press Herald* 3 Aug; *New York Times* 5 Aug 1984.

● On 6th August, 11-year-old Robert Crespi was swimming in the St Lucie River in Florida when he was seized by a twelve-and-a-half-foot alligator, and carried down the river. Police shot at the creature and the boy was released – but he was already dead. Later the reptile was bagged. It was the sixth alligator death in Florida since 1957. Once an endangered species protected by stringent state and Federal laws, the Florida alligator has made a spectacular comeback over the past decade. Their number is now believed to exceed a million. (AP) *New York Past* and Portland, Maine, *Evening Express* 7 Aug; *USA Today* and *St Louis Post-Dispatch* 8 Aug; Belleville, IL, *News-Democrat* 19 Aug 1984.

● On 10th August, police in Aurora, Colorado, arrested a three-foot-four-inch alligator as it crawled across a street. The

Highline Canal was about a mile away, while the nearest large body of water, Cherry Creek Reservoir, was over five miles (UPI) Plattsburgh, NY, *Press Republican* 11 Aug 1984.

● On 14th August, two men angling for catfish in the Humbolt Park Lagoon, Chicago, caught a two-pound, one-and-a-half-foot-long South American caiman, a smaller but meaner cousin of the alligator. It was taken to an isolation tank at the Lincoln Park Zoo. The fishermen reported seeing another one, twice the length, but this was treated as "a traditional fish tale". (AP) *USA Today,* Duluth, MN, *Herald,* Belleville, IL, *News-Democrat,* and *Boston Globe* 16 Aug 1984.

● On 31st August, Susan Turek, 30, dived into her swimming pool in Plantation, Florida, and surfaced to find a two-and-a-half-foot alligator staring her in the face. Her pool is about two blocks from a canal. (AP) Waterville-Winslow, Maine, *Morning Sentinal* 1 Sept 1984.

KANGAROO AGGRO

A large red kangaroo, over 6 feet tall, appeared at a barbecue at the village of Nungaloo (?Narngulu) near Geraldton, Western Australia, on 10th April 1985, and chased some children. Then it grabbed the throat of Katie Schmidt, 12, with its paws and sank its teeth into her head and ear. Her father Wayne Schmidt, 40, rushed to the rescue and was bitten twice on the right arm and had his clothing ripped. Finally Kevin Hopper pulled out a fence post and bludgeoned the 'roo to death. He pointed out that Katie was very lucky it was backed up against a car. If it had been able to use its back legs, it could have killed her. (AP) *Standard, Middlesborough Evening Gazette*, 10 April; *D.Express, Times,* 11 April 1985.

■ I'm reminded of another attack by a six-footer three years ago. Train driver Danny Pocock, 59, left his home in Wycheproof, Northern Victoria, at 6am to walk the 60 yards to the station when he saw the 'roo in the garden. It bounded up behind him and knocked him to the ground. He warded it off with his lunchbox, ran along the tracks to the station and hid in the stationmaster's office, *but the 'roo waited for him outside.* It was shot by a local policeman, who commented that the drought was making them aggressive. *Guardian* 20 July 1982.

TREASURE AND THE LIZARD

Mario Angelucci, 67, was convinced that the two-tailed lizard he found while repairing the foundations of his house in Bachero di Cingoli, near Florence, was a sign of good luck. He refused to hand it over to Authority, in the form of biologists at the local university, and would not even let them near his house. Keeping his lizard as a companion, Mario dreamt one night that Roman soldiers were marching past his house, as indeed they had done 2,000 years before.

In the dream, one of the Roman soldiers said to Mario: "Go 15 meters into your field behind your house and dig down 60 centimeters." When Mario awoke he followed the instructions...and – you guessed – treasure! A hoard of Roman gold coins, now worth £30,000. Said Mario: "I knew that lizard was a good luck sign. I might never have believed the dream if I hadn't believed in the powers of a lizard with two tails." *S.Express*, 30 Dec 1984.

This story sounds rather too pat to be true, but we keep an open mind as usual. We are put in mind of Liu Hai's encounter with the three-legged toad, and the good fortune which followed his acceptance of the creature as his Ally.

A FAUSTIAN ORDEAL

William Faust, 25, of Torrance, California, was driving along Topanga Canyon late on Sunday, 20 January, when he pulled over at a rural building site for a pee. He kicked idly at some plywood and fell into a 30-feet-deep cesspool. Not long afterwards a gopher fell in as well, and Faust spent the next 13 hours fighting off the irate creature. "It kept charging me. I had to fend it off all night." Workmen rescued him in the morning.(AP) St Louis *Post-Dispatch, Standard,* 22 Jan 1985.

CHIMP CAPERS

A chimpanzee stowed away on a Danish freighter at an African port, and thrived on bananas and whisky during the voyage to Hamburg. It played with the crew at sea, but once land was sighted it climbed a mast and evaded capture. *Guardian*, 10 Nov 1984.

● Zippy, another chimp, escaped in New Orleans wearing tennis shoes and blue underwear. Police found him riding around with four teenagers in a van. They had found him outside a grocery shop puffing at a cigar. *Express & Star*, 6 Dec 1984.

SNAKE SNACK

George Cabasco, 27, had a hearty meal in a restaurant in Baguio City, Philippines. Then he went into the kitchen and dropped a nine-inch snake into a bowl of soup, hoping to get his meal for free after lodging a complaint. He was caught by restaurant staff, but while a policeman was taking down his statement he swallowed the snake, and said "Where is your evidence?" He was set free. (R) St Louis *Post-Dispatch*, 14 Oct 1984.

MORE PHOTOS OF THE GODS

Our feature – in FT36 – on some varieties of photographic images, believed by many people and religious organizations to be, literally, photographs of Jesus or other divine entities, was well received. Our inevitable conclusion, while appraising the many conflicting claims about the origin of these images, was that they formed a genre of rumour, and have all the characteristics of what we have taken to calling 'foaflore' – ie the principal in the story is always an unfindable friend-of-a-friend (foaf) or equivalent, no matter how seemingly genuine are the foaf's credentials. Well, our interest in the subject continues, and we have a further two variations – one familiar, and one new – to add to the collection.

CHRIST

★ Firstly – as you'll see from photo A – we have another version of the image Bob Rickard called 'Christ in the Clouds II'. This one is obviously an enlargement of the figure of interest – a robed man, head obscured by clouds, with arms outstretched downwards – the surrounding areas having been heavily cropped. The shape and detail of the image differs from the versions labeled 'Image K' and 'Image L' on p39 of FT36. The new version we present here, was sent to us by reader Heather Zais, of Kelowna, British Columbia, in business as a psychic. Heather writes that according to her information the photo was "taken by a fellow in Edmonton, while he was flying in Kamloops, BC."

Photo A. Fortean Picture Library.

★ This is an appropriate place to correct two errors in the 'Photo of the Gods' piece in column two of p38 in FT36. On line 4, 'Fig K' should be **'Fig A'**; and in the first line of the paragraph headed 'Tattler Tales', **'[Fig K]'** should be inserted after '....this image'.

BUDDHA

★ Photo B was – according to our Bangkok reader, Peter Bennett – widely circulated in Thailand at the end of 1982 and throughout 1983, and was believed to be a genuine photo of the Buddha. Peter managed to obtain one of the postcard-sized photos for us which includes a halo-like circle around the head which was not included in the illustration in the Thai magazine article he also sent. Peter also commented on the pose and robe of the figure, and the face of the figure, being more Indian-looking than Thai.

The original magazine article on this phenomenon, sent by Peter, was quite impenetrable to us, and he very kindly had a friend translate it for us. The Englished version was complicated by poor handwriting, so perhaps it is best if we summarize it from 'The Mystery of Buddha's Image' in issue 1 of *Saksidhi Magazine* (March 1983). Apologies are offered in advance if we get the strange Thai names wrong. . .

The author of the article, Chedi Thong, refers to the general excitement created by the image; many people have framed it "for the purpose of paying their respects", and framed copies are even to be found on altars and tables among other "relics" in temples. Because of the general interest in the image, *Saksidhi* assigned reporter 'Tripeteh' to find out what he could, but – and this point will seem significant to foaflorists – instead of discovering a single origin he found no less than *eleven* different accounts! Briefly, they are. . .

1) Mr Boonmei Methangkura, chairman of the Mongkolthip Foundation School, denied the rumour that he took the photo.

2) Dr Ard Ong Choomsai, a professor at Sri Nakarintaravirajna University, in Arachinburi province, also denied the rumour that he took the photo.
3) that a Buddhist monk at Somana Viharn Temple took the photo on a trip to the Sri Maha Bodhi Temple in Buddha Kaya, India, revered as the place where Gautama obtained his illumination.
4) that Luang Poo Sim, leader of the Buddhist Tham Pha Plong group, of Chiengmai District, a follower of the prominent exponent of meditation, Pra Acharn Man Bhurithat, is rumoured to have taken the photo at Chieng Dow Cave. He has denied this.
5) that another monk, Luang Por Maharvira Thavaro, of Tha Soong Temple, in Uthai Thani district, took a photograph in the Sri Maha Bodhi Temple, which after developing showed the Lord Buddha sitting on a platform.
6) that a woman of Arachinburi province took the photo.
7) that the 'photo' is in fact a painting by His Highness Krom Luang Chumporn Ket Udomsakdi, hanging in the royal palace. 'Tripeteh' comments that His Highness had a reputation for "supernatural powers" but artistic skill is not known to be one of them.
8) that, according to a rival magazine, a highly educated man took photographs in a cave in Krabi district, famous for its 'Buddha's footprint', at the same time praying for proof of Buddha's existence. When developed, his colour film showed 12 black and white frames of the Buddha, one of which showed "the heart on the left side of the chest". Is this a bit of Catholic imagery creeping into Buddhist iconography? The man has since renounced his profession and entered the priesthood.
9) that the photo was taken on top of the Wong Pa Chandra mountain in Lopburi district, on the night of Saturday 13th November 1982, at 7.40pm. The photographer was a young boy, of a prominent Thai family, among a group of pilgrims led by a medium. They paid their respects to the images of five devas, erected by the family in the temple at the foot of the mountain. The medium then invited the devas to possess him, and the group received instructions "through the medium" to take photos on the peak which should be made available to the public for worship. The group ascended the peak, performed rituals and took photographs, during which lightning struck the ceremonial site. Mysterious delays dogged the development of the film, and the prints could only be made after blessing ceremonies. Again we hear of B&W prints emerging from colour film.
10) that in 1981 a physician at a hospital in Bangkok attended a seminar in New Delhi. Although he was not a Buddhist, when the seminar was over he made a tour of holy places, ending up at Buddha Kaya, where he took accommodation at a Thai temple. The next day he observed a number of different ceremonies, one of which – a large group carrying candles – seemed so ridiculous to him that he could not refrain from a loud, mocking laugh. (This is the second story to equate a modern education with religious backsliding.) Later he fell asleep near the Maha Bodhi and heard a voice admonishing him for his ignorance and aimlessness. He awoke feeling resentful and turned to see a monk sitting with folded legs on a platform under the Maha Bodhi. "Who are you, and why did you wake me?" he asked. The monk's answer, says author Chedi Thong, "will give Buddhists a thunderous shock." The monk said: "I who know the Truth lives here." [That's as written here. It seems ambiguous. Perhaps "I, who knows the Truth, live here" or "I, who knows the Truth (still) lives here" is meant?] The atheistic doctor was shocked. The monk taught him various sutras until the doctor was converted to Buddhism. He asked for permission to take a photo, and the monk raised his hand in agreement and shortly after "faded away". The doctor was so convinced he

Photo B. Credit: Peter Bennett.

had encountered the Lord Buddha that he fervently practised his faith on return to Thailand. His family were socially embarrassed by the change in him and rejected him until he told them what had transpired and showed them his proof. This story, it is said, was revealed by Phra Kru Sratha Sopon, abbot of Wat Mai Sitthavas temple, in Uthong, Supanburi district, in whom the doctor had confided.

11) and finally that, according to Phra Kru Ba Wongsacharu, abbot of Wat Pra Buddhabat temple, Lampang district, one of his followers who lived in Dowkanong, Bangkok, visited the holy site at Buddha Kaya and took a photo of the stone platform in the Sri Maha Bodhi. As he did so, he wished he could see what the Buddha looked like. [This request features frequently in the folktales of the Far East.] The result was this photo. When he showed it to some Buddhist monks they agreed it was a miracle of faith and the Buddha's power. They pointed out that the figure's features were those of a "White Indian" being "elegant like a god". This account is given in a leaflet being sold with the photo at Wat Mahathat temple, Bangkok.

Note: the place transcribed as Buddha Kaya throughout this text is more usually known as Bodh Gaya.

A giant squid caught off the southwest coast of Japan, 10 feet 6 inches long, 35 inches in circumference, and weighing 112 pounds. The man lying beside it provides some idea of scale. [Photo © Le Provencal, *6 Feb 1985.]*

FALLING FISH

★ **Bonita, California** – Sometime in the third week of August 1984, A.D.Ellmers, his wife Neva, and a neighbour, Walter Davies, were whiling away the evening in the driveway of the Ellmers' home when small fish began falling all around them from a cloudless sky, with "harsh wet splats". They also fell into nearby gardens. Ellmers scooped up a few and put them in his freezer. Richard Rosenblatt, a marine biologist at Scripps Institute of Oceanography, heard the story on the news and contacted Ellmers to examine the fish. He identified them as a freshwater fish – thread fin shad, *Dorosoma petemense* – commonly used in lakes as food for bass. It was quickly established that the Sweetwater Reservoir, about two miles from the Ellmers' house, has a population of these fishes. Dan Floyd, a worker there, said he saw nothing like a funnel cloud which might have lifted them. The report favoured pelicans "dropping" the fishes during an aerial flight – but surely this would have been noticed by the picnickers below? San Diego (CA) *Union* 29 Aug; *Newsday* (NY) 30 Aug 1984.

★ **Los Angeles, California** – On the morning of 19th December 1984, drivers on the Santa Monica Freeway, near Crenshaw Boulevard, were making their way through a rainstorm when "fish and live crab suddenly appeared at the side of the road." – see photo. California Highway Patrol officers supposed that they fell off a restaurant supply truck. Although no one saw the fish fall during the rain, that is what we suspect happened. But...oh! that Joke God and his phenomenal puns. Fish and CHiPs...get it? *Los Angeles Times* 20 Dec; AP 21 Dec 1984.

These fish appeared on a Los Angeles freeway during a rainstorm on 19 Dec 1984. [Photo © Marsha Traeger, Los Angeles Times.*]*

★ **Yeovil, Somerset** – Golfers found a 7lb carp flopping in a puddle on the 17th fairway of the town's golf course. Officials of the club blamed recent flooding due to the melting snow swelling the River Yeo. They expect us to believe that the carp leapt out of a reservoir, about ten miles away, into the river which runs alongside it, and was beached on the course as the flood receded. The report does not confirm that the 17th fairway was actually under water for a while. We suppose anything is possible, but, equally the carp could have fallen. Stranger things have happened. *D.Mail* 1 Feb 1985.

★ **St Cloud, Minnesota** – Falls of starfish are very rare in the annals of strange showers. Last issue [FT43 p11] we told of a single starfish found after a rain of winkles on a garage at Thirsk, Yorkshire; now we can tell of a whole rain of them. As far as we can decipher from the report, there was a heavy rainstorm on the evening of 21 April 1985 in the St Cloud area. One couple noticed "a white thing with five legs" in their backyard, and turning on the outside lights noticed more on the lawn. "We even had one on the garage roof," said Lynn Dirks. Neighbour, Dr Mark Moberg, also found some in his garden. He explains in terms of a prank by students at St Cloud State University, about a mile away, suggesting that they threw the starfish off the top of Sherburne Hall there, the nearest tallest building when the winds were very strong. That sounds quite fishy to us. A University fish biologist, Steve Williams, who identified the creatures as ocean-dwellers from down Florida way, gave a different implausible explanation for fresh ocean starfish found west of the Great Lakes – he thinks they were stored frozen until an opportunity came up for a practical joke. Seems pretty pointless! Needless to say, we think they fell. Minneapolis (MN) *Star & Tribune* 24 April 1985.

PRIESTLY PREMONITION

Waking suddenly from an afternoon nap, Father Stanislaw Wenerski jumped up and yelled "Quick, get everybody out!" He hustled his housekeeper into the street from the vicarage (somehwere in Austria, unspecified) and then dashed into the 200-year-old church of St Jakob's next door. A few minutes later after he had ushered out worshippers and fellow priests, the church and the vicarage collapsed in a heap of rubble. Investigations showed that they were built above a cave, part of an ancient brickworks which nobody knew existed. *S.Express,* 9 Dec 1984.

ONCE MORE WITH FELINES

Our last round-up of alien big-cats (ABC) – we have decided to adopt this acronym – was in FT42 [p40-42], and there's been a lot of rustling in the undergrowth since then. Now some readers have expressed guarded objections to the amount of ABC material in previous issues. Those not interested in it have felt it was boring, irrelevant and took up space which might be better devoted to their own interests. Our task, as editors, is to balance those interests, so that in time everybody's interests are catered for. In another respect, it is out of our hands. We have always felt that FT should be a 'mirror for contemporary phenomena' (to paraphrase a subtitle of a 19th century periodical), and so we feel it our duty to reflect whatever is happening. The fact that mystery big cats are so frequent and so widely distributed (we haven't even touched upon the many US reports!), must surely indicate that this topic remains one of the biggest of contemporary unsolved mysteries. It is certainly one of the longest running, as our readers will know.

Nevertheless we have a huge mountains of clippings, and perhaps the best way to deal with them is to condense them drastically – and so, below, you'll find the essentials tabulated for those cases which have come to our attention since we left off in FT42. The only embellishments I'll add are the following brief notes:

- 1) among those cases which have featured killings of sheep and lambs, a striking feature is the almost complete demolition of the carcase, the bones picked clean, or remains almost completely devoured. See cases 4, 8, 19 20 (see photo), and 38.

These remains of a fully-grown lamb, found at Buckfastleigh, Devon [Case 20] seem typical of the spate of almost totally devoured livestock in the listed incidents. [Photo © Torbay News.*]*

- 2) Many livestock depredations are undoubtedly due to the ravages of dogs, foxes, etc., and these are represented here too. See the mini-saga in Somerset (cases 43-46), for a well-defined instance. Farmers can usually recognize the signs when dogs are the cause of livestock killings. Which makes the near-total devourings (1, above) something out of the ordinary.

- 3) In case 19, Devon naturalist Trevor Beer had been called to a site on Exmoor where he found the carcases of 12 deer, killed at different times; one very recently. While he was investigating Beer made his own sighting, which converted him from the ranks of those who dismissed the 'Exmoor Beast' as a feral dog. Beer was now in no doubt that the Exmoor Beast is a panther, and appealed publicly for sightings – the results appearing in his booklet (reviewed elsewhere in this issue). This new evidence altered his view even further, to the idea of there being more than one ABC in the area. He was widely quoted as saying: "We are getting reports of sightings far apart at almost the same time. And while many of the sightings are of a large, black panther-like creature, there are quite a lot of reports of a fawn-coloured beast. I believe there is a puma and a panther on the moor." See the List for the variety in descriptions (as reported).

- 4) The Isle of Wight ABC – cases 25-39 – stimulated two further invasions of the island; one led by ASSAP's regional coordinator, Clive Seymour, and the other by Terry Newton, both from London. Mr Newton was investigating on behalf of the British Big Cat Research Group, set up in Di Francis in the wake of her book on the subject. Despite extended camping in the rough, nothing much was established.

- 5) In the last months of 1984, the biggest ABC story by far was the encounter between Di Francis and what is claimed to be a big cat of a previously unknown species of wildcat. The 43 inch-long jet-black creature was allegedly shot while caught in a snare on Strathspey Estate, West-Moray, and later frozen. Several weeks later a similar creature was also trapped and stuffed, also on Speyside. A full report on these incidents is regretfully deferred to next issue.

● 6) The Devon village of Bere Alston (not listed below), near Plymouth, seems plagued by large unidentified cats, probably (but not certainly) of feral origin. The news of sightings, mostly old, was no doubt stimulated by the recent sightings of ABCs around Newton Abbot (cases 14-16). One 83yr-old man said he and his wife saw *two* jet-black ABCs in their garden about 15 years previously. When he was young, he said, he used to hunt semi-wild cats with his uncle and father. He said he first saw the large ABCs at Tregantle firing range, in south-east Cornwall, while on military guard duty *in the 1920s*. If this is verifiable, then the ABC problem is much older than we had anticipated. *Western Morning News* 1 Oct 1984.

● 7) At Ashurst, Surrey, (case 56), one of the "dogs" being sought for a deer killing was said to be like a collie with a white tip to its tail. White-tipped tails are quite common among dogs, but, according to Di Francis, are also a characteristic shared by one of her types of ABC.

● 8) The ravenous beast which ate most of a 70lb lamb at Buckfastleigh, Devon (case 20), chose the town made famous in Conan Doyle's *Hound of the Baskervilles*.

● 9) Since the famous puma capture at Cannich, Inverness-shire, in 1980 – see FT34p24f – there have been faint rumours that that was far from the last of it. Recently, Janet Chisholm, a 70-yr old retired post-mistress, who lives in the near-wilderness 20 miles west of Loch Ness, told of being a prisoner in her own home at night because of several ABCs which prowl around her cottage and hen-house. She claims: "From the different sizes and groups I've spotted, I reckon there could be up to 20 of them in the forest." It was Janet who made the first reports of the Cannich puma, and she was disbelieved then too. (Case 38). See also para 11, below.

Naturalist Trevor Beer's drawing of his own sighting of a greeny-yellow-eyed black panther-like beast on Exmoor [Case No 19]. From West Country Mysteries *reviewed elsewhere in this issue.*

● 10) In the midst of the Isle of Wight sightings (cases 25-39) an equally strange and un-cat-like sighting was made. On the morning of Sunday, 17th March 1985, a theatre critic for the island's *Weekly Post* (according to their edition of 22 Mar 1985) was jogging on Whitely Bank and was crossing a field when he came face to face with a wolf-like creature. At first he thought the animal was an Alsatian, but it wasn't. It was the size of "a massive dog", "greyish with traces of brown", and a "wolf-type head". Wolves have been extinct in the British wild, officially, since the 18th century. Another conundrum.

● 11) Two deaths, connected in some way or other... A few days after a good sighting in Scotland (case 57), and on the same day as, or the day after, the sighting on Exmoor (case 18), a "vandal" broke into a wildlife park in Bristol and shot dead a rare Scottish wild cat (*D.Telegraph* 30 Oct 1984). The Cannich puma (see note 8, above) was found dead in her cage at the Highland Wildlife Park, near Aviemore, Scotland, in the 1st week of February this year. The origin of this American puma was a mystery. She died in her sleep, "from old age". (Scottish *Daily Record* 7 Feb 1985.)

● 12) Finally, two coincidences (a word which hides the truly mystifying). Firstly, we note from a letter from Doc Shiels, dated the day of the Tehidy sheep killings (case 11): "Our Cornish 'mystery cat' hasn't been seen for a few weeks, but a Cornish naturalist has just been killed by a tiger in India. He was from the Scilly Isles, sometimes thought to be part of Lyonesse (lioness?)." And lastly, we had to smile when we noted that the principal witness in the Chiddingfold, Surrey, sighting (case 49) was a Di Francis namesake, a farmer named D. Francis!

•

THE LISTING

See the end for key to code usage, and sources.

ARGYLL

1– 84.? .? – **Kilmichael Forest.** Puma, C)black • 6) 27 Jan 85.
2– 84.? .? – **Knapdale area.** Puma, C)tawny.• 6) 27 Jan 85.
3– 84.D .? – **Lochgilphead area.** Puma, livestock killings, 2 sightings in 6 months, believed to be 3 animals. • 6) 27 Jan 85.
4– 84.Oct.? – **Craignish area.** Puma, sheep almost totally devoured, 14th in 6 weeks.• 6) 27 Jan 85.
5– 85.Jan.,C – **Achnamara.** Puma/leopard/jaguar, C)dark with a light stripe, big pawprint. • 6) 27 Jan 85.

CORNWALL

6– 84.Dec.A – **Stithians.** Leopard/puma, L)4ft, small head. •11) 8 Dec 84.
7– 84.Dec.A – **Truro.** Big-cat, C)sandy brown, long tail. • 11) 8 Dec 84.
8– 84.Dec.A – **Fraddon.** Sheep found almost completely devoured. • 11) 8 Dec 84.
9– 85.Jan.B – **Stithians.** Big-cat, C)dark, ref to two earlier sightings in 2 weeks. • 25) 17 Jan 85.
10– 85.Feb.?3 – **St Austell.** Puma, 2nd report in a week. • 12) 4 Feb 85.
11– 85.Mar.4 – **Tehidy.** 2 alsatians found savaging flock, one shot, the other traced to owner. 20 lambs and sheep killed.• 25) 7 Mar 85.

DEVON

12– 84.Apr.? – **Holcombe, nr Dawlish.** (Feral?) cats, plague of wildcats, S)twice normal, one big as dog. • 10) 4 May 85.
13– 84.Jly.C – **Yelverton, Dartmoor.** Black animal, S)large, hundreds of chickens killed.• 12) 30 Jly 84.
14– 84.Aug.5 – **Mile End, nr Newton Abbot.** Huge cat, C)tawny, S)fox. • 11) 14 Aug 84.
15– 84.Aug.6. – **Mile End, nr Newton Abbot.** Huge cat, C)tawny, S)fox.• 11) 14 Aug 84.
16– 84.Aug.13 – **East Orwell, nr Newton Abbot.** Leopard, C)brown, S)small, chasing pony. • 11) 14 Aug 84.
17– 84.Oct.C – **Brayford, nr Exmoor.** Panther C)black, watched for 5 mins by 3 men, S)alsatian. • 23) 26 Oct, 11)24) 27 Oct 84.
18– 84.Oct.28 – **North Molton, nr Exmoor.** Large-clawed paw-prints photographed. • 26) 1 Nov 84.
19– 84.Sep.D – **south edge of Exmoor.** Panther, C)black, sleek, long hind legs, small ears, green-yellow eyes, seen at location of 12 deer carcases, W)investigating naturalist. • 12)24) 2 Oct, 23) 5 Oct 84.
20– 84.Nov.?2 – **Buckfastleigh, nr Dartmoor.** Lamb almost totally devoured (see photo). • 11) 31 Oct, 3) 1 Nov 84.
21– 85. ?.?. – **Bish Mill, nr Exmoor.** Panther, C)black, powerful, W)naturalist. • 23) 21 Mar 85.
22– 85.May.? – **Wistlandpound Reservoir, nr Exmoor.** Panther, S)labrador, small ears, green/yellow eyes, leapt 8ft hedge. • 23) 31 May 85.

HAMPSHIRE: MAINLAND

23– 84.Oct.24 – **Warnford, Meon Valley.** 4 sheep killed, 9 injured. • 8) 26 Oct 84.
24–85.May.21 – **Bedhampton, nr Portsmouth.** Lynx, black tufted ears, puma-like, C)tan, L)4-5ft, in field. • 8) 21 May 85.

HAMPSHIRE, ISLE OF WIGHT

25– 85.Oct.B – **St Mary's Hospital, nr Parkhurst Forest.** Big-cat, C)dark grey, L)2.5ft, long tail. • 10) 1) 12 Oct 84.
26– 84.Dec.C – **Ryde.** Puma, S)half-grown alsatian, C)light sandy, pointed erect ears, long tail. • 8) 20 Dec, 10) 28 Dec 84.
27– 85.?.? – **Calbourne.** Big-cat • 8) 5 Mar, 1)10) 8 Mar 85.
28– 85.Jan.A – **Ryde area.** Big-cat, pointed erect ears, bright eyes, S)alsatian, C)dark. • 1)10) 11 Jan 85.
29– 85.Jan.C – **Merstone.** Big-cat, C)black, small erect ears, long tail, W)policeman. • 10) 25 Jan 85.
30– 85.Jan.29 – **Binstea.** Terrifying animal noises. • 1) 1 Feb 85.
31– 85.Feb.? – **Brightstone Down.** Big-cat. • 8) 5 Mar, 1)10) 8 Mar 85.
32– 85.Feb.AB – **Ningwood.** Big-cat, L)4ft, C)light brown, long ears, seen twice by 13yr-old cyclist. • 1) 15 Feb 85.
33– 85.Feb.D – **Ningwood.** Big-cat, horrible cries. • 8) 5 Mar, 10) 8 Mar 85.
34– 85.Feb. 3 – **Ryde area.** Big-cat, C)dark brown + vague pattern, S)4 times cat-size, round pug face, long tail. • 8) 5 Feb, 1) 8 Feb 85.

35– 85.Feb.28 – **Newbridge area.** Big-cat, loud scream from two locations. •8) 5 Mar, 1)10) 8 Mar 85.
36– 85.Mar.A – **Cowes.** Leopard-like, S)labrador, C)black, thick tail. •8) 13 Mar 85.
37– 85.Mar.6 – **Littleton Down, nr Ventnor.** Young lion, C)golden sandy, S)alsatian, loping down hill, clawed pawprint 3ins. •1)10) 15 Mar 85.
38– 85.Apr.B – **Northwood, Parkhurst Forest.** Lamb killed, skeleton picked clean & head missing, spoor. •8) 15 Apr, 1) 26 Apr 85.
39– 85.Apr.C – **Oakfield, nr Ryde.** Large & small pawprints, suggestive of puma & cubs! •1) 26 Apr 85.

INVERNESS-SHIRE

40– 84.Nov.? – **Tomich, nr Cannich.** Pumas & cubs, believed to be 20! •27) 2 Dec 84, 4) 27 Jan 85.

LANCASHIRE

41– 84.Aug.? – **Whitewell Bottom, Rossendale Valley.** Mountain lion, sheep killed, cow attacked. •3)16)17) 16 Aug 84.

NORFOLK

42– 85.Apr.19 – **Barnham Common, nr Thetford.** Panther, surprised in woods, frightened dogs. •3) 23 Apr, 9) 21 Apr 85.

SOMERSET

43– 84.Jly.C – **Rodney Stoke, nr Axbridge.** 19 lambs killed, blamed on escaped alsatian named 'Percy'. • 15) 30 Jly 84.
44– 84.Jly.29 – **Charterhouse.** 16 lambs killed, blamed on 'Percy'. •15) 30 Jly 84.
45– 84.Aug.1 – **Tarnock, nr Axbridge.** 30 lambs killed, blamed on 'Percy'. •15) 2 Aug 84.
46– 84.Aug.3 – **Tarnock, nr Axbridge.** Dog shot while attacking flock, identified as 'Percy' from collar-tag. •15) 3 Aug, 3) 4 Aug 84.

SUFFOLK

47– 85.Apr.17 – **King's Forest, nr Elveden.** Panther, pawprints, birds killed. •2) 20 Apr, 4) 21 Apr, 29) 26 Apr 85.
48– 85.Apr.19 – **Honington nr US airbase.** Big-cat, L)4ft, C)light brown, long ears. •2)12) 20 Apr, 5) 21 Apr, 29) 26 Apr 85.

SURREY

49– 84.Sep.6 – **Chiddingfold.** Big-cat, C)sandy, L)3.5ft, long tail. •19) 14 Sep 84.
50– 84.Nov.28 – **Witley Park.** Big-cat, C)buff. •18) 7 Dec 84.
51– 84.Dec.27 – **Camberley.** Big-cat, S)alsatian, small head, long tail. •20) 3 Jan 85.
52– 85.Jan.A – **Esher.** May be same as #53 (below). Puma, tracks identified. •2) 8 Jan 85.
53– 85.Jan2 – **Esher, road to Cobham.** Puma, C)black, big, tracks. •21) 9 Jan 85.
54– 85.Jan.6 – **Milford, nr Godalming.** Big-cat, C)black, S)alsatian. •Letter from Chris Hall.

SUSSEX

55– 84.Oct 2 – **Danehill.** Large wildcat, S)collie, C)dark reddish with tabby stripes, large pointed ears. • 22) 5 Oct 84.
56– 85.Feb.? – **Ashurst.** Many sheep & deer savaged in last 3 months, 2 dogs blamed & sought. •28) 28 Feb 85.

SUTHERLAND

57– 84.Oct.26 – **Dornoch area, on Mound-Embo road.** Puma, C)jet black, S)bigger than wildcat, W)fireman. •14) 30 Oct 84.
58– 85.Mar.C – **Ardchronie Quarry, nr Ross boundary.** Puma, C)glossy black, blunt tail, L)3ft, W)policeman. •7)14) 6 Apr 85.
59– 85.Mar.? – **Shin Falls, nr Bonar Bridge.** Puma, C)glossy black, S)bigger than wildcat, W)policeman. •7) 14) 6 Apr 85.

•

CODES & SOURCES

C) = colouring; L) = length; S) = size comparison; W) witness (where occupation lends authority to observation). A, B, C, D indicate a vague date for the first, second, third, or fourth quarter of a month or year.
•1) *County Press,* Isle of Wight. •2) *Daily Mail* •3) *Daily Mirror.* •4) *Sunday Express.* •5) *Sunday Mirror.* •6) *Sunday Post.* •7) *The Journal,* Aberdeen. •8) *The News,* Portsmouth. •9) *Mail on Sunday.* •10) *Weekly Post,* Isle of Wight. •11) *Western Morning News.* •12) *Daily Telegraph.* •13) *Daily Express.* •14) *The Scotsman.* •15) *Evening Post,* Bristol. •16) *The Guardian.* •17) *The Sun.* •18) *Farnham Herald.* •19) *Haslemere Herald.* •20) *Surrey-Hampshire Star.* •21) *News & Mail,* Esher. •22) *Mid-Sussex Times.* •23) *North Devon Advertiser.* •24) *Express & Echo,* Exeter. •25) *The West Briton.* •26) *North Devon Journal-Herald.* •27) *Sunday Mail.* •28) *West Sussex Gazette.* •29) *Bury Free Press.*

•

Bob Rickard

Weird Lives

by Paul Sieveking.

THE TELEPORTING ASTROLOGER

This is the first of a series of thumbnail sketches of peculiar historical characters, unearthed by the editor in the course of his researches in British biography.

"He was the most *Saturnine* Person my Eyes ever beheld. . . of a middle Stature, broad Forehead, Beetle-brow'd, thick Shoulders, flat Nosed, full Lips, down-look'd, black curling stiff Hair, splay-footed; to give him his Right, he had the most piercing Judgement naturally upon a Figure of Theft, and many other Questions, that I ever met withal; yet for Money he would willingly give contrary Judgements, was much addicted to Debauchery, and then very abusive and quarrelsom, seldom without a Black Eye, or one Mischief or other."

The famous astrologer William Lilly [1] thus describes Evans of Gunpowder Alley [2], his first teacher in the magical arts, whom he met in 1632. Evans studied for several years at Oxford, where he became interested in astrology. Lilly says he was a master of arts, but Wood [3] could find no record, and suggests that he took his degree at Cambridge. He entered holy orders, and became a minister in Enfield in Staffordshire, where he began publishing almanacks. The one for 1625 advertises lessons in English, Latin, Greek, Hebrew, calligraphy and mathematics, although Lilly asserts he knew no Greek. "He was well versed in the Nature of Spirits," Lilly tells us, "and had many times used the circular way of invocating."

Lilly relates the following story from this period. A young Staffordshire woman married for money. Her aged husband bought her some lands, but in the name of a gentleman, "her very dear Friend". At length the husband died, but the widow's friend refused to give her the deed of purchase for the lands. She went to Evans and paid him £40 to procure her document. "*Evans* applies himself to the Invocation of the Angel *Salmon*, of the Nature of *Mars*, reads his Litany in the Common-Prayer-Book every Day, at select Hours, wears his Surplice, lives orderly all that Time." After a fortnight Salmon appears, is given his task, soon afterwards returns with the deed and, being dismissed, vanishes. It had been kept by the gentleman with other documents in a large wooden chest at one end of the house. When Salmon removed it, that whole wing of the house blew down and all the documents were torn to pieces.

Some time after this episode, Evans fled to London after some scandal connected with divining for stolen goods, which Lilly calls "the only Shame of Astrology" – hinting, presumably, at mundane dishonesty. Evans settled with his family at the Minories near Aldgate, where he made his living by the sale of antinomial cups (vessels made of glass of antimony to communicate emetic qualities to wine, for curative purposes, and protection against poisoning and sorcery).

In 1630 or 1631, "he then living in the *Minories*, was desired by Lord *Bothwell* [4] and Sir *Kenelm Digby* [5] to shew them a Spirit, he promised so to do; the time came, and they were all in the Body of the Circle, when lo, upon a sudden, after some time of Invocation, *Evans* was taken from out of the Room, and carried [five miles] into the Field near *Battersea* Causeway, close to the *Thames*. Next morning a Countryman going by to his Labour, and espying a Man in black Cloaths, came unto him and awaked him, and asked him how he came there: *Evans* by this understood his Condition, enquired where he was, how far from *London*, and in what Parish he was; which when he understood, he told the Labourer he had been late at *Battersea* the Night before, and by chance was left there by his Friends."

Meanwhile Digby and Bothwell had gone home, and returned the next day to discover what had become of Evans. Just as they arrived in the afternoon, a messenger arrived from Evans and told his wife to come and fetch him home from Battersea. Lilly asked Evans why he had been carried off, to which he replied that he had offended the spirits at the time of invocation by failing to make a due fumigation. I have so far been unable to locate any confirmation of this outlandish tale in the writings of Digby, or anywhere else. The ultimate fate of Evans is unknown, "because", says Wood [3], "he lived in several places, and in an obscure condition".

NOTES

[1] William Lilly: *Mr W. Lilly's History of his Life and Times from the Year 1602 to 1684 Written by himself* (in 1667). First published, with notes and a continuation, by Elias Ashmole, London, 1715.

[2] Lilly does not give his Christian name, but Wood [3] says his name was John Evans or Evance. Lilly gives oblique confirmation of this when he states that Evans had only two books: "*Haly de judiciis Astorum,*

and *Origanus* his *Ephemerides*". The British Library has a copy of David Origan: *An Ephemerides for Five Years to come,* revised by John Evans, 1633. As Katherine M. Briggs says in the Folklore Society's reprint of Lilly's *Life* (1974): "Evans may even have been at work on this when Lilly met him in 1632." This work is catalogued in the library under John Evans, *Philomath*, along with an almanack of 1630, which doesn't mention his first name, but was composed for the longitude and latitude of Shrewsbury. Wood[3] saw almanacks by John Evans for 1613 and 1635. Catalogued under John Evans, *Minister and Preacher of God's Word*, are two works: *The Sacrifice of a Contrite Heart*, a massive work of 1630, and *The Universall Medicine: or the Vertues of the Antinomiall Cup* (1634), where I found the clinching evidence of our astrologer's name. A note opposite the title pages states: "The Antinomiall Cups herein mentioned are made and sold by John Evans Minister of God's Word dwelling in Gunpowder-Alley near fetter lane."

The Dictionary of National Biography is perpetuating an eighteenth century error when it identifies Lilly's teacher as Rhys Evans, the religious fanatic who called himself Arise Evans, born in 1607, and thus only six when John Evans brought out his 1613 almanack. Arise Evans was a tailor's apprentice at Chester and Wrexham, and came to London in 1629 to practise his trade. In March 1633 he heard a sermon in Blackfriars which led him to discover his prophetic gifts and embark on his career as a visionary. He was unmarried until 1635, while John Evans was already married in 1632. Arise Evans was born in Merionethshire "in the parish of Llangluin, a mile from the Bearmouth". Wood [3] states that John Evans was born in Wales, but whereabouts he couldn't say, the name being so common. I think Robert Williams is confusing John with Arise when he states that the former was born in Llangelynin, Merionethshire (*Biographical Dictionary of Eminent Welshmen* 1852).

[3] Anthony à Wood: *Athenae Oxonienses* (1691). New edition by Philip Bliss, 4 vols, 1813-20.

[4] Wood says "one who called himself Lord Bothwell". Francis Stewart Hepburn, the illegitimate grandson of James V of Scotland, became fifth earl of Bothwell on the death of his uncle James Hepburn, the husband of Mary Queen of Scots. James VI expelled him from Britain and he died in Naples in 1624. His son Francis Hepburn was restored to his estates, but not to the title. He may, however, have used it as a courtesy.

[5] Sir Kenelm Digby (1603-65) was an author, naval commander and diplomatist, and by turns royalist, republican, protestant and catholic. He was a founder member of the Royal Society, discovered the necessity of oxygen in plant life and dabbled in alchemy and 'radionics', having claimed the discovery of a 'sympathetic powder' which could cure wounds at a distance.

[6] James Caulfield: *Portraits, Memoirs and Characters of Remarkable Persons, from the Reign of Edward III to the Revolution.* 3 vols, 1813.

IOHN EVANS,

the Ill favor'd Astrologer of Wales.

Published by I. Caulfield Feb. 1 1794

This engraving, published by Caulfield [6] in 1794, is based on an original drawing first published in 1776.

Clipping Credits for This Issue

David Ainslie, APRO Bulletin, Larry Arnold, Bob M.Barter, Chester Behnke, Peter Bennett, Janet & Colin Bord, Claudia Boulton, Jean-Louis Brodu, David Burns, Steuart Cambell, John Chalke, Peter Christie, Jerry Clarke, Alan Cleaver, Loren Coleman, William E. Collins, R.E. Cotton, Jim Darruck, Paul Devereux, Mike Diamond, Geoffrey Featherstone, Dave Fideler, Alan Gardiner, G.M. Garner, R.I. Gillham, Joan Good, Richard Goulding, Dick Gwynn, Brian Hain, Chris Hall, Mark A. Hall, John Holliday, Tuuri Heporauta, John Hitchens, Chris J. Holzhausen, Peter Hope Evans, John L. Hughes, J. Lang, Alexis Lykiard, Richard A. Leshuk, Nick Maloret, Valerie Martin, Colin Mather, Ian S. Murray, Roger Musson, Ray Nelke, Cory Panshin, Scott Parker, Nigel Pennick, Frank Pollack, Jenny Randles, Michel Raynal, Rickard pere, Ron Rosenblatt, Rita Sandstrom, Ron Schaffner, Paul Screeton, Doc Shiels, Bob Skinner, Anthony Smith, Geoff Smith, Henry Stanton, Rod Stevens, Paul Swan, Joe Swatek, A L Thomas, Haz Thomas, Paul R. Thomas, Joseph Trainor, UFO Newsclipping Service, Mark Velentine, Roger Waddington, Nigel Watson, Dwight Whalen, Roslyn Whitford, Ion A. Will, Heathcote Williams, Jake Williams, Steve Wrathall, Joe Zarzynski.

Science Frontiers

Compiled and Annotated by William R. Corliss.

The Immune System As A Sensory Organ

John Maddox, the editor of *Nature,* has written a remarkable editorial on psychoimmunology; that is, the science of the brain's effects on the body's immune system. It is basically a running commentary on new discoveries that are helping us to understand this poorly appreciated relationship. Maddox begins by mentioning the 20-plus-year collection compiled by Professor G.W. Brown, University of London, of life-events that affect the health of outwardly normal people. Typical life-events are the death of a spouse, imprisonment, personal bankruptcy, etc. Everyone seems to recognize – if only through anecdotes – that mental states affect health, but how this brain-body link is maintained is hard to pin down. D.Maclean and S. Reichlin (*Psychoneuroimmology*, 12:475, 1981) have reviewed some of the possible connections. One potential link is through the interaction of the hypothalamus on the pituitary. The pituitary is a source of materials that influence the immune system. Maddox lists several specific candidates, and then observes, "The more radical psychoimmunologists talk as if there is no state of mind which is not faithfully reflected by a state of the immune system."

So far, not too radical! But then Maddox comes to an article by J.E. Blalock, University of Texas (*Journal of Immunology*, 132:1067, 1984), bearing the title, "The Immune System as a Sensory Organ". Blalock argues that the interaction between the central nervous system and immune system must be reciprocal. By this he means that the immune system's response to infection, through the secretions of disease-fighting lymphocytes, gets back to the central nervous system and produces physiological and even behavioral changes in the infected animal.

Applicable studies of animals have been reported recently. For example, rats under stress are found to have less easily stimulated immune systems (*Science*, 221:568, 1983). Also, men who have recently lost their wives to breast cancer have immune systems less responsive to mitogens (*Journal of the American Medical Association*, 250:374, 1984). (Maddox, John; "Psychoimmunology Before Its Time," *Nature*, 309:400, 1984)

This is an appropriate time to suggest that "psychoevolution" may be physiologically possible. If the brain can fight disease and even control cell growth why not a role for the mind in stimumlating the development of new species, perhaps in response to extreme environmental pressures, and perhaps not on the conscious level? The body's sensory system would detect great external stresses, the brain would process the inshuffling. The genetic inheritance of an organism is not sacrosanct. Radiation, chemicals, and various other mutagens are recognized. There seems to be no a priori *reason why the brain-body combination cannot generate mutagens – possibly not randomly but intelligently! (We ignore here selfish DNA and Sheldrake's morphogenic fields.) Does this mean that if we wish to mutate, we can? Well, it's probably not as simple as wishing warts away, but Maddox's editorial underscores the complexity and subtlety of the brain-body combination.*

At Last! Someone Who *Can* Predict the Future!

More psychics claiming to know what's ahead down the road of time draw up rather long lists of predicted events. They may score a hit or so, but their records are generally very poor. The present article records the astounding performance of Emory Royce, a New Zealander. "The whole thing is preposterous," says Richard Kammann, the author and noted skeptic. Royce made four predictions and four only, on a radio talk show. Some of the predictions were a bit vague on details, but the overall outcome was unbelievable: all four events occurred! The predictions were Brezhnev's death (very close time-wise); naval disaster in the Falklands (prediction made well before the surprise invasion by Argentina); a New Zealand political scandal; and the completely unexpected cancellation of a New Zealand aluminium factory. (Kammann, Richard; "Uncanny Prophecies in New Zealand: An Unexplained Scientific Anomaly," *Zetetic Scholar*, no. 11, p. 15, August 1983.)

The Tsunami Tune

Tsunamis are giant sea waves set into motion by earthquakes on the sea floor. Some 322 tsunamis have been recorded in the Pacific between AD 83 and 1967 – or about one every six years on the average. The surprising thing is that tsunamis are more common in November, August, and March, but rarer in July and April. Off hand, no good explanation comes to mind why sea floor quakes should favor some months over others. (Anonymous; "The Times for Tsumanis," *Science News*, 127:88, 1985)

Two Snowflake Anomalies

Rarely is there anything in the scientific literature suggesting that anything about snowflakes could possibly be mysterious. Surprisingly, two articles on snowflake anomalies have appeared recently.

To form at all above -40°F, snowflakes supposedly require a solid seed or nucleus around which ice can crystalize – or so scientists have assumed for many years. It was long believed that airborne dust, perhaps augmented by extraterrestrial mirco-meteoroids, served as the necessary nuclei. But cloud studies prove that there are about a thousand times more ice crystals than dust nuclei. Now, some are convinced that bacteria blown off plants and flung into the air by ocean waves are the true nuclei of atmospheric ice crystals. Remember this the next time you taste a handful of snow! (Carey, John: "Crystallizing the Truth," *National Wildlife*, 23:43, December/January 1985.) *The possibility that the fall of snow and all other forms of precipitation is largely dependent upon bacteria brings to mind the Gaia Hypothesis; that is, all life forms work in unison to further the goals of life.*

The second item is from *Nature* and is naturally more technical. After reviewing the great difficulties scientists are having in mathematically describing the growth of even the simplest crystal, the author homes in on one of the fascinating puzzles of snowflake growth: "The aggregation of particles onto a growing surface will be determined exclusively by local properties, among which surface tension and the opportunities for energetically advantageous migration will be important. But the symmetry of a whole crystal, represented by the exquisite six-fold symmetry of the standard snowflake, must be the consequence of some cooperative phenomenon involving the growing crystal as a whole. What can that be? What can tell one growing face of a crystal (in three dimensions this time) what the shape of the opposite face is like? Only the lattice vibrations which are exquisitely sensitive to the shape of the structure in which they occur (but which are almost incalcuable if the shapes are not simply regular). *Maddox, John;* "No Pattern Yet for Snowflakes", *Nature*, 313:93, 1985. *It is amusing that this usually fairly open-minded journal* Nature *once blasted Sheldrake's* A New Science of Life *as a good candidate for burning. It is in this book that Sheldrake proposed morphogenetic fields as the explanation of crystal growth. Morphogenetic fields seem at least as reasonable as "vibrations".*

Pouring a Pyramid

The ancient Egyptians may have been more clever than we thought. Instead of chipping away laboriously in limestone quarries to precisely shape the stones constituting the pyramids, they may have cast the stones from a slurry of crushed limestone and a special mineral binder. Polymer chemist Joseph Davidovits has examined the limestone casing stones that were used to face some of the pyramids. (Most of the casing stones were removed for use in modern construction projects.) Davidovits claims that the casing stones contain mineral not found in the quarries, and that they contain as much as 13% binder material. In addition the casing stones have a millimeter-thick coating of this binder. This theory might help explain the precise fitting of the stones. Others have analyzed the stones, too, and oppose Davidovits' claims. (Peterson, I.: "Ancient Technology: Pouring a Pyramid," *Science News*, 125:327, 1984)

Geophysics: The Sick Man of Science

"In order to be a famed geo-scientist and belong to the inclusive club of fully accepted geophysicists in their *unknown* thousands, one must kneel on the hassock and swear allegiance to the following tenets regardless of any scientific considerations:

Tenet 1. That the moment-of-interia of the Earth has never changed.

Tenet 2. That the Earth contains a large central core composed of iron.

Tenet 3. That the continents are drifting as a result of unknown forces.

These must be held with religious fervour, dissenters are just not to be tolerated, the devotees feeling it their right, and indeed duty, to defend the creed against all criticism by any means of chicanery and of sharp-practice within their power, however crude and improper, so long as they judge they can get away with it, but all the time representing themselves to the world as acting with judicial calm in the best interests of their science. It will be shown that all three of these tenets are wrong, and how their (naive) acceptance has hamstrung the believers from making progress in the deep waters of terrestrial science, though not of course in the wordly world of 'modern science'. Shades of Sir Cyril Burt."

So begins a long technical article by R.A. Lyttleton, author of many scientific books and papers. (*He may lose his union card after this paper!*) Lyttleton proceeds to demonstrate the incorrectness of the first two tenets above. Demolition of the third is promised in the still-to-be-published second part of the paper. Lyttleton's reasoning is buttressed by many scientific observations and so much quantitative reasoning that it is impossible to encapsulate it all here. Suffice it to say that it all looks correct, serious, and above-board. (Lyttleton, R.A.; "Geophysics: The Sick Man of Science," *ISCDS Newsletter*, 5:3, December 1984.) *Now this is interesting. The ISCDS is the International Stop Continental Drift Society. The Society's* Newsletter, *if you don't already know, is usually a tongue-in-cheek publication. Not so here, Lyttleton is deadly serious. Either that or the joke is lost amid all the equations! ISCDS address: Star Route Box 38, Winthrop, WA 98862.*

Science Frontiers ***is extracted from William Corliss' bimonthly collection of digests from current literature, which is sent free to regular customers of his publications. For more details write to*** **The Sourcebook Project, Box 107, Glen Arm, MD 21057, USA.**

Tales from Africa

Pater Kavoi's house, scene of the flying stones. [Photo © David Barritt.]

Peter Kavoi [Photo © David Barritt.]

KENYAN STONE SHOWERS

On 23 December 1982, showers of stones, which seemed to materialise from thin air, began to terrorise Peter Kavoi, 53, and his family, who live near the town of Machakos in Kenya. Six months later, the stones were still falling. The following account was sent to us by journalist **DAVID BARRITT.**

Stones attacked Mulnegeta Abate, a Protestant theologian from the nearby Scott Theological College in Machakos who led the family in prayer to try and stop the phenomenon. "It is the work of the evil one," he said. "I actually saw the stones flying."

"From a theological point of view things like this are quite acceptable," said Japeth Muvengei, another Protestant theologian from the college who investigated the mystery. "This case is unusual because so many people have seen the flying stones. It is exceptionally well-documented."

"All I know is that I and my family are terrified," said Kavoi. "Since December 23 the flying stones have been terrorising us. I have been struck by them and my face cut. My son and his children were so frightened they fled and our neighbours are saying we are be-witched. I don't know why this is happening to us but it must have a supernatural cause. There is no other explanation."

The terrorised family are ordinary working-class Kenyans. Peter Kavoi, head of the family, is a truck driver. His son Wilson, 33, is a clerk at a garage in the nearby town of Machakos. Wilson shares the four-roomed house with his father, as does Mr Kavoi's 100-year-old mother Mrs Martha Kutui. Wilson is married with five children. The house itself is set about two miles outside Machakos in a quiet semi-rural suburb. It is a small, neat dwelling surrounded by banana palms.

At eight o'clock on the evening of December 23 the family were eating supper when they were startled by a sudden rattle of stones falling on the roof of their house.

"I thought perhaps the neighbourhood children were playing a prank so I rushed outside to see what was going on," recalled Peter Kavoi. "While I stood there more stones started raining down on the roof and on the ground near where I was standing. I picked them up and found them to be ordinary stones such as can be found lying all over the area.

After a few moments the stones stopped falling and because it was dark a search would have done no good at all. I went back in the house and forgot about it until the next morning.

Then when I left the house to go to work a shower of stones crashed on to the house roof. I immediately remembered the events of the previous evening and started running around to see who was throwing the stones."

Sarah Munyao, 34, Mr Kavoi's neighbour, also saw them falling. "I saw Peter running around like a mad thing trying to see where they came from. Even as he searched the area more fell on to the roof. At first I thought somebody must be throwing them but they came from many different directions.

I stood there gaping with my mouth open. I could not believe my eyes. Within a few moments people from all over the area were gathered in front of the house and we all saw flying stones. Sometimes there were one or two, sometimes a dozen or more. After a few minutes they stopped. Then about twenty minutes later they started again. The stones were mostly small, about two to three inches in diameter but occasionally larger ones the size of half bricks would fall.

Sometimes they seemed actually to fall straight down from heaven as if it were raining stones. At other times they would come whizzing along horizontally almost at ground level. We all believe that Peter must have been bewitched and that an evil spirit has been sent to torment him. I have heard of such things happening but I never saw anything like this in my life."

Mr Kavoi reported the matter to Sub-chief William Mutisya Ndunda. "At first I thought it was someone trying to terrorise the people" he said, "and I hoped it would just stop, but three days later he returned to my office and told me the stones were still flying and that nobody was throwing them."

Ndunda said that at first he did not believe Mr. Kavoi, but he went to the house to investigate. "Then I saw for myself that stones were falling on the house. We tried to find out what was causing the phenomenon but we did not succeed. We took

Chief Timothy Musinse and sub-chief William Ndunda examine some of the flying stones. [Photo © David Barritt.]

20 men to the area and had them thoroughly search it. Even as we searched the stones continued to fall, sometimes seemingly from places where my men were actually searching. We left the men there for 42 days trying to get to the bottom of the problem but we could find no explanation for what was happening.

When the stones fell they came from all angles, not just from one point, and some came from the ground. With my own eyes I saw a big stone fly up from the ground and hit the roof with such force that it shattered."

Ndunda also said that once while he was sitting inside the house at the Kavoi's he was struck by a flying stone. "One struck me on the right arm. It happened when I was sitting at a table inside the house with all the doors and windows locked. There were other people in the house but they were seated and could not have thrown the stone. As far as the government is concerned we have tried to help but we found no solution. It's a complete mystery."

"My life has become an unbelievable nightmare," said Mr. Kavoi. "The stones fly without warning from constantly changing directions. Our neighbours spread the word that we were bewitched and the entire town came to stare at our misfortune. It seemed that the stones were only interested in my house and my family because they never fell on my neighbour's property and only strike my neighbours if they come into my yard.

Sometimes I actually saw the stones seemingly materialise out of thin air. They would suddenly appear out of a tree or over a roof and plunge into our yard. Sometimes they would fall very gently, just pitter onto the ground. At other times they would fall with such force that they shattered. We never know when they are going to fall and sometimes they even

cont. on page 40.

HUNT EMERSON:

PHENOMENOMIX

THE ILLUSTRATED LONDON NEWS... 9TH FEB. 1856

"LIVING FOSSIL"

We have reports from France of the discovery, during blasting for a railway tunnel, of a Living Being embedded in Jurassic Limestone. The creature is said to be a Pterodactyl ...a flying dinosaur extinct for Seventy Million Years!

THE SCENE IS TYNESIDE... NORTH-EAST ENGLAND.... ...THE NORTH WALBOTTLE PIT, 1861....

GRABBED GEORDIE BODIES GRUNT AND SWEAT AT A COALFACE DARK, DANK AND DONK... A COALFACE HUNDREDS OF FEET BELOW THE SURFACE.....

...HUNDREDS OF FEET... MILLIONS OF GEOLOGICAL YEARS!

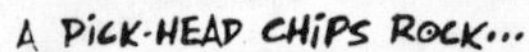

THE SIMPLE GEORDIE PITMEN AUTOMATICALLY AND QUITE NATURALLY ASSUME THAT THIS CREATURE, PRISTINE AMIDST THEIR GRIME, IS ONE OF THEIR ARISTOCRATIC MASTERS....

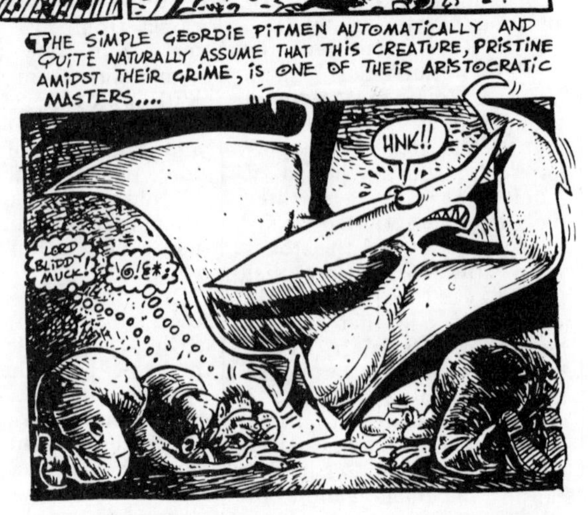

INDEED, THEY GET AS MUCH SENSE FROM THE THING AS THEY EVER DO FROM THEIR SO-CALLED BETTERS!
HAAK! HAARRGK! HAWWWW? HAW!
DO YE KNAA WHAT HE'S ON ABOOT?
NAW.. AA C'N NEVVA UNDERSTAND WHAT THEM TOFFS ARE SAYIN'....
BUT, BEING CANNY LADS, THEY TAKE THE ANIMAL TO THE SURFACE, WHERE THEY OFFER IT REFRESHMENT, IN THE FORM OF A WHIPPET SANDWICH AND A GLASS OF NEWCASTLE EXHIBITION ALE (THE BEST BEER IN THE WORLD).
HERE Y'ARE, YOUR WORSHIP... GET IT DOON YA!
HORKL?!
AAHM SORRY, HINNY, BUT HE'S A LORD OR A DUKE OR SUMMAT!
THE ANCIENT REPTILE, AFTER 70 MILLION YEARS WITH NOTHING TO DO BUT WATCH ITS NAIL VARNISH DRY, IS UNABLE TO COPE WITH THE CULTURE SHOCK BROUGHT ON BY THE BEER, AND DIES ON THE SPOT!
phew!
KLONK
Hik!
THE GEORDIES, STILL TAKING THE CRITTER FOR A VISCOUT, EARL OR SQUIRE, AND HAVING THE CORPSE AT THEIR DISPOSAL, CAREFULLY HACK IT TO PIECES AND FEED IT TO THE REPRIEVED WHIPPET, ACCORDING TO CUSTOM....
LORD BLIDDY MUCK....
yumyum! Gamey!
...THUS SAVING THE WISE MEN OF THE DAY THE NECESSITY OF EXPLAINING HOW AN ANIMAL BELIEVED EXTINCT COULD LIVE ENTOMBED IN THE EARTH FOR 70 MILLION YEARS!
HOW SHOULD I KNOW?!
SUPERSTITION! HALLUCINATION!! I DIDN'T SEE IT THEREFORE IT CANNOT EXIST!
I THINK WE HAD A CLOSE SHAVE THERE, FELLOW EGGHEADS!
MEANWHILE, 70 MILLION YEARS IN THE PAST....
TAP
GASP!
I SOMETIMES WONDER WHERE THEY GO TO...

cont. from page 37.

find their way inside the house. I have become afraid to open the door of the house in case one comes hurtling inside.

After a week I was too sick to work and Wilson sent his wife and children away. It was as if we were under siege in the house. I am a Christian so I asked the people at the theological college if they could help me. They came and said prayers and sung hymns but the stones still kept flying even when they were here.

Sometimes the stones stop for days at a time and then just as we think it's over they start again. I can tell you honestly that we are being driven mad by what is happening.

Hundreds of people have come to the house promising help but nobody has been able to do anything. We have prayers said and we have had witchdoctors performing strange ceremonies. Nothing has helped. Even the government say they don't know what else they can do. All I am doing is placing my trust in God. If I keep praying sooner or later I believe the stones will stop."

GOLDFISH DELIVERY

Douglas and Gladys Stowe were at home on the afternoon of 14 August 1982 in the Cape Town suburb of Plumstead when they heard a thump in the lounge. They discovered a beautiful, fat, soot-covered goldfish in their fireplace. Once in a bucket of water, it flapped its tail instantly.

Said Mrs Stowe: "It's about twelve centimenters long with a wonderful feathery tail and it's so fat that I am certain that it's pregnant." They knew of nobody in the immediate neighbourhood who kept goldfish, and speculated that it had been dropped by a crow. *Rand Daily Mail* 16 Aug 1982.

ELEPHANT RAIDS

In the summer of 1983, herds of marauding elephants were 'terrorizing' villagers – they were fearful anyway – in north-eastern Zimbabwe. "They are convinced that the animals have been sent by ancestral spirits" reported the South African *Star* (4 July 1983).

The Zimbabwe information Service reported that the elephants were operating mostly by night, moving in herds of 15 or so, coming in from Mozambique and the nearby district of Mutoko. Villagers were afraid to leave their homes. National Parks' wardens called in by the villagers had not seen them "because ancestral spirits had not wanted the elephants killed", a local council official was quoted as saying.

A 72-year-old villager, Mr Jonas Sambiyano, said: "Marauding elephants have been unknown since I was born." Game wardens had shot four in the area, but had seen no herds, according to a spokesman from the National Parks. The odd behaviour could be the result of the drought... I am reminded of the stories of vicious kangaroos in the Australian drought.

THE WATER SEER

With the soil cracked and dry, Joep Joubert, 74, great-grandfather of two, is one of South Africa's most sought-after men: he can 'see' water. Farmers have been visiting his Grootvlei plot outside Pretoria for 30 years.

"I am grateful for this gift and humbled by it" he said. He believes the gift is handed down from grandfather to grandson. "My grandfather was well-known as someone who could tell where to dig a well. I think my grandson also has this gift, though it has not yet been revealed. I have never advertised, and I never will. People hear that I have these powers and I find it hard to refuse them. In the old days I used to go all over southern Africa, but now I like to stay closer to home." But he is away from home nearly every day of the week, helping a farmer or giving advice to land buyers. South African *Star* 7 Oct 1984.

THE WALKING DEAD

Mr Abednego Machoba of Senaoane in South Africa was said to have died in January 1982 after being run down by a car on the Golden Highway. His wife and two brothers identified him at the government mortuary in Diepkloof and gave him a decent funeral.

In August 1982, Mr Machoba walked into his house. The children locked themselves in their bedroom and his wife would not allow him to touch her. They refused to sleep in the same house as the 'dead' man.

Records showed that Mr Machoba had been admitted to the Baragwanath Hospital in December, and was transferred to Sterkfontein Mental Hospital ten days later, where he remained until August. The scar on his head was the result of burns he sustained after falling on a stove in the hospital, he said.

Mrs Machoba insisted that she had buried her husband. She believed the man at her home had risen from the dead in her husband's form. "He is so different from my husband, although the features are the same," she said. The man she had buried had a head scar similar to the one on the living man. *The Sowetan* 18 Aug 1982. (For another case of misidentification, see FT42p26.)

BABY MONSTERS

In a semi-humorous story, the *Sunday Times* of 22 April 1984 referred to a credulous Swaziland Sunday newspaper called *The Observer*. What had them smirking was a headline: WOMAN GIVES BIRTH TO REPTILES. A woman named Jabulile Zwane claimed to have given birth to two fair-sized iguana-like creatures which then terrified the staff of the Raleigh Fitkin Memorial hospital. Easily checked, one would have thought?

In a way, this highlights the problem we have with some of the material we get, it being quite difficult to ascertain such pecadilloes as facts and truths at such distance. In the same vein we recall that our South African correspondent, Chris Holtzhausen, told us several years back he'd seen or heard of a magazine story in which a woman was said to have given birth to a human-headed spider. Needless to say, we frantically urged Chris to track it down, which he did to no avail. Perhaps we have a genre of foaflore forming here; if so, it is an old one re-establishing itself, as witness this old woodcut from a ballad sheet of 1654, illustrating the alleged birth of a child, a snake and a lapping toad to a woman near Colchester. It is from HE Rollins' marvellous compendium of early printed broadsides, *The Pack of Autolycus* (1927) which refers to a number of similar cases.

Woodcut of a 'monstrous birth' in 1654, of a child, a serpent, and "a lapping toad", (from Rollins' *Pack of Autolycus*).

REPORT FROM MBABANE

A young Swazi schoolboy who was struck by lightning while sitting in a classroom at the Gege School, on 13 September 1984, was struck down and killed instantly by *another* bolt on his way home. (Sapa) South African *Sunday Express* 16 Sept 1984.

AND DID THOSE FEET...

A giant left foot print, 4 feet 3 inches long, 2 feet wide and 6 inches deep, is to be found on a granite outcrop in a densely-forested region of the Transvaal, 28 miles from the Western border with Swaziland. Everyone agrees the impression is not a hoax: the granite is just too hard to carve. The individual toes and curve of the arch are clearly visible. It looks as if a giant stepped in mud, which later hardened into granite. One can even see where the 'mud' was squished up between the toes.

The Swazi's history records that the footprint was there when the first men settled the area. They call it 'the footprint of God' and no-one will build a hut within ten miles of the place. The first white man to see it was farmer Stoffel Coetzee in 1912. His son told writer David Barritt that he had read of a right foot print of roughly the same size impressed in granite near the summit of Adam's Peak in Sri Lanka. Our roving reporter Ion Will says that the Adam's Peak print is very unconvincing. The Far East is littered with giant footprints, supposedly made by the Buddha, but evidently carved out. There are at least four in Thailand. *Weekend* 23-31 Jan 1984.

MEANWHILE IN KENYA...

A Massai tribesman went into the Ministry of Tourism offices in Nairobi, broke into a glass cage containing a stuffed lion and began "stangling" it. When arrested, he explained that his brother had been killed by a lion and he wanted revenge. (UPI) *Telegraph* 14 Feb 1984.

☐ A man accidentally speared his 10-year-old daughter to death after mistaking her for a wild animal. (Kenya News Agency) *Standard* 16 Aug 1984.

☐ A giant monitor lizard wandered into a Mombasa court room, touching off a stampede among spectators and police that allowed twenty criminal suspects awaiting trial to escape. The lizard was beaten to death by court bailiffs with chairs and benches. *Standard* 2 Oct 1984.

THE REPORTING OF A LAKE MONSTER

Recent research in the US has added to the number of American lakes which are allegedly hosts to aquatic monsters of varying descriptions. One such is Wallowa Lake in north-eastern Oregon, a body of water 5-6 miles long, a mile wide and about 270 feet deep. What follows is drawn from information sent to us by Gary Mangiacopra, who has researched the reports.

Marge Cranmer, a 60-year-old local housewife, claims a ten-minute long sighting on the afternoon of 30 June 1982. She reported "seven dark coloured humps with a wake preceding each one" in the NE part of the lake. She thought the total length of the humps was around 50 feet. Another witness, 18-year-old Kirk Marks, was nearby. He was quoted in the press as having seen only high waves going towards shore, travelling the length of the lake, with dark shadows 30-40 feet long under the water. "I didn't see anthing above the water" he told the local paper; "I've seen things like this before, and I've seen it about five times this summer."

One explanation was that the witnesses had seen a fish, but Marge Cranmer added a defiant note to the sighting report form she filled in for Gary – "I don't believe it was 7 sturgeon as some people insist!" But the non-specific report and frequency of sightings raises the possibility that the objects were 'windrows', shadows created by the action of wind on the water surface. Certainly the witnesses were some distance from the water but at only a slight elevation and not in a good position for observation. None of the numerous boaters in the vicinity took any notice of the object; Marks "wondered why no-one else seemed to notice –?" *Wallowa County Chieftain* (Ore.) 12 Aug 1982; *USA Today* 19 Sept 1983; (sighting report on file with FT).

John T. Bryant and his wife Janice, a retired teacher, both aged 59, reported sightings in July of 1979 and 1980 – the first lasting two or three minutes and the second ten.

(Though it is not clear from their sighting report forms, it appears that the following descriptions refer to the latter event.)

"We both saw an unexplained wake in the lake," wrote Mr Bryant. "3 mounds or half loops came up out of the water. They were of dark colour, shining in the sun – 1 preceded the other 2 – in a row some feet apart. The object we saw seemed to be 15 to 25 feet from beginning to end – did not see any head or tail. Observed 10-15 minutes. Have no idea of what it was, or is..."

His wife wrote, "It swam up the lake, and then crossed back through its own wake. We finally got tired of watching and drove on to our destination... There was a large white wake all around the creature." The animal was described as "serpent-like", and the loops or coils were about 20 inches in circumference. The skin was smooth and the object "swam with an undulating motion", covering 40 yards in five minutes. "The creature just seemed to be enjoying the swim," reported Mrs Bryant. (Sighting report on file.)

Other sightings from Wallowa have been recorded in the local paper, the *Chieftain*, over the years.

★ November 1885: "A prospector, who refuses to give his name to the public, was coming down from the south end of the lake on last Friday evening in a skiff shortly after dusk, when about midway of the lake he saw an animal about fifty yards to the right of the boat, rear its head and neck up out of the water ten or twelve feet, but on seeing him it immediately dived. He ceased rowing and gazed around in astonishment for the strange apparition which he had just seen, when it rose about the same distance to the left, this time giving a low bellow something like a cow. It also brought its body to the surface, which the prospector avers was one hundred feet in length... It was too dark to see the animal distinctly, but it seemed to have a large flat head, something like that of a hippopotamus, and its neck, which was about ten feet in length, was as large as a man's body..."

The same report makes reference to an Indian tale concerning a big sea cow in the lake which "came up one evening and swallowed a young warrior and his dusky bride..." *Chieftain,* 5 Nov 1885.

★ July 1952: Three "somethings", said to be large sturgeon, seen "basking and playing" on the lake by a couple from a hill on the west side of the lake. (Undated

1980s clipping – see below).

★ July 1955: A 15 minutes "exhibition" by two "big fish" circling in the middle of the lake, witnessed by a shore party of six. (*Just Rambling* by Vance Orchard, Robert Bennet books 1981, p.73; ?*The Wallowa Record* 7 Aug 1955).

☆ An undated sighting in August from a *Chieftain* clipping probably between early 1981 and August 1982, of something "about 32 feet long with a neck and head sticking up at one end about three feet", not fish-shaped but rather like a serpent, seen by two locals, Bert Repplinger and Joe Babic.

The Wallowa Lake monster thus follows what has become a well-established pattern in America – a 'monster' known locally, decribed in widely differing terms by witnesses, reported only spasmodically, and said to date back to Indian legend.

There do seem to be many such lakes in the US, whose legends come to light either because of one well-reported case (the Cranmer sighting) or the activity of an investigator. It is interesting to note, for example, that Peter Costello's *In Search of Lake Monsters* (1974) says of Lake Champlain, "I have notes... but not in enough detail to write about them here." (p.239, paperback edition). Joe Zarzynski's tireless work there has since turned the lake into America's Loch Ness.

Of course, the same pattern can be observed in the UK, but here local research reveals a greater continuity in frequency of report and description of object than seems to have been the case in most US lakes.

A note of sceptism must be sounded about Wallowa; it has many of the ingredients of self-perpetuating local folklore, and the reserved *USA Today* account referred to above, headlined 'County has monster promotion', makes reference to attempts by the local Chamber of Commerce to attract tourists to the area by promoting the monster.

These include the sale of 'Monster Burgers', a painting competition, and the annual selection of a 'Sacrificial Maiden' – "a female between 14 and 101 who is to be offered to the monster should he show up and ask."

●

Mike Dash

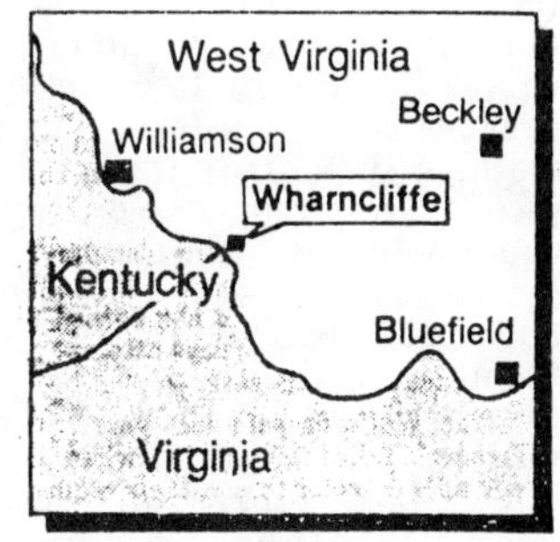

THE WHARNCLIFFE FIRES

In the summer of 1983 the tiny West Virginia coal town of Wharncliffe and nearby Beech Creek were plagued by mysterious outbreaks of fire. The first indication for visitors that something was very wrong came when they saw the wasps. Their wings were burnt off and they were walking.

The 200 residents of Wharncliffe first began to fear fire on 27th May. At 4.30pm a flash fire engulfed Bobby Queen's split-level home, three miles from the church. By the time firemen arrived the house was an inferno, and Queen barely escaped. About 4am on 9th June, firemen arrived in time to see fire destroy William Murphy's home, about 100 yards from the church. Murphy, asleep and attached to a respirator, also barely survived.

On the hot muggy afternoon of 13th June, fire returned – this time to the home of Eugene Clemons, 40, a lay minister at the Ben Creek Church of Christ. Eight separate fires broke out in a four hour span, burning articles in nearly every room of the ranch-style house, and flames shot 6 inches out of the electrical sockets. By now the Gilbert Volunteer Fire Department was really mystified. Believing the fires were caused by an electrical malfunction, Appalachian Power Co. employees cut all the lines going into the house and the church next door. The next day, fires broke out in the church's basement and its nearby all-purpose centre.

'Some of the clothing from the house was still good', recalled Clemons, 'so I gathered it up and gave it to my wife and told her to go to my mother-in-law's. And as they got up the hill, some of the clothing in the trunk was on fire.' Since then, most of the fires occurred at the Beech Creek home of Chloe Kennedy, Clemons' mother-in-law.

Chemical analysis of some of the burned clothing from

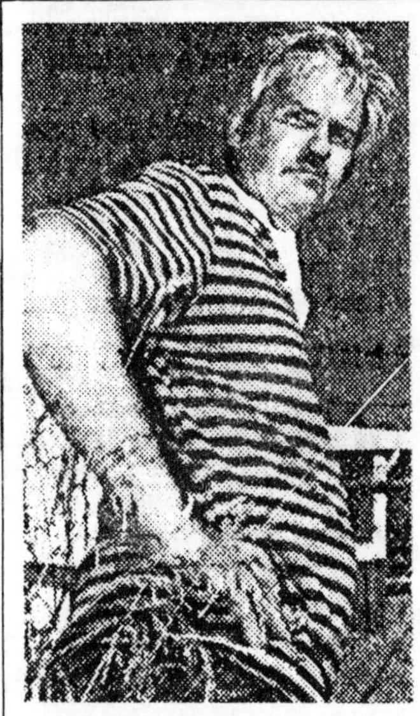

Eugene Clemons, chief victim of the Wharncliffe fires. [Photo Columbus © Dispatch.*]*

Bobby Queen's fire-gutted home. [*Photo*©Columbus Dispatch.]

the 13th June fires, conducted by a Columbus company on 11th July, only deepened the mystery. The clothing showed no traces of gasoline or other accelerant, and a company official stated he had never seen similar burn patterns. On 19th July, Clemons began to move back into his home which he had vacated a month before. Three fires broke out the same day, and he moved out again, having decided it was safer to live in Beech Creek.

Several different explanations have been put forward, all with passionate supporters. Robert R. Hall, supervisor of the arson section of the West Virginia fire marshall's office, was convinced the fires were intentionally set. At the beginning of July, his office gave lie-detector tests to Clemons' daughters, Lisa, 18, and Melissa, 15. Lisa passed, but the results of Melissa's test were inconclusive. This approach enraged Kendell Simpson, assistant chief of the Gilbert Fire Department. 'The fire marshall has said that he has several suspects, why doesn't he charge them?'

Also discounting the possibility of arson is Larry E. Arnold, director of Para-Science International of Harrisburg, Pa., which specialises in spontaneous human combusion research. 'It's inconceivable to us that those fires were set by human means. The Clemons episode, in part, falls very nicely into the poltergeist experience.'

The prevailing theory among Wharncliffe residents, however, is that they are microwave radiation fires caused by a 120-foot Norfolk and Western Railroad communications tower on Horsepen Mountain. The tower has five microwave relay dishes, which it uses to communicate with other N & W facilities 40 miles away. Governor Jay Rockefeller became worried enough to despatch researchers from the state health department on 8th July to test the area for microwave radiation. The tests were negative. 'The wavelength on the relay is so long it just won't start fires,' said Beattie Debord, the department's radiological health specialist.

'I'll be honest with you: a lot of people are saying we're just a bunch of dumb hillbillies,' said Kendall Simpson to the *Columbus Dispatch*. 'But I'm out of aces. I've been in the fire service for twelve years and I've never seen anything like it.' Houston (TX) *Post* 16 June; *Columbus Dispatch* 24 July 1983.

WITCHDOCTOR'S POSTHUMOUS REVENGE?

The same summer as the Wharncliffe fires, the house of the late millionaire witchdoctor, Khotso Sethunsa, in Kokstad, Transkei, South Africa, was the scene of six apparently spontenous fires within five days. The house was occupied by about 39 coloured people who rented it from one of Khotso's 26 wives.

At midnight on 6 August, an outbuilding leased by Mr

P. van Wyk, who was away at the time, burnt down. On the 9th August at 9 am Mr P. Olivier was lying on his bed when a carton under the bed caught fire. At 9 am the next morning, in a room occupied by Sergeant Pakkies and his wife, two mattresses began to burn of their own accord.

At 9am on the 11 August, a box of shoes in a room occupied by Mrs C. Booth began to burn. Mrs Booth is a non-smoker and there was no fire in the house at the time. At 8.30am the following morning, flames came out of a hole in the floor of a room belonging to Mr P. van Wyk who was outside at the time (he seemed to know when not to be around!) A plastic washing bucket full of clothing caught fire in the back yard while police and municipal officials were present. They could offer no explanation, and the fire brigade was quite baffled.

All the occupants agree, however, that the fires were caused by the spirit of the late witchdoctor. At the time of the report in the *South African Star* (13 August 1983) all the occupants had left the house and were camping in the garden surrounded by furniture and possessions.

A Wharncliffe wasp with fire-damaged wings. [photo © Columbus Dispatch.]

PHANTOM SKIRT-BURNER IN ROME OFFICES

In the summer of 1984, a series of spontaneous fires broke out in the Rome offices of the Institute of Health Assistance magazine, according to Len Stone, writing in the *Globe* (28 August 1984). "There is no earthly reason for the outbreaks," said Dr Duilio Ranalletta, the chief researcher.

It all began when Adelia Lioe, a 19-year-old secretary, was working at her desk when her skirt burst into flames. She was rushed to hospital with serious leg burns. Another blaze erupted in the archives while two clerks were going through files in a cabinet.

"I looked up and saw the fire in the door blocking their exit," said Ranalletta. "It looked like a campfire, but had started all by itself. The flames burnt fiercely for serveral minutes, but the fire was contained in a small area between filing cabinets. Suddenly it went out, but at that moment the double doors of the archive room slammed shut, and a gust of wind sent papers flying. Throughout the day, there were two more fires in the archive, each lasting just a few seconds, but each time the wind followed."

Lioe, who returned to work after treatment, added: "There was no work done during the whole week. We were terrified. First you could feel the heat coming from somewhere, then see the flames, and then the gust of wind came."

Maria Valdini, a 22-year-old clerk, added: "I had been in the archive for a minute and had just walked out when the door shut behind me. The wind blew through the office, and even the shutters outside the windows rattled. We were in such a panic that at first nobody noticed flames at the main door. There was this icy cold from the wind, then I felt the heat from the flames, even though the fire was small and I was 25 feet away. It lasted about 10 seconds. It was terrifying. You could feel a presence in the office."

The fire brigade was being called to the office as often as three times a day. In desperation, they put up warning notices: Beware of Sudden Fire. "There are 20 witnesses, including myself, who can testify they start for no apparent reason." The Institute compiles statitistics on work-related diseases. "Our work is centred on death and its causes," said Ranalletta. "A ghost is obviously the best explanation for our probelms."

As Far As We Have Vouchers..

Thomas Short and His History of the Air.

by Roger Musson.

The history of Science is a more interesting subject than many might think. True, the most exciting discoveries of times gone by may seem today outdated or old hat, but the scientists themselves of times past tended to be more interesting people than many of the leading scientists today: their interests were so much more varied. Today it is possible for a scientist to devote his entire career to say, gas chromatography, ignore all other scientific developments, and still make a reputation for himself. But in the 18th century a scientist was one who studied science – all of it. He may have had a specialisation, or we may remember him chiefly for his work in one field, but his interests are activities would have covered a much wider scope than that of the average scientist today. Besides the well-known work on elasticity, Hooke also wrote on earthquakes among other things. Isaac Newton even studied alchemy.

Furthermore, since the general body of scientific theory was less well-developed then than it is now, scientists had more open minds with respect to unusual phenomena. The boundary line between respectable data and "damned" data had yet to be drawn. Many common phenomena were still without accepted explanation, so there was no harm in accepting a few unexplained phenomena of a less common nature. Whereas, of course, today we expect to be able to explain virtually anything, so something inexplicable causes much more concern to the conventionally-minded. Witness the number of strange falls and entombed toads that appear in scientific periodicals even of the late 19th century. Where are they today (apart from in *FT*)? Try sending to *Nature* today the sort of material Charles Fort culled from its own pages in his lifetime, and see how far you get.

The result of all this is that the papers of scientists of earlier times can be an interesting hunting-ground for the Fortean, rather more interesting than those of say, the last umpteen Nobel-prize winners for chemistry. I want to consider here one person in particular – Thomas Short.

He was actually a physician rather than a pure scientist. His interests were very wide, but they always had medicine as a touchstone, though the connection might sometimes seem a little remote today. He was born in 1690, somewhere in the south of Scotland?[1], but after training as a doctor (where is unknown) he took up a practice at Sheffield. Very little is known about him other than can be gleaned from his own writings, and a few letters (to his patron Sir Hans Sloane, president of the Royal Society) which survived[2]. He seems to have been a sober, conscientious man, considerate of the poor, strongly opposed to alcohol, and with an amazing capacity for work. This shows up first in his work on bills of mortality. He sent agents up and down the country collecting material from parish registers, and then collated huge tables of births and deaths, virtually becoming a one-man census in the process. Some of his contemporaries seem to have doubted that one man could gather so much data, but one of his note-books has survived[3], and there it all is, page upon page, column upon column of figures.

His best known work is possibly that on mineral springs, another careful and thorough survey. This was a topic of enduring interest to Short – his first published work was *A Rational Discourse on the Inward Uses of Water* – and he published also medicinal considerations of other drinks, notably tea. (He particularly advocates an infusion of sage and water.)

However, the most interesting of Short's works is on quite a different topic. In or about 1731 he acquired a copy of the weather diary kept by Clifton Wintringham, a physician living in York, who had made some attempt to correlate prevalent epidemics with the weather at the time. This idea had good foundation (in the work of Hippocrates) and appealed to Short, who acquired some other weather

A contemporary woodcut of the enormous meteorite that fell at Ensisheim in Alsace on 7 November 1492, before the entire army of Maximilian I. By kind permission of the Mary Evans Picture Library.

diaries, notably that of Francis Say, an Ipswich clergyman, and started keeping his own. But he also hit upon the notion of expanding the idea on the grand scale, to cover not just England in his own time, but the whole world as far back as the Creation. He began serious work on this ambitious project around 1733, and in 1749 finally published the result, which was called: *A General Chronological History of the Air, Weather, Seasons, Meteors &c in Sundry Places and Different Times; more particularly for the space of 250 Years. Together with some of their most Remarkable Effects on Animal (especially Human) Bodies, and Vegetables*[4]. The work fills two thick volumes. It is, by the way, extremely rare; only a very few copies are known to exist. The most accessible is probably that in the possession of the Royal Meteorological Society.

After a couple of prefaces stating the aims of the work and the principles behind it, Short plunges in with all his data, laid out chronologically, starting with the flood in 1657 AM (*Anno Mundi*, i.e. from the Creation in 4004 B.C.) The early entries, not surprisingly, tend to be irregular and brief, but they fill out as the work progresses (particularly with long and grisly descriptions of the symptoms of various plagues and diseases) and become very long and full in the 18th century where Short has got contemporary weather diaries to quote *in extenso*. I shall quote one of the early years in full to give you the flavour.

"1009 (AD) This Year set in with often and

A

GENERAL CHRONOLOGICAL

HISTORY

OF THE

AIR, WEATHER, | SEASONS, METEORS, &c.

IN

Sundry Places and different Times; more particularly for the Space of 250 Years.

Together with ſome of their moſt

REMARKABLE EFFECTS

ON

ANIMAL (eſpecially HUMAN) BODIES, and VEGETABLES.

In TWO VOLUMES.

VOL II.

LONDON:

Printed for T. LONOMAN, in *Paternoſter-Row*; and A. MILLAR, in the *Strand*.

MDCCXLIX.

Some of Thomas Short's manuscript notes.

extraordinary Rains; in the End of May a Comet shone forth, followed by a terrible Plague in Saxony."

Well, you can see instantly one of the problems – where's the reference? Short does give some references in the text, but they are not as full as one would like, nor are they always very clear. They tend to be cryptic abbreviations which are nowhere set out in full – for instance, many data are referenced *Func.* The modern reader can be forgiven for not recognising what this cryptic reference refers to. Some are easier, though; for instance *Sim. Dunelm.* refers to the chronicle of Simeon Dunelmensis, which is published in the Rolls series. Short himself had this to say about his resources: "these Scraps of Histories lay scattered in a vast Multitude of Authors of different Designs and Professions, as Historians civil, ecclesiastical, and political; Physicians, Divines, Naturalists, Monks, Fryars, Journalists, Travellers, &c...they lay dispersed...in and endless Number of Books, and frequently in small Fragments..." Presumably much of the unreferenced material is that from the small fragments.

Short's other main failing is his difficulty with dates. He has a bad habit of taking two references to the same occurrence, which have different dates owing to a disagreement between sources, and citing both as though they were separate occurrences. Sometimes he notices the similarity and comments on it, but often it escapes him, so many of the dates he gives are highly unreliable, unless confirmed by other sources. Which makes it difficult to treat of that information which is not confirmed by any other sources.

Things become really curious, though, when we reach p165 of volume two. Before going on with his own weather diaries, he sums up what has gone before in a series of chronological tables of different phenomena. The purpose of these tables was two-fold; firstly, to enable a quick comparison to be made between a year's diseases and its meteorological phenomena, so that one could test the hypothesis that, say, comets cause disease (not so stupid – a recent issue of *New Scientist* carried an article entitled "Can you really catch a cold from a comet?"[5], so Short's ideas live on!). Secondly, they act as an index to the whole.

The titles of the lists are as follows: Earthquakes, Comets, Heavens on Fiery Flames, Fiery Meteors; Battles between Armies seen in the Air; Prodigies reducible to no Certain Class or Kind; Mock Suns and Moons, Strange and Common Parelia; remarkable Aurorae Boreales; Sun or Moon darkened with Eclipses; Rivers dried up; Irregular Tides; Stars raining down in Showers; Falling of Clouds; Sun or Moon red like Blood; Unnatural Rains; Uncommon Springs; Battles between Beasts; Breads reckon'd ominous; Sun or Moon naturally increased or decreased; Moon seen some days too soon; Land-Spouts (like those at sea); Locusts & Worms &c; Eruptions of Burning Mountains; very terrible Thunder and Lightning; Tempests; Hurricanes; Great Hail; Great and remarkable Snows; Great or long Rains; most remarkable Floods; Notable Frosts; Droughts; Famines; and Plagues and Diseases[6].

You can see the Fortean slant. I particularly like the phrase "Breads reckon'd ominous" – surely a good title for an FT column? Some items Short was disposed to take with a pinch of salt. "I would not be so credulous as to admit of every Thing for Truth I read in many Histories; so neither would I be such an Infidel as to discredit and deny the whole, because some Things appear monstrously incredible (which I have mostly omitted in this Collection) as raining of red and green Crosses, Ghosts knocking at Peoples Doors that were to be next infected, &c." However, "Some things either cannot, or may be falsely accounted for, nevertheless be true. The God of Nature most certainly has the Universe in his own Hands, and can dispose of his Creatures as he sees proper... He can turn Seas, Rivers, and Springs into Blood...or cause his Clouds to pour down ready Grain..." (and a long list of other things).

All the same, these tables are rather curious. For a start, not all the data that appears in the tables appear in the text. And many of those that do not are very odd indeed. For instance, would you believe "Dunbarton greatly shaken by an earthquake" – in 12 AD? How about Pickering burnt by lightning four years before that? At Carlisle, a hurricane blew down 420 houses in 349, and several families in Edinburgh were drowned by flooding in 155. That's according to the tables, anyway, but one might doubt legitimately whether there were 420 houses in Carlisle at that time. Even if Edinburgh (built on a steep hill) were much subject to flooding, would reference to such an occurrence in 155 have survived nearly sixteen centuries later? And if it did, where is it? For though Short has references in his text, there are no references in the tables.

The first sentence in the text that follows the tables begins with the following words: "Having gone now as far as we have

A fish fall from Erasmus Francisci's Der Wunder-Reiche *(Nuremburg 1680),*

vouchers..." But where are they? I am quite certain that Short had sources for these items; for him to have made them up seems quite out of character. He certainly had access to a great deal of information too, some of it from foreign sources (there is a good deal of east European weather data), but his original notes for this work don't seem to have survived. One possibility is that one of Short's acquaintances was a bit of a wag, and passed him some made up data, which the Doctor, distrusting sufficiently to exclude it from the text, nevertheless included in the tables. It seems unlikely now that we will ever know the answer, so the very early material that appears only in the tables must be regarded as dubious.

As an illustration of the unreliability of the dates that Short gives, the great storm of 1361 (possibly the worst ever to hit the British Isles[7]) does not appear under that date, but does appear both under 1360 and 1362. It will also be noted that for many records, Short gives no place. This is understandable, since localities are often missed out in the early chronicles from which the data were obtained.

I shall now present to you Short's list of "unnatural Rains, Dews or other Downfalls", in print here for the first time in over 200 years, and the first compilation of Fortean falls in history. I will give it first exactly as it appears in the table, and then some notes on it derived from the text.

A fall of meteorites near Oxford, 9 April 1628. The chronicler reports that "one of them was seene by many people to fall at a place called Bawlkin Greene, *being a mile and a half from Hatford. Which thunderbolt was by one Mistris Greene caused to be digged out of the ground, she being an eye witnesse, among many others, of the manner of falling." [By kind permission of the Mary Evans Picture Library.]*

UNNATURAL RAINS, DEWS, OR OTHER DOWNFALLS

A.M. (*Anno Mundi*, i.e. since 4004 BC)

2553 It rained Stones on the 5 Kings confederated against Joshua, and discomfited them
3505 It rained Flesh
3736 It rained Milk at Rome
A.D.
4 It rained Blood above 5 hours in London
89 It rained Blood three Days together in England
324 Rained Blood 6 Hours in Somersetshire
442 Rained Blood in York
452 or 58 Rained Ashes at Constantinople
461 Rained Blood at Tholouse
535 Rained Blood; a sad Epidemic after
652 Ashes and Fire fell from Heaven on Constantinople, a Plague quickly after
685 Rained Blood in England
688 Rained Blood 7 Days together through all Britain; Milk, Cheese, and Butter, turned to Blood
722 In Campania, Wheat parched, Barley, &c, rained down
744 Ashes rained down
755 Little red Crosses fell out of the Air at Constantinople
766 Rained Blood 3 Days, then venemous Flies, then Mortality
782 or 7 Blood both rained down and sprung out of the Earth
825 Like Wheat and all Sort of Grain rained, but fatal to the Eaters
828 The like Rain in Gascoigne; or the same
874 Rained Blood in Italy
951 With a Tempest, and Thunder, a prodigious great Stone fell out of the Air red-hot, a fiery Dragon seen at the same time
987 Like Wheat, rained, in Saxony
989 In Saxony it rained small Fish, stinking
1014 A Heap of Clouds fell, and smothered Thousands
1017 or 18 It rained Blood in France
1057 It rained Stones mix'd with Hail
1060 Blood rained in the Neighbourhood of Paris
1113 June, at Ravenna, &c, it rained Blood
1163 June, it rained Blood, and a Spring in Britainy run Blood
1165 In Dolanus, Blood rained down
1176 or 7 It rained Blood in the Isle of Wight 2 Hours
1178 It rained Blood in England
1198 May, it rained Blood in England; on St John Baptist's Day fell a Dew, like and as sweet as Honey
1222 It rained at Rome, Dusk and Blood mix'd
1223 A Cloud burst, and choaked many People with Water
1226 In Syria fell Snow that turned to Blood; at Rome it rained Blood three Days
1270 It rained Blood 3 Days in Silesia
1274 It rained Blood in Wales
1346 It rained Toads and Rain mix'd
136- In Burgundy a Shower of Blood
1459 A bloody Rain in Bedfordshire
1552 Fell a Honey-dew at Basil, May 12
1556 May 15. a Shower of Blood
1568 June 6. rained Blood at Brabant
1571 A Shower of Blood
1618
1632 Dec. rained Ashes in the Gulf of Volo
1649 Feb. rained Blood at Gloucester
1656 May 20. rained Wheat near Oxford
1678 On St. Joseph's Day at Genoa fell a bloody Snow
1683 A small Shower of Blood at Thistleyholm near Moffat
1695 or_ A Dew, like yellow butter, fell at Limerick
1720 A Shower of Blood

The following items from the table appear in the text but with no reference: 3736 AM, 535, 744, 766, 775, 1060, 1113, 1178, 1274, 1361, 1459, 1678. The source for the Biblical fall of stones is fairly obvious. *Func.* (actually the *Chronologia* of Ioannes Funccius[8]) accounts for the following: 3505 AM, 874, 951, 987, 1346. The *Magdeburg Chronicle* is well-represented, and is cited for 652 (the fire), 782, 825,

989, 1057, 1163, 1165, 1198 (the dew – no reference for the fall of blood this year), 1270. *Zonaras* is quoted for the fall of ashes in 458, and *Siegbert* probably Siegbert of Gembloux) for 461, 722 and the ashes in 652. The referencee for the strange fall of clouds in 1014 is given as the *Anglo-Saxon Chronicle*, but the reference is misplaced, and really refers to the next item in the text, a marine inundation, which does appear in the Anglo-Saxon Chronicle for that year. The fall of clouds does not appear in the Anglo-Saxon Chronicle, or, as far as I know, in any other. Speed's *Isle of Wight* is cited for 1176, and *Trithem*. (the *Annales Hirsaugiensis* of Trithemius) for 1222 and 1223. The blank space after 1618 is "bloody rains" in the text, and the reference is given as "History of the Iron Age" (which I have still been unable to trace). The 1695 butter-dew is from *Phil. Trans.*[9] The degree of unintelligibility of the references is further compounded by the fact that sometimes Short strings them together at the end of a paragraph so that one cannot tell which reference applies to which item, and sometimes it is not readily apparent how many references have actually been strung together when the abbreviations are not familiar. The text entry for 1226 is "Snow fell in Syria, and presently turned to Blood... It rained Blood three Days at Rome. *Chr. Fuld. Magdeb. Chr. Germ. Baleus.*" Sort that out! Similarly we have "*Isac. Chron. Clark's Mirrour*" (688), "*Pantal. Chron. Func.*" (874), "*Sigbert Fuld. Episcop.*" (1017/18). The 688 item *is* in the Anglo-Saxon Chronicle, so presumably that is the decoding of "*Isac. Chron.*" The other items in the table do not appear in the text (rather fewer, proportionately, than in some of the other lists).

Just to complicate the issue, there are some items in the text that are not in the table. "A bloody Snow fell" in 864 (*Magdeburg Chronicle*), and an item without reference for 1007 states that "Drops of Blood fell on People's Cloaths".

Some of the items above deserve further comment. As to the fall of little red crosses in 775, Short adds "if some Historians are to be credited". Quite. The 825 item is worth quoting in full. "In Gascoigne, a Grain like Wheat, but much shorter, rained down. In other Places, great Heaps, and all Sorts of Grain were found; but if Cattle tasted it, they died presently; or if Meal was made of it, it vanished under the Hand."

With regard to the "fiery Dragon" of 951, this phrase appears often in early chronicles and is generally taken to refer to a meteor – sometimes the aurora borealis, but clearly the former is correct in this instance. As to the fall of blood in Wales in 1274, this is at least well-documented even if Short gives no reference. However, most chronicles give the date as 1247. It occurred concurrently with an earthquake in Wales[10]. At least one chronicle gives 1274[11] as the date – in which year there is also reported an earthquake in Wales[12], which is odd, not to say suspicious.

It's nice to see one classic fall of toads in the list, in 1346. Finally, the penultimate item, the dew like yellow butter at Limerick in 1695, brings us right up to date, for you will find this very item in Chapter 5 of *Book of the Damned*[13], thus nicely dovetailing Short's list of Forteana with Fort's own work 170 years later.

NOTES

[1] For biographical information on Short, see the entry in the *Dictionary of National Biography*. **[2]** In the British Museum Dept. of Manuscripts *Add. MSS* collection. **[3]** Ditto. **[4]** Published in London by T. Longman. **[5]** By S. Senn; in *New Scientist* for 22 October 1981. **[6]** I have adhered to Short's spelling and punctuation throughout, including the 18th century practice of using a capital for almost every noun. The one change I have made is to substitute modern "s" for the old long s ("ſ"). **[7]** See, for instance C.E. Britton, *A meteorological chronology to AD 1450* (HMSO, 1937.) **[8]** Published in 1554, later extended to 1601, and published in that year in Germany. **[9]** This abbreviation at least is still in common parlance. In full: *Philosophical Transactions of the Royal Society*. **[10]** For the earthquake, see either *Brut y Tywysogyon* or *Brenhinedd y Saesson*, both in the *Rolls Series*. The fullest account of the fall of blood is in the *Chronicle of the Abbey of St Werburg in Chester*. **[11]** One of the versions of *Walter of Guisborough's Chronicle*. The other two give 1275. **[12]** John Capgrave's *Chronicle*. The earthquake was felt chiefly in the west of England and probably occurred in 1275 not 1274. **[13]** Page 63 in *The Complete Books of Charles Fort* (1941, 1974).

POSTSCRIPT

Since writing the above I have discovered further accounts of the butter-dew, known as "fairy butter" in the north of England:

"*Tremella mesenterica.* A substance occasionally found after rain on rotten wood or fallen timber; in consistency and colour it is much like genuine butter. It is a yellow gelatinous matter, supposed by the country people to fall from the clouds. Hence its second popular name of star-jelly." (*The Denham Tracts*, vol 2, p111 note 3.)

[There are many records of such falls known to today's Forteans. The 'fairy butter' also went by the Celtic name of Pwdre Ser *or 'Rot of the Stars', and among other sources its fall, or at least discovery, was repeatedly included in the annual* Report of the British Association *(particularly in R. Gregg's great catalogue of 'meteorites' in the 1860 volume), and* Notes and Queries. *The day we received this article from Roger Musson we also received the December 1981 edition of* Fate *with a fine article on 'Blobs from Space?' by another FT reader, Ted Schultz, dealing in part with* Pwdre Ser *– Ed.]*

Heavenly Showers:

A Cursory Glance at Chinese Falls.

by Steve Moore.

This meagre collection of material fallen from Chinese skies can hardly claim to be more than a first scratch at the surface of a vast subject. The Chinese have an enormous literature... meteorological records, official and unofficial histories, local gazeteers, etc...which would doubtless produce thousands of similar cases if thoroughly researched. Such a task is unfortunately beyond my capabilities, this brief collection being limited both to source material in the English language, and by the vagaries of my exceedingly eccentric reading habits. It may, however, provide a starting point for future researches. Any further reference would be welcomed (and credited) for a possible supplement at a later date. Please write care of the *FT* address.

The cases have been divided up into sections fairly arbitrarily, and where possible some attempt has been made to evaluate the 'quality' of the source material in the notes. Unfortunately, this source material is extremely diverse, and some of it uses old systems of English transliteration with which I'm not entirely familiar. With apologies, I have felt unable to attempt standardising the transliteration to the modern system. Place-names, etc. generally appear as they were spelt in the original references.

DUBIOUS TALES

We begin with a few instances from myth, legend and folklore. Evidentially, of course, these are quite useless; but contextually they may be of some interest, in that they give some indication of how the *idea* of falling material has penetrated the Chinese mind.

1st Century BC: a strange tale. Chang Ch'ien was a historical figure who led expeditions to the far west of China and beyond in 138–126 BC, and again a few years later. As such, he was tramping the steppes of Central Asia, and had, as far as I know, no connection with the sea whatsoever. Our tale records, though, that he discovered "the end of the celestial ocean" and never returned. But there fell down from the river of heaven (i.e., the Milky Way) a skulling oar. Nobody knew what it was, until a spirit descended and declared it to be Chang Chi'en's oar, and that the rest of his ship would fall down as it decayed. (1) entry No 84.

8th Century AD: a folk tale explaining the name of Cassia Peak, west of Hangchow. In the reign of Emperor Xuan Zong (713–756 AD), at the time of the Moon Festival (15th day of the 8th lunar month) a monk, De Ming, who served as a cook in the Lingyin Temple, heard a sound like the gentle rustle of a silken gown outside his window. It was after midnight on a clear, cloudless night; but millions of small pearl-like pellets were falling from the moon over the surrounding hills. He collected a rice-bag full of the many-coloured, fragrant pellets, which were the size of soy beans, and showed them to the abbot, Zhi Yi. The abbot told him about the mythical Wu Gang, the man supposed to be exiled in the moon and forever trying to chop down the giant cassia tree which grows there; the tree growing faster the more he chops at it, of course. Zhi Yi supposed that Wu Gang was drunk that night and chopping away like mad, the result being that an immense number of cassia seeds had been shaken loose and tumbled to Earth. The seeds were planted, and thrived, on the local hills. (2) p35-36. (3) p94-95.

8th Century AD: an extremely mythical account. Erh-hsiang, the brother of Chin-ku (born 766 AD and later deified as Ta-nai Fu-jen, The Matron who hastens childbirth), was requested to free the district of Ku-t'ien Hsien, Fukien Province, of a child-eating supernatural snake. Erh-hsiang was drunk at the time of the encounter, and the snake was about to devour him; whereupon his Master, Yu Chia, appeared in the air and let fall a golden bell, which covered him and protected him from the snake. (4) p474.

No date: A legend relates that an old woman of Kiangsi Province had her arm broken by lightning. A voice from the clouds (inferred to be that of Lei Kung, the God of Thunder) said: "I have made a mistake." A bottle fell from the sky, and the voice continued: "Apply the contents and you will be healed at once." This being done, the local villagers wished to take the divine medicine away and hide it for future use, but several men together could not lift it from the ground. It suddenly rose up of its own volition, and returned to the sky. (4) p243. (5) p202.

No date: In an extremely mythical account of the origin of one of the spirits of the sea, the Buddha Shih-chia-wen appears in the clouds, bringing relief to a heat-tormented dragon. As the Spirits of the Mountains and Waters bowed before this violet-haired, shining-faced apparition, the air was filled with the odour of incense and a rain of flowers fell from the sky. (4) p435.

RELIGIOUS PHENOMENA

Just as miracles abound in the lives of Christian saints and mystics, so they do also in the lives, and especially deaths, of Buddhist monks; these tales therefore have to be treated with the same amount of caution and respect that we would accord to Christian hagiography.

Frenquently mentioned are falls of "relics", *She-li*, which is apparently a Chinese transliteration of the Sanskrit *Serira*, or *S'arira*; but precisely what these objects are is uncertain. Giles (6) p254, defines She-li as parts of the body of a (Buddhist) saint, gathered together after cremation and preserved; which would suggest a fall to consist largely of bones and ashes. However, Waddell (7) p497, mentions that the Tibetans, having burned a paper mask of the deceased, mix its ashes with clay to form a tablet, equivalent to S'arira. So the possibility of these falling relics being clay tablets should not be excluded, although the usual meaning is that of bodily relics.

Between 420 & 450 AD: At the Lung-ch'uan Ssu (Temple) in Hupei Province: a visiting monk, Hui Kung, being asked by the abbot, Hui-yuan, to demonstrate the efficacy of his prayers to Kuan Yin, recited so effectually, that the room was filled with a delicious fragrance and celestial melodies. Outside, flowers fell from the sky and covered the ground. (4) p191.

Date unknown (after 8th Century AD): The Buddhist monk, Tao-ming Ch'an-shih, having died at the K'ai-yuan Ssu (Temple), was cremated; during which process a shower of precious stones fell from the heavens. (4) p490.

Between 830 and 870 AD: During the burial of the Buddhist monk Tsung-mi Ch'an-shih, probably at Sui-chou, Ssuch'uan Province, there fell from the sky precious relics, She-li. (4) p525.

843 AD, or shortly thereafter: The Buddhist monk Kuang-hsui Tsun-che, a native of Chekiang Province, died in 843 AD, and was buried in the Chin-ti Tao-ch'ang monastery. Some time afterwards, his disciple Liang-hsu cremated the corpse, and a thousand precious relics, She-li, fell from the heavens. These relics were placed in a tower over his tomb. (4) p230.

10th Century AD (?): The Buddhist monk Ch'uan-hsu Ch'an-shih, living in the O-chou department of Hupei Provoince, having been killed by rebels, his disciples cremated his body; at which point 49 precious stones fell from the heavens. (4) p101.

1028 AD: place unknown. The Buddhist monk Fa-chih Tsun-che (secular name Chin Chih-li) having died, his disciples kept him unburied for 24 days, during which his corpse remained undecayed. On his burial, five-coloured She-li (i.e. multi-coloured relics) fell from the sky "in abundance". (4) p120.

18th Century AD: the Buddhist monk Hsiang-an Fa-shih (died 1734 AD), a native of Kiangsu Province, made a pilgrimage to the mountain O-yu-wang Shan. There, before a statue of Buddha, he burned his fingers as an act of penance and made 48 vows. A shower of precious stones fell from the heavens. (4) p170.

SWEET DEW

We have numerous references to falls of "Sweet Dew" (*Kan Lu*, or *Gan Lu*), but unfortunately no one seems to have any solid idea of exactly what this substance is. Balfour (8), p161 mentions the appearance on the ground on "various occasions" of dew as sweet as sugar to the taste. Dennys (9) p128, speculates that it is some sort of secretion of animal origin, but goes no further. Rogers (10) p207, gives a Chinese description of the substance: "the semen of spirits, viscous as fat, sweet as sugar." In religious terminology, Kan Lu is frequently associated with the nectar of compassion and mercy, or to the water of life, Amrita. But we also learn of a *Kan-lu Ssu* (Sweet Dew Temple) at Chiu-hua Shan in Anhwei Province, where this "ambrosial brewage of the gods" is bottled and sold by the monks to pilgrims, for both faith and physical healing purposes (11) p105.

Whatever its substance, the significance of Kan Lu is well known; such a fall is believed to symbolise peace, prosperity, benevolent rule and harmony between heaven and earth. Thus a report of its fall was often considered good reason for changing the title of the Imperial reign-period to 'Kan Lu'.

53 BC: The reign title of the Han Emperor was changed to Kan Lu. As we have other cases where such a change followed immediately on a fall of such Sweet Dew, we would conjecture a similar fall for 53 BC; but so far have found no actual reference. (10) p207.

256 AD: in the 5th lunar month (i.e. 10 June–9 July), both the districts of Yeh and Shang-ku reported that Sweet Dew had fallen; as a result of which, on 10 July 256 AD, the reign title of the Emperor of the Wei dynasty was changed to Kan Lu (12) Vol 2, p245.

265 AD: In the 4th lunar month (3rd-31st May), the district of Chiang-ling reported that Sweet Dew had fallen, as a result of which the reign title in the kingdom of Wu was changed to Kan Lu. A separate report from the same source, of the same date, says that the district of Nan Shen-tse-hsien had also reported a fall of Sweet Dew. Whether these cases are identical, or not, is not known. (12) Vol 2, p509.

359 AD: In the 6th lunar month, Fu Chien, ruler of the Former Ch'in state, changed his reign-title to Kan Lu after Sweet Dew fell from the sky. We have no location or further details. (10) p117, 207.

5th Century AD (?): At the Shaolin Temple, Song Shan, Henan Province, there is an earthen platform called the Gan Lu Tai (Sweet Dew Platform). It is said to have been built by Ba Tuo (Buddhabhadra) who, according to our source (13) p54-44, founded the Shaolin Temple in 496 AD. Sweet Dew drops are said to have fallen on the platform while he was translating Buddhist scriptures there, thus giving the platform its name. But Werner (4) p137-138, makes no mention of Buddhabhadra having any connection with Shaolin, and states that he died in 429 AD, aged 71.

1109 AD: In the 3rd lunar month, a sweet dew descended on the chancellory, at the Imperial capital of Bianjing. (14) p23.

1728 AD(?): Dennys dates this case to 1788, but a typographical error seems likely, as he also states specifically that it occurred in the reign of Emperor Yung Cheng (1723-1736); I have thus conjectured 1728 to be the more likely date. The Emperor was memorialised to the effect that Sweet Dew had fallen for three days in the Sung-kiang prefecture (9) p128.

ICE, HAIL, etc.

Balfour (8)p161, mentions falls of hailstones the size of a man's fist, but gives no details whatsoever.

155 BC, Autumn: At Heng-shan, a fall of hailstones five inches across, which penetrated two feet into the ground. (15) Vol 1, p368.

149 BC, 31st May, or thereabouts: At Yuan-tu, in Heng-shan, a fall of hailstones reaching a size of one foot and eight inches. (15) Vol 1, p370.

181 AD, 18th July: Place unknown. A fall of hailstones as big as hen's eggs. (16) p1.

384 AD: the forces of the Eastern Chin Empire, under Yao Ch'ang, were surrounded and trapped at Pei-ti, in Shensi Province, in the 6th lunar month. The surrounding forces (of

Drawing by Steve Moore

the Former Ch'in Empire) had cut off Yao's water supply. His men were dying of thirst when, with the situation at its most extreme, there seems to have been a spot rainfall directed on his camp. Within the camp, the water was said to be three feet deep, while a hundred paces outside it was only something over an inch. Yao Ch'ang's men recovered sufficiently to win the following battle. (10) p177.

1590 AD: on the 18th day of the 6th lunar month (approx July), snow fell one summer night from the midst of the moon. The flakes were like fine willow flowers or shreds of silk. No geographical location given (9) p118.

1773 AD: the Chinese record runs thus: on the 20th day of the 7th lunar month (approx. August), a group of dragons burnt paddy in the field, drew houses into the air and travellers also, and hail-stones of two or three catties weight fell, killing horses and animals. A Chinese catty is equivalent to one and a third pounds, so these hailstones would have weighed between two and two-thirds and four pounds each. Dennys interprets this as a description of a water-spout, but I never heard of water setting fire to paddy-fields before. (9) p127.

1885 AD: "summer snow" was reported as having fallen near Soochow, causing great terror to the local populace. This occurred two years before publication of Balfour's book, so is presumably to be dated to 1885 (8) p161.

1983 AD: 11th April, 12-50pm, at Wuxi, Jiangsu Province (near Shanghai). An ice meteorite landed by the side of the road, producing a thin fog and causing nearby powerlines to sway. Some 60 centimetres in diameter, it broke into pieces, the biggest being 10 centimetres across. The largest ice-fall since modern meteorology began in China, 150 years ago, it is believed originally to have been two metres in diameter, and to have weighed nearly a ton. For once, there is no mention of passing planes or illegal toilet-flushing. An extraterrestrial origin seems certain: the meteor was picked up by satellite photographs, entering the Earth's atmosphere at 23-24°N, 130-132°E, and leaving a heat-trail toward Wu Xi. A dozen millilitres of the melted meteorite were handed over to scientists for study. (17) p41.

COLOURED RAINS

Dennys mentions that rains of blood have frequently recorded in conjunction with earthquakes, but gives no cases. (9) p126.

481 BC: An apocryphal text of the Han dynasty, the *Ch'un-ch'iu-wei Yen-k'ung-t'u* (Apocryphal Treatise on the Spring and Autumn Annals: Expository chart on Confucius), records this very apocryphal story: in 481 BC, it rained blood which formed into writing on the main gate of the capital of the state of Lu. This gave a message prophecying the death of Confucius and the subsequent history of his school of thought; the prophecy extending no later than the Han dynasty, of course. (18) Vol 2, p129-130.

300 AD: A red rain at Nanking, or in its immediate neighbourhood. The water which fell is said to have stained cloth the colour of blood. (8) p159.

1108 AD: 7th month: There was a drought between the Yellow and Huai rivers. The Taoist adept Wang Wenqing, after some unsuccessful attempts to solve the problem, prayed to the Lord of the Yellow River, asking to borrow three feet of the Yellow River. The following day a sweet rain fell, of a yellow colour. (14) p23. This tale sounds unlikely, but we also have it from a second source (4) p548: here the same Wang Wen-ch'ing, also known as Wang Shih-ch'en, is said to be a specialist rain-magician and protege of the Emperor Hui Tsung (1101-1126 AD); the drought is said to have been in the Yang Chou district, and Wang, by seizing his magic sword and blowing water from his mouth, is said to have *raised* the Yellow River by three feet. Some days later, the magistrate of Yang Chou reported that rain of a yellow colour had fallen at that place. See notes on both these sources.

1336 AD: a red rain fell in the neighbourhood of K'ai-feng Fu, the water being said to have stained cloth the colour of blood (8) p159.

Between 1368 and 1399 AD: No geographical location. Black rain, "as black as ink", fell during the reign of the first Emperor of the Ming dynasty, Hung Wu (8) p159.

1879 or 1880 AD: A red rain reported to have fallen in certain districts of Kiangsi Province, "seven or eight years" before the publication of Balfour's book, in 1887. (8) p159.

DUST, SAND, EARTH, STONES.

Balfour mentions, again without examples, violent gales, charged with so much dust as to make it impossible to distinguish a man two paces away (8) p161.

1231 AD, 9th April: Hangchow, Chekiang Province. Yellow clouds laden with sand plunged the city into semi-darkness. It rained, and all the roofs were covered with a yellow dust which penetrated everywhere and went up the nostrils of people in the streets. Visibility was restricted to a few yards. The sun, giving no light, was "like a metal mirror that has not been polished". At night, as the sand-fall continued, a fire broke out in a house east of the Bridge of the Immortals and spread in all directions. The next day the air was so thick with dust that it was impossible to see the glow of the fire. When the fire was extinguished at mid-day, ten thousand houses in the southeast of the city had been destroyed. (19) p180, quoting *Kuei hsin tsa chih.*

1511 AD: no geographical location. A rain of earth fell in the 5th year of the Ming Emperor Cheng-te (1511 AD). Balfour interprets this as a dust-storm of preternatural violence. (8) p161.

1626 AD, 31st May: Peking. A sudden earthquake. A sound like thunder rose in the northwest, shaking heaven and earth, and "black clouds flowed over confusedly". Dwellings were destroyed to such an extent that for several *li* (3 li = 1 mile) nothing remained. "Great stones hurtled down from the sky like rain". Smashed skulls, broken limbs and death resulted for humans and animals alike. Gunpowder in the Imperial Arsenal exploded, alarming the Imperial elephants, which ran amok and trampled people. 537 dead. (20) p65; a translation of *K'ai-tu ch'uan-hsin.*

ASTRONOMICAL EVENTS

Many of the cases in this section may be nothing more than colourful accounts of ordinary meteors/meteorites, but they have been thought worth including anyway. Modern accounts of accepted meteorites have been omitted.

211 BC: Ssuma Chien records, for the 36th year of the reign of Chin Shih Huang-ti, the

first emperor of China, that a "shooting star turned into a stone" when it fell to earth at Tungchun. Upon the stone was inscribed: "After the First Emperor's death the land will be divided", and one presumes that the story got about that a prophetic stone had fallen from heaven. However, it is Ssuma Chien's opinion that someone had written the characters on the stone after it had fallen (he does not seem to doubt the actual fall), and such an opinion was apparently shared by the Emperor's chief councillor, who went to investigate. Regrettably, no one would admit to the deed, so everyone in the vicinity of the stonefall was executed, and the stone destroyed by fire (21) p182. Balfour concurs in the opinion that the whole affair was probably a plot; he, however, doubts even the veracity of the original fall (8) p40-41.

238 AD: The City of Hsiang-p'ing, held by Kung-sun Yuan and his son, was under siege by the troops of the Wei kingdom. In the 8th lunar month, on the day "ping-yin" (3rd September, 238 AD), a long shooting star, white in colour and with a tail several hundred feet in length, streaked over the city. According to the *Chin Shu* (History of the Chin dynasty), it moved from the south-west of the city toward the north-east, and plunged into a river called the Liang Shui. But according to the *San Kuo Chih* (Chronicle of the Three Kingdoms), it came from the north-east of the mountain Shou Shan, and fell south-east of the city. This event terrified Kung-sun Yuan into seeking surrender terms, which were refused. On 29th September (or even on the 3rd; the chronology is confused), Hsiang-p'ing fell. Kung-sun Yuan and his son, attempting to break out, were killed on the bank of the Liang Shui, where the star fell. (12) Vol 1, p574, 595-597.

616 AD: 14th January: a "flowing star" (meteor) fell on the camp of the outlaw Lu Ming-yueh (place unknown), destroying some of his military engines and killing a dozen or so men. The same Chinese source mentions two examples of similar phenomena for 617 AD, but no details. (22) p94.

620 AD: 29th November: a meteor fell within the city walls at Loyang, with a thunderous roar (22) p94.

653 AD, between 27 October and 25 November: a "star" fell on the camp of the woman rebel Ch'en Shih-chen at Mu-chou, in Chekiang Province. (22) p94.

708 AD, 17 March: A meteor fell with "a thunderous roar", "in the south-west", causing all the pheasants to scream. (22) p94.

712 AD, between 9 July and 6 August: As the marshal Sun Ch'uan set out on a punitive expedition against the Manchurian tribes, a "great star" fell into his camp (22) p95.

744 AD, 7 April: a meteor "like the moon" fell south-east of Ch'ang-an, followed by a noise (22) p95.

757 AD. 19 May: a "great star", coloured reddish-yellow, with a train several hundred feet long, fell in the camp of the rebel general Wu Ling-hsun, as he laid siege to the city of Nan-yang (22) p95. Note the great affinity that Chinese falls have for military camps, especially those of rebels and bandits.

811 AD, 31 March: Shantung Province (?). A great meteor fell out of the sky with a thunderous roar. A red vapour like a snake arose from the place where it fell. The wild pheasants cried out. (22) p95.

837 AD, 18 December: a star fell at Hsing-yuan, in Shensi. (2) p96.

887 AD, between 27 May and 24 June: a great star fell out of the daylight sky into the military camp of Ch'in Tsung-ch'uan at Pienchou (i.e. K'ai-feng). (22) p97.

894 AD, summer: A star fell in Yueh-chou, in Chekiang Province, followed by a light more than ten feet long and shaped like a serpent. (22) p97.

896 AD, between 14 July and 12 August: place unknown. A star like a tea-cup rose in the south-west and fell in the north-east with a sound like a flock of ducks (22) p97.

1561 AD: place unknown. A meteor, having lain where it had fallen for several days, suddenly moved of itself. No further details (9) p120.

MISCELLANEOUS DROPPINGS

Grain falls: I've been unable to trace the falls in question, but Rogers mentions, in his notes, a quotation from the *Lun Heng* by Wang Ch'ung (27-97 AD) to the effect that the phenomenon of grain raining from heaven was considered to be an evil omen in ancient times; the reasoning being that any peak is inevitably followed by a decline: thus when heaven showers down grain, it provides a super-abundance of blessings, which can only portend imminent disaster. (10) p271.

340 BC (approx?): a rain of metal fell at Li-yang, in the state of Ch'in (15) vol 2, p22.

4th Century AD (prior to 382 AD): a long, involved tale concerning a mysterious vessel named the "Life-protecting Precious Tripod", allegedly originating from the legendary Emperor Chuan-hsu (traditionally, 2514-2437 BC). It was made of jade, and inscribed upon it were genealogical tables of all the emperors, kings and famous liege-men, from antiquity until the time of Fu Chien, Emperor of the Former Ch'in dynasty. Its finding was predicted by Wang Tiao, just prior to his execution for offering "treasonous" advice and prophecies, and it was duly found at the predicted place (Hsin-p'ing commandery in Shensi province) at the predicted time (382 AD). The date of

Drawing by Steve Moore

Wang's execution is not certain. In giving his prophecy, Wang remarked that he had studied under Liu Chan of Ching-chao (Shensi) who told him: "Once when I was practicing asceticism in my apartment, at midnight there was a shooting star as big as a half-moon which fell in this place." Wang Tiao proposed that this shooting star referred to the jade vessel, but it is not clear from the context whether the shooting star simply marked the location of the vessel, or actually was the vessel falling from heaven. No date is given for Liu Chan's sighting. (10) p154.

519 AD: no place mentioned; Fish fell from a shooting star. No further details. (9) p120.

Pre 10th Century AD: According to the *Yuh t'ang hien hwa*, a work surviving only in fragments but attributed to Wang Jen-yu (880-956 AD), something resembling a poltergeist haunting occurred at the Tung-ko Buddhist monastery, Lung-ch'ing district; at present Tsin-an, in Kansu province. Potsherds were thrown down from the air and dust was whirled up. A Taoist priest attempted to exorcise the place, only to have all his clothes stripped off by the spirits. The prefect of the district visited the place, and was showered with written leaflets in countless numbers, mostly written with complete sentences, full of insults and malice. Another man, relying on his own strength, attempted to revile the spirits, and was promptly struck in the groin by a large stone. What happened after that is not known; neither is there any fixed date for this story. (23) Book 2, Vol 5, p471-473.

No date: on the subject of written messages: Maitreya (known in Chinese as *Mi-lo Fu*), the coming Buddha, is due to appear either 3,000 or 5,000 years after the historical Buddha Sakyamuni (6th Century BC), when the world will have become utterly corrupt. However, his early arrival has frequently been announced, along with instructions to prepare for his appearance, in letters said to have fallen from heaven. (4) p303.

1107 AD: In Luzhou, it rained beans. This was considered an auspicious omen. (14) p22.

1782 AD: a formless body as large as a house bounded over the dykes near Yuling, furrowing the ground as it went, before ending up in the sea. From the context, it appears that this object originated in the sky. (9) p120.

REFERENCES AND SOURCE-NOTES

1. *Extracts from Histories and Fables to which Allusions are frequently made in Chinese Literature,* translated from the *Arte China* of Pere Goncalves, by Sir John Bowring. *The Chinese Repository*, 1851; reprinted in *The Chinese & Japanese Repository,* 1863-4. This particular entry published 3 March 1864, p391. Pere Goncalves was an uncritical collector, to put it kindly. His material is totally unreferenced, and subject to the wildest distortions.
2. *Folk Tales of the West Lake* by Wang Hui-ming (Foreign Languages Press, Beijing, 1982). Folk-tales. Chinese folklorists are not at all averse to "tidying up" their material for political or social purposes.
3. *West Lake, a collection of folktales,* translated by Jan & Yvonne Walls (Joint Publishing Co, Hong Kong, 1980). Folktales. See note 2.
4. *A Dictionary of Chinese Mythology* by E T C Werner (Kelly & Walsh, Shanghai, 1932; reprint: Julian Press, N.Y. 1961). This vast and monumental work is marred by the author's uncritical and unreferenced collecting. Material from genuine mythological texts is mixed with material from novels, histories, religious works and folklore without distinction. The material given above in the "Religious Phenomena" section seems all to be derived from religious histories, and is thus as reliable or unreliable as such works tend to be; with the other entries, it is almost impossible to make any judgement.
5. *Myths and Legends of China* by E T C Werner (Harrap, 1922). See note 4; the same criticisms apply.
6. *A Glossary of Reference on Subjects Connected with the Far East* by H A Giles (1878; reprint: Curzon Press, 1974).
7. *The Buddhism of Tibet, or Lamaism* by L A Waddell (Heffer & Sons, Cambridge, 1967).
8. *Leaves from my Chinese Scrapbook* by Frederic Henry Balfour (Trubner, 1887). A short chapter on portents, which skims the subject, frequently mentioning things that have happened without giving specific cases or references. Those he does give, however, are presumably fairly reliable.
9. *The Folklore of China* by Nicholas B Dennys 1876; (reprint, Oriental Press, Amsterdam, 1968). Poorly referenced and patronising; what sort of Chinese literature he's quoting is unknown, so the cases have to be taken at face value.
10. *The Chronicle of Fu Chien* trans. by Michael C Rogers (University of California Press, 1968). An excerpt from the *Chin Shu*, the Official History of the Chin dynasty. As such, it ought to be reliable, but Rogers is of the opinion that the narrative has been fictionalised and mythicised to turn it into an exemp-

lary piece. However, this opinion seems to be based largely on the number of portents it records, which raises an interesting point. If one believes portents do not occur, the narrative obviously appears fictionalised; if they *do* occur...

11. *The Nine Sacred Mountains of China* by Mary Augusta Mullikin and Anna M Hotchkis (Vetch & Lee Ltd, Hong Kong, 1973). The travel record of two ladies in China in the 1930s. Lightweight.

12. *The Chronicle of the Three Kingdoms* trans. by Achilles Fang (Harvard University Press, Cambridge, Mass. 2 vols, 1952, 1965) A translation from the *Tzu Chih T'ung Chien* of Ssu-ma Kuang (1019-1086 AD). Ssu-ma Kuang's massive work is a compilation from the official histories, to give a chronicle from the earliest times to his own period. This translation gives a great deal of his original source material as well, and so should be a thoroughly reliable text.

13. *Shaolin Temple* by Zhang Jiata (Zhong Zhou Arts & Classics Press, Henan, 1983). A locally produced guidebook. The English "translion" (sic) is frequently amusing.

14. *Proclaiming Harmony* trans. by William O. Hennessey (University of Michigan, 1981). A translation of a 13th or 14th Century romance, *Neglected Events of the Reign Period "Proclaiming Harmony"*. Like many such early works of "Faction", it is an expansion of the official histories and chronicles. It falls into two halves; most of the fictionalising is in the second half; the first, which contains the cases quoted here, is little more than a bald and laconic historical chronicle setting the scene for later events. As the events quoted seem to have no relevance to the development of the story, I assume they have been included because they are a matter of historical record and so, with obvious hesitation, I've decided to include them here.

15. *Records of the Grand Historian of China* trans. by Burton Watson (Columbia University Press, N.Y., 1961. 2 vols). A partial translation of the *Shih Chi* of Ssu-ma Ch'ien (145?-90? BC). This is the first of the Chinese Official Histories, and as such should be reliable.

16. *The Last of the Han* trans. by Rafe de Crespigny (Australian National University, Canberra, 1969). Further chapters from the work of Ssu-ma Kuang. See note 12.

17. *China Reconstructs* (Beijing) Vol 32, No 9, Sept 1983.

18. *History of Chinese Philosophy* by Fang Yu-lan (Princeton University Press, N.J. 2 vols, 1952, 1953). A reliable work, quoting an extremely unreliable text.

19. *Daily Life in China* by Jaques Gernet (Allen & Unwin, 1962). Reliable.

20. *Two Studies on Ming History* by Charles O Hucker (University of Michigan, 1971). Despite the wretchedly ungrammatical title of the book, the text seems reliable enough.

21. *Records of the Historian* by Szuma Chien, trans by Yang Hsien-yi & Gladys Yang (Commercial Press, Hong Kong, 1974). Further translations from the *Shih Chi.* See note 15.

22. *Pacing the Void* by Edward H Schafer (University of California, 1977) An excellent compendium of T'ang dynasty astronomical lore. Chapter 6 contains an excellent compilation of reports of meteors and apparent meteors. With apologies for so blatantly hijacking Schafer's material, I have sifted out those cases where something actually hit the ground.

23. *The Religious System of China* by J J M de Groot (reprint, Literature House Ltd, Taipei, 1964. 6 vols). De Groot was a man not entirely averse to quoting acknowledged works of fiction to demonstrate his point. Knowing nothing further of the work he quotes here, I can only assume it to be a factual report.

Books quoted above were published in London, unless otherwise stated. Remarks on the quality of material are personal opinions, naturally.

SILLY MID-OFF

The following item comes from *Cricketer International*, July 1984. We suspect that the name Charles Fortune is too good to be true....but you never can tell!

Raining cats and frogs

DUDLEY Schoof has, for a decade, been a leading umpire and is vice-president of the S.A. Cricket Umpires' Association.

I recently received from him a paragraph which may be of interest to cricketers and umpires generally. Mr Schoof had stood in the final of our day-night Benson & Hedges series at The Wanderers on the evening of Friday, March 30. His letter runs:

"You will be very interested to learn that, shortly after 9.00 pm, I was standing at square-leg and received a sharp blow on the top of the head. On looking in front of me, I found a small frog of approximately 1.5 inches in length on the grass, recoving from having hit me on the head. This is certainly the strangest phenomenon that has happened to me on a cricket field and I can only assume that it fell a few hundred feet from the heavy black clouds which were over the ground.

Would your English cricketers know of any similar experience?

CHARLES FORTUNE

PO Box 55009
Northlands 2116
South Africa

Forum

The Werewolves of Devon.

by Richard Gwynn.

Recent issues of FT [FT40 & 42] have chronicled the extraordinary depredations of livestock in Devon, mainly around Exmoor, attributed to a mystery animal dubbed 'The Beast of Exmoor'. [See p28 this issue for the latest news – Ed] With a little lateral thinking a quite different, and if true, more disturbing solution offers itself, and I offer these ideas for general discussion.

Since ancient times humans have been victims, willingly or otherwise, of the plague of werewolfery or lycanthropy. It can be a disorder, a disease, a curse or a cult. Plato mentioned it, but the earliest record of a werewolf cult I could find was in Pliny's *Historia Naturalis*: "Demaenetus, an Arcadian, transformed himself into a wolf by partaking of the entrails of a boy who had been sacrificed at Mount Lycaeus, since the Arcadians used to offer human sacrifice to Zeus Lycaean. After a space of ten years he recovered his original form, and overcoming all others in boxing, was crowned a victor at the Olympic Games." (Book 34, ch. 22).

Possibly closer, culturally and racially, to Britains than the Greeks are the Norse berserkers, followers of Odin in one of his more terrible aspects. Berserkers dressed in wolf and bear skins, and when transformed by Odin, through drinking a magical draught of beer, they would kill and devour anything or anybody who got in their way. They were members of a warrior cult which entered Britain with the Viking invasions; although there is some evidence that a Greco-Roman lycathropist cult was in existence in Britain by the first century AD.

There were also other cults in early Europe which centred on lycanthropy or vampirism. The distinction between the two has always been blurred. Douglas Hill, in his article 'Werewolf', in *Man, Myth and Magic*, described some interesting differences: "It has long been recognized that the mental illness known as lycanthropy is associated with a pathological condition in which the sufferer believes himself to be a wild beast and, as the old case histories show, develops a taste for raw or putrid meat, a desire to howl and run naked through the woods, and sometimes a wish to kill, rape and eat young girls. Assuredly, the werewolf is just as sexual a figure as the vampire but he lacks the sado-erotic subtlety of the vampire – werewolves are crude rapists and murderers with a few ghoulish or cannibalistic overtones."

In all the metamorphic or transformation cults I've looked at, there seems to be a common denominator: consumption of special food or drink *before* the change occurs. The man, or more rarely, the woman, after consumption becomes a werewolf or werebear, sometimes even a toad or a reptile. *Were* is an old Saxon word that simply means 'man'.

It is now known that the lycanthropic syndrome can be induced by eating the ergot fungus, *claviceps*, which grows on the ears of barley, blackgrass, rye, wheat and a number of other cereal grains. It contains an indole alkaloid chemical closely related to lysergic acid diethylamide, or LSD as it more widely known. There are a number of different types of ergot, and in ancient Greece it was *Claviceps paspati* which was given to the worshippers of Zeus Lycaean in the form of a large cup of *kykeion,* a foaming brew of ergot-infected barley. The ergot which infects England, and most of western Europe from France to Russia and Scandinavia, is *C. purpurea*, which also contains large quantities of two poisons: ergotamine and ergometrine. These two chemicals modify the effects of the alkaloid, giving the eater an almost limitless nightmare, after which he remembers nothing except the exhilaration.

The physical effects of *purpurea* poisoning include frothing at the mouth, paralysis of the salivery glands, uncontrollable rage, a construction of the vocal cords creating wolf-like howls, a burning sensation in the limbs, and as mentioned a feeling of tremendous excitement. The intoxicated 'victims' have shape-shifting hallucinations, easily imagining themselves to be wolves or other wild creatures. Because the wolf is a particularly European obsession, especially during the Middle Ages, it is no wonder that outbreaks of werewolf or vampire activities were more common then.

So what has this got to do with the Exmoor Beast? The link has been provided by Professor John Grange in his article 'Werewolvery' (*Devon Life* June 1984), in which he reveals that Devon and southern England have suffered more outbreaks of ergot-infected crops than any other areas of the country. Prof Grange writes: "Most people in medieval Devon ate bread which was tainted with ergot. An epidemic of mass-hallucinatory madness – St Anthony's Fire – occurred whenever there was a wet, cold ergot (growth) year. Many thousands of people died in a hallucinatory delirium. St Anthony's Fire took several forms, the most terrible being werewolvery. In 1195 Devon suffered an outbreak of what. . .modern doctors and psychologists would call ergot-induced lycanthropy. Demented lycanthropes – persons acting like wolves and really believing themselves to be wolves – ranged through the great forests which still covered much of Devon attacking shepherds and lonely farms. . .filling the world with a heart-stopping fear of were-wolvery." Gervase of Tilbury refers to the 1195 epidemic, in his *Otia Imperialia* (1212), writing that "frequently. . .men in England transformed into wolves for the space of a month. . ." Another historian, known as 'Walsingham', described a further two outbreaks in 1340 and 1362.

No one could explain these strange epidemics until recently when research into the pathology of ergot poisoning, and the discovery, in 1982, of ergotized grains dating back in the 1360s, helped unravel the mystery. Exmoor and Dartmoor are both ergot infested areas, and the grains grown there are very susceptible. The last major outbreak in England occurred in Devon in 1700. A Dr Freind recorded that many people in villages fringing Exmoor "were taken with frequent barking and howling like wolves and foaming at the mouth". But perhaps the most famous case was that at Pont St Esprit, in the Rhone valley of France, as recently as 1951, affecting 300 people, leaving five dead. The religious, unaware of the ergot explanation, might have thought it was a case of mass denomic possession.

In the cold, damp years of 1981, 1982 and early 1983, the winter wheat crop in south-west England became heavily infested with ergot fungus. Millers and Ministry of Agriculture officials destroyed many tons of contaminated grain. Did they find it all? Or did some people deliberately keep some precisely because it was infected? Are there now, on Exmoor, willing victims of *C. purpurea*? These periods correlate well with findings of 'Exmoor Beast' livestock mutilations. Of old, there are always some humans who will take any kind of mind-altering drug, regardless of the danger, and a fungus which has the power to turn a man into a wolf would be irresistable temptation to a few. Is it not possible then that the 'Exmoor Beast' is none other than a member or members of Lycanthropes Anonymous?

I shall be doing more research on this idea, and hopefully will get the chance to examine, forensically, a 'Beast'-killed animal. Any comments or suggestions would be very welcome.

●

Dick Gwynn
'Woolsack', Woolsery, Bideford,
N. Devon, EX39 5QS.

Elsie and The Liddell People.

by Doc Shiels.

Once upon a time, an old dodderer called Dodgson met a pretty little maid on a train. Her name was Elsie Wright, but the perverse old dodo insisted on calling her 'Leslie' because, for him, the name Elsie would always mean L.C., the initials of his nom-de-plume, 'Lewis Carroll', or Lorina Charlotte, known as Elsie, sister of Dodgson's heart-throb, A.L.P. or Alice Pleasance Liddell. Dodgson loved little girls (he was not so keen on boys or babies), thinking of them as 'human elves and fairies'. He was an expert photographer, and his favourite subject was 'pretty maids'. . .especially in what he called their 'favourite dress of "nothing"'.

On a warm July day in 1862, three little Liddells. . . Alice, L.C., and Edith, the littlest. . .listened to the 'fairytale' of *Alice's Adventures Underground.* Then, 55 years later, on another warm July day, a pretty young girl called Elsie Wright took the first of several fairy photographs at Cottingley Glen, West Yorkshire. Of course, this was not the same Miss Wright that the dodderer had met on the train, but he would have surely approved of Cottingley Elsie's interest in fairies and photography. I think he would have liked her cousin Frances, too, especially as she had the same first name as his mother and his sister 'Fanny'.

Another famous old writer with a keen interest in fairies and photography of Elsie and Frances was Sir Arthur Conan Doyle. When certain people suggested that the Cottingley pictures were fakes, Sir Arthur strongly defended the 'innocence' of his young friends. Dodgson thought Alice Liddell was 'innocent' too, though she bewitched him entirely.

Consciously or unconsciously, Alice dabbled in witchcraft. When 'Lewis Carroll' sent her chasing a trickster-rabbit into the Underworld, his shape-shifting heroine underwent a shamanic, oneiromantic experience. She drank the magic potion, ate the magic mushroom, uppers and downers. She grew a long serpentine neck, and repeatedly invoked the name of her familiar, Dinah, a black cat. Dinah sounds like Diana, a witch-name, and the name of Alice

Liddell's mother. Yes, Alice is a witch-name, too. As Alice was told, when she passed *Through the Looking Glass*: 'With a name like yours, you might be any shape, almost.'

The hare is a lunar animal, a companion of witches, and the hat is a symbol of authority. White hares and rabbits are known to pop out of wizards' top-hats. In Looking-glass Land, Alice's mad Hare and Hatter become Haigha and Hatta, punning the witch-spell, 'Horse and Hattock', spoken when one wishes to make a broomstick fly. 'I love my love with an H', said Alice. One day, in 1921, a psychic gentleman named Hodson visited Cottingley Glen and saw lots of elves, gnomes and fairies. He wrote about this enchanting event in his book, *Fairies at Work and Play*. Hodson and Dodgson. . .what can it mean?

Riddle: Hoddy doddy,
With a round black body,
Three feet and a wooden hat,
Pray tell me what is that.
Answer: a three-legged cauldron with a wooden lid.

In 1922, Conan Doyle's book, *The Coming of the Fairies*, was published by Hodder. 'Hod-ma-Dod, Hod-ma-Dod, stick out your horns,' said the witch-girl to the snail. Dicky Doyle, Sir Arthur's artist uncle, drew fairies riding on snails. He worked for *Punch*, up to 1850, when John Tenniel, illustrator of the 'Alice' books, replaced him. A curious piece of street naming makes Doyle Gardens lead us to Liddell Gardens in London, NW10.

Oh, we know the fairies in the Cottingley photographs were, as 'Lewis Carroll' would say, 'made entirely of cardboard'. . .just like the King, the Queen and their playing-card court in Wonderland. . .but that's not really the point. Elsie Wright copied her first cut-outs from a picture of dancing fairies which she found in *Princess Mary's Gift Book* (Hodder, 1915). This was an illustration for a poem by Noyes (No-Yes!) called *A Spell for a Fairy*. . .an invocation, no less. Elsie's cardboard fairies were, perhaps, decoys, with which she hoped to lure the *real* fairies and to capture them, photographically. If so, her technique was a mixture of sympathetic magic and hunting guile. If we believe Hodson, the Cottingley fairies were there to be seen by those who could see. The cardboard decoys, as they appear in the photographs, could also be 'red-herrings', diverting attention from authentic paranormal happenings at Cottingley Glen. Look into the backgrounds of *all* those pictures, and maybe you will catch a glimpse of something weird in the foliage. Remember, there's more to this business than meets the eye. . .which is exactly what Alice thought about the Looking-glass.

The Fairies Were Real.

by Leslie Shepard.

Although the famous Cottingley fairy photographs are now known to be fakes, it would be premature to write off the fairies themselves as fraudulent. There are various aspects of the Cottingley case that deserve closer examination.

According to Joe Cooper (*The Unexplained*, Issue 117), Frances told him that she had often seen fairies. She was scolded by the grownups for falling in the stream and getting her clothes wet. When she explained that she had been playing with the fairies she was not believed. It was Elsie who dreamed up the strange idea of getting their own back on the Wright adults by proving the fairies real by faked photographs. As she explained later, it was to be "Santa Claus in reverse" – playing a prank on adults who sneered at fairies but told fibs about Santa Claus.

The adults were meant to be overwhelmed by photographic proof of the reality of fairies, after which the girls would triumphantly reveal the hoax. In fact, the adults refused to believe in the photographs right from the start and the joke fell flat on its face.

It was revived fortuitously when Elsie's mother attended a Theosophical lecture a year later at which fairy folklore was mentioned. She remembered the Cottingley photographs and in due course showed them to the lecturer, who passed them on to Theosophist Edward L. Gardner. Having convinced himself that the photographs were genuine, Gardner in turn interested Arthur Conan Doyle in the story.

Gardner asked the girls to try to take more pictures and provided a camera. This development placed the girls in a dilemma. They would either have to confess to the hoax or else prolong it by making more fakes. In the event, they provided three more 'fairy photographs' which finally convinced Doyle of their genuineness. The publication of Doyle's *Strand* magazine article in March 1921 and his book *The Coming of the Fairies* (1922) created a sensation, and by now the hoax was too big and involved too many important people for the girls to confess.

One critical phase of the story which has not received sufficient attention was the visit to Cottingley in 1921 of clairvoyant Geoffrey Hodson, a friend of Gardner. Hodson visited the glen with the girls, and claimed to see gnomes, fairies and elves which were confirmed by the girls themselves. These observations were mentioned briefly in Hodson's book *Fairies at Work and at Play* (1925) and detailed at length in Gardner's book *Fairies; the Cottingley Photographs and their Sequel* (1945).

However, at the time of Hodson's visit, the girls were growing up quickly and it is unlikely that Frances was seeing fairies any more. Flushed with the success of their additional fake photographs, the girls had some fun with Hodson, gravely pointing to imaginary fairies which Hodson duly confirmed that he also saw. To this day, they believe that Hodson was a phoney. This would seem to be a simplistic view. The 'imaginary' fairies may have been projected to Hodson as thoughtforms, or they may indeed have had some tenuous reality of which the girls themselves were unaware. Even before the original faked photographs, Elsie had painted pictures of fairies, and had a psychic experience at an early age. It is possible that Elsie developed a mocking scepticism about the occult as a defence against its believed dangers. In a letter to Gardner's son Leslie (quoted by Geoffrey Crawley) she wrote: 'I hate to think there is a fringe of people who could get carried away into taking up spiritualism should they take our photographs very seriously... I got a very bad fright when I was about five years old which I never forgot.'

Whether the girls perceived Hodson's clairvoyance as vaguely menacing or just the self-deception of a silly man is not important. Hodson's clairvoyance is best evaluated by his extensive observations in many different locales as reported in his book *Fairies at Work and at Play* and his further book *The Kingdom of Faerie* (1927). Gardner's own book stated that Hodson had met the great Irish poet "AE" (George W. Russell), who also reported seeing and even painting nature spirits. In addition to the testimony of folklore, many reputable individuals throughout history have also claimed to see fairies.

So far as the Cottingley fairies are concerned, it is by now very difficult for either Elsie or Frances to remember accurately incidents and feelings that belong to the magic world of childhood. The photographs are really an oversize red herring. The conflicting emotions raised by a prank over sixty-five years ago have overshadowed their lives ever since. At various times the girls have been heartily fed up with the continuing controversy. Elsie now seems to have taken refuge in scepticism about fairies, coupled with some pride in sustaining the hoax for so long. Her grown-up son is also a sceptic. Frances has largely avoided too much publicity and seems to be more embarrassed by the hoax. Her daughter Christine shares her belief that she did indeed play with fairies, and has collected a number of reports of fairy sightings in Ireland.

The curious mix of genuine and fake phenomena in the Cottingley case is reminiscent of the complex problem of genuine and fake mediumship in Spiritualism, and points to the need for careful sifting of motives and attitudes as well as evidence. An out-and-out sceptic like Ruth Brandon in her book *The Passion for the Occult in the 19th and 20th Centuries* (1983) only succeeds in debunking the paranormal by an inexcusable manipulation of evidence – selective reporting, suppression of key facts, innuendo, quoting tainted gossip as honest statement – all with an air of practical commonsense. (For an excellent exposure of Ms. Bandon's methods, see the review of her book by Brian Inglis in *Journal of the Society for Psychical Research*, Vol. 52, no.795, October 1983).

In dealing with the paranormal, invincible scepticism is as misleading as uncritical belief, and many investigators are hindered by conscious and unconscious commitment to belief or disbelief. As well as fake mediums, there have been others who mingled genuine and fake phenomena to a degree which blurred their own perception of which was which. Genuine phenomena seems to be elusive and unpredictable. The fake not only fills the gap when genuine phenomena fails, but sometimes seems to prime the pump so that paranormal phenomena is facilitated.

In the Cottingley case, the belief of Frances that she *did* see fairies as a child is obscured by the long drawn out controversy over the faked photographs and the complex motives and attitudes involved. Of course, her belief may be an honest fantasy of childhood, but her clear distinction between the real fairies and the faked photographs argues for genuineness. Geoffrey Crawley's excellent and sympathetic series of articles in the *British Journal of Photography* was written from the viewpoint of a committed sceptic, and his bias is persuasive, particularly in view of his careful research. In contrast, Joe Cooper's article in *The Unexplained* is brief and anecdotal, but his account of conversations with Frances in which she claimed to see real fairies is impartial and carries conviction. Fair-minded readers must draw their own conclusions after a careful study of this case.

For myself, I think the balance of evidence is that the fairies were real, even though the photographs were fakes.

The UFO as Geopsychic Artifact:

Geophysical Causes, Biophysical Effects & Psychosocial Influences

By Hilary Evans.

It is a very clever trick to ride round a circus ring with this leg on one horse and that leg on another, but if your intention it to travel anywhere, you will do better to harness the two animals together.

For some while now, ufologists have suspected that in their stable they have two potential winners: the 'feet-on-the-ground' geophysical hypothesis, and the 'all-in-the-mind' psychosocial hypothesis. At first sight, no two creatures could be less compatible; but some recent studies show that first sight, here as so often, may be deceptive.

Some of those who have carried out these studies have had presentiments of their potential implications, others have been working in isolation: some might not be at all pleased to find their work used out of context in this way. This is one reason why, though in principle it would be best if a qualified scientist were to do the work, in practice we are unlikely to find a suitable candidate, for necessarily it extends beyond any single discipline, and geologists who recognise the psychological implications of their work, or psychologists who perceive the relevance of geophysical factors, have yet to make their existence known. One day, I hope they will appear to take over the work; but for the moment, the angels fear to tread in this no man's land, and unless a fool rushes in, nobody will.

Since a start must be made, I propose to present a number of findings, propositions and influences, arising from a number of disparate research efforts, and indicate how together they may form a valid avenue of approach.

1

There is an apparent correlation between some kinds of geological feature – for example: faults in the rock structure; subterranean deposits of water or oil; ores, especially those with electromagnetic properties; reservoirs with their stress-creating potential – and an above-average share of UFO reports. While we should beware of a simple cause-and-effect relationship – concluding that the UFOs are themselves a direct manifestation of the geological phenomenon – it would be equally foolish to dismiss the correlation as a coincidence without examining it more deeply. (1,2,3)

2

Certain geophysical events – notably the imminence of earthquakes (themselves the outcome of the interplay of geophysical forces as yet not fully understood) – cause an increase in electromagnetic activity. In particular, the proportion of electrically-charged particles in the atmosphere can be augmented to a degree where, though still negligible by 'conventional' standards, they can affect animal behaviour and the mental state of humans. The pre-storm and pre-earthquake depression and anxiety states are an example of these psychological effects which have yet to be properly explored, let alone recognised, by science, but which are real enough to those who experience them. (4,5)

3

That certain external factors can induce altered mental states or trigger mental processes is well enough known, if far from well enough explored. Among the effects which can be induced are hallucinations, which occur spontaneously as the result of pathological states such as fevers, or can result from taking specific drugs or from physical interference with the brain, and so on. Since hallucinations can be induced in so many different ways, it is reasonable to theorise that they may be one of the consequences of the geophysically-generated phenomena we are discussing. (6)

4

Hallucination may be loosely defined as believing you see something when there is nothing for you to see, from which it is generally, and reasonably, assumed that it consists of the exteriorisation of material which is either already extant in the percipient's unconscious mind, or has been fabricated by it for this occasion. It should not be confused with misinterpretation (mistaking one thing for another). However, the dividing line is sometimes deceptive. If, for example, you look at the sky and think you see an alien spaceship, this is likely to be hallucination, pure and simple. If you see the planet Venus and suppose it to be an alien spaceship, this is misinterpretation, pure and simple. But if you see Venus with a row of windows and flashing dome, this is, in part at least, a case of hallucination. In considering the possibility of geophysically-generated hallucinations, we must retain the option that they may or may not be associated with a physical object. (7)

5

It is generally assumed that hallucinations

originate in the subconscious mind of the percipient; if so, they must be made up of material which is to be found in that mind. This is true even if we happen to believe that the illusion of, say, a UFO sighting has been 'fed' into the percipient's mind by some external agency, for whatever educational or more sinister purpose. The material used for the fabrication of the hallucination will derive from three sources:

★ The individual's own preoccupations, expectations, wishes, hopes, fears etc., which could reflect an on-going attitude or a momentary crisis.

★ The cultural climate in which he was brought up and that in which he now lives. Catholic communities in which visitations by the Virgin Mary are an accepted possibility, and space-age cultures which envisage exchange visits between different worlds, will each provide what has been termed an 'authorised myth' within whose parameters the individual will feel free to create his own fantasy.

★ The data to which he has been exposed – pictures and statues of the Virgin, for example, or movies about space exploration.

The combination of these three variables will have the result that no two hallucinations will be alike; each and every so-called UFO sighting will be unique, just as every 'Virgin' will be distinctive. (8,9)

6

Though many hallucinations are extremely elaborate, it may be objected that it is stretching the definition too far, to ask it to accommodate those elaborate UFO-related experiences in which the percipient not only sees the UFO but meets its crew, accepts – voluntarily or otherwise – an invitation to go on board, is subjected to medical tests, enjoys a journey in space, and acts as a channel for elaborate messages, often of a complex metaphysical character.

Fortunately, we can progress from the hallucination to a more elaborate mental process, the 'induced dream', even if the boundary where one shades into the other is an uncertain one.

Since our knowledge of what brings about the dream state is rudimentary and largely conjectural, it may seem presumptuous to introduce a category of dreams which are 'induced' as opposed to occurring spontaneously. However, the concept is a useful one to describe dream-states which result from conditions other than normal sleep: examples are side-effects of drugs, physical probing as in brain surgery, and the like.

It is known that there exists a component in the brain, the *locus coeruleus*, which interacts with a serotininergic system, the *Raphé* system, to release hallucinations, dreams, delirious visions and so forth. This component performs the function of a switch giving a choice between the 'reality' of radio or the 'unreality' of a recording.

It is important that we bear in mind that our brain is fundamentally an electrical system whose functioning is regulated by chemical processes. Whatever may be involved in the *content* of our dreams and hallucinations, in the way of individual feelings, emotions and memories, it remains a fact that their *processing* is a physiological matter, and so subject to physical factors.

One of those factors is the air we breathe. If that air contains an abnormally high or low proportion of electrically-charged particles, this, like variations in the foods or drugs we take into our bodies, is liable to have a physical effect on our internal processes. One of those effects could be to operate the 'switch' which sends the brain into an altered state of consciousness or into the dream state. (10,11)

7

The 'dreamlike' quality of many UFO events is so frequent in reports as to be a cliché. The scenario here presented shows it to be a precise description. We know, from the amazingly involved adventures of our 'normal' dreams, how ingenious and how elaborate a dream-production can be, so there is no reason to doubt that even the most complex UFO-incident is within the capability of our dream-producer.

Provisionally, then, I propose that it is at least a scientifically valid possibility that certain geological events may, under appropriate conditions, cause mental changes in some percipients which would induce them to have hallucinations or dreams, whose form, given the appropriate personal make-up and cultural context, could well take the form of an apparent UFO-experience.

8

Parallel with the studies which have led to the scenario just presented, have been other studies which, though comprising many identical elements, introduce an additional element: a physical object or substance, generated by the geophysical conditions, which acts as a visual stimulus on the percipient.

It is known, for example, that rocks, under certain conditions, will, if crushed or fractured or otherwise subjected to stress, generate short-lived sparks or flashes: it is argued that a similar process could lead to the generation of something more stable and longer-lasting than a spark or a flash, perhaps something along the lines of ball lightning.

The fact that no such extrapolation from the

unstable flash to the more durable phenomenon has yet been scientifically demonstrated should not discourage us; for the frequent observations of 'ghost' and mountain lights, and also of 'earthquake lights' before and during quakes, is evidence that geophysically-generated light phenomena, more substantial than momentary flashes, certainly exist. And if they exist, they could, no doubt, be responsible for mental effects such as we have been attributing to geophysically-generated changes in the atmosphere. Many who have come close to such phenomena have reported physiological after-effects, such as headaches, vomiting and the like: if they can have these gross effects, they can certainly be supposed to exert the subtler mental changes we have been considering, though for the moment supposition is all we have to offer.

Another variation on the foregoing is a proposal that seismic stress produces, via the piezo-electric effect, ionized gases which could be released by earth tremors and form luminous phenomena. Such a process could lead either to simple visual reports, or to the more complex hallucination and induced-dream effects. Either way, it is certainly a promising line of research. (12)

9

Another potential line of research is the often-noted association of UFOs with power lines. Two diametrically-opposed explanations have been offered:

* The power lines create the 'UFO' by some kind of electrical discharge effect creating something akin either to ball lightning or to the piezo-electric flash.
* The UFOs are alien spacecraft which are interested in our power supplies, perhaps to the extent of themselves obtaining power from them, occasionally to the extent of causing an overload leading to power failures such as the 1965 North American black-out.

10

Since we have no right to disallow any clue, however bizarre, it is worth referring to a phenomenon of which, so far as I know, only two instances have been reported, one in an electrical laboratory and the other in a power station, when (presumably) discharge effects from the machinery caused the formation of cloud-like shapes in the air which assumed the appearance of human faces or figures. Here we seem to have the production, by purely material means, of phenomena similar to those more generally associated with psychological or parapsychological processes, and it is for that reason that, bizarre as they are, they should be taken into account. As to what process was involved, whether from the technical or the psychological angle, I can scarcely speculate, but once again we seem to have an interface between the material and the mental realms. (13)

That ultimately, is what this paper is concerned with. Every one of the propositions presented here is based on serious research, even if none of them is yet incorporated into the body of accepted scientific fact. It may seem presumptuous to construct a scenario composed of so many doubtful or unsubstantiated elements; but it may be that their strength in combination is greater than as isolated findings. All over the world, individual researchers are patiently pursuing their private paths, but it may be that, without realising it, they are walking side by side along a broad avenue of progress.

REFERENCES

1. Devereux, Paul, *Earthlights,* Turnstone, 1982.
2. Persinger, Michael A., and Lafrenière, Gyslaine F., *Space-Time Transients and unusual events,* Nelson Hall, 1977; *Possible infrequent geophysical sources of close UFO encounters*, in Haines, Richard F., *UFO Phenomena and the behavioral scientist*, Scarecrow, 1979.
3. Reservoir-associated UFOs are frequent in the literature, but I know of no catalogue. A useful starting-point would be Sanderson, Ivan T., *Invisible residents,* Crowell, 1970.
4. Tributsch, Helmut, *When the snakes awake*, MIT Press, 1982. This is essential reading for this field of research.
5. Playfair, Guy Lyon, and Hill, Scott, *The cyclesof Heaven,* Souvenir, 1978.
6. Evans, Hilary, *Visions, apparitions, alien visitors,* Aquarian, 1984. This covers many aspects discussed in this paper.
7. Hendry, Allan, *The UFO handbook*, Doubleday, 1979. Cites many cases though contains no discussion along the lines of this paper.
8. Guérin, Pierre, *Le probleme de la preuve en ufologie,* in Bourret., J.C., *Le nouveau défi des OVNIs,* France-Empire, 1976.
9. Monnerie, Michel, *Et si les OVNIs n'existaient pas?* Humanoïdes Associés, 1977; *Le naufrage des extra-terrestres,* Nouvelles Editions Rationalistes, 1979; Scornaux, Jacques, *Et si Michel Monnerie n'avait pas tout a fait tort?* in *Inforespace 39,* 1978.
10. Rifat, Claude, *Is the locus coeruleus involved in the most bizarre aspects of UFO reports?* in *UFO PHENOMENA Vol 11 no 1,* 1978; interview in *OVNI-présence 25*, 1983.
11. A layman trying to understand what goes on in the brain could not do better than read Taylor, Gordon Rattray, *The natural history of the mind*, Secker & Warburg, 1979.
12. Frizzell, Michael A., *Investigating the Brown Mountain lights,* in *UFO Journal 43*, 1984. Includes brief account of Wagner's seismic stress hypothesis.
13. Gaddis, Vincent, *Electrical ghosts*, in *Fate*, April 1951: Steiger, Brad, *Mysteries of time and space,* Prentice Hall, 1974.

On The Rocks.

by Nigel Watson.

Unlike Hilary Evans I am not so certain that research into the geophysical causes of UFO events is marching us down the road of progress and greater insight. I agree that geological events *could* produce luminous phenomena in the sky, but the evidence for this is extremely tenuous to say the least. Even if such an hypothesis is correct, probably ten times as many observations of lights in the sky could still be attributed to misidentifications of Venus alone.

This leads us to the more problematical area of earth light research which suggests that geological events can effect the physiological functioning of our brains in such a way that it will cause us to experience hallucinations, misperceptions and induced dreams moulded by cultural, social and individual psychological factors. It is certainly an entertaining idea worthy of any science fiction writer. Indeed, in the films '2001' and '2010' the black monolith seems to have the role of the mind manipulator instead of our Earth itself.

Alternatively we might consider that this theory validates the paranoid fantasies of those contactees and ufologists who believe that we are being manipulated by some sinister external force(s). The difference is that the ray beams from Shaver's Hollow Earth, or the enigmatic Ultraterrestrials postulated by John Keel, have changed into rocks merely rubbing together. Some might think that great progress. I am not so sure.

My concern is that ufologists seem all too happy to embrace theories that are on the fringes of science. The earth light hypothesis is a byproduct of behaviourism; the birth trauma hypothesis came from the psychoanalytical approach to the study of human behaviour; the ETH came via the popular perception of rocket technology and the fantasies of science fiction writers, etc. One year Jungian archetypes become fashionable, the next parapsychology becomes all the rage. Yet from my own limited studies I feel that much of the UFO phenomenon can be explained with the aid of conventional physical and psychological science. Unfortunately, many ufologists prefer to revel in mysteries or point to Government cover-ups that prevent us from getting at the truth.

In a paper distributed by Hilary Evans at the Franco-Anglais meeting held in Hardelot on 23 and 24 March 1985 entitled *The "Signal" of Michael Persinger* he notes that this hypothesis does contain several weak links. Despite them I will admit the earth lights controversy does help us in several ways. First of all it has encouraged the collection and analysis of UFO waves pre-and post-1947. It encourages sceptics like myself to present counter-arguments and to carry out research which might show why the earth lights hypothesis is not as valid and all-embracing as its supporters suggest. Lastly, it is more accessible to testability than Ultraterrestrials and their kin. However, the earth lights hypothesis is still very difficult to test. UFO sightings are not reported and/or investigated in the same detail or quantity throughout a single town, county, city, state or country. The data is often buried in private files or ignored because it doesn't fit the ufologists' view of what a UFO sighting should be like. Nonetheless I welcome the attempts by Persinger, Devereux, and others to prove their case.

Basically we have to ask ourselves if this is a UFO fad which will be immediately abandoned as soon as someone comes up with a new hypothesis that looks exciting and scientific enough for our jaded brains to respond to with renewed enthusiasm. Devereux et al do point out that:

> *Earth lights have never been witnessed without being interpreted in the light of whatever the prevailing cultural prejudice happens to be.* (*Anomaly*, No 1, 1985, p16.)

Which should make them aware that their own hypothesis is subject to the same kind of prejudices. So on reflection I would rather have my destiny in the stars than on the rocks.

A photograph of Astor College, London, reveals a strange face filling one window. [Photo ©The Times, *28 Nov 1984.]*

Book Alert!

by Janet Bord

1985 seems to be producing a mixed bag of Fortean books, some pot-boilers and some of great originality – and I am not giving any clues as to which books go into which category. Books which have already appeared in the early months of the year include: Joe Fisher's *The Case for Reincarnation* (£9.95) and *The Paranormal*; An Encyclopedia of Psychic Phenomena by Brian Inglis (£12.95), both from Granada Publishing. Robert Hale published Peter Underwood's *The Ghost Hunters*: Who Are and What They Do (£9.95), and New English Library published *The Mind Race* by Russell Targ and Keith Harary (£8.95) on psychic abilities, with details of scientific research in the USA and USSR. Four books on psychic phenomena described so far, and still more to come – it is amazing that so much is written on this subject, yet so little real progress appears to be made. (No letters please – I realise that is a controversial statement, and it is a personal opinion only!)

What sounds like a weighty tome, if the price (£30.95) is any guide, has been published by Praeger – *With the Eyes of the Mind*: An Empirical Analysis of Out-of-Body States – scientific analysis of altered mind/body experiences using data from a large-scale study of those reporting such experiences. More accessible to the ordinary mortal is Elizabeth Sunderland's *Ravens and Black Rain*: The Story of Highland Second Sight (£9.95), a survey of precognition and paranormal experiences in the Highlands of Scotland, published by Constable in April, in which month Andrew Collins published his newest book, *The Knights of Danbury* (£2.20 incl. p+p from Earthquest Books, 19 St David's Way, Wickford, Essex, SS11 8EX). Among the conclusions the book presents are that the hilltop encampment on which Danbury is situated was once a place of sun worship and midsummer celebrations. Also, that its medieval landowners, the mysterious and powerful Knights of St Clere, perpetuated and kept alive the old traditions, the evidence for which is presented in the book.

One intriguing book published in the spring is called *Genisis*: The First Book of Revelations, by David Wood (£15 from The Baton Press). According to the advertising, 'David Wood has singlehandedly, and with a breadth of vision few have achieved before, unearthed some of the world's most jealously guarded information. The conclusions he draws about the Christian faith and its history are as startling as they are controversial.' He brings in many old favourites – the Temple of Solomon, Atlantis, the Ark of the Covenant, the Holy Grail, and ancient Egypt too, if the cover illustration is any guide. It all seems too much – can it be a spoof??

By comparison we come down to earth in the second half of the year, when there are several books due which I shall certainly want to read. Among them is William Broad and Nicholas Wade's *Betrayers of the Truth*: Fraud and Deceit in Science, coming from Oxford Paperbacks (£3.50) – 'How the lure of fame and fortune has led even the most eminent of scientists to cheat and fabricate evidence.' How the dead can communicate with the living is the subject of John G. Fuller's *The Ghost of Twenty-Nine Megacycles* (Souvenir Press, £10.95), and from the same publisher comes a welcome book from Don Robins, *Circles of Silence* (£10.95) about the energy experiments at Rollright and elsewhere. Jenny Randles and Peter Warrington's delayed book *Science and the UFOs* will hopefully put in an appearance from Basil Blackwell (£9.95) in the second half of the year; likewise Paul Devereux and Nigel Pennick's *Earth Mysteries* (Turnstone Press). Colin Wilson writes of out-of-body and edge-of-death experiences in *Afterlife* (£9.95 Harrap); he also wrote an introduction for *West Country Mysteries* (Bossiney Books). Nevill Drury's *Dictionary of Mysticism* (Harper & Row, £8.95) includes nearly 3,000 cross-referenced entries to make it, according to the publishers, 'the most comprehensive one-volume reference work on mysticism and the occult available'.

The best, or at least the funniest, is saved till last. If you are tired of serious books, try some of those listed in Russell Ash and Brian Lake's *Bizarre Books* (£7.95, Macmillan) – 'Dentologia or Poems of Diseases of the Teeth', 'Harnessing the Earthworm', 'The Fangs of Suet Pudding', 'The Toff Goes Gay' – all 100% genuine titles.

Finally, I have details of one title of great interest to fans of the writings of the late Ted Holiday. Llewellyn Publications of Minnesota, USA, are planning to publish two hitherto unpublished manuscripts, one about men-in-black and the other his final book on Nessie and Co., both together in one volume. The title will be *The Goblin Universe* and the book will have an introduction by Colin Wilson, but I do not have a publication date – however it will certainly be reviewed in *FT* when it appears.

LETTERS
Cont from p3.

organism, still alive and well, that *only* grows on native British elk dung, even though elks have been extinct in Britain since the Bronze Age. Should make the unknown mould Britain rarest and silliest living species.

Peter Roberts
36 Western Road, Torquay
Devon, TQ1 4LR

[Thanks for correcting me, Peter. The bird stories were written up – like most of our stories – .from the clippings to hand. We're not so daft as to claim, therefore, that our 'facts' are accurate. We really do try to be accurate, but you are only as good as your sources – and, as I've said before, the standard of modern journalism in this regard is quite deplorable. Nevertheless, we do it mainly to inform those interested of an occurrence which might repay investigation. Even so, we're always grateful for corrections, and we'll always pass them on for the benefit of everyone.

As for that bear... my unwise pronouncement was merely intended to indicate that we heard no more of the story in the media. If there is any truth to the claim of 'Bob' then somewhere in a woodland grave on Exmoor are the remains of a bear. If anyone follows this up, please keep us informed. Meanwhile, the latest Exmoor sightings are summarized on p30. RJMR]

MONSTROUS SQUIDS

I was interested in Ole Brix (nice name!) and his ideas about ole Architeuthis [FT42 p8], but can't agree that the creatures . are slow movers. Heuvelmans, and others, report sightings of giant squids moving at pretty high speeds (20-25 knots, for example, quoted on p.78 of *ITWOTSS*). Also, Heuvelmans (and, again, others) write of these giants expiring when they leave their 'warm habitat' and enter cold waters...just the opposite of Brix's notion. The fact that the blood pigment is haemocyanin doesn't have to slow the creatures down, and it is highly concentrated in cephalopods. G.C. Robson reckons that Architeuthis seeks a temperature of 10 degrees C and 'It s natural reaction when it finds a lower temperature is to rise near the surface into warmer water'... which seems to contradict Brix. There are, of course, several different species of Architeuthis, and very little is known about any of them. Also, by the way, certain mulluscs have developed haemoglobin (for instance, some weird slug-like things which live underground in a low oxygen environment). Cute cookies, molluscs!

You've done a nice job with my piece on the 'elephant squid' theory, but I really can't take the credit for the name, *Dineteuthis proboscideus.* That was the name given to the Kerry Kraken, by A.G. More, which was rather different. How about *Dinosepius* or even *Elephanteuthis*....... if not *Rynchoteuthis shielsi*!?! Then there's *Nessiteuthis* or *Nessiteuthis proboscideus* to describe the freshwater type as opposed to a strictly marine version. Great game, but I'll leave it to the ICS lads. Also, I'm not the first to suggest that Nessie could be a type of giant squid. If I remember rightly, back in 1933 the director of the New York Aquarium (I think) came up with this notion...he was quoted by Gould, but I don't have his book on Nessie to hand right now. Interesting though, don't you think, that the freshwater problem didn't seem to bother him? Also, you may remember that Roy Mackal had a similar theory back in 1966 when he proposed something 'between the giant squid and the slug' – that is, a giant gastropod with cephalopod leanings – as a probable Nessie.

The main reason that I'm so convinced that the Loch Ness creatures and sea-serpents are very closely related (probably the same type of animal) is, of course, that I've been lucky enough to actually see Morgawr *and* Nessie, and I'm sure they are very similar beasties. Dave Clarke, who has seen Morgawr, agrees that the animal was like Nessie (in my pix, and those of Wilson, etc). This first-hand experience goes much further than academic theory (of the Binns kind, for instance)...but it presents me with one problem: Our creature has to be able to live in either fresh or seawater, or both. I am not a zoologist, so I leave the problem up to sympathetic experts. It *is* a problem, I know, and it's the shakiest part of my 'elephant squid' hypothesis. All the same I'm convinced it has much more going for it than all the other Nessie notions put forward so far, and it's a fact that many molluscs have successfully adapted to freshwater, (though they tend to be smaller than their closest marine cousins). Cephalopods *have* been reported in rivers...and Loch Ness is connected with the sea.

The important thing, or one of the important things, about the 'elephant squid' notion is that, unlike other theories concerning Nessie's identity, it seems to encompass a great variety of different sighting reports and just about all the well-known photographs. My creature could, quite easily, appear as shown in Hugh Gray's picture, Wilson's, Lachlan Stewart's, Rines', etc etc. Seemingly contradictory eye-witnesses (quoted gleefully by Binns & Co) could all be telling the truth if they are describing an 'elephant 'squid', a colour-changing shape-shifter. As far as I know, *nobody* has succeeded in filming or photographing a *living* adult (that is, fully grown!) Architeuthis......not even Cousteau, who spent a lot of time trying. . .but even Binns would have to admit that they exist. The few that have been captured and examined were either dead or dying. Yet they can't be all that bloody rare... we're told that they form an important part of the sperm whale's diet, which implies that there are a lot more giant squids than sperm whales in the ocean. The fact that the sperm whale population is much lower than it used to be should suggest a related increase in the giant squid population, but very few have been seen since the mass suicides in Newfoundland over a hundred years ago .....which established their reality.

On re-reading Heuvelmans, I'm struck by the fact that, although he is a great fan of Architeuthis as a Kraken, he doesn't like the idea of a giant cephalopod as a 'sea serpent'. For example, on p.526 of *ITWOTSS,* discussing the 1963 Vopnafjörthur monster, he says that the creature couldn't possibly be a giant squid because: 'First of all the tail of an Architeuthis, when placed horizontally, is not shaped like the ace of diamonds, as in some smaller squids, but lanceolate like an ace of hearts, so that a giant squid could never show a triangular fin when swimming on its side'. This is quite untrue. First of all there are several different kinds of giant squid and one of them, stranded at Yorkshire in 1925, is illustrated in Graham McEwan's *Sea Serpents, Sailors & Sceptics.* The photograph clearly shows an 'ace of diamonds' triangular tail fin. Anyway, the smaller of the two fins illustrated (of the 1963 thing) could form half of a lanceolate tail, and that was the leading fin (or hump!), suggesting that, if the creature was a kind of cephalopod, it was travelling backwards, as usual, under jet power.

Heuvelmans is also wrong to suggest that a squid would be unlikely to swim on its side. Squids often do this..... they are quite acrobatic...and, anyway, there's always the possibility that the animal was injured. (Heveulmans uses injured creatures to 'explain' several unusual monster sightings...so why not allow an injured squid?)

Don't think for a moment, that I'm knocking Heuvelmans.....I admire him enormously...but I think he's guilty of some slightly blinkered judgements (aren't we all?). See the report (p.269 etc) on the 'Nestor' sea serpent. Heuvelmans attempts to explain it as a whale shark, but I think Dr Andrew Wilson came much closer to the truth in suggesting that it was a kind of giant cuttle fish. I think it was a giant striped Dinoteuthis, a beast with many cuttlefish characteristics (not least, the 'lappits'!) Heuvelmans says 'who ever saw an Architeuthis striped like a zebra?' I think Capt Webster did...at least he saw a huge sepia-like monster, with a long proboscis (not a tail), striped and coloured *exactly* like the common cuttlefish. *Sepia officinalis.* So many of the serpents described by Heuvelmans could be gigantic cephalopods. I'm not saying that 'normal' (?) giant squids are the answer to everything – though poor old Henry Lee doesn't deserve the bashing that most sea monster buffs give him – but giantism in the cephalopods is not confined to Architeuthis-type squids.

Now you've published my theory I would like some unprejudiced marine biologists to consider its possibilities.

Congratulations on FT43. Just a couple of tiny teuthological criticisms: That so-called 'giant octopus' on p5 is obviously a squid, in spite of its caption; and, on p25, *Loligo vulgaris* is 'identified as a cuttlefish' which it ain't... *Loligo* is a common squid. Squids rule!

Doc Shiels
Ponsanooth, Cornwall

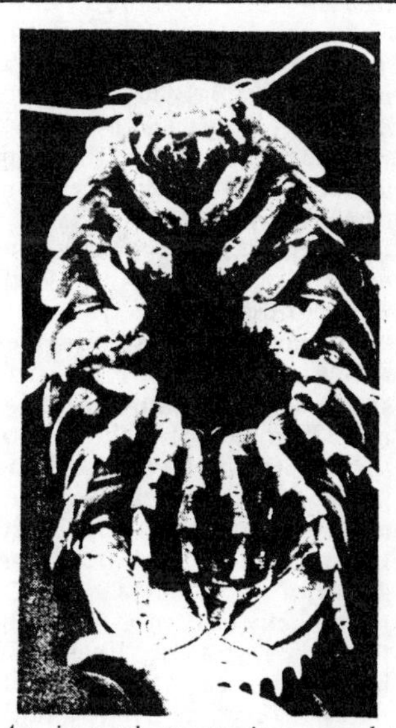

An isopod crustacian, caught 350 fathoms down in the Gulf of Mexico, previously known only from fossils. [Photo ©Grit, 22 Feb 1976.]

RED RAINS & RADIO WAVES

I enclose a clipping, from *Practical Wireless* (March 1985, p69), about the effects of 'space dust' on TV reception in East Anglia. It seems that 'red rains' bring Spanish TV!

[The clipping discusses the "remarkable VHF and UHF opening to Spain and southern Europe" in south-

east England early in the evening of Friday, 8th November 1984, in which strong signals from Spanish TV, and signals from Spanish radio hams, were overriding a local Anglia TV transmitter. Likewise, TV hams in southern Europe were getting strong signals from Anglia. The writer then briefly describes how, the next morning, his yellow Lada Estate, parked somewhere on the East Anglian coast – he was not specific – "was found to be brick red, as were many vehicles, windows and ledges in the area", the dust turning to red mud in the rain later. For more discussion of the dust fall of November 8/9, please turn to SANDY SKIES on p19 – Ed.]

It was only after thinking about it that this seems to be even more curious than at first sight. Perhaps I should explain a little about VHF radio propagation.

Normal radio frequencies above about 15 mhz (the short wave on your radio) do not bounce off the ionosphere (or F-layers, as the jargon goes). So radio waves in the broadcast FM (100 mhz), amateur 144 mhz and 430 mhz bands and UHF television (600 mhz) mostly travel in straight lines and have a range of about 50 miles. Very rarely (perhaps twice a year) they *do* bounce off the ionosphere and come down 2000 km or more away. This is held to be due to 'sporadic' ionisation of the E-layer (hence 'sporadic-E' or 'Es'). Frankly, no one seems to know what causes sporadic-E. One recent occurrence, on 17 June 1984, was put down to a violent thunderstorm over the South of France (see *Practical Wireless* Feb 1985). Since the ionisation is supposed to be at 100 km, this must have been a hell of a storm!

[The author of the PW article refers to a current theory that sporadic-E might be created by the infall of dust from meteor showers, and suggests the same might happen when sand is elevated to the upper atmosphere, creating "sudden and unexpected openings" – Ed.]

If Spanish TV is going to appear in East Anglia, presumably it must have bounced off the ionosphere halfway, somewhere over Brittany. The question is: why did it rain red dust in East Anglia rather than in Brittany? Or perhaps it did? Have the Fortean Files anything to offer for 8 Nov 1984, or for that matter 17th June? Radio hams are perhaps a good source for this kind of anomalous information because any disturbance of the silence of the 144 & 430 mhz bands is avidly recorded, timed and written about.

Bob Everett
(callsign: G1DWC)
73 Fordwych Rd,
London NW2

[We might just be able to answer Bob's questions plausibly. Although we don't have any record of a sandfall over France on 8th Nov, from what we know of the event (see SANDY SKIES on p19) the particles fell out over southern England only when the transporting high altitude winds lost their sustaining power after *traversing France. Which means that about the time of the VHF "openings" to Spain, the sandcloud could well have been over Brittany en route to England. As for the "opening" of 17th June... all we have is a brief note of a sandfall in Spain on the 19th, but an investigation of weather conditions might well bring out some relationship, perhaps a slow and circular route which passed over northern France on the 17th? But that's only a guess. If TOAD was operational and contained the data, we could obtain a chronological listing of sand and dust fall reports quite easily. This could then be compared with a list of sporadic-E events confirming or not the possibility that the hitherto unexplained sporadic-E can be created, perhaps not exclusively, by aerial sand clouds. Until then we'll have to do it by hand. Meanwhile, Bob Everett has expressed an interest in pursuing this topic and requests that anyone with relevant information writes to him at the above address – Ed.]*

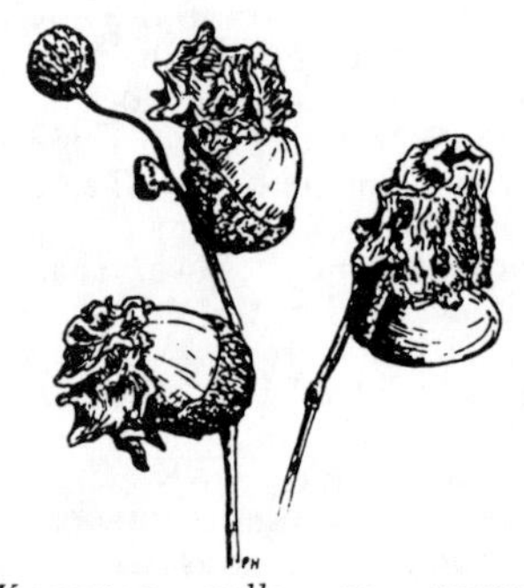

Knopper galls on acorn. Drawing by Pamela Hadden.

OAKS – GOOD NEWS!

Re **Andricus and the oaks** [FT43,p43]: Autumn 1983 was indeed very bad for knopper galls on oaks, but press reports were exaggerated. The wasps tend to knopper about the same number of acorns each year, irrespective of crop size, and 1983 was a small crop, hence most were ruined. The following year had a normal crop and so it appeared the wasps had declined. Another point is made by tree expert Alan Mitchell. The English oak has 284 species of insect living on it and has adapted to cope quite happily with this vast community; only unhealthy trees suffer. He does not believe there is any threat to the future of the oak.

Chris Hall
Fleet, Hampshire

Reviews

THE WOMEN'S ENCYCLOPEDIA OF MYTHS AND SECRETS

By Barbara G. Walker.
Harper & Row, London & NY: 1984; pb £11.95/$19.95; pp1121, bib, photos.

For once the blurb lives up to the book. I quote: "...this unique, comprehensive sourcebook focuses on...precisely what other encyclopedias leave out or misrepresent... it offers 1350 entries...on magic, witchcraft, fairies, elves, giants, goddesses, gods and demon possession...the mystical meanings of sun, moon, earth, sea, time and space; ideas of the soul, reincarnation, creation and doomsday; ancient and modern attitudes towards sex, prostitution, romance, rape, warfare, death and sin...a thousand hidden pockets of history and custom; myths, superstitions, fairy tales, folk songs and dances, nursery rhymes, traditional games and holidays, magic symbols, sagas, and scriptures both original and revised, apocryphal and otherwise – in addition to the valuable material recovered by archaeologists, orientalists, and other scholars." It is, proudly, a one volume feminist encyclopedia, with a scope so all-encompassing that I wouldn't be surprised if the kitchen sink were in there as well. As one who can appreciate the work and scholarship I can only stand in awe and admiration of this fat book, twenty-five years in the making. I agree again with the blurb when it calls the book "a browser's delight" – dip into it anywhere and it's hard to get out again. All the entries are cross referenced, and refer to a 13-page bibliography. Delightfully unexpected connections arise from the material accumulated under each heading, not the least because it is written up from a viewpoint consciously distanced from patriarchal morality. No selection could do justice to its quality. I know this will turn out to be one of the most used reference works on my shelves, and I recommend it to serious researchers of all persuasions and interests. If you can't afford it, it is essential to get your local or school library to obtain a copy. *RJMR*

INCREDIBLE PHENOMENA

Orbis Publishing Ltd., London: 1984; hb £12.99; pp256, index, photos.

THE AGE OF THE UFO

Orbis: 1984; hb £9.99, pb £7.00; pp208, index, photos.

GHOSTS

Orbis: 1984; hb £9.99, pb £7.00; pp207, index, photos.

CULT & OCCULT

Orbis: 1985; hb £12.99; pp240, index, photos.

Not content with the publishing success of their part-work, *The Unexplained* (TU), Orbis have tried to milk their winner in as many ways as possible, and TU has already been released several times. Then came the 'mini-volumes': about 23 articles extracted from TU on a particular theme (eg volume 11 is 'Appearances and Disappearances'). To top that Orbis have now bound extensive selections from TU into the handsome thematic books listed above. By cutting production costs in this way Orbis have been able to publish very lavish books indeed, with good quality paper and full-colour printing on every page; to do the same in a conventionally published book would push the price beyond the affordable.

Generally the standard of writing and research in TU was very high. Most of its writers are well-known to you, and many have contributed to our own pages. If you have TU already, you might not want these volumes, but certainly they are in a form which public and school libraries should have. If the reader is new to the subjects they will serve as an excellent introduction, especially for the young inquiring mind. These volumes are so attractive they will make ideal presents.

Incredible Phenomena, in fact, is a wonderful introduction to the Fortean Universe, not the least because of my own two articles on Charles Fort therein (no false modesty here!). Also included are spontaneous combustion, fish falls, fire walking etc, electric people, live burials, the Cottingley saga, mermaids, mysterious manuscripts, historical mysteries, the Hexham heads, toad-lore, coincidences, cosmic jokes, the unhangable man, the Barbados coffins, the Tunguska fireball, weird China, armpit-vision, the 'money pit' mystery, moving rocks, and many more mysteries.

RJMR

OCCULT/ PARANORMAL BIBLIOGRAPHY: 1976–1981.

by Thomas C. Clarie.
Scarecrow Press, Metuchen, NJ: 1984; hb £42.00; pp561, index.

Basically, this is an annotated list of just under 2000 books, based on reading over 8000 reviews. They are listed alphabetically by author, with full bibliographical data, and indexed by subject and title. This volume continues from the authors *Occult Bibliography* which listed 2000 books for the period 1971-1975.

If the shallow treatment given to my book with Richard Kelly, *Photographs of the Unknown*, [see last issue's editorial for Paul Sieveking's protest about this] is typical of Clarie's 'research' standard, then it would be hard to assess the *real* value of this work. He acknowledges his dependence upon the reviewer of books and this has frequently led him astray. Clarie sets out his criteria at the beginning: he seems to understand why he includes occultism, paranormal and "supernatural pheneomena" but excludes religion, mysticism, "wonders /curiosities" and "mysteries" generally. He does not help us decide where the acceptable phenomena stops and the unacceptable begins. He says he excludes fiction and "highly personal testimonies" but includes, say, Castaneda's books because they are "allegorically real". A book like this one is intended mainly for the use of reference librarians and buyers for libraries, and this gives it a certain influence. To indicate Clarie's own value judgements on books essential for libraries and "collectors", he has a rating system of one to three stars. According to this scale the works of Castaneda get three stars and the priceless works of Corliss are grossly undervalued at one star, and poor old Fort doesn't get any. And as for its research value: knowledgeable researchers usually follow references in specific works back to source. That leaves only reference librarians and new enquirers, both of whom will have to rely on Clarie's jusgement, based, he admits, on other people's opinions. It all seems so arbitrary.

RJMR

CHAMP – BEYOND THE LEGEND

by Joseph W. Zarzynski.
Bannister Books; 1984, $8. pb, pp224, index, bib, notes, illustrations, tables.

UK price: $11.70 (incl. p+p) from M–Z Information, Box 2129, Wilton, NY 12866, USA.

This is the first book to deal with the monsters of Lake Champlain. As such it should be welcomed, but though it is in some respects an admirable work, the book is disappointing considering its source.

Zarzynski has been working at Lake Champlain for a decade, and has been almost single-handedly responsible for elevating the topic to its present status as 'America's Loch Ness Monster'. Unfortunately, the book is an extended version of a pamphlet, and it shows. Excluding the extensive appendices, it is only 123 pages long, and more than half of that space is taken up by the numerous illustrations.

Only just over one page of text deals with eyewitness sightings. (The details of these 224 reports are set out in a tabulated appendix, but such a format does not allow for their critical examination.) Given the inconclusive results of sonar work at the lake, and the debatable nature of the only photo of Champ used in the book, sighting reports deserve much better treatment.

The appendices are the best part of this work, and they deal not only with witness reports, but with the analysis of the 'Mansi photograph' and with the recently-held 'Champ seminar' addressed by many leading cryptozoologists.

The Mansi photo is one with which most readers of FT will be familiar; it has been published in Michell and Rickard's *Living Wonders* and shows a large hump and a thick head-and-neck curving away from the camera. The picture was taken at a range of 150 yards, and it is unlikely that it represents any known object. It is almost certain that it is either a fake, or the real thing.

It is unfortunate that the photographer, Sandra Mansi – an otherwise convincing witness – is unable to relocate the spot from which the photo was taken, and it cannot even be proved that the location was Lake Champlain. Photo analysis reported by Zarzynski has ruled out a montage or superimposition, but has revealed what may be a sand bar close to the object – suggesting that a model may have been placed there. (It is interesting to note that in this case 'scientific analysis' meant the researcher in question showi- the picture to a local resident and asking her opinion.)

On the other hand, the witnesses' estimates of size have been confirmed, and the mechanics of constructing and placing a model at least 15ft long in a lake are so formidable as to deter most aspiring hoaxers. More study is needed before the photo can be accepted – but it is at least encouraging that detailed work has been carried out.

Elsewhere in the book, Zarzynski discusses well the possible identity of the creatures without committing himself to specific conclusions. He includes sections on local legislation concerning the monsters, sonar work at the lake, the place of the Champ tradition in Americana and the future direction of the monster hunt.

Certainly Zarzynski is capable of writing an excellent – and definitive – book on the subject. He has yet to do so. *Mike Dash*

THE QUAKERS AND THE ENGLISH REVOLUTION

by Barry Reay
Temple Smith, London; 1985, £12.95 hb; pp184, index, bibliography, illus. Foreword by Christopher Hill

Unconventionality in Nature (Forteana) is often echoed in human affairs by eccentric behaviour or curious ideas. Through the ages, efforts have been made to harmonise this apparent disharmony. The best-known systemisers, the 17th century Puritans, have been scorned, condemned, ignored and worshipped – according to the mood of the times. Cromwell was a hero to the Victorians, missionaries of sturdy individualism. Come the Russian revolution and Cromwell became the ancestor of collectivism. Since the hippies, our historians have focused on the weird sects beyond Cromwell and the orthodox Puritans. Hill's *The World Turned Upside Down* showed the way, and his protegé, Reay, has followed with two books previous to *The Quakers and the English Revolution*, which develops the process. The blurb tries to tailor these 17th century weirdos to current obsessions and causes: radicals, militants, feminists, paranoid authoritarianism. . . (*The World Turned Upside Down* even hinted at parallels to psychedelic drugs.) The new orthodoxy rescues much buried truth but it still offers a single vision, however alternative, not a total vision. Inside this materialist context Reay is excellent at exploding the contrived stereotype of pacifist separatists by showing it was feared that Quaker soldiery would spearhead a putsch, possibly in 1656, certainly in 1659.

Before 1660 Reay proves Quakers were ferociously anti-authoritarian and the byword for perversity: in religion, politics and sex. These outward attitudes derived from their mysticism. They relied solely on 'the light within' which manifested itself in visions, revelations, signs and providences. In the heady days of the Reign of Saints, there were calls for universities to study Bohme, Alchemy, Rosicrucianism and other Baconian subjects. A pre-Fortean College would collate such Prodigies and apply them to worldly affairs. Quakers scrupulously recorded signs "whether in the form of stones or flies", and applied this divine pattern to their lives, turning themselves into prodigies. Their "extravagant behaviour" symbolically set them apart from the ungodly. Though Fox began the transformation to respectability from external revolution to internal regeneration, his beliefs were still based on prodigies. He exploited his own reputation for oddness by wearing a bizarre leather suit, and cultivated a penetrating (bewitching) gaze. In his *Book of Miracles*, Fox recorded his dreams, revelations and miraculous cures: some 150 including smallpox, convulsions, blindness and a broken neck. Quakers even tried to raise the dead – by faith not necromancy.

The most famous sign was their quaking, trembling, wailing and incantatory witnessing. Armed Quakers might present a wordly threat but their supernatural powers caused a greater terror. Faced with this inhuman behaviour people wondered if the inspired voices were the tongues of angels or devils.

The act was cleaned up politically in 1660. Discipline, in organisation and doctrine, was introduced and justified as survivalism – as with the Muggletonians. By the 1690s even Fox's writings had to be sanitised. The very act of quaking went: silence and stillness became the measure of godliness. Mystified inaction could be mistaken. As Reay says "The Seekers had become sleepers."

John Nicholson

THE EVIDENCE FOR THE BERMUDA TRIANGLE

by David Group
Aquarian Press, Wellingborough, Northants; 1984, £2.95 pb, pp160, index, bib. illus.

THE EVIDENCE FOR PHANTOM HITCH-HIKERS

by Michael Goss.
Aquarian Press; 1984, £2.95, pb, pp160, index, bib, notes and references, illus.

The two recent additions to the excellent ASSAP (Association for the Scientific Study of Anomalous Phenomena) *Evidence For. . .* series – dealing this time with the Bermuda Triangle and the Phantom Hitch-Hiker – display the strengths and weaknesses of the series in general. The authors' brief is to provide, in a standard 160-page format an introduction and critical overview to a phenomenon. This is a realistic aim, but limiting, and it naturally favours the more limited topic.

Here Goss is at an advantage, since he is studying a subject borrowed by Forteans from folklorists comparatively recently, and which is all the better for it. His book is able to display the range and content of the Hitch-Hiker 'myth' for the first time.

David Group is forced to adopt a perhaps less rewarding approach; the components of the Bermuda Triangle legend are the books on the topic rather than the losses and disappearances themselves, and Group has had to compile factual case-histories from many sources and discuss the numerous theories put forward to account for the phenomena.

He does it well. Having shown that almost all the Triangle stories are exaggerations, misinterpretations or the products of inadequate research, Group is free to dispense with the more colourful theories advanced to meet equally lurid 'facts'. In the section 'A personal assessment', he breaks down the cases into three categories. There are those which are inconclusive, the result of poor investigation or the passage of time, and included in this category are wartime losses, many of the pre-20th century cases and several of the smaller craft lost since. Many more Triangle cases can be explained in natural terms, and among these Group stresses losses to the modern-day pirates who hijack small boats for drug-running operations. This leaves only a tiny residue to be classified as truly mysterious – five of 211 cases. Two of these are not dealt with in the text, and the other three rest on the testimony of a single source. Finally, Group emphasises the tiny ratio of the disappearance of ships, aircraft and divers in the Triangle to the total activity in the area.

This does not mean that anomalous disasters do not take place at sea, simply that there is no evidence that they happen in clearly defined areas.

Group is quick to point out, too, that less than half of the cases credited to the Triangle actually occurred within the original boundaries specified by Vincent Gaddis in the early sixties. Writers who have stretched the 'Triangle' into a square, 'blob' or trapezium have done so only to include the maximum number of cases. The most famous ship thus included amongst 'Triangle' victims is the *Mary Celeste,* which was found derelict off the Azores.

Group could hardly hope, in 160 pages, to deal with the subject in as much depth as Lawrence Kusche, whose seminal *The Bermuda Triangle Mystery – Solved* began the debunking trend. Instead he has chosen to deal with two dozen representative cases and with a similar number of witnesses, mentioning several of the better-known but in fact easily explicable cases only briefly. Perhaps the highlight of the book is an excellent section on the human factors which occasioned many of the disasters. However the specially commissioned illustrations are of a very poor quality.

Michael Goss has had the priceless advantage of being able to define his own subject. He deals well with the variations which occur in the classic tale of the driver who picks up a hitch-hiker, only for the passenger to vanish disconcertingly while the driver's attention is on the road, usually leaving some sign or token with which it is possible to identify the passenger as deceased.

The story has been routinely written off as modern folklore, but Goss's central point is a good one. He believes that some PH-H cases belong to parapsychology rather than folklore, and suggests that the acid test is the apparent purpose, or lack of it, in a tale. To be good folklore, the passenger must be 'proved' to be a ghost, and the story provided with a 'moral' in the form of a good reason for the hitch-hiker to be frequenting the road at a particular place – whether it is the scene of death or because the ghost has some warning to import.

As Goss makes clear, Forteans rarely allow the researcher the luxury of making much sense of a subject, and he feels that the comparatively few stories that lack satisfactory endings are likely to fall within the parapsychological canon.

The author is particularly good on 'lies and mistaken identities', on the psychological aspects of the phenomena – why the percipients see the hitch-hikers, and why hitch-hikers at all – and on the sexual element in reports. Here he points out that in almost every case the phantom is of the opposite sex to the driver.

The Evidence for the Phantom Hitch Hiker is, I feel, the best book yet in the series, certainly in terms of being the most nearly complete and satisfactory treatment of its subject.

Mike Dash

THE EVIDENCE FOR ALIEN ABDUCTIONS

by John Rimmer
Aquarian Press; 1984; £2.50, pb, pp160, index, bib., photos.

Abductions are becoming recognized as something different from mainstream ufo sightings. Hilary Evans has dubbed them pseudo-UFOs for they seem to be more like vivid dreams, psychological or mystical experiences than *real* abductions by *real* aliens. Many cases are soundly and perceptively examined, and it is significant that they seem to be similar in kind to tales of abductions and molestations by fairies, demons, phantoms, deities and mythical beings of most religious cultures. Rimmer concludes, in the now obligatory personal assessment, that beneath the overlay of UFOs (which are merely the appropriate current cultural images) the phenomenon is basically psychological and universal. Again, we have an excellent summary of a complex subject in which we have no answers and are only just learning to ask sensible questions. *RJMR*

WEST COUNTRY MYSTERIES

by various authors. Introduced by Colin Wilson. *(1985, £2.25 pb, pp 104, drawings, photos). Bossiney Books, St Teath, Bodmin, Cornwall.*

Latest in a growing catalogue of Bossiney titles concerned with strange goings-on in Britain's south-west peninsula. In his perceptive introduction, Colin Wilson suggests that the Westcountry's 'earth itself' provides the power or 'force' behind many seemingly supernatural happenings in this myth-ridden part of the world. *Fortean Times* readers will be especially interested in detailed chapters on the 'Exmoor Beast' and Cornwall's 'sea-serpent', Morgawr. Recommended.

Doc Shiels

STONEHENGE: its Druids, custodians, festival and future,

by John Michell *(Radical Traditionalist Papers No 6, 1985, 23 pages, illus, £2.20 incl p+p from 2 Blenheim Crescent, London W11.)* A timely booklet, appearing shortly after the police riot, outlining the significance of Stonehenge and the illegal infringements over many years by English Heritage of the 1918 Deed of Gift, when Cecil Chubb gave the monument to the nation.

Paul Sieveking

THE FOUR MAJOR MYSTERIES OF MAINLAND CHINA

by Paul Dong
Prentice-Hall Inc., Englewood Cliffs, New Jersey; 1984, $8.95/£8.05, pb, pp223, index, photos.

These four mysteries will be somewhat familiar to readers of FT, being: Chinese UFOs; psychic phenomena, or as the Chinese call them, Exceptional Human Functions (EHF); qi gong; and Wildman. Paul Dong is a Chinese-American journalist who is also an editor of the Chinese *Journal of UFO Research*, based in Gansu and thus is in the best of positions to present the material; and any book on anomalous phenomena in the Middle Kingdom is most welcome.

The main emphasis is given to the first two subjects (about 70 pages each) and, as much as anything, these sections are a personal history of Chinese UFO and EHF research, the personalities involved and the controversies aroused. Despite the rather gosh-wow style and the unwholesome note of triumph when conservative opponents fail to carry the day, these sections contain much of interest, being based largely on material gathered personally by Dong on visits to the country, and painting a picture of widespread and enthusiastic research by members of the scientific establishment which would be the envy of western Forteans. The last two sections are more lightweight, and that on Wildman is rather disappointing. More than half this section duplicates material translated in the first FT Occasional Paper, and the section as a whole is entirely undocumented. And that is the book's major fault: poor referencing...a fault made even more pointed by the fact that Stanley Krippner's brief afterword is copiously documented. True, many of the stories must have been gained by personal collection or correspondence, but which ones were is not clear. True, most of his readers would have neither the access to, nor the ability to read, the original source material. True, there are *some* references. But items preceded by "a newspaper report said..." or "according to historical records..." (if anything at all) simply will not do, and one can only hope for improvement in Mr Dong's future works. Nonetheless, the book is well-produced, well-illustrated and well-worth having. Unfortunately, British distribution seems lamentable; the book has been published almost a year now, and I've yet to see copies in the shops...

SM

BOOKLETS

- **The Beast of Exmoor: Fact or Legend?** by Trevor Beer *(48 pages, 4 plates, £2.75, 1984, from the author at 'Tawside', Park Avenue, Barnstaple, Devon.)* This book was inevitable, given the long lifetime of the story and its many bizarre twists and turns. Readers of FT will be aware of the saga of the Exmoor Beast that has now extended from 1982 into this year, one of the longest running and most heavily witnessed of recent 'out-of-place' animals in Britain. The author, Trevor Beer, is a local field naturalist whose 'nature chat' columns are printed in three local newspapers in North Devon. As such he clearly had an interest in the 'Beast' as he calls it. What seems to have convinced him of its real existence, is his own brief sighting in summer 1984, which also prompted him to produce this booklet.

It is written in an impressionistic/journalistic style with numerous anecdotes (some of great interest) and few dates. To be fair, this is partly the result of how the data was collected – via an appeal in the local media. The writing shows the need of an editor's hand, as Beer seems content merely to print verbatim his rough data. The main drawback of the booklet, however, is the author's apparent lack of knowledge about the 'mystery big cat' phenomenon in general. He writes as if the Exmoor Beast is a genuine and unknown animal with no effort to place it in the British or European context. He mentions Di Francis and her book, *Cat Country*, but it doesn't seem to have made him aware of the extent of the phenomenon. Beer concludes, fairly but unsatisfyingly, that "there are some big-cats loose on Exmoor and elsewhere", but he doesn't know what they could be. If you want serious converage of the story, then I suggest you keep reading FT.

Peter Christie

● **Les Felins-Mystere** by Jean-Louis Brodu & Michel Meurger. A brief account of sightings of mystery cats in France over the last few years, with an essay (by Meurger) on the mystery animal in modern French mythology and psycho-sociology. *36 pages. 1984. 25 Francs. Pogonip: BP 195 75665, Paris Cedex 14, France.*

Help!

WANTED – Hollow and flat earth books and magazines, also copies of the British *Fate* magazine. Will trade *Search*, American *Fate*, and other occult books and magazines. Also, information requested on the following and their writings on the inner earth: Albert McDonald, Guenther Rosenburg, Wilfred A. South, Madeline Argo, W.C. & Gladys Hefferlin, Antonin T. Horak, O.C. Huguenin and Gottfried Messerschmidt. **F.D Brownley, 29 McCall Road, Rochester, NY 14615, USA**

I'm engaged in some research on **HOLLOW EARTH** theory, largely on behalf of an American correspondent who placed an ad in this column a few issues ago. It is probably a long shot, but does anyone remember or know of a Hollow Earth Society run by someone called **Duerson**, or something similar? Contact **Alan J. Rooke: 2 Shen Field Place, Brentwood, Essex.**

I'm interested in obtaining information on the infamous character **SPRINGHEEL JACK,** his rise and fall in the UK and USA. Will exchange what I have for what you have. Contact: **Jesse Glass Jr, Box 11538, Milwaukee, WI 53211, USA.**

I would like to hear from anyone interested in the **SHAVER MYSTERY** and other inner earth ideas, with a view to forming a research organisation here in the UK. Write to: **Ray Archer, 134 Humer Ave, Stoke, Coventry, W.Midlands CV1 2AT.**

Somehow my copy of **WILD TALENTS** has vanished. I've been trying to get another copy, but it seems to be the only one of Fort's books that is not available outside collected editions. Do you know if it can be obtained *solus*? Also, do you know of anyone in the Fortean network who has an interest in **Geneaology** and lives in Cornwall? Why? I'm benighted by the problems of tracing my husband's family (before they started to disrupt the colonies) by the shortcomings of clerical attention to enquiries. Despite the resources of contacts through the Society of Australian Genealogists, the Cornish side of things remains obfuscated. Offers of help to **Alyson Lander: Box 18, Tullamore, NSW 2874, Australia.**

[How sad to have lost a relatively rare edition of WILD TALENTS, published in 1932 by Claude Kendall. The only other edition we know of is the 1972 paperback, by Ace Books of NY, but that can be just as hard to find. Our only advice is to keep trying through second-hand bookshops or book-finder services – RJMR.]

Small Ads

Bibliography.

There follows a gleaning from that great happy hunting ground of the bibliomaniac, *The British Library Catalogue of Printed Books to 1975*. All 180,000 pages in 360 hefty volumes can be yours to fill your living room for £11,800 from K.G. Saur of Munich/London/New York/Paris/Oxford (try the phone book). They can rush you everything up to S, the rest following shortly.

BALFOUR (Blayney Reynell Townley) *See* London. —iii. *Association for the Prevention of Premature Burial.* Premature Burial and its Prevention . . . With preface by B. R. T. Balfour, *etc.* [1911.] 8°. 7307. aa. 6. (7.)

COLES (Richard Bertram) and **KINMONT** (Patrick David Clifford)
—— Skin Diseases for Beginners, *etc.* pp. 43. *H. K. Lewis & Co.: London*, 1957. 8°. 7643. f. 45.

COLLINS (Sewell)
—— The Rubáiyát of a Scotch Terrier . . . With drawings by the author. *Grant Richards: London.* 1926. 8°. 011645. h. 91.

ḌOSĀBHĀĪ FRĀMJĪ KARĀKĀ.
—— Freedom must not stink. (2nd impression.) *Bombay. Kutub*, 1947. X. 708/16638.
pp. 29. 18 cm. △

EDISON PORTLAND CEMENT COMPANY.
—— The Romance of Cement. pp. 128. *Livermore & Knight Co.: Providence*, [1926.] 4°. 07822. d. 13.

ENGLAND.—*Ministry of Defence.*
—— An Introduction to space. pp. vii. 103. *London*, 1968. 4°. B.S. 88/53.

FERRETS.
—— Ferrets and Ferreting . . . With chapters on working and shooting by Arthur Niblett. Fourteenth edition. pp. 57. *Bazaar, Exchange & Mart: London*, [1951.] 8°. 07209. a. 2.

FIVE HUNDRED HOUSEHOLD HINTS.
—— Five Hundred Household Hints. By 500 Housewives. pp. 121. *Country Life: London*, 1926. 8°. 07943. k. 73.

FOX (Marion C.) The Supernatural History of Worms. (Compiled by M. C. Fox. Second edition.) *Friends' Book Centre: London.* [1931.] 8°. 4380. h. 29

GANNETT (William Channing)
—— Blessed be Drudgery . . . With preface by the Countess of Aberdeen. 1897. *See* Books. Worthy Books. vol. 1. 1897, *etc.* 8°. 3622. df. 1.

GREAT UNKNOWN. The Great Unknown; a mystery. [In verse.] (Legal indignation; a hotch-potch.) *London*, 1826. 12°. 993. d. 39.

GRUNDY (Fred)
—— A Study of Hospital Waiting Lists in Cardiff, 1953–1954. A report prepared for the Board of Governors of the United Cardiff Hospitals by F. Grundy . . . R. A. N. Hitchens . . . E. Lewis-Faning. pp. 58. [1956.] 8°. *See* Cardiff.—*United Cardiff Hospitals.* 7689. bb. 39.

HARAKIRI.
—— Harakiri? Eine groteske publication. (Direction: fried-hardy worm.) *Berlin: Romal-Verlag*, [1920]. 48 cm. Cup. 21. g. 14. (51.)

HARRIET, *Aunt.* "Chains for the Neck." A text-book of heavenly truths . . . for the young. [Compiled by Aunt Harriet.] *London*, [1867.] 16°. 3129. a. 28.

HARRIS (Elmo Golightly) Compressed Air: theory and computations. pp. xii. 123. *McGraw-Hill Book Co.: New York, London*, 1910. 8°. 08766. d. 37.

HENDY (David Ponting)
—— Thirty-six reasons for believing in Everlasting Punishment. pp. 15. *Marshall Bros.: London; Bishop's Stortford* [printed], 1887. 8°. 4372. df. 31. (8.)

HIGGINS (Alex)
—— Boiler Room Questions and Answers. pp. vii. 139. *McGraw-Hill Book Co.: New York & London*, 1945. 4°. 8771. d. 33

HOCH (August) *M.D.* Benign Stupors. A study of a new manic-depressive reaction type. [Edited by John T. MacCurdy.] pp. xi. 284. *University Press: Cambridge; New York* printed, 1921. 8°. 07660. ff. 56.

HOLYOAKE (George Jacob)
—— Public Performances of the Dead, *etc.* *London*, [1865.] 8°. 12273. k. 7. (12.)

HOWSON (Geoffrey) Handbook for the Limbless. Edited by G. Howson. Foreword by John Galsworthy. pp. 225. *Disabled Society: London*, [1922.] 8°. 08282. aaa. 60.

HUTTON (Thomas) *F.G.S., Captain, Bengal Army.*
—— Pre-Adamite Death proved to be a geological delusion. *Agra*, [1863.] 8°. 4373. aaa. 43 (3.)

IAMS (Jack)
—— Prematurely Gay. pp. 191. *Rich & Cowan: London*, 1951. 8°. 12730. p. 18.

IDE (Jacob)
—— The Nature and Tendency of Balls, seriously and candidly considered in two sermons [on 1 Thes. v. 21] preached in Medway, *etc.* *Dedham*, [1818.] 8°. 4486. aaa. 94. (9.)

KLINE (Burton) Struck by Lightning: the comedy of being a man. pp. 308. *John Lane: London, New York* printed, 1916. 8°. NN. 3813.

KUENKEL (Fritz) Let's be Normal! The psychologist comes to his senses . . . Translated by Eleanore Jensen. pp. 299. *Ives Washburn: New York*, 1929. 8°. 8404. df. 30.

LARGE (Jean Henry) Nancy goes Camping, *etc.* pp. 215. *D. Appleton & Co.: New York, London*, 1931. 8°. A.N. 837.

LARKIN (Brand)
—— Learn to Croon. pp. 88. *W. Foulsham & Co.: London*, [1936.] 8°. 07899. de. 34.

LEAKE (Frederic) Historic Bubbles. pp. 217. *Suckling & Galloway: London [America printed]*, 1896. 8°. 9072. bbb. 24.

LING (Ting) *See* Ting (Ling)

LONDON.—ii. *Sessions.*
—— Select trials. vol. iii. From April, 1726, to May, 1732. I. Margaret Clap, for keeping a sodomitical house. *Penzance: Triton Press*, 1973. Cup. 550. cc. 36.
pp. 9. 10 cm. △
An extract from the 1762 edition of "Select trials".

LONDON. —*Thames Barrage Association.*
—— Tideless Thames in Future London. By J. H. O. Bunge . . . With articles on the Thames Barrage from a health aspect by Lieut.-Col. Wm. Butler . . . the Thames Barrage in a replanned London, by Sir Charles Bressey. [With maps and illustrations.] pp. 121. *London*, 1944. 4°. 8803. cc. 21.

MOYES (Vernon)
—— The Nurse's "Nasty" Nightmare; or, Patients in uniform. [A one-act play.] pp. 16. *London*, [1940.] 8°. [*French's Acting Edition.*] 11791. t. 1/635

OLISAH (Sunday Okenwa)
—— The way to get money. The best wonderful book for money mongers. By the Master of Life (Okenwa Olisah). *Onitsha: Okenwa Publications*, [1963?] X. 0909/588. (141.)

OMER (Lewis) Hand Grenade Throwing as a College Sport. pp. 9. *A. G. Spalding & Bros: New York, Chicago*, [1918.] 8°. D-7911. de. 33.

FT Backissues.

ALL AT SINGLE ISSUE PRICE

31

32

33

34

35

36

37

38

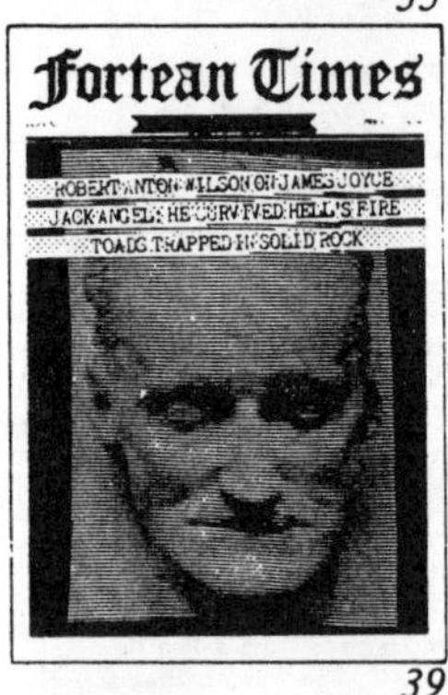

39

40

41

42

SUBSCRIPTION RATES – UK:£6; Overseas: $12 (US) or equivalent. This is for 4 issues, which we try to get out in one year. FT is a 'sporadical'.

SINGLE COPIES – UK: £1.50; Overseas $3 (US) or equivalent. We can send a recent issue and our flyer to a friend. (Overseas mail is sent by accelerated surface post, which ought to arrive within six weeks.)

PAYMENT – Payable to FORTEAN TIMES. Dollar cheques acceptable; for other currencies we prefer a sterling cheque drawn on a bank with a London office. PLEASE no Euro cheques or Irish Postal Orders. European readers may prefer to remit through GIRO services to our National Giro account – **No 50 782 4008 (Fortean Times)** – but if you do so please notify us directly, so that we know what you intend the money for.

96 MANSFIELD RD, LONDON NW3 2HX, UK.

Fortean Times

ISSUE NO.45 The Foremost Journal of Strange Phenomena PRICE:£1.50 $3.00

PLUS WEIRD TALES FROM
FINLAND, IRELAND & RUSSIA

Fortean Times

Cover art by
ADCO

The Journal of Strange Phenomena.

Winter 1985
ISSN 0308.5899

Contents

Annie Taylor, stunt woman (page 62)

Fortean Times

96 Mansfield Road, London NW3 2HX, UK

GANG OF FORT

Editors Robert J.M. Rickard
Paul R.A. de G. Sieveking
Consultants Richard Adams (art)
Hunt Emerson (comix)
Dick Gwynn (print)

SPECIAL CORRESPONDENTS

Australia Greg Axford (Vic.)
Paul Cropper (NSW)
Rex Gilroy (NSW)
Tony Healy (ACT)
Richard King (Vic.)
Belgium Henri Prémont
Canada Dwight Whalen (Ont.)
Mister X (Ont.)
England Bruce Chatterton
Peter Christie
Mike Crowley
Mike Dash
Peter Hope Evans
Alan Gardiner
Brian Hain
Chris Hall
Nick Maloret
Valerie Martin
John Michell
Steve Moore
Nigel Pennick
Paul Screeton
Bob Skinner
Anthony Smith
Paul R. Thomas
Finland Tuuri Heporauta
France Jean-Louis Brodu
Dr Bernard Heuvelmans
Greece Anastasios D. Panos
Ireland Doc Shiels
Japan Jun-Ichi Takanashi
Malaysia Ahmed Jamaludin
Roving Ion A. Will
Scotland Roger Musson
Roland Watson
Jake Williams
South Africa Chris J. Holtzhausen
Sweden Ake Franzen
Anders Liljegren
Sven Rosen
USA Larry E. Arnold (PA)
Tom Adams (TX)
Loren Coleman (MA)
Richard T. Crowe (IL)
David R. Fideler (PA)
Mark A. Hall (MN)
Steve Hicks (KS)
Michael Hoffman (NY)
Phil Ledger (CA)
Kurt Lothmann (TX)
Gary S. Mangiacopra (CN)
Ray Nelke (MO)
Ron Schaffner (OH)
Joseph Swatek (NB)
Joseph Trainor (MA)
Robert Anton Wilson (CA)
USSR Vladimir Rubtsov
Wales Janet & Colin Bord
West Germany Ulrich Magin
Yugoslavia Milos Krmelj

Typesetting Cecilia Boggis, 11 Ashburnham Road, Bedford, MK40 1DX.
Overseas Mailing Overseas Postal Services Ltd. 2-8 Hornsey Street, London N7 8HF.
Sub & Label Computing Anagram, 316A Richmond Road, Tickenham, TW1 2PD.

I offer the customary apology for the lateness of this issue of *Fortean Times*. We do try to be quarterly, but have only managed three a year for some time. I hope that the extra number of pages offers some compensation: the printers couldn't fold the magazine if it were any fatter!

★ Answering post, sorting clippings, writing up the news items, preparing the lay-out and organising the mail-out all take a toll on my time, and have to be fitted in around my job, not to mention eating, sleeping and the essential moments of slack. Next issue will be edited by Bob Rickard, while I'm preparing FT 47. We plan to edit alternating issues from now on, relieving some of the pressure on our lives.

★ "For every expert there is an equal and opposite expert" Bob was quoted as saying, in a long article on the front page of the *Wall Street Journal* (30 Sept 1985.) This, and articles in *Whole Earth Review* and the *San Francisco Chronicle*, have brought in many new American subscriptions. Another distant place for publicity was the back page of *Arab News*, a Saudi publication, which talks of one Charles Forte, presumably an anomalous restauranteur. Where will we read of FT next we wonder. . . *Pravda? The South China Morning Post?*

★ The data has been pouring in as usual, enough for a hefty monthly, if only we had time. Stocks of some back issues, from FT 31 onwards, are running low, so don't delay ordering. FT is really a part-work, and many items refer back to write-ups in previous issues. Summaries of contents and subscription information appear on page 37.

★ Many readers have been inquiring about the reprint, in book form, of back issues 21 to 30, mentioned some time ago. So far, we haven't found an independent publisher, and may have to do it ourselves. We'll keep you posted. Meanwhile, do send advance orders, if you haven't done so already.

★ I conclude with a quotation from William James: "Anyone will renovate his science who will steadily look after the irregular phenomena. And when the science is renewed, its formulas often have more of the voice of the exceptions in them than of what was supposed to be the rules."

Paul Sieveking

Letters

PREPUCE FOOTNOTE

I was interested to read the little piece on 'Preposterous Prepuce' [FT44,p.8]. Perhaps I can add a curious little historical footnote to this article. At least one Catholic writer devoted a treatise to Christ's circumcised foreskin, asserting that it ascended, like Jesus Himself, and expanded into one of the rings of Saturn! (Leo Allatius: *De Præputio Domini Nostri Jesu Christi Diatriba*).

Another curious historical reference to this singular object is noted in a book published on the Portuguese Inquisition published in 1761 which recorded that the real Santo Prepucio was kept at Rome, subsequently falling into the hands of some invading soldiers. It would not allow itself to be touched by these profane wretches, until one soldier suspecting the truth sent for a pure virgin, where upon it readily expanded! (G.W. Foote and J.M. Wheeler: *Crimes of Christianity*, London 1887.)

Michael Conway
Ilford, Essex

BIG CAT ENCOUNTER

On Saturday, 30th August 1985, at about 9.30 in the evening, I decided to put our corgi pup outside. I put on the kitchen and outside lights and looked out the kitchen door. Standing and staring at me about 6 feet from the door was a sandy-coloured cat-like animal, about 2 feet 6 inches tall, lithe with long legs, and a long thin tale held vertical. The eyes were huge, round and bulging. It turned and disappeared up the garden steps. It definitely wasn't a panther, and was nothing like anything I've seen before.

A.Grizzell
Faversham, Kent

EXPLOSIVE QUESTION

Do you have any information about explosives that have been kept top secret from the general public without a good logical reason in relation to nuclear types?

Robert Beach
Skelmersdale, Merseyside.

[If it's been kept top secret how would we know about it Mr Beach? – Eds.]

TRUTH ABOUT KANGAROOS

I am somewhat annoyed by the irresponsible reporting reaching for a vicarious immortality in the pages of FT44 as "Kangaroo Aggro".

Mr Kevin (W)Hopper might have had his own reasons for clobbering a pet kangaroo with a fence-post, but it seems a trifle gratuitous to embroider his viciousness with a virtual admission of the macropod's disorientation.

That the "large red kangaroo" was almost certainly a pet is suggested strongly by its size (over seven feet is adult male – Red females are blue/grey – "Blue Flyers"); that it approached a group of adults and children; the location; and its lone state. But, most importantly, that it failed, if it was indeed "backed up against a car", to take advantage of this, the best defensive fighting position for a kangaroo.

Settlers last century learned, at the cost of embarrassing numbers of torn and disembowelled dogs loosed on to kangaroos backed up against trees or rocks, that protection and physical support from the rear rather enhances the effectiveness of the downward rip of those nails on the hind feet.

Can we inject a little sanity into future kangatales? I know the marsupial macropods are a source of fascination, particularly if they don't exactly live on your doorstep, but their characteristics are interesting enough without embellishment.

Alyson Lander
Injune, Queensland.

UNFAIR EXCHANGES

I discovered that the play "Unfair Exchanges", based on *Fortean Times*, was due to be screened on Sunday 20 January 1985. This was by way of my newspaper (*The Daily Mail*) on the Saturday morning. *The Mail* seemed to express astonishment or disbelief that the *Fortean Times* was a *real* magazine, a point which will sadly have escaped many.

My memory being jogged by the title of the play, I called up a couple of fellow investigators and suggested they watch. After a few hours I wished I hadn't bothered!

Firstly, I discovered that I could not get in touch with Dot Street (one of my fellow authors on *Sky Crash*.) Her phone simply gave out an incessant whining. I needed urgent consultation as our publishers had just given me 10 days notice they were "retiring" and would cease to exist. However, after much frustration I discovered that her line was disconnected. I later gathered, from Dot, that she had been so threatened for several weeks and had staved them off with the prospect of sufficient to pay the outstanding (horrendous) bill when some due money came from our publishers. Gleeful at its arrival she picked up the phone and was calling through to accounts when the exchange snipped the line dead!

Undaunted I tried other

Cont. on p. 43

OPERATION CONGO

We had hoped to carry a report on the preparatory stages of this cryptozoological initiative by four young Britons – Bill Gibbons, Mark Rothermel, Jonathan Peacock and Jonathan Walls – to track down a dinosaur-like creature, but Bill's departure for the Congo was brought forward unexpectedly, to 13th November, and we are without his notes.

Their attempts to raise sponsorship from major British companies and institutions were met with a wall of indifference. As Bill kept us informed of these rebuttals almost daily it made us feel ashamed to be British. If the team shows the same dauntless spirit in the jungle around Lake Telle as he did in the face of this negativity they should do well. Pretty much the same attitude was shown by the British media at first, although later on, mainly due to Bill's persistence, interviews with the lads appeared in numerous national and regional papers. Being their first exposure to the crassness of British journalism, they were taken aback by the inability of the reporters to treat their efforts with the seriousness they felt they deserved.

It is regrettable also that the nature documentary departments of the major TV companies lacked the vision to take up the opportunity to loan them special lightweight video equipment, or even to send a cameraman along. One would have thought that, however skeptical they might have been about the *mokele mbembe*,this would have been a good chance to film a rarely visited part of the world with unique scenery, indigent and secretive pygmies and a large number of rarely seen animals (including an extremely rare type of gorilla). Only the news company ITN responded with a clockwork cine-camera and a donation in return for a one-day right on any successful footage. The team have also signed a deal with Robert Hale Ltd, to do a book on their return, and Tim Dinsdale has agreed to write the forword to it.

The team have prepared themselves by reading everything they could on the *mokele mbembe* in our files, and in the books by Dr Bernard Heuvelmans and Dr Roy Mackal. Meetings with these leading cryptozoologists, and especially several long transatlantic conversations with Dr Mackal on the problems the team will face, proved very helpful. In the last two weeks before Bill left by ship for the Congo, several things went wrong. One scare involved a panic dash to the Congolese Embassy in Paris for their visas. Another heart-stopping moment came when the shipping firm offering them free passage came up with only one berth, not the expected four, and brought forward their departure date. Yet another came when Bill, out jogging, saved a young girl from being run over and fractured his ankle in the process. Nevertheless he felt fit enough to undertake the journey by ship, with their equipment (including many different kinds of cameras), in order to make advance contact with Dr Macellin Agnagna, who will lead the official Congolese half of the expedition. The rest of the British team will fly out at the end of November.

Bill has promised to send us a progress report (if possible) and a full report whether Operation Congo is successful or not. Meanwhile, if you'd like to help their efforts, please turn to the T-shirt offer on the outside back cover.

BOLTS FROM THE BLUE

The Rev. Ray Hewett had just concluded the burial of Liza Poteete, 91, in Blairsville, Georgia, with the words "we never know who's going next" when a bolt of lightning struck dead her grandson, Donald Metcalf, 27. *Guardian, D. Telegraph*, 14 July 1982.

● Alan Weatson, 31, was quarrelling with his wife Debbie, 24, about how to cut the lunchtime joint in Keynsham near Bristol at the height of a thunderstorm. He exclaimed "May God strike me down if I'm wrong", there was an almighty bang, he was thrown across the kitchen and blinded for a few minutes. *D. Mirror*, 10 Aug 1982.

● A church in Salford, Lancs, was struck by lightning in late August 1982 as the vicar joked with friends about the Second Coming. Three weeks later the Rev. Bill Lister, 73, stand-in preacher at Sawley, Yorks, was taking a service. He raised his arms and said in a loud voice: "We must all do as the Lord commands!" when there was a huge bang. A nearby electricity sub-station had been struck, and 15 square miles of countryside were blacked out. *D. Star*, 13 Sep 1982.

● Jack McPherson, 55, a farmer in Ganmain, near Wagga Wagga in Australia, was mixing calf feed in a light drizzle when he was struck by lightning on 13 February 1983. He survived, though suffering from burns, paralysis and memory loss. Twenty years earlier, in 1963, he had been struck while standing in exactly the same place: he was milking a cow when the bolt knocked him out and killed the cow. *Canberra Times*, 15 Feb 1983.

• Mrs Betty Meggitt, 31, of Swinton near Rotherham, was flung across the kitchen when her sink lit up during a thunderstorm. Two weeks earlier, her TV blew up after a lightning strike. *D. Telegraph*, 20 May 1983.

• A woman accused with 33 other villagers of stoning a man to death for allegedly manipulating lightning, was herself killed by a lightning bolt in Pietersburg, South Africa, on 16 February 1984. *Aberdeen Press & Journal*, 24 Feb 1984.

• Vebi Limani, 34, was struck dead by lightning near his home on Sara Mountain, in southern Yugoslavia. Reporting his death, the newspaper *Politika* said that his father, a brother and an uncle had suffered the same fate in the past few years, and lightning had also struck a sister, making her an invalid. *D. Telegraph, Sun,* 17 Aug; *S. Express*, 26 Aug 1984.

• A local Boston radio station was broadcasting a phone-in show with city councillor Dapper O'Neill. In assuring an irate caller that he would launch an enquiry into complaints about a hospital, he said: "I'll get to the bottom of this. May lightning strike me dead if I don't." Lightning struck immediately and knocked the radio station off the air. *Standard*, 21 Aug 1984.

• Villagers in an area of West Donegal in Ireland have petitioned Dublin for lightning conductors on the rates. In the last two years they have been terrorised by a spate of freak lightning bolts. Roofs have been stripped off houses in 10 villages, windows smashed, pipelines wrecked, telephones and TVs blown up. The latest bolt, on Christmas Day 1984, turned the area's first white Christmas in 20 years into a three-day blackout. No-one knows why the storms have chosen to blast this area in particular. *S.Express*, 30 Dec 1984.

• Zimbabwe has been suffering the worst electrical storm season on record. By the beginning of February 1985, the season's death toll was 116. The country holds the record for the most people ever killed by a single bolt – 21. *D.Express*, 8 Feb 1985.

STRANGE SWARM

Every spring, Lufkin, Texas is invaded by a scenario from a science fiction horror movie. Creeping crawfish swarm by night in their thousands, crawling into offices and lurking in the streets, and ruining crops and machinery with their clay mounds.

The crawfish (aka crawdads, mudbugs or crayfish) are nocturnal, land-based relatives of the lobster which have particularly infested plains across ten counties in East Texas and some parts of Louisiana. On spring nights they swarm from their holes, having hibernated underground most of the year, to mate. The females build hollow mounds of clay, about 18 inches high, which are soon filled with rainwater. While the hot Texas sun bakes the mounds rock-hard, the crawfish retreat to water-filled hollows beneath the mounds and elsewhere in the ground. By summer they no longer surface, and have sealed themselves into their subterranean colonies until the next spring.

The problem is getting worse, say the farmers, who, apart from the nightmare of a landscape carpeted with crawling crustaceans, are suffering considerable loss due to tilling or mowing machinery being damaged on the hard mounds and thereby the inadequately tended crops. Federal and state officials monitoring the swarmings say that approved pesticides have failed to stop the creatures' increase. Farmers try to fight back by pouring crushed mothballs, carbide or burning oil down the holes. But despite that the eerie scenes return each year. One farm near Lufkin had 27,000 mounds per acre, and in worst-hit Angelina County an estimated 200,000 acres are infested. "It's like a horror movie," said Hal Brockman, district conservationist for the US Dept of Agriculture. AP/Portland (ME) *Press Herald* 13 May 1985.

EAGLE ATTACKS

Sweden's reindeer population suffered its worst year for depredation last year (1984/5). The worst predators were wolverines, but some were killed by lynxes, bears and even. . .eagles. In the Lapp village of Idre, one eagle has become a serious threat to their reindeer. The villagers' petition for permission to shoot the pest was recently refused because the golden eagle is a protected species.

Sigvard Jonsson, village spokesman, says he has seen, with his own eyes, the eagle carrying off a six-months-old reindeer calf. The eagle managed to transport the calf, which weighed between 20-25kr (44-55lbs), about 200 metres. According to Jonsson, the eagle has snatched ten young reindeer like this, and has killed the bigger heifers, which it could not lift, by apparently learning to bite into the carotid artery. *Sydsvenska Dagbladet* 10 May 1985. [For more accounts of animal behaviour changes, see SHELDRAKEANA on p19]

Aerial abductions by eagles, particularly of humans, are discussed more fully in *Living Wonders* (1982) by John Michell and Robert Rickard, and also in their *Phenomena* (1977).

CADAVER CONFUSIONS

Fifteen days after a road accident near Sioux City, Iowa, Patricia Noonan, 16, awoke from a coma in hospital and found that another girl had been buried in her name. The dead girl was Shawn Lake, 14. The fathers of both girls had also been killed. Shawn's mother Colleen had sat beside Patricia's bed thinking it was her daughter. The girls were of similar build and colouring and bandages on Patricia's face obscured her identity. (UPI) Belleville IL *News-Democrat, Standard,* 26 Nov 1984.

● In the 'Great Blow' of 1913 on the Great Lakes, 12 lake vessels vanished and 250 to 400 sailors perished. Many bodies, some from the Canadian steamer *J.J. Carruthers*, washed up along the eastern shore of Lake Huron. Thomas Thompson of Hamilton, Ontario, received a telegram from his daughter, Mrs Edward Ward: "John has been drowned. Come at once." Mrs Ward believed that her brother, a 27-year-old marine fireman, was among the dead from the *Carruthers*, which listed a "J. Thompson" on the payroll.

Thomas Thompson travelled to Goderich and viewed the body. Like his son, it bore the tattooed initials 'J.T.' on the forearm. Distinctive scars on John's nose and leg corresponded with scars on the dead man. Also matching were two deformed toes and some dental peculiarities. Mr Thompson, his wife and daughters all agreed it was John, and the body was sent to the undertaker. One daughter was not convinced, however. She knew that her brother's 'J.T.' tattoo was topped by an anchor, which was missing on the corpse – but she was overruled by her father.

Scanning a newspaper in Toronto, John Thompson read of his own death, and returned home to Hamilton to find his family in black and a flower-bedecked coffin in the parlour. His mother was overjoyed, but his father, who had bought a graveyard plot and incurred other expenses, was able to contain his elation. The dead man was never positively identified, and was interred in Hamilton's Holy Sepulchre cemetery. This story, with its striking parallels to that of Albert Steer (FT33 p19 & FT42 p26) was told by our correspondent Dwight Whalen in *What's Up Niagara,* June 1983.

● A similar tale was published in the *Farnham Herald* (6 July 1984) in the "80 years ago" section, which dates it to approximately 1904, three years earlier than Albert Steer. The weekly *Letter from London* related an 'extraordinary experience' that befell a family from Greenwich. After John Gobbett, a lighterman, had left Greenwich, his barge was delayed by bad weather from Southend, and a body found in the Thames was identified as Gobbett by his wife, his father and several others. The dead man shared the following characteristics with Gobbett: a long scar on the leg, which had been broken and mended badly; a scar on the bridge of the nose; and a peculiar birthmark. The corpse was interred at Nunhead. A day or two later the wife received a letter, supposedly from Gobbett, though not in his handwriting, stating that he would be home on the following day. And in the morning he did indeed turn up. (For yet another variation on this theme, see TALES FROM AFRICA (FT44,p40.)

THREE-LEGGED MOUSE BITE

As some kind of arcane footnote to the Pied Piper legend, we report the following: that while on a British army adventure holiday in Hamelin, teenager Glen Aspinall from Barnsley was bitten by a three-legged mouse and was undergoing a three-month course of injections as a precaution against rabies.

"We had wanted to keep the mouse to carry out tests for rabies," said an army spokesman, "but it escaped from the guardroom where we had locked it." *Laboratory News* 3 Sept 1982.

A MOVING EXPERIENCE

On 14th February 1985, around noon, about 30 children left their school and went next door to pray, as is their daily custom locally, in the small church of St Mary, in Asdee, on the coast of Co. Kerry. At least four of them (see photo) were among the first to glimpse two almost life-sized statues, of Jesus and Mary, moving. Elizabeth Flynn, 7, said: "I saw Jesus moving. His hand moved and called me. Then I saw the eyes of the Blessed Virgin move." Elizabeth's sister Mary, 12, and their brother Connie, 9, and his friend Michael Scully, 9, also said they saw the right hand of Jesus beckoning and the eyes of Mary moving. They ran back to the playground with their exciting news, and since then the tiny 300-seater church has been packed with the pious and the plain curious.

Although no pronouncement has been made on the phenomenon, the Bishop's office was said to be taking the claims "very seriously", which, as those Church watchers amongst you will realize, neither approves nor condemns the apparitions. The parish priest, Father Michael O'Sullivan, interrogated the children, then sent a report to the acting Bishop of Kerry, who sent an envoy to further question the witnesses. "They have shown amazing consistency in their accounts," said the priest. Nevertheless, countless of the faithful have already jumped the gun and ensured Asdee's place on the list of pilgrimage sites. Already there have been visits from American clergy.

As Forteans we know from experience how optical illusions can quickly be incorporated into a belief system, and children have fewer analytical obstacles to such assimilation. We had mused about the obvious objections to actual movement of the statues – and the most obvious was that the movements were a product of afterimages caused by staring at brighter objects first, then looking at a darker one. Now, the statues stand on an altar, about waist height, about ten feet apart, and between them is a small round window – as can be seen in the *Sunday Press* photo we reproduce here. The feet of the statues are surrounded by candles – so whether looking up or from one to the other the children would be looking past a bright light. We don't usually indulge in explanation either, and we are only going into this to set the scene, as it were, for a comment by Irish journalist Cal McCrystal. In the *Sunday Times Magazine* for 7th April 1985, he wrote: "I go into the church which is small and unremarkable. Dozens of people crowd round a candelabra, lighting candles and reciting rosaries. I decide to try an experiment. The circular window has three horizontal and four vertical bars and the sun sends a shaft of light on to the devout faces in the church. I stare at the window for a good 20 seconds, then switch my eyes to a statue. An illusion of movement is produced." (p40).

The four principal witnesses to the moving statues (behind them) in St Mary's Church, Asdee, Co. Kerry – from left; Michael Scully, Connie Flynn, and his sisters Mary and Elizabeth. [Photo © Dublin Sunday Press.]

We don't know if this is how the children saw the movement, and we probably never will. But we can note a couple of observations which may have contributed towards a general contemplation of piety and perhaps even miracles. Firstly, Asdee is in the area of western Kerry rocked by an affair known as 'The Kerry Babies' which has highlighted the plight in this region of unmarried women who find themselves pregnant, and are frightened by social, religious and male intolerance and double standards into hiding the pregnancy, and even, in the current case, the eventual birth, with equally inevitable, again in this case, tragic and fatal consequences. For a full account, read Cal McCrystal's article in the *Sunday Times* from which the above quote was taken. The "sinful" Kerry Babies affair, dominating the Irish news-media for the last year, and sharing front-page headlines only with the ferociously debated issue of whether or not to legalize the general availability of contraception, has stirred up religious feelings and issues of all sorts, creating "a form of national shock", as McCrystal describes it. It is against this local and national background of religious and moral tension that McCrystal places the 'apparitions' at Asdee and their rapid acceptance.

Be that as it may, another fact is that the night before the children saw the statues move, the community saw a film on the life of the stigmatic saint-in-waiting, Padre Pio. Other sources: Dublin *Sunday Press* 17 Feb; *D.Express, Times* 18 Feb 1985.

■ We wrote this Asdee story for inclusion in FT44, but due to pressure of events and space we had to postpone it. Little did we know then that it would be followed by a veritable epidemic of meandering masonry. For this sequel, see THE MOVING STATUES OF IRELAND on p30.

HAZARDS OF XMAS PUDDING

Marie Hefferman was 13 when she celebrated her first Christmas in Australia after her family had emigrated there from England in 1972. Unknowingly, she swallowed a 1959 silver threepenny piece which her mother had put in the Christmas pudding. She developed laryngitis and lost her voice six weeks later. Doctors were mystified. X-rays failed to show the coin which lay horizontally in her throat between vocal chords, preventing their vibration.

Twelve years later, Marie had not uttered a word but was married and working as a secretary in Canberra. She had a coughing fit and brought up a little black lump which turned out to contain the unsuspected coin. After some speech therapy, she found she could speak again – and had acquired a broad Australian accent in her years of silence. *USA Today, D.Telegraph, Guardian, D.Express, Scotsman,* 21 Dec; *D.Mail*, 22 Dec 1984.

▲ We have lots of clippings on things stuck in people. For instance: Julie Ford, 11, of Hucknall, Notts, went to see her dentist, who discovered a screw stuck up her nose, which had been there about ten years without anyone knowing. Ruth Clarke, 23, of Mansfield, Notts, went into hospital with breathing problems, and a yellow tiddlywink which had been stuck up her nose for 20 years was removed. *D.Telegraph*, 19 July 1979 & 5 Feb 1981. Can there be some special propensity of Nottinghamshire noses?

▲ Doctors in Cannes could scarcely believe their eyes when a routine X-ray of a man complaining of headaches showed a seven-inch screwdriver embedded in his skull. On further investigation, they found the tool was in the X-ray machine where it had been left by a careless technician. *Shropshire Star*, 22 Feb; *Scotsman*, 23 Feb 1985.

▲ Writing in *The Lancet* (17 May 1985), Dr Richard Warburton, serving as a British Aircraft Corporation medic in Saudi Arabia, describes how he removed a shirt button that had been lodged up a woman's nose for 32 years.

DEATH IS A BAD HABIT

Musyoka Mututa, 60, had been lying for a day in his coffin in the village of Kitui, 100 miles from Nairobi, when pall bearers came to his home, sprayed the supposed cholera victim with insecticide to ward off flies – and he sat up asking for a drink of water.

Musyoka had come back from the dead twice before, according to reports in the Kenyan newspapers, the *Daily Nation* and the *Standard*. When he was three, his body, wrapped in sheets and blankets, was being lowered into a grave when he let out a cry. Nineteen years later, his family reported him missing and a six-day search ensued. Shepherds found his apparently lifeless body in a field. As he was again being buried, he forced open the coffin lid.

After his third kiss of death, he told reporters: "There appeared to be a row over why I was picked. Some angels decided to return me. I sat thinking under their wings, then they escorted me back to earth. Death shall finally come. This I am certain about." And he was right. Four months later he 'died' again, was left unburied for two days in case of revival, but this time the angels let him in. *D.Express* 27 May; *D.Mail, Sun* 1 June; Philadelphia *Enquirer* 2 June; *D.Mail* 23 Sept 1985.

SOLES OF BLASPHEMY

Thousands of Chinese shoes have been seized in Egypt and other Arab states because the anti-slip treads reverse out as the Arabic for Allah. Ding Guoyo, Chinese Ambassador in Cairo, insisted that it was accidental and the makers in Nangyshen didn't know Arabic.

G.B.Britton, boot manufacturers in Kingswood near Bristol, were also in trouble for blasphemous boot treads, and 15,000 were impounded. The boots had been on sale for 12 years without any trouble. A French firm had similar problems. *D.Telegraph, Scotsman* 15 Mar; *Evening Post* (Bristol) 26 April 1985.

SOUTHERN SATIRE

A man drowned while attending a party for New Orleans lifeguards celebrating their first drowning-free season in living memory. The victim was Jerome Moody, 31, who was not a lifeguard and had not been swimming. He was fully dressed. More than half the 200 people there were certified lifeguards, and four were on duty at the pool. [AP] Lincoln (NB) *Journal* 1 Aug; St Louis *Post-Dispatch* 2 Aug 1985.

KILLER PHONES

Jason F. Findley, 17, of Piscataway, New Jersey, passed a stringent all-day physical examination for acceptance into the US Military Academy at West Point on 16 May 1985. On 21 May he was at his grandmother's house after a day's work at Muhlenberg Hospital, Plainfield, NJ, waiting for his mother to pick him up. He was talking to his girlfriend, Marsha Stevens, on the phone when she heard an odd click on the line. This was followed by a gasp and the sound of the television in the background. Jason's grandmother found him unconscious, still holding the phone in his left hand. He was pronounced dead shortly afterwards at Muhlenberg hospital.

A preliminary autopsy failed to determine the cause of death. The New Jersey Bell Telephone Company found the telephone properly grounded and working normally. "There was no indication of any extraordinary charge of electricity," said a spokesman. "If there had been a large electrical charge, the phone would have been damaged and the lines burned – and there is no evidence of that having happened." Findley was lying on a wooden bed which couldn't conduct electricity.

The case was referred to Marius Lombardi, special forensic investigator with the New Jersey medical Examiner's Office, who told AP wire services on 31 May that *about six people had died in the United States in similar circumstances.* A New Jersey woman contacted his office to say she was knocked unconscious for two hours in 1984 by a high-voltage shock from her telephone. Several weeks before the Findley death, a man from Whitehouse Station NJ was found unconscious with a telephone in his hand. He said later that he had experienced an electric jolt.

In 1984, nearly 12,000 people in the USA were taken to emergency rooms because of injuries related to telephones, according to the Consumer Product Safety Commission in Washington. Of those cases, *100 people died*, although the Commission didn't know (or reveal) the exact details.

Lombardi said that Findley had a haemorrhage of the inner ear, leading him to suspect that he had died either from an acoustic shock, an inaudible high-pitched sound capable of stopping the heart; or from an electric surge. Lombardi disagreed with the telephone spokesman, saying it *was* possible that a lightning bolt had travelled along the phone wires without leaving visible damage. There had been an electric storm over Scotch Plains NJ the night Findley died. [AP] Huntsville (AL) *Times* 30 May; AP newswire 2 June; NY *Times* 11 Sept 1985.

Richard Adams

Fred Wehner's report in the *Sunday Express* (7 July 1985) quotes Lombardi as saying: *"This is the first time I've heard of it being fatal."* Is this dim-witted sub-editing or a cover up?

● Two people were killed in Toulouse, France, by lightning travelling along telephone wires, according to police reports. One was a fireman being alerted by a colleague to deal with storm damage, and the other was a young girl telephoning her boyfriend 100 yards away. The boyfriend was thrown to the ground. *Neue Zurcher Zeitung* (Zurich) 18 Aug 1984.

● Telephones can kill in more indirect ways. A 28-year-old Brooklyn woman speaking on a public telephone was killed when lightning struck a flower pot on a ledge 8 storeys above her, causing it to fall about 115 feet onto her head. A passer-by had to tell the victim's mother, left hanging on the phone. *D.Express* 17 July; *Canberra Times* 18 July 1985.

● For more clues about what the dastardly phones are up to, see Jenny Randles' letter on p3 , and IT'S FOR YOO-HOO (FT43,p26). I can also recommend *Phone Calls From the Dead* by D. Scott Rogo and Raymond Bayless (*Prentice Hall*) published in 1979, the year that Ion Will and myself wrote a prolegomenon to a proposed study of telephathic telephones. As we said then: "It is only now that unmistakable evidence can emerge of a complex machine behavioural psychology and self-consciousness. . .Telepathic telephones who know you better than you and try by wrong numbers and crossed lines to connect you to whom you *need* to speak to. . .evidence that the Network is evolving a transistorised electronic version of the Akashic Records. . ."

Paul Sieveking

THE BLACK BEASTS OF MORAY

●*1 – Gazette editor David Morgan (right) and Tomas Christie (left) examine the body of the mystery cat shot at Kellas in 1983. [Photo © Les Hester.]*

●*2 – This newsprint photo is the only image left of the mystery cat shot at Grantown in September 1984.*

Over the years we've chronicled many outbreaks of alien big-cats (ABCs) in Scotland – the most consistent sightings of black ABCs have come from Argyll, on the west coast, Sutherland in the far north, and the counties adjacent to the Moray Firth, eastwards from the tip of Loch Ness. It is from this latter region that the latest sensational news comes of the shooting of not one cat-like animal, but four.

On the 17th October this year many British papers headlined the shooting of a large unidentified animal near Dallas, in Moray. This creature was shot through the body by a gamekeeper, while it stalked pheasants on land adjoining the estate of Tomas Christie at Kellas. It was not like a lynx or puma, or other big cat, not did it resemble a wildcat. It was described as taller and slimmer than a domestic cat, with long legs and a long bushy tail -- see photo 3. It was a young male, probably about a year old. It's body was about the size of a spaniel, and it measured about 36 inches from nose to tail. It's coat was jet-black with long, stiff, white guard hairs.

Leading up to the period of the four shootings there were sporadic reports of black cat-like beasts in the Inverness-Moray area for many years. We have an unrecorded note, from the Scottish *Sunday Post* 12 August 1984, that such a beast was seen a number of times "in the past few weeks" in the Forres area, including three times in one day on the outskirts of the town. Here are the details of the first three shootings. . .

The first happened sometime in 1983, probably late summer or autumn. It was trapped and shot by Tomas Christie, who owns the Kellas estate at Dallas. Mr Christie had been concerned for some time about unusual livestock killings, and stated that he had himself seen at least four of these animals since 1982. The jet-black beast he shot clearly differed from a wildcat. It was dog-sized, about 42 inches from nose to tail, with a long tail and large fangs. It had another peculiarity: it walked with its claws out, unlike most other cats, and left clawed footprints which had fooled locals into thinking the depredations were made by a dog. Mr Christie had the animal stuffed – see photo 1. This specimen was briefly examined by the Natural History Museum, South Kensington (BMNH) later in 1984.

The second black animal was shot in mid-September 1984, after it was caught in a snare at Revack Lodge, near Grantown-on-Spey, some 15 miles to the south of Dallas and over the foothills of the Grampian mountains. The overall description is similar to the first one, except that it measures 43 inches from nose to tail. The dead beast was passed to an incompetant taxidermist, whose neglect caused the remains to be so useless they had to be disposed of. All that remains of this animal is a rather poor newsprint photo – see photo 2 – the originals of which are irretrievable. It was news of this second kill that brought big-cat hunter Di Francis to Forres from Devon. A photo of her and the first specimen appeared in the major national dailies in mid-December

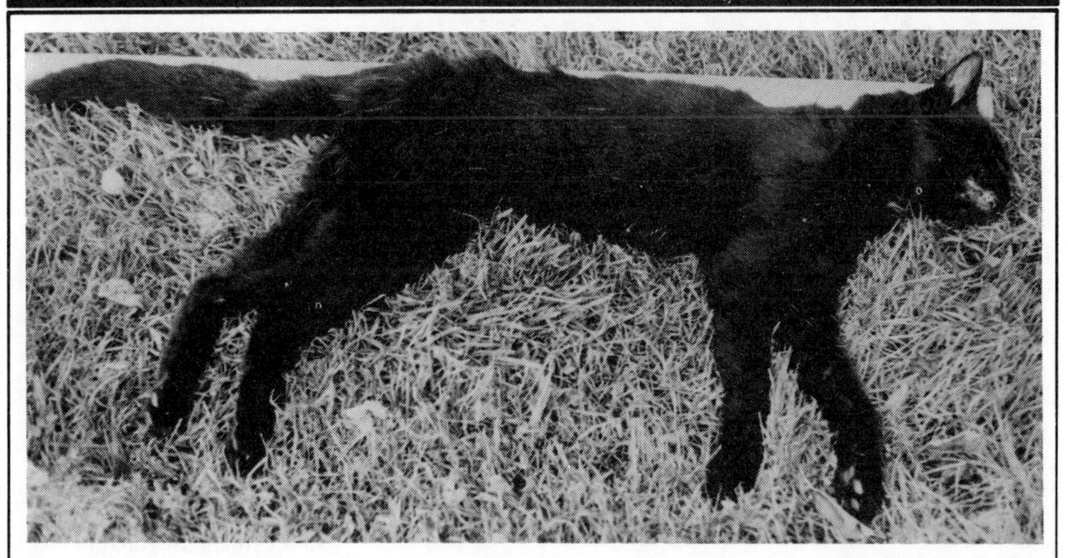

●*3 – The body of the latest mystery cat, shot at Dallas on 14 October 1985. It measures 36 inches from nose to tail. [Photo courtesy of* Forres Gazette.*]*

1984 as Miss Francis publicized her attempt to get the BMNH to identify the Kellas creature. Despite having the stuffed cat for half a day, and x-raying it, the BMNH resisted pressure from the media to make a pronouncement on the mystery animal's identity; however this did not deter Di from asserting that it was proof of the validity of her theory that Britain's remote areas are inhabited by a large strain of wild cat which has not yet been scientifically described.

The third big cat was shot in early May this year at Advie, northeast of Grantown. We believe the remains were sent to the BMNH.

The latest specimen, the second killed in the Dallas area, has not yet proved useful in identifying the species. Within two hours of its death it was examined by a local vet and David Morgan, editor of the *Forres Gazette*, who has investigated each incident and many other sightings of the black cats. Morgan and the vet took a blood sample and sent it to Douglas Leighton, a PhD biologist at Aberdeen University. Unfortunately the sample was contaminated and proved useless for identification. The carcase is still in a freezer on the Kellas estate pending suitable transportation to the BMNH. It is hoped the skin and skeleton can be sent to the Royal Scottish Museum in Edinburgh for proper mounting.

What can we say about the identity of these beasts, which have stumped local, and apparently national, zoologists? Attempts by several sources, including Di Francis, to label them melanistic wildcats were clearly not thought out: a black wildcat would be a curiosity indeed, but these creatures have many features which are not shared by the Scottish wildcat, *Felis silvestris grampia*, whose home region this is. A more enduring notion, favoured by many of the naturalists cited in the reports, is that we have a new strain of wild cat, from several generations of mating between feral cats and wildcats. Even so there are some characteristics still to be explained, among which are the tendency to large size, the long legs and the extended claws. As far as we know the cheetah is the only cat which can walk with its claws out, and this prompts the thought that somewhere along the line our new breed has mated with one or more possibly melanistic exotic big cats, which as you know are also sighted regularly, particularly in central Scotland. The detail of the clawed-foot print, which we have observed before in the reports from the Bettyhill area of Sutherland, suggest the new breed of wild cat may be quite extensive in the Highlands. Certainly the farmers around Dallas believe they have a whole family of them locally.

With all the evidence available, the silence from the professional biologists is deafening. Concerned zoologists are far from ignorant about the matter, so we can only assume that some very low-profile research is under way. With the possible glory of describing a hitherto undescribed large mammal, and a native one at that, as the prize, we're not surprised the investigators (if they exist) are keeping quiet. In the meantime David Morgan and his colleagues are keeping vigilant, and kitted-out with proper blood-sampling kits, are confident they will sooner or later be able to provide more conclusive evidence.

Primary sources for this summary are: the *Forres, Elgin & Nairn Gazette* 3 Oct 1984 and a few subsequent undated clippings; Scottish *Daily Record*, Birmingham *Eve. Mail*, Dundeed *Courier & Advertiser* 17 Oct; *Mail on Sunday* 20 Oct 1985. Additional sources include: *Western Morning News*, *D.Mail* 27 Sept; Aberdeen *Press & Journal, D.Record, D.Telegraph, Shropshire Star, The Scotsman, D.Mirror, Western Morning News, Shields Gazette* 15 Dec 1985.

Our thanks go to David Morgan, editor of the *Forres Gazette*, and Mike Goss for providing additional information, and to Andrew MacGregor for pointing out the name of a sports-shoe, the Puma Dallas! News of other ABC sightings will have to wait until next issue.

MIND THE HOLE

A team of astronomers at six radio telescopes linked for simultaneous operations, using the new techniques of very long baseline interferometry, have (more or less) confirmed the existence of a black hole at the centre of our Milky Way galaxy, first suggested by Doctors Lynden-Bell and Martin Rees of Cambridge in 1971. (*Nature*, vol. 315, 9 May 1985.)

Besides the extremely intense and unusual radiation, which is believed to be generated by material before it is sucked into the void, the team has studied the very high velocities and irregular motion of gas in the vicinity, using infrared detectors.

Sgr.A., as it is known, is approximately five million times more massive than the sun, with a diameter of about 20 astronomical units, or the size of the solar system within the orbit of Saturn. It is thought to be continuously growing as it devours stars in the constellation of Sagittarius. Adrian Berry in the *Telegraph* points out that if the earth were compressed into a black hole it would be under half an inch across; but we needn't be too worried yet, since this cannibal star is 30,000 light years away. *D.Telegraph, Times* 11 May; (UPI) St Louis *Post-Dispatch, Detroit News* 7 June 1985.

ARCHEOLOGICAL BOMBSHELL?

Very large banded stone axes – so called from the grooving caused by cane binding – have been discovered on the northern New Guinea coast north of the city of Lae. They were in creek beds running through limestone and interbedded with volcanic ash, which enabled accurate dating by the Australian National University in Canberra, showing that the tools were at least 38,000 years old.

Associate Professor Les Groube, a New Zealander working in the Department of Archaeology at the University of Papua, New Guinea, said that the axes were too heavy to be used as hunting tools. "They are of a kind which archaeologists have found modern primitive people using elsewhere for ploughing and gardening," he said.

Current archaeological orthodoxy places the invention of agriculture in the Near East about 10,000 years ago. If Professor Groube is right, then farming is almost four times as old. UPI newswire, 19 June; *Detroit News* 20 June 1985.

THE BLIND AT WORK

Doctor John Bongiovanni has been blind since March 1980, but performed eight operations in late 1980 or early 1981, including urinary, bladder and prostrate surgery, in Ogdensburg, NY. During one operation, he had to be told that a patient has begun bleeding upon insertion of an hydraulic extension. In March 1984, the State Board of Regents deciplined the doctor and barred his guide dog from areas where patients were treated. The ruling "may make it impossible for me to perform" said the doctor. There was no evidence that his patients had complained about their treatment. (AP) *Guardian* 3 Mar 1984.

☐ Blind Edward Bennett, 32, of Nuneaton, was had up in Warwick Crown Court for acting as a lookout for his burglar friend Peter Hiatt. As soon as Mr Bennett heard a car, he called his dog, which was the warning signal, and then fled. *D.Telegraph* 6 July 1985.

☐ Percy Moorby, 52, of Barrow-in-Furness, a former sheet-metal worker who had been blind for 10 years, achieved his ambition to judge a beauty competition, even picking the eventual winner, Debbie Clarke, before the last round of the Miss Lakeland contest at Windemere. He had a private meeting with each of the 12 finalists, and was allowed to caress their hair and touch their faces and shoulders. *D.Telegraph* 8 July 1985.

☐ Police who stopped a car after a 60mph chase found a blind man in the driver's seat and a drunk sitting next to him. The drunk was afraid of being given a breath test, so he gave the wheel to his blind friend after drinking in a bar in Landsberg, Bavaria. "My friend operated the foot controls while I steered from the passenger seat" he said. *D.Mirror* 19 April 1985.

LONG SHOTS

John Brownhill, 43, was celebrating his first hole-in-one in the clubhouse of Shortlands Gold Club when his wife Ena, 40, dashed in saying that she had just done the same – at the same hole. He used a seven iron, she a seven wood. *The Guinness Book of Records* was investigating whether the double was unique. Even if another couple have already bagged their first hole-in-one at the same hole on the same day, it's unlikely that they share the same birthday, as the Brownhills do. And they are both insurance brokers. *D.Mail*, 27 Mar 1985.

● Joe McCaffrey scored his first hole-in-one after 25 year's golf at the 12th hole at the Vale of Leven Golf Club in Dunbartonshire. Later the same day, his son Gordon, 29, holed-in-one at the same hole. *The Golfer's Handbook* records that the last time a father and son holed-in-one in the same competition was in 1909 at West Bowling Club, Bradford, *S.Express,* 5 April 1984.

● Les Smith, 68, was dealt all thirteen spades in a game of full-deck brag at the Moor Park Veterans' Club in Bradford. Two days later he came up with the same hand. Experts reckon the chances are hundreds of billions to one against it happening once, let alone twice. *D.Mirror*, 19 Nov 1984.

● Among the Christmas cards sent out by Irene Winstone, 80, of Weston-super-Mare in Somerset, was one to her old friends Major Jay Plain and his wife Margaret at 1 Severn Road, Weston. It arrived eventually, having travelled the few hundred yards from Mrs Winstone's house – via Canada. In Canada, it had found its way to the doormat of one Kathleen Bagley of 1476 Sixth Lane, Oakville, Ontario, who just happened to have been brought up in Weston, and had a sister who used to live on Severn Road. *D.Mail*, 15 Jan 1985.

● Myra Murray of Huntingdon phoned a friend who lives on a farm in North Yorkshire. The friend answered the phone, but what she said made no apparent sense: "I'm sorry, but Hilary is out for the evening." It emerged that her friend was not at home, but out baby-sitting at a farm two miles away. Miss Murray had misdialled the number, and had no idea who Hilary was, or where the farm was situated. Letter in *S.Express,* 3 Feb 1985.

● Teacher Anthony Cleaver, 36, plunged 30 feet during a climbing trip at Wintour's Leap, near Coleford, Gloucestershire, and landed next to ambulancemen on a mock rescue. He was given first aid for head and leg injuries. *Sun*, 7 Feb 1985.

Krause and Blue Moon on 31 July 1984 [AP Photo]

MULE NEWS

We have more details on Krause, the Nebraska wonder mule [FT43,p16]. She gave birth to a foal called Blue Moon on 6 July 1984. The father was a donkey called Chester. Mules, bred from male donkeys and female horses, are normally sterile. Blood tests showed that both Krause and Blue Moon were bona fide mules with 63 chromosomes. Horses have 64, donkeys 62.

While most sources quote expert opinion that this is the first documented case of mule fertility, the Burlington (VT) *Free Press* (24 Sept 1984) claimed there have been about six earlier documented cases of mules foaling, but these were bred by stallions. In March 1985, Krause was reported to be pregnant again. The Silvesters, who own the mule, have been solicited by a congressman to support a motion to make 28th October Mule Appreciation Day. Lincoln (NB) *Journal* 1+2 Aug, 27 Dec 1984, 3 Mar 1985; Belleville (IL) *News-Democrat* 4 Mar 1985.

BATTLE FOR A PATENT

Joseph Westley Newman may be the new Tesla who will free humanity from electric bills and petrol pumps by harnessing the unsuspected power of the common magnet.

Newman, 48, of Lucedale, Mississippi, has spent 20 years developing the Newman energy generator. He has written a 281-page book explaining (nearly) all about it. His claim is that it produces more energy than it consumes. His first application to the patent office in March 1979 wasn't even read after a skimming reviewer concluded that "it smacked of perpetual motion" and thus contradicted the second law of thermodynamics.

Newman is already an accomplished inventor, with plastic-coated barbells, an orange-picking machine and several other creations to his credit, all of which are patented. More importantly, he has affidavits from 30 engineers and physicists attesting that his generator works as claimed. He has built several prototypes, the largest of which is a squat 9,000-pound cylinder. Inside is a 100-pound rotating magnet surrounded by 50 miles of coiled copper wire. A row of ordinary light bulbs fastened into lamp sockets is perched on the top and a fan is lashed to its side. A handful of Ray-O-Vac dry-cell batteries powers the machine, but it's the speed-of-light gyroscopic spin of subatomic particles within the magnet and coil, Newman says, that produces the energy leaping out the other end. The energy produced is up to 10 times what the batteries pump in, with no waste products or pollution. He insists that it's not a perpetual motion machine. The material of the magnet and coil is slowly turning to energy. When commercial, the generators would be the size of a window air conditioner that might run everything in a house for 50 years.

Dr Roger Hastings, an expert in magnetic sensors for Sperry-Univac Corporation in St Paul, MN, tested the machine in Lucedale in 1981, and about 120 times since, and concludes that "there's a probability that his theory is correct". A group of investors put up over half a million dollars for research, and at least one electronics manufacturer, Commercial Technology Inc. of Dallas, is making its own Newman generators for possible future marketing. The company's president, Mort Zimmerman, an electrical engineer who holds four patents in the field, says that there are some problems in converting the machine's unusual pulsating output into usable electricity, but they may not be insurmountable.

Twice Newman has taken a prototype to experts – at the national Bureau of Standards near Washington and at Auburn University in Alabama – but he says there was no-one in either place competent to run tests. Enraged by the continued refusal to grant him a patent, he filed a federal suit in 1983 to have his case reviewed. The suit has not gone well. Pleading ignorance of the science involved, Judge Thomas P. Jackson appointed patent attorney William Schuyler as "special master" to advise him on the case. Schuyler had headed the patent office from 1969 to 1971 and could hardly be expected to favour an alchemist like Newman. After reviewing the case, however, he concluded that, since no evidence had been submitted to contradict Newman's "overwhelming evidence (that) the output energy exceeds the external input energy", the inventor should get his patent. Jackson rejected the recommendations, despite a requirement of patent law that Newman's supporters' claim obliges the court to accept a special master's decision if one is named.

The inventor refused Jackson's subsequent order to deliver one of his prototypes to the National Bureau of Standards (again!) by the end of May 1985 for testing, claiming that this would endorse the judge's violation of the law, and anyway, patent law did not require him to do so. He had reason to be wary, since both the bureau and patent office were part of the Department of Commerce. He argues that the patent office is stifling rather than stimulating inventive genius. A few times a week he sings a song he composed to his son, Gyromas, 2, about individual potential. "I intend to get a patent," he said, "and I'll fight till hell freezes over." Conway (AR) *Log Cabin Democrat* 14 Mar; Belleville (IL) *News-Democrat* 15 Mar; Charlotte (NC) *Observer, Detroit News* 23 May; *New York Times* 4 June; Little Rock (AR) *Arkansas Democrat* 5 June; *Guardian* 11 June 1985.

FALLING FISH

★ Fort Worth, Texas – Louis Castorano, 30, was working in his backyard, on the morning of 8th May 1985, when several 2-inch long fish plopped at his feet. "I thought someone was playing a joke on me," he said. "Then I looked up and had to move out of the way because a whole bunch came at once time." He counted: there were 34 of them, identity unknown. Castorano said he noticed no planes, but that the fish fell "right after a dark cloud passed over." Al Moller, a meteorologist with the National Weather Service at Forth Worth, had predictable fun with the whole silly notion of fish falling from the sky, saying "I haven't heard of it happening in the past year." He should read *Fortean Times*! But he did confirm that the area had thunderstorm activity that morning. Ft Worth (TX) *Star-Telegram* & UPI 9 May 1985.

★ Calne, Wiltshire – Maintenance man Roy Clarke was called in to clear blocked guttering high on the town hall roof. To his surprise he found a large trout wedged in the downpipe. Peter Brown, the town clerk, supposed it had been dropped there by a bird. We think it could have fallen with the recent torrential rain! Bristol/Somerset *Eve.Post* 5 Aug; *D.Mirror* 7 Aug 1985.

STRANGE FALLS

★ As Mrs Marthe Kistner, 65, lay in her bed listening to the Fourth of July celebrations in Mad River Township, near Dayton, Ohio, she heard a loud boom which did not seem to be part of the fireworks. "It scared me to death," she recalls. "I jumped out of bed and felt blood coming out of my ear." She stuck her finger in her ear and prised out a bullet. Police think someone may have fired a gun into the air and the bullet fell through the open skylight of her trailer home to land in her ear. [AP] Cincinnati (OH) *Enquirer* 7 July 1985.

★ Two housewives sunbathing on a beach 100 miles south of Perth, Western Australia, had a lucky escape when a meteorite hit the sand only a few yards away from them on 2nd October 1984. The husband of one of them, who retrieved the hot rock, said it looked like a black potato. It is said to be of great value to science because it was recovered so soon after impact. *D.Telegraph* 3 Oct 1984. Another source gives the ladies' names as Janice Stokes and Mrs System. Mrs Stokes said: "Mrs System was about to pick up the crumpet-sized blob when a man rushed up shouting, 'Don't touch it! I am a scientist and this will lead to new knowledge about the formation of the universe.' Then he ran off and we have seen nothing of him since!" We recall something similar happened once on a beach by the Caspian Sea, with an excited scientist and a fallen blob. Could the story be a new folklore theme making the rounds?

★ On 17th April 1985, an engine fell off a jetliner flying over the New Mexico desert. The engine was recovered and showed "evidence of foreign object damage". Investigators are on record speculating that a block of ice must have hit the engine and knocked it off. If this is so, the ice, or whatever the 'foreign object' may have been, must have fallen from *above* the plane. [AP] Lincoln (NB) *Journal* 3 May 1985. See back to FT42p23 for a similar incident in which something smashed into the tailplane of a Chinese military jet. The Chinese still haven't answered our enquiry about it.

Look out ! Here comes another one !

MEXICO QUAKE MYSTERIES

Just after 7.18am on Thursday 19 September 1985, the biggest of several quakes shook Mexico City. When we get our quake clippings sorted out we'll be able to tell you more precisely how many people, especially babies, were rescued from the ruins 10 days or more later. As we recall there was one story, well-reported by the media, about a young boy who survived well into the second week and who communicated with the rescuers, painstakingly making their way towards him, by tapping out replies to their questions. Eventually the rescuers broke through to the chamber he was believed to be in, only to find it empty. Was it a cruel hoax as some suggested? Were the boy's sounds deflected by debris, giving a false location? Did he teleport out? We shall never know.

However, we can add, thanks to the vigilance of Joseph Trainor, that just two weeks before – on Monday 2nd Sept – another natural disaster struck Mexico City, as the worst hailstorm in 50 years there, left some streets more than a foot deep in ice. At least one person was killed, and 185 injured. There was a power blackout, and traffic jams which took until midnight to clear. The hour-long pelting was so severe that 25 old buildings collapsed under the weight of ice, and an estimated 4000 roofs were damaged. They were repaired just in time for the quake to complete the destruction more thoroughly. [AP] Boston (MA) *Herald* 4 Sept 1985.

ICE FALLS

★ **Easton, Maryland** – further to the fall on 8 Sept 1984 recorded last issue [FT43 p20]. The "part-time" Fortean investigator mentioned is one John Lutz, who paid for the ice to be analysed at the University of Maryland and the University of Pennsylvania, where the smelly blue ice was revealed to be "a sanitizing agent combined with urine." Lutz who had been backing the ice theory, commented: "It looks like it was from a passing plane after all." Washington (DC) *Post* 2 Oct 1984.

★ **Perryman, Maryland** – the same report (above) says that Lutz (see above) was also investigating the fall of a two-foot diameter chunk of ice that fell here on 23 Sept 1984. A brief check with last issue's listing (FT43 p20f] reveals another fall on that same date at Leominster, Massachusetts. Is it part of the same event? Was someone pelting the East Coast?

★ **Stock, Essex** – Perhaps this is a non-ice fall story, but we record it here anyway. On the morning of Saturday 29th Sept 1984, William Hull, manager of a chicken farm on Broomwood Road, was walking his pony in his garden when he found a strange hole, which, he has since been told, must have been made by a falling chunk of ice. As soon as he saw the hole he remembered that his son had told him that during the night he (the son) had heard "a whistling noise and then a thump". From the report there does not seem to have been any obvious sign of fallen ice when he found the hole, but linking it with the noise and fearing there might be some radioactive metal down the hole, Mr Hull called the police, who found nothing suspicious. If it had been ice, could it have melted in the few hours between the noise and the discovery? But was it ice at all? The hole is said to be "not wide" but four feet deep! Must have been a quick-melting icicle. *Essex Chronicle* 5 Oct 1984.

★ **Somewhere in northern Australia** – the wacky *Weekly World News* (13 Nov 1984) has come up with a story which true or not [surely they can't invent *all* they print?] is a favourite in our ice-fall department. According to the *WWN* a "wild-eyed witch doctor" called Willi Bumguli did a rain-dance for three days to relieve the drought on his people's land. We are not told where – the *WWN* thinks accuracy and detail interferes with their story-telling. Suddenly a 13lb chunk of ice fell from the sky, glancing off the back of Willi's head, knocking him out. *WWN* says this was witnessed by a German anthropologist, Eva Schindler. Later, when Willi came-to, he was less concerned about his lucky escape than he was about this obvious admonition from the gods. "I forgot the ways of the dance," he said, vowing to try again.

★ Chippenham, Wiltshire – An ice bomb smashed through a roof. The ice was "pink". No other details. *D.Mirror* 19 March 1985.

★ Cadnam, Hampshire – Mrs Joyce Penny escaped injury, on 4th July 1985, when a block of ice crashed through her kitchen ceiling. *D.Express, D.Mail, Shropshire Star* 5 July 1985.

More ice-falls, including USA ones, next issue.

A MODERN NOAH

John Roeleveld, a Dutchman of 72 living in the village of Eerbeeck, 55 miles east of Amsterdam, said that God had instructed him to collect and mount two of every species in preparation for the end of the world, which was imminent. God had promised more than forty years ago that his collection would rise up and live again after Judgement Day, and that the scrap iron fragments and old furniture that littered his garden would also be made new.

In April 1982 police raided Roeleveld's house in response to complaints, and were astounded to find a rabbit warren of concrete bomb shelters which he had built in the backyard of his shabby home. In the shelters were an estimated 250,000 stuffed animals and birds, including crocodiles, ostriches, kangaroos, panthers, apes, a bear, an elephant skull and a camel. Some had been stuffed in the last century, but most were the work of Roeleveld himself. A great many belonged to protected species, and it was not clear how they had come into his possession. The collection also included thousands of eggshells, bones and insects preserved in formaldehyde.

Roeleveld wasn't upset when 40 police and firemen began to remove his collection. "They will return to me of their own accord," he said. "Let them take the animals. For each one they take I will get a hundred back."

The Lincoln, Nebraska *Journal* (17 Apr. 1982) informs us that the police were investigating a number of possible charges including possession of unlicensed firearms, danger to the public health, unlicensed taxidermy and hunting of protected species. And an Eerbeek municipal officer said the town council would consider building a special museum to house the collection if sufficient examples could be rescued from the ravages of mould and rot.

THE UNICORN SHOW

Ringling Bros. Barnum & Bailey Circus and the American Society for the Prevention of Cruelty to Animals butted heads over a goat unicorn on display, and three others, which the ASPC claimed were goats with surgically implanted bulls' horns. Allen Bloom, vice-president of the circus, claimed they arrived exactly as they look now, except that the horns have grown a bit. The Agriculture Department was called in to adjudicate, and decided that the goats had undergone a simple graft in which one of their own natural horns had been made to grow in an unnatural position. [AP] Houston *Chronicle* 30 Mar; Glens Falls (NY) *Post-Star* 6 April; *D.Telegraph* 6, 8, 11 April; Beaumont (TX) *Enterprize* 9 April; Lincoln (NB) *Journal* 10 April; Cincinnati *Enquirer* 11 April 1985.

● An earlier goat-unicorn, called Lancelot by his owners Morning Glory and her husband Otter G'zelle (that's what it says here), was on display at Marine World near San Fransisco in 1982. He was a year-old Angora goat and the horn, ten inches long, was said by "animal science professors" to be "just a rare abnormality". (This horn with its crinkles, strikes me as more convincing – the clipping is unreferenced.)

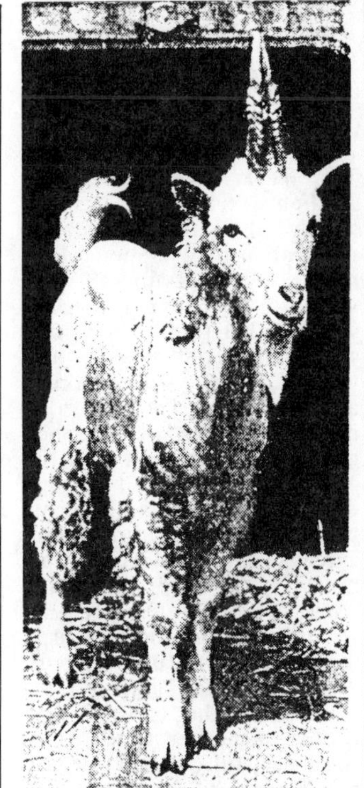

Lancelot, the goat-unicorn, 1982.

One of the goat-unicorns of Barnum & Bailey's Circus. [AP Photo]

HUMDINGER

News of an underwater hum which has maddened the 1,500-strong houseboat colony of Sausalito, located at one end of the Golden Gate bridge on San Francisco Bay. A new theory has it that the "loud and audible mechanical raspy hum" heard nightly every summer for 11 years is – wait for it – the mating call of the Singing Toadfish.

Local harbourmaster Ted Rose said, "It's like an electric razor noise, only 10 or 15 times louder. The noise is coming through the water and people are picking it up in the concrete houseboat hulls."

Describing the sound for reporters, Rose said: "It's like this – mzmzmzmzmzmzmz.

"Sometimes it gets so loud you have to talk above it. It can drown out conversations and wake people from a dead sleep."

Acoustical engineers said the hum was "a vibration in the water. . . It sounds like a mechanical spectrum." Some blame a nearby US Navy torpedo range, others "the sunken wreckage of an old turntable from a railway trestle". Similar underwater noises have been reported from other bays north and west of Sausalito, frequented by USN submarines.

The hum begins at around 8–9pm and goes on until 6am during the Summer months. It has a frequency of between 50 and 130 herz and has been measured at 40 decibels.

John McCosker, an aquarium director, proposed the Singing Toadfish theory in August. The male fish burrows into mud during the mating season and attracts females by emitting a droning from muscles surrounding the swim bladder.

Quite a few Singing Toadfish have been caught in the area. "It's the best theory so far," said the acoustical engineers.

San Francisco *Chronicle* 29 July; UPI/AP St Louis *Post-Dispatch* 30 July + 9 August; San Diego (CA) *Union* 30 July; Christian Science Monitor News Service/St Louis *Globe-Democrat* 20 August; *USA Today* (Arlington, VA) 8 August 1985.

BABY TALK

The *Weekly World News* of 21 Feb 1984 carried a story which it claimed "makes medical history". Shen Xian-mei, a 27yr-old doctor who works in a Shanghai factory, was startled to find that the seven-month-old baby she was carrying was making audible crying noises from her womb. She went to her gynacologist, Dr Jin Xue-ying, of the Peoples Central Hospital in the city, who "laughed at first" but agreed to try to record the noises. "The sounds were coming more frequently and we didn't have long to wait," said Shen. Dr Jin declared: "I was amazed. I have a tape filled with the cries of the foetus. At other times, it is the lusty, fully-formed cry of a living infant."

So far so good. The *WWN* then quotes Dr Jin: "There is no record of anything like it in the annals of medicine. It has always been believed that an infant made no sound whatever until the moments after birth... But now we know that unborn babies are capable of making sounds. The Chinese government is undertaking an investigation to learn what other sounds they can make." In Western medicine at least, it is common practice to listen to the foetal heartbeat using a microphone in contact with the mother's belly, but we don't know to what extent the electronics used to mask the mother's own heartbeat would also eliminate any other sounds from the unborn baby. More anciently, midwives have used a form of funnel, like an ear-trumpet, to listen to the baby's heartbeat, and that would certainly pick up any additional noises in the area, but mentions of cries heard by these methods is not findable by us. Consequently we can agree to the rarity of the phenomenon. The phenomenon might well be rare in China, but Dr Jin is wrong when it comes to Western annals. Our indispensible reference, Gould & Pyle, says that many of the pioneers of medicine have referred to the phenomenon of 'Antepartum crying of the child'. But G&P are quite skeptical, calling them "fabulous stories", offering instead the suggestion that the child was making noises during the actual delivery, which has been more often and better observed by doctors themselves.

But how does that help us with Dr Shen's baby, who was making sounds some *two months* before his birth (a normal boy of 7lbs 4ozs)? We suspect this is another subject, like spontaneous combustion, in which official ignorance is at odds with little-known observations. Among the many valuable curiosities sent to us by Bob Skinner, culled from Victorian natural histories, are two pages from an early and very Fortean book, called *The Wonders of the Little World, or a General History of Man* [I forgot to note author and date – blushing RJMR]. Chapter 1 of book 4 is entitled 'Of such infants as have been heard to cry while they were in the wombs of their mothers.' Admittedly the eight cases fall between the 16th and 17th centuries, but some of them were respectfully witnessed. We summarize them: 1) Holland, crying heard "almost continuously" for 15 days before delivery, many witnesses; 2) Argentina, cries heard "some days" before birth, a few witnesses; 3) Rotenburg, cry heard 42 days before birth and two more the day after, mother died in labour but daughter lived; 4) Witenburg, pregnancy lasted "more than 11 months", cries heard prior to labour, baby born healthy; 5) Belgium, pregnancy lasted "three years", many heard cries; 6) Holland, cries heard "a few days" before labour; 7) Holmiana, in 8th month, many heard cries on three occasions, healthy daughter; 8) Cheshire, in 7th month, at dinner with guests "extra-ordinary stirring in her belly" at same time as cry heard, guests observe closely as it happens twice more.

Such antenatal cries would certainly impress people of earlier times, who might think it ominous. But what are we to make of another *WWN* item, for 10 April 1984, which it calls a "reincarnation nightmare"? The report cites a Dr Eloise Pilot, of an unnamed and therefore unfindable hospital in the north of France. Dr Pilot "told the *News*" that seconds after the birth of an infant girl, which she attended, the baby issued a blood-curdling scream, and while it was writhing the voice of a woman in torment came from it: "Satan has abandoned me, yet unto the fires of Lucifer thou condemn my soul. I am not a witch...no longer am I the mistress of Incubus. Still now do the flames scorch mine naked feet. In Salem there be no mercy." There was more in the same vein. With another scream the baby subsided into the normal wailing of a newborn baby. As cited, Dr Pilot seems convinced that, for a moment, a girl who was burned at the stake during the infamous witch persecutions at Salem, Massachusetts, somehow transmitted her agony across time, at the same time reincarnating herself. Dr Pilot refuses to disclose the identity of the infant. That's all that can be said about this uncheckable story.

SHELDRAKEANA

Rumours concerning the commando-style antics of the sheep of the Welsh valleys have been around for years. The animals were said to negotiate cattle grids by tiptoeing across or in some cases rolling over the obstacle. Now a film has been taken to prove it. 82yr-old Skip Morgan, of Shennybridge in Gwent, took the film in the Brecons in June 1983. "I was amazed," he said. "I saw the sheep on the one side and thought they shouldn't be there, and then the ram started coming back. He picked his way along and across the bars as though he were walking a tightrope." The 16mm film (see photos) was shot from Mr Morgan's car.

A local councillor said the design of the grids would have to be changed. "Sheep are not as daft as people think," he said. A Ministry of Agriculture spokesman commented: "Sheep from the Welsh hillsides are particularly nimble and athletic, but the rolling-over-the-grids business is more difficult to understand. I would like to see it happening." *Western Mail* 17+23 June 1983.

A writer in the *Guardian*, for 28 Feb 1985, points out that the sheep in no other region of the British Isles seem to have yet picked up the Welsh sheep's trick of rolling across grids. Outside Britain only the lowland sheep of Sweden's Malmoehus region have manifested the technique. In allusion to Dr Rupert Sheldrake's controversial ideas on the development of non-corporeal systems governing form and behaviour, this writer says: "Among the questions which immediately arise are how long it will take the Swaledales of Yorkshire to learn, and whether, when they do, they will be demonstrating the theory of formative causation." To eliminate the remote possibility of learning by observation, the writer suggests the sheep of the Falklands be monitored as a control group. "If Sheldrake is right it is only a matter of time before the Falklands sheep assert themselves."

■ Another glimpse of new behaviour patterns came to light when the Asda superstore in Castleton, in Greater Manchester, was prosecuted after bird droppings were found in its ham. According to the *Daily Telegraph* 23 July 1985 the manager explained that the local sparrows and starlings were cleverly beating all attempts to keep them out of the large building. It was, he said, a common problem these days when the large covered open-plan spaces offered warmth, food, water, perches and no predators. "No wonder they want to stay," he added. When strong blasts of air at the doors failed to keep them out, the supermarket installed heavy ribbon curtains. This worked for a while, but the crafty birds now ride in on the backs of forklift trucks. The store lost its case and was fined on two counts.

■ In the meantime Rupert Sheldrake has asked if *Fortean Times* readers know of any occurrences of simultaneous action among plants or animals similar to what happened to the musk (*Mimulus moschatus*), a flowering plant discovered in British Columbia in 1824. It was widely cultivated as a house-plant for its lingering musk-like scent, used to relieve the musty damp of houses before the invention of the damp course. Suddenly, in 1913, the flowers of musk plants all over the world completely lost their perfume, as far as anyone can tell, at the same time. Roy Genders, author of *The Cottage Garden* (Pelham, London, 1969), thinks this might have happened because the plant reverted to its original scentless and hairless form, but this does not explain how it should have happened "in all gardens at the same time."

If you know of any other examples of this kind of simultaneous change, please write in.

UNLUCKY!

◆ Ralph Claridge, 29, jumped to his death from his tenth-floor flat in Mitcham, Surrey, when he found his wife, Janice, had taken an overdose. Within minutes, she regained consciousness, but unlike Shakespeare's Juliet, she then refrained from killing herself. *D.Telegraph* 30 Jan 1985.

◆ A Los Angeles business-man, identified only as Arnold G., proposed marriage to his girlfriend Carol and asked her parents for their consent. After the engagement had been announced, Carol's father took Arnold aside and confided that his daughter was born by artificial insemination because he was unlikely to father a child. He named the sperm bank, to which Arnold had donated as a student. Arnold obtained a court injunction to inspect the records and found that he was the father of his bride-to-be, and of 806 other children. The wedding was called off. *S.Express*, 21 Oct 1984.

◆ James McIntire, 59, who was running half the distance of a 10 kilometer run to raise funds to combat heart disease, collapsed and died of a heart attack, less than two blocks from the finishing line, in Glendale, California. A few days later, Edward Hill, 57, declared fit after three weeks in a Houston hospital with a minor heart complaint dropped dead as he was about to leave. He has just been given the bill – 38,000 dollars. (UPI) St Louis *Post-Dispatch*, 11 Nov; *S.Express*, 25 Nov 1984.

◆ Staff at the Center for Devices and Radiological Health, part of the Food and Drug Administration in Washington, held a Christmas party on Friday, 14 December 1984. More than half the party-goers had nausea and other symptoms of food poisoning by the following Monday. They referred the matter to the appropriate authorities – their colleagues. St Louis *Post-Dispatch*, 25 Dec 1984.

◆ The imitation duck calls made by Dimitris Thomasinas, 19, to lure birds his way when he went shooting in Salonika were so lifelike that two of his colleagues fired at the bushes where he was hiding and shot him dead. *D. Telegraph*, 28 Jan 1985.

◆ Woodrow Kreekmore had a narrow escape when his car skidded off the icy road and slammed into a telegraph pole outside Chickasha, Oklahoma. He climbed out and strolled into the road to hitch a ride. He had walked only a couple of feet when the pole keeled over behind him and struck him dead. *S.Express*, 3 Feb 1985.

◆ Schoolteacher Timothy Bode, 39, stopped his car and went to protest to a driver that she might have killed him by pulling out in front of him. He was then struck and killed by a car driven by Lucy Dolling, 79, *D.Telegraph*, 15 Feb 1985.

◆ A cocked pistol stuck in the belt of Gonzalo Martin, mayor of Candaba in the Philippines, shot him dead when he slammed his car door on it. His driver ran out of petrol while trying to get him to hospital. *D.Telegraph*, 21 Feb 1985.

◆ At least 48 people drowned when a boat capsized while carrying sight-seers to look at a shipwreck near the port of Cuddalore in Tamil Nadu state, southern India. About 50 others were rescued by fishermen. *Guardian*, 8 Mar 1985.

◆ Harry Dale, 62, removed the roofrack from his car after dreaming that thieves tried to pinch it. Someone stole his car instead at Hunstanton, Norfolk. *D.Mirror*, 5 Feb 1985.

◆ More than 50 villagers in southern Taiwan who walked over burning charcoal in a ceremony intended to bring good luck and wealth were hospitalised for burns. St Louis *Post-Dispatch*, 9 Mar 1985.

◆ And now, a classic story from 1839. A boy from Gideon Hunt, near Allentown PA, fell into his father's mill pond while sliding on the ice. One of his brothers fell in trying to rescue him. A third and fourth brother, and then the father, also fell through the ice. The father and one boy managed to climb out, but the others were drowned. At the funeral of the boys, the carriage of their uncle was dashed to pieces, the horses becoming restive, and the uncle's collar bone was broken or dislocated. Those who had been in the carriage got into another, which was also overturned and broken; and the horses ran against the vehicle of another uncle, upset it, and threw out those who were inside. When the father returned from the funeral, he found his house on fire. *Trenton State Gazette*, reprinted in the *St Catherine's Journal*, 14 Mar 1839.

BEWARE THE RED MONSTER

An inquest in Exeter, Devon, heard how a 6yr-old boy had a premonition of the blaze which killed his two younger brothers. Anthony Raynor ran in terror to his parents' room during the night, telling them: "A red monster is coming to burn the house down – he's got purple eyes!" Six hours later, as he slept in his parents' bed, a fire, the origin of which was not explained, broke out in the bedroom he shared with Jason, 4, and Richard, 2. They were rescued by their father, Andy, but died later from their burns. *Sun* 11 Oct 1985.

CROSS IN THE SKY

Two postmen saw a huge cross in the sky over Bideford, Devon, on the morning of 7th December 1984. Bill Taylor was cycling to work towards the town from Horwood, at 6.00am, when, looking up, he saw: "Two huge beams of light, like searchlight beams, [which] formed a perfect cross. The moon itself was the centre." After about ten minutes, the arms, which seemed to him to be thousands of feet long, faded, leaving only the moon in the sky. He said he did not think it had any religious connotation, but agreed that it was "awe inspiring". When he got to work at Bideford PO, he found that a colleague, Paul Downing, had also seen it.

Plymouth meteorologists, asked to explain the phenomenon, said it was an optical illusion caused by moonlight refracting through thin cirrus cloud containing ice crystals. From our own work we know of several different kinds of phenomena which may give rise to similar appearances, but a quick flick through the works of Flammarion and Corliss show no clear cross-shape associated with the moon or sun. There are pillars of light, and partial crosses centred on sun, moon and on their mock-counterparts – but in this case we seem to have a rare observation of a complete cross. *Bideford Gazette* 14 & 21 Dec 1984.

The dip into our files also revealed a remarkably similar case from 1977, when, just before 7 am on Christmas morning, Mrs Alice Camburn, looked out of the living room window of her Whitstable, Kent, home. Against a grey sky she saw "a large black cloud with a distinct crucifixion-like cross in...the centre." The cross was white – "It looked just as if it were illuminated." – and lasted 20 minutes. *Whitstable Times* 30 Dec 1977.

Crucifix seen over Whitstable, Kent, on Christmas Day, 1977. Sketch by Valerie Martin from the painting by a witness, Mrs Camburn.

Our industrious correspondent, Valerie Martin, who lived near Mrs Camburn and who "has a knack of just missing interesting things", investigated. She found Mrs Camburn was doing a painting of what she had seen, and we reproduce here Valerie's own sketch of the painting. Could this too have been the product of moonlight shining through ice-crystals in the black cloud? Of less concern to the meteorologists is the coincidence of it. Like Bill Taylor later, Mrs Camburn's feelings on viewing this timely apparition were ambiguous: "I'm not really religious. It was just because it was Christmas morning that it seemed so significant." Valerie found, in asking around, that more than one person thought the aerial cross was a portent of the "recent" extraordinary high tide. One of Mrs Camburn's relatives vaguely remembers a similar cross in the sky seen over Folkestone "around Easter a few years ago."

HINTS OF LIMBO

- Seven years after it went missing, one of Bernard Lince's racing pigeons came back to his house in Costessey, Norfolk. *D.Mail, D.Mirror* 22 April 1985.
- In 1981, a battered imitation silver cigarette case arrived by post at Eric Bettis's old address in Long Lane, Hillingdon, Middlesex. Eric had emigrated to New Zealand 12 years before, and had never smoked in all his 58 years. The case had been posted 6 miles away in Ealing, 31 years earlier in April 1950. There was no message with it. *S.Express* 4 Oct 1981.

A WHALE ON THE ROCKS

In Alluitsup, a tiny settlement on the southern Greenland coast, astonished biologists and other scientists are studying the remains of a 59ft (50ft) whale found frozen inside an iceberg, 13ft (12ft) above sea level. Speculation is divided about the origin of this curiosity.

The first supposition was that this was a "prehistoric" specimen which had been preserved for thousands of years in the ice cap which makes up the greater part of Greenland, and which drifted off as its iceberg tomb broke away. The chief difficulties here are the mystery of how it became entrapped in the first place, and the widespread, but unconfirmed, belief that the whale is, or resembles, a modern male sperm whale. There is also the little matter of the cylindrical hole in its neck, about 15 inches across and three feet deep, suggesting it was the victim of harpooning. The *Sunday Express* (19 May 1985 – the source of the bracketted measurements above) suggests that the iceberg was once part of a glacier, but that makes even more problematical how the whale might have entered the glacier inland and at a higher altitude.

So the scientists have been forced to suppose that the whale, however it came to be dying or disoriented, found itself in shallow waters over a submerged portion of the iceberg, and was lifted up when the berg's bulk shifted. How the whale was sealed into a block of ice is not explained. Some wag suggested the whale must have leaped out of the water and landed in a crevice in the berg. What, 13 feet up?

The iceberg drifted towards the settlement in the last week of February. Photographer John Rasmussen, one of the first on the scene, says: "It stank like an overturned latrine. We could smell it long before we could see it. We located it just by keeping downwind." Tugs pulled it into the settlement, which has a small scientific community. But before the scientists could get to the berg it had been attacked by the locals seeking to get at the whale's teeth. Long ago Greenlanders had a thriving art of carved whale teeth, also used by sailors for scrimshaw work, but since the protection of the sperm whale, such teeth were rarely available. Little wonder, then, the locals' eagerness to get at this treasure trove despite the stench. Rasmussen said that villagers "had their heads and elbows buried deep in the whale's gaping jaw, hacking away with saws, hammers and crowbars." The *Express* adds a curious footnote: that in the night, eskimos paddled out to the berg, carved a tunnel through the ice and "stole the whale's single 15ft long horn" to grind it up for an aphrodisiac. Are they talking about the same animal? Narwhals have horns, but the *UPI* report of 15 May 1985, from which we take most of our details, makes no mention of a horn, preferring to liken the creature to a sperm whale.

A nice mystery, this. We await news of a more detailed report.

As a footnote of our own, this would be an appropriate place to mention the discovery, in July this year, of the body of a woman entombed in a glacier near Verbier, in the Swiss Alps. She was identified as Regina Spring, from England, who disappeared on 2 August 1981, aged 34. London *Standard* 30 July 1985.

NAZI NEWS

The daughter of Lord Redesdale, Unity Mitford, who had a crush on Hitler, was conceived at a place called Swastika in Ontario. It was here that the Redesdales owned a goldfield, where they would go panning for their summer holidays. *Standard* 16 Nov 1984.

ASTROLOGY OF PLACE?

ABOUNDING BOUNDERS

This summer past was jumping with mystery marsupial sightings. We tabulate. . .

- First week in January – Westward Ho!, Devon – William Phillips discovered a great number of prints in his garden in Beech Road. He was convinced they were made by a wallaby because "they were long, deep and in pairs, which indicated that they were made by an animal jumping with two feet together." a local animal welfare 'expert', asked by the newspaper to examine the tracks, pronounced them to be made by a large rabbit. *Bideford Gazette* 4 Jan 1985.
- 25 or 26 May – Teignmouth, Devon – a wallaby escaped from an animal santuary at nearby Holcombe. It was tranquillised and returned. *D. Telegraph* 27 May 1985.
- 14 August – Crowmarsh, Oxfordshire – student Greg Caswell, driving home late from a party saw a wallaby (a kangaroo in some reports) bounding along the Benson to Crowmarsh road on the pavement outside the South Oxfordshire district council offices. He got out and chased it but it was too quick for him. A Wallingford policeman also chased and lost it. Earlier that evening a cyclist was knocked off his bike by what might be the same animal which then bounced off

across the fields. No clues as to the origin of this mystery marsupial. See also 27 Aug (below). We have to mention that the next day, in another part of Oxfordshire, a hippo was caught sniffing roses in a garden at Little Tew, was caught and returned by Banbury police to Chipperfield Circus which was quartered at Heythrop, two miles away. Emma, the 2yr-old hippo, had been left in a field at dawn, but escaped by a river. There is no obvious connection with the wallaby; the circus hadn't lost one, although a spokesman said darkly: "There've been one or two missing recently." "Two or three" wallabies are known to have escaped from the McAlpine estate at Fawley, near Henley, about eight miles down the road from Crowmarsh, before Christmas 1984, but they were all believed to have been killed in road accidents before. Oxford *Mail* 15+19 Aug; *D.Mail, D.Express, Sun* 16 Aug; Oxford *Times* 30 Aug 1985.

• 21 August – Chipping Camden, Gloucestershire – Mrs Julia Brooks, of Hoo Lane, putting out scraps for birds in her garden was shocked to see them eaten by "a wallaby". *D.Mirror* 22 Aug 1985. If this is the same animal as the Crowmarsh wallaby, it has travelled some 33 miles to the north-west, across Oxford itself, without being seen, and will have to travel back to Crowmarsh again (see next item). No wallabies missing locally, but *D.Telegraph* 23 Aug 1985 says one reported missing (no date) at Whipsnade, about 80 miles away.

• 24 or 25 August – Crowmarsh, Oxfordshire – a wallaby found drowned in a private pool near Wallingford; thought to be same one seen on 14th August (above). Oxford *Mail, D.Telegraph, Sun* 28 Aug 1985.

A policeman from Chipping Norton Oxon, just misses a wallaby near the railway line at Finstock Halt. [Photo © Clive Postlethwaite, Mail on Sunday *6 Oct 1985.]*

• 25 August – Charlbury, Oxfordshire – Workers on the Cornbury Park estate saw a kangaroo in nearby fields. One man thought it was a deer at first and got within 50 yards, then it reared up and jumped towards him. The witnesses are insistent that they saw a kangaroo and not a wallaby. They describe it as "between five and six foot tall and grey-coloured". Charlbury is about 15 miles south-east of Chipping Campden, between that town and Oxford. If the Crowmarsh animal had travelled to Chipping Camden it would have passed through or close to Charlbury – but this sighting comes after the drowning at Crowmarsh. One possibility is that the Chipping Campden and Charlbury animals are the same, but then it was a wallaby and not a kangaroo that Mrs Brooks is supposed to have seen. Back at Charlbury, there was another sighting by more estate workers coming home from a pub. Oxford *Mail* 27 Aug; Oxford *Times* 30 Aug 1985.

The Oxford *Mail* for 17 Sept 1985, says that a police constable, Jon Badrick, of Chipping Norton police, had been assigned to track down the creature. He reveals that the animal is most likely a wallaby that once belonged to Mr Dennis Washington, who keeps several wallabies at Middle Barton. It is not said whether any of Mr Washington's animals had escaped, and if so, when. There have also been several more sightings, at least two by train drivers, says PC Badrick, along railway cuttings. He thinks the wallaby is running along the railway unable to escape the high embankments. We don't know any more. If you want a progress report ring PC Badrick at Chipping Norton police station.

• mid-Sept – Hungary-Czechoslovakia border – at least one kangaroo, perhaps several, are frightening unsuspecting villagers in northern Hungary. An explanationist reporter on the Hungarian Sunday paper, *Vasarnapi Hirek,* is cited as suggesting they were boxing kangaroos which "must have" escaped from a circus in Czechoslovakia. [UPI] Plattsburg (NY) *Press-Republican* 23 Sept 1985.

CLOUD OF UNKNOWING

Not since the 1908 Tunguska blast and the south Atlantic atmospheric flash of 1979 has there been an explosive event as stubbornly enigmatic as the mushroom cloud off Japan in 1984. [see FT42,p20.]

☐ The 1979 flash was recorded by American Defence Department Vela satellites, whose sensors pick up many flashes from lightning bolts and meteors, most of which are very brief. The south Atlantic flash was more like the prolonged sequence from a nuclear blast; but there was no evidence of fallout or atmospheric pressure waves, and a White House 'panel of experts' concluded that the most plausible explanation was that a small meteoroid had knocked debris off the satellite which then reflected sunlight back to the sensors.

☐ The 1984 mushroom cloud appeared 200 miles east of Japan, shortly before midnight on 9 April. It was reported independently by four crews of commercial airliners flying above a 14,000 foot cloud deck, who saw the mushroom erupt, expand to a diameter of 200 miles, well up to above 65,000 feet at an estimated 500mph, thin out and disappear. No radioactivity was found on the planes, or in dust samples collected from the area shortly afterwards; no flash or other tell-tale effects of a nuclear blast were seen; and there was no disruption of aircraft electronics.

Dr Daniel A. Walker of the Hawaii Institute of Geophysics operates an array of hydrophones near Wake Island in the western Pacific used to monitor nuclear tests and seismic events. These recorded a swarm of underwater earthquakes commencing in March somewhere west of Wake Island, and peaking on 8 and 9 April. Although several candidates for the site of disturbance emerged from his analysis (*Science* vol. 227, p.607), the 'best buy' was the subterranean volcano Kaitoku Seamount, located at 26-0°N, 140-8°E, 80 miles north of Iwo Jima. But how could this cause a cloud 900 miles northeast at 38.5°N, 146.0°E? Wind charts from the National Climatic Data Center showed that the wind was in the wrong direction. The two events were "purely coincidental".

Another theory was put forward by André C. Chang and James A. Burnetti in *Nature* (vol. 314, p676): that a meteor may have encountered the cloud deck just as it shattered, producing heat which warmed the cloud layer over a large area. Convection would then have produced a cloud plume. Walker maintains that this hypothesis doesn't explain the mushroom shape, nor the energy needed to force a cloud upwards at 500mph. NASA spokesman Arlin Krueger was also skeptical, stating that a meteor would probably burn out at a higher altitude. In May 1985, Walker was assessing such admittedly far-out proposals as an explosion of a tanker laden with liquid hydrogen, which might not produce a very bright flash, and so would not be seen through the cloud cover. However, there is no maritime record of such an explosion.

FT readers will not be surprised that Tom Bearden, a retired army lieutenant colonel who worked on high energy lasers and surface-to-air missiles for the American Defence Department, believes the cloud is evidence for a Russian psychotronic beam weapon based on the physics of Nicola Tesla. The scientific establishment in general agrees with Dr Kosta Tsipis, MIT arms specialist, that "Bearden is off the deep end". However, according to the *New York Times*, the Soviet Union had warned of impending weapons tests before April 1984, but far to the north of the enigmatic mushroom. Boston (MA) *Sunday Globe* 13 Jan; *New Scientist* 25 April + 9 May; Beaumont (TX) *Enterprize* 5 May; Chicago (IL) *Tribune*, Milwaukee (WI) *Journal* 12 May; *New York Times* 21 May; Greensboro (NC) *News & Record* 26 May; London *Times* late June 1985.

SOME INSIDE STORIES

Surgeons from a hospital in Peshawar, Pakistan, claim to have removed six foetuses from the body of a two-month-old boy, Awwal Khan. Crowds who believed he heralded the end of the world were flocking to the hospital. *Sunday Mail* 29 Jan 1984.

▲ Margarita Valenzuela, 86, was X-rayed at a Mexican hospital after complaining of stomach pains. A 28 week mummified foetus was found, which she had carried since she was 27. [AP] *Guardian, Star, Western Morning News* 9 Feb; *Canberra Times* 10 Feb 1985.

▲ Helen Hollenbaugh, 57, weighed about 600 pounds, but lost 200 pounds with the removal of an ovarian cyst in Lewistown Hospital, PA, in December 1984. The cyst contained 20.8 gallons of fluid. We have in the archive a similar 200 pounder from 1970, which was even more extraordinary, since the 30-year-old woman in that case weighed a mere 380 pounds before surgery – so the growth was heavier than her. Lincoln (NB) *Journal* 17 Dec; St Louis *Post-Dispatch* 18 Dec 1984; Lincoln (NB) *Journal*, Omaha *World-Herald* 8 June 1979.

THE STRENGTH OF NEED

Rique Schill was underneath the family Ford when it slipped off a jack, pinning his chest with the rear axle, in the driveway of their Jamestown, North Dakota, home. His son, Jeremy, aged 9, playing nearby heard the screams but didn't panic. The 65lb boy lifted the 4,000lb car. Unfortunately it wasn't high enough for Dad to slide out and the boy had to let the car down again. He had the presence of mind to call his mother, and then remember that another jack was buried under snow near the front steps. His father was rescued and taken to hospital with bruised ribs. UPI/Schenectady (NY) *Gazette* 28 Jan 1984.

● Ola Erixon, 15, weighing only 6 stone 10 pounds, managed to lift his 17 stone father out of the icy waters of Lake Rorvattnet in northeast Sweden. Leif Erixon, 41, a non-swimmer, had been clinging to an inflated seat cushion for three hours after his fishing boat had capsized and his two companions drowned. When his father had failed to return, Ola rowed his own boat out on the lake and found him by torchlight. Doctors said he would not have survived another 15 minutes. *S.Express* 11 Nov 1984.

● A weight-lifting welder, Robert Hauser, 32, of Fairfield, Conn., saw D'Andria Harris, 10, knocked down by a car and dragged 70 feet. She was trapped under a wheel, and Hauser, who weighs 200 pounds, lifted the 2,400 pound car off her while she was dragged out. Detroit *News* 18 Jan; Houston *Chronicle* 19 Jan; NY *Post* 28 Jan 1985.

● Sven-Olaf Ling, 39, from Stockholm, returned from work to find his son Lars, 18, trapped under his Simca car after a jack had collapsed two hours earlier. The chassis rested on his chest, and only his hands prevented the exhaust pipe pressing down on his throat. Despite a recent operation for a slipped disc, Sven lifted the 1,700 pound car while his wife pulled Lars free. *S.Express* 14 April 1985.

● Terry Siddons, lifted a Ford Granada, weighing 2,240 pounds, off Jonathan Cotterill, 3. Terry's wife Lynne had run over the child in their driveway in Stocksbridge, Sheffield. *D.Mirror* 19 April 1985.

SPORTS OF NATURE

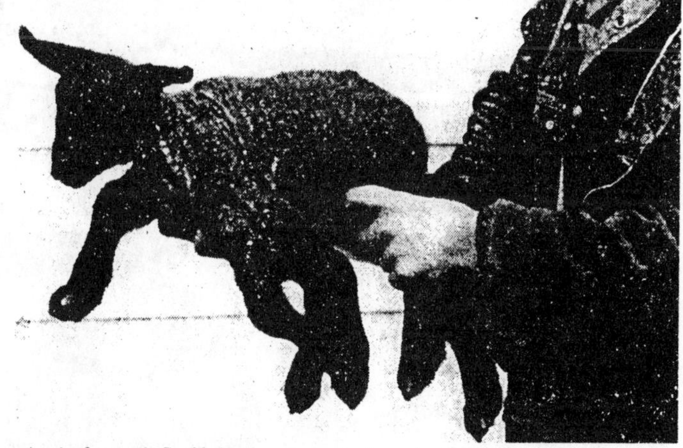

A six-legged Suffolk lamb, a twin of an ordinary quadruped, held by its owner Richard Brakhage from Tobias NB. It was first such offspring among about 1000 births in the 14-year-old herd. [Photo © Dean Terrill, Lincoln (NB) Star *11 Mar 1980.]*

Another six-legged lamb born on a West Wales farm sent in to Amateur Photographer *(31 Aug 1985) by O.G.Jeremy of Manselton, Swansea.*

MASS DEATHS

Some of the dead pilot whales at Eastham, Cape Cod – the biggest mass-beaching in the area in recent years. [Photo © Frank Paparo, Boston Herald, *8 Oct 1984.]*

The exact cause of mass beachings of whales and dolphins has eluded the study of marine biologists for decades. In the accounts of the recent events chronicled below, 'experts' were cited as believing in a number of theories: that the animals were unfamiliar with the territory; that they were pursuing prey so fast they were in shallows before they knew it; that they all followed a sick and disoriented leader; that they were disoriented by violent storms; or that parasitic ear infections drove them all crazy.

The facts give the lie to all of these. In the first case whales cruise well-known migratory routes between feeding and breeding grounds, and their navigation is usually pretty good.

Secondly, there are many cases – eg. Cape Cod 20 Nov 1984, and Spurn Head 15 Jan 1985, below – in which the pods of whales were observed before beaching, not rushing headlong but rather obviously (at least enough to alarm experienced observers) drifting somewhat aimlessly, or dazedly, on a collision course.

Thirdly, we find it hard to accept that creatures of such vaunted and demonstrable intelligence should be thought capable of following a sick leader to their obvious doom. But we'll not push this one because human beings have shown themselves to be pretty daft in this area.

Fourthly, not all beachings occur during or after storms. Cape Cod Bay has strandings most years, and the last big disasters there – at Eastham in December 1983, and at Wellfleet in November 1982 – were both during severe storms. Yet the current disasters at the same two locations (listed below) are higher in casualties and took place in relatively calm weather. Clearly some other factor is operating.

Lastly, all the cetaceans and many other marine creatures have parasites of the ear - it is as normal a state as the bacterial colonization of the human gut – and there is no evidence suggesting it is a disorienting condition. If it was, one would then have to explain why so many individuals could suddenly become disoriented simultaneously.

But evidence is beginning to accumulate, supporting the notion of some kind of disorientation of a magnetic sensing mechanism in marine mammals. One clue comes from Cheryl Cornwell-Huston, gathering data on the whale beachings of New England for a master's thesis (the St Louis (MO) *Post-Despatch* 9 Oct 1984 does not say which university), who says "I have found a definite correlation [between] steep (magnetic) gradients and the mass stranding locations. There is a very steep (magnetic) variation running right through the middle of Cape Cod Bay, from northeast to southwest through Wellfleet Harbor and Eastham." Mrs Cornwell-Huston's theory is that whales come into the bay from an area with a low magnetic field and are disoriented by the sudden change in the strength of the magnetic field. At Wellfleet Harbor, apparently, the tidal area is only navigable for an

The beached whale at Bexhill, Sussex. [Photo © Mark Power, Observer, *25 Oct 1984.]*

hour, and she suggests that in trying to escape from the magnetic disorientation the whales blunder into shallows and are quickly stranded. But she admits that "How the [sensing] mechanism works is still the big question."

More substantial evidence that whales and dolphins exploit the geomagnetic variations of the earth beneath the ocean floor to navigate comes from the California Institute of Technology, where Dr Joseph L. Kirschvink has plotted the locations of hundreds of beachings along the US east coast. He told the annual meeting of the American Geophysical Union, in San Francisco, in December 1984, that the 212 strandings, ranging from individuals to pods of up to 100 animals, correlate closely with regions where the earth's geomagnetic field has been diminished or masked by the magnetic fields of local rocks. Kirschvink also found that these locations are at the ends of long troughs in the geomagnetic field, suggesting that dolphins and whales use these channels of magnetic minima as "geomagnetic highways" – and like Mrs Cornwell-Huston, he thinks that the animals cruising the lanes that led, fatally, shorewards become too disoriented to extricate themselves. Kirschvink adds that this does not explain why the animals came so far into shallow waters in the first place.

In reviewing Kirschvink's work – as reported in *Science News* 126:389 (1984) – William Corliss, compiler of SCIENCE FRONTIERS (see p40) writes: "If Kirschvink's theory is correct, the magnetic sensors of the whales and dolphins are extremely sensitive, because the deepest magnetic troughs are only about 4% weaker than the background magnetic field. Magnetite crystals have been found in birds, fish and insects, where they are thought to contribute to a magnetic sense of some sort. So far, no magnetite has shown up in whales and dolphins."

1984

● **? May – Ortaon, Italy,** 39ft sperm whale found dead on nearby Adriatic coast. Had suffocated on 50 plastic bags wedged in throat. A bullet and industrial waste found in stomach. *Times* 7 May 1984.

● **21 Sept – Portland, Dorset.** 10-12ft "rare deep-sea dolphin" trapped in harbour. For four days all attempts to coax it out failed. Fishing firm foreman, Terry Studley, convinced his company to shut down their underwater pumps. Almost immediately the dolphin stopped going round and round, "did a tremendous leap out of the water and off he went." *D.Express* 22 & 25 Sept; *S.Express* 23 Sept; *D.Mirror* 22, 24, 25 Sept; *D.Telegraph* 24 Sept; Bristol *Eve. Post, D.Mail* 25 Sept 1984.

● **6 Oct – Eastham, Cape Cod, Massachusetts.** 94 pilot whales (up to 70ft) found dead and dying on the ironically named First Encounter Beach. Rescue attempts fail, so whales killed by sodium pentabarbitol injection. One young whale survived and swam away. Providence (RI) *Journal-Bulletin* 7 & 8 Oct; Attleboro (MA) *Sun-Chronicle*, Pawtucket (RI) *Evening Times*, St Louis (MO) *Post-Dispatch* 8 Oct; Boston (MA) *Herald* 7 & 9 Oct 1984.

● **4 Nov – Brighton, Sussex.** 6ft whale dead on beach. Brighton *Eve.Argus* 5 Nov 1984.

● **6 Nov – Rustington,** Sussex. 15ft "killer" whale. Already dead before washed up on beach. West Sussex *Gazette* 8 Nov 1984.

● **20 Nov – Wellfleet, Cape Cod, Massachusetts.** A lone 16ft pilot whale, and a 14ft bottlenose dolphin found dead on a beach a few miles north of the massive beaching of 6th Oct (above). Officials of the Wellfleet Bay Wildlife Sanctuary were also monitoring the pod of 15-20 other pilot whales swimming close to shore between Wellfleet and Eastham. Boston (MA) *Herald* 21 Nov 1984.

- **21 Nov.** During the night 19 whales from the offshore pod beach themselves just two miles north of First Encounter Beach. Nine were dead before they were discovered. By the end of the day workers were caring for a lone survivor – and two more whales, presumed members of the same pod, were found on beaches about 15 miles away. Boston (MA) *Herald* 22, 23, 24 Nov; Providence (RI) *Journal-Bulletin* 22 & 23 Nov 1984.
- **23 Nov – Bexhill, Sussex,** 40ft pilot whale. Brighton *Eve. Argus* 24 Nov; *Observer* 25 Nov; *Guardian, D.Mail* 26 Nov; *D.Telegraph* 26 & 27 Nov 1984.
- **23 Nov – Portyerrock, Isle of Whithorn, southwest Scotland.** 30ft whale found dead on rocks. *Scotsman* 24 Nov 1984.
- **2 Dec – Weymouth, Dorset.** 20ft whale found dead on beach – the third in the area in four days. Same day: hundreds of dead fish washed into Poole harbour, near Bournemouth (about 20 miles away). Officials of Southern Sea Fisheries District investigating possible links between these and drums of chemicals washed ashore "daily". Bristol *Eve.Post, Express & Star, D.Telegraph* 3 Dec 1984.

1985

- **15 Jan – Spurn Head, North Humberside.** 34 whales, singly and in small groups, were found dead and dying in a 3-mile stretch of beach between Holmpton and Easington. At least eight were killed by barbiturate injections given by vets. It's the first known stranding at this location. *D.Star, Express & Star* 16 Jan; *D.Mail, Times, D.Mirror, D.Telegraph, D. Mirror, D.Express, Guardian* all 17 Jan 1985.
- **18 Jan – Venice, Florida.** Six pilot whales beached. One died, the rest taken to Sea World at Orlando. Providence (RI) *Journal-Bulletin* 20 Jan 1985.

(We'll list more recent beachings another time.)

DOLPHINS RESCUE WHALES

As a heartening footnote to the generally depressing subject of mass deaths of whales, we must mention an incident from September 1983, in which a pod of 80 pilot whales were stranded by the ebbing tide at Tokerau Beach on New Zealand's north island.

Local people tried an increasingly common technique in rescuing beached whales, wading out to them, stroking and talking to them soothingly, and keeping their skins wet until the tide came in again. But when the refloated whales were pointed seawards they turned around and grounded themselves again. On this occasion – as reported in *Oceans* 17:50 (1984) – a school of dolphins fishing offshore appears to have comprehended the situation, and in a remarkable demonstration of species aid, came into the shallows and guided the whales back out to sea. A similar incident is recorded happening five years earlier, at Whangarei – also on NZ's north island – in which dolphins rescued 76 stranded pilot whales.

But the question arises...if there is anything to the magnetic disorientation theory, why weren't the dolphins affected in these cases? Undoubtedly the matter is more complicated than it first appears – or perhaps there is more than one cause of cetacean beaching.

FROZEN ALIVE

On the morning of 19 January this year, and while his parents slept, two-year-old Michael Troche wandered out of their Milwaukee, Wisconsin house. Nothing unusual about that, except that he was wearing only light pyjamas and the temperature outside had plummeted to 60 degrees below zero during a cold spell which broke low temperature records from Michigan to Texas. He soon collapsed in the snow. When his anguished father found him several hours later, he was literally frozen stiff. His limbs were hardened, ice crystals had formed on and beneath his skin, and he had stopped breathing for an unknown time. He was rushed to the city's Children's Hospital where 18 doctors and 20 nurses worked on him for six hours. Dr Kevin Kelly, a specialist in hypothermia, described Michael as "dead, extremely dead". One report says that doctors actually heard the ice crystals in his body cracking as they lifted him onto the operating table. As his blood was warmed in a heart-lung machine, and his body thawed, drugs were used to prevent his brain swelling. His arms and legs began swelling as fluid leaked from ice-damaged cells, and incisions had to be made to allow the tissues to expand. Dr Thomas Rice said that they knew of no one who had survived when the core of their body had dropped below minus 16 degrees C, as Michael's had done. He remained semi-conscious for over three days and then made rapid recovery. There is minor muscle damage to his left hand, and he has had some skin grafting on his limbs to cover the deep incisions, but he avoided critical brain damage. This is attributed to the wind-chill which effectively quick-froze him so rapidly that his metabolism had very little demand for oxygen. Our last report shows him leaving hospital after a good recovery. Detroit (MI) *News,*

AP and major English dailies of 4 Feb; *D. Mail*, 1 March; *D. Telegraph*, 30 March 1985.

As remarkable as Michael Troche's story is, it is by no means the only such tale from the 1984/85 winter. We briefly chronicle some recent ones. . .

■ After 20 minutes under the icy waters of Lake Michigan, four-year-old Jimmy Tontlewicz was pronounced dead on arrival at Children's Memorial Hospital, in Chicago. He was sledging on the lake-front when the ice gave way, plunging him into the cold (35C degrees) water. His body temperature had fallen to 80F degrees when he was fished out. Instead of reviving him immediately, doctors kept him in a drug-induced coma to control brain pressure. A week later he was recovering well without obvious signs of brain damage. Dr Robert Pozos, director of a hypothermia safety lab at the University of Minnesota, says the smaller you are and the faster you are chilled, the better your chances for survival. A year later Jimmy is relatively normal, but is still receiving treatment for "a minor speech problem". Omaha (NB) *World Herald*, 22 Jan 1984; Belleville (IL) *News-Democrat*, 13 Jan; *Int. Herald Tribune*, London *Standard*, 16 Jan 1985.

■ Two-year-old Matthew Traines was submerged for at least 20 minutes in an icy pond before a neighbour discovered him and administered resuscitation for 15 minutes. The boy's body temperature had dropped nine degrees below normal. Very ill but recovering. *D. Mail*, 20 Dec 1984.

■ When the Robinson family's car plunged into an icy pond in the North Humberside village of Warter and sank upside down, the adults were saved by residents. The survivors told the rescuers that baby Katie was still underwater, strapped into her car seat. When she was brought out she was blue and not breathing – revived after several minutes' resuscitation. *D. Mail*, 3 Jan 1985.

■ Three-year-old Megan Birmingham was clinically dead on arrival at the Community Hospital in Olathe, Kansas. She was found curled up, unconscious, in light clothing in a snowdrift only 100 yards from a house on the town outskirts. She had been abandoned by her mother. She was making a "fair" recovery from frostbitten extremities. She was released from hospital into the care of an uncle, but will need months of observation to determine the extent of brain damage (if any). St Louis (MO) *Post-Dispatch*, 20 Jan; Belleville (IL) *News-Democrat*, 21 & 23 Jan 1985.

■ Another story from Wisconsin. 57-year-old taxidermist David Kostichka, of Forestville, was found slumped in an armchair when his brother and a neighbour broke into his house to investigate his 'disappearance'. He had been sitting there, unconscious, for seven days after a shot through a window lodged a bullet in his head. He was also suffering from hypothermia, malnutrition and dehydration, but survived because the unheated house kept his body temperature low. Sydney, Australia *S. Telegraph*, 3 March 1985.

■ Paul James, 24, visiting Amsterdam from Ireland, "died" for 15 minutes after plunging into a frozen pond to rescue his dog, becoming trapped under ice. Recovering. *Sun*, 29 March 1985.

■ In the *Weekly World News* (19 March 1985) Michael Troche's defrosting is compared to that of two-year-old Vicki Mary Davis, about 30 years previously. Vicki was found lying with her grandmother on the floor of their unheated home in Marshalltown, Iowa, when the temperature dropped to 24 degrees below zero. Although she had a faint heartbeat, she was as hard as a rock. Even her eyes were frozen. Her case was considered hopeless when she was taken to a hospital, so for the next hour the doctor fought to save the grandmother and the baby girl was left on a trolley. When Vicki eventually received attention her body temperature registered 60.8F degrees (slightly higher than Michael's), but this was after lying in a warm hospital for an hour. She was so hard, remembers Dr Harold E. Sauer, that "the only place we could get a needle in was between the thighs". Vicki was placed in a tub of water at 70F degrees and after ten hours her body temperature had returned to normal. An hour after that she was well enough to ask for something to eat, suffering only minor swelling and blisters in her extremities.

■ Finally, an irreverent footnote. . . The *D. Mail* and *Sun* for 9 July 1983 mention Esmeralda, a chicken which had been mistaken for dead, thrown into a sack with some genuinely dead chickens, and then tossed into a deep-freeze by Bob Allcott, a shopkeeper in Frome, Somerset. Two weeks later Mr Allcott gets out the sack of frozen chickens and notices one still alive, the very same Esmeralda, who was then given to a chicken-farmer to nurse back to health. As *AG*, 'the newsletter of compassion on world farming', states in its Sept 1983 issue: the mystery of how the chicken survived two deeply frozen weeks is one thing; the purpose of freezing sackfuls of ungutted, unplucked chickens is another.

THE MOVING STATUES OF IRELAND

The epidemic of moving statues in Ireland this summer provides one of the most interesting manifestations of religious phenomena for many a year, and we hope to see a detailed study of it one day. In so far as we can tell, it began with the apparitional movement at Asdee, Co Kerry, in mid-February – see A MOVING EXPERIENCE on p6, followed, about a month later by a similar phenomenon at Ballydesmond. Sporadic apparitions continued to be reported throughout the spring, gradually dwindling towards summer. The event which seems to have triggered off the wave of gesticulating statuary, was an incident well-publicized in the Irish paper *Sunday World* for 14 July 1985, in which some Irish pilgrims and the paper's reporter saw a "solar miracle" (sun dancing in the sky) at BVM vision site at Medjugorge, Yugoslavia. (We will have more on this in our vision round-up next issue.) Within two weeks of this news the first and biggest sensation began at Ballinspittle. At the time of writing there are reports of statues bleeding and weeping, as well as moving, from over 40 sites all over Ireland, including full-scale aerial apparitions at Carns. Mostly these have been at roadside shrines, as at Ballinspittle (see photo), modelled on the Lourdes grotto, and established in 1954, which had been designated a Marian year.

The "religious and moral tension" to which we referred in the Asdee write-up was sustained throughout the summer and must have contributed to the proliferation that followed. The Catholic Church dominates Irish affairs as it does in no other European country, and any event which can turn the public's conscience towards matters of religious tradition only makes the task of progressive government that much harder, particularly on the subject of divorce, abortion and contraception. The strengthening of religious feeling also stokes up the sort of nationalism which obstructs the orderly reunification of the Irish people and their provinces. Inevitably, those who believe this avalaanche of animated alabaster as a sign of divine favour towards the Republican claim on Northern Ireland see as equally significant the lack of similar dispensations in those northern counties.

The affair has serious religious undertones too. Although the sight of so many of their flock "regenerating their spiritual batteries" (as one reporter put it) must be gratifying, few of the faithful have stopped long enough to realise that not a single incident has received official blessing, even on a local level. In almost every case the reactions of the local priests have fallen between urging caution over claims of divine origination to unequivocal rejection of the phenomena. There were also subtle pleas to the people, which were reassertions of the ages-old tactic, so useful in domesticating superstitious pagans: why worship a statue in a field when you can worship a statue inside our church building?

Yet despite the regular *ex cathedra* warnings ordinary religious people have flocked in their thousands to see the meandering masonry, many waiting for hours in uncomfortable conditions and some of them, perhaps inevitably, seeing what they came to see. Of the two main interpretations of the phenomena it is the believers, naturally, who claim the events to be the work of God, and for them the ambiguities of this esoteric and essentially clumsy way of reaching His faithful have little importance. And yet they will have to be faced, for as we shall see, the whole affair has developed what those same faithful might describe as demonic aspects. To the rest of us the whole saga is an exciting illustration of suggestion, rumour and panic. That the witnesses have seen something has rarely been doubted; the central question is whether the movements of the statues were objective or subjective.

The most concise way of summarising the post-Asdee incidents is to present them geographically. Forgive us any errors in duplication: modern reportage begets misinformation enough without having to cope with the complexity of local place names in Ireland. Our chief sources are an excellent list in the *Sunday Tribune* (15 Sept 1985), sent to us by Harold Covington; and some first hand enquiries made by Lionel Beer. Even so, we do not have precise enough data to offer a chronological list. Here goes. . .

Co CARLOW

★ **Carlow** – A small statue, which used to be down a coalmine and resited on Rossmore Hill 15 years ago, alleged to have moved inside its glass cover.

★ **Killeshin** – Moving statue; details unknown.

★ **Spink** – Moving statue; details unknown.

★ **St Dympna** – Moving statue at a hospital; details unknown.

Co CLARE

★ **Bridgetown** – Moving statue; details unknown.

★ **Broadford** – Moving statue; details unknown.

★ **Cartloe** – Two women from a local prayer group claim a statue moved. Later another witness saw a "Christ-like" face superimposed

upon the BVM's, while yet another saw a face like that on the Shroud of Turin. Children say they have seen the faces of Padre Pio and one of the Popes upon the same statue. Large crowds pray nightly.
★ **Clarecastle** – Moving statue; details unknown.
★ **Corofin** – Moving statue; details unknown.
★ **Ennis** – Two moving statues: one inside cathedral, the other in grounds of Friary. No other details.
★ **Glenbrien** – On 7th or 8th September, two local women see BVM statue move. Nightly vigils of crowds.
★ **Kilkee** – Moving statue; details unknown.

Co CORK

★ **Ballinspittle** – On the evening of Monday 22nd July, 17yr-old Clare Mahoney and her mother praying at the shrine were convinced they saw the 3cwt statue of BVM rocking on its heels. The next night they returned with about 40 friends and relatives, many of whom saw something to gratify them. Since then the shrine's sacristan, local people and scores of pilgrims, including some self-confessed skeptics, have seen the statue rock back and forth and side to side, bowing, moving its eyes, shoulders and hands. Others have seen Christ's face in place of the Virgin's. An estimated 200,000 people thronged the village in the first two months; and special coach trips operate from most parts of Ireland. A local committee appointed crowd-control stewards and mounted a 24hr guard against relic hunters. A middle-aged woman claimed she was cured of crippling arthritis by praying at the shrine (*Sunday Post* 18 Aug 1985).
★ **Ballydesmond** – In early March, barely a month after the Asdee events, some children said they saw a statue move in a local church. Pilgrims came, even though the children's parents put the vision down to over-active imaginations.
★ **Belgooly** – Moving statue; details unknown.
★ **Cork City** – On Friday 13th September, three school children see a BVM statue move in the Church of the Resurrection at Farranree. They said it almost toppled onto them. The mother of one child said the statue's eyes

The Lourdes-style grotto at Ballinspittle stands 20 feet up on a hillside. At night its halo is backlit for effect. Those who see the statue move, for instance open its eyes, from the viewing area below must have pretty good eyesight! [Photo © Lionel Beer, with kind permission.]

became red and her cheeks and feet black.
★ **Courtmacsharry** – Date unknown. A group of tourist said they saw a statue sited near the town move. No subsequent reports. No great influx of pilgrims.
★ **Dunmanway** – Moving statue; details unknown.
★ **Mitchelstown** – In the first week of September, four teenage girls said they went into a trance during which the statue spoke to them, calling for peace. On the 14th Sept the girls felt "drawn" once gain to the shrine and heard it utter "Peace". At least 20,000 pilgrims have come to see for themselves. And sure enough, some of these also claimed visions of movement and eyes changing colour.

Co DUBLIN

★ **Dublin** – On 11th September, a statue in the grounds of the Oblate church at **Inchinore** was reported to have animated. Despite priests dismissing it as "just messing" by local children crowds have gathered nightly.

Co KERRY

★ **Killarney** – Worshippers at a BVM grotto gasped as the statue rocked and turned. Two boys were later accused of playing a cruel trick, but whether they confessed voluntarily (always suspicious) or were seen and caught is not clear.
★ **Rathmore** – **Pilgrims at the shrine** here were attracted by reports of strange sounds from the statue. When a spotlight was turned on the shrine a startled owl flew away.

Co KILDARE

★ **Monasterevin** – Since late August a BVM statue has moved at "regular intervals" and displayed Padre Pio's face, as well as "other visions".

Co LAOIS

★ **Abbeyleix** – A statue is seen to move in the grounds of Knock church, outside the town.
★ **Stradbally** – Bloodstains were reported on a BVM statue also seen to move. Face of Padre Pio and iamge of Sacred Heart also seen on statue.

Co LEITRIM

★ **Carrick on Shannon** – A young girl on way home from school sees BVM statue move in grounds of convent, first week in September. No crowds so far.

Co LIMERICK

★ **Cahermoyle** – Early September. Statue in grounds of Oblate monastery seen to move. Crowds pray every night.
★ **Coolard** – BVM statue in Marian shrine seen by local child-

ren to move at end of August. Crowds gather every night.

★ **Foynes** – Women sees BVM statue move in first week of September. Many pilgrims since.

★ **Limerick City** – Large crowds gather day and night to view the BVM statue at **Garrytown**, near the greyhound stadium. Several witnesses claim that blood poured from the BVM's hands.

Reports of moving statues also come from two housing estates in the city, at **St Mary's Park** and at **Moycross.**

★ **Mainster** – Early September – Statue seen to move. Crowds pray every night.

★ **Mountcollins** – At the end of August some women and children say the BVM statue in their local grotto swayed. Later witnesses claim blood flowed from the statue's eyes, and the image of the Sacred Heart was superimposed on its breast. Crowds continue to keep vigil.

Co MONAGHAN

★ **Doohamalet** – Moving statue inside a church near **Castleblaney;** no other details.

Co SLIGO

★ **Carns** – On 2nd September four local schoolgirls had a vision of the BVM in a field at **Culleens.** Since then others have seen apparitions of St Bernadette, BVM and a crucifix in the night sky. There is a makeshift shrine at the site, but no-one has reported the BVM statue there for movement – yet! This place is second only to Ballinspittle for numbers of pilgrims – 20,000 were expected on Sunday 15th Sept.

Co TIPPERARY

★ **Roscrea** – BVM statue in the grounds of St Anne's Convent was seen by locals to move on the night of 10th September. The nuns within have not accepted the claim.

Co WATERFORD

★ **Dunkitt** – At the end of August a statue of BVM in Our Lady's Grotto on the main Waterford/Kilkenny road, was seen to breathe, move its hands and shimmer. A face of Christ was also said to move. Hundreds gather to pray and sing each night, and thousands have visited the shrine.

★ **Mooncoin** – Several youths claim to have seen a BVM statue move on 4th September. One girl, Bernadette O'Hanlon, said she saw a tear fall from its right eye and the left one open and close twice. A small boy saw the Sacred Heart and an infant Jesus superimposed on the statue's face. Nightly gathering of prayers and songs.

★ **Mount Mellary** – Three children allege that a BVM statue, near the Cistercian Abbey, got down from its pedestal to tell them: "God was very angry with the world". The statue, newly erected in August, is now attracting thousands of pilgrims.

★ **Waterford City** – On 9th September a BVM statue outside the Mercy Convent school opened its eyes, cried, and spoke of an assassination attempt upon Pope John Paul II, according to two young boys. Hundreds of pilgrims maintain vigil since then.

Co WEXFORD

★ **Camolin** – Large crowds gather nightly around a BVM statue said to have moved.

★ **Enniscorthy** – A group of women leaving the House of Missions building, in the evening of 9th September, saw the BVM statue move. Large crowds continue to gather nightly.

IS IT ALL HYSTERIA?

If you can think of the possibility that hysteria might play a part in all this you are obviously not among the faithful. That is perhaps a gross oversimplification, because many of the voices urging caution and inquiry came from the bishops and leading Catholic scholars. For example, the two cases from Co. Kerry (above), which were 'exposed' as the work of hoaxers and an owl, both came from a priest who used them to illustrate the perils of jumping to pious conclusions too soon.

Dr Jurek Kirakowski, a psychologist at Cork University, blames "the way our visual systems work" as he seemed to be trying to explain in terms of tricks of the light. "These grottoes are all very similar in terms of the background which merges into the sky when you look up at them in the twilight. The glare from the illuminated halo on the statue means that you cannot easily see the head and shoulders in relation to the rockface behind." The movement itself was merely an optical illusion, he thought.

But hoaxes and misperceptions alone cannot account for the contagious excitement which swept, like an illness a skeptic might say, throughout Ireland. Dr Thomas McDonnell, Bishop of Killala, Co. Mayo, made a curiously ambiguous plea for the incidents to be regarded as "psychic phenomena" until sure signs of a supernatural source were found. "The people who see these things are in no way abnormal or hysterical," he added. A certain amount of misperception is indeed a normal part of everyday perception, but surely not to the extent we see manifested here under conditions which invite direct comparison with cases of so-called 'mass hysteria'. It is our guess that Dr McDonnell was seeking to protect the witnesses from the taint of 'hysteria', a term for which the Catholic Church has a history of abhorrence, fearing as they do, persistently and wrongly, that otherwise many a saint would thereby be lumped with madmen, liars and exhibitionists. "These people are good people, and no one has the right to look down on them," he says.

Most psychologists today accept hysterical mechanisms as part of normal psychic functioning. Hysterical personalities do not always behave in the exaggerated manner popularly attributed to them. Some extensive public re-education needs to be done here if any progress is to be made in a fascinating subject which spans the unconscious mimicry of almost every functional and pathogenic disease, hypnotic conditions, psychosomatic phenomena, multiple personalities and a bewildering variety of *beneficial* effects. Even Dr McDonnell accepts the role of suggestibility, a significant factor in hysteria, when he says that the witnesses "may not be aware of what the expectation of marvels can do to the human mind or senses." Consequently, we must say that the "expectation of marvels" was there, as well as the conditions appropriate to optical illusions. But that is not to say the proliferating visions were meaningless, for as Dr Anthony Clare, the Dublin-born professor of psychiatry at St Bartholomew's Hospital, London, commented: "So many people reading so much significance into such banal events. . .suggest a very deep need indeed for simple reassurance." Whatever their origin, no one can detract from the value the witnesses themselves place upon their experiences.

An interesting example of the subjective nature of some or most of these apparitions came on the evening of 31st July. Many people watching the 9pm news on the Irish TV station, RTE, were convinced they saw an image of Christ during a report on the Ballinspittle shrine. Following the phone and letter enquiries, the company's engineers examined the videotape thoroughly but could find nothing unusual.

In the meantime, the Church deliberately procrastinates. All possible explanations must be investigated, the bishops say, before any pronouncement can be made as to the validity of the incidents. The bishops held a meeting to discuss the matter in early October, during which some of them were said to be "at variance". Later, their spokesman said: "Without wishing to poke fun at anyone or to be

"Patrick claims the whole of Ballinspittle's moving."

facetious I can say that the Church moves much more slowly in these matters than do the statues." Here, one of the great Irish virtues, their irrepressable wit, shines through, as it has done down on the street. According to *The Scotsman* (24 Oct 1985) an irreverent folklore has sprung up, circulating such stories as ". . .how church lights are now left on at night so that the statues don't bump into each other. . .how the Ballinspittle Virgin is no more, having been knocked down while crossing the road . . .how the statue in Co Waterford of Master McGrath, a famous greyhound, has had to be caged in as it was worrying sheep."

DEMONIC VISIONS

But all is not humorous or well. On the night of 31st October, three youths armed with axes and iron bars attacked the Ballinspittle statue's head and halo while the worshippers could only scream helplessly. One of the iconoclasts shouted to the shocked crowd: "You stupid fools, worshipping a stone statue," before fleeing. Whether this was a simple act of vandalism or an action more sinister we cannot divine. But there is worse. . .

On the night of Thursday 5th September the nature of the apparitions at Mitchelstown, Co Cork, began to change. According to a huge feature in the *Sunday World* (15 Sept 1985) there was panic in the crowd. Teenagers and younger children began screaming and crying that they had seen a devil. One 16yr-old boy, unnamed, went home crying and trembling, telling his mother he had seen "shocking things". His mother told the paper: "While looking at the statue of the Blessed Virgin he saw it changing into various forms and he saw the face of the devil. The thing he saw had horns and was a dark figure. He was terrified. Then he saw the face of Jesus and a Pope with glasses." The panic seems to have started with this boy and quickly spread to a group of three girls. Mrs Eileen Graham, who was present, told the paper that it was as though the children were "tuned to something". They began shouting "He's here! He's here!" She said the kids were roaring; some fainted and were carried out. The local priest, Fr Denis O'Connor, confirmed that several of his altar boys also claimed to have seen demonic figures, and he urged his flock not to go expectantly to the shrine but to pray in his church.

This sort of unexpected development shows the prudence of the Church's attitude. As the news of this incident spread many adults expressed their own fears openly. Pilgrims who had been to Ballinspittle first spoke of the noticeably different atmosphere at Mitchelstown, that it was not as comforting but cold and frightening. Even more curious is the revelation by Mrs Graham, that a woman she refused to name had seen a vision of a devil at the shrine some *six weeks previously*. Of her own experiences, Mrs Graham said: "I saw the face of an old woman in a nun's habit. Another woman saw the same thing. Then I saw Our Lady's face and half of it growing old. There was a huge big bag under her left eye, then there was a tear running down her face. I cried."

We will continue to monitor the situation.

The sources for this summary are too numerous to list here; they are on file should they be needed.

•

Bob Rickard

ELECTRO-OSMOSIS?

Joseph Orchard and his wife June of New Cottages, The Street, Adisham, Canterbury, Kent, lost their High Court damages claim against the South-East Electricity Board on 8 March 1985 after a 12 day hearing.

Their story was that after a power supply cable was attached to their home in 1976, metallic objects, including a cooker door and a bath tap, flew around the cottage, and they fled next door. The cottage became flooded and the ceiling fell down. They blamed *electro-osmosis*.

Mr Justice Steyn, rejecting their claim, blamed the Orchards or their son David, 15 at the time. David, he said, had suffered problems at school and his interest in electricity "was fuelled by pseudo-scientific matters" (Hmm...) The phenomena could not have been caused by electricity, pronounced the judge, as power had been supplied to houses for more than 65 years without similar effects. The water damage could only have been caused by a crack in the structure of the cottage, but none was found, and water could not have come from the ceiling unless poured from above. Concluded the judge: "It is no job of mine to determine the reason for their extraordinary behaviour, but the Orchards have been untruthful". *Guardian*, 9 Mar 1985.

TALKING BEAR

Greg and Stephanie McKay from Enumclaw were camping in Pierce County about 5 miles off Highway 410 near Greenwater in Washington State. Before dawn on 6 July 1985, according to their report to the Pierce County Sheriff's office, their campsite was attacked by a bear-like animal, 8 feet tall, ugly and smelly with curly brown hair.

"You may think this sounds crazy, but the bear talked to us," Stephanie, 35, said in a telephone interview. In a very high-pitched voice that didn't sound human it asked them their names and whether they had permission to use the campsite. They said they had permission, but the bear told them to get off the property immediately. While they gathered up their belongings, the bear stood on its hind legs and began throwing stones at them. "It must have weighed almost a ton," she said. "We ran like anything."

Greenwater Fire Department officials visited the site, but could find no signs of a struggle. The only visible tracks were those of a large dog. The case was eventually dismissed as a product of over-active imagination. According to Deputy Bob Hoffman of the Pierce County sheriff's office, the couple had been told earlier (by humans) that their campsite was on private property and the fire danger was high. (UPI) Boston (MA) *Globe*, Houston (TX) *Chronicle*, San Francisco *Chronicle*, San Diego (CA) *Union*, Pawtuxet Valley (RI) *Daily Times* 8 July; Seattle (WA) *Times* 10 July 1985.

GETTING THE POINT

■ Motorcyclist Richard Topps, 21, was happily riding along at Ogston Reservoir, near Chesterfield, in Derbyshire, when his bike collided with a car. His passenger was badly injured while Richard was thrown in the air onto a wooden fence, where a 4ft-long, 2x3ins post speared him diagonally from chest to hip. He hung there, fully conscious and completely unable to help himself, for over over an hour until he was discovered by his brother. After help arrived, it was another 30 minutes before the post was sawn through. It took another two-hour operation in hospital to remove the rest of the stake. Amazed surgeons found that his vital organs had all escaped damage. and he recovered quickly. It was said that his size – he is well over 6ft, and 17st – probably saved him. *D.Telegraph*, *D.Express* 14 Aug 1979.

■ Tibursio Gonzales, 21, was driving his tractor-trailor onto the shoulder of a road, at Cotati, California, when a branch of a tree smashed through the cabin window and impaled him diagonally through the left side of his chest. He remained fully conscious throughout his rescue. AP/Framingham (MA) *Middlesex News* 7 June 1980.

■ Driving a pickup truck on her way home from work in Quincy, Massachusetts, 18yr-old Kimberly Lotti swerved out of control into a chain-link fence and one of the 2-inch thick aluminium fence posts rebounded through the windshield and through her upper left chest. "It was eerie," she said later. "I didn't feel any pain at all. I thought the pipe was just pressing against my arm. I guess I was in shock." Rescue firefighter Alan Predella said:

"She was still conscious when we arrived, and she was very calm. We cut the pipe about five inches in front of and behind her body, and took her to hospital where it was removed. Once again we hear of the penetrating object narrowly missing heart and lungs. *Globe* 20 Dec 1983.

■ Just eight days after being pierced completely through his chest by a wooden stake, miner Charlie Bethell walked out of hospital. Charlie was working in the Whitwell Colliery, near Worksop, Notts, when a 9ft post was dislodged from a conveyor belt and impaled him. Luckily, the two-inch-thick stake passed his lungs, missing his heart. After morphine shots, the post was cut short, and Charlie was taken to hospital with the remainder protruding from his front and back. Surgeons were amazed to find his only injury, apart from the holes, were a few torn muscles. *Sun* 25 April 1985.

■ The most astonishing story of this little collection of skewered people comes from India. On 15 April 1984, 28yr-old Muchaki Ayatu had an argument with his best friend, Kuhrami, while they were both out hunting. As he walked away, Kuhrami turned and fired an arrow at Muchaki and then walked away. Muchaki says he felt a sharp pain in his "middle" and fell to the ground. He tried to pull out the arrow but it wouldn't budge. As the pain and loss of blood increased he fainted. He awoke in the morning and again failed to tug the arrow out, so, finding he could stand, decided to try the four miles to his village. He met relatives out searching for him and they helped him back. His wife and children were, naturally, horrified by the sight of him – see photo.

The village elders told him he must go the nearest police station – a mere 10 miles – to report the incident, and only then go on to the hospital in Jagdalpur. And after a short rest, this is what he did. Even though a fellow tribesman supported him, the pain was so great he thought he would die. At the poice station he rested overnight, and in the morning set out again, this time with an officer. You might think the worst was over for him, but not yet! It was a 20-mile hike over hills along narrow jungle paths, simply to get to the main road, which meant an overnight camp in the jungle. In the morning the officer flagged down a bus. When they got to town there was another mile to trudge to the hospital, but after what Muchaki had been through that was easy. By the evening the arrow, which had been his closest companion for three days, was separated from him, and almost at once the pain stopped. According to the *National Enquirer* 4 Sept 1984.

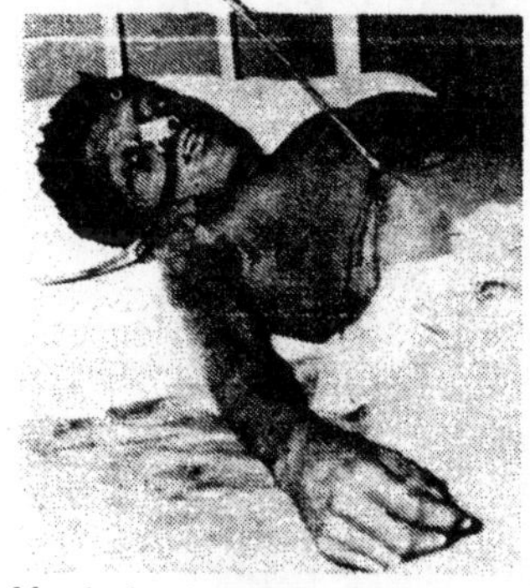

Muchaki Ayatu in hospital at last, three days after being shot by a friend. [Photo © National Enquirer.]

TWO GRAND MASTERS DIE

From Italy comes the story of the strange death of Masahiro Oki, reputed to have been the only samurai to have refused to prostrate himself before Emperor Hirohito. Oki, aged 64, died while performing extreme yoga austerities as Pesaro, on on the Adriatic.

Oki was the sort of character rarely found outside *ninja* novels. He was an acknowledged expert on yoga and various martial arts, holding a 36-dan, three degrees in Western medicine, and degrees in Oriental medicine. He was a top linguist and was once personal physician to the Japanese Emperor.

Oki was said to have reached a level of ritual in which the elements are regarded as a form of illusion. To meditate on this he wore a lead-weighted jacket and assumed the lotus position underwater. He died during the fourth immersion. The length of time he stayed submerged is not stated. His students were unable to resuscitate him, our report says, "using ancient Samurai methods". His body was flown back to Japan. If any of our readers can shed more light upon this evocative incident, please write in. *Sunday Express* 4 Aug 1985.

■ The same week that Oki died, there was an army crackdown on the kung fu fanatics in Madagaskar in which 31 were injured and 20 killed, including the cult's Grand Master, Pierre Misael Andrianarijaona. Kung fu had been outlawed in 1984 after its supporters attacked a youth camp, killing 60 people. The cult is believed to have 10,000 members, mostly living in the capital Antananarivo and other cities. [R] *Guardian, D.Telegraph* 3 Aug 1985.

A KNOTTY PROBLEM

When John Michell and Bob Rickard wrote their closing chapter of *Living Wonders* on the subject of Rat Kings, they knew of no cases of any other animals found in small groups, tied together by their tails. Well now we can add a new category to the annals of unexplained zoology with the discovery, in Brunswick, Maine, of seven squirrels fastened by their furry extremities.

On Monday 13 May, Mrs Carol Robbins' attention was attracted by a group of squirrels behaving a bit differently, or oddly, at the base of a pine tree in the backyard of her home in River Road. They stayed as a group and each was trying to run or escape in a different direction. "It was like a committee," she said. "None could decide which way to go." Seeing the animals in such distress, she called her husband, and they decided the tangle should be helped or killed. By the time Jack Robbins went into action, the group was halfway back up a tree after falling to the ground. He knocked them out of the tree with a pole into a bed of leaves. Mrs Robbins thinks one of the squirrels came free at this point and made its escape. John put the remaining bunch of six into a pail and drove the 12 miles to the office of veterinarian Dr Ray S. Youmans.

Youmans anaesthetised the animals and untangled their tails. He thinks they were about six weeks old, "about ready to go out on their own", and perhaps all of one litter. He surmised that some pine pitch stuck to their tails "and as they became more active their tails became all tied in knots". He does not say he found evidence of 'pine pitch'; nor does he clearly state whether the tails were glued together by the resin or actually tied in a knot. Later Mrs Robbins returned them all to the tree in their backyard. "I never saw anything so weird in my life," she said.

Nor is this the only case. *Press Herald* reporter Sara Hammond told Loren Coleman (who sent us this story) that a Naval Public Affairs Officer told her of a similar group of squirrels that had been discovered "a year ago" at the Brunswick Naval Base. And Dr Youmans told John Robbins that he had seen a tangle of squirrels the previous year, but we are not sure if this is the same as the one seen at the naval base. Is this a new phenomenon? If not, does anyone know of any earlier records? Portland (ME) *Press Herald*, Portland (ME) *Evening Express* 14 May 1985.

SNAKE DIET

Wang Biao, a young peasant from Jinlin province in north-eastern China, ate more than 1,800 live poisonous snakes over two years to cure himself of convulsions, reported the *Canton Daily*. The cure was effective, but Wang became addicted to the snakes and needed to swallow one before every meal. He has started breeding them to ensure a regular supply. [R] *D.Telegraph*, *Scotsman*, *D.Mirror* 21 Sept 1985.

FELINE PRODIGY

A kitten with six legs and two tails, born in Kandana in Sri Lanka. It only lived a day, but the owner has preserved the body. Large crowds were still gathering to see it. Sri Lanka Daily News *11 Mar 1985.*

IF PIGS COULD FLY

Something, apparently a very large something, has been wandering around a first-floor balcony in the harbour area of Huntingdon Beach in California. And whatever it might be, it was leaving a huge turd behind, described by condominium resident Holly Craig as "What you might expect from an elephant".

Neither the police, the Humane Society of Huntingdon Beach nor the county Health Department, had solved the riddle of the Craig family's late-night, unseen and unheard balcony visitor. But a vet analysed a sample and concluded it was the work of a huge pig.

Few agreed with him, as pigs are scarce in the harbour community, and anyway how could it manage to reach the balcony? And the Craig family at 325B Sparkler Drive was left wondering what manner of creature it might be that, up until the end of February 1982, had visitied and left its calling card three times in the previous two months. *The Register,* Santa Ana, California, 26 Feb 1982.

Back Issues

• FT31 – The Chinese Wildman; Gateways to Mystery; The Touch of Death; UFO muggers; mystery big cats; ball lightning; synchronous names; little people; fake doctors; Forteana from China; comix.

• FT32 – The Mississauga Blob; Old Ives' Tales; Gateways (pt 2); occult murder; mystery big cats; fairy tales come true; Forteana from India and China; child sacrifice; mystery panthers in USA and Australia; comix.

• FT33 – The Enfield Poltergeist; mythology of UFO abductions; Gateways (pt 3); mass hysteria at Nottingham; simulacra; coffin stories; Jeoff Watson's Nessie pix; UFOs; Forteana from China; giant snakes; comix.

• FT34 – Congo dinosaur hunt; lake monster names; phantom hitch-hikers; interview with Dr Jean Bolen on synchronicity; the Welsh 'puma'; mystery big cats; beached whales; animal saboteurs; nature follows art; ice falls; inept crimes; Trashkashic records; odd Irish doings; giant squids; comix.

• FT35 – The Myth of Darwinism; an SHC from 1744; The Runamo Runes; Forteana from Malaysia and China; spontaneous combustions; antiquities; strange trees; magic fuels; frog and stone falls; mystery big cats; bizarre bacteria; TV science; occult murder; Fortean travel in USA.

• FT36 – Anomalistics; Photos of Jesus; Runamo Runes; Gent's Mag extracts; hermits and wildmen; strange tales; toads in holes; bleeding statues and visions; the Buddha's UFO; DIY surgery; coin, ice and sand falls; ASSAP and CSAR; jellyfish in the sky; Forteana from China; USA monitor lizards: Nessie; comix.

• FT37 – Australia's Lizard Monsters; energy from space; encounters with Greek gods; interview with Dr Rupert Sheldrake on a New Science of Life; a female prophet; Irish oddities; mystery USA kangaroos; UFO hallucinations; falls of crabs, frogs, peas, fish; visions, stigmatics and fasting; plants in odd places; mystery UK bear scares; talking polts; reflections; homing rings; locked-up by friends and relatives.

• FT38 – Psychometry of cattle mutilations; Isotope myth; synchronicity of clowns and 22; Sieveking's Selection; two BVM visions; talking polts; recent discoveries of old and new species; objects penetrating brains; double image; strange fires; Rasta folklore; comix, columns, letters.

• FT39 – Robert Anton Wilson on Synchronicity in Joyce's *Finnegans Wake;* SHC Survivors inc Jack Angel; The ET Law; Entombed Toads; Gentlemans Magazine Extracts Pt 2; Mystery Cats; Chinese Hair Clipping Panics; Homing Wallets, Snippers & Snatchers Etc; Death Tableaux; Ice Falls; Updates on Material in Previous Issues; + Columns, Letters, Comix.

• **FT40** – More *Living Wonders* (Rat Kings, Hibernating birds, Winged cats, Falls of wheat & tadpoles, Dinosaur survival, Animal loyalty, Long returns, Avian abductions & more); Chronology of the Exmoor Beast; Fortean Follow-ups; *Gent's Mag* extracts pt. 3; Name synchronicity; Chessie; Chinese hair-clipping panics; End Times Bulletin; Ball & Bead lightning; Snakes & Bugs in tummies; Un-conscious births; Japweed; the mystery of the Wiltshire cornfield holes; Ice falls; Vatican-Masonic connection; Creatures from the Black Lagoon; comix; letters; in a thick 72 page issue.

• **FT41** – Our 10th anniversary Special Issue. 76 pages of articles by the Bords, Peter Christie, Jerome Clark, Loren Coleman, Peter Costello, Hilary Evans, David Fideler, Bernard Heuvelmans, Michael Hoffman, John Keel, John Michell, Steve Moore, Nigel Pennick, Michael Persinger, Bob Rickard, Leslie Shepard, Doc Shiels, Ron Westrum, & Mr. X; and art by Hunt Emerson and Pokkettz.

• **FT 42** – Another jumbo 76 page issue, to include our *Strange Days* section, a news round-up of the whole spectrum of strangeness. Plus Doc Shiels' giant squid hypothesis for lake monsters, an interview with Dr Michael Persinger, author of *Space-Time Transients and Unusual Events*, and a new regular feature, gleaned from William Corliss' excellent bimonthly *Science Frontiers*. And the Exmoor Beast, the fire nanny case, world sightings of the Blessed Virgin, more bleeding statues and coffin humour, mermaid controversy.

• **FT 43** – Janet Bord summarises the downfall of the Cottingley fairy photographs, Wilford Anderson casts strong doubt on the identity of Christopher Columbus, and John Michell examines the York Minster fire mystery. Plus human horns, modern folklore, strange trees, drunken animals and Forteana from France, Iceland and the Philippines – and Science Frontiers, comix by Hunt Emerson and Pokkettz, and lots of recent enigmas in Strange Days.

• FT 44 – Study of Thomas Short, 18th cent. portent chronicler, by Roger Musson, Steve Moore on Chinese falls, Dick Gwynn on lycanthropy and ergotism, Doc Shiels and Leslie Shepard on fairies, Hilary Evans and Nigel Watson on UFO hypotheses; plus spontaneous combustion, Oregon earth divot mystery and lake monster, weird tales from Africa, British alien big cat survey, teleporting astrologer, wolf boy and much else.

WILDMAN. Specially translated articles on the Chinese wildman, edited by Steve Moore. FT Occasional Paper No.1. UK £1.00. Overseas surface $2.50.

PUZZLING QUESTIONS – Some Observations on the History of Prodigies.
A gripping little book on society's reaction to, and use of, prodigies, including Fortean phenomena, in the last 2,000 years. By John Nicholson, one of England's few remaining pamphleteers. 52 pages. UK: £1.80; overseas surface: $3.00 (or equivalent).

BACK ISSUES £1.50 / US$3.00 each.
SUBSCRIPTIONS 4 issues £6 / US$12.
8 issues £12 / US$24.

FORTEAN TIMES, 96 MANSFIELD ROAD, LONDON NW3 2HX.

Weird Lives

by Paul Sieveking.

Portrait of Francis Battalia, originally engraved by Hollar in 1641.

Francis Battalia, Stone Eater.

The main account of this prodigious youth is to be found in John Bulwer's *Man Transform'd* (1653) [1]:

"Man naturally both cometh in, and goeth out of the world empty-handed; yet I saw in *London* the other day an *Italian*, one *Francis Battalia* by name, about thirty yeares of Age, who was borne with two stones in one hand, and one in the other; who, as soon as he was borne, having the breast offered unto him, refused to suck; and when they would have fed him with Papp, he utterly rejected that also, whereupon the Midwife and Nurse entring into consideration of the strangenesse of his birth, and refusall of all kinds of nourishment, consulted with some Physicians what they should do in this case. They when they saw the Infant rejected all that they could contrive for nourishment, told the women, that they thought the Child brought its meat with it into the world, and that it was to be nourished with stones, whereupon they wish'd the Nurse to give him one stone in a little drinke, which he very readily tooke into his mouth and swallowed down, and when he had swallowed all the three stones, and began to want his hard-meat, the Physicians advised the nurse to get some pebles, as like those which he was borne with as they could, with the which kind of nourishment he was brought up, and now, in this stone-devouring-age, lest pebles should be too plentifull and cheape, he subsists here among us with the same kind of aliment. His manner is to put three or four stones

AND THE APE BENEFITS FROM THE ARRANGEMENT BY LOOKING EXTREMELY BUSY WHEN TEDIOUS CHORES LOOM!

OI! YOU! HOWS ABOUT COMING OVER HERE AND HELPING THE REST OF US EVOLVE INTO INTELLIGENT CREATURES!

...er... SORRY... HAVE TO DELIVER THIS.... ..hehheh...

THINK THINK PONDER

into a spoone, and so putting them into his mouth together, swallows them all down one after another; then (first spitting) he drinks a glass of beer after them, he devours about half a pecke of these stones every day: and when he chinks upon his stomack, or shakes his body, you may hear the stones rattle as if they were in a sack; all which in twenty foure hours are resolved, and once in three weekes he voids a great quantity of sand by siege; after which digestion of them, he hath a fresh appetite to these stones, as we have to our victuals, and by these, with a cup of Beere, and a pipe of Tobacco, he hath his whole subsistence; He hath attempted to eate meat, and bread, broath, and milke, and such kind of food, upon which other Mortals commonly live; but he could never brook any, neither would they stay with him to do him any good. He is a black swarthish little fellow, active and strong enough, and hath been a Souldier in *Ireland*, where he hath made good use of this property; for, having the advantage of this strange way of alimony, he sold his allowance of provant at great rates; for he told me, that at *Limerick* in *Ireland*, he sold a sixpenny Loafe and two pennyworth of Cheese for twelve shillings six pence. It seems the fellow when he came first over, was suspected for an Impostor, and was by command of the State shut up for a month with the allowance of two pots of Beere, and halfe an ounce of Tobacco every day, but was afterwards acquitted for all suspicion and deceit."

Robert Boyle, the distinguished scientist, mentions Battalia in his *Experimental Philosophy* (Part II, Essay III): "Not long ago, there was here in England a private soldier, very famous for digesting of stones; and a very inquisitive man assures me, that he knew him familiarly, and had the curiosity to keep in his company for twenty-four hours together, to watch him; and not only observed that he ate nothing but stones in that time, but also that his grosser excrement consisted chiefly of a sandy substance, as if the devoured stones had been in his body dissolved, and crumbled into sand."

[1] "Anthropometamorphosis: Man Transform'd: or, the Artificiall Changling Historically presented, In the mad and cruel Gallantry, foolish Bravery, ridiculous Beauty, filthy Finenesse, and loathsome Loveliness of most Nations, fashioning and altering their Bodies from the mould intended by Nature; With Figures of those Transformations, etc." By John Bulwer, London 1653. pp.306-309.

Science Frontiers

Compiled & Annotated by William R.Corliss.

Hypnosis and Memory

Hypnotic hypernesia is the unusually vivid and complete recall of information from memory while under hypnosis. The present article reviews the extensive literature on the subject and the long-standing controversy as to whether hypnosis can enhance memory at all. One fact does seem clear, hypnosis does not help subjects recall nonsense data or information without meaning, such as random numbers and words. When it comes to meaningful phrases, sentences, paragraphs, etc., hypnosis does aid recall to some extent. If the words evoke considerable imagery, as poetry often does, hypnosis seems to help recall even more. Finally, the recall of meaningful visual images and connected series of images is helped most of all by hypnosis. In fact, there is some evidence that eidetic imagery, that vivid, near-total recall of images, which is almost exclusively a talent of childhood, can be recovered by mature subjects under hypnosis. There do not seem to be any theories that explain all these effects of hypnosis on memory (Relinger, Helmut; "Hypnotic Hypernesia," *American Journal of Clinical Hypnosis* 26:212, 1984.) *Of course, memory shorn of hypnotic effects cannot really be explained either. The results of Relinger's survey make one wonder whether the human brain is specially "wired" or built to efficiently handle visual imagery that is 'meaningful' in the context of human experience and theoretical expectations. This kind of construction is quite different from computer memories which process meaningless data as easily as meaningful data. UFOs, sea monsters, N-rays,, etc might just be eidetic images from human memories evoked by certain stimuli and encouraged by suggestion.*

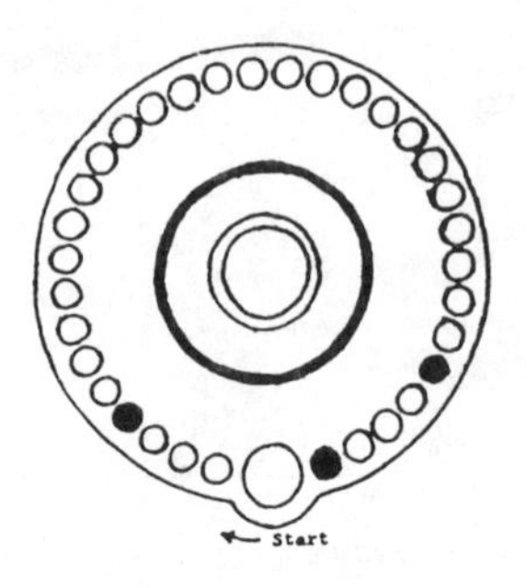

Diagram of the Mallia disk, with intercalation cups in black. Diameter: about 3 ft.

The Mallia Table

The Mallia Table was discovered in the Central Court of the Minoan Palace of Mallia in Crete. It is a large limestone disk 90cm in diameter and 36cm thick. Around its circumference are 33 cups of equal size. A 34th cup is larger and is located in a sort of ear that extends beyond the normal circumference of the disk. The larger cup is oriented due south. The disk is set in the stone pavement of a small terrace that is slightly elevated above the level of the Central Court. This strange monolith, which dates circa 1900-1750 BC, has been a puzzle to scholars since its discovery in 1926 by French excavators.

Herberger's thesis is that the disk is a lunisolar clock. The 33 small cups provide a convenient and symmetrical division of the 99 lunations of the 8-year cycle. By moving markers from cup to cup with each lunation, one could have a fairly accurate lunisolar clock. The 34th cup by virtue of its larger size would announce the need for an intercalated month. This sort of clock, even though arrived at empirically, represents a remarkable innovation for a period almost 4,000 years ago. (Herberger, Charles F.; "The Mallia Table: Kernos or Clock?" *Archaeoastronomy*, 6:114, 1983)

The Inka Road System

An important new archaeological book bears the above title (and alternate spelling of Inca). As one reviewer puts it: "The Imperial Inka road system must rank alongside the Great Wall of China and the Egyptian Pyramids as one of the greatest achievements of any ancient civilization. Yet despite this, relatively little is known about the nature, extent and functioning of this vast communications network." Some impressive statistics: the Inka Road System runs for more than 23,000 kilometers through Peru, Bolivia, Ecuador, Chile and Argentina. Generally, the roads were 11-25 meters wide. They were greatly superior to anything built in Europe at that time. One reviewer notes that many of the so-called Inka highways had a non-Inkan origin – and then leaves us hanging. What pre-Inkan civilization built such roads? (Saunders, Nick; "Monumental Roads," *New Scientist*, p.31, June 8, 1985. Also: Lyon, Patricia J.; "Imperial Connection?" *Science*, 228:1420, 1985.)

Shrimp Trains Are A'Coming

In March's "Gallery" pages of *Discover*, several incredibly colored and patterned shrimp stun the eyes of the reader. Some of these shrimp put the gaudiest butterflies and birds to shame. We won't stop here to dwell on why some shrimp are so colorful while others are so tasty. The anomaly at hand is buried in the caption describing the red-and-white striped peppermint shrimp, which decorates the Great Barrier Reef. It turns out that this shrimp, like the Atlantic spiny lobster, sometimes joins up with others of its species to form long, moving trains or chains of animals. This behaviour remains very puzzling to biologists. ("Shrimp You Won't Find in Your Cocktail," *Discover*, 6:55, March 1985.)

Multiple Whirlwind Patterns

English meteorologists are spending some of the lazy summer days out in the countryside tracking down whirlwind patterns engraved on fields of wheat and other crops. (See FT40,p27 and FT43,p31.) One eye-witness account of the formation of a single spiral pattern has been found. However, the multiple spiral patterns excite the most interest because of their geometric regularity. Between 1980 and 1984, eight quintuplet patterns have been found, consisting of a large central circle and four smaller satellite circles. Triplets were also discovered. Although the origin of the multiplet patterns are still unexplained, some interesting generalizations have emerged: (1) The whirlwinds responsible for the flattened circles of crops have lifetimes of only a few seconds, whereas dust devils may persist for many minutes; (2) These whirlwinds seem to occur around eveningtime instead of during the heat of the day; and (3) They are all anticyclonic, while tornados are almost all cyclonic and true heat whirlwinds are split about evenly in their spin direction. (Meaden, G.T.; "Advances in the Understanding of Whirlwind Spiral Patterns in Cereal Fields," *Journal of Meteorology, UK,* 10:73, 1985.)

Subterranean Electric Currents

We have little appreciation of the immense electrical currents that flow through the rock formations beneath our feet. These "telluric" currents are primarily those induced by the earth's changing magnetic field, as it is affected by the solar wind. Telluric currents do not flow uniformly through the earth's crust. Rather, they seek out low resistance rocks, in accordance with Ohm's Law. Such current concentrations can be detected at the surface with magnetometers.

The present paper announces the discovery of a regional telluric current flowing in the vicinity of the San Francisco Peaks volcanic field in Arizona. The shallow part of the current flows in an unidentifiable "geoelectrical" structure not more than 10 kilometers below the surface. There are no surface hints as to what this geoelectrical structure could be. (Towle, James N., "The Anomalous Geomagnetic Variation Field and Geoelectric Structure Associated with the Mesa Butte Fault System, Arizona," *Geological Society of America, Bulletin,* 95:221, 1984) *Similar anomalous magnetic fields exist in many areas, indicating a vast subterranean system of poorly understood geoeletrical structures. Some of the channelled earth currents are man-made, being the return paths in electrical power transmission systems. The return paths may be far-removed from the actual power lines because they tend to follow the geoelectrical structures.*

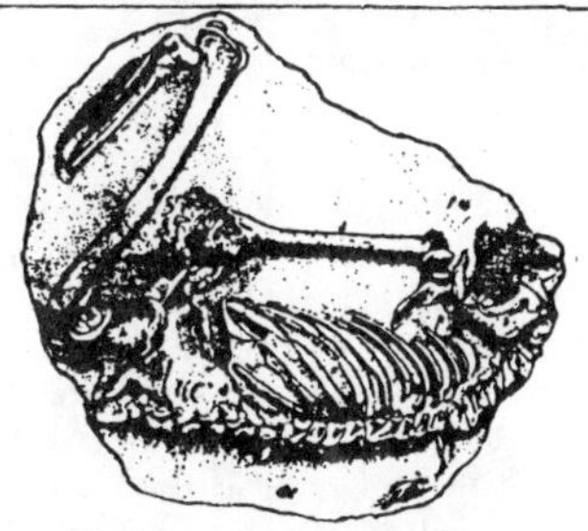

Fossilized human skeleton from Guadeloupe. The Paris specimen.

Back to Guadeloupe Again

Just how old are those modern-looking human skeletons in those chunks of Guadeloupe lime--stone? Opposing views were discussed in FT42,p.33 and FT43, p28. The basic problem is the dating of the limestone in which the skeletons are embedded. If the limestone is truly of Miocene age (about 25 million years old) the presence of human skeletons represents a major scientific anomaly, since modern man apparently arrived on the scene only about 5 million years ago. Most scientists say the limestone is only recently formed beach rock a few hundred years old, and that radioactive dating proves this. Doubters have pointed to 3-million-year-old coral reefs stratigraphically above the limestone. In a recent issue of *Ex Nihilo*, a few more cans of gasoline have been thrown on the fire: (1) The radioactive date usually served up actually came from another island in the area; (2) Beach rock is not now forming at the skeleton site, rather the skeleton limestone is harder than marble and not loosely consolidated beach rock; (4) True Miocene limestone does exist in the area; and (5) Geologists have carefully described and mapped the rest of Guadeloupe but have omitted the skeleton site – presumably because of the anomalies involved. (Tyler, David J., et al; *Ex Nihilo,* 7:41, no.3, 1985.) (Keep tuned to this station and in the interim read Jacques Barzun's *Science: The Glorious Entertainment.)*

False Pregnancies in Males

This is a very rare psychosomatic condition. In the past 45 years, about 100 cases of false pregnancies in females have been reported, but only 3 in males. A fourth has now come to light. It is the story of 40-year-old, married man, who wished to have another child but his wife didn't. Subsequently, the man's abdomen began to protrude and his weight increased by 20 pounds. Symptoms similar to those of morning sickness also developed. The conditions eventually subsided as he and his wife "talked out" their disagreement. The man had a previous history of depression and schizophrenia. (Evans, Dwight Landis; "Pseudocyesis in the Male," *Journal of Nervous and Mental Disease*, 172: 37, 1984.)

Science Frontiers ***is extracted from William Corliss' bimonthly collection of digests from current literature, which is sent free to regular customers of his publications. For more details write to*** **The Sourcebook Project, Box 107, Glen Arm, MD 21057, USA.**

U·F·O Commentary by Nigel Watson

THINGS IN THE AIR

"Heroes in battle with heroes,
And above them the wrathful gods."

Have you heard about the invisible airship? The Ontario, Canada, newspaper, the *St Catherines Standard* of 18 April 1913 (credit: Dwight Whalen) claimed that Captain Faber, MP, told everything he knew about this remarkable craft at a Navy League meeting held in London, England.

Apparently, this airship had already made a 29-hour-long flight with a 28 man crew which covered a distance of 1,600 miles. It was, of course, a German airship. A German officer, who had been on this mission, told Captain Faber all about the wonderful new inventions it carried to help it reconnoitre enemy landscapes without being detected.

First of all, it could eject vapour so that it could be hidden from view – presumably people on the ground would mistake it for a noisy cloud. To aid the helmsman in his navigation of the craft a map of the countryside automatically unrolled to show him exactly where he was positioned (surprisingly the Japanese are still working on such a device for car drivers!). And, finally, it carried a camera with a Goerz lens which enabled the crew to take snapshots of the land beneath them.

To drive home the danger of such aircraft the newspaper added that, 'Germany has now 38 airships, and 30 more on order'.

In Britain a phantom airship scare had swept across the country throughout January, February and March 1913, which amply revealed the fear the British had of German aeronautical superiority. Even the most ardent sceptics (the sort of people who might today edit *Magonia*) thought that Britain should do something about defending the country from aerial attack.

The Scarborough *Daily Post* of 20 February 1913 (credit: Granville Oldroyd) contains a summary of an article by Mr Alfred Stead published in his magazine *Review of Reviews*. Under the headline 'What German Airships Can Do' it is noted that 'Today the danger of this country is not on the sea nor on the land – it is very decidedly in the air'. Then the capabilities of the German airships are detailed. Reading them it is likely that Mr Stead was the source of Captain Faber's invisible airship story, rather than a treasonous German officer.

After informing us that one German airship can carry 27 tons a distance of 1,550 miles at a speed of 50mph, and stay aloft for 4 days, the author then highlights the kind of armaments it could carry. Besides several machine guns, the vehicle could deliver 2,000 lbs of incendiary bombs very accurately to its target because German 'bomb dropping now approaches an exact science'. Not content with such revelations, the author goes on to tell us about the marvellous bombs the Germans have developed for the benefit of Britain. This weaponry included a fire bomb which illuminates its own flight down to the ground and continues to burn after it has struck the target so that the airship gunners could see what they had hit. Another bomb carried a poisonous gas which on impact would kill anyone in a 100 yard radius. To make the airship invisible whilst it unleashed these deadly toys, dense, heavy smoke which would sink slowly towards the earth could be dispersed in great quantities.

These features and the fact that Germany intended to spend £1,000,000 on airship development, lead Stead to say that every town in England should collect £1,000 each to pay for an aeroplane which they could present with the necessary spare parts to the Army. In addition, larger towns should collect money in order to buy airships.

As I have already noted (in *MUFOB* No.10 and *Magonia* 3) during the British 1909 phantom airship scare similar concerns were expressed about the German threat. This prompted the *Daily Mail, Hull Packet* and *East Yorkshire and Lincolnshire Courier* of 21 May 1909 to publish the following (humorous, I think) proclamation:

Notice is hereby given. The Lords of the Admiralty offer a reward of £100 to the first person who sights an airship, and doesn't have a fit; £500 to the person who doesn't run away; and £1,000 to the person who controls himself sufficiently to send a telegram to the War Office. A pension for life will be given to the sighter if the airship is of German manufacture.

The *Sheffield Daily Telegraph* of 21 May 1909 (credit: David Clarke) even suggested that the Suffragettes would swarm down from the rope-ladders of airships brandishing crowbars. Crying out 'Votes for Women! Votes for Women! Hark the glad triumphal sound', they would hook Mr Asquith (the Prime Minister) with a balloon anchor and fly him away. But that seems to have been wishful thinking!

Sir George Doughty MP, however, took the matter seriously. A report in the *Grimsby News* of 28 December 1909 informs us that he had a rowdy election meeting in Grimsby. Whilst insisting that we spend more on the navy to protect ourselves from the Germans, a voice from the audience said "speak the truth" to which Sir George replied, "Yes, that's another German or some foreigner". The 'voice' then aksed "Are we all Germans?" Sir George answered, "You soon will be, if you don't mind." When he was asked to talk about the Budget, Sir George stated that "You have got to listen to what I like to speak about." As the report noted, "it was quite an entertaining meeting".

At a Liberal party demonstration reported in the Grimsby *News* of 20 August 1909, the Tory ideology of Sir George's was derided. Mr. F. Maddison, Labour MP for Burnley said:

"Why, if those Englishmen who saw those wretched airships were typical of our race, the Germans need not bring many battalions, for we were done already."

Whilst Mr Tom Wintringham, the prospective Liberal candidate for Grimsby, said that "every unnecessary Dreadnought (battleship) they got postponed the possibility of social reform... Do not let them lose their heads and, by losing their heads, lose social reform."

Seventy-four years later there are just as many political leaders more concerned about war than social reform. The only difference is that phantom airships have turned into flying saucers; and Dreadnoughts and airships have turned into cruise missiles and nuclear warheads.

Letters

Continued from p3.

routes to get information to Dot that Saturday, including talking with Brenda Butler, our other author. Whilst Brenda and I chatted another voice came on the line and proceeded to join in our conversation. Then our line was cut dead in the midst of discussion, although I got the dial tone and I had made the call. (This being so, Brenda could not have accidentally cut us off and I knew that I had not done so.)

We spoke again later, with no problems. But on another call (about a ghost investigation in Yorkshire) two voices came onto the phone and began a four way debate. Obviously this was a crossline, although the call was from London and I was speaking to Sheffield! Resolving to call the engineers on Monday I quit for the Saturday night and no more calls occurred.

By Sunday lunchtime I was mildly intrigued as to why there had been no calls now for about 20 hours. The phone *was* working, as I had made one outgoing call and tried again to get Dot, without success. Then my brother turned up and said he was concerned enough at our not answering the phone (as he knew us to be in) to have driven all the way from Manchester to find out why.

Eventually we discovered, by getting a neighbour to call, then trying again and picking up the phone anyway, when it did not ring, that calls were coming through and it was just the bell which was not working. So, I picked up the phone to have a look, and the whole thing promptly fell to pieces!

I spent the next hour putting it back together again and discovered that there were a few screws loose. This had broken the bell circuit connection and led to total collapse when I had unwisely moved the instrument. Once all tightened up the phone worked perfectly and still does. The engineers found no problems and the cross-line effects have not returned, but obviously were nothing to do with a loose bell.

A few hours later when "Unfair Exchanges" came on, with its constant motif of telephonic malevolence, I knew exactly how Julie Walters must have felt.

Anybody who studies synchronicity (as I do) knows that the act of collating coincidences generates coincidences in your own life. I have been told (in one book review) that I have an obsession with them and tend to make too much out of nothing. Perhaps so – although its darned good fun anyway. But I do wonder if the process of making a phone call to advise someone to watch a television programme about paranormal effects involving telephones did not somehow (in the mind of our great cosmic joker) create paranormal effects.

Maybe I just asked for it!

Jenny Randles
21 Whittlewood Close,
Gorse Covert, Warrington,
Cheshire WA3 6TU.

[When the editorial team of FT attended a preview of 'Unfair Exchanges', we were surprised to note the lack of any acknowledgements whatever. We put it to the producer, Kenith Trodd, that, from the context, interested viewers will be convinced FT is a fictional magazine, which might prejudice our own publicity in the long term. Although the BBC did not screen the full notice that we hoped for, they did include a brief – almost subliminal! – acknowledgement among the credits, in the broadcast version, and for that we're grateful, even if the expected flood of interest has not yet materialized. See our review of the play, FT43 p26. –Ed.]

News from the Wild Frontiers

In the wake of wolf-boy Shamdeo's death in February 1985 [FT44,p5], it seems appropriate to survey the recent news of *Homo sapiens ferus*, and the stirring record of the noble beasts that foster our young round the planet.

Kunu Masela with Poppy, his canine mother [Photo © National Enquirer *27 Dec 1983.]*

■ In January 1982, an Indian army expedition, trekking 2,000 miles along the lower Himalayas, encountered a group of naked people above the snow line. The expedition had crossed the forests of Geeling, and were trudging through 10 to 16 feet of snow covering the 14,000 foot Chetak pass near Rai village, on the border of Arunachal Pradesh with Bhutan, when they saw two women running away. They were naked, with Mongoloid features and long hair. Once they were convinced that the soldiers were not hostile, they invited them back to their cave. The men were also naked. The deputy leader of the expedition, Captain Harbhajan Singh Chauhan, told UNI wire services that these cave people ate raw flesh, not knowing how to cook food, or even how to make fire.

One of the world's leading specialists in Himalayan ethnography, Professor Gerald D. Berreman of Berkeley, was quick with the skeptical retort: "It is inconceivable that any group of people in the world who have existed in the past 200,000 years don't know the use of fire and don't know about cooking. The army must have been seeing the Yeti and not human beings." The 'raw' meat might actually have been dried, he suggested; adding that the only humans who go naked in the snow are yogis and acestics. . . who presumably don't renounce cooking . . .questions and answers go begging, the sign of a stirling fortean puzzle. (UNI) 20 Jan; Calcutta *Statesman*, 21 Jan; Philadelphia *Daily News*, 22 Jan; Albuquerque (NM) *Journal,* 23+25 Jan; Houston (TX) *Chronicle*, 25 Jan 1982.

■ In March 1982, a wildman was found by charcoal and wood gatherers in the rugged Lambwe Valley Forest on the eastern shore of Lake Victoria, about 175 miles northwest of Nairobi. He was carrying the tattered remains of a blanket, and was taken to the Homa Bay hospital nearby, where he was named 'John'. He was about 26, and ate bananas like a monkey, skin and all, as well as meat on the bone and leaves. He shunned vegetables, and when he drank from a bowl he rotated it to ensure that he drank from all sides. He preferred squatting to sitting, even sleeping in that posture. Dr Paul Maundu, the District Health Officer of Homa Bay, said John had "nibbling silly behaviour" with fast monkey-like movements, and that it was not impossible that he had been abandoned as a child and raised by monkeys. He communicated with grunts, quick animal-like gestures and a few sounds that seemed related to words in the languages of the Kuria and Kisii tribes of the area. He spent his time in the hospital yard gathering wood and leaves. (UPI) Rome (OH) *Herald-Star*, Lincoln (NB) *Journal, D.Telegraph,* etc., 6 May 1982.

■ Joel Zacarias, 2, a starving slum child in the outskirts of Manila, Philippines, was nursed back to life by a mongrel dog that allowed him to suckle her milk for more than a year, according to the *Weekly World News* (17 Aug 1982). Adults who tried to interfere were snarled off. The dog came every day to suckle Joel, who would sleep in the afternoon with his head resting on the dog. He was eventually taken to a rehabilitation clinic. The sounds he made were identical to a dog's bark or growl, and he bit and clawed in canine fashion.

■ Back to Kenya for another boy-and-dog story. Kunu Masela, 6, had been seen for three years scavenging for food round the town of Machakos with a dog. Eventually a Mrs Grace Kubuu realised that he was never seen with adult humans, and asked him where he lived. "With Poppy" was all he would say. One evening she followed them out into the bush and saw the dog dragging together some banana leaves to make a bed for them.

The local press ran the story, after which his real mother came forward. Mrs Rukia Ali Murefu, 29, a coffee plantation worker who had moved to Nairobi, said that her husband had left her when Kunu was born, and she had struggled for three years to care for the child. She was very poor, and eventually abandoned him in the bush. "I knew that Kunu would be cared for by God – and I was right." "Poppy my mother. Poppy give me milk" Kunu told a reporter. David Barritt in the *National Enquirer* (27 Dec 1983) reported that the boy was in a juvenile home run by the government, and Poppy was being cared for by Muthua Nzoica, a market trader in Machakos, who hoped that boy and dog could be reunited.

Imiyati, the Indonesian feral girl [Photo © News of the World *13 Nov 1983.]*

■ In the Autumn of 1983, hunters discovered a naked 12-year-old girl in a swamp in southern Sumatra. At first they thought she was an orang-utang, because she was covered in moss and couldn't talk. It turned out that her name was Imiyati and she had not been seen since February 1977, when she went on a fishing trip with her younger sister and three other children. While crossing a river, their craft capsized in the strong current, and the four other children were drowned. Imiyati was given up for lost, presumed dead, but somehow she survived and was only 12 miles from her home when she was found 6 years later. This was the story reported in the British press on 28 Oct 1983 (*Express, Mirror, Star* & *Sun.*)

Many details differ in two subsequent reports. In the *News of the World* (13 Nov 1983) the girl is called Emmiyati, and is 18 years old. When found "she was naked, with thorns matted in her hair. Her teeth had become razor sharp, her fingernails were like three-inch claws, and she walked in ape fashion. She had forgotten how to talk, laugh or even cry." Her family had spent months looking for her. In the intervening six years they had moved 120 miles away, but one of their other daughters heard about the discovery of the jungle girl, went to see her, and knew instantly it was her sister. Her father is named as Firdaus, her mother Hotomoa. She looked no more than 10, and was only 4ft 6ins tall.

In the American tabloid, the *Globe* (22 Nov 1983), the girl is 12-year-old Imiyati again, but was swept from the family raft by a giant wave two miles out to sea, and couldn't swim. Before her capture, she had been seen swinging in the trees with a pack of apes. Her diet was entirely fruit and leaves. An 'official' stated: "she is watched constantly, but escapes and climbs trees to screetch for her ape family." According to hunters who patrolled the area where she was found, the apes were going berserk looking for their lost sister. Sounds like sub-editing embroidery to me.

■ Six Christian children aged between 3 and 15 lived in a cave eating only wild fruit and berries in Lebanon's central mountains for 75 days after their mother was killed and their father vanished during the fighting between Druze and Christian militias in September 1983. A Druze patrol found them on 24 November and took them to the Red Cross. (Reuter) *D.Telegraph*, 28 Nov 1983.

■ Mrs Shirley Austin, 37, was found in a barn three miles from her home in Claverdon, Warwickshire, in August 1984. She was covered in bruises and scratches, had lost two stone in weight and could hardly stand. She had survived for four weeks on wild fruit and water from animal troughs. She vanished from home on 11 July, after telling her husband and daughters that she was going to post a letter. *D.Express*, 7 Aug 1984.

CHO-LEE

■ Six weeks later, Thomas Mazvipedza, 2, disappeared from the outskirts of his village near Battlefields, 110 miles west of Harare in Zimbabwe. The next morning, his parents consulted a spirit medium who directed them to a hill 15 miles away, police said. There they found baboon tracks, which led the searchers to Thomas, lying between two rocks, stripped of his clothes but asleep and unhurt. Winona (MN) *News*, 22 Sept 1984.

■ In FT42 (p9) we reported the discovery in early 1984 of a 7-year-old 'monkey girl' in Sierra Leone. I suspect that the anonymous tale of the Gabon Tarzan in the *Weekly World News* (8 May 1984) is a recycling of this case – it reads too much like a novelette. Anyway, let me summarize:

A team of German geologists searching for uranium deposits in the republic of Gabon in West Africa encountered a tall white man "with ice-blue eyes and a long mane of platinum blond hair", dressed in a hide loin cloth and surrounded by apes. He had a large sheath knife at his hip and a smaller one strapped to his right leg. The team were unable to communicate with him.

Making enquiries, the Germans found a tribal elder who told them that the jungle man had crashed into the Ogooue River in a small plane with his family when he was a baby. Three adults, one a woman, were killed in the crash. The plane drifted ashore and the baby's cries could be heard that night. But when the wreckage was examined, only the three corpses were there. The elder said that the child was often seen in the arms of a she ape as he suckled at her breast. The elder took the Germans to see the decaying aircraft wreck with the bones of three people still inside. About as likely as the lost London tube train full of skeletal passengers in Victorian clothes. . .

■ Chinese doctors were studying the case of a 10-year-old peasant girl in Liaoning province who lived with pigs, according to a report in the *Canton Evening News* which reached Beijing on 29th December 1984.

She was suckled by sows, shared their swill and slept in their sty at nights. "The pigs never bite her and, in fact, the temperamental porkers had only to hear her cry and they would come running to her side" said the report. When neighbours tried to tear her away from the pigs, she screamed. Her speech was unclear and she grunted and snorted when hungry. (Reuters) *Guardian, D.Star*, 29 Dec; St Louis *Post-dispatch*, 30 Dec 1984.

More details (though uncorroborated) appeared in a report by Derek Clontz in the *Weekly World News* (29 Jan 1985). Animal behaviour expert Dr Chou Lai-Myung said that tests indicated that the girl, who was called Cho-Lee, had normal or even above normal intelligence, and appeared to think and act like a pig by choice. She continued to push food away with her forehead, unless it was spoiled rice and vegetable leftovers served in a trough. She was healthy, weighing 10 to 15 pounds more than the average for her age, and appeared to have no nutritional deficiencies. She had three normal brothers and a twin sister.

Her father, Chiang Nang-Lo, said that pigs fascinated her as a baby, and once she was old enough to walk she couldn't be kept away from the sty. The pigs wouldn't let her family near her, and they gave up trying to get her back. She lived exclusively on sows' milk until she was almost five. Then she graduated to pig swill. She was always first at the trough when it was filled in the mornings. At least two contingents of outraged villagers tried to separate her from the pigs, but on each occasion they encircled her, daring anyone to come near. We are not told how she was eventually taken away. The father concluded that if the doctors could do anything with her, he would gladly bring her back home; and if they couldn't, there would always be a home for her out back in the sty.

Paul Sieveking

Tales from Finland.

HOLES IN THE ICE

A bubbling hole, 8 feet by 10 feet, appeared in the 8 inches thick ice of Säkkiä Lake near Länkipohja in the district of Längelmaki, southern Finland, on 8 December 1983. It was carefully marked, as there is a lot of motor traffic over the lake in winter. Master builder Olavi Tuominen, who reported it to the police, said the oval opening had clear, even borders and bubbled mainly in the middle. The water at that point was 26 feet deep. Police stated that there were no traces or tracks near the opening.

Villagers in nearby Hiukkaa had noticed whirling lights in the sky in the previous few days, and naturally connected the phenomena. A similar strange hole had appeared the previous winter in a lake near Virrat, among other places. Jämsä *Koillis-Häme*, 10 Dec; *Helsingen Sanomat*, 13 Dec 1983.

It was happening again in the winter of 1984. The *Courrier de l'Ouest* (22 Feb 1985) reported that the Finnish army had been sent to find out about the strange luminous phenomena and unexplained hole in the frozen lake about 43 miles east of Helsinki. According to witnesses, a strange light appeared at the beginning of the week, and then a hole in the ice, 12 inches wide. A group of military *plongeurs* (presumably skin-divers rather than dish-washers) arrived on 21 February to sound the water. Late in 1984, a Soviet missile crashed on another Finnish lake. [For further ice holes, see FT24 p41.]

Tiina Lamminen looks on as her uncle Heikki Karlsson holds up the hawk that attacked her. [Photo ©Ilta-Sanomat, *Helsinki.]*

HAWK ATTACK

Three-year-old Tiina Lamminen was playing in the courtyard of her grandmother's house in Liljendahl, near Loviisa on the south coast of Finland. A goshawk circled a long time above her. After she went inside, it kept an eye on the courtyard from a high fir. Later, Tiina was playing in the living room, with her back to the window, when the hawk crashed through the 3mm thick glass and grabbed her head with its claws. The glass broke around the edges, splinters flying onto the kitchen table more than 16 feet away.

Tiina's mother Alli heard the bang, rushed in, grabbed the bird and threw it against the wall. Its claws had pulled out a tuft of Tiina's flaxen hair, leaving a visible wound. The bird was stunned and her father covered it with a jacket, keeping it quiet with a wooden brush. Luckily for Tiina, she was not facing the bird which might have gone for her eyes – or she might have been hurt by flying glass. Her uncle Heikki Karlsson, an experienced bird hunter, supposed that the bird took her blond hair for a prey. The bird was to be

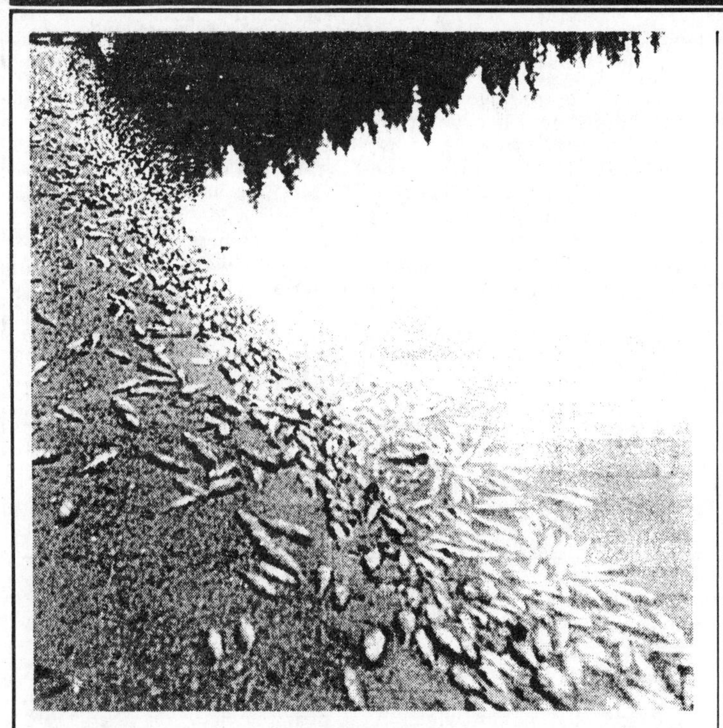

A layer of decaying perch covering the shore of Niemisvesi Lake, Finland. [Photo ©Mika Putro, Helsingen Sanomat.]

stuffed and added to the collection of the Karlsson family.

The curator of the Natural History Museum in nearby Porvoo, Raimo Luoma, said he had never heard of anything like it, and proposed two even more outlandish alternative explanations. Either the hawk was chasing another bird which dodged aside just before impact with the window; or it was confused by the reflection in the glass. Helsinki *Ilta-Sanomat*, 28 Aug 1984. For more avine aggro, see EAGLE ATTACKS on p5

FISH MASSACRE

Something odd was going on in Niemisvesi Lake, Ähtäri, central Finland, in the summer of 1984. In August, masses of dead ruffs were washed up, and waves of other species of small fish followed, ending up with perch in October. Quite large quantities too: farmer Timo Karkonen noted 500 kilos of fish on one beach in a single weekend. Investigations by the State Institute of Veterinary Science showed that the livers and air bladders of the fish had burst, and coagulated blood was found in the cavities, indicating a sudden change of pressure.

The lake is renowned for its clear and oxygen-filled water. There are no diseases, no sewer has its outlet there, and the algae are sound and healthy. In general the lake is very shallow, but it sinks to 47 feet in places. The official assumption is that someone had been fishing with explosives, removing the larger fish, and leaving the smaller ones to drift ashore. But police could find no witness among the angry local people to any explosion, which would have had to be quite powerful to cause the kind of damage seen in the fish. No boat had been seen, and a small fleet would have been needed to collect all the big fish from such a large lake, The nights are very dark in August (no Northern Lights) so the operation would have had to be carried out in daylight... *Helsingen Sanomat*, 6 Oct 1984. Our thanks to Tuuri Heporauta for the translations, and to Sven Rosen for the translations of *Nordic News* (FT43 p45).

AN INTERNATIONAL INCIDENT

A Finnish tourist was walking down a Stockholm street with a relative on 17 July 1984. Suddenly, a knife-wielding Swede stepped in front of them and raised his weapon threateningly. The Finn fled into the road and was run over by a Dane. He escaped with a broken leg. *Helsingen Sanomat*, 19 July 1984.

EASY MONEY

In 1917 or 1918 a Finnish woman, Mrs Ester Hallio, nee Jäntti, was witness to the following remarkable events; this is a paraphrase of her account.

"I was studying at the Athenaeum and lived with my fellow student Miss Inni Siegberg at her parents' home. The family was away in the country, except for Inni's sister, a nurse working at the eye clinic. I was at home with one of my fellow students. It was autumn, and the wind was blowing furiously. We started to tell ghost stories. Suddenly a faint click was heard, and then another one. We looked around and found two large overcoat buttons on the floor. We suspected each other, protesting that this was not a proper time for jokes.

The next click sounded clear, metallic. A coin had fallen on the parquet floor, rolling and revolving before coming to rest. More coins fell at intervals of five, ten or fifteen minutes. Pale with fear we went next door to ask an Estonian lady to join us and witness the miracle. By now coins were falling in the adjoining dining room, which also had a parquet floor, making the clicking noises clearly audible. With growing fright we went to fetch Mr Arttu Brummer who had a planning office with Mr Topi Viksted nearby. They returned with a third gentleman named Vainio.

The Estonian lady suggested that her brother-in-law, a deeply religious man, should be asked to stop the phenomenon. He came with his Bible, read some incantations and commanded the phenomenon to cease, but after his "Amen", a coin fell on his Bible, he panicked and escaped. Some of the gentlemen suggested we call in Professor Arvi Grotenfeldt, a member of the Society of Sciences, and he came together with a couple of his students. The professor compiled a report, including the names of all the witnesses, which is still in the Society's archives.

The coins continued to pour down. There was already more than ten marks, a considerable amount at that time. We placed them on the mantelpiece. We dared not stay overnight, and spent the night in our friends' office.

In the morning the coins were still on the mantelpiece. Inni's sister, the nurse, who had been at work all night, telephoned and told us that she had been disturbed during the night at the clinic by curious noises resembling the tinkling of coins. We told her what had happened, and at that moment another fifty penny coin fell onto the telephone table. As soon as Inni arrived, we went to the Bank of Finland to show the money. The coins were genuine. As nobody claimed them, we went to Bronda (a popular restaurant) with all our friends to celebrate, and had coffee with apple pie. Arttu Brummer thought the coins were fine, but that we should have asked for some rustling (banknotes) too!"

SOURCE:
Ihmistiedon rajamailla (On the fringe of human knowledge), edited by Mrs Aikki Perttola-Flink, published by Tammi, Helsinki, Second impression 1972. Thanks to Tuuri Heporauta.

HELSINKI MISSILE

At 9.50pm on Friday, 30 August 1985, the 45 bus was at the Ruskeasuo roundabout in Helsinki. There was a loud crash at the back of the crowded bus and a missile whizzed between the passengers, showering them with glass. It made a fist-sized hole in the thick plate-glass on entering and a hole about one foot six inches wide in the window opposite (see picture).

Police thought it was a stone, though none was found; as there was no injury they took little interest in the case. Our correspondent Tuuri Heporauta comments that it looks like a gunshot from the pictures, but the calibre must have been enormous, and such weapons are not at large in Finland. A single rifle theft from an armoury is an instant news item. Helsinki *Iltalehti* 31 Aug 1985.

The hole made by the missile leaving the bus. [Photo by Antti Kauranne.]

Soviet Signs & Wonders

In February 1984, the Russians set up a commission to investigate all sightings of moving objects or flashing lights in the sky, headed by Pavel Popovitch, a retired Soviet cosmonaut, announced *Trud*, the organ of the Trade Union Council. Pavel said that most reports could be explained but that scientists had been disturbed by an event on 27 March 1983: A wingless, cigar-shaped object as big as a jumbo jet zig-zagged over the city of Gorky and was tracked for forty minutes on Gorky airport radar before vanishing. Observers said it made sharp turns impossible for conventional aircraft. (R) *International Herald Trib.* + *Guardian* 30 May 1984.

Further UFO sightings are listed in the *National Enquirer* (4 Sept 1984), but we have seen no corroborative reports. We give them here anyway, subject to the customary FT *caveat lector:*

○ 21 June 1983 – Another cigar-shaped something circled for 18 minutes over strategic nuclear research installations in the city of Dubno.

○ 20 September 1983 – A monstrous 'jellyfish' surrounded by a glowing fiery mist hovered over the city of Petrozavodsk for 14 minutes, sending down a shower of what was described as 'luminous rain'. Panic erupted in the streets as many terrified residents tried to flee. Army troops were ordered to seal off the local railway station and restore order.

○ 2 December 1983 – A squadron of seven luminous, globe-shaped UFOs in V-formation circled the city of Minsk and was seen by hundreds of people.

○ 12 January 1984 – A similar squadron of UFOs flew over the city of Vladimir.

○ 6 February 1984 – Dozens of frightened eye-witnesses described an eerie formation of triangular and round lights flying across the night sky over Gorky.

○ 26 February 1984 – A huge explosion in the atmosphere, about 60 miles above Siberia, in the same area as the Tunguska mystery explosion of 1908.

○ 14 March 1984 – Six UFOs, described as a brilliant orange 'string of sausages', zipped through the skies over Sverdlovsk, then suddenly changed colour simultaneously to fluorescent blue, red, and then back to orange.

■ Six days after this last sighting, a huge earthquake (7.1 on Richter scale) struck the Soviet central Asian republics of Uzbekistan and Turkmenistan, shaking towns and cities on a 500 mile line from Tashkent in the south-west to Ashkhabad on the Soviet-Iran border. Older buildings were destroyed in the Uzbek city of Bukhara, the Turkmen city of Chardzhou, but damage was heaviest in the desert town of Gazli (population 10,000) in the middle of a natural gas field. 30,000 tents and 50 field kitchens were set up there shortly afterwards: no figures of casualties were announced. Tashkent and Samarkand were also shaken, as was the Iranian city of Mashhad.

Tashkent was struck by the biggest earthquake of recent Soviet history in 1966, while 10,000 were made homeless in Gazli in the quake of May 1976.

On 29 (or 30?) October, a strong quake struck the Soviet republic of Tadzhikistan, causing much injury and damage. It measured 7 on the 12-point Soviet scale (the March quake had been over 9 on this scale.) (AP) *Standard* 20 Mar; *Guardian* 21 Mar; *Telegraph* 21+23 Mar, and (R) 31 Oct 1984.

The highest active volcano of the Eurasian subcontinent, Klyuchevskaya Sopka, 15,912 feet, in the Kamchatka peninsula, was erupting and sending up ash and gases in early September, announced *Pravda;* (R) *Telegraph* 8 Sept 1984. The following month, Soviet geologists announced that Mount Elbrus, a dormant volcano and the highest peak in the Caucasus, was slowly building up for its first eruption in a thousand years. *Standard* 17 Oct 1984.

■ A UFO event which got wide press coverage happened, presumably, in January 1985, and was reported in the newspaper *Trud* on 30 January. The four-man crew of a TU-134 airliner with 27,000 flying hours between them were flying from Tbilisi, Georgia, to Tallinn, Estonia, on a clear night (Aeroflot flight 8352). At 4.10am, about 75 miles from Minsk, capital of the White Russian Republic, they saw what looked like a large unblinking yellow star which shone three beams of light onto the earth from a height of 25 to 30 miles (one report says 40 miles). The brightest beam formed a 'radiantly luminous cone' of white light which lit up houses and roads.

A ray of light from the object suddenly lit up the plane. "The pilots saw a dazzling white spot surrounded by concentric coloured rings" reported *Trud*. The object "flared up, leaving a green cloud in its stead", which descended with extraordinary speed and crossed the flight path, dropped below, then came up level at 33,000 feet and accompanied the plane at 300mph for the rest of the flight. Passengers also spotted the cloud, which changed shape into a plum, then a square, and finally 'solidified' as a giant, needle-nosed, wingless aircraft with a curious animal-like tail illuminated by a green and yellow light; and it was seen by the crew of another airliner flying in the opposite direction. Ground control at Riga and Vilnius picked up two blips when flight schedules showed only one aircraft airborne at the time, and tracked them all the way to Tallinn, where the intruder was again picked up by radar.

Nikolai N. Zheltukhin, a vice-chairman of the Commission on Anomalous Phenomena and a member of the Academy of Sciences, told *Trud* that the occurrence "is indeed of interest, although the Commission already knows of similar cases." Skeptics at NASA claim that strategic weapon tests that violate the 1963 outer space treaty are concealed as UFO sightings – but the Minsk encounter seems too outlandish to fit this scenario, *New York Times, D.Telegraph*, Greensboro NC *News & Record*, 31 Jan; *D.Mirror, D.Record*, 1 Feb; *S.Times*, 10 Mar 1985.

According to the report in the *New York Times*, a 1976 underground document attributed to a professor at Moscow's Aviation Institute, referred to 300 UFO sightings. The report was not confirmed, but the professor in question did not publicly refute it. The most dramatic sightings mentioned are a 1961 UFO that appeared above a railway crossing stalling engines for 45 minutes, one in 1976 that hovered for 36 hours over Nalchik, and an object that, like the latest one, trailed an airliner from Vorkuta all the way to Omsk.

■ The Soviet Union is being terrorized by wolf-dog hybrids, who are now well established in parts of the Russian Republic, Siberia, the Buryat Republic and Kazakhstan. They are much bolder than the country's 60,000 wolves, who avoid humans. They make dens near highways, in old farm buildings, and on suburban construction sites. A wolf-like creature was recently reported 'watching traffic' on the edge of central Moscow. *Observer* 28 Oct 1984.

Two wolves are said to be living in Moscow Park and scavenging city dustbins by night, and a female badger was found in the basement of St Basil's cathedral in Red Square. "A fox stalking wild ducks on Moscow River was shot dead outside the capital's biggest hotel, the Rossya", reported the *Komsomolskaya Pravda*. "Owls and hawks regularly visit the city and there are roes, muskrats, martins and minks." Elks and wild boars are also rampant. "Recently, three wild boars panicked when chased through the city streets and rushed into an apartment house and got to the fourth floor before they were caught."

■ Wild boar are also roaming the streets of Turin in Italy, and 400 have been killed in the surrounding countryside. City councillor Teoboldo Fengolio believes the boar population has exploded because wild females are mating with domestic pigs, thus producing three litters a year instead of one. *S.Express*, 18 Nov 1984 & 6 Jan 1985.

■ The Russian winter of 1984-5 was the worst since 1979, when temperatures fell to minus 40c and the huge public thermometer in Gorky Street, Moscow, broke under the strain. The cold spell this time swept across the whole country, bringing emergencies to sub-tropical places like Alma Ata with the temperature at minus 30c for days on end. Blizzards covered the entire country with six inches of snow. A shortage of anti-freeze in Moscow led drivers to improvise with vodka in their washer-reservoirs. Enterprising drunks developed complex home-made tools to get at it; so drivers added detergent, but the drunks persevered, frothing green at the mouth. *Guardian*, 14 Jan 1985.

■ The search for the Soviet wildman continues. Sometime between 10 and 15 December, 1984, an article was published in the daily *Socialist Industry* by Andrei Kozlov, a medical worker from Perm, who had led expeditions of the Alpine Expedition Department of the Soviet Geographical Society for 13 years. Since the 1960's the Department has gathered information on the 'relict hominid' from uninhabited regions of the Caucasus and the Tyan-Shan mountains. Kozlov said there have been 5,000 sightings of the creature, and about 50 plaster casts have been made of its footprints.

Based on the sightings and other research, Kozlov believes the creatures are about 6 feet 6 inches tall, weigh about 440 pounds, and have a long stride, up to 5 feet. They live alone in the mountain forests, shunning groups, and sleep in the day on beds of branches. Towards dusk, they go hunting. They are not aggressive, and there are only five occasions on record when they have attacked humans, always in self-defence. Kozlov hopes for a face-to-face meeting, having lured one with 'aromatic bait'. He then plans to tame him – or her. *Detroit Free Press*, 17 Dec; *Int. Herald Tribune*, 18 Dec 1984.

■ Finally, we read that the new Soviet leader, Mr Gorbachev, has called for the party to rid itself of 'alien phenomena', whatever that means! *D.Telegraph*, 1 April 1985.

FORTY TWO YEARS IN THE WILDERNESS

Karp Lykov (or Lyokov) began his flight from civilization in 1922 for religious reasons. His extreme Christian fundamentalism, based on teachings from before the reign of Peter the Great (1672-1725), whom he described as his enemy, called on him to shun all contact with other people. Moving from village to village during the next decade with his wife Akulina and their two small children, he finally left society in 1936 after his house was attacked by a gang.

He retreated to the wilds of the Siberian Taiga, and built a log cabin into the side of a hill near the Abakan river. It was 220 miles to the nearest village, through dense forest. Two more children were born in the wild, and his wife died in the 1950s. The Lykovs lived without meeting another soul for 42 years, surviving waist-deep snow and temperatures of minus 50 degrees centigrade. They had no books or entertainment, except for an old bible – on discovery, the children could read, but their speech was difficult to understand. They had no proper footwear, and dressed in old sacking. They lived on potatoes, onions and turnips from their garden and nuts and berries from the forest. They slept on dry leaves and made fire by rubbing stones together. Lykov and his sons grew long shaggy beards, in defiance of Peter the Great's edict against beards.

Karp Lykov, who has shunned civilization.

Agafya Lykov, who had never seen civilization.

According to the account in the *Globe*, they had somehow tamed the surrounding animals. The only trouble came from a bear that ravaged their food supply, and which they were obliged to kill with spears and stones.

In 1978, four Soviet geologists on their way to Siberian oil deposits by helicopter discovered the "Stone Age family", who had never heard of World War Two. The daughters were frightened and prayed hysterically. As the news spread round the region, many recalled the famous legend of the White Guards officer who killed his elder brother and eloped with his widow into the forest.

Their discovery by the outside world was disastrous for the Lykovs. The two sons, Savin, 56, and Dmitri, 40, died within a few weeks of each other in the autumn of 1981 from a mysterious intestinal ailment, and Natalia, 46, from pneumonia. In October 1982, when the story appeared in the western press, the only surviving members of the family were 84-year-old Karp himself, white-bearded and exceptionally vigorous for his age, and his daughter Agafya, 38. They were still living in the log cabin.

Komsomolskaya Pravda, the Young Communist League newspaper, published a book-length account of the Lykovs by Vasily Peskov, and initiated a nationwide debate on whether they should be forced to rejoin society and enjoy the dubious benefits of 'civilisation'. Karp Lykov said the most difficult aspect of their spartan existence had been the absence of salt. *Standard*, 11 Oct; *Omaha World Herald*, Houston *Chronicle*, 21 Oct; *D. Telegraph, Weekly News*, 23 Oct; *Shropshire Star*, 2 Nov; *Globe*, 16 Nov 1982.

Golden Oldies

The following wonderful tale, alas unreferenced, comes from an album of Nessie clippings made in the 1930's, found under some floorboards and presented to the FT Archives by Bruce Chatterton.

GIANT FLY

"Pursued by British Warships"

A story of how British warships pursued a giant fly across the North Sea, and finally shot it down, is told by a Bulgarian paper (says Reuter).

The paper quotes the London "Daily Step" for its facts, and it is explained that the case occurred last February but has only just been reported because a panic might have spread in London nad they been known at the time. Here is the story, as given by the Bulgarian paper:—

An expedition brought back from Tanganyika territory an incubator containing three gigantic eggs (each about 26 inches long) of some unknown creature, which a member of the expedition had found in a bush. The incubator was placed in the laboratory of a learned society.

One night the caretaker was roused from sleep by a loud noise, but thought it was an aeroplane. Soon after he heard his watchdog barking frantically, then become suddenly silent.

This alarmed him and he went to investigate. He found the dog dead, poerced as if by a rapier. The metal incubator was burst, the window smashed, and two of the eggs were on the ground. There was only the shell of the third egg.

A professor of the Society was called, and he declared that the eggs were those of a large bird. But when one of them was broken an immense fly was discovered within, three feet in length and with a tongue like a dagger, eighteen inches long.

The professor at once reported the matter to the Home Office, and the police were ordered to find the fly which had escaped.

Its habit was to sleep in trees by day and fly by night, so few people saw it. It flew to Yorkshire, where it killed many sheep before it was located. The police advanced against it in armoured cars; but it rose into the air with a great noise and flew out to sea.

The resource of the British Navy, however, was too much for the monster fly, units of the Home Fleet dashed off in pursuit and shot it down.

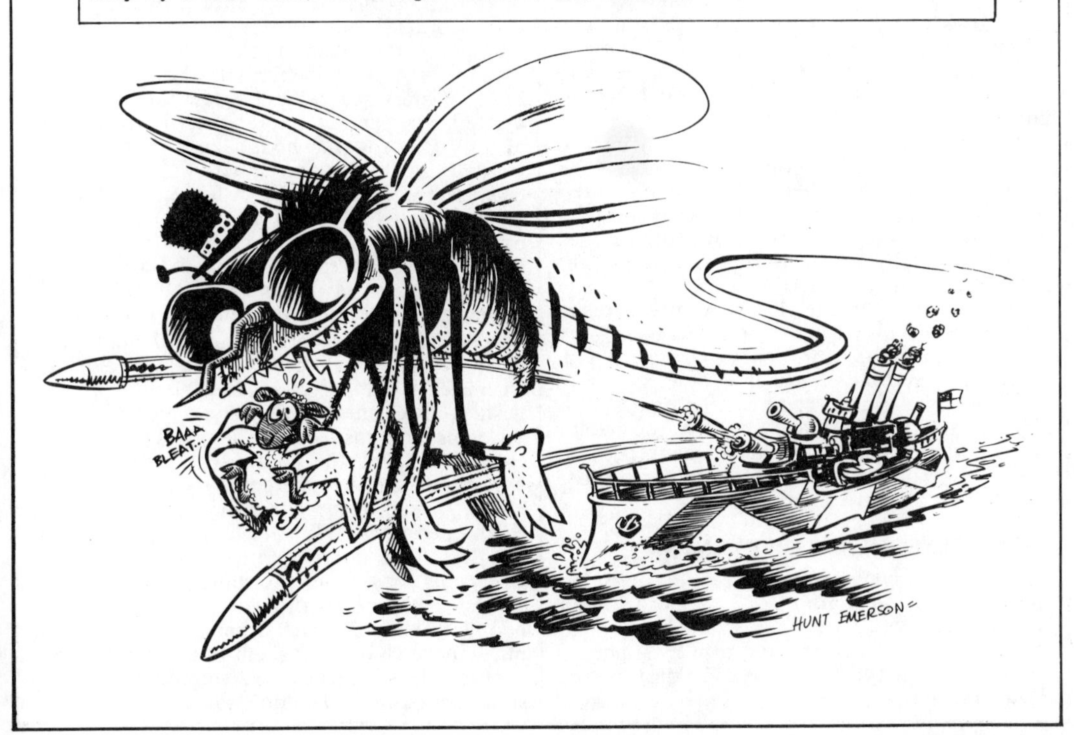

Phantom Attackers.

by Ron Westrum.

THE SEIGE AT LOWELL, MICHIGAN

INTRODUCTION

This case is extremely complex, and the two days I spent investigating it could easily have been extended into a week. Several leads could not be followed up, but it is unlikely that the case could have been resolved completely.

I became involved in the case through the work of investigators David Fideler and Jerome Clark. Shortly after the arrest of the protagonists, news stories appeared which intrigued David Fideler, but since the charges were serious it was very difficult to get anything from either prosecution or defence. I managed to get access to the case by offering my 'expert' services to the defence in return for being able to interview those involved. I went to Grand Rapids for two days, talked to the protagonists and examined briefly (the temperature was sub-zero) the scene of the events. I am extremely grateful to Patrick Bowler and Douglas McKinney of the Grand Rapids Public Defender's office for their help.

Exactly what happened and when cannot be established at this point. The events took place in early November 1978 and the interviews in early January 1979. Some sketchy information was obtained by the Public Defender's office at the time, and it is evident that much 'rational reconstruction' has taken place. It is also possible that some of the participants, especially those on the fringes of the action, know more than they have disclosed. I have four hours of taped interviews in which there are many gaps and inconsistencies. For reasons that will become obvious, the names of the participants have been changed, and, for the sake of brevity, a large number of non-essential details have been omitted.

A ROUGH SEQUENCE OF EVENTS

Of the three main characters – Cordell, 29; Masters, 24; and Hamby, 23 – Cordell and Masters had been living in a small house in a sparsely settled area near Lowell, Michigan – Cordell for three weeks and Masters for about a week – before the events of the 7th and 8th of November. For about a month before this, Masters had been acting cautiously to the point of paranoia, and the more time Cordell spent with him,the more he felt himself becoming fearful.

Exactly what Masters was afraid of is unclear. Some suspected he was engaged in drug dealing, and it might be that he was afraid of arrest, or of violence from the competition. This possibility may also have something to do with the mysterious siege of their house. Whatever the reason, both Cordell and Masters were on the lookout around the house. About a week after he moved in, Cordell found half a grape bubblegum wrapper on the flat roof and the other half near the wood pile – this made him more suspicious. Both Cordell and the owner of the house had feelings that there were peeping toms at the windows at times.

It was in this atmosphere of quasi-paranoia that Cordell and Masters went out to the house on the afternoon of November 7th. Walking out from behind the house at about 3pm, Masters saw what he described as "bow-hunters" in camouflage fatigues. Disturbed, he went back to the house and told Cordell. Cordell did not think much of the incident because there were quite a few hunters in the area. About 4.30pm, Masters saw some people on the hill behind the house, but Cordell was unable to see them. An hour and a half later, Masters again saw some "kids" (children?) behind the house, and this time Cordell thought he could see them too. About dusk (6.30pm?) Masters saw what he thought was a "kid" (teenager?) in a camouflage suit, playing with a dog outside the house. Cordell also saw this and rushed outside. He was not fast enough to catch the youth, who scurried away with great speed, apparently *on his hands and knees.* Cordell returned to the house and yelled to the people he felt were hiding but could not see that if the nonsense did not stop somebody was going to get shot. A short time after that, Cordell and Masters thought they heard several people outside the back door. Cordell thinks he might have shouted at them to leave. Obviously frightened, he "racked" his shotgun and fired a shot at the top of the door frame.

In the meantime, Masters had called the police, who arrived shortly after the shot, questioned both men and left. Masters called a friend who brought over an assortment of guns. He left, but returned an hour later with two others, including Hamby. Things seemed to quieten down. All five went over to Hamby's house but, after some discussion, Masters, Cordell and Hamby went back to Cordell's house. At about 1.30am on the morning of the 8th, Cordell and Masters again saw individuals around the house; Hamby did not, but they decided to switch off the lights to see what would happen. They thought they saw figures outside and fired off about 10 shots. After a few minutes Hamby insisted that he had not seen or heard anyone outside, and said they ought to put their lights on again. They did so and began to wonder if their imaginations had not got the better of them. At that moment all three heard someone run across the roof and apparently drop down in front of the front windows. They turned the lights off again.

The action continued in this on-and-off fashion. Towards 5am, however, things really began to happen, according to all three men. Cordell, the oldest and probably the most level-headed of the group, felt that there was a co-ordinated assault by some six people at least. He personally shot someone hanging from the roof in front of one of the bedroom windows – he saw the figure hang for a moment and then drop. He is a skilled deer-hunter and had shot to kill. Hamby fired a .44 magnum through a refrigerator – I saw the hole myself – at a person in the kitchen, whom he heard slam against the sink, fall on the floor, and make gurgling noises, as if critically wounded. Cordell said: "I was very sure the person in the kitchen was dead." All three were extremely scared; Masters to the point where he was re-loading spent cartridges into the revolver. At 5.30am, they called the sheriff's department. Because one of them was on parole, and had a real interest in not being associated with fire-arms or drugs, it demonstrates the degree of their desperation.

Calling in the law proved to be a mixed blessing. The police drove by the house twice, apparently missing it. Hamby then fired what he thought would be an alerting shot out of the top of the front window with a shotgun. Some of the pellets from the shot, however, hit one of the police cars. Suddenly the three found themselves to be the object of police attention, instead of their mysterious attackers. After some not-very-successful negotiating, the three came out of the house and were arrested. The police refused to approach the house until they had reinforcements and had gassed it.

The three expected the police to find at least one body and probably some blood, but they found nothing except the evidence of considerable shooting, all of it from the inside. On reflection *none* of the three remembers being shot at by the mystery assailants. The three were then taken away, under the cameras of the media, and booked on charges of assault with intent to commit murder. In later weeks the charge was changed to misuse of a firearm, With this serious felony charge against them, their complete bafflement as to what had transpired had to take second place. It is no less baffling for us too.

WHAT REALLY HAPPENED?

The best guess as to what happened has to be that the three men suffered an hallucination due to the effect of fear and drugs. They never actually saw their assailants. They saw silhouettes and heard noises, although very distinct ones. The entire sequence took place at night and in a context of fear, suspicion and insecurity. One would be tempted to leave the matter here were it not for the Shelbyville case (which follows).

But could there have been real assailants? Unlikely, but not impossible. The Lowell, Michigan area apparently does have some "crazies" who dress up in military fatigues and take shots at each other with real bullets. The possibility of some drug-related violence cannot be ruled out either. However, the persons engaged in such a desperate venture must have been extremely hardy or very foolish, because the three men shot to kill with weapons which would have been fatal (I counted five large .44 holes in the back wall of the house.) Furthermore, the three remembered having shot and *hit* the people they were shooting at – even taking into account their state of mind, it is hard to discount their testimony about this entirely.

Another possibility is that the events at Lowell and Shelbyville (see below) are linked in some way, but this leads off in an unknown direction. The assailants at Shelbyville attacked only a week earlier, showing the same indifference to the threat of bodily harm. The two sites are only 25 miles apart, and both houses are in sparsely populated areas. There are disturbing parallels, too, with a case of phantom attackers in 1692, recorded by Cotton Mather (see below) who also showed themselves to be impervious to gunfire, and who are said to have spoken in an *unknown tongue* (this is underlined in the original). Cordell thought he heard his assailants speaking in a language he did not understand, but this may have been due to its inaudibility. Then there is the problem that UFOs were reported in both Shelbyville and Grand Rapids areas about this time. Did the UFOs have anything to do with the phantom attackers? Or could both have had a common cause?

THE SEIGE AT SHELBYVILLE MICHIGAN

INTRODUCTION

Unlike the Lowell case, the incident at Shelbyville took place almost without context, unless American society in 1978 is to be considered a context. The couple involved, Jack, a 24yr-old carpenter, and 22yr-old Laura, still do not understand the motives of the attackers and have no idea who they were.

At the time, the (unmarried) couple were living in the tiny and sparsely populated community of Shelbyville, between Grand Rapids and Kalamazoo, and within a quarter of a mile of the home of Jack's parents. Jack and Laura's house is a small, square, one-storey ranch house, set about 300 yards from the main road (124th St.) Across the road sits a large supermarket, and next to it a lumber company. It is about a quarter of a mile from other houses, and is partially circled by woods.

THE INCIDENTS

At dusk, on November 4th, 1978, Jack was alone in the house when he thought he heard someone whistle. Thinking it might be Laura unable to open the door while loaded with groceries, he went to the door, but there was no one there. He looked out of the window but her car was not in the driveway. She did not return until later. Between 9.30pm and 10pm, the couple were watching television in the darkened house when Laura throught she could see someone outside. Jack ignored her and cotinued to watch television. Laura went into the bathroom, and looking out of the window noticed a green light up in a tree. When Jack went up to bed later and looked out of the same window, he too began to notice green lights. The couple were now more vigilant, and, unable to sleep, began to peer out of the windows. Green lights were seen from time to time, both stationary and moving slowly. Jack described them as being like the eyes of deer reflecting a bright light. They were small, and about the brightness of a lit cigarette seen outside at night. Whenever Jack would tell Laura to come and look, or when either of them yelled, the lights would stop moving.

At about 2am, Jack opened the living room window. A creek runs near the house, and Jack thought he could hear splashing sounds from it. He thought he could see the figure of a man by one of the trees. Jack could see him clearly through the telescopic sight of his rifle. He yelled that he was armed and the man had better identify himself. At 5am Jack was standing by the living room window when he noticed a man crouched below the window holding something in his hands; he could not see what it was. Aiming a pistol at the figure, he said: "You'd better get away from here or I'll blow your head off." The man, who appeared to be wearing a uniform of dark fatigues and a baseball cap, did not move a muscle. Suddenly Jack realized he was framed by the window, making an excellent target for anyone outside. He moved away from the window and ordered Laura to retreat to the bathroom.

While still watching the window, Jack became aware that a man had come through the back door and was approaching the living room. Jack put the gun to his shoulder and aimed at the man. Although he could easily have killed the man at that range, Jack did not fire. He "panicked" and chased the man out of the back door, shouting: "I'm going to kill you, if you don't get away from my house!" By now Jack was very excited. He called the state police at Wayland, Michigan, who told him they had no car to send out immedaitely. He then called his brother-in-law before going into the bathroom with Laura and locking the door.

Just before he secured the door, Jack experienced the most peculiar aspect of this case. About to enter the bathroom, he noticed what appeared to be an orange "lens", about four inches wide and two and a half high, move up in the window and then down. The bottom sill of this window is six feet above ground level outside, and at its highest point the lens would have been eight feet from the ground. The lens [like a car tail light?] rose up again but ducked down immediately Jack aimed his gun at it.

From inside the bathroom, they heard someone walking across the tiles of the kitchen. A shadow passed under the foot of the door. Jack yelled again that he was armed and that he wanted the people to leave. The door handle began jiggling, and fearing someone was trying to get in, Jack put his arm against the door to keep it from opening. Suddenly Laura said someone was trying to get in through the window. Jack reached up to check whether the window was open; it was locked. Then the door started to open, and a pushing contest ensued between Jack and whoever was on the other side. . . Curiously, Jack felt they were not putting their full weight against the door; Laura said they would not have been able to resist if they had done so. There was no shadow under the door, so Jack and Laura guessed the person must be off to one side. Jack yelled to Laura, who was holding the pistol, "Shoot both sides of the door!" Laura fired a shot, but at the back wall. The door closed and Jack locked it. About ten minutes later Laura's brother arrived, yelling that he had the police with him. Jack yelled back that there was still someone inside the house, and asked them to kick the back door in. No sooner had he said this than the police burst open the front door. The siege was over.

WERE THE POLICE INVOLVED?

A number of factors come together to raise a serious question as to whether or not the police were responsible for the events. During an early phase of the affair, Jack had seen first one, then another, Allegan county sheriff's patrol car in the parking lot of the supermarket. The second car was shining its spotlight around the premises as if searching for a prowler. Then a large van with red, yellow and orange lights on top, stopped in the lot. Jack described it as brown and about the size of a United Parcel Service van, which is quite large. A man got out and walked to the back end – Jack saw him clearly in the 'scope of his rifle.

The figure crouching below the living room window appeared to be wearing a S.W.A.T. [a police special weapons and tactics task force] uniform, similar to the one used in the television programme *S.W.A.T.* It was for this reason the couple delayed calling the police – they believed the police were already outside.

At this point, it would be well to consider the role that Federal Investigators, particularly from the Drug Enforcement Agency (DEA), play in contemporary American folklore, which unhappily corresponds with many real incidents. The 'drug police' have been known to burst into a house without announcing themselves, tie people up, point guns at the occupants, and threaten lives if the whereabouts of drugs are not divulged. Some instances of this behaviour have come to light as a result of raids upon innocent households. This tradition of covert and essentially illegal activity often makes it hard to distinguish the police from prowlers. Added to this is the tendency to shoot at the slightest sign of resistance, a habit gained through interacting with equally fast-shooting drug pushers.

The reason why the couple never fired directly at their attackers is because they believed they were being besieged by the police, and that if they fired at all they would both be killed. In actuality, however, the behaviour shown by the phantom attackers is too bizarre, even for the drug police. DEA agents simply do not show the sort of restraint seen here. For instance, if the crouching man had been a real DEA agent, Jack would have been shot the moment he brought his rifle to bear on the man. If is also very unlikely that a drug agent would allow himself to be chased out of a house; he might feel panic for a moment but he would surely have turned and shot, or his companions would have shot to cover him.

The possibility that the attackers might have been police agents was apparently taken seriously by the officers who questioned Jack and Laura, when they offered to testify in the Lowell case. When Laura asked one of them what the green lights might be, he suggested "starlight scopes", light amplification devices used by commandos and increasingly by federal investigators. He too thought the attackers might be federal agents.

The state police had arrived at the house some minutes before the brother-in-law. They waited and watched, apparently waiting for reinforcements. One officer claimed he was just outside the bathroom when Laura fired the shot, and this may explain why Jack and Laura were severely grilled by the officers. One of them told Laura that he spent the following night in their basement, to see if anything unusual would take place. Jack and Laura were very suspicious of the actions of the officers; but my own feeling is that they were behaving well within the normal range to be expected in an ambiguous situation where there had been shooting. (Another officer once told me: "The one call you don't want to get is just 'Trouble!' You never know what you're getting into.")

Nonetheless, the presence of police near the supermarket is unexplained. Jack and Laura said they see Allegan county sheriff's vehicles only very rarely. There is also the question of what affected the dogs.

ANIMAL REACTIONS

Two nights before these events, two dogs of a neighbour had behaved strangely. When taken to a veterinarian, he found they had been drugged by hallucinogen or amphetamine, according to Laura, who talked with the neighbour. Jack and Laura's belief that they were being attacked by federal agents was strengthened when friends told them that it was a common police practice, where stealth was necessary, to "put dogs to sleep" with drugs.

On the night of November 4th, another neighbour's dog began barking at 4am. This dog was known to bark at the approach of strangers. Two weeks after the main incident, this dog barked again, causing its owner, who had heard of the mystery attack,to phone Jack and Laura in case something was again happening – it was (see below).

Early in the evening of November 4th, Jack had let out his own dog to relieve itself. Once outside something caught its attention. Suddenly Jack lost sight of the dog. Later a scratching was heard at the back door, as was the dog's habit, but it soon stopped. Later still, Laura peered out of the back door but could see no sign of the dog. It finally returned after Jack had chased the intruder out of the back door.

Unusually, the dog vomited. After the second incident (see below) the dog urinated in Jack's lap, again unusual behaviour for it. It is now disturbed by anyone wearing a stocking cap, and barks loudly at the wearer.

THE SECOND SHELBYVILLE INCIDENT
Two weeks after the first mystery siege (the date is uncertain), Jack was alone in the house when he again noticed green lights outside. Of the three lights, two were found later to have routine explanations; the third was mysteriously moving while blinking on and off. The neighbour whose dog had barked about the time of the earlier attack, phoned to ask if anything unusual was going on because his dog was acting up again. Jack called Laura to tell her about the lights. As he put the phone down, something slammed against the front door and made a strange noise which he could only liken to the mooing of a cow. Jack went outside and shouted that he would not be scared by these tactics. Back inside he called his father and a friend who agreed to come over, but he got in his own car and left.

AN HISTORICAL ACCOUNT
These cases may be the result of unusual human activity, or they may represent instances of a still unknown psychological or physical phenomenon. The only similar occurrence I have been able to locate took place in Gloucester, Massachusetts, in July 1692, and was recorded by Cotton Mather in his *Magnalia Christi Americana* (1702: Silas Andrus & Son, Hartford, 1853) volume 2, page 620. According to Mather the events centred on an Ebenezer Bapson, and concerned seemingly real people, described as Frenchmen and Indians, who were repeatedly shot at for three weeks, defying all attempts to kill or capture them. The bold appearance of these phantoms, their general lack of concern about the gunfire, their seeming invulnerability when convincingly hit, and their skulking, are all familiar elements in these stories. Many of these elements also have similarities to some poltergeist events.

DO YOU KNOW OF OTHER CASES?
I have reported these accounts to determine whether similar cases exist elsewhere, and readers are invited to notify me of any known to them.

Ron Westrum,
929 Fifth St, Ann Arbor,
MI 48103, USA.

More Phantom Seiges.

by Bob Rickard.

Taking up Ron's invitation I would like to add notice of two other cases – a venerable one from the annals of ufology, and a more recent one involving bigfoot-like creatures.

THE GOBLINS FROM SPACE
The close encounter between members of the Sutton family and the "little men", whom everyone agreed were like nothing on this earth, on 21 August 1955, at the hamlet of Kelly, near Hopkinsville, Kentucky, has been told and retold many times in the UFO literature. My facts come from the exhaustive report made by Isabel Davis, a model of UFO investigation [*Close Encounter at Kelly and Others of 1955* by Isabel Davis & Ted Bloecher, Center for UFO Studies, 1978].

At 8pm on the night of 21st August a family friend getting water from the backyard well saw what he described as a silvery object with a rainbow-coloured exhaust fly low over the Sutton farmhouse and land in a tree-shrouded gully about 300 feet from the house. The family and friends, totalling eight adults and three children, regarded the witnesses' story of a "flying saucer" as a joke – he had a low credibility with the family, so no-one investigated. About half an hour later, one of the sons and the UFO-witness went outside to check on their wildly barking dog and saw, coming towards them with arms raised, a strangely misshapen faintly-glowing figure which seemed to be floating rather than walking. The men both fired their guns at the creature, which "flipped" over backwards and scurried into the darkness.

For the next three or four hours the creatures were seen at windows, in trees, or on the roof and repeatedly fired at to no effect. At one time a claw-like hand on a long spindly arm reached down to touch the hair of the UFO-witness standing beneath a porch roof. One of the family fired from the yard and knocked the creature from the porch roof up and over the ridge of the main roof. At another time, two shots knocked a creature out of a tree, but instead of falling it *floated* down. Another, shot from the roof, floated some 40 feet to the back fence, upon which it perched like a bird until it was knocked off by another shot only to scurry off on "all fours". About 11pm the terrified family fled the house in two cars, driving directly to the police station in Hopkinsville.

Davis notes that folk of this region tend to reach for their guns first when threatened rather than call the law, and so this flight alone was an indication of their desperation. All the officers and others involved in the subsequent investigation, whether they believed the story of the weird little men or not, were struck by the obvious terror of the family. There were sightings and shots again the next night, after the investigators had left – by sunrise they had gone for good.

Although later news accounts described a dozen or more of these creatures, only once were two seen together, or rather under conditions which suggested two creatures. Their other pecularities were striking: their invulnerability to gunshots; the way they "did a flip" when hit (one sounded like shot hitting a metal bucket); their locomotion after flipping was fast although most of the propulsion seemed to have come from their long spindly arms rather than their stiff knee-less legs); their eyes did not turn to follow movement; their faintly-glowing dull metallic skin; they made no noise at any time; they made no hostile moves, nor retaliated (Davis comments: "We do not even know that they recognised the shooting as a sign of antagonism."). The origin of the creatures is a mystery too, because there is no evidence they came from a "saucer".

Subsequent police investigation found no evidence of the creatures – no bodies or blood, no marks or footprints, and no sign of the "saucer" in the gully. They did find, however, considerable evidence of shooting damage to window screens and frames, and some shotgun shells. Curiously, one of the Hopkinsville police cars en route to the farmhouse to begin investigation noticed meteors in the sky in the direction of Kelly.

At the time of the incidents, only five interpretations were available to the investigators: that the story was a hoax; that it was a shared hallucination; that it was a fabrication to cover up indiscriminate shooting; that the family had been terrified by escaped monkeys; or that it was an actual, if incomprehensible, alien

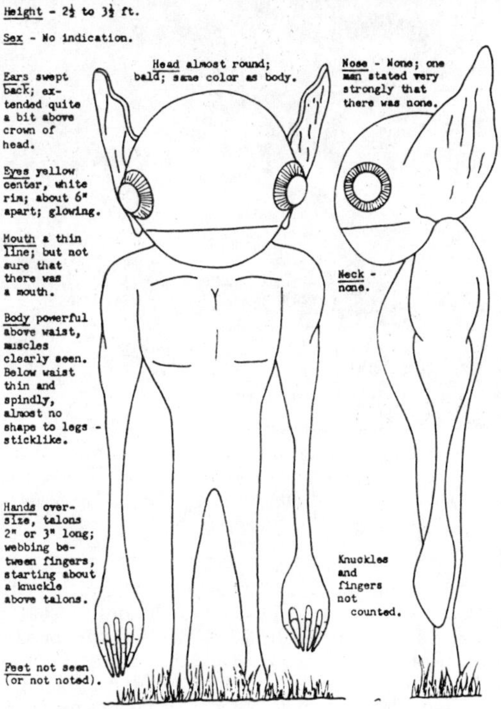

Artist's reconstruction of the Kelly creature, based on artist's interview with key Sutton family witnesses. [© CUFOS/Isabel Davis – page 51 in Davis' report.]

visitation. In her construction of the report, Isabel Davis, who had interviewed all the principal characters the following summer (June 1956), while carefully avoiding endorsement of visiting aliens from the "saucer", adequately disproves the remaining alternatives. Consequently, whatever happened at Kelly on 21 & 22 August 1955 has remained a mystery. I omit Davis's dismissal of the suggestion that hallucinations may have been involved because it is the one weak point in the report, showing a fairly limited understanding of the subject. I, for one, would have liked to know a lot more about the psychological dynamics of the group and their beliefs. While no less easy to understand, we can see, in comparison to the other cases here, that the phenomena of the Kelly siege are not unique, even though the imagery is.

THE SIEGE OF THE GIANT APE-MEN

When it comes to high strangeness it is quite unhelpful to compare cases, and each case must be examined according to its own evidence. While we are used to high strangeness in UFO cases, it also features in some bizarre bigfoot encounters, especially those in which several different kinds

Artist's reconstruction of the dark humanoid forms and strange horse seen from the roof of Robert S's farm, Ohio. [© Dennis Pilichis – reproduced by kind permission.]

of phenomena (eg UFO sightings and psychic phenomena) also figure. The example that is relevant to the theme of attackers who behave like phantoms was investigated by Dennis Pilichis, a long time fortean, and presented in his report *Night Siege: The Northern Ohio UFO-Creature Invasion* [published by the author at Box 5012, Rome, OH 44085, USA]. It is marred by the author's awkward prose which leads to ambiguities in some details. Critics might also think the report is dubious because in visiting the 'besieged' group Pilichis himself witnessed some of the events, and this could be interpreted as becoming party to the collective hysteria (or whatever) and thus a loss of objectivity. But I believe Pilichis has presented an extraordinarily complex and confusing situation truthfully.

At the centre of events are a family – Robert S., his wife and sons, some friends and neighbours and, later, Pilichis and some of his colleagues from Ohio bigfoot and UFO research groups. Again we learn of a lonely farmhouse in a rural wooded area; this time on the Johnson Road in Ashtabula County, near Rome, Ohio. According to Pilichis, the area has a history of bigfoot activity – or rather mysterious livestock killings, tracks and attacks on food stores, and noises in the woods suggestive of bigfeet in the minds of the investigators.

The events in question began on the night of 25th June 1981, when Robert and his sons noticed a huge dark (featureless) form with "two big red glowing eyes" in their front yard. It seemed to be "on all fours" [this has been a detail occurring in at least three of our stories], bothering his ducks. While one son shone a flashlight at it, Robert fired his shotgun; he was sure he hit it because it fled screaming across a field. The next night (26th), Robert investigated the wild barking of his dog in the yard. While shining his torch around, he noticed another huge figure standing by a hoist. The dark gorilla-shaped form had shining red eyes and stood about nine and a half feet tall (as measured later against the hoist). It was growling, and by the light of his torch, Robert saw it had pointed fangs and was covered in dark fur. Recovering from his fear, he ran inside for his gun. He emerged again with his boys, and they heard the creature crossing a field, clambered into their truck to pursue it, and lost sight of it. On the way back,noises were heard in the brush adjacent to the road they were on, and suddenly their engine died. Pilichis compares this to the so-called electro-magnetic engine-stopping effects observed in some UFO close encounters. Later the engine started perfectly.

On the night of 28th June, at least two black forms were seen in the field adjacent to the house. They were felt to be different from the giant red-eyed creatures – more like mobile human shadows – and they waved blue lights back and forth. A hairy giant standing by a pond was shot and observed to fall, and shot at again. Suddenly two more red-eyed forms emerged from the woods towards the pond, and then split off in different directions. In the diversion, if that is what it was, the 'dead' creature by the pond vanished. The next day the sheriff, called by the panic-stricken family, found strange large footprints which were too indistinct to be useful.

The family began a regular vigil up on the roof. On the night of 1st July, square box-like lights, which changed colour, were seen hovering over the trees – one of them directed a beam which lit up half an acre "as bright as day". Screams were heard and the lights went out. Many times red-eyes were shot at and heard to scream, while others were noticed to lurk about the woodline as though they were observing the house. At one point two giant forms and a dark horse-like shape were seen in the field. Two people shot at the 'horse' which screamed and growled before fleeing. At about 3.30am, a white light appeared and one of the family, who nearly fell off the roof, said he felt that the glow had "hit him in the head". Shots were fired at the light and it winked out. Then something even more curious happened: a glowing red light seemed to flit among the trees like a bird going from branch to branch; some felt it was made by an owl-like form. When shot it fell to the ground and after a pause seemed to scamper away on all fours. Also, a small object, like a "cigarbox" ringed with blue and red lights, flew across the clearing and over the house. As it went over Robert shot it and heard a sound like breaking glass, but it continued its flight unaffected. No evidence of the object was ever found.

The strange seige continued. As in our other cases, the figures showed no sign of aggression or even concern despite being repeatedly shot at. Their appearance would be preceded by flashes of blue light in the woods, and one night three members of the research team saw the woods "light up as bright as day" three times in five minutes. "Footprints" were found – many with splayed toes – which remain unidentified. There were also many chilling screams and strange smells. Yet, despite all this activity, there was no convincing evidence that the attackers were physically there. Like the other cases, too, there is no clue as to why the siege began, or why it stopped. Unfortunately Pilichis doesn't say how this story ends, but I get the impression of sporadic incidents, progressively more infrequent.

CONCLUSION

These cases contribute to the feeling that Ron Westrum has identified a distinct manifestation which cuts across the categories of phenomenal types. The single common thread linking these cases is a kind of collective panic; a shared experience of mounting anxiety and fear, in which it is reasonable to expect misperception and hallucination to be operating. To the reductionist that is all these cases might amount to. After all, in each of the above cases the only unambiguous evidence was the damage created by the trigger-happy reactions of the 'besieged', with no clear sign of the physical reality of the attackers. But our new genre has other aspects which would repay study. For example a psychologist might be interested in the contagious effect of the hysteria demonstrated here; a sociologist might identify the prevailing fears and expectations of the group; while a folklorist might be able to interpret the incidents in the light of current folk traditions. To the fortean, all of these angles are important, and we must add our own inquiry as to the origin of the imagery involved, what triggered the events, and what significance, if any, can be attached to the underlying similarity of the cases. Most of all we need to know a lot more about the witnesses. As a curious and relatively rare form of collective human experience, the 'phantom siege' deserves our study.

Artist's reconstruction of the 9 foot tall hairy giants seen at Robert S's farm, Ohio. [© Dennis Pilichis – reproduced by kind permission.]

Clipping Credits for This Issue:

Norman Adams, Bob Barter, Janet & Colin Bord, Jean-Louis Brodu, David Burns, Peter Christie, Loren Coleman, Steven Cooper, Richard Cotton, COUD-I (Collectors of Unusual Data—International), Jim Darroch, Peter Hope Evans, George Featherston, Larry Fiander, John Fullerton, Stuart Gary-Thompson, Robert Gifford, R.I.Gillham, B.F.Greene, Brian Hain, Chris Hall, Mark A. Hall, Tony Healy, Tuuri Heporauta, G.H.Hill, J.Hitchens, John L. Hughes, Amad Jamaludin, Richard King, J.Lang, Alexis Lykiard, Nick Maloret, Valerie Martin, John Michell, Steve Moore, Ian S. Murray, Kevin J. Neilson, Ray Nelke, Nigel Pennick, Maureen Porter, Cory Panshin, Sven Rosen, John P.Ramsay, Michel Raynal, Robert M. Rickover, Ron Schaffner, Paul Screeton, Rupert Sheldrake, Doc Shiels, Bob Skinner, Anthony Smith, Dennis Stacy, Joe Swatek, A.L. Thomas, Paul R. Thomas, Joseph Trainor, UFONS, Roger Waddington, Nigel Watson, Dwight Whalen, Owen Whiteoak, Jake Williams, Ion Will, Steve Wrathall, Joe Zarzynski.

Stoned on Annie Taylor.

by Dwight Whalen.

"There shall not be left a stone upon a stone, that shall not be thrown down" *Mark XIII,2.*

When Mrs Annie Edson Taylor, a dancing teacher of 63, packed herself into a wooden barrel to waltz over Niagara Falls, October 24, 1901, everyone feared one thing: rocks. Impact on the big rocks below the Horseshoe Falls would shatter her keg like an eggshell. By the greatest luck she plunged into unobstructed water and was safely rescued.

Notoriety assured, Annie expected to reap a fortune telling her tale to captivated listeners across America. But while her body had not been dashed upon the rocks, her hopes of money-making were. The pot of gold she saw at the end of Niagara's rainbow was anything but a stone's throw away.

Stones. In researching this remarkable woman's story for a book I'm writing, *The Lady Who Conquered Niagara*, I find myself repeatedly, unexpectedly, stumbling over stones. Or should I say, bombarded by them. I can't seem to dodge discovering strange stories of stones falling from the heavens, falling in ways as wildly unlikely, frightening, and dangerous – in one case, fatally so – as Annie's own fall. Reading an old microfilmed newspaper, rooting out information on "The Queen of The Mist", as she dubbed herself, I seem inevitably to find a Fortean gem (stone) like the following report from the *Buffalo Express*, October 27, 1901:

WHO THREW STONES?

Mysterious Fusillade Scares People
In An Ohio Town

Missiles Came From Where No One Knows
Seemingly From A Clear Sky

Pomeroy, O., Oct. 26 – The little village of Harrisonville, eight miles from this city, is terribly wrought up over the mysterious stoning of houses and people there in broad daylight. It began on Sunday afternoon, October 13th, when a small boulder came crashing through the window of Zach Dye's house, a half mile out of town. The family were all at home, and at once ran out to see who had thrown the stone, but no one could be found, notwithstanding the house stands in the open and several hundred yards from any object large enough for a man to hide behind. While the members stood about in the yard in open-mouthed wonder, other stones pelted the house, coming from where no one knows.

On Monday afternoon, at about the same hour, a shower of stones fell right in the heart of the little village. The first intimation the citizens had of it was when a piece of rock came through the plate-glass door of a store, and when the proprietor and the customers ran outside to see who had thrown it, there was no one in sight. An alarm was given and the citizens came out with their guns, and, notwithstanding the stones continued to fall about them, they were unable to tell whence they came. One man, William Alkire, was hit a glancing blow on the arm, but was not seriously injured, while James Clay, a one-legged man, who was standing in front of his house shouting to the excited populace that it was probably nothing more than a lot of mischievous boys, had his crutch knocked from under him and broken by a large boulder, which struck it about midway.

On the third day, when the stones began to fly through the air, the entire population thronged the streets. They were lined up and counted, to see who it could be that was throwing the stones. Every man and boy in the village was found to be in the line, and still the dangerous missiles flew through the air.

After her business manager absconded with her barrel in January 1902, Annie spent time in the Auburn, N.Y., area, plotting to get it back. I found this item in the *Auburn Daily Advertiser* of March 20, 1902:

STRUCK BY A METEOR

Near Indianapolis, Ind. – Thomas Sloane had a close call when a meteor about as large as his fist struck in the opening of his right overcoat pocket, passed through it, burned his leg in a painful manner and then entered the earth to such a depth that his neighbors are still digging for it.

Annie's manager sold her barrel to a Chicago theatrical company for use as a promotional gimmick for a play called "Over Niagara Falls"

* A slightly shorter version of this article appeared in *Pursuit* (Vol 16, No.4), the journal of the Society for the Investigation of the Unexplained (SITU), PO Box 265, Little Silver, NJ 07739, USA.

On August 15, 1902, a police raid snatched the cask from a department store window. Scanning the *Chicago Tribune* for this period I came across:

MAN KILLED BY A METEOR

San Antonio, Tex., Aug. 17 – (Special) – a sheep herder named Ramon Cruz was killed in Edwards county by a fragment of a meteor that was shattered by coming into conflict with a huge boulder on which he was seated last Friday. Details as to the exact time and the circumstances are not known. A piece of meteoric stone weighting an ounce was imbedded in his skull. Near the body was found a piece of the meteor weighing five pounds, and seven small fragments.

The odds against anyone being struck by a meteorite are – duck! – astronomical. The odds against it occurring to two people in the United States within a six-month period are ultra-astronomical. But perhaps the strangest part, coincidentally, is that Annie Taylor's life is linked to the locales where these murderous meteorites fell.

The first struck "near Indianapolis". In an autobiographical sketch which she published in 1902 called "Over The Falls", Annie claimed to have lived for a time in Indianapolis, and "taught dancing in La Fayette, Ind.," which is near Indianapolis.

Edwards County, Texas, where Ramon Cruz was struck in the head and killed by a meteorite, is not far northwest of San Antonio. According to her own account, Annie served as an associate high school principal in San

Continued ☛

Annie Edson Taylor. A portrait from the Chicago Chronicle.

AEROLITE

Found By Comic Paper
Turns Out To Be A Piece Of Blast Furnace Slag
Expose by Prof. Lindahl

The aerolite, it was alleged, had fallen on June 23, and landed in the middle of Yale Avenue, between Park and Elmwood Avenue, Walnut Hills, turns out to have been nothing more than a piece of iron slag from an iron furnace.

A morning paper told how this alleged aerolite had fallen from the clouds and how its descent had been witnessed by one or more persons.

Prof. Lindahl of the Natural History Society, who examined the alleged meteoric stone, was seen yesterday be a representative of The Enquirer and asked about the matter. He said:

"I examined this so-called aerolite and found it to be a piece of slag from a blast furnace. I suppose some enterprising reporter threw it off a housetop in the vicinity where it fell and then had the material from which to weave a story about the falling of an aerolite."

The Cincinnati Enquirer
July 6, 1901

STONES

Thrown At Senator Hanna As He Was Leaving Canton After The Funeral Of McKinley

Special Dispatch To The Enquirer

Canton, Ohio, September 20 – It is reported today that Senator Hanna had a narrow escape from serious injury at the hands of some unknown miscreant last night.

According to the story the attack was made just after Mr Hanna had left Canton for Cleveland, following the funeral of President McKinley. The Wheeling and Lake Erie train, on which the Senator, Myron T. Herrick and other politicians were riding had stopped at a siding a few miles outside of Canton when two big rocks, it is said, were thrown through the window. One of the missiles is said to have come dangerously close to the Senator and fell at his feet.

Secret Service men on board the train dashed from the car in search of the miscreant, but did not find him.

It is said that messages were sent back to Canton telling of the incident, and in this way the story leaked out.

The Cincinnati Enquirer
September 21, 1901

Antonio from 1878 to 1881. In fact, one of the reasons she gave for barrelling over Niagara concerned San Antonio. She owned a small ranch there, she said, and hoped to earn enough money lecturing about her Falls ride to update the property and make it her permanent home.

One time near San Antonio, she barely missed catching a fatal "meteorite" in the head herself. "A gang of Jesse James' men," Annie related, waylaid a stagecoach she was riding between San Antonio and Austin. When she refused the bandits' demand for money, one of them pressed a pistol to her head. "Blow away," she told him, "I would as soon be without brains as without money." He let her keep both.

Looking for a newspaper account of the stagecoach robbery I came upon this report in the *San Antonio Express*, May 3, 1876:

An aerolite which fell in Collin county (north of Dallas), some year or two ago, was ploughed up in a field a day or two since, and is now on exhibition at McKinney.It weighs about one hundred and fifty pounds.

I know of no connection between Annie and the stone-shower site of Harrisonville, Ohio, but Annie toured a number of Ohio cities with her barrel before it was stolen, and the Buckeye State has been stoned in strange ways more than once. In 1860 at New Concordia some 200 hot stones dropped out of the blue into a field in broad daylight. The *St Louis Republic* in 1899 said that a man was once killed by a meteorite in Ohio, and the paper claimed it was probably the only case of its kind ever authenticated:

Early one morning in August, 1870, David Misenthaler of Whetstone township, Crawford country, Ohio, was struck and instantly killed by a stone which fell from the sky. In this instance the aerolite was of about the size of a peck measure and weighed about 60 pounds. From the position of the remains of Misenthalter when found it is judged that the stone came down from a direction a little west of south. The man's body was cut entirely in two.

According to Annie, the urge to ride a barrel over Niagara Falls struck her sometime in August of 1901. "The idea came to me like a flash of light," she said. Late that same August, another flash of light – "resembling a huge ball of electrical blue, slowly unwinding a line of red fire" – rolled across the daylight sky of southern California and fell in the mountains northwest of Los Angeles. Witnesses said the big meteorite was 500 to 1000 feet in diameter. "When the vast form neared the ground", reported the *Buffalo Express*, September 1, "little stars burst forth in showers, and when it struck there was a violent tremor and a roaring like the firing of heavy artillery. It is believed to have detonated as it reached the earth, and there is no telling what the fragments may reveal, if ever found."

This dramatic picture of Annie Taylor, showing her being helped to shore by the outstretched arms of rescuers below the Horseshoe Falls, appeared in the Bay City Times, *December 7, 1941. The paper called the picture "a scoop 40 years late", claiming the photo had never been published before. Coincidentally, December 7, 1941, deadly missiles from the sky in the form of Japanese bombs rained on the US Pacific fleet at Pearl Harbor. A Lockport, NY, paper, reporting Annie's death in 1921, said she once visited Hawaii.*

In the matter of strange stone showers, Annie Taylor was once in the immediate proximity of one. Charles Fort, in his book *LO!*, describes "three showers of hot stones" which fell near the building of the Charleston *News and Courier*, September 4, 1886, four days after the devastating Charleston, South Carolina, earthquake (*Complete Fort*, p.563). Referring to details published in the *Richmond Whig*, Fort says the paper was informed "that stones, which were flint pebbles, ranging from the size of a grape to the size of a hen's egg, had fallen upon an area of 75 square feet, and that about a gallon of them had been picked up."

On the night of the earthquake, August 31, who should be one of those rocked in their chairs at Charleston but Annie Taylor. She said she was sitting in the parlor of a friend's home listening to a music recital when the cataclysm struck. She reacted with stony composure and scientific interest. "Her first thought was as to the effect an earthquake has on the temperature," said the *Buffalo Express* in 1901. "She got up and looked at a thermometer, noted the state of the mercury, and later observed that within an hour the temperature had fallen 26 degrees."

Having retrieved her barrel from Chicago in 1902, Annie hired a new manager and took the barrel on a tour that autumn. She was exhibiting at Trenton, New Jersey, the first week of October. A farm near Trenton, says Fort in *LO!*, was the scene of a stone shower in June 1884 (*Complete Fort*, p561). The *Trenton Evening Times*, October 2, reported:

SHOWERS OF STONES SCARE PEOPLE IN LITTLE VILLAGE

By Publisher's Press Direct-Wire

Wheeling, W. Va., Oct. 2 – The suburban village of Parkview, four miles east of this city, is the scene of great excitement over fifteen showers of stones.

During the last two days showers have been frequent and some damage has been done to property. A house was badly damaged. The stones are the size and shape of cobblestones.

The larger that have fallen are jet black and very hard, while a number of snowy white ones have also fallen. The white coating has the appearance of lime.

Many of the people from here have visited the village and have brought some of the stones to the city.

I am unable to connect Annie with Wheeling, West Virginia. However, the same October 2 edition of the *Trenton Evening Times* reported the following from a town 20 miles north of the New Jersey capital:

BELIEVE IT RAINED FISH AT BLOOMSBURG

Fleminton, Oct. 2 – After the heavy shower Sunday afternoon many small fish were discovered in the streets. As no stream of water could have overfloweed its banks and reached the place it remains a mystery how the fish came to be there. Many, however, have accepted the theory that they came down with the rain.

It is interesting that a probable fishfall took place that close to Trenton while Annie was there, and interesting that I should discover it. I have documented numerous instances of rainfalls of fish in the Niagara Falls area ("Niagara Fishfalls", *Pursuit*, No. 62, Second Quarter 1983).

In 1903 Annie spent several days in Orange, N.J., negotiating with the Edison Manufacturing Company to have a motion picture made depicting her tumble over Niagara Falls. Looking to find a report of her in the *Newark Evening News*, I found the following dated July 24:

HAS FIVE-POUND METEOR

Fell At Doorstep, Just Missing Woman As She Passed In The House

Special Dispatch to the Evening News

Annie Edson Taylor with the barrel in which she went over Niagara Falls, the first person to do so and live.

Jackson, Mich., July 24 – During a terrific storm of electricity and rain last night a piece of a spent meteor, weighing a little less than five pounds, fell within three feet of the doorstep of the residence of Frank B. Thayer, in North Gorham Street, and embedded itself in the earth. The son, Montford, saw it, and after the storm went out to pick it up, but it was too hot to handle, and for thirty minutes retained its high temperature. Mrs Thayer had just stepped into the house as the meteor went into the ground.

The strange stone, which is of a reddish brown color, and oblong in shape, has attracted considerable attention.

I wonder if Frank B. Thayer was related to Tiffany Thayer, Secretary of the old Fortean Society.

The meteorite that killed a shepherd near San Antonio struck on the very day Annie made "the kill" of recapturing her barrel in Chicago.

The Harrisonville stone showers began on October 13, 1901, the same day Annie arrived at Niagara to begin preparations for her barrel-ride.

The 15 stone showers outside Wheeling occurred during Annie's exhibition at Trenton – where again her barrel was stolen by an unscrupulous manager, this time for good.

Jackson, Michigan, site of the near-fatal

Thayer meteorite, is 25 miles from Lansing, where lived Annie's brother Montgomery Edson, whom she spitefully scolded in 1901 for revealing her true age to the press. She wanted people to believe she was 43, not 63. Jackson, too, is about 100 miles as the crow flies from Bay City, Michigan, where Annie was living when she conceived her Falls-shooting scheme and had her barrel built.

Reports of Annie Taylor in the Niagara press become fewer and fewer after 1903, and with them disappear my findings of stories of strange stone showers and deadly meteorites during the declining years of her life. It is remarkable that these phenomena occurred, not only so frequently during a relatively short time-span in the US, but at times, and/or near places, of significance to Annie, as if laying cosmic emphasis on her struggle to make money telling the story of her escape from death on the rocks below Niagara Falls.

"AFTER-THE-GRAVE STONES"

Annie Edson Taylor died, stone-blind and stone-broke, in the Niagara County Infirmary, Lockport, N.Y., April 29, 1921. But stones from the heavens have continued to fall in places associated with her.

On March 22, 1953, an object believed to be a meteorite plunged into the upper Niagara River, two miles upstream from where Annie was cast adrift on her trip over the Falls. Riverfront witnesses (two blocks from Edison Avenue) saw a blinding flash of light over the river, accompanied by an explosion like a gunshot. Fragments of the object reportedly struck two houses, but no one, apparently, attempted to retrieve the pieces.

At Skaneateles, NY., fishermen John Cazzola and Robert Moore were the target of a mysterious stoning, October 27, 1973. Most of the stones were small, dark, "like railway cinders or something", said Cazzola. They started falling around the pair as they sat in a boat on a lake, and when the men fled in fear, pursued them for miles, pelting their car (INFO, No.14). Annie claimed to have once taught dancing at Skaneateles.

Her name returned to the headlines in February 1980. Chamber of Commerce officials in Bay City, Michigan, desiring to honor their town's legendary lady, sought permission to have her remains removed from Oakwood Cemetery in Niagara Falls, NY., and reinterred in Bay City, where a fancy mini-Niagara Falls memorial stone, complete with falling water, would mark her resting place. The plan fell through – and not too many miles from Oakwood Cemetery, something else fell. On the night of February 8, a flaming meteor, streaking across the eastern US coast, landed in Lake Ontario at a point between the western New York communities of Wilson and Newfane. (Annie delivered a temperance lecture in Newfane in 1901).

Later in 1980, in a violent May storm, large hailstones containing tiny iron pebbles fell at Orange, New Jersey (*Pursuit* No. 52, Fall 1980, p.173). Orange was where Annie came in 1903, hoping the Edison people could make her a "movie star". Instead, Annie's fortunes, following her Niagara triumph, plummeted like a falling star.

Fortean Extracts From *The Gentleman's Magazine*:

...being the third installment from the pages of ***The Gentleman's Magazine,*** founded in 1731, and compiled chronologically for us by **Peter Christie.**

1747

- In April another example of water diet came to light.

At Astonby near Carlisle, a girl, aged 10 or 12 years, has lived since the 30th of November last meerly upon water. Her mother attempted to force her to eat, but in struggling the girl's nose bled much, which made her desist; the girl walks about and does some business, but her strength decays daily. (page 199)

A six months' fast is difficult to believe although a decaying strength seems to indicate some truth to the story. The case becomes extraordinary when we read an August entry, printed below.

- On July 8 Bristol experienced,

a violent storm of rain, attended with thunder and lightening (sic), and a fall of hailstones, several inches round, one in particular measur'd above 5 inches round, which put into a bason and dissolved, produced near a quarter of a pint of water. Several shocks of an earthquake, attended with a considerable noise, and succeeded by claps of thunder, were felt in different parts of Devonshire. (page 341)

The conjunction of storms with earthquakes bears out many similar occurrences, noted, amongst others, by Corliss in his *Sourcebooks* series.

- In August the magazine editor returned to the non-eating girl, this time giving some more details. Thus we are told that she was named Ann Moses, the 11-year-old daughter of Robert who was a farmer at Astonby near Carlisle. In October 1746 she had been ill but soon recovered. From this date, however, she swallowed nothing but water until May 1747. During this period she had no excreta yet actually grew faster than her contemporaries! By July 1747 she was eating – but only a few spoonfuls of oatmeal per day. The similarity of this case with earlier examples – the fast after an illness – is worth noting. Does this phenomenon still happen today? (page 376)
- Also in this month one Anne Dent of the hospital at Appleby – presumably in Westmoreland – cut 4 teeth – hardly a major news item except when you realise that she was over 100 at the time. (page 398). Those interested in name synchronicities will find something here to get their teeth into!
- In October the magazine published a long report of catalepsy in a young girl in France. Whilst in a coma she talked and the locals took this as a sign that she was masquerading as a cataleptic. To test their theory they resorted to extreme measures,

A blow was given her on the face with the palm of the hand, a finger was suddenly pushed so near her eye as to touch the cornea, and a wax candle also held so near it as to singe the lashes; a person suddenly starting into the room screamed as loud as he could in her ear; brandy and sal ammoniac were put into her eyes and mouth, Spanish snuff was put up her nostrils, she was pricked with a needle in several places, and the joints of her fingers were distorted, without producing the least sign of sensibility or interrupting her discourse. (page 459)

Apart from wondering what she actually talked about this case indicates the force of one of the many unknown facets of our brains and bodies. How can the autonomous nervous system be 'turned-off' yet a stream of verbalisation be maintained?

- This month also saw the report of a ghost sighting which had first occurred some 12 years previously. A servant of William Lancaster reported seeing a spectral army marching over a precipitous ridge on Souter-fell in the Lake District but "as no other person in the neighbourhood had seen the like, he was discredited and laugh'd at." (page 524)

Some 2 years later Mr. Lancaster himself saw the ghost army on Midsummer eve. He called his family and they all witnessed a force of cavalry marching 5 abreast with now and then a rider galloping out and 'regulating' the march of the rest. The vision was seen from about 8.30 p.m. until dark. The ghost army was not seen again until the Midsummer eve before the 1745 rebellion, when 26 witnesses saw the spectral procession. A search the next morning revealed no sign of hoofprints on the path the army had followed.

The writer of the report suggests a fairly fanciful idea of mass hallucination sparked-off by a slow moving meteor! The editor added a note about a similar event seen in 1707 in Leicestershire by 2 people – this might be added to the many other ghost stories from this county reported in the article by Paul Devereux and Andrew York in *FT11* and *FT12*.

- On November 7 in this year died Mrs. Ball of Bishopsgate in London. She had carried a dead foetus for 16 years and managed to have four other children normally whilst doing it. (page 545).
- The year ended with a letter from J. Dixon of Chesterfield who wrote concerning a double hen's egg – one complete egg inside another. (page 573)

1748

- The letter concerning a double egg caused two other correspondents to write in about their experiences. One letter related the birth of a monstrous chicken and the other dealt with a double lemon – ie one complete lemon inside another. (page 82)
- In May there was "An authentic Account of a Hail-storm and the figure of a Hail-stone, eleven Inches in Circumference, that was taken up at Seighford in the County of Stafford, after the dreadful Tempest that happened there, July 4, 1719." (page 210). The "Account" was as follows,

The day before the hail-storm, the air was dusk and cloudy, and the sun through the dense vapours appeared of a colour as red as blood. The next morning was hot and clear, and the day so continued till about two in the afternoon when suddenly, in an instant, the clouds began to rise in the West, and a soft shower followed. After this a storm came out of the North which soon overspread the sky, and a little past four ended in a most dreadful tempest of hail. The stones were of various shapes and figures, and of a monstrous and immense size. They seemed to be fragments of some huge cylindrical body of ice, broken and dashed to pieces in the fall, vast numbers of which measured five or six inches in circumference, and several measured nine, ten and eleven inches, even a considerable time after the storm was over. E.B. Seighford, May 7, 1748.

- This month also saw the publication of a letter from "J.J.B." of Devon,

In digging a vault, very lately, in this parish church of Axminster in the county of Devon, were found several bones of a human body, very ponderous, which, when opened, appear'd to be full of lead, particularly the thigh bone. This, so surprising a thing, has puzzled the most curious in these parts . . . (page 214)

I have come across several other examples of this phenomenon. The suggested explanation usually concerns a burning church and molten lead dripping into graves – not a very likely occurrence I would have thought, though in December a correspondent recalled a fire at Gravesend parish church in Kent in 1727. Here the roof lead melted and dripped down and lead filled bones were found after the fire. (page 577) In November of this year the *Gentleman's Magazine* printed an extract from Weever's *Funerall Monuments* concerning a similar case in Newport Pagnell, Bucks in 1619 where the lead filled skull weighed 30 lbs!

My own idea concerns the deliberate preservation of bones by this method as pre-Reformation holy relics. If other readers have come across any similar cases I would be delighted to hear from them.

- On June 12 the Home Counties and the Midlands were hit by a massive storm. At Springfield near Chelmsford in Essex a boy was struck dead by lightning during a church service, also,

. . . at Addington Place, Surrey, fell hail 7 inches in circumference, rebounding 2 foot from the ground, which much damaged the gardens and windows . . . Near Reading was a storm of broken ice, in flat pieces, about 2 inches broad. (page 281)

- Also in June a very lucky man survived a lightning strike in Yorkshire – he recounted his experiences which included deafness and loss of feeling in a long and detailed letter to the editor. (page 283)
- In July another letter was printed which dealt with one of the favourite Fortean topics,

I saw in Staffordshire, in my way to this place, the cavity on a stone, which being lately broken a toad came out alive; the stone was solid, and I could see no manner of perforation by which the animal could breathe or take in the outward air. (page 295)

I know that Bob Skinner, who published an article in *FT27*, is now actively researching this topic and has, I believe, now located well over 250 cases. I look forward to reading an article from him on this controversial subject soon.

- At the end of July a swarm of locusts appeared near Bristol after appearing earlier in Shropshire and Staffordshire. If nothing else they appear to have provided a vast feast for local rooks. (page 331)
- Also in July but at an unspecified date a storm hit Howfield and brought with it so much rain that it tore up the local churchyard and, "14 bodies . . . were found hanging upon hedges some miles from the church." (page 376) Not a pretty sight!
- Just to round off a year of oddities a monstrous birth was announced. Admittedly it took place in October – but news travelled slowly in those days.

Two months ago, J.H. a poor woman, belonging to this town, was delivered of a monstrous child, which besides the usual form and parts of a female, has adhering to, or rather contained on it, as in its capsula, a rude and imperfect subject whose shape is somewhat conical; at the birth it resembled a large cyst, or bag, extending itself from the fundament quite down to the toes of the child . . . A few days after the birth the membrane bursting, discovered to view an irregular mass of flesh, perfectly human, with a smooth skin of florid colour;

The writer goes on to describe in detail what is clearly a parasitic body with its head buried in the child's body. Apparently the body,

receives fluids, and increases in bulk, tho' whether it enjoys an animal or vegetable life is uncertain. I saw the child myself yesterday, which feeds heartily; many hundreds besides myself have likewise seen it; and 'tis allowed to be one of the most surprising instances of the kind ever seen or heard of. Such phenomena, as they are remarkable displays of divine almighty power, so they are undoubtedly visible proofs of God's displeasure against sin (the parent of the child has been remarkably vile, and her offspring is spurious), in that contrary to the established laws of nature, He sometimes permits such uncommon lusus naturae *to exist among the human species; for in general harmony and proportion are the beuty of all his works. (signed) J.D. – Beminster, Dorset December 21.* (page 535)

The canting religious overtones in this letter are nothing unusual for the eighteenth-century. As to the child itself one can only assume from the description that the poor thing lived but a short time.

To be continued.

Classified Exchanges

FT welcomes an exchange of publications with those of mutual interest. This listing represents exchange publications received since last issue. Symbols: # = issue number; Pay = to whom cheques should be made if different from title, O = overseas rate; E = European rate; all rates inland or surface unless indicated; NFC = no Foreign cheques, many offer airmail rates, so inquire. Please mention FT when writing to listings.

FORTEAN

◆ **ANOMALY** [unnumbered, presumably the first issue!] ASSAP's Journal of Record (see ASSAP News, below).

◆ **ASSAP NEWS** [n16, Dec 1984 – n20, Aug 1985] Newsletter of the Association for the Scientific Study of Anomalous Phenomena. 6/yr. Free to members. Enquiries to: Caroline Wise, ASSAP Membership Secretary, 56 Telemann Sq, Kidbrook, London SE3.

◆ **BULLETIN OF THE TYCHONIAN SOCIETY** [n38, Sept 1984 – n39, Jan 1985] Dedicated to a geocentric cosmology. Free on request, but donations appreciated. New address. BTTS: 4527 Wetzel Ave, Cleveland, OH 44109, USA.

◆ **CLYPEUS** [n83, Aug 1984 – n85, March 1985] Fortean journal in Italian from the group Clypeus. Enquiries to: Clypeus: Box 604, I–10100 Torino, Italy.

◆ **CRUX** [n1, Summer 1985] A vibrant personal commentary on Fortean events, loosely connected with editor Tom Adams' two main themes, Texas and cattle mutiliations. Much of humour and interest. ?/yr. $5. O:$6. NFC. Pay: Thomas R. Adams: Box 1094, Paris, TX 75460, USA.

◆ **INFO JOURNAL** [n46, June 1985] One of the handful of essential journals for Forteans. $10/yr. International Fortean Organization: Box 367, Arlington, VA 22210, USA.

◆ **JOURNAL OF METEOROLOGY** [v10 n102, Oct 1985] Frequently has items of Fortean meteorology. 12/yr. Has a variety of sub rates from £15.50. J.Met: 45 Frome Rd, Bradford-on-Avon, Wilts BA15 1LD.

◆ **JOURNAL OF VAMPIROLOGY** [v1 n1, 1984 – v2 n2, 1985] Editor John L. Vellutini, who writes most of the material, is developing a fine exposition, covering every aspect of historical, criminal, mythological, pathological and psychopathological vampirism. 5/yr. $10. NFC. JOV: Box 881631, San Francisco, CA 94188, USA.

◆ **MURDER EXCHANGE** [n1 – n2] Supplement to *Journal of Vampirology* (see above), transcribes newsclippings on bizarre and cult murders.

◆ **PURSUIT** [v18 n1, 1985] The journal of the Society for the Investigation of the Unexplained, and essential reading for informed Forteans. 4/yr. Memb: $12. O.rates on application. SITU: Box 265, Little Silver, NJ 07739, USA.

◆ **THE SEARCHER** [v5 n4, July/Aug 1984 – v7 n3, May/June 1985] Journal of the Society for the Research and Investigation of Phenomena, of Malta, edited by Ivan Sant. 6/yr. Inquiries to: SRIP: Box 318, Valetta, Malta.

◆ **THE SHAMAN** [n9, Jan 1985 – n11, mid-1985] Editor Paul Screeton has decided to change the format of his invaluable book and magazine reviews. No 11 is the last under the present title – the new title will be *Folkore Frontiers* and its brief will be to monitor the many aspects of modern folklore and myths. No doubt it will be essential reading as always. Our guess at the new details. . .4/yr. £3. O:$8(surf), $12 (air). Pay: Paul Screeton: 5 Egton Drive, Seaton Carew, Hartlepool, Cleveland TS25 2AT.

◆ **SHAN** [v4, Dec 1984] Italian esoteric magazine with brief English & French summaries. 3/yr. 6 issues for 10,000 lire. Shan: via Avigliana 13, I–10138, Torino, Italy.

CRYPTOZOOLOGY

◆ **CHAMP CHANNELS** [v3 n2, 1985] News of the Lake Champlain monster and related information; edited by its energetic investigator, Joseph Zarzynski. 4/yr. $8. O:$9. NFC. Lake Champlain Phenomena Investigation: Box 2134, Wilton, NT 12866, USA.

◆ **CREATURE CHRONICLES** [n8, 15 March 1985] Fortean news from Ohio. ?/yr. Inquiries to Ron Schaffner: Box 335, Loveland, OH 45140, USA.

◆ **CRYPTOZOOLOGY** [v3, Winter 1984] Essential for serious cryptozoologists. Articles, research reports, expedition reports, reviews, debates. 1/yr. Apply to International Society of Cryptozoology: Box 43070, Tuscon, AZ 85733, USA.

◆ **ISC NEWSLETTER** [v4 n1, Spring 1985] Report of a new expedition to investigate the (mermaid) Ri of New Guinea, identifies them as a species of dugong, thus vindicating Jon Erik Beckjord (see FT42p34). Many other item of cryptozoological news. 4/yr. You get this and *Cryptozoology* (above) when you join the International Society of Cryptozoology: Box 43070, Tucson, AZ 85733, USA. Annual membership is $25.

◆ **NESSLETTER** [n67, Dec 1984 – n70, June 1985] The latest news of sightings, expeditions and controversies about Nessie and her cousins from the Ness Information Service. 12/yr. £2.50. O:$9. NIS: Rip Hepple: Huntshieldford, St Johns Chapel, Bishop Aukland, Co Durham DL13 1RQ.

PSI

◆ **JOURNAL OF THE SOCIETY FOR PSYCHICAL RESEARCH** [v53 n799, Feb 1985 – v53 n801, Oct 1985] 3/yr. Membership: £13/$34. SPR: 1 Adam & Eve Mews, London W8 6UG.

UFO

◆ **APRO BULLETIN** [v32 n1 – v33 n1] Essential reading for current US investigations from the venrable Aerial Phenomena Research Organization. 12/yr. Memb: $15. O:$18. APRO: 3610 E. Kleindale Rd, Tucson, AZ 85712, USA.

◆ **BUFORA BULLETIN** [n17, May 1985 – n18, July 1985] Magazine of the British UFO Research Association; lately more informative and better produced. 4/yr. Memb: £12.50. BUFORA Membership Sec: Pam Kennedy, 30 Vermont Rd, London SE19 3SR.

◆ **CENTRE UPDATE** [n5, June 1985] newsletter & reviews from the Resources Centre of the Organisation for Scientific Evaluation of Aerial Phenomena (OSEAP). 3/yr. *New address.* OSEAP: 15 Edmondson St, Barnoldswick, Lancs, BB8 5EY.

◆ **JOURNAL OF TRANSIENT AERIAL PHENOMENA** [v3 n4, March 1985 – v4 n1, Sept 1985]. 2/yr. Free to BUFORA members, and for exchange. See 'BUFORA Bulletin' above.

◆ **FLYING SAUCER REVIEW** [v29 n5, 1984 – v30 n6, 1985] Still essential reading for ufologists after 30 years on the front line! 6/yr. £7.50. O:$15. NFC. Pay: FSR Publications Ltd: Snodland, Kent ME6 5HJ.

◆ **MAGONIA** [n19 May 1985] Essential for informed ufologists and forteans. 4/yr. £2. USA:$5. O:£2.50. Pay: John Rimmer: 64 Alric Ave, New Malden, Surrey KT3 4JW.

◆ **NORTHERN UFO NEWS** [n112, March/Apr 1985] Vital news & investigations from the north of England, including the thoughts of Jenny Randles. 6/yr. £4.50. *New address.* NUFON: 8 Whitethroat Walk, Birchwood, Warrington, Cheshire WA3 6PQ.

◆ **UFO 21** – Belgian/Dutch UFO magazine. Inquiries to Marc Broux, Koning Albertstraat 40, 3500 Hasselt, Belgium.

◆ **UFO NEWSCLIPPING SERVICE** – Monthly collections of clippings from all over the world, with several pages of Forteana too. 12/yr. Apply for rates. UFONS: Route 1, Box 200, Plumerville, AK 72127, USA.

◆ **UFO NEWS FLASH** [n12, March 1985] Italian news and sightings in English. ?/yr. Details from: Massimo Greco: Box 29, I–25121 Brescia, Italy.

◆ **UFO RESEARCH AUSTRALIA NEWSLETTER** – Essential for keeping infomed on Australian research and cases. 6/yr. A$15; O:A$18(surf)/A$30(air). NFC. UFORAN: Box 229, Prospect, SA 5082, Australia.

EARTH MYSTERIES

◆ **ARCHAEOASTRONOMY** – The bulletin of the Center for Archaeoastronomy. Academic studies of cultural and historical evidence of ' tive' systems of astronomy. 4/yr. $15. US:$12. CA: University of Maryland, College Park, MD 20742, USA.

◆ **CAERDROIA** – This well-illustrated and enthusiastically produced journal, pioneering research into and cataloguing the world's mazes and labyrinths, shows what you can do with scant resources. Apx 4/yr. £3.50. E:£4.50. O:$10. The Caerdroia Project: 53 Thundersley Grove, Thundersley, Benfleet, Essex SS7 3EB.

◆ **EARTHLINES** (n4, 1985] Welsh Border earth mysteries, with snippets of historical regional Forteana. 4/yr. £4. O:$10. Earthlines: 7 Brookfield, Stirchley, Telford, Shrops TF3 1EB.

◆ **EARTHQUEST NEWS** [n13, Feb 1985] Editor Andy Collins investigates energetically fortean, psychic and earth-mystery phenomena in Essex (mainly). Essential reading. 4/yr. £3. E:£4. O:$8. Earthquest: 19 St Davids Way, Wickford, Essex SS11 8EX.

◆ **THE LEY HUNTER** [n96, Summer 1984 – n98, Spring 1985] 3 issues + separately edited supplement/yr. £4. E:£6. O:$20(air) $15(surf). T L H: Box 13, Welshpool, Powys, Wales.

◆ **NORTHERN EARTH MYSTERIES** [n28, May 1985 – n29, Autumn 1985] Journal of the Northern Earth Mysteries Group. No.28 includes a facsimile of the first issue of *The Ley Hunter* (1965). 4/yr. £2.50. Pay: Philip Heselton, 170 Victoria Avenue, Hull HU5 3DY.

◆ **QUICKSILVER MESSENGER** [n10] 3/yr. £5. $16. NFC *Temporary new address*: Chris Ashton, c/o EEP. Jln Kapten Tendean 18, Jakarta-Selatan, Indonesia.

◆ **STONEHENGE VIEWPOINT** Each issue is filled with informative and imaginative explorations of every aspect of megalithic culture. 6/yr. £5. US: $8. Can:$10. SV: 2821 De La Vina St, Santa Barbara, CA 93105, USA. UK Agency: c/o 3rd Floor, 35 Gt Russell St, London WC1.

◆ **TOUCHSTONE** [n7, Sept 1985] Newsletter for Surrey Earth Mysteries, edited by Jimmy Goddard. Enquiries to: Touchstone: 25 Albert Rd, Addlestone, Weybridge, Surrey.

OTHERS

◆ **BLACK CHIP** – A journal of computing for anarchists. 4/yr. £2. Pay: Richard Alexander, 55 Dupont Rd, London SW20 8EH.

◆ **CRITIQUE** – "A journal of Conspiracies & Metaphysics". A weighty journal of great interest, in its fifth year of publishing. Quarterly. $14. O:$21 (air). *Critique* c/o Bob Banner, PO Box 11451, Santa Rosa, CA 95406, USA. Sample (150pp) $6.0 (air): $9.0.

◆ **LIGHT TIMES** – Unclassifiable, certifiable, sporadical. Enquiries to: Light Times: Box 85366, Los Angeles, CA 90073, USA.

◆ **MAGGIE'S FARM** – Australia's alternative network magazine; with some coverage of occultism & PSI research, and Abo resistence to the erosion of their beliefs and sacred sites. Inquiries to MF: Box 29, Bellingen, NSW 2454, Australia.

◆ **NEW ALBION NEWSLETTER** [n1] a sporadical comentary on the contemporary pagan scene. Free to UK inquirers who send an SAE; those abroad should sent Int. Reply Coupons. Editor: Nigel Pennick: 142 Pheasant Rise, Bar Hill, Cambridge CB3 8SD.

◆ **NEW INSTANT** – Free alternative adsheet. Freedom Press, Angel Alley, 84b Whitechapel High St, London E1 7QX.

◆ **RESURGENCE** [n109, Mar/Apr 1985 – n112, Sept/Oct 1985] "A thoughtful voice of decentralist, spiritual and ecological outlook," incorporating *Undercurrents*. 6/yr. £9. O:£11. Resurgence Sub. Dept.:Worthyvale Manor Farm, Camelford, Cornwall PL32 9TT.

◆ **THEOSOPHICAL HISTORY** [v1 n1, Jan 1985] An independent journal studying the Theosophical movement, edited by Leslie Price. 4/yr. £5. O:$10. Pay: Leslie Price: 46 Evelyn Gardens, London SW7 3HB.

◆ **WHOLE EARTH REVIEW** – Continuation of the *CoEvolution Quarterly* and the *Whole Earth Software Catalog.* A broad-based wise-up New Age review of tools and ideas for the Computer Age. Essential to keep up weih the times and techniques. 6/yr. $18. O:$22(surf)/$34(air). WER: Box 27956, San Diego, CA 92128, USA.

●

Small independent magazines are labours of love and need your support. Please mention **Fortean Times** *when you respond to these listings.*

Reviews

ENCYCLOPEDIA OF OCCULTISM AND PARAPSYCHOLOGY

edited by Leslie Shepard.
Gale Research Co, Detroit; 1985, $245 hb, 1,617 pages in 3 volumes, indexes.

A hearty welcome to the second edition of the single most valuable reference work in the combined fields of occult science, magic, demonology, superstitions, spiritism, mysticism, metaphysics, psychical science and parapsychology. It is a major work in every sense.

The project started out to amalgamate the old encyclopedias by Nandor Fodor and Lewis Spence. Leslie Shepard the fortean and well-known scholar of mysticism and paranormality was an ideal choice of editor, and he added many new entries bringing the material up to date. Since then Gale issues two updates and a supplementary volume. Now these have been amalgamated into a single series, completely reset into a uniform format, and completely reedited with hundreds of new entries covering recent events and research, concepts and theories, cults and personalities, organizations and publications, spanning three solidly-bound volumes.

Many entries have been rewritten in the light of new knowledge. In controversial areas, well-balanced encapsulations put the case for and against, with key sources for further study. Bibliographic data has been added to many entries, including paperback editions where these are original sources. As if that were not enough, the reference value is increased by the quality and extent of the indexing. Besides the General Index, there are indexes for Animals, Birds, Insects, Demons, Gems, Geographical (places of events), Gods, Periodicals, Plants & Flowers, and Societies & Organizations. Also included is an index for Paranormal Phenomena with 51 separate categories.

We at *Fortean Times* have found the *Encyclopedia* an invaluable companion in our work and we have no hesitation in recommending it to anyone, whether they are beginners searching for footholds of understanding in the vast edifice of the paranormal, or more seasoned researchers following specific lines of inquiry. At $245 it is, perhaps, beyond the individual pocket, in which case every fortean has a duty to insist his local library buy a set.

RJMR

THE MOON AND THE PLANETS

compiled by William R. Corliss
The Sourcebook Project: Box 107, Glen Arm, MD 21057, USA; 1985, $18.95 postpaid, pp383, indexes, illus. refs.

The fifth in the projected 25 volume 'Catalog of Anomalies'. The reference value of these works is, literally, phenomenal. If the Catalogs are new to you, Corliss has salvaged historical and modern anomalies from the scientific literature and catalogued them in a hierarchy of topics with references, examples and an anomaly rating. The present volume is devoted to astronomical anomalies involving all the solar system planets and their satellites including this earth of ours and its moon.

A sample of category headings cannot do justice to the richness of the material, but to hint at its range you will find here anomalies of orbit and spin; surface and composition curiosities; telescopic observations; anomalies of transit, atmosphere, radiation and magnetic field; possible and temporary satellites and anomalies of any 'rings'; ambiguous surface markings (eg bands, lines, streaks etc); topographical features (eg canyons, craters and mountains) and anomalous luminous phenomena.

These books are essential for researchers, but in order to encourage new generations of forteans they must also be available in every school and local library.

RJMR

CURIOUS ENCOUNTERS

by Loren Coleman.
Faber & Faber, Boston & London; 1985, $11.95 pb, pp166 , index, illus, appendices.

Close on the heels of his first solo book, *Mysterious America*, comes another collection of American forteana and Loren Coleman's best book yet. Like the true fortean he is, Coleman begins with an acknowledgement of the difficulty of grouping his material because of the way the phenomena and investigations merge into one another. So he has chosen to organize his material loosely around major landscape and topographical features – the oceans, the sea and the air, the sky, the jungles, the cities, the swamps, the hills, etc – which well indicates the vast and changeable nature of the backdrop against which the selected mysteries are acted out. For example, in the chapter on phantom trains you will find these ghostly engines lead onto a discussion of spook lights, UFOs, and various humanoid apparitions, all with some railroad connection.

As before the whole cast of the fortean parade is here with some new additions: giant birds, aerial serpents, frog-like monsters, snake-like denizens of lakes and rivers, hairy giants, gill-men, phantom big-cats and kangaroos. "They pass and pass and keep on passing," as Fort wrote. Coleman has added discussion of stone forts, 'magnetic' hills, and many other hard-to-define mystery sites, including some classic haunted houses. Of particular interest to me were the chapters on the mysterious little people of Yucatan and the enigma of the Thunderbird (evidence of the giant birds in Indian legends surviving into the modern era).

Most of the material will be new to the majority of readers and that is what really absorbs the fortean interest. It also has immediacy, because Coleman has investigated the cases personally or had direct access to the investigations of others. And because he is developing a good story-telling style, you learn unobtrusively while being entertained. The frequent dollops of Fort's philosophical asides make an interesting leavening: the old boy would have noted with some amusement that while some mysteries from his day are still recurring, his words are equally applicable to the newer mysteries, like alligators-in-the-sewers and the girl in Newport, Oregon, who, in April 1966, saw "three tiny tree stumps walking across a meadow". I feel Fort would have like this book.

The British edition will be on sale from late January 1986 from Faber & Faber Ltd, priced £6.95 (pb) – so there's no excuse for any of you not getting your own copy.

RJMR

GLOWING BIRDS
Stories from the edge of science

by Patrick Huyghe
Faber & Faber, Winchester, Mass: 1985; pb $9.95; pp241.

This is a collection of popular science articles the author has written for glossy American publications such as *Science Digest, Omni, The New York Times Magazine* and *Psychology Today*. The title comes from a piece on the accomplishments of Bill Corliss and his amazing rescue project for obscure Fortean-type data (for more info, see page 40 in this issue). The wide-ranging subject matter is divided into four categories: Mind, Life, Universe and Frontiers. The first deals with our earliest memories; imaginary companions; dream psi; alexithymics (people who lack the ability to express their feelings and emotions in words); diaries of all sorts; awareness under general anaesthetic; manias for cleanliness, and self-mutilation, biting people; people who jinx equipment; and artificial intelligence. Life features thoughts on the 'primordial soup'; healing plants; amoeba lethal to humans; medical diagnostic; the health risks of going to hospitals; heart disease; new remedies for poor vision; and sudden deaths from fear, anxiety, stress etc. The Universe section assays old records of stars; the mysteries of precognition and ELF radiation; our knowledge of the sun; what goes on at the heart of our galaxy; and the energy "fountains" in space. Frontiers looks at the 'science' of cycles; the Sasquatch; technology forecasting; the Society for Scientific Exploration, a sort of Fortean society exclusively for established scientists; the US government's record of supressing information on UFO incidents; and the article on Fortean anomalies generally which gives the book its title. On the whole, an entertaining and informative read.

RJMR

SCIENCE AND THE UFOS

by Jenny Randles & Peter Warrington.
Basil Blackwell, Oxford; 1985, £12.50, pp215, index, bib, plates.

In recent years Jenny Randles and her co-author have offered a series of books with the triple aim of improving the public attitude towards contemporary investigative ufology, improving the standards of investigative ufology itself, and making some of the unique and varied case-material of

British investigators available to the ufological community worldwide. This book is expressly different: the authors describe it as "not an appeal for ufology's acceptance into the scientific community" but a demonstration "that there are sound reasons for scientists to investigate the subject for themselves."

The book's success depends upon its audience. If they are 'demonstrating' the fact to members of the public, the book is well done and convincing -- but the public have little sway over the direction of scientific research. If they are speaking to scientists themselves their reception will be mixed: those who oppose the very idea of UFOs, and they could be the majority, will not even deign to read this book, much less properly ponder the evidence; those who are sympathetic to the idea will inevitably, because of the social stigma still attached to the subject, pursue it unofficially, if at all.

Pessimistically, then, there seems little point to the book. It is, however, an excellent assessment of the tangible evidence of UFOs, the problems of evidence and investigation generally, and a good review of what might be called the 'serious' side of ufology (governmental attitudes towards the subject, official and military inquiries, and investigations led by accredited scientists, etc). Perhaps the most important part of the book is the final chapter, in which the authors spell out what a 'serious' investigation might hold for cosmology, astronomy, geophysics, physics, psychology and sociology, when the UFO-anomalies which involve these aspects are eventually solved. While this might not appeal to orthodox scientists, whom, history shows, tend to resist the influx or even threat of new ideas, especially those from *outside* their discipline, it will undoubtedly give some sense of direction, if not hope, to a new generation of budding ufologists.

RJMR

THE SECRET POWER OF MUSIC

by David Tame.
Turnstone Press, Wellingborough, Northants; 1984; pb £5.95; pp304, notes, bib.

David Tame has written a very creditable occult history of music and its overt and covert influence on the development of both individuals and society. He charts how the power of music has been used and abused by musicians, philosophers, scientists and mystics. He explores its effects on heat rate, metabolism, digestion, stress, and our physical, mental and emotional well-being, and concludes that the ancients indeed understood well the recuperative power of music. Particularly interesting are the explorations of the almost Pythagorean philosophy of music in ancient China and India and the cosmological significance of fundamental tones and harmonies; and these are critically (and unfavourably) contrasted with the spiritually empty forms of jazz, modern rock and computer music.

On the way, Tame aims a broadside at behaviourist explanations of music as purely bio-mechanical stimulation. This official view is enshrined in the concept of 'muzak' and denies the role of music as a vehicle for creativity, inspiration, morality, regeneration, and even worship. Far from being a cultural curiosity of little consequence, Tame shows how music may shape civilizations as well as (perhaps) chromosomes. Towards the end of the book, as the discussion is dominated by esoteric theories of vibrations, it is clear that Tame is equally in the grip of neo-theosophy and a belief in the teachings, if not the existence of El Morya, Master KH and other members of the Great White Brotherhood, for whose reality he offers no proof. But whether the reader accepts or not the source of such teachings, and Tame's dependence upon them, does not detract from the value of their insights, and this book is good enough to stand *despite* my own skepticism in this direction. Nor is there any doubt about Tame's grasp of ancient musical philosophy, the history of music, or current musical trends. It could all have been so dry and humourless; instead Tame shows a dry wit, and a good Fortean grasp of the absurd.

RJMR

THE GENIUS OF THE FEW

by Christian O'Brien
Turnstone Press, Wellingborough, Northants: 1985; pb £9.95; pp320, index, bib, fold-out map.

Convincing attempt to place the original 'Garden of Eden' near the Dead Sea. O'Brien argues, from close study of Sumerian and Hebrew texts, that a technologically advanced people settled there in the 7th/8th millenia BC, founding a laboratory for breeding animals and plants. Called the *Anannage*, or 'Shining Ones', they finally dispersed when their base at Kharsag was destroyed by the Great Flood, migrating to Scandinavian and Celtic countries via Greece, inspiring local cultures, technologies and religions. Just who these 'Shining Ones' were, with their genetic engineering, electrical technology and flying craft, who were skilled enough to have created a race of men (from Adam to

Noah), and who were revered as gods by the races of men (Neandertal & Cro-Magnon) they visited? O'Brien is deliberately vague on this subject which he is keeping for a sequel, though he does comment, at one point, that they "were not of our species – possibly not even from our planet..." (p137). He keeps such 'ancient astronaut' speculation to a minimum, and this has helped greatly to keep the presentation of his ideas free of the "Gee whiz!" hysteria with which some other writers have damned these and similar prehistorical enigmas. I found the book to be one of the most thought-provoking and enimently sensible statements, on the enigmas presented by what appear to be descriptions of high-tech sciences in man's most ancient texts, that I ead for a long time.

RJMR

ATLANTIS RECONSIDERED

By Michael Baran.
Exposition Press, 1701 Blount Rd, Pompano Beach, FL 33069, USA: 1981; hb $6.00; pp85, refs.

INSIGHTS INTO PREHISTORY

by Michel Baran.
Exposition Press: 1982; hb $7.00; pp114, refs.

TWILIGHT OF THE GODS

By Michael Baran.
Exposition Press: 1984; hb $10.50; pp144, refs.

The general concern of these books by 'Michael Baran' is the prehistoric period symbolized by legendary "lost" continents of Mu, Lemuria and Atlantis. Baran has put an enormous amount of efforts into expressing his thoughts, and his sections (in the earlier books) on the remains of Atlantis-like myths in the traditions of American Indians are interesting and regrettably brief. Instead Baran's main discussions rest almost entirely on completely dubious sources. Atlantis and Mu are pretty much like blank canvasses upon which the contemporary dreamer can portray whatever society he likes, using as colours the unverifiable and (deliberately?) evocative imagery provided by Madame Blavatsky, James Churchward, Edgar Cayce et al. As a Fortean, I cannot accept Plato's account of Atlantis on his eminence and antiquity alone; the story was at least fifth-hand when he heard it! God only knows what proof was destroyed with the library at Alexandria, but the fact is that here and now we have none that would convince even the fair-minded. Blavatsky's authorities were the Great White Brotherhood and the Akashic Record, neither of which/whom I have been able to consult; Cayce's word pictures – you could hardly call them information in the useful sense – were 'revealed' to him while he was unconscious; and there is nothing to gainsay the idea that Churchward's Mu existed only in his imagination. What a palette for today's discontented musings about the Golden Age! What brave new age societies we can imagine; what marvellous races of beings peopled those ideal lands, and what science-fiction technologies they *must* have had!

There was a time when I too was caught up in such fantasizing. Books like these and others of the Daniken, Berlitz, Colosimo, Charoux, Tomas ilk, in which there is typically very little hard referencing or factual underpinning, serve no real purpose except as creative therapy for the expressing author's emerging cosmology. Baran's book is at least an honest statement of belief, where others have had more commercial motives. However, there is a growing use of 'creative imagination' in the exploration of historical and prehistorical enigmas, especially in the USA where it is called 'psychic archaeology'. Only time will tell its value. In my Fortean work I have found such books to be of no value at all.

RJMR

THE BIBLE CAME FROM ARABIA

by Kamal Salibi
Jonathan Cape, London; hb £10.95, pp223, index, maps.

Salibi's linguistic and geographical research led him to conclude that the land of Abraham and the site of the first Temple lie not in Palestine but in a coastal strip south of Mecca. (I summarised his evidence in the last issue, FT44,p14.) The destruction of Judah by Nebuchadnezzar in 586 BC put an end to the Israelites as a political force in south-west Arabia, although Judaism survived there as a religion into the present century. As long ago as 1946 the British Arabist, Gerald de Gaury, prophesied: "In the valleys of Asir, and the Hijaz, there are ruins which one day will reveal the meaning of references in the early books of the Bible and those of the Koran". Not surprisingly, the Saudi authorities forbid any archaeological investigations in the area – they need a relocation of the Promised Land within their borders like they need a hole in the head!

Paul Sieveking

Also Received

- **Arkana** – new paperback imprint of Routledge & Kegan Paul for reprinting classics of "exploration of inner space, mind and psyche". First releases are: **The pocket I Ching** translated by Richard Wilhelm and Englished by Cary Baynes (£3.50); **The secret of the golden flower** by Richard Wilhelm (£3.95); **Views from the real world** (£4.50) and **Meetings with remarkable men** (£3.95) both by G. Gurdjief; **A new model of the universe** by P D Ouspensky (£5.95); **The book of the dead** by E A Wallis Budge, with plates and 420 vignettes (£7.95); **A course in miracles**, being half a million words of "inner dictation" to Dr Helen Schucman, a professor of medical psychology at Columbia University (£9.95); **The magical arts** by Richard Cavendish (£4.95); **The power of the pendulum** by T C Lethbridge (£3.50); **The Conference of the birds** by Farid ud-din Attar (£3.50); **The western way** by Caitlin and John Matthews (£4.50); and **Don Juan, Mescalito and modern magic** by Nevill Drury (£4.95.)

● **The body's recollection of being** by David Michael Levin *(RKP, 1985; hb £29.95, pb £9.95; pp390, index notes, bib)* – a phenomenological psychology and philosophy applied to the problem of nihilism.

● **Survival and disembodied existence** by Terence Penelhum *(RKP: 1980; pb £2.25; pp116, index, bib)* – a deep and difficult philosophical discussion of the logical problems created by the notion of disembodied existence. Written in 1970, before the explosion of interest in so-called Near Death Experiences.

● **Numbers: their history and meaning** by Graham Flegg *(Pelican/Penguin 1984; pb £4.95; pp294, index, bib, diags)* – everything you wanted to know about the history of counting systems.

● **Atlantis** by Charles Berlitz *(Macmillan London: 1984; hb £9.95; pp223, index, bib, colour plates)* – you might have thought Berlitz, after three books using this subject, had nothing new to say, and you'd be right. This is a re-hash of his old material.

● **Mindreach** by J H Brennan *(Aquarian Press, 1985; pb £2.50; pp160, index).* An overview of psychic and psi phenomena, suggesting how you can do them. Contains a test programme in Basic for Apple computers.

● **The bond of power** by Joseph Chilton Pearce (*RKP, 1982, pb £3.95; pp177, notes)* – an exploration of the latent potential of human consciousness in which the siddhi meditational philosophy of Muktananda meets the holonomic physics of David Bohm.

● **The book of Hu & the book of Tyana** by John Gibson *(Philosophical Library, 200w 57th St, NY, NY 10019, USA: 1984; hb $15.00; pp136)* – the author's own synthesis of the Truth, gleaned from many sources, predicated on a theosophy-type belief in reincarnation and the Great White Brotherhood. Mostly unreferenced, plenty of jargon. If you can accept such notions as 200 million giants currently residing "inside planet earth" you should have no difficulty with this.

● **Nostradamus 2: Into the twenty-first century** by Jean-Charles de Fontbrune *(Hutchinson, 1984; hb £7.95; pp172, bib).*

● **God and the new physics** by Paul Davies *(Pelican/*

Continued ☛

Booklets

★ **THE HUGHENDEN DRAGON** – by Clive Harper. A brief account of the dragon-like creature seen near High Wycombe, Bucks, in 1578. *(Torsdag Publications: 7 Malmers Well Road, High Wycombe, Bucks HP13 6PD. Price 65p inc postage.)*

★ **THE COSMIC SHEEPDOG** – by Robert C Girard. Ufology's most famous bookseller condenses the thought of several years' musings on the ontological problems raised by anomalous phenomena (including UFOs). Just as the actions of humans can affect the other forms of life with which we share this planet, so might the strange things that happen be the results of the unwitting actions of beings in a "larger reality" who might be as blissfully unaware of us. Before you dismiss this as another form of 'special pleading', Girard's ideas deserve a hearing. *(Arcturus Book Service: Box 2213, Scotia, NY 12302, USA. Price $5.95, signed.)*

★ **SKYWAYS & LANDMARKS REVISTED** – by Philip Heselton, Jimmy Goddard & Paul Baines. A re-evaluation of Tony Wedd's 1961 paper on the Kentish leys and their markers. The authors suggest that the re-emergence of leys and other 'earth mystery' topics in recent years was sparked off by the 1954 belief in 'orthoteny', or lines which could be seen by craft in the upper atmosphere. These lines, or leys, were laid out by extra-terrestrials, precisely to educate us about the mysteries of our planet. *(Published jointly by the Northern Earth Mysteries Group and the Surrey Earth Mysteries Group. Price £1. Available from Jimmy Goddard: 25 Albert Road, Addlestone, Weybridge, Surrey.)*

★ **THE BRENTFORD GRIFFIN** – investigates the alleged griffin sightings in Brentford. *(£1.25. Earthquest Books: 19 St Davids Way, Wickford, Essex SS11 8EX).*

A drawing by Nick Maloret in response to Dick Gwynn's musings on lycanthropy and ergotism [FT44,p59.]

REVIEWS

Cont from p 75.

Penguin: 1984; pb £3.95; pp255, index, notes, bib).

- **The cosmic code: Quantum physics as the language of nature** by Heinz Pagels *(Pelican/Penguin: 1984; pb £4.50; pp336, index, bib).*
- **The origins of man & the universe: the myth that came to life** by Barry Long *(RKP: 1984; pb £6.95; pp300, index).*
- **Space, time & medicine** by Larry Dossey *(Shambala/RKP: 1982; pb £5.95/$8.95; pp248, index, notes/bib)* – another synthesis of eastern philosophy and Bohm's holonomic physics, this time seeking implications for the health and healing of mind and body.

Truss Fund

our thanks to the following for their kind donations: C.H.D'Alessio, Mrs K.Francis, Mia Gerhardt, Michael Hine, D. Lowdon, Nick Maloret, Sven Rosen, P. Wilson.

Small Ads

Fortean Book Club

WOOLSACK, WOOLSERY, BIDEFORD, DEVON, EX39 5QZ.

Selections for November 1985.

1. **Railway Ghosts** by William Barry Herbert. Well-written stories of ghosts and haunted lines, specifying place, person and circumstance. HB £6.50
2. **Curious Facts** by John May with Michael Marten, John Chesterman, David Brittain and Lee Torrey. First published in 1981 and reprinted twice. Wide-ranging if occasionally over-brief. Headings such as "The Great Bengal Frog War" gives some idea of contents. PB £3.25
3. **The Ghost of 29 Megacycles** by John G. Fuller. One of the best books on electronic communication with the dead. Lacks index and more technical detail. Newly published. HB £9.75
4. **The Occult Roots of Nazism** by Nicholas Goodrick-Clarke. The most serious study of the occult side of Nazism yet produced. Photos. HB £11.00

To join the book club, choose one or more of the above and send the order with remittance, **plus £1.20 postage**, to us. All books are offered below published price. For outside Europe, the US$ price is twice the UK£ price, i.e. £6.50 = $13.00. This covers our cheque encashment costs and increased postage. All books have a money-back guarantee if you are not satisfied.

CRITIQUE

A Journal of Conspiracies & Metaphysics

– – Subjects Explored – –

High-Tech Murders
Gnostic Gospels • Psychic Warfare
Global Elites • Russian Spy Schools
High-Tech Mind Control
Weather Warfare • Anomalies
Secret Societies • the Occult
UFOs, Sufis, Mossad
Ideological Indoctrination
Nazism and the Occult
Assassinations • The Middle East
Cosmic Mysteries
Cover-Ups • Revisionists
Pearl Harbor • The Vatican Scandal
Electromagnetic Fields: ELF waves
Media Monopolies • Mass Hypnosis
Book & Zine Reviews

Send for free literature;or sample ($6. Air: $9.) Critique, PO Box 11451, Santa Rosa, CA 95406, USA.

WANTED: *Fortean Soc. Magazine* Nos 4&5, *Doubt,* 59 onwards, *Rosicrucian Digest,* pre-1955 only. Write to 54 Monks Rd, Exeter, Devon EX4 7BB.

Help!

INFORMATION & CORRESPONDENCE, please, on any cryptozoologocial matter. Special interest in Australian giant lizards, African dinosaurs and the maybe monsters of South America. Howie Pine, 359 Taylor Mills Rd, Englishtown, NJ 07726, USA.

HELP WANTED: information on the mystery of the lost Pleiades. Who can sell me Prof. Piazzi Smith's book on pyramids, or photocopies? Special interest in Haliburton's material contained therein. Who can sell/lend me other material about the lost Pleiades? Please write to: J. Langbein, OT. Niese, Auf dem Felde 11, D-4927 Lügde, West Germany.

INFORMATION, please on helicopters in relation to UFOs: phantom 'copters, 'copters changing into UFOs, and vice versa, and 'copter "mythology". Write to: Dennis Stillings, c/o Archaeus Project, 629 12th Avenue SE, Minneapolis, MN 55414 USA.

INFO OF ANY KIND on the Springheel Jack phenomenon. Write to Andy Roberts, 84 Elland Rd, W.Yorks HD6 2QR.

TREPHINATION – I am collecting data on this operation, especially on those (including self-trephinees) whose motive has been consciousness expansion; the extent of the practice in modern societies; and the reported effects. Anonymity assured. Write to: Peter A. Kels, Lot 41 Repeater Stn. Rd., Springbrook 4213, Queensland, Australia.

★ **IRISH FORTEANS** are invited to contact Harold A. Covington who wishes to start an Irish fortean group and newsletter. Write to him at: 77 Knockmoyle, Tralee, Co Kerry, Ireland.

COUD – I (Collectors of Unusual Data – International) is a free association of clipsters with no expense and no meetings, whose purpose is to exchange data worldwide. The more stuff COUD – I gets, the more we can pass on to the Fortean journals. New members wanted. Write to COUD – I, Ray Nelke, 2312 Sheilds Ave, St Louis, MO 63136, USA.

Fortean Times

SUE No.46 The Foremost Journal of Strange Phenomena PRICE: £1.50 $3.00

SPECIAL ISSUE: LAKE MONSTERS OF CONTINENTAL EUROPE

Fortean Times

Cover art by **AdCo.**
See caption on p55

The Journal of Strange Phenomena.

Spring 1986
ISSN 0308.5899

Strange Days

Features

Forum

Usual Stuff

Fortean Times
**96 Mansfield Road,
London NW3 2HX, UK**

EXECUTIVE EDITORS
Robert J.M. Rickard
Paul R.A.de G. Sieveking

STAFF WRITERS THIS ISSUE
Mike Dash
Bob Rickard (Editor)
Paul Sieveking

SPECIAL CORRESPONDENTS
Australia Greg Axford (Vic.)
Paul Cropper (NSW)
Rex Gilroy (NSW)
Tony Healy (ACT)
Richard King (Vic.)
Belgium Henri Premont
Canada Dwight Whalen (Ont.)
Mister X (Ont.)
England Bruce Chatterton (Lond.)
Peter Christie (Devon)
Mike Crowley (London)
Mike Dash (Herts.)
Peter Hope Evans (Lond.)
Alan Gardiner (Sussex.)
Brian Hain (Glos.)
Chris Hall (Hants.)
Nick Maloret (Hants.)
Valerie Martin (Kent)
John Michell (London)
Steve Moore (London)
Nigel Pennick (Cambs.)
Paul Screeton (Clvlnd.)
Bob Skinner (Surrey)
Anthony Smith (Staffs.)
Paul R. Thomas (Avon)
Finland Tuuri Heporauta
France Jean-Louis Brodu
Dr Bernard Heuvelmans
Greece Anastasios D. Panos
Ireland Peter Costello
Doc Shiels
Robert Anton Wilson
Japan Masaru Mori
Malaysia Ahmed Jamaludin
Scotland Roger Musson
Roland Watson
Jake Williams
South Africa Chris J. Holtzhausen
Sweden Ake Franzen
Anders Liljegren
Sven Rosen
USA Larry E. Arnold (PA)
Tom Adams (TX)
Loren Coleman (MA)
Richard T. Crowe (IL)
David R. Fideler (PA)
Mark A. Hall (MN)
Steve Hicks (KS)
Michael Hoffman (NY)
Phil Ledger (CA)
Kurt Lothmann (TX)
Gary S. Mangiacopra (CN)
Ray Nelke (MO)
Scott Parker (TX)
Ron Schaffner (OH)
Joseph Swatek (NB)
Joseph Trainor (MA)
Joseph W. Zarzynski (NY)
USSR Vladimir Rubtsov
Wales Janet & Colin Bord
West Germany Ulrich Magin
Yemen Ion A. Will
Yugoslavia Milos Krmelj

CONSULTANTS: Richard Adams (Art); Hunt Emerson (Comix); Dick Gwyn (Print). **TYPESETTING:** Cecilia Boggis, 11 Ashburnham Road, Bedford, MK40 1DX. **COMPUTER SETTING:** Serious Software, 55 East Road, London N1 6AH. **GRAPHIC SERVICES:** Adco, 2 Blenheim Crescent, London W11 1NN. **LABEL COMPUTING:** Anagram, 316A Richmond Road, Twickenham TW1 2PD. **OVERSEAS MAILING:** Overseas Postal Services Ltd., 2-8 Hornsey Street, London N7 8HF.

THANKS PAUL!

Hasn't Paul Sieveking done well? Paul stepped behind the editorial desk at very short notice and managed to put out issues every bit as good as mine. He worked hard on them and it shows. I'm sure you'll join me in thanking him.

BACK IN THE HARNESS

When I handed over to Paul, just 15 months ago, I was moved by the number of letters from well-wishers, and especially the pre-Christmas Fortean bash in my honour. Things had become very tough for my little family because of severe excema in both my boys; my wife and I were exhausted by four years of daily nursing and sleepless nights. The time available for work on FT dwindled rapidly and I was relieved when Paul made his offer to keep FT going for a while to give me a break.

It was just in time because my family suffered a blow that has been hard to accept. Within a few months my youngest son, Freddy, aged two and a half, would be dead. The cause was a herpes virus, which would ordinarily produce a cold sore, but which is devastating to vulnerable excematous skin. Freddy fought valiantly but could not overcome it. Our love goes with him into the next stage of his life. As if in a personal demonstration of the balancing forces, in which I believe as a fortean, we had been blessed with a baby daughter, Kim, just five weeks earlier. She too is covered with excema, presenting all the familiar problems, but to us she is beautiful.

There was much to keep me occupied: the fortean database project, as well as the work at which I earn a living and the relentless demands of excematous children. My debt to my wife, Sam, is enormous; together we have found the strength to cope with our problems. So my sabbatical was no holiday, but the sheer relief of not having to put FT together for a while was as good as a rest. I feel able to resume; as witness this issue.

TYPESETTING FT

Another experiment in this issue is the use of our word processor to code the text for typesetting. The results you see have taken many hours of wrestling with ponderous codes. We could save a lot of time and expense with special software, but this will cost about £2000. The long-term results would be well worth it. **Could YOU help with a donation towards this software?**

OCCASIONAL PAPERS

We are pleased to announce the revival of our series of occa-

Continued ☛ 65

Letters

KINGS & A PEARL OF A COINCIDENCE

In answer to your query on other cases of 'Squirrel Kings' [FT45p36], I find the details of five cases of the phenomenon in Martin Hart's book *Rats* (Allison & Busby, 1982) in the chapter on Rat Kings (pp80-81). Three of these cases were in America (two of which were at a zoo in South Carolina), and two cases in Europe.

Another coincidence has occurred in connection with my writing to you. On the last occasion I cited Fort:

"But it is not that I take numerous repetitions as a standard for admission – the fellow who found the pearl in the oyster stew – the old fiddle that turned out to be a Stradivarius – the ring that was lost in a lake, and then was found when the fish was caught –

"But these often repeated yarns are conventional yarns.

"... Out of dozens of reported pearls in stews, most likely there have been instances..." (THE BOOKS p864.)

I was delighted to see, the other day, when doing a clipping search in the *Daily Mirror*, the following report in the paper for the *very day* I wrote to you:

PLENTY OF FISH...BUT GO STEADY ON THE PEARLS! A fish pie special was going down a treat until a customer crunched into a pearl. But astonished businessman Hilary Chittenden didn't complain. ..he just finished his meal and took the pearl to a local jeweller who confirmed it was genuine. Cook Alison Bench thinks the perfectly-formed pearl was among the mussels she put in her pies at the White Hart Hotel in Fairford, Gloucestershire. 'We are proud of our pies,' she said, 'but they aren't usually so exotic.' Hilary added, 'I thought I had lost a filling when I bit on the pearl'. (D.Mirror 28 Nov 1985.)

Although Fort calls such stories "often repeated", I must admit that I haven't come across this one before, to my recollection, which makes this coincidence all the more remarkable.

Bob Skinner
Farnham, Surrey

OF MERMAIDS AND MONSTERS

I note in vol.4, no.1 of the *ISC Newsletter* that a group from the Eco-sophical Society of California went to Papua New Guinea after the other expeditions, and anchored in Nokon Bay just as the natives were pulling a netted creature out of the water, which they identified as the *Ri* or *Ilkai* creature that Wagner, et al, had photographed the previous trip. These Californians correctly identified this creature beyond any doubt as being a mere Indo-Pacific dugong, which verifies my own findings from 1983 on my trip there. Once more, sailors as well as scientists were fooled into thinking the humble sea-cow was a mermaid.

However, all was not wasted on my trip – I uncovered a number of sighting stories about large sea serpents, and little men, a crashed UFO (now swallowed up by jungle) and a sailing ship that appears and disappears mysteriously in the sea twice a year, just off the coast of a village in northern New Guinea. I even ran into two men who claimed to have, separately, pulled in mer-men and a mer-maid, respectively, while fishing. Like the mermaid-on-a-fishing line stories that Tim Dinsdale has recorded from the seas around Scotland, each fisherman quickly let the creature go, for fear of bad luck. Maybe we really don't want to catch a mermaid after all. ..maybe we'd better not.

Erik Beckjord
Malibu, California

WATER HORSES & FAIRIES

In FT43 (p43) you wonder about a sighting of two strange horse-like creatures in an Icelandic lake, guessing it could be "the most exciting cryptozoological discovery" of recent years.

In fact these animals are

Continued ☛ 75

PURGE ON SUPERSTITIONS

As we slide into the Year of the Tiger, Chinese officials have posted their new year's resolutions on the front page of the influential Communist Party newspaper *Guangming Daily*. The notice from the Public Security Ministry urged: "We must crack down with determination on witches, sorcerers and other criminal elements who practice feudal superstition to engage in hooliganism, swindling and even go so far as to kill people." The outburst was in part aimed at the popular festivities which traditionally accompany the Chinese lunar New Year (on Feb.9th this year).

Western countries have seen the horrible consequences of officially condoned witchhunts, and politically motivated persecution of folk-religion, and it is frightening that there is no hint of moderation in the declaration. The official line is that 'superstitious' activities provide opportunities for criminals and con-men. The example is given of a 73yr-old woman, last spring, "who claimed to be a witch, pretended to die and then shocked hundreds of mourners by sitting up in her own coffin, all in a ploy to boost her witchcraft business." Will the next luckless person who recovers from a mistaken diagnosis of death be persecuted as a witch-criminal upon awakening?

Even more sinister, in the opinion of the Ministry, were "superstitious sects formed as a shield for carrying out counter-revolutionary activities," and which must be "completely outlawed".

But to those of us interested in such things, pronouncements like these are a fascinating indication that ancient folk beliefs are still a part of everyday life in China. The report says that only last year (1985) "a young woman believed to be possessed by a 'fox spirit' responsible for reducing the sexual ability of young men, was battered to death in the southern province of Guangdong." Albany (NY) *Times Union* 4 Feb 1986.

As an indication of the deep-rooted awe of the Chinese people towards portents, see GIANT FISH on p 28 , where the appearance of these monsters is related to earthquakes. Now comes the news -

NIGERIAN MERMAID PANIC

From the Nigerian town of Enugu comes a story of a strange panic which has a similar character to it as the rumour of marauding smurfs in **FT42p14**. In this case there was general circulation of a rumour that an evil female spirit, known as the ' mermaid', was to visit schools in Enugu to avenge the killing of her daughter. When several children at the Idaw River primary school, screamed that they had seen the mermaid, pandemonium broke out. According to one pupil, the mermaid had entered the classroom and, when asked by the teacher what she wanted, replied: "The children." In the ensuing panic, nine schoolchildren were killed on a staircase as they fled from a classroom. Reuters. *New York Post* 1 Nov 1985.

Guardian 4 Feb 1986 - that the reappearance of Halley's comet, visible in China in late February, is stirring a certain belief in coming floods and other natural disasters. And because of the rarity and unusual nature of celestial visitations like Halley's comet - which they call *Saozhouxing*, or the 'broom star' - which are thought to portend the fall of dynasties or emperors, there is concern for their current leader, 81yr-old Deng Xiaoping, who has not been seen in public for months.

Justification of this view was seen by all in July 1976 when 'the mantle of heaven' was shaken by the huge earthquake in Tangshan, in which 242,00 people died. Six weeks later, Chairman Mao, who had not been seen in public for several months, died, aged 83.

It is not clear to what extent the purge on superstitions affects popular belief in such 'coincidences'. Prof Wang Yongqian, however, does take them seriously. This member of the Chinese Academy of Sciences, researching flood prevention schemes for the Yellow River, has studied Chinese records of comets going back 2,240 years, and found that on at least nine of the 29 appearances of Halley's Comet since 240BC, which were sighted before April, there were huge floods, especially in south and south-east China. This year, says the professor, we should expect further natual calamities and unpleasant weather because it is also a peak year for sunspots.

OPERATION CONGO

The continuing story of four lads' search for a dinosaur-like animal in the Likouala swamps of the Congo. Well, Bill Gibbons, Mark Rothermel, Jonathan Walls and Joe Wella arrived in the Congo on 30th December, and were immediately faced with problems which no amount of forethought could have prevented. Fearing an attempt on his life, the Congolese President had removed a number of ministers, including the man who gave Operation Congo the go-ahead. Consequently, our lads were told, they did not have the 'proper documents'. It took about five weeks of meetings and waiting for meetings in Brazzaville, because officialdom there is slow, disorganised and paranoid about paperwork. Further panic ensued when their passports were "lost" for three weeks while applying for a visa extension. Eventually the lads had to agree to kitting out, feeding the Congolese members of the expedition, and pay each of them 600,000 CFA **in advance**, before the Secretariat-General would allow the expedition to proceed. Bill, in his depressing letter to us (dated 31 Jan, arrived 22 Feb!) said they also had to sign a 'protocol' setting this out, and agreeing to photograph the *mokele mbembe* only.

They also experienced dishonesty and bare-faced corruption that seemed to be the way of life in the Congo. It had also taken five weeks to get a signature from the Ministry of Finance on a form exempting them from paying tax on their five cases of equipment, under customs bond in Point Noire. After another week's delay (because a clearance had not arrived from the shipping company), and "bribes" of about 67,000 CFA to get the cases out of bond, they found two had been broken into and £1000 worth of equipment missing. The customs denied liability, and still demanded 37,000 CFA rent.

As you can expect, their funds were running out. Mark telexed London for help, and was told in reply that £1000 was being sent. Astonishingly, when he went to collect it, the Commercial Bank of the Congo told him they had only received £100. And so on.

Perhaps the blow that hurt the most came from Dr Roy Mackal. The day after signing the protocol, the Minister of Economy and Forests received a letter from Mackal "urging" him to cancel Operation Congo because it "does not have the financial backing, nor are any of the members experienced in conducting this kind of expedition. I strongly urge you not to allow this expedition to proceed." Dr Marcellin Agnagna, the Congolese appointed leader of the expedition, spoke up for it, assuring the minister that the plans and equipment were "excellent", as were the skills of the British members. Besides Agnagna himself was providing the zoological expertise. It is difficult to understand why Mackal, who had seemed so encouraging during the preparatory stages, should make such a

Continued ☛

☛ *Continued*

trecherous attempt to sabotage this effort. Inescapably, we are drawn to suspect he fears its success would steal the thunder from his own expedition planned for later this year. I hope Mackal can convince us he acted not from personal jealousy. If not, his action is both shameful and unprofessional.

As we go to press the word is that the team is assembling at Imphondo prior to setting out for the Likouala swamps. Because of the remoteness of the area, and difficulties in communication over the distance, we do not expect to hear from them for a few months - unless, of course, they get lucky.

Our special 'Operation Congo' T-shirts, advertised last issue, have been a great success and completely sold out. The money is being forwarded to Operation Congo's London agent. On behalf of them, though, we thank you for your support.

LAKE MONSTER: SIBERIA

A snake-headed, long-necked, carnivorous creature is said to live in the frigid waters of Lake Labinkir, in the Siberian province of Yakutia. According to Anatoly Pankov, author of *The Oymyakonsky Meridian*, on the curiosities of the region, the first reliable sightings were made in the 1950s, although there are many earlier stories. About that time, a group of geologists saw the long neck rising from the murky lake, after they were alerted by splashing sounds. The animal uttered "a sound much like a child's cry," and vanished back into the 150ft-deep waters. Another group of geologists actually saw its form below them, through clear ice, reporting that the greyish creature was like nothing they had seen before.

Some reindeer hunters once saw the creature lunge out of the water to snap up a low-flying bird. Pankov claims that a hunter, who had shot a goose and sent his dog into the water to retrieve it, likewise saw the beast emerge from the depths to gobble first the goose and then his dog. The hunter, it seems, was a trickster, equal to any in European folktales. He got his revenge by putting hot coals on an animal-skin raft, floating it out and watching the creature gulp that down too. A short time later the monster reappeared, thrashing the water and "making terrible sounds".

An article on the monster of Labinkir appeared in *Komsomolskaya Pravda* in the 1960s, inspiring "many" expeditions to the lake, about 150 miles south of the gold-mining town of Ust-Nera, but they all failed to see any sign of the animal. Some biologists have explained it as a giant *schuka* or northern pike, which can reach up to nine feet long. AP. Schenectady (NY) *Gazette*, Framingham (MA) *Middlesex News* 9 April 1979. For more on GIANT FISH, see p28.

IF YOU GOTTA GO...

The sheer ingenuity of many suicides makes the manner of their going a kind of gruesome performance art. Here are some recent examples of a dying art...

● Jehovah's Witness, Donald Allanson, 41, beheaded himself with his chainsaw after hearing of a friend's adultery. Suffering from depression, and believing himself to be under surveillance by British Intelligence, the Yorkshire resident reportedly tied the saw to a tree and walked into the blade. *D.Mirror, D.Express* 30 April 1985. For other chainsaw stories, see **FT43**p17.

● According to the police, in Hobart, Indiana, the death of James Cooley, 52, was suicide. His method was rather obvious: he kept on pounding his head with a claw hammer. 32 times! Lake County coroner, Daniel D.Thomas, thought this was so "ludicrous" that he publicly asked the police to think again. *Sun* 26 Oct; Houston (TX) *Chronicle* 29 Oct 1985.

● A 45yr-old man, in Hamilton, Scotland, has created a puzzle for local police. He seemingly committed suicide in a field, on 20th May, by swallowing 3lbs of cow dung. *Hamilton Advertiser* 24 1985.

Inspired (if that's the right word in this case) by the ghastly fate of this man, we dug into our files and found that dung deaths (what else can we call the folder?) are not as uncommon as one might presume. According to the *Detroit*

News (MI) of 10 Oct 1985, three bodies were found in a manure pit near Ionia, Michigan. Cause of death of the two men and a woman was not established.

In Henniker, New Hampshire, the superintendent of the local rainwater treatment plant fell into raw sewage and drowned. *Pawtuxet Valley Daily Times*, West Warwick (RI) 19 Dec 1985. A 92yr-old retired bishop died after falling into a septic tank (*D.Telegraph* 22 March 1983); and an Islamic student at Essex University committed suicide by drowning himself at the local sewage farm (*Cantab*, Cambridge 15 Feb 1983).

● Can it be called suicide when a man burns himself to death fully believing he will come alive again? For this story, see CULTISH CURIOSITIES on p 18.

COINCIDENCE CORNER

★ 24yr-old Kevin Fisher rescued Tracy Watkiss from a blazing car in 1979. Tracy, then 17, was a passenger in the car when it crashed near Kevin's home. Six years on, in 1985, there was a repeat performance when hairdresser Tracy's car hit a tree at Redditch, near Worcester. Unknown to her, Kevin was in the car behind. She lives in Solihull, and her rescuer in Wythall, West Midlands. "I was dumbfounded," she said. "We hadn't met since the first crash." *Sun* 25 May 1985.

★ Peter Bacon of Eyam, Derbyshire, crashed into a car driven by Peter Bacon of North Anston, Sheffield. *D.Mirror* 9 Feb 1985.

★ A couple of months later, John Stott, whose car crash was witnessed by Bernard Stott (no relation), and investigated by WPC Tina Stott, was taken back to a police station where the trio was met by desk sergeant Walter Stott. *Weekend* 8-14 May 1985.

★ Golfers Bert Campbell and Dave Young both scored holes-in-one at the same hole - the short 14th - in the same match at Ballochmyle, Scotland, in April 1985. After searching the area around the green, they found Bert's ball in the hole, resting on top of Dave's. *D.Mail* 27 April 1985. A month later, three members of the West Sussex Golf Club each scored holes-in-one at different holes within 90 minutes of each other. *S.Express* 19 May 1985.

★ The actor originally hired to play John Lennon in the recent BBC TV dramatization, 'A Journey in the Life', was fired when Lennon's wife, Yoko, discovered that he bore the same name as the Beatle's assassin, Mark Chapman. Actor Chapman had changed his name from Lindsay in the year Lennon was killed. *D.Mail* 26 June 1985.

★ An earth tremor shook Cairo, on 23rd July 1985, while the film *Earthquake* was being shown on Egyptian TV. *Sun* 24 July 1985.

★ In the same vein...Horror film fans Dave and Babs Perry were watching an old Dracula film on the video in their Tondu home, Mid Glamorgan, when suddenly a bat flew into their living-room. "It was the shock of our lives," said Babs. "We've never been so frightened." *Sun* 16 Jan 1986.

RETURN OF KING BEE

Chalicodoma pluto, or "king bee" as the Indonesians call it, compared with a common honeybee. This bee, at one and three-quarter inches the largest in the world, was first reported by A.R. Wallace in the North Molluccas in 1859, and a specimen was sent to the British Museum. It was thought extinct for over a century until Adam Messer, a biologist from the University of Georgia (Athens) found two on Hamaher Island recently, gathering tree resin with their weird, plier-like mandibles. The sting in not serious, as the stinger is not barbed. © *Popular Science*, Oct 1984.

THERE'S GOLD IN THEM THERE VARMINTS

Some sequels to the sheep that was too rich to eat [see **FT43** p14]...

● The wife of Sioux Indian, Benny Left Hand, was cutting up a chicken she had recently killed, and discovered the kind of chicken nugget you *won't* find at McDonald's. Mrs Left Hand was in her kitchen on the Standing Rock reservation, when "she felt something hard in the chicken's gut, like a stone," said Benny. "She cut it open and that thing popped out." That thing was a nugget of gold, about an ounce in weight, and with an estimated value of $500. The Left Hands have no idea how it came to be there, and add that since the news got out there have already been attempts to steal their other chickens. Beaumont (TX) *Enterprise* 26 Aug 1985.

● Li Yunzhong, a Chinese farmer, from Hunan, found a 1.18 carat uncut diamond in the gizzard of a chicken he was preparing for dinner. He sold it for 950 yuan (apx. £300), or three times the average peasant's annual income. It was suggested the bird picked up the gem from paths spread with gravel from a diamond mine. *Shropshire Star* 24 Sept; *Guardian, D.Mirror* 25 Sept 1985.

● When Ken Holdaway tucked into his fried egg for breakfast, at his home in Merthyr Tydfil, South Wales, he forked up a nine carat gold ear-ring. *Sun* 17 Nov 1985.

SHC ON TV

It's nice to know BBC TV is even further behind in its reporting of weird stuff than we are. It may take us going on a year to get a story into print, but when *Newsnight* (13 Jan 1986, 10.40pm) covered a fascinating case of possible spontaneous human combustion (SHC), the story was six years old. As written up in *The Listener* (16 Jan 1986), by the programme's reporter Steve Bradshaw, the tale goes like this:

In 1980 CID officer John Haymer was called to a mysterious fire "in a South Wales valley". Speaking of his experience publicly for the first time, Haymer told *Newsnight* that "it was a very cold day, but I was struck by the warmth of the house, and the living room was like an oven."

Entering the room, the policeman noted smoke stains on the wall. "[The room] had a strange glow, orange-red. Condensation was running down the window. The walls were generating heat; the window and light bulb were covered in an orange substance. The light bulb was bare because the plastic shade had melted. There was an open grate, but it was undisturbed. The settee still had its loose covers. The carpet was largely undamaged. The knobs of the TV had melted, but it was still on."

"On the floor was a pair of human feet clothed in socks. They were attached to the lower portion of the body; this was clad in trousers, undamaged as far as a distinct burn-line. From the trousers protruded the calcinated bone, and just beyond the knees this disintegrated into an amorphous mass of ash. My first thought was, 'This is just how Dickens described the death of Mr Krook - spontaneous human combustion.'"

According to this well-read peeler, the remains were those of an elderly man who lived there. No reason for the fire or cause of death was ever established.

Newsnight was surprised to find that SHC was not an uncommon phenomenon, and set out, as Bradshaw admits, to debunk the 'paranormal' explanation. The orthodox medical line of pathologist, Prof. David Gee, was trotted out. According to Gee, "The person collapses and dies for some reason...they fall into the fireplace, or some other form of ignition. Since this usually happens to old ladies, in wintertime, they're probably wearing a lot of clothes. Once the clothing burns, it melts the body fat, which soaks into the clothing...like a candle, with the wick outside. Of course when it gets to the knees, the clothing effectively ends. And that's why the extreme end of the body is rarely damaged."

A nice try, but as any fortean will quickly realize, as an explanation it has more holes than a golf course. Even allowing for the improbable ignition, it seems legitimate to ask how the corpse moved itself from the grate; why the head and hands were totally destroyed; and why the trousers were not totally consumed by the fire? - assuming that mere body fat can indeed generate the intense and sustained heat needed to completely incinerate bones. Even *Newsnight* could not quite swallow the theory whole: noting that in many fire disasters "the human body is still recognisable as a burnt corpse - yet in apparent cases of SHC, it is reduced almost completely to ash, in rooms that are virtually undamaged by flame." This is the distinctive signature of the phenomenon called (we are still awaiting a more precise term) SHC.

Bravely admitting that they had abandoned the attempt to debunk SHC, Bradshaw and his producer consulted "one of Britain's most experienced crematorium managers". The man was perturbed by the photos of alleged SHC victims, which he had not seen until Bradshaw confronted him with them. What they accomplish with temperatures over 800 degrees - "six times hotter than a domestic oven" - and with "carefully regulated oxygen supply", was accomplished in an open room almost undamaged by fire. "It looks as if the fire comes from within," the bemused manager concluded. "Don't ask me how - I've never heard of spontaneous human combustion. But it wants a lot of explaining...and must be frightening."

After viewing the programme, we realized Haymer's case was vaguely familiar. Sure enough, we covered the inquest in **FT35 p10-11**, where the victim's name is given as Henry Thomas, 73, of Ebbw Vale, and the incident occurred on 6 January 1980. Nevertheless, this new testimony is valuable and welcome.

For more SHC news, see STRANGE FIRES on p 24.

LAKE MONSTERS: SWEDEN

★ An old clipping this, but appropriate to this issue. Our Finnish correspondent Tuuri Heporauta sent a translation of a story in the Hameenlinna *Hameen Sanomat* for 22 July 1981 of a monster seen in Lake Tornea, in northern Sweden, which in turn had been taken from the Swedish paper *Norrlandska Socialdemokraten* of the day before (21 July 1981). Anton Stockel, of Kiruna, had taken his son's family to their summer cottage in Salmi, near Lake Tornea. They had just begun boating when his grandson, Per, cried: "Grandpa, what is that moving on the lake?" Stockel said: "We saw, about 400 metres away, a creature which slowly moved towards the deeper waters. Its colour was coal black, and its length about 15-20 metres." Stockel said his father had seen a monster in the lake "well over 60 years ago".

★ Sweden's most famous monster - the *Storsjoodjuret* (= the monster of Lake Storsjon) - has been seen again, wriggling in the water with serpentine movements. A family of three, from the town of Gavle, spotted its humps just above the surface at about 23.30 one evening. They estimated its length at 10-20 metres. It left a huge wash when it finally disappeared. *Arbetet* 17 July 1985.

Our correspondent Sven Rosen comments that at this time of year the sun is above the horizon most of the night, so it is reasonable to suppose there was enough light, at half past eleven, for a good sighting. Sven also adds that 'Storsjon' means 'The Great Lake', so the monster might also be called 'The Great Lake Monster'. For more comments on this monster, see **note 11** to Michel Meurger's article in this issue.

HUBBARD DIES – AGAIN

The låtest - we hardly dare say the last - word on the life and death of cult leader, L.Ron Hubbard, is that he is dead. As Heber Jentzsch, president of the Church of Scientology, put it, at their Los Angeles HQ: "He no longer had need of the encumbrance of the physical identity we have known as L.Ron Hubbard."

It's not the first time for Hubbard, 74, the guru of Dianetics and founder of the $300 million Scientology movement. As well as claiming a prior visit to heaven in his writings, the former pulp-SF author was the subject of an extensive law-suit, brought by his estranged son in an attempt to prove that Hubbard was dead. Although the guru did not appear in person, had not been seen in public since 1976 (another source says 1980), and even refused to speak to the judge by telephone, written submissions persuaded the court to deliver its 1983 judgement that he was alive.

The Hubbard family have been at the centre of numerous controversies. Another son, Geoffrey, was found comatose in a car at Los Angeles airport in October 1976, and died a fortnight later. Cause of death was not established. **[See FT21 p11.]** Hubbard's first wife divorced him in 1951 on the ground that he was a paranoid schizophrenic. He remarried, and in 1979 his third wife was convicted, along with ten Church members, of burgling federal offices in an attempt to recover documents accumulated by US government investigators.

Hubbard published his *Dianetics: The Modern Science of Mental Health* in 1950. Dianetics - the word comes from the Greek for 'thought' - holds that all mental aberrations, including neuroses and psychosomatic illnesses, are caused by 'engrams', recordings made by the subconscious mind while the conscious mind is turned off, either in sleep, during pain or periods of unconsciousness, and before birth. In dianetic theory the conscious mind is a flawless but literal analytical machine which can be misled by data from the nonliteral subconscious. It is therefore vital to 'unkey' all engrams, usually by a lengthy - and expensive - process of 'auditing'.

The Church of Scientology, a spin-off stressing the spiritual nature of the individual, claims 6 million adherents worldwide, about 200,000 of which are in Britain. Cynics suggest that it was founded to allow Hubbard to exploit the exemptions allowed to religious bodies under US tax laws. An obituary in the *Guardian* of 29 January 1986 quotes Hubbard from a lecture he gave in 1949: "Writing for a penny-a-word is ridiculous. If a man really wants to make a million, the best way would be to start a religion." Recent analysis suggests that much of dianetics and scientology is based on the ideas he used in his science fiction stories.

Hubbard's chequered early career included stints as an engineer, a radio crooner and a naval officer. The *D.Telegraph* (29 Jan 1986) says: "He commanded an escort ship that distinguished itself off the coast of Oregon by shooting up a log in mistake for a Japanese submarine, and in another occasion opened fire on Mexico." According to defectors from the movement, Hubbard was a mediocre high-school student at the time he claims to have been learning the "secrets of life" from lamas and priests in Asia.

Hubbard's death, in California, from a stroke - the *Telegraph* says he died in his sleep! - was confirmed by the San Luis Obispo coroner's office; his body was rapidly cremated and his ashes scattered at sea.

RIVER MONSTER: BORNEO

A creature known as the Lawas monster, with a neck as big as a 40-gallon drum, eyes like electric light bulbs and a head like a cow, has been seen again, said Bernama, the Malaysian news agency. A boatman, crossing the Lawas River, in Borneo, said he saw it near where it was first reported several months earlier. Wildlife 'experts' dismiss the monster as a dugong. Madison (WI) *Capitol Times* 15 May 1985.

GLAD TIDINGS

After the doom-laden section on telephones last issue [**FT45 p8**], the following tales are offered to redress the balance. Sometimes the infernal machines are on our side...

★ Hilton Martin, 41, was cleaning his lavatory in Satellite Beach, near Cape Canaveral in Florida. He used Comet brand cleanser in the tank, and hung a Sani-Flush block inside. As the water started bubbling the telephone rang. He rushed to answer it, but it stopped before he could pick it up. Then he heard behind him a noise "like a hand grenade going off". The special-order oblong porcelain lavatory and tank were blown to pieces.

Fire officials were stumped, but someone suggested the calcium hypochloride in Sani-Flush had combined explosively with hydrocarbons in Comet. Spokespeople for both products denied that this was possible. Huntsville (AL) *Times*, Duluth (MN) *News-Tribune & Herald, Shropshire Star* 20 Sept; *Times, D.Star* 21 Sept 1985.

★ Kris Tamer, an office manager at the Westland Convalescent Center in Detroit, mis-dialled a number by transposing two digits, and hung up when she heard a gasping voice at the other end of the line. A colleague suggested someone might be in need of help, and Tamer rang the wrong number again. Alex Johnson, 81, who was suffering from congestive heart failure, was just able to give her his address. She rang the police and thus helped to save his life. Houston (TX) *Chronicle* 2 Nov 1985.

★ Lexilinkers will have noted the Comet connection, but perhaps not all will register the Westland name, referring to a small farce involving the British Conservative Party.

VIRGIN BIRTH?

A human egg has defied scientific convention and divided without waiting for fertilization by a sperm. The egg, from a woman receiving treatment in the fertility clinic at Monash University, Melbourne, did so 12 hours after removal from the woman. It spent the intervening time well away from any fertilizing agent.

Although the egg stopped after the first division, a host of interesting possibilities have been raised. Virgin birth, and the potential existence of daughters who are clones of their mother, are just two of the implications doctors will have to ponder. Dr Donna Howlett said: "God only knows what happened." Just so! *Guardian* 21 Nov 1985.

A FESTIVAL OF FETISHISM

HAIR TODAY, GONE TOMORROW!

▶ A hair fetishist, nicknamed 'Jack the Crimper', caught the imagination of the British press in a big way last year. We have nearly 20 clippings detailing the activities of Keith Everitt, 29, a Hertfordshire security guard, whose MO was to sneak up behind women and rub washing-up liquid or shampoo into their hair for two or three minutes. He made over ten attacks between September 1984 and March 1985; all of them near his home. The victims were aged between 12 and 34.

Everitt pleaded guilty to two specimen charges of assault and two of criminal damage to clothing in April and was sentenced to a year's imprisonment at St Albans crown court. Pleading for clemency, his defence lawyer said: "Clearly he needs treatment. These attacks are so unusual and have attracted so much publicity that if any similar attack occurred, Everitt would not only be the prime suspect, he would be the only suspect." We say the crime is certainly not unique: see **FT39p20** for the story of the Danish shampoo fetishist who murdered a hitch-hiker after washing her hair five times. *D.Star* 23 April; *Scotsman* 18 June; *D.Telegraph* 6 July 1985.

▶ There are plenty more orthodox hair freaks around too. RAF corporal Anthony Stewart, who hankered for long locks, already had a conviction for 17 previous offences, when he struck again at the Notting Hill carnival. He cut the waist-length hair of Christine Brannan, 25. Police found four cuttings of hair from other people in his pockets and 106 locks of hair, some two feet long, at his home. Fined £75. *Sun,D-.Mirror, D.Star* 8 Nov 1984.

▶ A month earlier, Oxford police were seeking a 'demon barber' who offered women free haircuts in the streets of the city's Westgate Centre. Those who fell for the con man's line ended up with bizarre and unwanted " punk hairstyles". Police said the fetishist, who claimed to be an unemployed hairdresser, was not breaking the law. *S.People, News of the World* 7 Oct 1984.

▶ A young man attacked two women with shears in Duluth, Minnesota, in mid-November 1984. He fled with his samples and evaded pursuit. The local paper had previously covered the story of a Californian fetishist. This one was a cyclist who pedalled up to long-haired women and squirted glue in their hair. He had carried out at least five attacks in the 18 months to April 1984. Duluth (MN) *News Tribune & Herald* 9 April + 17 Nov 1984.

▶ Another hair-snipping was committed in the Jolly Cut, of Hamilton, Ontario, back in February 1984. Daniel Calligan took a seat on a bus behind long-haired Cathy Starcevic and cut off 30cms of her hair. He repeated the attack on March 6th, lopping off schoolgirl Rebecca Brown's ponytail. Hamilton (Ont) *Spectator* 10 Oct 1984.

▶ 'Jack the Snipper' struck three times in Plaistow, east London, in July 1984. On the 11th, he attempted to hack the plaits off a pregnant woman with a craft knife, but ran off when chased by passers-by. The next day he successfully removed locks of hair from a woman at the tube station, and a schoolgirl at the bus station, using scissors. We

HINTS OF TELEPORTATION

Two bulls, which seem to have obeyed natural urges rather than the laws of nature, are puzzling horny handed sons of toil on both sides of the Atlantic.

At Chillerton, on the Isle of Wight, farmer Derek Steedman locked 12 Hereford calves in a cattle shed one evening, in mid-January 1984. Returning early next morning he found that they had been joined by a three-week-old cross-bred white bull. It lacked the usual ear tag or hide markings used by farmers, and no-one has turned up to claim the valuable animal . *S.Express* 5 Feb 1984.

In Clifton, Kansas, a similar incident has baffled Lawrence Alexander. He was perturbed by a 1,400 pound Black Angus bull which moved in with eight of his Holstein heifers during the night of 9/10 May 1984, and which is also unclaimed. "I've tried to get close enough to see if he has any markings, but he's pretty wild," Alexander told the reporter. "Besides, I don't have any intention of getting stranded out in the middle of a pasture with a bull. I can't run that fast." AP. Lincoln (NB) *Star* 24 July 1984.

have no record of his arrest, but no further news of snippings, until...on the 6th Jan, this year, a young "pervert" clipped a chunk of hair from a woman at a bus stop in Stratford, not far from Plaistow. When she felt her hair tugged, the woman turned and on seeing the scissors, screamed. The man fled. *Newham Recorder* 18 July 1985; 9 Jan 1986.

KNICKER NICKERS KNICKED

▶ Ian May, 19 and unemployed, admitted he stole women's underwear to fulfil his sexual fantasies. His downfall was doing it while breaking into houses to steal valuables. *D.Mirror* 12 Nov 1985.

▶ Army lieutenant John Luckins, 22, was jailed for a year at Salisbury crown court after admitting two charges of burglary. He had stolen £20,000 worth of silk knickers and bridal gowns. Luck ran out for Luckins when he dumped frillies he didn't want on a rubbish tip, but inexplicably left a shirt with his name on among them. When police raided his room in the barracks at Tidworth, Wilts, they found more than 100 dresses, neatly kept in boxes, and photos cut from bridal magazines; there was even a roll of silk, cut out to make a dress, with the pattern still pinned to it. Sandhurst-trained Luckins was described as a "promising officer" who had served in the Falklands, said he had been dressing as a girl since the age of six, when he used to borrow his sister's clothes. It beats us how he kept this secret on an army base! *Sun* 3 Dec 1985.

ABOMINABLE TOE MEN

▶ Back in **FT39p19** we reported on 'Leonardo da Toenail', the L.A. student with a compulsion to paint college girls' toes. He was finally arrested with 16 pots of nail varnish about his person, but charges were dropped. Leonardo might like to know that his is the kink of royalty. According to the *Daily Mirror* (18 Jan 1986), HRH Prince Andrew gets his kicks this way too; indeed "much of his courtship of Miss Kathleen Stark was spent painting her toenails." Now Andrew's new girlfriend, Sarah Ferguson, has splashed out on a pedicure. "It must be love," coos the *Mirror*, which goes on to reveal that Edward VIII spent so much time grooming the feet of his mistress, Mrs Simpson, that his butler quit in disgust. Yes, you get the real low-down with **FT**!.

▶ In New York, Richard Hunter, 21, received a 3-month sentence for breaking into a house to tickle Oyra Ostad's feet and steal her shoes. He was caught when he returned three weeks later to do the same to Oyra's older sister, Farbia. UPI. 1 June 1985.

▶ In Nashville, Tennessee, George Mitchell can't help plying his old trade by now. He has spent much of the last 15 years in prison for a series of about 40 foot-stamping offences - see **FT39p20.** Due for release in May 1985, he pleaded to be kept in jail, saying: "I'd rather be dead than stamp on another woman's foot." *Sun, D.Express* 7 May 1985. The inevitable happened. In September he was jailed again. After his release he committed two offenses, and a third while on bail for the first two. AP. *Guardian* 5 Oct 1985.

▶ The foot fetishism of a mystery Chinese man is both milder and culturally understandable. He knocked at the door of Margaret Edwards, in Stepney, east London, saying he was doing a survey. She said: "He made me shut my eyes and he lay on his stomach on the floor, asking me to say which foot he was touching. When I opened my eyes he was writhing and really sweating." At the sound of passing police sirens he panicked and ran out. *Sun* 10 Dec 1985.

BUM RAP

▶ Birmingham police were searching for a "pint-sized pervert" who has made nine attacks on women, stabbing them in the buttocks. *News of the World* 14 Oct 1984. After a gap of over a year, the attacks begin again; police fear it is the same man. Two girls in

Continued ☛

HEADY STUFF

An Egyptian parliamentary committee studying drug abuse has revealed that cocaine sold in Egypt is being cut with a secret ingredient, to increase its weight - powdered human head bones. One snort and you can be out of someone else's skull! *Guardian* 4 Jan 1986.

☛ Continued

their late teens, both had their bottoms slashed as they were walking in the city's Sparkhill area at dusk on different days. Although no one has seen his face, police believe the menace, who uses a craft knife, is a young Asian who jogs up behind a victim, attacks, and jogs off without looking back. Birmingham Eve.Mail? 27 Nov 1985.

▶ Just as unpleasant is the 'Acid Splasher' of Anchorage, Alaska, who squirts hydrochloric or sulphuric acid on the backsides of women in parking lots. He struck six times between August and December 1985. UPI: 20 Dec 1985. By the time the story reached the UK a week later, the number of attacks cited was 17 - which might be an error, we can't say. All his victims had long hair and wore dresses; all but one were in their 20s. Wolverhampton *Express & Star* 28 Dec 1985.

▶ Lately, we heard of a Chinese case. Wang Jinhou, described as "crazed", was sentenced to death in northern China, for slashing 25 women on the buttocks and breasts with a fruit knife. *Sun* 4 Feb 1986.

MIRACLE HOAX

The 'miracle of the eternal roses' drew thousands of pilgrims to St Mary's Church, at Heaton Norris, near Stockport, in Cheshire. For three years from 1947 the flowers mysteriously appeared on the head of a statue of the Madonna, and then seemed to stay fresh for months without a single petal falling. Now Arthur Clare, 60, a former altar boy, has revealed that it was all a trick devised by the parish priest and a local florist. He said, at his home in nearby Bramhall: "Now I can face death with a clear conscience." *D.Mail* 5 Sept 1985.

CAT STUFFED

Remember Felicity? That was the name given to the famous puma, captured in October 1980 by farmer Ted Noble, at Cannich, Inverness, close to Loch Ness. She had been taken to the Highland Wildlife Park, near Kingussie, where she was a main attraction before dying in February 1985, at the ripe old age of 16. Director, Eddie Orbell, repeated his view that she could not have been long in the wild because she was "too tame and too well fed...Obviously, she had been someone's pet." *Scotsman* 7 Feb 1985.

Now, Felicity's mystery is to live on. She has been stuffed by an Edinburgh taxidermist, and will be on permanent display at the entrance to Inverness museum. *Scotsman* 23 Sept 1985.

Felicity reclines (stiffly) on a bench, prior to being shipped to Inverness Museum. *Photo © **Scotsman** 23 Sept 1985.*

BEAR ACTIVISTS

Last issue we told of a couple's frightening encounter with a huge bear-like animal who ordered them off their campsite, in Washington State, and threw stones at them - see FT45 p34. Later, we heard, via the *Denver Post* of 1 Sept 1985, of the activities of a group, in the Yellowstone National Park, Wyoming, who call themselves Earth First!, who are protesting against the exploitation, and damage to, the ecology of the Park area. The group practices a weird mixture of paganism, conservationism and animal-liberation idealism expressed in a form of "street theatre" they call "ecotage".

By day they dress in bear-suits. For example: to attract attention to their pamphlets against the controversial Ski Yellowstone winter resort, two or three, dressed as bears, lie on the roadside while another member wearing skis stands on top of them. Their biggest success, in terms of publicity, drawing attention to the plight of the Park's bears, was when 30 protesters, all dressed as bears, some with children dressed as cubs and others holding teddy bears, were stopped by police from handing out pamphlets outside the Park's Grant Village Hotel. The whole furry tribe then tried to check into the hotel, demanding berries for room service. We did wonder if the hapless couple in the Washington wilderness had not encountered one of these fancy-dress conservationists. There is some precedent in the Bigfoot field, where the antics of humans in monkey-suits caused little amusement and much annoyance to serious researchers.

However Earth First! take it further. By their own boasting, their acts of 'ecotage' have included sabotaging oil-rigs, logging sites, road-building machinery, ranch fences, fouling the petrol-tanks on vehicles at such sites, and following survey crews to uproot their stakes as soon as they are out of sight. The sheriff of Teton County, Roger Millward, said they had caused $10,000-worth of damage in one incident alone by cutting several miles of power cable into 3ft sections.

STATE OF DISGRACE

An astonishing controversy is fluttering cassocks in the Vatican with the discovery that the body of Cardinal Schuster of Milan shows no sign of corruption 31 years after his death. Normally wise heads would be nodding at this extraodinary, but not unknown, sign of God's Grace towards his faithful servants.

The trouble is that Cardinal Schuster is still remembered as an open admirer of Fascism, a friend of Mussolini up to the dictator's death in 1945, and an enthusiastic supporter of the Abbysinian War. That the heavenly powers should have looked down with such favour upon such a right-wing Cardinal was said, by one commentator, to be "the most embarassing discovery since Eve noticed her nakedness."

Already there is a movement for Schuster's beatification, which is countered by allegations that "injection marks" have been found on the body - the implication being that "the Archbishop's doctor" had injected a preservative after death. But would such a tiny puncture be detectible after all that time? London *Standard* 27 Feb 1985.

IT'S JUST NOT CRICKETS

News of animal invasions:

● Thousands of salamanders caused consternation in Goodrich, North Dakota, by invading in such numbers one weekend that "the roads became skid pads". UPI. Houston (TX) *Chronicle* 16 Sept 1984.

● The greatest gathering of sea turtles seen for years appeared on Raine Island, part of Australia's Great Barrier Reef, staying for what was luridly described as "a mass egg-laying orgy". Between 50,000 and 150,000 female green turtles appeared, laying up to 1,000 eggs each. 11,500 turtles were counted in one night alone. No-one has any idea just why the turtles are congregating on Raine. The USA's "leading turtle researcher", Archie Carr, of the University of Florida, commented: "It's just incredible. We've seen large concentrations of other species at times in the Caribbean, but not this big." *Detroit News' (MI) 4 Dec 1984.*

● *Millions of crickets infested the northern Kenyan town of Garissa in March 1985, putting the power station out of action by gnawing through cables. "We cannot tolerate this any longer," said chief engineer Gilbert Oloo, whose workers were taking three hours each morning to clear out all the crickets that crept in during the night. Houston (TX) Chronicle* 30 Mar 1985.

● "Voracious toads the size of dinner plates" are spreading rapidly across Northern Australia. The Cane Toads were introduced to Queensland from Hawaii 50 years ago, to combat sugar cane destroying pests. Now they have become a major pest themselves, eating almost anything, and are even suspected of hitching lifts in cars to speed their migration. Local conservationist, Bill Freeland, says: "Toads have appeared up to 60 miles ahead of the main toad front. The bloody things eat some sorts of native wildlife into extinction." Reuter. *Times* 5 July; *The Scotsman* 6 July 1985. Latest news: scientists have failed to come up with a poison to stop them. *S.People* 16 Feb 1986.

● In contrast the migration of toads through the Chinese village of Wangjianan, in Sichuan Province, was "perfectly orderly". Hundreds of thousands of toads hopped "in procession" in two lines about a foot apart, towards hills. They took five days to pass. *S.Express* 1 Sept 1985.

● Carpet snakes are seen "ankle-deep" at Inwwod, Manitoba, which now sees an annual migration to and from nearby limestone pits and swamps. Ken Stewart, a University of Manitoba zoologist, says the half-dozen limestone pits now contain, between September and May, the world's largest concentration of reptiles. A single hole may spawn 10,000 snakes, which mate in the late spring sun and then migrate to the swamps to hunt frogs. The journey of several dozen miles can take up to two weeks. Some residents of Inwood have got used to finding hundreds of these harmless snakes in their cellars, and one family made friends with one which lived in their shower. An annual two-week 'snake picking' season recently netted 50,000. In May, up to 100 males will strive to twist themselves around a single female, and the writhing cabbage-sized ball will flow to and fro, over rocks and up into trees, for up to two hours, until the female has mated. The mating season has become a major tourist attraction, as the pits literally seeth with rippling clots of frenzied snakes. *Wall Street Journal* 11 June 1985.

● In Sri Lanka, a vast army of ants, numbering "billions" is advancing on the administrative capital of Sri Jayawardenpura, southwest of Colombo. Power supplies are cut off as the insecticide-resistent ants short-circuit switches and wires. Work on the new Parliament buildings and a hospital may have to be abandoned if the army cannot be stopped. *S.Express* 1 Sept 1985.

● Millions of snails have infested a farm in Sormland, Central Sweden, swarming over trees, bushes, vegetables and flowers. They have been identified as members of the *Arianta arbustorum* species, very rare in Sweden, but more common in Central Europe. One farm-worker, Anna Hardh, said she could pick 5000 snails a day. She had removed about 100,000 already, without seeming to diminish their numbers. The owner of Taffsnas Farm, Borje Klangestem, is in despair, as the invaders munch even his potatoes while experts are at a loss to explain the swarming. One French specialist, however, suggested Mr Klangestem should feel blessed rather than cursed. To the French, he says, the eggs of this snail are a delicacy comparable with Russian caviar; one kilogram fetching at least 6000 French francs. This is what Fort would call an irony of Providence! *Arbetet, Sydsvenska Dagbladet* 25 Aug 1985.

MEDIA VISITATIONS

► GOD VIDEO-TAPED - Police in predominantly Moslem state of Malacca, Malaya, are said to be concerned about the activities of a strange unnamed religious group who have distributed pamphlets throughout the state. They claim that the God 'Yehobah' [sic] had descended in person upon "Mt Sion" in Taiwan, to appoint one Elia Hong as his prophet, saying all nations should worship him. The writings claim the visitation was video-taped and rays of spiritual light emanated from Yehobah's "entire body". AFP. Sri Lanka *Daily News* apx 11 March 1985.

► VIRGIN MARY GIG TAPED - An Italian priest claims to have recorded the voice of the BVM, joining 12 children in singing a hymn. Monsignor Giuseppe Amaro, a episcopal vicar of a diocese near Naples said this happened on 1st November 1985, but the story begins back in May when "A peasant girl called Mafalda first said she saw the Holy Mary at the entrance to an old castle," he said. The apparition told the girl to build a shrine on the spot, dedicated to world peace. The priest said: "When I learned of the apparition, I went with a class of Sunday school children to the spot and we saw the figure of the Mother of Jesus. The children all broke out into a song and I recorded the song on tape at the same time as the figure was seen." Two healings have also been credited to the site. *S.Mail, S.People* 10 Nov 1985.

Next issue we hope to review developments at Medjugorje, Yugoslavia.

FISH-BOY

A 3yr-old Chinese boy has developed hard black scales which are defying medical treatment. The *Guardian* (22 July 1985), quoting the *Farmers' Daily* of Peking, said that the boy tries to rid himself of the severe itching caused by the scales by washing them off, but they return within two days.

This sounds like an unpleasant and extreme form of excema known as icthyosis, which as the name suggests produces an itchy, scaly skin. Although the condition is thought to be congenital, there is at least one case in which it has been cured using hypnosis.

CJS Thompson, in his *Mystery and Lore of Monsters* (University Books, NY, 1968), p109f, refers to three 'fish-boys' who were exhibited in London: an Italian boy born in 1684 (see illustration); a 'merman' taken on the coast of Denmark in the time of Queen Anne; and most famously, Francis Lambert of Suffolk, in 1820.

For a note on a European 'fish-boy' see Ulrich Magin's article, under HUNGARY. See also India's amphibian boy - **FT32 p40** - on which we will have an update next issue.

CULTISH CURIOSITIES

MORE PHILIPPINO MADNESS

Our last helping was in **FT43p24.** We will lightly skip over the annual public voluntary crucifixions and floggings each Easter - Catholicism's equivalent ofthe Kataragama festival in Sri Lanka - to mention an incident reminiscent of the Jim Jones massacre. The *S.Telegraph*, of 22 Sept 1985, simply reports that in the remote Mindanao village of Davao, after a "reputed magician" told villagers that drinking an insecticide concoction would "free them from all hardships". He was right; nearly 70 died. The *Guardian*, two days previously (20 Sept), had slightly different 'facts'. According to them, 69 people died from eating insecticide-poisoned porridge, urged on by a "high priestess", who then stabbed herself to death.

But if we want a fuller story we have to go back another day, to the London *Standard* (19 Sept). Here we learn that Davao is a region, and that the mass suicide occurred on September 9th, at the mountaintop village of Gunitan, 600 miles south of Manila. It seems that the "high priest" of the Ata tribe, Datu Mangayanon, had promised the dried leaves of a tree, which he had ritually killed by hacking, would turn into money. The tribe waited for days, and when the miracle did not happen the priest sulked as his people muttered. He responded with the laced porridge, saying whoever ate some "would see the image of God." His wife balked at the meal, and so Mangayanon hacked her to death also. Marines flown to the village found 68 bodies, including women and children. Seven survivors could not say if Mangayanon was among those who died. One curiosity is how the later news reports could get their stories so muddled!

THEY DID NOT RETURN

Followers of Brian Coupland, 40yr-old founder of a nameless group, kept a vigil for four days and nights around his body, believing he would rise again by the power of his faith. When it was clear that he had abandoned them for good, they reported his death to the police. Coupland, of Abbey Wood, south London, had died of a lung infection while on holiday near Newquay, Cornwall, with his four childern, pregnant wife and three followers. One of them told the inquest: "We trust Jesus as our healer. We do not consult medical science, as we have no need for it." *D.Mail* 15 March 1985.

A more spectacular demise was that planned by Philippino Rodrigo Maneja, 33, of Cebu, 350 miles south-east of Manila, who headed a cult called 'Kahal ha Masiyac', which believes it will survive a nuclear war. Maneja gathered hundreds of followers and spectators to demonstrate

BELOW THE BELT

● A Samoan woman was jailed for three years by a court in Sydney, Australia, for slicing off her husband's penis and throwing it into a rubbish bin. Surgeons successfully reconnected the recovered organ in July and the unnamed man was said to have tested it, triumphantly,in the city's red light district. *Guardian* 15 Oct 1985.

● Same city, same month - Nem Moeurn, a Kampuchean woman, was tried, in Sydney, with maliciously wounding her 5yr-old son. She had cut off the boy's penis because she believed it held the spirit of her estranged husband. Although surgeons had reattached the penis, it was too early to say if the join will hold. *Shropshire Star* 21 Oct 1985.

● ...and just to prove its not simply a story making the rounds, the *Guardian*, of 21 Sept 1985, refers to a recent medical book entitled *Recent Advances in Burns and Plastic Surgery - The Chinese Experience* by R.H.Baker (MTP Press, Lancaster; Oct 1985). Of one experience in particular, Baker writes: "The penis in question is Chinese and was removed by a disgruntled wife with a pair of dressmaking shears while her husband slept. It was reattached by Chinese surgeons, possibly aided by the serrated edge." A case of "Aieeeee! No corrida."

● ...and finally - A young accountant was receiving treatment in a Johannesburg hospital after being shot in his penis by a woman demonstrating her prowess with a gun at a cocktail party at Rundu, in Namibia. *D.Telegraph* 20 Dec 1985. Ah, but could she do it at 200 yards?

he could return from death within four hours. His brother-in-law poured petrol over him and ignited it, as Maneja called out to the crowd that "Elohim will protect me". After the appointed time had passed with no sign of life, police took his charred remains to a funeral parlour. At his burial, his mother said: Some members of the family may not follow me, but I will continue worshipping the God who asked my son to sacrifice his life." *Guardian* 12 Aug 1985. For other bizarre suicides, see WHEN YOU GOTTA GO on p 6

VENEZUALAN EARTH MOTHER

A fast-growing 'earth mother' cult is seen by Venezualan sociologists as a reaction to the rapid urbanization of the country. It venerates a 16th century Indian maiden, Maria Lionaz, who fled to the mountains to escape the Spanish invaders [so how come the Spanish name?]. A combination of Catholicism, Amerindian religion and voodoo, it lacks a formal doctrine, being unitarian rather than moral. The cult stresses the importance of nature, and is a focus for a form of radical traditionalism and feelings against the evils of modern society and technology. Its activities include magical medical practices, similar to those performed by the 'psychic healers' of the Philippines. Although the 40,000 or so followers of Maria Lionaz consider themselves a Catholic sect, the Church has denounced their beliefs as witchcraft. *Guardian* 5 July 1985.

LOVELAND FROG LEAPS BACK

Rumours of a giant frog lurking in Ohio's Little Miami River, near Loveland, go back at least to the 1950s, and are probably more ancient. It came to national prominence in the first week of March 1972, when two police officers encountered the dog-sized, frog-faced creature climb over a guardrail between the road and the river, on two separate occasions. For the fullest accounts read Ron Schaffner's *Creature Chronicles* No.4, and Loren Coleman's recent book *Curious Encounters*, p75f. Coleman also refers to sightings of other frog- or lizzard-like creatures in the USA.

The two officers' real names have been revealed by the Loveland (OH) *Herald* (18 July 1985) as Ray Schocke (known previously as Williams) and Mark Matthews (Johnson). Their name-change had not protected them from the huge amount of ridicule they had to endure: Schocke refuses to discuss the case still and Matthews migrated to Florida. Their treatment has made other witnesses, who have sighted the creature before and since 1972, reluctant to come forward. However, due to the increase in sightings "in the past two years" - probably due to the opening of a bike trail along the riverside - local businessmen have offered a $2000 prize for its capture, and $50 for its photograph.

Early in July 1985, two boys were skipping stones across the river when they saw what they described as a very large frog. "I thought it was a boulder at first," said an 11yr-old who did not want to be identified. "Then it jumped and I was sure it was a frog," He described it as about the size of a big dog and about four feet wide. "There is no way a frog could grow that big," said David Jardine, head of reptiles for the Cincinnati Zoo. *Creature Chronicles* No.9 (1 Aug 1985).

The frog-like creature of Loveland, Ohio, according to witness Mark Matthews. *Photo © **Ron Schaffner/FPL.***

OVER-REACTION

Farmer Pantelis Vizonis, 54, of Palea Vigla in northwest Greece was in a local taverna when a friend jokingly accused him of never buying a round of drinks. Vizonis left and returned with a shot gun with which he shot dead two friends and the owner. He returned home and shot his wife and two other friends who tried to restrain him. *D. Telegraph*, 18 Mar 1985.

THE BEAST IS BACK!

Not Editor Bob, but our old friend the Exmoor Beast. More Devon sightings from 1985, followed by a few feline frolics from elsewhere.

★ Last week of May: Beast prowls just 20ft from car of tourist couple, then jumps 8ft hedge, at Wistlandpound Reservoir, between Barnstaple and Lynton. *Western Morning News* 1 June 1985.

★ End of August: A feline "black animal the size of a large dog with a tail longer than its body" seen in fields near the Newberry Lodge Hotel, Combe Martin, by a holidaymaker. *Western Morning News* 31 Aug 1985.

★ September or October: Richard Stevens, an estate agent in Dunster, sees the Beast in Dunster deer park. "I can only describe it as a large cat, about two to three feet long, much bigger than a domestic or wild cat. It was jet black with yellow eyes and stood about three feet high." It moved into bushes and out of sight. Bristol *Eve.Post* 3 Dec 1985.

★ 17 September: A couple and their 26yr-old son saw "a black panther walking along the road in front of their car just below Simonsbath." The animal crossed the road then leapt a stone wall and was lost to view along riverbank. Report from naturalist, Trevor Beer, who is regularly cited as believing there are at least three such animals locally. *North Devon Gazette* 27 Sept 1985.

★ 30 October: A South Wales couple on holiday saw the Beast in the car park of the Hunter's Inns, at Heddon Mouth. They describe it as "black, about four feet long with a curved tail, small round head and small ears". *N.Devon Advertiser* 1 Nov 1985.

★ Late November: reference to sightings of two black cat-like animals, and two sets of tracks near Luxborough, on the east moor of Exmoor, seen by park officer, Gerry Belton. *Observer, Mail on Sunday* 1 Dec; Bristol *Eve.Post* 3 Dec 1985.

★ Early December: A mystery animal which has haunted woodlands around Mrs Brenda Cornish's Woodcombe Farm, near Minehead, Somerset, with its hideous screaming, left clear tracks when it stole some tripe from the farm. 'Experts' say the four-clawed tracks have been made by a wolverine, and this is proposed as the true identity of the Exmoor Beast. *D.Express* 7 Dec 1985.

...and in 1986...

★ First week, January: Sightings at Trentishore, Holdstone Down (twice). *North Devon Advertiser* 10 Jan 1986.

★ Early January: Black cat-like Beast seen twice, at Muddiford, and at Combe Martin. *D.Express* 8 Jan 1986. According to *Western Morning News* (15 Jan 1986), two farmers both see puma-like creature in separate sightings near Muddiford; but not clear if these are same two sightings as given in the *Express*.

★ Mid-January: A lynx-like animal, coloured "greyey, greeny, tanny" came face to face with 13yr-old Graham Mugglestone in a field, 200yds from his parents' Broomhill Farm, near Muddiford. The frightened creature was followed by Graham's dad, but it got away in the darkening evening. Exeter *Express & Echo* (? Jan), *North Devon Journal-Herald* 23 Jan 1986.

★ First two weeks, February: Two separate attacks on ewes on the farm of David Rawle at Parracombe, near Lynton, by "something large and powerful". *Shropshire Star* 13 Feb 1986.

ISLE OF WIGHT

★ Builder John Ball and four colleagues watched a large cat-like animal for 15 minutes on farmland off Forest Road, Newport, from the first floor of the building they were working on. "It was black, like a panther, about five feet long with a long tail and pointed ears. It moved like a lioness or panther," said Mr Ball. The animal seemed to be carrying something in its mouth, "like a rabbit", which it dropped as it searched for a way out of a field. Isle of Wight *Weekly Post* 31 May 1985.

★ Mick Ford, 42, was walking his young Alsatian dog in a field near his home in Parkhurst, at about 10pm, when he heard a "blood-chilling" howl, then a "sickening...deepthroated howl" from some bushes. Suddenly, "a big cat jumped out. It was the size of a Labrador dog." They all ran off in different directions, frightened. Said to be more than 120 sightings of the island's mystery cat in past two and a half years. Portsmouth *News* 7 Sept; Isle of Wight *Weekly Post* and *County Press* 13 Sept 1985.

CORNWALL

★ On 12th Dec 1985, a motorist saw a "puma-like" animal leap a 15ft hedge near Liskeard. *D.Mirror* 13 Dec 1985.

GLOUCESTERSHIRE

★ Farmers in Westbury on Severn, were hunting a "mysterious tiger-like black animal, said to be four times the size of a domestic cat." *Shropshire Star* 7 Nov 1985.

NORTH YORKSHIRE

Police and animal welfare officials in N.Yorks were on the alert, on 30th October 1985, for "a large black panther-like animal" seen, on three separate occasions, stalking farmland around Harrogate and Knaresborough. These were at Starbeck, near Harrogate; Bilton Hall Lane, Knaresborough; and close to the A59

York-Harrogate road. Knaresborough Zoo announced that police were satisfied that all their panthers and big cats were secure in their cages. Flamingo Park Zoo reported the same. That same day, a farmer's wife at Kirby Misperton, 30 miles away, telephoned the local radio station to say that on the 29th a party of five Young Farmers saw what they described as a "black panther", with orange eyes and a long black tail, disappearing into a cornfield near her home. *Yorkshire Eve.Post* 30 Oct; *Yorkshire Post, D.Mail* 31 Oct 1985.

★ The next day, 31st October, the search shifted to the Abbey Road area of Knaresborough, after a man was terrified by a big black cat-like animal, ran to the nearest phonebox and put in a breathless call to the police. Nothing found. *Yorkshire Post* 2 Nov 1985.

SOUTH WALES

★ Farmer's wife Susan Howells, 35, clearly saw a huge cat while riding near her parents' farm at Kenfig Hill, mid-Glamorgan. "It was fawn in colour and savage looking. Forestry Commission has taken plaster casts of paw prints. *D.Express* 13 Sept 1985.

ELECTIVE AFFINITIES?

★ John Corfield from Manchester wrote to the *Sunday Express* (29 July 1984) about his Ibiza holiday the previous week. He and his wife Mildred were given the wrong hotel room, which had in fact been booked for a Jack and Mildred Corfield who had travelled out on the same flight.

★ On 11 August 1984, Karen Dawn Southwick, 22, was married at St Michael's and All Angels, Tettenhall, near Wolverhampton. She was given away by her father, Alfred G.Southwick. Three hours later another Karen Dawn Southwick, aged 22, was married in the same church, given away by her father, Alfred G.Southwick.

The two brides had not met before the preparatory get-together with the vicar. There was a slight flaw in the congruity, however, the fathers' middle names were George and Gordon. Alfred George had never met Alfred Gordon, but believed they might be distant cousins. *Shropshire Star*, Wolverhampton *Express & Star* 8 Aug; *Sun* 9 Aug 1984. (For another story of synchronicity involving Karens, see **FT42 p20.**)

★ Victor John Foti, 64, of Fairbanks, NY, checked into a hospital in Rochester for a quadruple heart bypass operation. He was surprised to find, in the adjoining bed, another Victor John Foti, also from Fairbanks, but aged 59, had been admitted for the same operation. To avoid confusion the hospital decided to distinguish them by their weight. Victor the lesser, the first one to be admitted, said they had been getting each other's mail for 20 years, and actually met seven years ago, but "we have never had anything like this before." AP. *Die Rheinpfalz, D.Express* 11 Feb 1986.

HALLOWE'EN CAPERS

★ The lower half of a left arm, embalmed about 50 years ago, was thrown out of a car in a downtown street of Wheeling, West Virginia, at 6.35pm on the 27th October 1985. Officials were busy checking crypts for signs of a break-in. Duluth (MN) *News-Tribune & Herald* 29 Oct 1985.

★ Six days later, two skulls, without their lower jaws, were hurled from a speeding car at Harold Hill police station, London. For some reason we cannot fathom, detectives believed they belonged to two East End gangsters, called David Elmore and Jimmy 'the Wad' Waddington, who were supposedly hacked to pieces with swords in a restaurant on St Valentine's Day in 1984. Tests showed the skulls were too old. Six days after the skull-hurling, storeman Frederick Wardrop, 24, was charged with stealing three skulls from Lord Petre's family crypt in Brentwood as a Hallowe'en stunt. *D.Mail* 6,7,8,9 Nov; *D.Telegraph, Guardian* 8 Nov 1985.

BELGIAN WRECK CLUSTER

The French nuclear cargo ship, the *Mont Louis*, wallowing in 40 feet of water seven miles off the Belgian coast with its barrels of uranium hexafluoride, lies just above the wreck of a World War II ammunition ship, the *Washaba*, which sank in 1944 with its highly combustible cargo intact. The proximity of the two wrecks is potentially lethal, according to the secretary of the Ostend North Sea Yacht Club. The Chairman of British Nuclear Fuels, Con Allday(!), scorned the scare stories. *Observer* 16 Sept 1984.

FEARS FOR TEARS

We don't really know how or when the fire jinx was first attached to a hideously tasteless, yet obviously popular, printed icon known as 'The Crying Boy' (TCB). As you can see from our illustration, it exists in a number of different versions, all of them mass-produced 'paintings'. It first came to our attention in the *Sun* (4 Sept 1985), with the jinx already established. A Yorkshire fireman, Peter Hall, is quoted as saying that copies of TCB were frequently found at the scenes of fires, and usually untouched by flames. He and his colleagues were serious about this enough to promise that they would never allow the painting into their own homes. Peter's own brother, Ron Hall, had refused to take the firemen's warning, and while fire damaged the kitchen and living-room of Ron's Swallownest, South Yorkshire, home, the TCB on the living-room wall was not harmed. Ron's son put his boot through it in revenge, and his wife has banned its replacement.

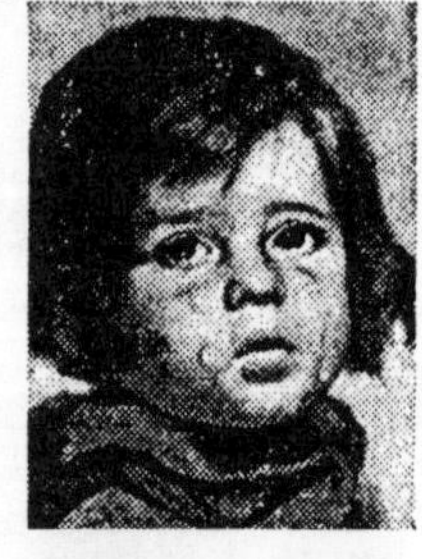
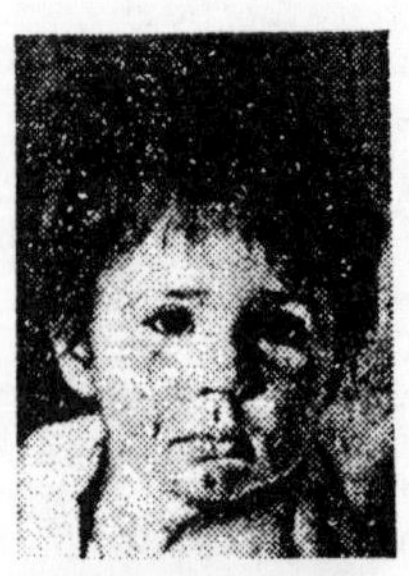

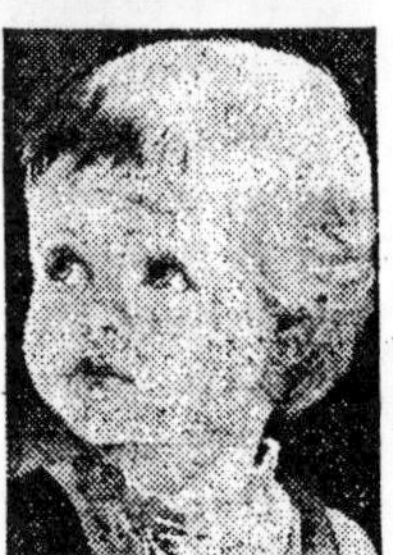

Some of the variations of 'The Crying Boy' picture.

The next day's *Sun* (5 Sept 1985) said they had "a flood" of calls in response to the TCB story, and gives four cases: Dora Mann, of Mitcham, Surrey, said "Only six months after I bought the picture my house was completely gutted by fire. All my paintings were destroyed, except the one of the crying boy."; Sandra Craske, of Kilburn, said that she, her sister-in-law, and a friend had all had fires since buying the picture. She had also seen the TCB print swing from side to side; Linda Fleming, of Leeds, and Jane McCutcheon, of Nottingham, both had fires in which the print escaped. Janet Wyatt, of Wroxall, IOW, said she tried to burn her two copies after reading of the jinx, but they would not catch fire. Other stories followed thick and fast; we'll just abbreviate them...

★ Brian Parks, of Boughtor, Notts, was destroying his copy after a fire put his wife and two children in hospital. *Sun* 9 Sept 1985.

★ Grace Murray, of Oxford, taken to Stoke Mandeville hospital with severe burns. TCB "almost undamaged" in fire in her home. *Sun, D.Star* 9 Oct 1985.

★ The Parillo Pizza Palace, Gt Yarmouth, destroyed by fire. TCB undamaged. *Sun* 21 Oct 1985, which invites readers to send in their "cursed" copies for destruction.

★ Kevin Godber and family, of Herringthorpe, South Yorks, lose home to a fire. TCB "unmarked" while pictures on either side of it were destroyed. *D.Mail* 24 Oct 1985.

★ Explosion destroys the Amos family house, in Heswall, Merseyside. Two TCBs, in living-room and dining room, unharmed. They are unceremoniously destroyed by Mr Amos. *Sun* 25 Oct 1985.

★ House in Telford partially damaged by fire. The owner, ex-fireman Fred Trower, refuses to blame his TCB, hung in the hall. "Obviously, if there was another fire it would go. I'm not that open-minded," he adds. *Shropshire Star* 26 Oct 1985.

★ Six months after restaurant owner, George Beer, installs two TCBs in his Holsworthy establishment, they are severely damaged by two separate fires a year apart. Both times the prints were unsinged. He doesn't blame them, and wouldn't part with them. *Western Morning News* 26 Oct 1985.

Continued ☛

MORE HISTORICAL REVISIONISM

► Jesus lived in Britain with his mother, the Virgin Mary, who was born in Cornwall. She led an active sex life, had eight children, and is buried at Glastonbury, according to Victor Dunstan, author of *Did the Virgin Mary Live and Die in England?* "Jesus was the sort of guy who would have gone down well at the rugby club," claims Dunstan, who believes that mother and son sailed from Palestine to Burnham-on-sea in the Biblical gap between Jesus' childhood and the few months leading to his crucifixion. *S.Mirror* 17 Nov 1985.

► The story of William Tell has been removed from Swiss history textbooks to tighten up on pseudo-historical falsification. UPI. Belleville (IL) *News-Democrat* 7 Sept 1984.

► Pseudonymous barrister 'Peter Westcott' has published a 75 page booklet, *Whatever Happened to the Big Fisherman?* (Alvescot Press, Oxford; £6.95), in which he refutes the Roman Catholic dogma that the apostle Peter founded the See of Rome and the papacy after the death of Christ. (The Catholic claim to supremacy over other Christian faiths is partly based upon this belief.) Westcott quotes Biblical passages as 'proof' that Peter did not live in Rome for 25 years, as the Vatican asserts, and maintains that it is unlikely that he ever visited the city at all. Bones found beneath the High Altar at St Peter's in 1951, claimed to be the apostle's, were probably female remains from a 2nd century AD pagan tomb under the church, writes Westcott. Those interested in the deliberate Christian tactic of siting shrines and churches on the sites venerated by older traditions will find much food for thought in this. *S.Telegraph* 12 Aug; *Guardian* 14 Aug 1986.

► Working from the descriptions of an eyewitness - the 'Father of history', Thucydides - a doctor has put forward the theory that the mysterious Plague of Athens (430-427 BC), which triggered the downfall of the Greek city-state, was influenza complicated by toxic shock syndrome. Dr Alex Longmuir, ex-chief of the US Center for Disease Control, is the latest entrant into the lists, which already feature proponents of smallpox, scarlet fever, measles, typhus and bubonic plague. *Schenectady Gazette* (NY) 17 Oct 1985.

Continued

★ *Sun* 26 Oct 1985 reports on accumulating pictures for mass burning. Various improbable stories: a male stripper's fire-eating act goes wrong after he taunts his wife's TCB; one woman blamed the death of her three sons and husband on the picture. Dr Peter Baldry of City University, London, cited saying no reason why the pictures shouldn't burn. Roy Vickery, secretary of the Folklore Society, speculates whether the artist mistreated his model resulting in a vengeful curse. Several readers say that pairing the TCB with a Crying Girl picture has brought them luck.

★ Stella Brown, of Portsmouth, burns two TCBs successfully, blaming them for a long run of bad luck and family health problems. Her son trips while fetching water to put the fire out! *Portsmouth News* 30 Oct 1985.

★ After hearing of the curse of the TCB, Richard Reynolds and his wife, of Falmouth, dumped their two TCBs upon a bonfire that was being made for Guy Fawkes night. Twice they had given them away to friends, only to have them returned. *West Briton* 31 Oct 1985.

★ *Sun* 31 Oct 1985 - "thousands" of TCBs burned. Supervising fire officer Barry Davis cracks: "We all listened for muffled cries, but all we heard was the crackle of paintings burning." Topless beauty Sandra-Jane Moore said her home was flooded after drawing punk hair on her friend's TCB. Mrs Woodward, of Forest Hill, blames TBC for death of her son, daughter, husband and mother.

★ *Guardian* 1 Nov 1985 - Entertaining write-up of the *Sun's* big bonfire, tells that *Sun* editor Kelvin McKenzie, who believes in the picture's curse, "went bananas" when some wag hung a TCB in his office. It also notes the refusal of several fire brigades to participate in the burning.

★ Last we heard...Malcolm Vaughn's living-room blazed after he destroyed a frightened neighbour's TCB, in Churchdown, Glos. *Sun* 12 Nov 1985.

★ **ADDENDUM** - Having written the above we learn, from the *Sun* (24 Feb 1986) that the 'curse' has struck again, in the death of 67yr-old William Armitage in the fire that swept through his Weston-super-Mare, Avon home. The TCB was intact, lying on the floor near the pensioner's body. One fireman said: "We have all heard of this jinx, but when you actually come across the picture in a gutted room, it is most odd."

STRANGE FIRES

■ Mary Carter, 86, an elderly widow, was found dead in the hall of her flat in Ivor Rd, Sparkhill, Birmingham. Although she died from a heart attack, she had severe burns, yet there was no evidence of any fire in the flat, her inquest was told. A fire investigation team concluded that her clothing must have caught fire "elsewhere" and she had been running for help when she was engulfed by flame. There were candles and matches in some rooms but none near the body. If there was any evidence that these had been alight, or had ignited her clothes, it would not have been labelled a 'fire riddle'. Wolverhampton *Express & Star* 23 April 1985.

■ Paul Hayes, a 19yr-old London computer operator, is one of that select band who seem to have survived a spontaneous combustion - see photo. What happened to him, as he walked along a quiet road in Stepney Green, late on the night of 25th May 1985, remains a mystery to police and medical investigators, because he suddenly and inexplicably burst into flames. From the waist up, he was surrounded by intense flames, as though, in his own words, he had been doused with petrol and set alight. "It was indescribable...like being plunged into the heat of a furnace...My arms felt as though they were being prodded by red-hot pokers, from my shoulders to my wrists. My cheeks were red-hot, my ears were numb. My chest felt like boiling water had been poured over it. I thought I could hear my brains bubbling." Fearing more for his eyes, he instinctively shut them tight and put his hands over them. Screaming and shouting, "I tried to run, stupidly thinking I could race ahead of the flames." But he fell to the pavement. In distress and pain, he curled up into a ball. "I thought I was dying. Images of my parents, my friends, my girlfriend, came to mind." Then, as suddenly as it began, his half minute ordeal was over. "I opened my eyes. There was no flame, no smoke. For a few minutes I lay still, terrified. I began to shiver with shock." He felt himself gingerly. "I was numb in some spots, white-hot in others." Luckily he was only a few streets away from the London Hospital, and he stumbled into casualty, where he received prompt treatment for burns on his hands, forearms, face, neck and ears. Paul does not smoke. London *Standard* 31 May; *National Enquirer* 23 July 1985.

■ Earlier still last year was news of an "enigmatic explosion" in the mouth of a 61yr-old patient at the Innsbruck University Clinic. According to the accounts of other patients, the pensioner "suddenly spat fire" and suffered burns to the face. Only the speedy intervention of other patients prevented him from further injury. AP. *Soester Anzeiger* 15 Feb 1985.

Photo © *National Enquirer* 23 July 1985.

Paul Hayes holds up the shirt he was wearing the night he burst into flame unaccountably.

LAKE TAHOE MONSTER FILMED

In **FT43 p6**, we noted a series of sighting reports from this large lake on the Nevada/California border, and noted their somewhat dubious provenance.

Unfortunately it seems that new evidence from the area must be treated with equal caution. The *Tahoe Daily Tribune* of 17 April 1985 tells of a film sequence taken at Zephyr Cove. An object appeared in the water about 100 yards off the beach; Mike Conway and Virgil Anderson filmed it with a Panaflex cine camera fitted with a 1,000mm lens. According to Anderson: "I thought it was just a huge fish. The wake was probably 20 feet long. The fish was probably 15-20 feet long. There was a wake in front of the fin and a wake in back of the fin."

The film was developed and apparently came out well. However, the two cameramen were employees of the local Visitors' Bureau, shooting a commercial to publicise the area, and their footage is now owned by a syndicate of local casino operators.

Loch Ness investigator, Rip Hepple, who published the report in his *Nessletter* 70, comments: "it does seem strange that nothing else has been heard about this...with a 1,000mm lens at a range of about 100 yards the resulting film should enable you to count its scales, or eyelashes, even without enlargement."

In *Nessletter* 71 the subject becomes further muddied. The monster - by now dubbed 'Tessie' - was seen by 18 people and three sets of pictures were obtained, according to a report from Erik Beckjord. Conway and Anderson's film was a 20-second strip and it is still owned by the Visitors' Bureau, who refuse to release it on the grounds that it would turn Lake Tahoe "into a circus" and might scare off swimmers and water-skiers. One still photo did not come out, and the other - a 35mm shot by Conway - has been witheld by him for fear of angering his employees, the Visitors' Bureau, upon whom he is dependent.

For more news of big fish, see MONSTROUS FISH on p28.

IT'S A MIRACLE?

In 1978, a fisherman in the French town of Sierck-les-Bains put the carp he had caught in the River Moselle into his bathtub, but soon the fish escaped and wedged itself into the overflow pipe, causing an extensive spillage of water. Over the last six years the resulting patch of discoloration on the outside wall of the bathroom has assumed the form of a human face (see photo). According to venerable precedent, in which many a spontaneous face has been declared by the great unwashed to be an image of Christ (or whoever), some residents of Sierck are convinced this 'acheropite' (a naturally occurring image) is of divine origin. The local priest has refused to visit the shrine of the overflow, and the French national media reports, without exception, identified this visage of the spillage as an apparition of Jesus Christ! Paris *Liberation*, *Le Republicain Lorrain* 12 Sept; *Nice Matin* 14 Sept 1985.

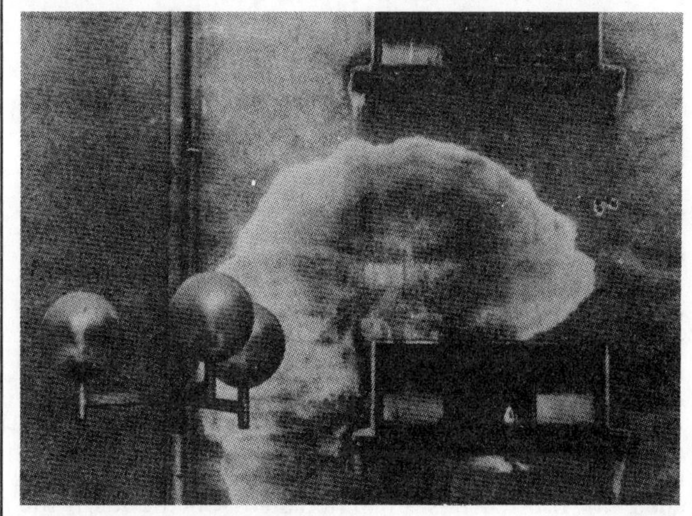

Is this the face of Jesus? In the stain of a bathroom overflow? *Photo © AFP.* ***Telerama*** *29 Oct 1985.*

CITIES, LOST AND FOUND

■ BRAZIL - Aurelio Abreu, vice president of the Sao Paulo Archeology Institute, said that he and two colleagues had found "ruins of a structure of stone giving the impression of a fortress, dating from ancient times" in Bahia state. The nearest town is Brumado, 25 miles away, where the ruins had been known "for decades" as Ingrejil, after the mountains where the ruins are found. State authorities had asked the Institute to inspect the site and this was first done between 31st August and 2nd September. Abreu said the ruins of Ingrejil "are nothing like the structures built by Indians known to inhabit Brazil in pre-Columbian times...[using] precision-cut stones fitted without mortar in the style of the Inca architecture of Peru. [They] may have been built by refugees from Incan [12th to 15th century] or pre-Incan Peru who found there the mountainous terrain and cool climate that suited them." Abreu added that he believed there were other such structures still to be found in Brazil's interior. UPI. Houston (TX) *Chronicle*, St Louis (MO) *Post-Dispatch* 10 Sept 1984.

■ PERU - Late in January 1985, two archeologists from the University of Colorado at Boulder (CU), Thomas J.Lennon and Jane C.Wheeler, announced that they had found one of the fabled 'lost cities' of the Andean rain-forest. It is an extensive, well-preserved pre-Inca site, often shrouded in clouds, with many two-storey stone houses, terraced mountain sides used for agriculture, paved roads "which disappear straight into the jungle", and intact tombs built into a sheer 1000ft cliff. CU promised an immediate expedition to investigate.

The following month CU had to withdraw the claim with some embarassment amid accusations of hoaxing. It seems the 'lost city' was not lost at all, but listed in guide books and encyclopedias as Gran Pajaten. It was discovered by a Peruvian team in 1963, but made known more widely through the work and writings of explorer Eugene Savoy, of Reno, Nevada, who actually gave the city-site its name during an expedition of 1964-1965. It was Savoy's Andean Explorers Club (AEC)that blew the whistle on what they called "the hoax of the millenium". For their part CU say the original reports in the *Washington Post* did not divulge their full statements, made in interviews with their exploration team, "which clearly referred to previous explorations..."

The announcement by CU was intended to publicize the fact that the university had been awarded a 15yr contract by the Peruvian government to study the site. A team of over 24 scientists will try to establish the identity of the city's mysterious builders, who seen to have occupied the area between 500 AD and 1500 AD. The Incas began their domination of the area in about 1476. "It is entirely possible," said Lennon, "that this is one outpost of a more complex civilization." Lou Whittaker, an experienced climber on the team, said they had an agreement with the government not to reveal too much about their findings. Whittaker and fellow climber, Greg Wilson, were needed to explore the cliff burial site. He would only hint at the existence of caves filled with bones and other artifacts, mummies, rock paintings, statues with animal and geometric designs. He said the weeks of mud, rain, cold and mosquitoes were among the worst he had encountered.

Regarding the criticism of CU by the AEC, Lennon says: "I don't deny

GHOST STOPS BUS

In Taiwan, a bus company in Tainan, 200 miles south of Taipei, has had to cancel its evening run to a remote village because frightened drivers are refusing to make the trip after dark due to a phantom passenger. It seems that a part of the route passes through a plantation of tall, shadowy sugar cane fields - which, as anyone knows who watches Chinese ghost films, is a typical and likely haunting place. On one trip a driver picked up a young girl at the spooky spot, only to discover she had vanished from the bus by the time he got to town. This is an interesting variation of the phantom hitch-hiker motif. *S.Express* 16 Feb 1986.

anything Gene Savoy says. But I do take exception to the idea that there is nothing left to do at Gran Pajaten because he did it all. He discovered the site. What we want to do is study it in a lot more detail." Story assembled from UPI bulletins. *Detroit News* 2 Feb; UPI 13 Feb; *Saginaw News* 16 Feb + 12 July; St Louis (MO) *Post-Dispatch* 21 Aug 1985.

■ PERU - Meanwhile, Eugene Savoy, on record as having discovered some 40 'lost' cities in South America, was at it again. This time he has found a pre-Incan metropolis in the jungle of northeastern Peru, on the eastern slopes of the Andes, between the Maranon and Utcubamba rivers. After recently spending 60 days at the site, 9000ft above sea-level, he has named it Gran Vilaya.

The site contains about 24,000 structures, including well-preserved circular buildings on platforms "like fortified towers", terraced pyramids, and other long buildings, in 80 interconnected city-like layouts covering 120 square miles. There is also a 25-mile-long defensive structure which runs for 25 miles along a mountain ridge. It is the most extensive building complex yet discovered in South America. "I have never seen anything quite like it in my many years of exploring, " said Savoy. Savoy agrees with Federico Kauffmann Doig, ex-director of Peru's National Museum of Anthropology and Archeology who now heads the Amazonian Archeological Institute, that the city could date to about 1000 AD, and could have been built by the warlike Chachapoyas Indians, who were defeated by the Incas in about 1480 AD. The Incas later told their Spanish conquerors that the Chachapoyas were a tall, fair-skinned people. Savoy thinks they may even have sailed to Africa. AP: *New York Times* 7 July 1985. UPI: 6 July; *Saginaw News* 9 + 12 July 1985.

■ HONDURAS - Britain's Col. John Blashford-Snell is no slouch at the discovery game, either. A team from his 'Operation Raleigh' have discovered one and a half square miles of ruined buildings, which may be a city of the Payan civilization, perhaps even the legendary Cuidad Blanca or 'White City'. The Payas inhabited the Patuca River, in the country's inhospitable northeastern jungle. Archeologists from the Honduras Institute of Archeology are examining the site. AP. *D.Telegraph, D.Mail* 11 May; Belleville (IL) *News-Democrat* 12 May 1985.

View of a wall in the 'lost city' of Gran Vilaya, in the jungle-covered mountains of Peru. *Photo © AP.* ***New York Times*** *7 July 1985.*

MONSTROUS FISH

We noted two giant fish, from California, in **FT43 p6** - here are more whoppers:

► Angler Neville Fickling, claimed a new British record, after landing a pike weighing 41 lbs 6oz, on the Norfolk Broads, beating the previous record of 40lbs. *D.Mirror* 14 Feb 1985.

► A new horror has invaded the rivers of the Macon area of France - a large flesh-eating catfish. Invading from the direction of eastern Europe, this ugly, stout-bodied carnivorous catfish is said to measure up to two meters (6.6 feet), and weigh up to 60kg (132 lbs). The fish's size has been attributed to its appetite for other fish; it is raising fears for the resident populations of bream, pike, carp, tench, crayfish, freshwater mussels, and even waterfowl and ducklings. In some areas there have even been rumours of attacks on swimming children, creating "jaws"-type panics. Our source goes further: "There are tales about fishermen's boats being picked up off the water by giant fish on the River Saone - and about divers inspecting bridge structures scared off by huge, dark shapes." These sound more like the river monsters discussed by Ulrich Magin; see his article on p52 AFP. *Jakarta Post* 2 Sept 1985.

► From the same paper comes news of a group of giant fishes inhabiting a remote lake in the far northwest corner of China, whose appearance is counted a bad omen. The official Chinese news agency, Xinhua, said that there were numerous local legends about the "monsters" in Lake Hanas, in the autonomous region of Xinjiang. One old Mongolian claims to have seen a "lot of big fish" in the lake in the 1930s just prior to a major earthquake in the area. It happened again in August 1985. Just a few weeks after a scientist identified the red monsters as a huge species of salmon - at 10 meters (33ft) long reckoned to be the biggest salmon on record - the province was rocked by a quake in which 80 people died. (For more on Chinese portents, see PURGE ON SUPERSTITIONS on p4.)

The fishes were first spotted in June by a group of scientists on a field trip on a nearby mountain, who said they saw a collection of "red boats and a mass of seaweed". Binoculars revealed the 'boats' to be large red fish. Xiang Ligai, associate professor of the Xinjiang University Biology Department, observed the fish for at least 10 hours on 23 July 1985. "Professor Xiang could clearly make out the head, spiny rays and tail fin," said Xinhua. He said it was a type of salmon known in China as *hucho taimen*, usually found in the rivers of Heilongjiang, China's northern-most province, usually measuring about 6.6 feet and weighing about 154lbs. UPI 28 Aug; Boston (MA) *Herald*, Schenectady (NY) *Gazette* 29 Aug; *Mainichi Daily News*, Tokyo 30 Aug; *Jakarta Post* 2 Sept 1985.

► Dreams of fish farming in Kenya's Lake Victoria, and thereby developing a new food industry for countries in East Africa, have been cruelly dashed by the appearance of giant cannibal fish. The huge carp-like Nile Perch, called by Lake fishermen the "elephant of the water" grows to the size of a man, weighing about 220lbs. They have practically cleared Lake Victoria of some 300 species of food and ornamental fishes, and crustaceans. One species of fish, now gone, was introduced to control the water snail responsible for spreading the disease bilharzia. "Now the fish are cannibalizing their own kind because there is nothing left for them to devour," said a spokesman for the International Union for the Conservation of Nature (IUCN). Alas for the locals, the giant fish is no delicacy, being so oily it requires heavy smoking, and fetches a low price in the market. The IUCN also expressed concern that similar fish farming plans are being made for other large lakes, like Lake Malawi, and they fear the same thing may happen again with dire consequences for local economies. UPI. 19 Dec 1985.

SLOW POST TO TORQUAY

A postcard, posted in Clevedon near Bristol, arrived in Torquay on 16 November 1984, fourteen years and one week after it was posted. We have dozens of such delays on file – evidence, perhaps, of some postal limbo. *D.Mail* 17 Nov 1984.

WATER MONSTERS: GREENLAND

Although this is an old report, we don't get much news about Greenland, so it's well worth giving here. Our source is the Finnish paper *Ilta-Sanomat* ? July 1954.

The fishermen of Godthaab, said its mayor, Nokolaj Rosing, will studiously avoid Lake Natsilik despite its abundant fish and game, because they fear a terrible water monster. The native "superstitious mind" has furnished most of the large lakes in Greenland with monsters, many larger than Nessie is said to be, he said. Rosing added that while "experts" were generally skeptical about such stories, they are very ancient, and seem to be reinforced by occasional sightings. Perhaps the most famous is the huge sea serpent seen in 1734, by the zoologist-priest Hans Egede, founder of Godthaab.

Most recently [date unknown] a group of women saw a huge fin, "as large as a sail" jutting out of the water of the 30km-long canal linking Lake Natsilik with the sea, north of Godthaab. According to Nokolaj Rosing, mayor of Godthaab, it belonged to an enormous creature which was "very, very angry." He said: "It whipped the water furiously and threw big stones into the air." The monster, which had been seen in the area two years before (1952), lost a few "saucer-sized" scales in this activity.

Rosing was speaking to a visiting party from a Danish parliamentary committee, who told the press when they returned home.

The report also mentions three other water monsters. The first resides in Lake Umanak, northwest Greenland, and is white in colour. A black monster haunts Disco Bay. Sometimes huge fins are seen, but not in every case. Lake Natsilik itself boasts a "boat-sized sea-scorpion", the *Kajanok Agdlinartok.* There is also a popular belief among fishermen about the *Imap Umassoursua*, a flatish creature "the size of an island". These sailors live in terror of taking soundings which indicate the water is rapidly becoming shallow, for it may mean the Imap Umassoursua is rising off the ocean floor directly under their boat. This sounds very like the 'Hide' or the blob-like creatures which merit a chapter in Michell & Rickard's *Living Wonders.*

FOOD OF THE GODS?

Four huge depressions, eight feet long, five wide and 16 feet across were found in a maize field outside Milan. Farmer Gianpiero Baizi told the police of his discovery, and they inturn noticed the whole area was covered by a grey powder. They could advance no explanation.

The terrified farmer found no consolation in this. Referring to his weird and unwanted tourist attraction, Baizi said: "They were the exact shape of a chicken's footprint, but enormous; as if some gigantic bird had swooped down, landed, and taken off again." It is not said whether any of his corn was missing. One can almost picture him, glancing nervously to the skies. *S.Express* 9 June 1985.

THE BIG SLEEP

★ On Christmas Day 1985, James McDonell rang the doorbell of his house in New York, to be greeted by his wife Anne. He had been missing for 15 years, and had been declared legally dead 7 years after his disappearance.

His fugue began in 1971 with two car accidents in which he suffered concussion and other head injuries. One day he complained to a friend of a headache, went for a walk and never returned. He 'came to' on a Philadelphia street, with no identification, knowing only that his first name was James. He took the surname 'Peters' off a nearby store sign and got a job at a cafe. The former postal supervisor said his memory returned when he bumped his head on Christmas Eve. He checked the telephone book to see if his wife of 20 years still lived in New York. New York *Daily News* 27 Dec 1985.

★ If, in the continuity of all things, there are fugues similar to self-hypnosis, this next tale would be a candidate. It concerns a 50yr-old lady dentist who put herself into a hypnotic trance and couldn't be woken up for two weeks. She had attended a course, run by a professional hypnotist, on how to use the 'fluence to help people overcome their fear of going to the dentist. Because part of his technique involved teaching self-hypnosis, the dentist decided to experiment. She was so successful that even

Continued ☛

☛ Continued
her family and friends couldn't rouse her. After two weeks in a coma-like state she partially revived but was plainly not her usual self. Several months of "intense psychiatric treatment" followed, which failed to remove her constant feeling of lethergy. When confronted with the effects of his technique upon the dentist, the lecturer would only say "No comment." *Sydsvenska Dagbladet* 16 Jan 1986.

CAT NEST

We've heard of bird-dogs and cats and cats with wings, but how about this! A tortoiseshell cat, owned by farmer's wife Pamela Fletcher, climbed a 15ft tree to give birth to three kittens in an abandoned magpie's nest, at Bradwell, Derbyshire. ***D.Mirror*** **28 May 1985.**

THE NELSON CURSE

Doreen Squires of Riverdale, Harbertonford, Devon, had reason to be apprehensive when her son Martin, 25, had a piece of steel fly into his right eye while working in a saw mill in Totnes. Her father, grandfather and great-grandfather had all lost their right eyes in accidents. They were all born on 29 September, the birthdate of Lord Nelson – and we know what happened to his right eye. Jim Chapple, a stone cracker, lost his eye to a stone chipping. His son Jim, a blacksmith, lost his to a piece of steel while making a horseshoe, and *his* son Adrian, Doreen's father, lost his in a quarry blast. Martin recovered from his accident, and his sight is perfect. It possibly helped that he was *not* born on 29 September. *Western Morning News, Sun* 27 April 1985.

ANIMAL GRIEF

▶ A polar bear named Hans, died just three weeks after his life-long mate, Helga. Dudley Zoo, West Midlands, said: "They were very affectionate. Hans was obviously lonely after Helga died. Then he collapsed." *D.Mirror* 22 Feb 1985.

▶ Koko, the famous 'talking' gorilla at San Francisco Zoo's Gorilla Foundation, fell in love with a white tail-less kitten and was allowed to keep it in her cage. Koko, who learned to communicate with her keepers in a special sign language, herself chose the kitten's name, All Ball. She had asked for a cat after being read children's fairy stories which featured cats. Early in January 1985 All Ball escaped and was run over. A zoo spokesman said: "Koko didn't say anything at first, when we broke the news to her in sign language. Then she started crying. She has been pining ever since." Luckily, All Ball's mother was expecting another litter, and the keepers plan to give Koko one of the kittens. *D.Mirror* 10 Jan 1985. The *Birmingham Post* of 3 April 1985 has a photo of Koko cuddling the replacement lovingly on her chest.

▶ For 27 years Inga and Raja lived happily together. They were Indian elephants, in the Zoo of Dushanbe, capital of the Central Asian republic of Tajikistan. During the "unusually severe cold" at the end of 1985, Inga contracted a lung inflammation and died, aged 30 years. Her death affected Raja badly. He dropped to his knees beside her, tears streaming from his eyes, and could not be moved from her side. When medical workers tried to use a crane to remove her body from the animals' enclosure, Raja angrily tore the rope to pieces and threw them away. With great difficulty, the keepers eventually managed to lure Raja into a thick-walled winter shed, but he soon broke free to stand guard by his mate once more. For 24 hours he would let no-one into the enclosure, until, it seemed, his mourning was over. Then he helped the keepers pick up Inga's body gently, and allowed them to take it away. *Soviet Weekly* 11 Jan 1986.

▶ A similar story is told of Toto and Moto. two African elephants who came to the Colchester Zoo together as babies, from the wild. After 17 years' friendship, Moto died suddenly, on 24th Sept 1985. For the next five hours Toto stood by her friend's body, allowing no-one near. Her keeper, Richard Spurgeon, said: "Watching Toto's efforts to revive Moto was worse than the death itself. Toto kept caressing Moto with her trunk and pushing at her." Now she keeps going over to touch the place where Moto collapsed with her trunk. *D.Mirror, D.Mail* 25+26 Sept 1985.

▶ Jean Ricord and her aging mongrel, Coco, were inseparable, and a familiar sight around their neighbourhood of Nice, France. When Jean died after a coronary, aged 59, a neighbour took in Coco, who moped all day, for seven days, on the fourth-floor balcony. Coco would not eat and hardly drank; "She just sat there looking down to the street where she and Jean used to walk for hours together," said the neighbour. On the seventh day, the funeral procession for Jean passed by in the street below, and as though that was what she was waiting for, the mourning dog leapt from the balcony to her death in front of the stunned mourners. With touching compassion, the mourners agreed to bury the dog with her master, and there and then she was placed in the coffin and so it was done. *Weekly World News* 31 Dec 1985.

WEST COAST SEA SERPENT

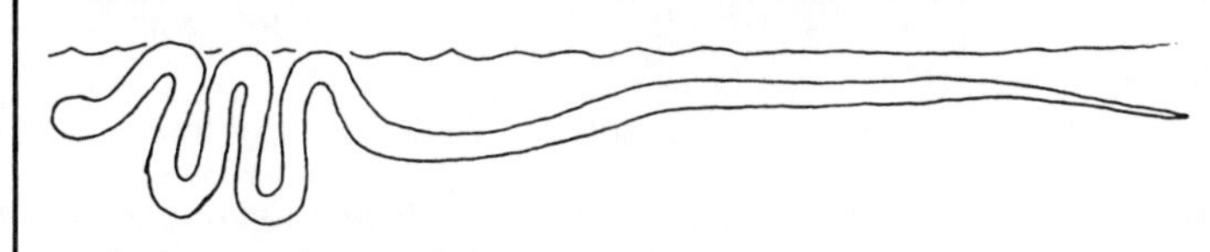

A view through the water showing the vertical movement of the monster. *Drawing in* ***Gate***.

The sighting of a serpentine creature of monstrous proportions in San Francisco's Bay, on 5th February 1985, is reported in *The Gate* Jan 1986, and vouched for as genuine - we have no clippings on this incident (yet!).

The witnesses, twin brothers Bill and Bob Clark, were sitting in their car enjoying a view of the Bay, when they noticed two seals, about a hundred yards away, panic and move inshore towards a sea wall. Then they saw what was chasing the seals. It was more like a snake and "moving strange", said Bill. "We watched it coming in, undulating in a vertical manner. Where most snakes undulate side to side, this was up and down, creating humps in the water." Though its head never broke the surface (see diagram) the water was so clear that they could see it

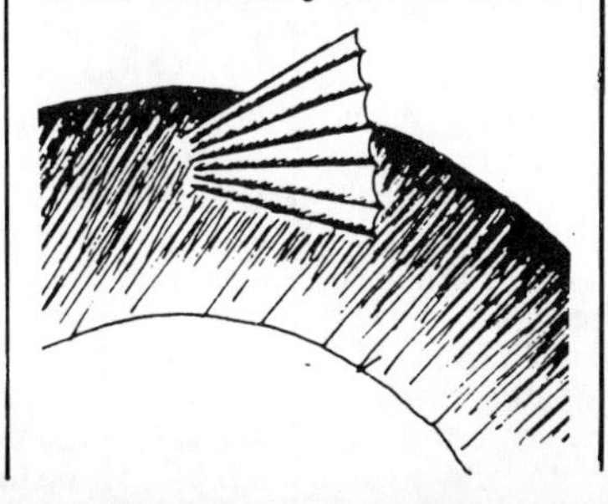

was "snake-like, short and stout, like a viper's type of head," said Bob. As it neared the sea wall, it seemed to get "tangled" in the rocks and "corkscrewed" trying to get free.

As it twisted, sections came out of the water, one rising out at least three feet. "I got an excellent view of a fin-like appendage which opened up like an accordian fan," Bob said. The twins estimated its length at close to 60 feet. Its dark green skin faded to a creamy underbelly. Bob said the underbelly reminded him of an aligator's.

The creature moved rapidly out towards the center of the Bay, using a "violent downward thrust of its neck." Later Bob and Bill contacted the coastguard, but there had been no other sightings. They went to the library to make an attempt at identification, and then took sketches to the Steinhart Aquarium. The director there said he had no idea what they saw. The twins stick to their story, and have received a lot of ridicule for it. But they are convinced and have had their accounts notarized.

Clipping Credits for This Issue:

OUR THANKS GO TO: Selby Anderson, Chris Ashton, Janet & Colin Bord, Jean-Louis Brodu, Colin Brown-Ross, Harold J.Butcher, Steuart Campbell, Bruce Chatterton, Peter Christie, Loren Coleman, Richard Cotton, Collectors of Unusual Data – International (COUD-I), AJ Dixon, Dr Franziska Dokter, Tony Egan, Richard Furlong, Ron Gauntlett, Robert I.Gillham, Mick Goss, Brian Hain, Chris Hall, Mark A.Hall, John Hitchens, Tuuri Hepaurata, Peter Hope-Evans, J Kain, J Lang, Kurt Lothmann, Alexis Lykiard, Ulrich Magin, Nick Maloret, John Michell, Steve Moore, Ian S.Murray, Roger Musson, Ray Nelke, Steve Parker, Rickard pere, Andy Roberts, Sven Rosen, Paul Screeton, Doc Shiels, Bob Skinner, Anthony Smith, Joseph Swatek, Paul R.Thomas, Joseph Trainor, RG Twine, UFO Newsclipping Service (UFONS), Roger Waddington, Owen Whiteoak, Ion Will, Steve Wrathall, Joseph Zarzynski.

TRANSLATION CREDITS: Jean-Louis Brodu (French); Ulrich Magin & David Metherell (German); Tuuri Heporauta (Finnish); Sven Rosen (Swedish).

Forum

A Picture is Worth 8x10^6 Bits.

by David M.Frost.

Your subscription renewal notices always advise the reader to "clip something strange today". Well, I believe that I may have found something way out here in Knoxville (in *Knoxville*?!?) wondrous enough to be of interest to FT readers. Please find enclosed a complete copy of the July 1985 issue of the *Whole Earth Review*, the periodical brought to us all (apparently) by the same Illuminati who invented the *Whole Earth Catalog*, the now legendary 1970's book index and all-around cornucopia of self-help, do-it-yourself, environmental, alternative culture, and other Third Wave topic resources. In an improvement over the *Catalog, WER*, today spends much of its time on subjects relating to science and advanced technology, reviewing new personal computer software well as books and "soft-tech" products (the publication is often found in computer-speciality stores as well as in the larger bookstores here in the US, which is how I managed to find something strange in Knoxville). And this month they came up with news that could leave every Fortean on the planet in a state of shock. One can now walk into a bookstore, buy a computer magazine, and read on the cover: *Flying Saucers in San Francisco – Digital Retouching, The End of Photography as Evidence of Anything.*

One glance at the cover photo says it all. The most that even the most hard-boiled viewer might suspect is that *WER* has somehow managed to fund and build airplanes that look like full-scale UFOs and get them off the ground long enough to buzz downtown San Francisco. That the saucers – basking in the California sun as they taxi in for a landing at the Transamerica Pyramid – are nothing more than mere *real* dinnerware adorned with parts cannibalized from model kits, is something no one would ever guess without looking inside the magazine. There, a feature article written by *WER* editors Stewart Brand, Kevin Kelly, and Jay Kinney describes the advent of the new mainframe-sized data processors – the Scitex machines made by Scitex of Israel, and the Chromacom by the (appropriately named) West German firm Hell – that "use high-tech page makeup processes that involve turning photographs into computer data, where it is so easy to fiddle with the images that the temptation is overwhelming."

Moreover, according to *WER*, these devices are already ubiquitous throughout the publishing industry, their use as page layout, reproduction, and transmission machines now standard practice in the windowless rooms of *Time, US Today, National Geographic, Popular Science, The New York Times,* and many other enterprises both here in the US and abroad (and although they don't mention them by name, they accuse ABC's *Nightline* – a news/interview show that airs around midnight in the US – of tampering digitally with their images too).

But what we've all got to understand is that all this goes way, way beyond anything that's ever been possible before. Certainly it's always been possible to "doctor" photographs in the past, but until now there had always been the hope of getting one's hands on the original negatives (as in the case of the 1920 Cottingley Fairy swindle reported by Janet Bord in FT43) and looking for the signs of tampering or re-photography that the old crude mechanical and chemical methods would inevitably leave behind.

And there were always certain technical limits as to what could be gotten away with. But now *everything* is up for grabs! Because not only do the Chromacom and the Scitexes make the most outrageous corruptions imaginable to a photograph child's play, they do so *without leaving any traces behind!* I've seen the actual Scitexed *National Geographic* covers *WER* refers to and the illusions are just as seamless as the authors say (moreover, the optimistic noises Kevin Kelly makes about future "machines that will sniff a photograph and say how real it is" is in total vain when one realises that it would no doubt be a simple task to get a upgraded retouching computer to wash the bogus details of a "slide" with fake "background noise", too).

And my amateur photographer brother, Doug, tells me that it would be an all too simple task for a swindler to rig up out of whole cloth on one of these machines whatever lake monster, UFO, BVM, or other impossibility he or she cared to claim extant, plop it down into the middle of an originally placid scene lasered off another photograph, and then zap the whole fraud onto a negative fitting exactly the kind of cheap pocket camera a sincere witness is liable to have out in the field; any evidence that all this was ever just a collection of pixels getting lost in the new "negative's" coarser grain. Provided that the *real* negatives and the computer files are destroyed, and the people involved keep quiet, there's no way any of this can ever be found out.

Continued ☛ 34

HOW THE *WER* PHOTO WAS MADE

Top left: Ted Schultz holds the intricately crafted UFO made of melamine dinner plates and "scavenged detritus". *Top right:* Schultz dangles the UFO on nylon line as Stewart Brand photographs the scene to get the light correct on the models. The photos – one general view and three of the UFO – are laser-scanned, turning them into digital information. The Chromacom's monitor *(left)* shows the 'hole' left by the middle UFO when its image is taken out of its photo. Gradually the desired image is assembled digitally and a set of high quality negatives are made for full-colour printing. The final result (below) must be seen in colour to fully appreciate it. *All photographs are copyright of **Whole Earth Review**, and used by kind permission.*

☛ Continued

So what it all boils down to is this: anyone with deep enough pockets and an axe to grind can walk right up to Gully Bull and offer up the "original, unretouched negative" of the photo (or film or tape) of, say, the Cottingley fairies dancing on Margaret Thatcher's hat; and there's not a thing that can be done about it. Since there's no technical means of telling if it's a lie, there's no real means of telling if it's not a lie. There's no way of telling once this technology gets rolling whether any such proof is, as *WER* puts it, "organic".

From now on, a belief in *any* photograph constitutes an unalloyed act of faith. The future is here. Right on top of us. From now on that perennial Fortean Holy Grail, The Ultimate Photograph of (you name it) That Convinces Everyone, is forever out of our reach.

The End of Photography as Evidence?

by Bob Rickard.

We originally planned to do a cover feature on the important subject of digital retouching (DR). We were very happy when our good friends at ***Whole Earth Review*** - Kevin Kelly, Jay Kinney, Ted Schultz and publisher Stuart Brand - agreed to let us reprint or precis the article and went to a lot of trouble to provide us with their copyright photographs, and we are grateful for their help. Alas, as things turned out, the next available 'slot' in our schedule was at least six months away and our choice was to wait or to bring you a cut-down version. Somehow the subject seemed relevant to this issue, and while pondering how to squeeze it in, we received David Frost's excellent summary of the ***WER*** article. [For the full version, with the UFO photo in full colour, read ***WER*** 47 (July 1985). **Whole Earth Review, Box 27956, San Diego, CA 92128, USA.** Single issue price is "[3.]

Firstly there is a difference between computer 'enhancement' of photos and digital retouching; although both involve digitizing an image into thousands of pixels (picture cells), an enhancement - eg. as carried out on Rines' 'flipper' photos (see Mike Dash's article on p60) - simply clarifies the existing image by sharpening vague edges and colour densities. Digital retouching deliberately manipulates the image at the pixel level in ways limited only by the operator's creative skill. Because an operator can now produce 'photographs' of an image as desired, not as seen, it is truly an artistic medium, but a hi-tech one.

If Rines had had access to a Scitex or a Chromacom back in 1972 he could have altered the image to show whatever he liked (or imagined!), instead of employing the services of an air-brush wizard. But the ensuing argument would essentially be the same as it is now: we can't accept the published photos as evidence because a subjective element has crept into them, however honest Rines' intentions. Elsie Wright and Frances Griffiths also claimed good intentions; they simply wanted to show the kind of fairies they "really" did see in that glen in Cottingley [see FT43 pp48-53]. But there were no digital retouching machines around in Yorkshire in the 1910s. Just imagine the amazing and convincing photos of fairies we'd be arguing over if there had been!

But there is a dark side too. Our human race has a perverse streak which inevitably finds expression in using the available artistic media for nefarious gain. As soon as photography was invented, for example, sharp charlatans were creating 'spirit portraits' - the first such photographs date from the 1860s! If it were not for the problems of access to these fabulously expensive machines, there would be a flood of convincing fakes. If a digitally retouched photo is all we have to go on, there would be no internal clue to its unreality, barring the clumsiness of the operator. Similar machines have been used in the film industry (eg. pioneered by the ***Star Wars*** special effects technicians) at least since 1979, so Fort only knows what an enterprising prankster could have put into the arena by now. It is certainly possible, for example, that the mystery Nessie photo discussed on p36. could have been created by a DR manipulation of one of Doc Shiels' own photos. But by whom, when, and why? The questions remain.

One event coming up, which would be an unbeatable opportunity for DR pranks, is 'Dr Crypton's Great Hoax Contest', announced in the November 1985 issue of ***Science Digest***. The offer two categories: UFOs, and "weird beasts". They describe the latter as "open-ended; we are looking for photos of (presumably) imaginary creatures, such as the Loch Ness Monster, a living dinosaur, the Abominable Snowman, a Martian, and so on." Like Joe Zarzynski says (in his ***Champ Channels*** v3 n4 1985), we will soon see how easy, or difficult it is to perpetrate a photographic hoax of a lake monster.

NOW YOU SEE THEM.

NOW YOU DON'T.

Altering photographs to suit editorial whims is not new. In 1924, the figure of Trotsky, then out of favour, was removed from a photo of Lenin making a speech. Today, according to the *WER* article, most of the big magazines and big-buck advertising agencies do it. In this demonstration photo for Pacific Lithographic (where *WER*'s UFOs were digitally retouched), it was relatively easy to remove three figures. The real magic of the DR machine comes in its 'cloning' facility, which doesn't so much duplicate any part of the scanned image as replicate it. For example, adding duplicate people is simple; the clever part is that textures can be imitated which are not duplicates. In this case it 'filled-in' the people-shaped holes with "sky and mountain paint" as *WER* put it. the edges of cloned areas are 'seamless' and undetectable unless the operator is too lazy to avoid duplicating the cloned image or texture.

In fact no fortean subject would be beyond the illustrative skills of a DR artist. A rain of frogs, a man in the act of combusting, or some spectacular feat of psychokinesis or levitation. It is conceivable that DR technology could one day be available to the personal computer market, especially since the Mackintosh has whetted the artistic thirst for better quality graphics and image manipulation software. But for now it is only affordable by big companies, institutions and perhaps even government departments. I'm sure the potential of DR technology for propaganda and 'disinformation' has not been lost on the 'dirty tricks' departments of various governments. What a sinister prospect that is! It is now within the power of DR to create false images with the express purpose of demoralising, confusing or discrediting 'targeted' organisations , beliefs or movements. An anti-Catholic organisation, for example, could circulate fake BVM appariton photos. Let the conspiracy buffs and ufologists ponder that!

Apart from the astonishing consequences of DR upon the nature of photographic evidence and proof, which we are now forced to consider, we are really no further forward or backward. Even if a photograph of a strange creature or phenomenon is proved beyond doubt to be genuine, a confirmed skeptic cannot be made to accept it.

But of one thing we can be sure: seeing (a photo) is no longer a simple yardstick for believing - if indeed it ever was. In these days of jaded palates overexposed to media tricks of all sorts, people have a residual suspicion. Recently, a book of UFO photos - ***UFO Contact from the Pleiades***, 1979 - printed in glossy full colour, immediately aroused suspicions. It was too good to be true! After all everyone knows that **genuine** photos of UFOs, ghosts, bigfoot etc are murky and misty. Not lyrical and composed, but hasty and unfocussed.

This Fish Story Still a Mystery

Women's News Service.

Marseilles, France — Francoise Monsergent was very proud of her one large goldfish that had won several prizes.

The other day she returned home to find the big fish missing and 90 tiny goldfish in the aquarium instead. The mystery has not been solved.

A strange story from the Hay Springs *News* 12 Jan 1923.

A Mysterious Portrait of Nessie.

by Bob Rickard.

To some skeptics and critics of the photographic evidence for the Loch Ness monster, the name of Anthony 'Doc' Shiels does not inspire much confidence. The fact that he managed to photograph both the Cornish sea monster 'Morgawr' [see **FTs19-23**], and Nessie herself [see **FT29**] weighs less with them than his flamboyant eccentricities. They feel he is not a good witness for the defense because he is an accomplished stage magician and a self-confessed practitioner of the 'real thing'. They are also made uneasy by Doc's claims – backed up by genuine sightings – to have joined with other magicians worldwide to raise the monstrous denizens in a few other celebrated lakes, aided by parties of naked young witches, his daughters among them. That Doc is also a Punch and Judy professor, a busker at fairs, a photographer, a painter, a surrealist, a playwright, a wit and raconteur, and a master of the 'black art' [making Guinnesses disappear] provides more fuel for their doubt.

But one gets the feeling that Doc's chief offence is simply that his Nessie photos of 21 May 1977 are the clearest and most detailed of all the known photographs. A good colour print of one (known as ANS-1) can be seen on p14 of *Photographs of the Unknown* (R.Rickard & R.Kelly, NEL, London, 1980/81). Doc himself will not be drawn into a public squabble in their defence. He acknowledges that they will never convince the deep-dyed skeptics like Steuart Campbell, Maurice Burton or Ronald Binns, adding, justifiably in my opinion, "I **know** my pictures are genuine, and that's all that really matters."

It is to his credit that Doc has never browbeaten his critics with the photos, or touted them with demands for money, though there must have been times he was tempted to do so. Doc has been a friend to FT from its early years, and in all that time he has been completely candid in his correspondence with myself and other forteans. Doc displays an admirable fortean attitude to phenomena; he is extremely well read, with a true scholar's integrity, and what he doesn't know about lake and sea monsters wouldn't fill a gnat's codpiece (as the Black Adder would say). Nowhere in all my dealings with him, do I find grounds for the slightest suspicion that he manufactured a hoax. And if Doc is not a hoaxer, it would be utterly reprehensible to reject his photos simply because he cuts an unorthodox figure. The universe has no obligation to us to present challenging evidence in ways acceptable to an arbitrary and local orthodoxy.

THE 'CUMBERNAULD NESSIE' PHOTO

Having said that, I do understand the consternation of those who cannot accept Doc's photos for what they are – the best yet of Nessie. But what will they make of a bizarre development that has even Doc wondering just what is going on? What I'm about to reveal is a complicated story about an even better photo (if authentic), which raises more questions than it answers. I have agreed not to reveal the identity of Doc's contact (whom we shall call 'H'), for personal and health reasons not connected with this affair. For the following account I rely heavily upon Doc's letters to Janet and Colin Bord, and to myself, from 12th April 1984 to the present, from which all the quotations are taken.

the Cumbernauld Nessie photograph. © *FPL.*

It began in the spring of 1984 – close to April 1st! – when H (who is well known to the Shiels family) went into a public library in Cumbernauld, Glasgow, looking for any books on the Loch Ness monster. H noticed a "smallish", blonde woman, in her mid-30s, holding a copy of Tony Harmsworth's small booklet (written for the monster exhibition at the Loch), and told the woman that H knew the man who had taken the photo of Nessie on the book's cover. The woman then blurted out that she too had taken a photo of Nessie, in September 1983. The woman agreed to show it to H, and they arranged to meet in a cafe a few days later. The meeting took place and the woman, whose name was McLachlan or McLaughlin (H can't be sure), gave H a 35mm colour slide "as if she was pleased to get rid of it".

Doc's first reaction to the picture – see photo – was astonishment, because it so closely resembled his own photo. "I was impressed...but suspected a clever fake, based on a reversed image, a mirror-version of my ANS-2 picture." As some readers might know, the original colour slide of ANS-2 was lost in the post when Doc sent it to his friend, the American magician Max Maven. It also crossed Doc's mind that someone had somehow got hold of the missing ANS-2 original and used it to create the 'Cumbernauld Nessie'. If the Cumbernauld Nessie could be discovered to be a fake, this whole affair would simply be a bit of nonsense – but alas! for certainty: a close examination reveals that it is indeed a different picture.

EXAMINED BY COLIN BORD

Doc sent the transparency to Colin Bord for his assessment. In order to make a comparison of the all-important image, Colin copied it (now designated CUM-1) onto B&W film, enlarged the detail of the monster, and printed it reversed and slightly rotated (see photos) to match the similar detail from ANS-2. I summarise Colin's findings, from his letter to Doc dated 12 July 1984:

SIMILARITIES

1) the shape of the 'head' and 'neck'.
2) the markings on the 'head'.
3) the markings of the 'mouth' area.
4) the 'musculature' of the 'neck'.
5) a V-shaped notch in 'neck' at water-level on left.
6) a roundish object at water-level, left of centre.
7) colour comparison with ANS-1 shows object to be a similar dark bronze colour.

DIFFERENCES

1) grain structure of CUM-1 more pronounced (due to greater enlargement or faster transparency film used).
2) wave structure in both pictures differ in pattern and definition.
3) angle of 'neck' to water is greater in ANS-2 than in CUM-1.

Detail of ANS-1. © ***Doc Shiels/FPL.***

Detail of ANS-2. © ***Doc Shiels/FPL.***

4) CUM-1 is lit from the left, whereas ANS-1/2 are lit from the right. If CUM-1 was taken from the same side of the Loch as Doc's, as Ms MacLachlan claimed, we would expect the creature's shadowy reflection to lie at a similar angle on the water.

5) the 'throat' of 'neck' in CUM-1 is paler, as if caught by light, and brightest near water-line, unlike ANS-2 in which the same area is uniformly dark. ANS-1, however, shows the same light effect as CUM-1, except that the right-hand edge of the 'neck' is darker, tapering away to the water-line.

Colin could detect no cut-out/paste-up or double exposure work. The similarities between the two pictures "although remarkable, are not quite close enough" to identify CUM-1 as a reversed version of ANS-2. Of course we cannot say that CUM-1 was not the product of airbrush retouching of ANS-2, but as Colin points out, the hypothetical artist would have to have been a master of his craft, and spent considerable time upon it, to effect such fundamental differences in fine detail in such an indetectable manner. To have such work done professionally would cost a great deal.

CURIOUSER AND CURIOUSER

Doc himself wondered whether the object in Ms MacLachlan's photo was "a cleverly constructed 'muppet'", based upon his 1977 photos and manipulated from a midget submarine or by radio control, "as part of a plot to discredit me and my own Nessie shots." Then his anxiety took off: "Maybe my 'success' in 1977 was some kind of bizarre set-up, planned and executed by the same people whoever they may be...Up to a couple of months ago, I believed absolutely that the 'thing' I photographed was the Loch Ness monster (plesiosaur, tulpa, elephant squid or whatever, but *real*), and I even swore an affidavit to that effect [We have it on file – Ed.], but now I'm not 100% sure. *If* the 'thing' was some kind of animated model it was beautifully made and it moved in an entirely 'natural' manner...a real Hollywood special-effects job...it must have cost a fortune. The hoaxer, if there is one (or more), must be wealthy." [The photo could have been generated by altering Doc ANS photo/s with computer imaging processes – some thoughts on this are given in my contribution to our FORUM discussion of digital retouching, see p32.]

To which one must add the obvious

Detail of CUM-1, reversed and rotated for comparison with ANS images. © *FPL.*

question, why go to such trouble to discredit Doc's photos? If that *was* the purpose, no one has come forward to shout "Yahboo!" to those of us who accept Doc's photos as authentic. They have passed scrutiny by a number of photographic experts [see **FT29**] and critics have consistently failed to substantiate their objections to the contrary. So, the next question must be, has Ms MacLachlan indeed photographed the same creature? This is the only other possible interpretation of the similarities and differences taken together.

THE MYSTERIOUS Ms MACLACHLAN

Ms MacLachlan told H that she had been on a cycling holiday in the Loch Ness area (we don't know if she was alone), around mid-September 1983. The photo was take on a sunny afternoon, from the shore below the A82, somewhere south of Achnahannet. The camera was a Canon, probably a 35mm SLR, with a zoom lens, which suggests to Doc the lady had more than a casual interest in photography, and perhaps even went to the Loch hoping for a portrait of Nessie. If we can believe her, she succeeded!

But genuine photo or not, there are still some nagging questions. We know nothing of 'Ms MacLachlan', if indeed that is her real name. Was it just coincidence (whatever that is!) that Ms MacLachlan met H in the library? Or did the lady who claimed to have taken a photo of the same monster as Doc, or at least was carrying a nearly identical photo to Doc's, somehow know that H would be there, and that H had a direct line to Doc. It turns out that the library does not have *any* books on Nessie, therefore Ms MacLachlan had brought the Harmsworth pamphlet (with Doc's Nessie photo on the cover) with her. If the aim was to discredit Doc's own photos then why choose this elaborate and risky way of doing it. Why not send the picture, with a description of how it was done, to one of Doc's critics, Campbell, say, or Binns? As it is Doc sat on it for a while out of sheer puzzlement.

Partly because of my own coaxing, Doc agreed to its publication in FT, both for the record (in case it *is* genuine), and in the hope that, if it is a fake, it will draw the perpetrators out of hiding. Doc admits that his request to protect the identity of H will add to the suspicions of the skeptics, but among other things H's health was not good, and the possibility of having been used in such a way by some obviously clever and resourceful people, was adding unwanted stress. Doc writes: "If it is a fake, it is a very convincing fake, and its publication will almost certainly call my own pictures into question." Personally, I cannot accept the argument that if the Cumbernauld Nessie photo was shown to be a fake, then *ipso fatso* Doc's 1977 pictures are fakes. This is innuendo, not logic, and no fortean will be convinced by it any more than they are by Mr 'Amazing' Randi when he asserts that because he himself can fake PK, Geller's phenomena *must* be faked! Doc admits he had a strong urge to keep quiet about Ms MacLachlan's photo, but to his credit he passed them on, despite his own anxieties about the circumstances in which it came to light.

We must be wary, of course, but also fair. Until evidence comes forth to the contrary I'm happy to say that these photos, by Doc and 'Ms MacLachlan' are the best yet of Nessie. I would be just as happy if I were proved wrong, because then the uncertainty would be resolved.

The Jabberwocks of Quebec.

Michel Meurger, a mythozoologist attached to the *Institut Metapsychique International* in Paris, studied Canadian lake monsters, and suggests the absurd range of monsters might indicate cultural differences among the witnesses, rather than the existence of many different kinds of monsters.

The number of books available on the lake monster problem continues to grow. Most of those writing since the days of oddity collectors like Rupert T.Gould sail under the flag of those searchers dedicated to zoological enigmas, the cryptozoologists.

Unfortunately, after years of searching, mainly concentrated in Loch Ness, the few inconclusive bits of evidence amount to some disputed sonar prints and several blurred photographs. In these disturbing circumstances cryptozoologists concentrate on the vast bulk of sightings, trying to find a coherent thread, chiefly in an attempt to validate one theory or another.

Alas! As Loch Ness specialist Roy Mackal stated, as early as 1967: 'No single animal fits all the Loch Ness data.' **[1]** Notwithstanding this bold affirmation, Mackal has tried successively to adjust some zoological coat or other to the variable humps of Nessie. But watch out for the tailor, for he is always forgetting the measurements for the suit! First he tried the 'giant mollusc' theory, neglecting among other considerations, Nessie's amphibian characteristics. **[2]** Next he proposed a new cloth, a reworking of Commander Gould's 'giant newt' theory, overlooking the sea-serpent brothers of the monster and the amphibian's dislike of salt-water. **[3]**

The newest fashion for the Scottish star seems to be an archaic form of cetacean, the zeuglodon. But this time the proposed clothes are too short for the famous swan-like neck. Mackal also pre-empted himself in 1976 by writing: 'Not even archaic (cetacean) forms, such as zeuglodon, though more serpentine in shape, had an elongated head-neck region.' **[4]** Today our modish zeuglodon has stretched his neck a bit, and this mammal can wait hours underwater without so much as a breath-bubble. I must say that I wait in considerable awe for the next costume: long-necked seal boots?

I have emphasized the Mackalian opinions because they represent, in my opinion, the best cryptozoological material available on the lake monster riddle. And if Mackal's flaws are that obvious it is best to say nothing about such popular ideas as the 'plesiousaur' hypothesis. By 1934, Dr Oudemans had formulated irrefutable arguments against it, based on a careful study of the plesiosaurian skeleton. **[5]** Yet today the plesiosaur remains the spoilt child of pressmen and popular reconstructions, mainly because of its obvious 'lost world' associations. It seems to me that the only evident result of this 'quest for the dragon' will be to provide the public with a modernized legend. The time for a study of this phenomenon of rationalization in a cultural context has arrived.

The horned serpent of the Iroquois (after H.M.Converse, *Myths and Legends of the Iroquois*, 1908).

In August 1981, I joined with Claude Gagnon, a professor of philosophy at Montreal University, in a project designed to 'hunt the hunters'. Quebec, the French-speaking province of Canada, was taken as our hunting ground because it seemed so full of potential. It is a land literally soaked with lakes and rivers, and at the beginning of our investigation it was an unexplored territory on the map of lake monsterdom.

George Eberhart's excellent *Geo-Bibliography of Anomalies* **[6]** mentions only one lake as monster-haunted, and the Bord's international lake monster listing **[7]** gives three, if we correct the duplication of one lake in two provinces.

By February 1983, our personal on-the-spot investigations had revealed the surprising number of fifty monstrous lakes, and we had only covered a small part of our map!

Some of our findings were published in Montreal, in our book *Monstres des Lacs du Quebec* **[8]**, the first part of which covers the fieldwork, complete with statements, photos and witnesses' drawings. In the second part of the book I present some of their European counterparts, chiefly bringing to light historical texts on an unknown lake monster region, the German Alps. And for a dessert, I destroy a cherished Press hoax, the so-called 'extract from the log of the explorer Samuel de Champlain' in which he is supposed to have described the monster in the lake which bears his name as 'a serpent-like creature with a head like a horse'. This description is completely apocryphal, but has been reproduced hundreds of times, not least significantly by *Life* magazine (August 1982). There is nothing of the sort in the original French text, which I include in my book (pp288-290). Writing of his discovery of the huge lake in 1609, Champlain spoke only of a common fish, the garpike; hardly a 'serpentine monster'.

If we return to Quebecian waters, it is possible to summarize some results of our quest as follows:

1) basic forms ('upturned boat', 'variable humps') are sighted in Quebec lakes, as they are elsewhere.

2) However the unity disintegrates after this promising beginning; **in the same lake**, witnesses gape at a number of totally different **general** shapes, primarily

i) the 'big fish', spindle-shaped with fins;
ii) the 'long-necked something', bulky and round with a giraffe-neck, waddling upon flippers;
iii) the 'alligator', short-necked, with clawed feet;
iv) and last but not least the 'great serpent' with no appendages at all.

Sometimes, the same witness gazes in amazement at the whole fashion parade and grunts: 'This lake is like a zoo!' The select few may see, **in those same waters**, the 'giant turtle' and the 'freshwater squid', a tentacled fortean impossibility. **[9]**

The 'Tete de cheval' of Blue-Sea-Lake. *Drawing by **Michel Meurger** from a witness' description.*

In vain we seek coherence in the details; we have a choice of features for each part of the body – head, neck, back, tail and appendages. Depending upon our cryptozoological theories, we can recognize fashionable mammals, acceptable saurians, and, for the more conservative, comprehensible fishes. The only problem is that *everything is available.* So help yourself and follow the cavalcade!

There are three sorts of heads: mammalian ('horse-like', 'cow-like'), reptilian ('serpent-like', 'croc-like') and piscean. Sometimes protruberances are seen ('horns') of variable number (one or more...). The neck may be short or long, and the back ridged or not, with no less than five different types of ridges mentioned. A ragged 'newt-like' ridge, a regular 'row of small pipes', 'long spines', a rounded 'croc-like' ridge or tall 'candle-stick' structures reminiscent of the external gills of some molluscs. If there are still any enthusiasts, we can offer three different tails: forked and fish-like, lizard-like, or flattened like a beaver's. Appendages vary in number (two or four) and form: sometimes fins, flippers or webbed feet, sometimes long toes with claws. The descriptions of skin range from something resembling seal-skin to being blotched and toad-like: the blotches themselves vary in size from tiny blisters to enormous bumps. There may be long or short hair, a 'scaly skin' or an 'armoured' one like a croc's. Refreshingly, some witnesses spoke of animals possessing hair **and scales at the same time!**

Every detective expects some variations in a collective description of a suspect, but in this case it is not the existence of variations which is disturbing but the extent of the discrepancies. But we should not exclude them from our consideration solely because the creatures seem to be composites – remember the *ornithorhynchus*, a mammal despite its duck beak, egg-laying and venomous toe! However, because the descriptions in the reports vary so much, it is impossible to make any definite identifications. The lake monsters themselves taunt us with elusiveness in their bodies as well as in their habitats. Their forms melt away like jelly or the fauna of dreams.

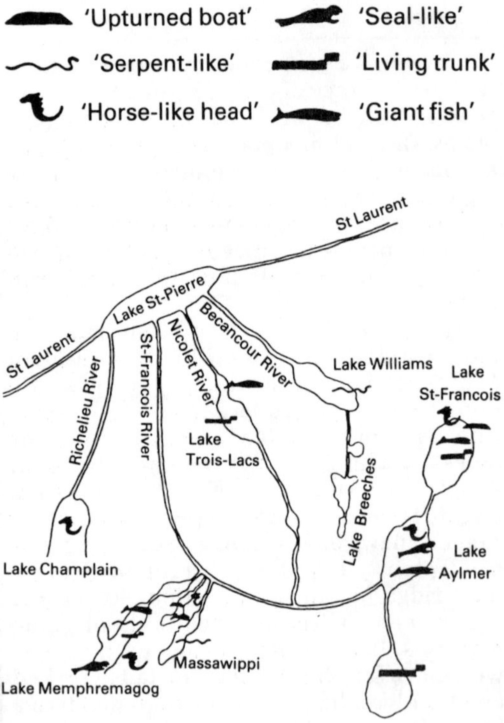

'Upturned boat' 'Seal-like'
'Serpent-like' 'Living trunk'
'Horse-like head' 'Giant fish'

A schematic map of a group of lakes feeding Lac Saint-Pierre in the St Laurence sea-way (Lake Champlain is the open-ended one on the far left), showing the locations of different types of monster-descriptions. Meurger points to the absurdity of four major types co-existing in the small Lac Saint-Francois (rightmost top).

It seems impossible that **four** (or more) quite different and totally unknown types of large animal could co-exist in some Quebecian lakes, many of which are of only average size and depth (see map). It is difficult to believe that such lakes could sustain a viable breeding population of each - even the resources of the giant Lake Champlain would not be sufficient!

But these small problems do not seem to worry the Quebecian critters, drawing on their inheritance of Gallic insubordination and nonsense. Poems and written allusions to them have been found dating back to 1850. At this point the reader has to ask himself if the Quebecois are over-imaginative or exaggerating. If so, perhaps they are not alone because the Ogopogo of Lake Okanagan, in British Columbia, is likewise furnished with a stimulating wardrobe: three sets of tails (fish-like, serpent-like and beaver-like), and sometimes jocularly exhibits a seal-like head *with scales!* **[10]** Champ, the Lake Champlain monster, also has many forms, as does the Scandinavian *Storsjoodjuret* **[11]**. Even Nessie has the bad taste to waddle ashore with the short neck of a hippo! Thus, it seems to me, that the solution to the lake monster puzzle, is more of a cultural than a naturalistic one.

If the aquarium were not so stuffed with scaly things it might also include yellow submarines. Indeed in some Quebecian lakes, where a few witnesses describe living forms, others speak of seemingly mechanical devices like mystery subs or flaming unidentified submarine objects (USOs). **[12]** In *Monstres des Lacs du Quebec* I have collected material to demonstrate that the European ancestors of the modern Canadians brought along with their luggage the water monster traditions of their home regions, which mixed fruitfully with the rich indiginous Indian folklore about lake serpents. For example: in both Indian and European traditions, lake monsters can transform themselves into fiery balls.

The mountainous part of continental Europe is well stocked with an ancient menagerie of alpine lizards, flying snakes and lake-dragons; the most interesting being a Swiss rival to Nessie which I exhumed from folklore and historical accounts. This creature – named 'The Big Elbst' – was sighted a great many times between 1585 and 1926. A kind of giant lizard, it lived at the bottom of a tiny lake, the Seelisbergsee, and could transform itself into a floating island, a 'green bough', a fiery ball or a fiery wheel. **[13]** It is not unreasonable, then, that the strange 'subs' reported in Quebecian lakes are a phase in the modernizing of an archaic mythology. The 'mystery sub' is , in turn, a rudimentary form of the USO.

Folklore studies, such as those of the Bords, or of Clark and Coleman, which explore the relationship between, for example, dragons and the new 'ET' monsters, are more useful to these researches than the hardcore tracts of cryptozoology. Formal cryptozoologists, like the 'nuts-and-bolts' ufologists, seem blind to the whole cultural background of their quest. Certainly, my fieldwork in Quebec seems to indicate that it would be more promising to study the inhabitants on the shores of a lake than to probe its murky waters. If lake monsters are indeed created in a cultural context then our research method should be properly called **mythozoology.**

The monster of Lac Saint-Francois. *Drawing by* ***Michel Meurger.***

NOTES

■ 1 – R.P.Mackal, 'Sea Serpents and the Loch Ness Monster' in *Oceanology International* (Sept-Oct 1967) p41. ■ 2 – ibid, 'Giant Molluscs: a Suspect'. ■ 3 – R.P.Mackal, *The Monsters of Loch Ness* (Futura, London, 1976). ■ 4 – ibid, p136. ■ 5 – A.C.Oudemans, *The Loch Ness Monster* (EJ Brill, Leydon, 1934). ■ 6 – *A Geo-Bibliography of Anomalies* (Greenwood, Westport, 1980). ■ 7 – Janet & Colin Bord, *Alien Animals* (Paul Elek/ Granada, London, & Stackpole Books, Harrisburg, 1981) p219. ■ 8 – M.Meurger & G.Gagnon, *Monstres des Lacs du Quebec* (Stanke, Montreal, 1982). *[The book is of great interest to both hard and soft cryptozoologists, not the least because it explores the continuity between the native Canadian and immigrant European traditions of lake monsters. Despite our attempts to interest an English-language publisher, it remains available only in French – Ed.]* ■ 9 – See also Charles Fort, *The Complete Books of Charles Fort* (Dover, NY, 1974) p597 for a discussion of a squid caught in the fresh water of Lake Onondaga, NY. There are other rumours about squids and octopuses in North American waters...perhaps some future work for Loren Coleman! ■ 10 – Mary Moon, *Ogopogo* (JJ Douglas, Vancouver, 1977) p55. ■ 11 – *[A recent letter from our Swedish correspondent, Sven Rosen, included the following animadversion on some Swedish lake monsters: 'On 17 July 1985, our newspaper* Arbetet *briefly mentioned that the monster of Lake Storsjon had been seen again. Three persons observed it; it was brownish black, had humps, and it swam in a serpentine way. The paper added that 'every year at about this time there are reports about this monster, and it is suspected that some of the stories are spread by PR-minded persons trying to attract tourists.' Which, of course, explains why the monster is as seasonal as the tourists – it is almost never observed in the winter. There is a folklore answer to this problem as well: the lake monsters of Norrland are seasonal 'because' they migrate from the Bothnian sea, where they spend the winter months, and sometimes in summer they have been observed on land moving between the different lakes.' Sven goes on to mention the little known study of the Storsjon monster by Dr Peter Olsson in 1899, a full account of which may be found more easily in chapter 8 of* Peter Costello's In Search of Lake Monsters *(Panther, London, 1975). Olsson wondered if the monster might be an unknown species of giant seal, but readily admitted that seals should have been more noticeable in the winter, and the lack of breathing holes in the lake's ice. Sven continues: 'So the monster was seasonal long before there were any tourists. I don't think people nowadays see exactly the same kind of monster as they did 100 or 150 years ago. In those days the* storsjoodjuret *was a 'water-horse-serpent', and even mistaken for a swimming horse at first glance. I have seen reports describing its head (when surfaced) surrounded by a long white mane of hair floating in the water. Nowadays witnesses don't seem to notice its horse-like head and mane, but 100 years ago practically no-one failed to mention it, which is the reason why Dr Olsson guessed it was a seal. Not that seals have manes (as far as I know, but reptiles should not be hairy at all!) Olsson is cited by Heuvelmans (*In the Wake... *p332.) as just one example of a scientist taking both a lake monster* and *Oudemans' sea-serpent solution (an unknown seal) seriously. Then Sven adds a comment relevant to Meurger's closing observations: 'Perhaps we are dealing with a 'camouflageon' (= a hitherto unknown species of highly developed amphibian chameleon) which any day now may even transform itself into a yellow (or Red) submarine?' – Ed.]* ■ 12 – *[The relationship between 'mystery subs', USOs and water monsters, especially in the continuing reports from Swedish fjords of unidentified objects which elude naval blockades, was discussed in* FT42 p7f *– Ed.* ■ 13 – *[See also under 'Switzerland' in Ulrich Magin's artilce on p 52 – Ed.]*

A Mari Usque Ad Mare.

Mr X. adopts quite a different approach from that of Meurger, when confronted by the baffling diversity in descriptions of the monsters in Canadian lakes. He cuts right through the absurdities by arguing from the salient facts of the geological history and geography of the monster sites, and establishes the most suitable zoological candidates.

According to the recently-issued *Encyclopedia Canadiana* (1985), Canada has only two monsters worth noting, the *Sasquatch* and 'Ogopogo'. In 1984, the Toronto *Globe and Mail* criticized any belief in the 'Yeti' or 'Loch Ness monster' as the product of a deranged mind; but apart from failing to identify the Canadian monsters which have been known far longer than their foreign cousins, the editor also failed to realize that both the mythical unicorn and kraken were found living in Canadian waters under their aliases of the narwhal and giant squid.

When the subject of lake monsters and sea-serpents arises, two impressions are formed in most minds: firstly, the visual image of a large aquatic animal, and then the question as to how much skepticism one will attach to the idea of the animal's existence. But the existence of monsters depends as much on popular attitudes and perceptions as it does upon scientific inquiry. What is imagined may not in itself exist, but the phenomenon which stimulates the mind into perceiving a monster may be very real, even if the end product is imaginary.

A century-and-a-half ago, the existence of sea-serpents was accepted by much of the public and most of the scientific community. The fossil remains of giant marine lizards had been publicly displayed in museums, and their survival from antediluvian times need not have depended upon Noah's Ark. In a world which believed in the divine creation of mankind, the independent creation of each species, and a world history measured in thousands of years, the existence of behemoths on the ocean's abyss was quite logical.

The excitement created by the claim of Captain M'Quhae and officers of *H.M.S. Daedalus* in 1848, that they had seen a 'sea-serpent' in the South Atlantic, illustrates the acceptance of such testimony in Britain. In the *Times* of November 2nd, one writer expressed his belief that the monster was a "plesiosaurus". The prominent zoologist, Richard Owen, responded doubtfully in the *Zoologist* with : "I regard the negative evidence from the utter absence of any of the recent remains of great sea-serpents, krakens, or Enaliosauria, as stronger against their actual existence than the positive statements which have hitherto weighed with the public mind in favour of their existence."

The transformation of popular and scientific opinion into skepticism about the existence of sea-serpents and lake monsters was brought about largely by Darwin's *On the Origin of Species* in 1859. The mutability of species and their extinction as a consequence of natural selection, the common ancestry of species, and a classification of species defined by their evolution and fossil remains of their ancestors cast the continued existence of sea-serpents into doubt. As astronomers and geologists pushed back the creation of the world beyond Bishop Ussher's 4004 BC., the extinction of the dinosaurs and disappearance of sea-serpents was assumed by scientists to be simultaneous, as stated by Owen. The realm of the sea-serpent and lake monsters was confined to museum displays of fossils and popular adventure fiction.

Sir Arthur Conan Doyle's *The Lost World* did much to stimulate the hypothesis that some prehistoric animals may have escaped the ravages of extinction into the modern era. If sheltered in a remote habitat, possibly dinosaurs and sea-serpents could still be found in jungle swamps and along unfamiliar coasts. The discovery of living coelacanths off the coast of Africa has helped to reinforce the belief that 'lost world' survivals may yet be found and identified as the source of sea-serpent and lake monster reports.

If lake monsters were only reported from the swamps of Africa, Loch Ness, Lake Okanagan, or relatively isolated regions, the 'lost world' hypothesis might be justified as the dominant explanation of the reports of lake monsters. However, the 'lost world' hypothesis is seriously jeopardized by the fact that more than ninety lakes and rivers across Canada have associated lake monster reports; and, given the geological and zoogeographical background of these locations, the origin of Canadian lake monsters must be sought either in the human imagination or another location.

Unlike birds, insects, mammals and reptiles, most of the inhabitants of freshwater lakes and rivers live in a very restricted territory. Except for occasional floods, geological changes altering a river's flow, and accidental introductions (such as fish dropped by birds), the migration of species is limited. the exceptions to this confinement of larger species are those who can tolerate both saline and fresh water, such as salmon, eels, lampreys and sturgeon. The island of Newfoundland is an excellent example contrary to the 'lost world'; for having lost its native fish and animals when it was covered by a relatively recent ice-sheet, its only fauna today are those which have negotiated the 16km channel of salt-water which separates it from the mainland. No strictly freshwater species is found in Newfoundland's lakes and streams. There are no reptiles; and the only amphibian – a frog – was introduced by man. Yet, several lakes on Newfoundland have been claimed as the homes of lake monsters.

The Arctic and Nearctic regions of Canada would also impose limitations upon any air-breathing lake monsters, because nearly all the lakes and rivers freeze over. Even the Great Lakes in the south become ice-bound. This leaves any such lake monsters with three choices: the use of air-holes (as done by seals), hibernation under the ice (as done by turtles and amphibians), or migration to the open sea across any obstacles in the river channel. If zeuglodons (primitive whales) were the explanation of Canadian lake monsters, their presence should be indicated by air-holes in the winter ice or sightings across river barriers to the sea before the freeze-up. The harsh climate would seem to discourage this possibility.

The glacial ice-sheets which covered nearly all of Canada only 20,000 years ago are responsible for the current formation of its lakes and the species which can still be

'The monster of Lake Eutopia' – a print by B.Kroupa. *Canadian Illustrated News* 30 Nov 1872. C-58905 ***Public Archives Canada.***

found there restricted to freshwater. Of 234 species found in the Great Lakes, most fish species are described as "living fossils" and "ancient relicts", having migrated from the St Lawrence, Albany, or Mississippi drainage basins following either the formation of glacial lakes during the retreat of the ice, or by escaping from the southward crush of the sheet's formation. Some parts of Northern Quebec and Labrador have yet to recover from ice-sheets which existed only a few thousand years ago, for the rivers and lakes lack any species of truly freshwater fish.

So the presence of lake monsters in Canada would have to be the result of migration, either in the glacial lakes produced only thousands of years ago or the result of recent incursions from the oceans. The Champlain Sea, Lake Algonquin (which occupied the Great Lakes), Lake Agassiz (which occupied the prarie provinces), and the interconnecting lakes of the Fraser and Colombia River valleys would have allowed large aquatic species easy access to the Canadian interior; and the diminishing size of these lakes into their present locations could have stranded some species beyond barriers now impassible. For example: a lake monster in Flathead Lake, in Montana, could have migrated in a glacial lake extending throughout the Rocky Mountain Trench, which also allowed access to the Nicola, Thompson, Shuswap and Okanagan basins, all of which have associated lake monster reports.

The best known example of a salt-water species invading Canadian lakes is the sea lamprey, whose invasion of the Great Lakes by way of the St Lawrence Seaway nearly destroyed the inland fishing industry. Fort cited the discovery of a squid and a sargassum fish in Lake Onondaga, near Syracuse, New York, reported in *Science*, but he failed to mention the discovery of a remora caught in a trout stream on the Michigan shore of Lake Superior. Two species of European flounder and China crabs have been found in Lake Erie, according to Dr Alan Emery, of the Royal Ontario Museum, who has also expressed a belief that sharks might survive in the lakes. In the late 1960s, author Farley Mowat and some of the passengers on his schooner *Happy Adventurer* claimed to have seen the dorsal fin of a shark on Lake Ontario. On July 14th, 1968, a shark attacked a line of fish belonging to Giovanni Pirollo, of Montreal, in Rivieres des Prairies and was captured by him, though he ate the evidence before experts could identify the species. And, in 1978, a shark was found in the water intake of Edison's Trenton Channel Power Plant, in Detroit. The passage of sharks into freshwater rivers can reach great distances. For example: live specimens have been captured at Arlington, Texas, (between Dallas and Fort Worth), and at East Lynn Lake, West Virginia, (some 800km from the Atlantic); and shark attacks at Azair and Basra, in Iraq, some 240km inland are mentioned in Wilfred Thesinger's *The Marsh Arabs*.

Even a familiar species could account for some lake monster reports in Canada and possibly explain the many reports of 'merfolk' by the early French settlers and Indians living along the Great Lakes. A "non-descript animal" with gleaming teeth was shot by George F.Kennedy, on April 28th, 1882, on the same Lake Onondaga where Fort's squid and sargassum fish were found. The creature lashed the water furiously before another three shots finished it. A taxidermist identified it as a "hair-seal", six feet long and 100lbs in weight. Apparently it had migrated up the Oswego River from Lake Ontario and the St Lawrence River. The sighting of a creature, half-human, half-fish, near Pie Island on Lake Superior, on May 3rd, 1782, by voyager Venant St Germain, may have been a seal which migrated from the Ombabiki River, 130 km away, Lake Nipigon, the Ogoki River, the Albany River and Hudson Bay – as Niagara Falls would prevent a migration from Lake Ontario. Similarly, a seal was said to have been the origin of bunyip reports at Lake George, in Australia, according to Lt WH Breton; and the bunyip seen in the River Molongo, in 1886, was said to be the size of a dog and have "the face of a child", which differs little from St Germain's creature seen near Pie Island.

Although excited imaginations and familiar animals seen in unfamiliar circumstances may account for many lake monster reports in Canada, the majority of sightings are of a large animal several meters in length, with a serpentine body of eel-like form. Another peculiar characteristic in both lake monster and sea-serpent reports (from both Atlantic and Pacific coasts) is the elevation of the creature's head and neck above the water. Although mirage phenomena could produce the illusion of a head and neck high above the water, as suggested by Prof. WH Lehn of the University of Manitoba, several such sightings are made at extremely close range and could not be ascribed to an optical illusion. Lake monsters which display this behaviour might well be air-breathers as well as gill-breathers.

Only a few known species display both an air-breathing and gill-breathing capacity, but none of these species are known to exist in the size range ascribed to Canadian lake monsters. The two prominent choices would seem to be the salamander and the eel; and though the possibility of a plesiosaurus migrating inland from the oceans would not be ruled out, their migration to some locations would prove most difficult to conceal and has seldom been reported.

In 1930, the Danish ship *Galathea* captured a giant *leptcephalus*, or eel larva, measuring 1.8 meters in length. The existence of this specimen was not revealed until 1949 after it had been lost at sea while being transported to France, though it had been long available as a specimen at the Marinbiologisk Laboratorium at Charlottenlund Slot. Were this larva to grow to ten, 20 or 30 times its length, as do other eel larva, one could expect an animal both in form and length similar to some lake monster reports. The eel's ability to move overland between bodies of water is well-known and could account for its presence in remote lakes and streams. Also, eels often migrate from the oceans to freshwater and back to the oceans in their life cycle.

Malcolm Burr suggested: "With the exception of the marine habitat and the great size, the general description of the sea-serpent does not differ fundamentally from that of the newts. I see no real reason why our sea-serpent should not be a hitherto unrecognized relative of the newts, adapted to life in the sea, developed to a relatively great size, timid and nocturnal in habit, and consequently seldom seen." Although Burr was trying in part to provide an explanation of FW Kemp's sighting of the 'Cadborosaurus' (British Columbia's more familiar sea-serpent), the only fundamental objection to salamanders (or newts) as prime candidates for lake monsters are their size.

The salamander explanation should be given serious consideration owing to the mutability of the species. Firstly, not all of the larval salamanders progress in their growth into land-dwelling adults. The existence of larval adults is a condition known as neoteny, and neoteny is a normal characteristic of some salamander species. Apart from these species, other environmental conditions may produce neoteny: a lack of thyroxine due to insufficient iodine in the water, high altitudes, and cold temperatures. Also, some Canadian salamanders demonstrate the 'Jefferson salamander complex' in which a hybrid species, a triploid mutant is derived from two distinct species. A triploid mutant has three sets of chromosones instead of the usual two. Tremblay's salamander *(Ambystoma tremblayi)*, and the Silvery salamander *(Ambystoma platineum)*, are regarded by zoologists as species parented by other species.

Canada's Pacific Giant salamander is known to reach 28cm in length, and the Giant Asiatic salamander of Japan has a recorded length of 1.8 meters. Prehistoric salamanders are believed to have reached lengths of 4.5 meters or more. Should the condition of neoteny prevent sexual maturity and permit the continued growth in size indefinitely, or should a polyploidal mutant (such as found in the Jefferson salamander complex) produce gigantism or revert by atavism to a giant size, the occurrence of giant salamanders might be more frequent in favourable environmental conditions, such as the cooler thermocline in Canada and Northern Europe. The isotherm of +10C found on the Canadian Pacific and Atlantic coasts, around the British Isles and Scandinavia also appears to have a greater number of associated sea-serpent reports, which suggests the salamander explanation may extend to sea-serpents as Burr had stated. **[1]**

If one is to assume the existence of lake monsters of large size in Canada, based on the testimony of witnesses, photographic and sonar evidence, their existence must therefore result either from the mutation of a species towards gigantism, or the breeding of a species of giants. The discovery of giant squid at Aalbeck, Denmark, by Japetus Steenstrup, by the French warship *Alecton* near Tenerife in 1861, and along the Newfoundland coast throughout the 1870s, it might be argued, only indicate the discovery of individual giants among a species of lesser size. However, in October of 1875, Capt. JW Collins of the *Howard* helped capture five giant squid found dying on the surface of the ocean at the Grand Banks. Altogether, the fishing fleet from Gloucester, Massachusetts, captured 25-30 giant squid, which were later cut up for fishing bait. This singular account of multiple giant squids helps confirm their existence as a species of giants. The infrequent reports of sightings of more than one lake monster or sea-serpent on the Pacific coast of Canada seems to indicate a breeding population may exist in some locations. Moreover, the continued sightings over a long time implies either a breeding population or environmental conditions promoting mutation towards gigantism.

A report from the Fish and Wildlife Branch in British Columbia once considered how many lake monsters could inhabit Lake Okanagan. It stated: "Okanagan Lake is about six times as large as Loch Ness (85,000 acres vs. 14,100 acres) so that on the basis of comparative surface area we may conclude that Okanagan Lake could harbour in the range of ± 60-120 Ogopogos up to a size of about 3300lbs (1500kg). This is interpreted as a maximal estimate of lake carrying capacity. If larger individuals do in fact exist in the lake, the numerical carrying capacity would be correspondingly reduced... It would be advantageous to have better estimates of the size of Ogopogo. If, for instance, monsters significantly larger than 3300lbs occur in Lake Okanagan, there would necessarily be fewer than 60-120 individuals indicated by the 'high' carrying capacity estimate." If Ogopogo were to measure 12 meters in length (or 40ft) as a full adult size, and if its shape were proportionate to that of an adult eel (the shape generally given by witnesses), its bulk would be at least 3300 kgs, (more than twice the Fish and Wildlife Branch estimate). From 1975 to 1981, the length of Ogopogo in sightings ranged from 10-22.5 meters; thus the population of monsters may be less than 30-60 animals, but still sufficient for a small breeding population.

Multiple sightings of Ogopogos have been reported. On February 26th, 1948, Don Nourse, of Penticton, saw four 'Ogopups' near the shore and brought the sight to the attention of passengers on his bus. On June 29th, 1950, Alvin Moorman thought he saw two Ogopogos in tandem, while other witnesses claimed seeing only one. On July 2nd,, 1952, Dr Stanley Underhill was able to distinguish two Ogopogos with binoculars when other witnesses claimed seeing but one. In 1958, on the last day of the Kelowna Regatta (July-August), William Marx claimed that a series of humps moving in line belonged to two monsters. And, on August 3rd, 1976, Edward Fletcher may have seen two Ogopogos when he took his photographs according to Mary Moon in her book, *Ogopogo*; yet there are no suggestions of multiple sightings in her article on the monster in the Toronto *Globe and Mail* in 1978, or in Arlene Gaal's report of the incident in the Kelowna *Courier* in 1977. On the other side of the continental divide, at Rocky Mountain House, an Ogopogo "with six little Ogopups happily trailing along in the wake" were seen going downstream before the freeze-up in 1943 or 1944, according to a report collected by Robert E.Gard. It would prove most interesting to identify how many locations, such as Loch Ness, Lake Okanagan, and the North Saskatchewan River, have had reports of multiple sightings and which might be considered breeding areas.

Apart form Lake Okanagan, whose reports of Ogopogo extend back to Indian legends, several locations in Canada have a long tradition of lake monster sightings. Lake Ontario has had sightings dating to the summer of 1829, when a "hideous water snake, or serpent, of prodigious dimensions" was seen near Grantham Township. Lake Erie and the Niagara River above the Falls have reports dating back to July of 1817. Lake Simcoe, in Ontario, has had reports dating back to 1880. And 'Old Ned' of Lake Utopia, in New Brunswick, has reports dating back into MicMac Indian legend. Although several lakes have older reports, these Canadian lakes have provided sightings up to the present. If we do not ascribe great longevity to individual lake monsters, more than one monster would be necessary to explain the continuing series of reports; and Canada's long tradition of published reports establishes a historical record which goes beyond that found in most other countries with lake monsters.

Old Ned first gained prominence in

1867, when first reported by the *St John Globe*. Both European settlers and the local MicMacs had known of Ned's presence for at least 40 years before this first report. In 1872, Ned found fame in the *Canadian Illustrated News*, and had already been the object of a joint stock company which tried to capture him with nets and traps. Canadian naturalist William F.Ganong collected reports of sightings, and in 1891 related claims were made by a lumberman who saw "great furrows in the sand" on Lake Utopia's shore. After 1873, the next reported sightings were made in 1951 and on July 9th, 1982. The presence of the monster has been assumed by area residents for many years, but the reluctance to report their sightings makes it difficult to establish whether Ned's appearances are due to the occasional giant mutant or whether the population of Neds migrate from the nearby Bay of Fundy. As Lake Utopia is not part of any major drainage basin, Ned would appear to be a salt-water incursion in recent times, and may be closely related to the sea-serpents reported along the Maritime coasts during the last century.

On Newfoundland, as already discussed, the lack of native species suggests that the island's lake monsters have most likely migrated from the sea. Also, different monster locations have no connection to each other, but drain into the ocean. A "giant conger eel" was seen by four loggers boring its way through a sandbank on Crescent Lake, in the summer of 1960. It was at first thought to be an overturned dory when spotted by Bruce Anthony, who claimed to have seen at least 3 meters of the "fish" before it disappeared. Crescent Lake drains into Notre Dame Bay, off Roberts Arm. An eel-like monster has been seen several times at Long Pond, which drains into the Salmon River and Bay D'Espoir; and the most recent sighting in 1967 described it as a foot wide and 30-40 feet in length, with a salmon-like head and trout-like tail. A more peculiar monster, named 'Maggot', has

A model of 'Ogopogo' at Kelowna, British Columbia. *Photo* © ***Rene Dahinden/FPL.***

twice been seen near Swanger Cove, in Bay D'Espoir, around 1952. No longer than a foot, it was described as similar to a lobster with fish-like eyes, three pairs of legs, and three-inch pincers but without the jointed tail of the well-known crustacean. Although giant squid have been found in the shallow waters and on the shores of Newfoundland, none of the descriptions of the inland lake monsters include squid-like characteristics – it is much more likely that a giant species of eel has migrated into several of the interior lakes.

In 1883, Prof. Addison E.Verrill, of Yale University, wrote of the giant squid he studied: "The pen of our *Architeuthis harveyi* seems to resemble that of the ancient genus *Tendopsis* found fossil in the jurassic formations, and contemporaneous with the huge marine saurians, icthyosaurs and plesiosaurs, etc., the sea-serpent of those ancient seas. May there not also be huge marine saurians still living in the North Atlantic, in company with the giant squids, but not yet known to naturalists? Such a belief seems quite reasonable when we consider how many species of great marine animals, both among the cephalopods and cetaceans, are still known only from single specimens, or even mere fragments generally obtained only by chance."

Verrill may have considered the North Atlantic and the waters off Newfoundland and Labrador an area where the 'sea-serpent' could still be found. His comment, though not directed at Owen's skepticism, indicate the kraken had survived into the present day from fossil times. We know salt-water incursions have taken place in several Canadian lakes and rivers, but as we have seen, it would be difficult to accept that all the lake monsters were 'plesiosaurs', as is the current popular preconception.The explanation of lake monsters must therefore be pluralistic in its approach. While hoaxes, optical illusions, excited imaginations, and misidentifications of other animals can be used by the skeptic to explain away the existence of lake monsters, the considerable body of sightings in diverse locations would suggest that an unknown species, if not two or more, may yet be found. In Canada, the fossil evidence shows that huge marine saurians swam in seas now turned to stone, but the geological history also shows that the country was swept clean of its natural fauna in the last glacial period. Therefore the only likely origin for some of the monsters is in the ocean, which also strengthens the possible relationship between sea-serpents and lake monsters.

The Canadian experience of lake monsters crosses cultural and temporal boundaries, as well as geographical ones. What has been described by natives as inhabiting the waters of Lake Utopia in New Brunswick, Lake Dubawnt in the Northwest Territories, and Lake Okanagan in British Columbia, has similarly been described by Scottish settlers at Lake Ainslie, on Cape Breton Island in Nova Scotia, by the French at Lac Pohenemagook in Quebec, and by British settlers on the Great Lakes and on Lake Simcoe. With every province and territory claiming at least one lake monster of its own, the phenomenon can truly be said to exist *a mari usque ad mare*.

The prevailing popular conceptions and attitudes towards lake monsters in Canada is one of skepticism. The witnesses who do report their sightings may attract attention from local news media, but how many people decide not to report their experience for fear of ridicule cannot be usefully estimated. The 'lost world' or 'plesiosaur' explanations, prevalent since the turn of the century, remain in disrepute. For the *Canadian Encyclopedia* to suggest that Ogopogo may have arisen from a frozen dinosaur egg which thawed at the bottom of Lake Okanagan is ludicrous, and demonstrates the lack of any scientific consideration. Although efforts have been made by a few scientists and researchers to document reports of lake monsters, most of these have ended up as ill-equipped fishing expeditions or studies of sightings from a single lake or region. No proper study has been made to indicate a direct relationship between reports of lake monsters and sea-serpents; and even Scotland's Nessie attracts more attention from the local news media and researchers than native Canadian monsters in nerby waters.

If due consideration were given to witness descriptions, the climate, geological history and the zoogeography of Canada, the prospect of mutable species, such as giant eels or giant salamanders, might be given more serious attention. Although Darwin's work may have discouraged belief in the sea-serpent, any study of unknown species must recognize what known species may account for observed traits and in what territories they are to be found.

How long the illusory vision of what lake monsters and sea-serpents should look like persists will depend on the human imagination. How long it will take for scientific inquiry and accumulated evidence to convince the skeptic that lake monsters and sea-serpents truly exist in the present day will depend on the doubt cherished by the scientific community over the last century. Unknown species of lake monsters and sea-serpents did not arise by the score from independent creation; and in Canada at least it would seem that lake monsters and sea-serpents are closely related species. The pursuit of lake monsters and sea-serpents must now be extended to a pluralistic review of what species may provide the characteristics which best suit them to their many habitats across many lands and across many seas.

NOTE: [1] *Heuvelmans (*In the Wake... *p449ff) credits Burr with the first realisation that sea-serpent descriptions often matched the characteristics of neotenous amphibians. Although Heuvelmans calls the theory "ingenious", he says it is open to a "good deal of criticism." - Ed.*

Weird Lives

by Paul Sieveking.

CROMWELL'S GIANT

M. Lauron ad vivum del. W. J. Taylor sculp

Oliver Cromwell's Porter

Published by I. Caulfield 1793

The surname of this man, who florished around 1650, is not recorded; his Christian name was Daniel. He was remarkably tall, his height being preserved by a large O on the back of the terrace at Windsor Castle. He was probably selected as porter to the Protector because it had become the fashion in previous reigns to have giants attending the royal gates. James Granger, author of *The Biographical History of England*, 1769-74, says Daniel was a plodder in books of divinity, especially those of a mystical kind, which are supposed to have turned his brain.

He spent many years in Bedlam asylum, where he was allowed to keep his library, "as there was not the least probability of his cure". The most conspicuous of his books was a large Bible given him by Nell Gwyn, Charles II's mistress, "a woman who appears to have possessed every virtue, excepting that of chastity."

Daniel frequently preached and sometimes prophesied; he was said to have foretold several remarkable events including the Great Fire of London (1666). Charles Leslie (in his *Snake in the Grass, or Satan Transformed into an Angel of Light*, 1696) tells us that people often went to hear him preach, sitting many hours under his window in wrapt attention. Leslie once asked a sober old lady among the audience what was the point of listening to this madman; and she replied, pitying his ignorance, that Festus had thought Saint Paul was mad.

A Brief Survey of Lake Monsters of Continental Europe.

Ulrich Magin, our West German correspondent, begins a long overdue survey of European lake monster traditions and sightings. Experience with modern reports of 'Sea Serpents', which later turn out to be very large fish, has made him generally skeptical; but it is obvious that a great many lakes and rivers have monster traditions stretching back into antiquity. Already Ulrich is compiling a second instalment. If you would like to contribute information, write to him at: **Stuhlbruderhofstr. 4, 6704 Mutterstadt, W.Germany.**

Most forteans and others interested in European lake monsters are aware that the majority of publicized sightings come from the British Isles, Ireland, Iceland and Scandinavia. Less well-known is the fact that these mysterious animals are also seen to the south and east of these countries. As far as I know this is the first published survey of lake monster sightings, historical and modern. It is far from complete, yet most of the places mentioned are not included in the Bords' gazeteer of lake monsters. **[1]**

FRANCE

Beginning in France, we find a monster in the River Rhone, which in the first century lurked between Arles and Avignon to swallow unwary passers-by. The creature was called Tarasque, looking like a cross between a turtle and a mammal. It had a scaly dragon-like body with six legs, a spiny shell and a bearded face. Saint Martha calmed it with a crucifix and holy water, and the local people then killed it. A model of the Tarasque is still shown in Tarascon at an annual festival. Its resemblance to the famous stranded 'sea-serpent' of Stronsa raises the possibility that its origin also might have been a decomposed basking shark. **[2]**

A similar monster lived in the River Huisne, near the town of Ferte-Bernard, during the Middle Ages. Known as 'the hairy one', it was as big as a bull with the head of a snake and turtle-like legs. Its ball-like body had green hairs and was covered in spikes. It spouted fire and killed people with its tail. When a strong, fearless hero cut off its tail, it became helpless and died. **[3]**

In 1304, a similar dragon inhabiting the Belchensee, at Grand Ballon in the Alsace, was killed, according to old chronicles. **[4]**

These stories may not have much value for scientific research, but to us they reveal the possibility that lake monsters were more widespread in the Middle Ages than today. However, there have been recent reports of "monsters" in the River Rhone in 1954/55 **[5]**; and in the summer of 1964 a sea-serpent with a long neck was seen by J.Borelli and his son at the mouth of this river. **[6]** Another monster in this region was described by the Provencal writer, Joseph d'Arbaud, as living in Lake Vaccares, a great pool in the Camargue, between the mouths of the Grand Rhone and

Petit Rhone; but it is not known whether this account is based on fact or entirely fictional. [5]

According to a report of 1933 or 1934 "The Allier at Vichy was suddenly visited by a black beast with three heads, which evoked a phenomenal crocodile." This reminds me of the monsters with two or three heads sighted in British Columbian waters, but I would prefer to regard them as folklore or hoaxes. [7]

SWITZERLAND

A legendary 'giant worm' was believed to live in the Rotsee, near Lucerne – and a dragon, called the Elbst, dwelt in Lake Seelisberg. [3] The Elbst, which seems closely related to the more famous Scottish monsters, sometimes looked like a drifting log, and at other times like a floating island or a swimming serpent. It created strong wakes at the surface, and sometimes crawled ashore to catch unwary people or animals. The name 'Elbst' comes from the old German for swan, 'albiz'. It was first mentioned by Renward Cysat (1545-1614). The strangest feature of the Elbst, and one which stimulates the fortean imagination, was its ability to transform itself into a fiery wheel. [14] There are no recent accounts, so I think that the Elbst is possibly a legend that Scottish or Irish missionaries brought with them when the came to the area in the Middle Ages.

A more conventional monster was seen in the River Doubs, in 1934, which has its source in Switzerland and then flows into the Rhone. Sightings refer to an animal with "an oval body, a long neck, small head, blue back and yellow stomach. It travels with an undulating motion." It is interesting that this report comes from a river connected with the Rhone, which, as we have seen, has associated monster reports of its own. Does it have a resident population of Nessie-type animals or is it a migratory route for them? [15]

The River Doubs rises in the Jura mountains, and there, according to the author Langelaan, all the fountains, rivers and lakes are filled with aquatic monsters. They are "known by the name *Vouivre* ... They are very peaceful creatures, which never harmed anyone." [16]

In the summer of 1976 something monstrous was seen in Urner Lake, a lobe of Lake Lucerne. On August 25th, a crowd of about 60 people watched what they thought was a long-necked monster, about 20-25ft long. It surfaced three times close to the resort of Brunnen, bellowing "like an ill cow". It was reported worldwide, being called a dragon, a "sea-serpent" and, inevitably, 'Urnie'. A week later Swiss TV declared it was a hoax; a model built for a popular Swiss TV show. It had been in the lake for at least a month, and had made several public appearances, but had not been reported in the press. As entertainer Kurt Felix put it: "I'm surprised that the thing was not discovered weeks earlier!" The TV channel, fearing that they were not getting their money's worth, paid someone to pose as a German tourist who had photographed the thing. Naturally their own camera team was on the spot when the fuss started. The story only really took off when the newspapers printed it in all seriousness. If nothing else it demonstrates how easy it is to start a myth. Interestingly, the model was over 60ft long, and the witnesses had **underestimated** the monster! But what do we make of the two German divers who said they had encountered something similar in the lake the previous spring? [17]

A monster is said to live in Lac Leman, but this too sounds like a hoax to me. [5]

Tarasque float hauled through Tarascon on festival days. *Postcard: Magin's collection.*

AUSTRIA

The lake dragons here are mostly legendary. One is supposed to bask on the shore of the Leermoser Drachensee; the name itself indicates an ancient association with dragons. The Urisee, near Reutte, and the Reiffinger See, in the Windische Steiermark, are both reputed to be the haunts of water-serpents. **[4]**

Austria's most famous monster is the Tatzelwurm, a creature resembling a cross between a worm and a giant newt usually seen in the mountain of the Alps. **[29]**

ITALY

Italy has modern sightings as well as the expected legends. A water-dragon lived in the Amadoier Lake, at Mount Rosengarten, in the Alps. **[4]** South of that location is Lago Maggiore, inhabited by a horse-headed, fish-eating monster, mentioned by the novelist Stendhal at the beginning of the 19th century. At least this was not only a legend, as the animal was seen again, by fishermen, at the mouth of the River Ticino, in 1934. **[18]**

Lago Como, just to the west of Lago Maggiore, has quite a similar ecological constitution, and both flow into the River Po. If a marine monster had reached Lago Maggiore through the Po we might reasonably expect Como to have a similar monster. It is no surprise, then, to learn, according to the Italian Bureau of Information, Ansa, that in November 1946, fishermen on Lake Como spotted a "marine monster". Van Hageland describes it: "Over its whole length of four metres (ie. circa 13 feet) it was covered with scales and red marks." **[19]**

In June 1975, just across the River Po from Venice, a monster terrorized Goro. Maurizio Trombini described it as a large snake with legs. It was over ten feet long and as thick as a dog. It had been seen several times in previous years, and experts claimed it was an escaped crocodile. Goro is close to the sea, so we wonder if a sea-serpent had come ashore. Could it have been the most southerly sighting of the Austrian 'Tatzelwurm'? A recent sighting of

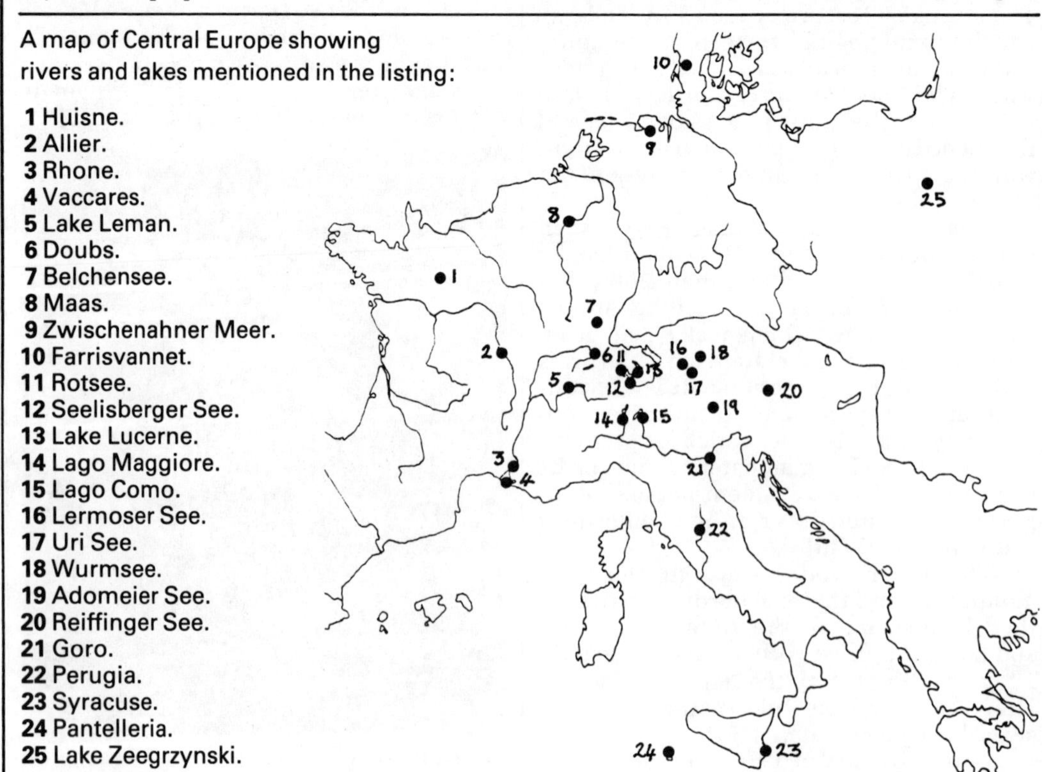

A map of Central Europe showing rivers and lakes mentioned in the listing:

this creature took place at Udine, in the summer of 1963. [20]

In 1933 or 1934, an aquatic monster appeared in marshes near Perugia. [21] These swamps are connected to the sea by the River Tiber, in which a sea-serpent was seen at the end of the 6th century. It looked "like a big log" and was supposed to have brought the plague to Rome. [22] It is significant that sea-serpents are often seen in estuaries of rivers which flow from monster-haunted lakes.

After an exciting hunt lasting several days, a reptilian monster was killed by two peasants, in a marsh near Syracuse, in Sicily, in December 1933. According to the *Times* the animal was snake-like, 11ft long and covered with scales. The creature was never identified scientifically because it was destroyed immediately by the superstitious peasants who thought it might be the *Colovia*, which folk-belief says is something like a cross bewteen a Chinese dragon and a crocodile, whose appearance presages disaster. "Scientists", however, speculated that it might have been a python or boa, escaped from or let loose from some collection, or else arrived in a boat from Africa. [23]

The most recent candidate for an Italian lake monster report appeared in July 1982, in the Venus Lake, on the island of Pantelleria. However, this monster was not seen, but heard making strange and "frightening" noises on the lake at night. [24] Several years before, in March 1980, a mysterious submarine object was caught in a net, by the Italian trawler 'Socrate I', close to the island. It was widely thought to be a Russian submarine, while a few thought it might be a sea-serpent and. Whatever it was , it escaped after several hours of struggle, breaking the nets. [25] Similar occurences prior to 1900 were interpreted as temporarily entrapped sea-serpents.

BELGIUM

An unusual animal in the River Maas, called 'Maasie' (what else), was seen near the village of Ombret. A man had seen a three-foot

Engraving from Athenasius Kircher's *Mundus Subterraneus* (Amsterdam, 1665/1678) illustrating a Swiss incident, said to happen in 1619, in which a winged dragon and a winged snake *(see cover illustration)* migrated from a cave on Mount Pilate *(top right)* to Lake Lucerne *(lower left)* and back.

The mysterious melusine of medieval European legends – usually represented as a curious mixture of half-woman half-serpent – is generally thought to be an imaginative variation of the mermaid, which in turn was based, it is argued, upon misperceptions of seals or manatees. It is not impossible that melusines were folk-memories of some unidentified lake creatures upon which the mermaid was grafted. *Left:* Eve tempted by Lilith in the guise of a melusine *Woodcut, Augsburg, 1470. Right:* Melusina discovered in her bath *Woodcut, Antwerp, 1491.*

"crocodile" August 6th, 1979. Police searched the river but it was not seen again. However, another man reported seeing someone throwing a 20cm-long crocodile into the river some three months previously. Biologists were quick to point out that the sighted creature could not have been the same animal, because it could not have grown so big in such a short period. Herpetologist Frank de Graat, of the Amsterdam Zoo Aquarium, believed the animal was a pet alligator thrown into the river, but predicted it would starve or freeze to death. No more news was heard of it. **[8]**

GERMANY

Also in 1979, on April 26th, two water-policemen claimed to see a slimy back, 12ft long, break the surface of the Zwischenahner Meer, near Bad Zwischenahn. Several other sightings followed and the animal, seemingly a giant catfish, was dubbed 'Germany's Nessie'. Stories about the creature appeared as far afield as in the *New York Times* and *Bangkok Post.* For a while the lake was crowded with hopeful anglers, some attributing their lost lines to the subsurface mystery. Even the disappearances of dogs were blamed upon the creature. Soon the monster had vanished from the newspapers, as well as the lake. However, this was not the first monster of its kind in German waters, for a 10ft long catfish had been captured in the Trintsee lake, in Brandenburg, in the 1930s. **[9]**

A 'sea-serpent' appeared near Frankfurt, in the River Main, in August 1983, and this time its body was found. Following a witness's report of seeing a giant serpent swimming in the river, the water-police found a seven-foot-long serpent, floating dead. It was taken to the Senkenberg Institution for identification. It was also believed to have been thrown into the river by its owner. **[10]** The previous year saw an incident in which such a supposition was justified. On a hot day in July 1982, bathers in a flooded gravel-pit, near Augsburg, were surprised to see a large snake sharing the waters with them. Policemen called to the scene recovered a boa constrictor, three and a half feet long, which had been brought there by its owner for a swim. **[11]**

The earliest dated incident involves a large pike, 19 schuh (literally, a shoe-length) long, was landed on November 6th, 1497, from a pond near Kaiserslauten, Palatine. It bore a golden ring around its neck commemorating the date, in 1230, that it was put into the pond, which may have been artificial. The pike was therefore assumed to be 267 years old; a fact definitely worth an entry in the *Guinness Book of Records*. I have heard that similar ancient pike stories are told of other German lakes, even with identical dates! **[12]**

The next item evokes the image of 'mermaids' in the lakes and rivers of Europe, and a possible relationship between serpentine aquatic monsters and 'mermaid' sightings. Some lake monsters, for instance, have been described as a mixture of the long-necked type of creature and a 'fish-woman'; like the first known report of Morag, the denizen of Loch Morar in Scotland. We will see later a Hungarian report of a 'water-man', which may have been a wild-boy, but more difficult to account for is the serpent-like mermaid seen in 1615. It inhabited a pool in the River Lahn, near Marburg, between 15-17 October. According to a local historian: "It is said to have had a serpentine form, with a thin body, built of water, and was multi-coloured. When someone tried to harm her, she just dived. She did no harm to anyone...so it was ordered to let her go in peace; whoever disturbed her would be penalized." **[13]** It is hard to imagine what the writer meant, in this account, published in 1697, by the description "built of water". Witnesses may have seen only wakes or unusual surface disturbances. It is not impossible that a seal or unknown animal made its way up the river, and actual observations were misinterpreted according to local superstitions. If the dragon of the Seelisbergsee in Switzerland (see below) could turn itself into a wheel of fire, a nymph could surely be made of water! I do not have the necessary insight into alchemical beliefs, but it may be that the local observations were reinterpreted in a symbolic manner by later Renaissance scholars. Interestingly, that same year (1615) produced the only known German sea-serpent sighting, at Hamburg.

Monsters are also said to inhabit the Starnbergersee (also known as the Wurmsee), and the Ziereiner See – but these are legendary, without definite or recent sightings. **[4]**

POLAND

A seemingly genuine sea-serpent was sighted in Lake Zeegrzynski, 1982. Bathers said they saw a 20ft monster with a "slimy black head, with rabbit-like ears". I think this might be another giant cat-fish, whose barbels could easily be mistaken for ears; in which case the length might well be an exaggeration. **[26]**

The Zeegrzynski monster is not Poland's first. Legend has it that a monster lived in the 'Black Lake', near Posen. Local people believed it was an incarnation of the Devil because it was cunningly successful in eluding all attempts to capture it, and because the fish caught in the lake were mysteriously inedible. One winter, a party gathered to fish through holes in the ice, but the net came up empty twice. On the third attempt, they hauled up with the net "the head of a goat with two big horns" (sounds like Rines' 1975 photos of Nessie!). The glowing red eyes of the animal frightened the men, who dropped the net and ran. Suddenly a storm blew up and a loud roar-

A hippocamp-like dragon swallowing a man; painting in the Catacombs of Priscilla, Rome. *Postcard in Ulrich Magin's collection.*

ing noise filled the forest surrounding the lake. The air became unbreathable (poisoned?) and some of the men became ill afterwards. According to Zedler, this was a real event and happened in 1578. **[27]**

HUNGARY

In the Konigssee, a curious human-looking water animal was seen and finally caught in 1776. It proved to be a human boy, well adapted to life in the water. After living among humans for a while it learned to talk, but ate nothing but fish and refused to wear clothes. When left carelessly unguarded on a bridge, the creature jumped back into the water. There was a further sighting of it, or something like it, in 1803, after which it was never seen again. It is difficult to know what to make of this story, but it rings true, and the 'water-man' may have been a feral child. **[28]**

OTHERS

Some lakes in the Alps, with monster traditions, which I was not able to identify, are the Muhl, the Wildensee, Ofeser See and Pilburger See. **[4]**

CONCLUSIONS

Though Europe cannot boast so many well-documented lake monster sightings as Iceland, Scotland, Ireland or Scandinavia, perhaps some of the more detailed and recent reports may have some basis in fact. Many of the lakes concerned have no direct connection with the sea, and lie in remote mountainous regions; but then this applies to many American and Canadian monster lakes too.

The reports I have collected seem to me to fall into two groups: firstly, giant fish; and secondly, animals similar to the Loch Ness monster. The reports of 'longnecks' seem to localize south of the Alps, either in large Alpine lakes connected to the sea by the River Po or the rivers of the Rhone basin. These waters might have a small resident population of monsters, or the rivers might be migratory routes to and from the Mediterranean. North of the Alps, and sometimes in the Alpine region, we tend to find hoaxes, or reports of giant fish (such as sturgeon, wels and pike). As these are also the biggest European fish, it is reasonable to suppose that captures of an exceptionally large fish would give rise to reports of monsters.

If long-necked unidentified aquatic animals inhabit waters south of the Alps, further investigation would be fruitful. My gleanings only scratch the surface, suggesting that it would be fruitful to conduct a more systematic search through local newspapers archives and histories, particularly with regard to the large Italian lakes and the rivers of the Rhone basin.

A German flyleaf illustration of 1590 shows a monstrous serpent associated with Lake Constance (Boden See), on the border between Switzerland, West Germany and Austria.

NOTES▶ 1 – Janet & Colin Bord, *Alien Animals* (Paul Elek/Granada, London, 1980), appendix 2. ▶ 2 – J.L.Borges, *Einhorn, Sphinx und Salamander* (Hanser, Munich, 1964) p85. *[Francis Huxley (in* The Dragon, *Thames & Hudson, London, 1979, p42) mentions three other similar dragons in Provence; at Aix, where it was destroyed by St Margaret; at the evocatively named Draguignan, "where the mayor has the right to have any of his godchildren christened 'Drac'"; and at Beaucaire – Ed.]* ▶ 3 – ibid, p119. ▶ 4 – Hoffman-Krayer, *Handworterbuch des deutschen Aberglaubens* (Gruyter, Berlin, 1929/30), see under 'Elbst', 'Drache' and 'Seeschlange'. ▶ 5 – Letter from Jean Jaques Barloy, 4/8/1984. ▶ 6 – B.Heuvelmans, *In the Wake of the Sea-Serpents* (1968), p585. ▶ 7 – A.Van Hageland, *Dans la Mer Magique* (Marabout, 1973), p141. ▶ 8 – *Saarbrucker Zeitung* 9 Aug 1979. *[Explanations like these, in response to croc-type sightings, seem to follow a pattern made familiar by studies of the 'Alligator in the Sewers' phenomenon – Ed.* ▶ 9 – *Die Rheinpfalz* 30 Aug 1979. The idea of a 12ft catfish sounds a bit fishy. The *Guinness Book of Records* (London, 1973, p48.) gives the largest known size as 11ft. It was a European wels (*Silurus glanis*) caught in Sept 1918 in the Desna River, Ukraine, USSR. A wels only 6ft long was called a "giant" by the *Bild* (25 Aug 1982); and when a Czech youth claimed to have caught an 8ft catfish, the story was headlined 'Hoax or Catch?' (*Die Rheinpfalz* 1 Sept 1983). It seems likely that the witnesses at the Zwischenahn Meer had overestimated the size of the fish, if they had seen it at all. It was known that catfish were put into the lake by anglers several decades previously, and so the existence of a big one is not unlikely. In May 1936 a "sea monster" was seen in the Maritza River, near the Bulgarian village of Korschiak, near Philippopel. Some brave men launched their boats and eventually caught it in their nets. It proved to be a giant sturgeon, 10ft long. *Neue Mannheimer Zeitung* 15 May 1936. Similarly, in July 1939, bathers in the River Nemel (now Njemen, in the USSR), in Litauen, thought a great back surfacing was a "water serpent". A hunt was organized and the creature netted. This too proved to be a giant sturgeon eight and a half feet long. *Neue Mannheimer Zeitung* 12 July 1939. One month later, a teacher on a fishing trip to an unnamed lake in east Lettland (now in the USSR), pulled in his catch to find a giant fish in front of him. The size is not given, but it was big enough to frighten him badly. Locals knew of a giant fish in the lake, and thought it was a giant pike. *Neue Mannheimer Zeitung* 12 Aug 1939. ▶ 10 – *Mannheimer Morgen* 23 Aug 1983. ▶ 11 – *Die Rheinpfalz* 13 July 1982. ▶ 12 – V.Carl, *Pfalzer Sagen* (Neustadt, 1977), p235. ▶ 13 – J.J.Winkelmann, *Description of the Counties of Hesse and Hersfeld* (Bremen, 1697). *[Surely there is good indication here for fortean zoologists that a comparative study of European 'mermaid' lore, as exemplified by the widespread tales of 'melusines', sirens, the French 'vouivre' (see under note 16, below), the Greek Nereids, and the traditions of other European* water-associated deities would yield useful *insights for lake monster studies – Ed.]* ▶ 14 – *[Michel Meurger devotes a whole chapter to discussing the Elbst and a few other European lake-associated monsters, in his book with Claude Gagnon: as mentioned in his own article in this issue – Ed.]* ▶ 15 – *New York Herald Tribune 20 June 1934.* ▶ *16 – Langelaan, Unheimliche Wirklichkeiten* (dtv 1975), p29. *[Francis Huxley (*The Dragon, *p13, see comment under note 2, above) does not agree that the* vouivre *were harmless, calling them the "sinister...wyvern of France," and like melusines with bad tempers, whose parents were proper dragons. Their form too was similar to the melusines; to the seductive torso of a maiden was added a bat's wings and a serpent's tail, very like Kircher's* flying dragons (see caption on p22). The voivre *lure men with the treasure they guard, devouring them in the depths where they lurk – Ed.]* ▶ 17 – *Die Welt* 16 Sept; *Times* 31 Aug, 1 Sept 1976. *Gong* Sept 1976. ARD (German TV station) 10 April 1980. ▶ 18 – Peter Costello, *In Search of Lake Monsters* (Panther, London, 1975) p321. Jean Jacques Barloy, the fine French cryptozoologist, whom I'd like to thank for his help in compiling this survey, tells me he has failed to trace this reference in Stendhal. ▶ 19 – Van Hageland (see under note 7, above), p150. ▶ 20 – Edoardo Russo, 'The Goro Monster', *Pursuit* summer 1976, p62. ▶ 21 – British *Morning Post*, cited in *Punch* 10 Jan 1934, p50. ▶ 22 – Heuvelmans (see under note 6, above) p88. ▶ 23 – *Times* 2729 Dec 1933. ▶ 24 – *Die Rheinpfalz* 21 July 1982. ▶ 25 – *Sonntag Aktuell* 16 March 1980. ▶ 26 – *Nessletter* 53, p4. ▶ 27 – Leander Petzoldt, *Deutsche Volkssagen* (CH Beck, Munich, 1970) p221. H.Zedler, *Grosses Vollstandiges Universal-Lexikon* (Leipzig und Halle, 1747), v.53 p681. ▶ 28 – *Berliner Abendblatter* 5 Feb 1811. *[For a note on a modern 'fish-boy' and some historical ones, see FISH BOY, on p 17 – Ed.]* ▶ 29 – *[The tatzelwurm is given a cryptozoological discussion by the pioneering science-writer Willey Ley, in The Lungfish and the Unicorn* (Modern Age Books, 1941). Ivan T.Sanderson also discusses the mystery creature in his *Investigating the Unexplained* (Prentice-Hall, NJ, 1972), suggesting that modern lake monsters might be "gigantic neotenous forms of some huge kind of tatzelwurm, the adult form of which is 'extinct' but which have left their larvae to carry on." (p37) – Ed.]

Murky Waters.

The recent controversies surrounding two of the most famous Loch Ness Monster photographs assessed by **Mike Dash.**

The walls of the Loch Ness Monster Exhibition, at Drumnadrochit, are covered with pictures of Nessie – representations of the loch's famous denizen culled from half a century of monster hunting. Two snaps stand out from the crowd; probably the two most familiar to the visiting public. The 1934 'Surgeon's photograph' and Robert Rines' 1972 'flipper' picture *are* the Loch Ness Monster for many. Now the claims of both to be genuine representations of the monster are being challenged as believers yield ground to a new generation of skeptics.

THE FLIPPER PICTURES [1]

In the early hours of August 8th, 1972 [2], the Loch Ness Investigation (LNI) crew moored off Temple Pier, in Urquhart Bay, noticed the beginnings of a large underwater trace being etched onto the recording paper of the sonar equipment they were monitoring. 35ft below the surface, a transducer belonging to the Academy of Applied Science team, led by Dr Robert Rines, had picked up an object as it intruded into the zone of coverage. The sonar transducer was mounted on the sloping loch bottom in such a way that it covered a 16mm strobe camera, also on the loch bed, in about 45ft of water and about 100yds off shore. The camera exposed a frame of colour film every 55 seconds in conjunction with a bright strobe flash which temporarily illuminated the heavily peat-stained loch waters to a range of 15ft. [3]

As the trace lengthened over a period of 25 minutes, Peter Davies, the LNI skipper of the research vessel *Narwhal*, from which the sonar equipment was mounted and monitored, rowed over to a chartered motor-cruiser, *Nan*, from which Rines had mounted the camera. Shortly afterwards Davies and Rines rowed back to *Narwhal* to find the trace still developing. "By now it was enormous, about the size of my thumbnail. We were all excited but we just sat there, hardly daring to move, and watched in fascination and awe as the trace got longer and longer," Davies told Nicholas Witchell. **[4]** At 02.10, a breeze sprang up, disturbing the "jelly calm" **[5]** loch surface. *Narwhal* swung around and the trace was lost. Later, however, film from the Egerton strobe camera yielded four shots, two of which responded to computer enhancement at the Jet Propulsion Laboratory (JPL) of Pasadena, who have the experience of working on the Mars and Voyager films for NASA.

The sonar record and the strobe photographs complemented each other. The published sonar chart **[6]** was accompanied by expert interpretations which referred to a "large object...intruding into the zone of the beam coverage!"; a "real...large...moving...trace indicating the possibility that the creature has several segments, [and] body projections such as humps"; and even "a sudden protruberence...[which] would appear to be an appendage." It is important to remember, however, that these interpretations were made on the assumption that the transducer was bottom-mounted and was therefore monitoring only open water. As we shall see, this was not the case.

The published photos were even more dramatic, and one clearly showed a diamond-shaped flipper **[7]** and part of a roughly textured body. The flipper was described as 6-8ft long, 2-4ft broad, and not mammalian. Indeed, the "general shape and form of the flipper does not fit anything known today." **[8]** It was, said LNI's scientific adviser, Prof.Roy Mackal, "positive proof".

There the matter rested until 1983. That summer, Alan Kielar and Rikki Razdan – chairman and president, respectively, of ISCAN Inc., an American company manufacturing underwater tracking systems – arrived at the loch. They brought with them an ambitious sonar rig which they anchored off Temple Pier, in roughly the same location in which the 'flipper' pictures were taken. The array operated for seven weeks.

Nothing happened.

A reinvestigation of sonar and photographic evidence **[9]** was initiated, with particular attention paid to the sonar traces made in the same place eleven years earlier. A number of important, and negative, discoveries were made and published in the *Skeptical Inquirer*[10], organ of the controversial Committee for the Scientific Investigation of Claims of the Paranormal (CSICOP). Rines and his associates have replied, notably in various issues of *Nessletter* **[11]**.

THE RINES PHOTO CONTROVERSY

The description of events given above is the traditional version, appearing in various books and articles since 1972. The principal challenges by the ISCAN team are to the status of the camera and sonar transducer. In the Academy's illustration of the operation, they are shown as fixed to the loch bed. In fact they were suspended from *Nan* and *Narwhal*, a little way off the loch floor, as virtually admitted in the statement that contact was lost because *Narwhal* was moved around by the breeze. **[12]** Camera and transducer may therefore have been out of alignment and so recorded different phenomena, destroying a vital part of Rines' argument.

At the top of the sonar trace is a jagged line. This probably represents a side-lobe or second-time-around echo, sonar side-effects, variations in which suggest the transducer was moving. If the camera and transducer were freely suspended from boats, currents - such as those from the nearby river mouth - could easily have moved them temporarily in any direction, including pointing to the surface or the bottom.

ISCAN claims that the jagged sonar trace resembles turbulance created by a boat wake, and postulate that it was caused by the passage of Davies and Rines in the rowing boat *Fussy Hen*. Remembering that the trace began before the first trip across the loch, evidence evaluaters from the Loch Ness & Morar Project (LNMP) – a British group with a decade's experience in underwater operations in those lochs – hypothesize that the first part of the famous trace is an echo from the loch bottom, side or surface created by movement of the transduc-

Continued ☛

FLIPPERS: REAL OR IMAGINED?

The original unenhanced photo. (NB: most of the subtle tones of murky green are lost in our b&w reproduction.)

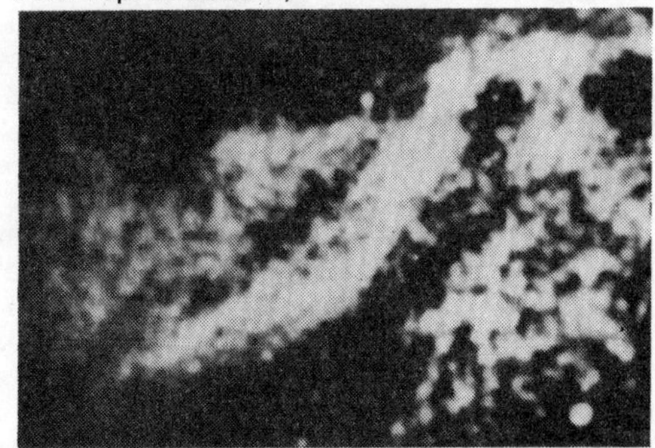

The JPL computer enhanced version (NB: we have taken this image from a secondary source – *Skeptical Inquirer,* see note ***[2]*** – again with the loss of some middle tones, but the blotchy character of the enhancement is evident when compared with the released version below).

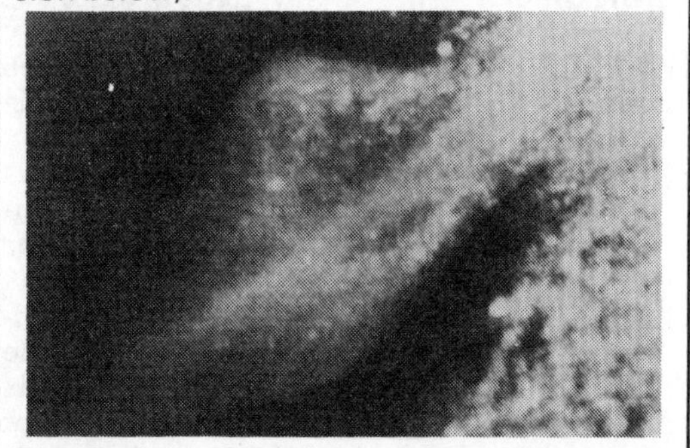

The final version of the photo, which Rines released without the information that it was a retouched version of the computer enhancements. *All photos* © ***Academy of Applied Science.***

☛ *Continued*

er. In this context it is interesting to note that a fuller version of the night's sonar chart shows an earlier trace, recorded between 1.05 and 1.20am. One has to wonder why this, admittedly weaker, signal did not alert the LNI crew. **[13]** Rines obtained similar patterns again in 1976, and these were immediately traced to turbulence made by a rubber raft manned by boy scouts, according to the Academy's press officer, Dennis Meredith. **[14]** Rines admits this, but also claims that such traces have been recorded when no boats were around. **[25]**

As part of their research, Razdan and Kielar applied to JPL for copies of the computer-enhanced photos they had returned to Rines. To their surprise the JPL enhancements bore little resemblance to the 'flipper' pictures that Rines published. There was scarcely a trace of the distinct edges which made the photos so impressive, and very little to gainsay the suggestion that the original image was of debris or even a poorly-lit section of the loch bottom.

According to the article which Razdan and Kielar contributed to the 'Skeptical Eye' section of the American science magazine *Discover*, Allan Gillespie of JPL told them, "the published pictures look a little suspicious around the margins", and Charles Wyckoff – Rines' photo interpreter in later years – went so far as to state that "after JPL finished with the photographs they were retouched. Rines is the only one who could know how much they were retouched or who retouched them." **[15]** This led the two Americans to virtually accuse Rines of deliberate fakery in the article; but his vigorous defence and a a clarification by Wyckoff caused ISCAN's remarks to be toned into neutrality by the time the *Skeptical Inquirer* went to press.

It seems altogether more likely that, as Wyckoff states, "versions were printed in newspapers and magazines with whatever 'retouching' the photographic departments of those publications considered appropriate to show in print in their media what the transparancies showed," **[16]** Perhaps it is too much to hope that the image was not 'improved' somewhere along the line. **[17]** The Academy did publish the original JPL prints later in *Technology Review*. **[18]** The published photos were composites, produced by marrying the products of several different enhancement techniques, but the pictures usually reproduced today as 'the flipper photos' are versions of the *Review* photographs which were retouched by a specialist in that technique. Consequently they must be considered unreliable as evidence.

To a certain extent the problem of multiple versions of the 'flipper' pictures is a red herring; the unenhanced originals – now lost, as seems typical of the fate of much original evidence – showed *something*. But unfortunately we cannot say what that 'something' is because of the unreliability of the sonar trace as corroboration. Rines himself has a tendency to view indistinct objects as 'flippers' **[19]**, and he is not himself expert in operating the equipment he uses, relying instead on the interpretations of fellow researchers. **[20]** This means that one should treat his technical pronouncements with care. No-one doubts Rines' sincerity, but it does now seem necessary to question his results.

Another of ISCAM's revelations – devastating to the *Inquirer*, but less likely to increase the anxiety of FT readers – was that Rines was guided to that location, that evening, by a local map-dowser and monster-witness, Mrs Winnifred Carey. She dowsed for the monster on a large-scale map of Urquhart Bay and flashed its location to the watchers by means of coded car headlight signals indicating a grid reference.

WILSON'S PHOTOGRAPH

This most famous of all monster images was secured by Dr Kenneth Wilson, a London gynaecologist, in April 1934. Traditionally, Wilson is said to have taken the picture with a quarter-plate camera fitted with a telephoto lens after being surprised to see the monster surface while he was engaged in relieving himself by the roadside at about 7.30am.

The surgeon exposed four plates in all, of which two came out when developed later the same day by George Morrison, an Inverness chemist. The better shot was sold to the *Daily Mail*, in which it first appeared on 21st April.

Although Dr Maurice Burton concluded, in 1962, that the main picture showed the tail of a diving otter, and Dr Roy Mackal, in 1976, identified it as the head and

The full version of the remains of Wilson's famous Nessie picture. *Photo* © ***Associated Newspapers Group Ltd.***

neck of a diving bird, little interpretation of the heavily-cropped version usually printed was thought possible. Recently, however, the Edinburgh-based ASSAP member, Steuart Campbell, found a much fuller print, languishing in the picture department of the *Daily Mail*, while researching for a book on the monster, commissioned for ASSAP's *Evidence for...* series. Campbell's full analysis of the picture was published in the *British Journal of Photography*. **[21]**

The new print – which appears here in its entirety for only the second time anywhere – with its inclusion of shoreline, does reassure those who doubted whether the picture was taken at Loch Ness at all. It also reveals that the object is in fact very small. This can be seen by a single comparison of the 'neck's' height with the relatively modest waves in the foreground. Campbell was able to measure the object's height above the water as 70cm (about 27.5 inches), and establish that it was probably only 16m off shore. The position from which Wilson took the photograph is tentatively established in the *BJP*, and the photographer's elevation estimated at 19.5m from the surface. This latter contradicts the surgeon's own statement that he was 100ft above the loch and snapped an object which was 150-200yds from the shore. Finally Campbell establishes that the photographs were not taken with a telephoto lens.

A combination of factors suggests that the surgeon's photograph *is* a hoax. There are major discrepancies in Wilson's accounts of how he came to take the pictures. The traditional story (above) was given to monster author Constance Whyte by letter in 1955. In 1934, however, the surgeon told the *Daily Mail* that the photos were taken at noon, and that far from being surprised by the monster's sudden appearance, he said: "I got my camera out of my car and made it ready in case I should spy the monster." **[22]**

Wilson never claimed that he *had* photographed "the monster", and later told Maurice Burton that he did not believe in it anyway. The doctor's son believes the pictures to be a hoax **[23]**, although other members of the family continue to think it is genuine. **[24]**

The date of the photographs – given by Rupert Gould as April 1st – has also been used to suggest they are fraudulent. It appears, however, that the main picture was sold to the *Daily Mail* on the date it was taken, and a 3-week delay to April 21st, in such a newsworthy item, seems unlikely. Wilson said the photos were obtained on a Thursday – the 1st was a Sunday – so Campbell has calculated that Thursday 19th April is the best candidate. This is supported by postcards still sold by the chemist's shop, where the originals were processed, which state that they were developed on the 19th.

Such contradictions suggest that the 'Surgeon's Picture' is unlikely to depict the Loch Ness Monster. Burton, Binns and Campbell – the leading skeptics – all feel that Wilson photographed the tail of a diving otter and passed it off as the monster; the second picture being a portrait of the otter's head. When I discussed this theory with Campbell at the loch in 1984, he added the refinement that the otter's tail was broken, producing the effect of the monster's 'head'.

My own opinion is that this hypothesis is needlessly complicated. Campbell suggests that Wilson's photographs were cleverly faked on the spur of the moment; he saw an otter and made it look like the monster, deliberately blurring the focus of the second photo to disguise the animal's head. Although it is *possible* to picture an otter this way, it it much easier to make it look like what it really is – a small mammal with a short neck. No-one else has taken pictures of an otter in the loch before or since. It seems altogether too good to be true that Wilson should get two 'monster' poses in a row, and even more unlikely that his otter should have a conveniently broken tail to enhance the 'head'effect. The object could be a model – the angles at the base of the neck suggest a bottle floating slightly on its side; in which case a second model could have been thrown further out into the loch for the second photo. What may be a pattern of three cylindrical floats around the 'neck' has also been pointed out.

The precise nature of the object is really unimportant. What matters is that enough doubts have been raised to render this well-loved photo unacceptable as evidence. One more photo down, and not all that many to go. Will Loch Ness photography ever produce positive proof?

FOOTNOTES

● 1 – Four shots were obtained on the night in question, of which three have been published. Two of these show 'flippers' and it has been suggested that the third shows tow tails. The best shot has become known as the 'Flipper Picture' and is usually referred to in the singular. However, according to Rines' interpretation of the sonar chart, there were two animals present, and the two 'flipper' pictures could be the limbs of different animals. ● 2 – According to the *Skeptical Inquirer* vol.9, pp47-58 (Winter 1984-5), it was on the 9th. ● 3 – The camera fired automatically at fixed intervals and was not triggered by the sonar, as suggested by Ronald Binns in *The Loch Ness Mystery, Solved* Open Books, 1983) p154 *[...and reviewed in this issue – Ed.]* ● 4 – Nicholas Witchell, *The Loch Ness Story* (Penguin, 2nd edn, 1975) p130. ● 5 – It had been calm all evening according to Rines; Davies says "it had been quite choppy until midnight." ● 6 – In Roy Mackal, *The Monsters of Loch Ness* (Futura, 1976) p281; and plates in Witchell, and Tim Dinsdale, *The Story of the Loch Ness Monster* (Target, 1973). A fuller version of the chart, showing the earlier contact, appears in *Wildlife* magazine (March 1976) p105. ● 7 – This led Sir Peter Scott to dignify the monster with the name *Nessiteras rhombopteryx* (= Ness beast with the diamond-shaped fin) in *Nature* (1975) vol.258, p466. ● 8 – Mackall, p111, and p277. ● 9 – When I met them at the loch in 1983, Razdan and Kielar told me that as scientists they could not accept eye-witness testimony. As a historian I found this a bit hard to swallow! ● 10 – An early version of their charges appears in *Discover* (Sept 1984). ● 11 – *[Nessletter is published by Rip Hepple: see our exchange magazine listing. Rines also replied in 'Retouching of Nessie Flipper Photo Claimed...Denied', in International Society of Cryptozoology* Newsletter *3:1, No.4 (Winter 1984). William Corliss'* Science Frontiers *noted that* Discover *had refused to publish any rebuttal of the allegations against Rines – Ed.]* ●

12 – Witchell, p130f. ● 13 – See note 6. In Dinsdale, p111, Rines refers to these traces as evidence for the monster; such references are not present in later books. If we are to accept that two monsters were swimming around the rig for over an hour, off and on, Rines must explain why more photos were not taken. ● 14 – Dennis Meredith, *Search at Loch Ness* (New York Times Book Co., 1977) p129f. ● 15 – 'The (Retouched) Loch Ness Monster', in *Discover; Nessletter* 67. ● 16 – Wyckoff's letter to the editor of *Discover*, quoted in *Nessletter* 67. There is still the problem of the "triangular appendage appearing to contain five digits" referred to in an LNI 'Confidential Newsletter' of October 1972 (Binns, p154). No such digits are visible in any published version of the photos. ● 17 – *[Retouching of Doc Shiels' 1977 photos of Nessie, by the newspapers, created similar problems – see* **FT29 p26-31.** *Fortunately, in his case, we had one of the originals to study; the other was 'lost', inevitably – Ed.]* ● 18 – *Technology Review* (March/April 1976). I have been unable to examine a copy of this American publication and base my account upon the exchanges in *Nessletter.* ● 19 – In 1971 the strobe camera was moored to a buoy in Urquhart Bay. It disappeared one night – perhaps removed by salmon poachers – and was found the next day drifting in the main body of the loch. When the photographs taken that night were developed, one snap was interpreted by Rines as a picture of a 'flipper'. In fact it was probably a photograph of a loop of rope from the mooring. Binns, p153f; and information from the LNMP. ● 20 – For example: Rines has never answered researchers who wonder why he used a narrow-angle lens (actually a standard lens with a flat port) quite unsuitable for the peaty waters. Rines is a patent lawyer, and his doctorate was awarded by a Taiwanese university for the submission of a paper on starting up high technology industries in under-developed countries. *New Scientist* (26 Aug 1982) p578. ● 21 – Steuart Campbell, 'The Surgeon's Monster Hoax', *BJP* (20 April 1984). ● 22 – *Daily Mail* 21 April 1934. ● 23 – Binns, p97. ● 24 – Tim Dinsdale, *The Loch Ness Monster* (RKP, 4th edn, 1981) appendix A. ● 25 – Harold Edgerton & Charles Wyckoff, in *Spectrum*, journal of the American Institute of Electrical & Electronic Engineers (Feb 1978).

AUTHOR'S NOTE

I would like to thank Adrian Shine and Ricky Gardiner – respectively, the field leader and the Evidence Committee chairman of the Loch Ness & Morar Project – for discussing the Rines and Wilson pictures with me.

Editorial

Continued from p2.

sional papers under the general editorship of **Mike Dash**. The papers are intended to present material of somewhat greater length and depth, or more overtly reference material than could otherwise be accomodated in *Fortean Times* itself. But an invitation is extended to any fortean with original and suitable material that they would like made available to other scholars, to write to Mike Dash at the FT address.

The series got off to a good start with Steve Moore's *Wildman*, a collection of essays on China's Yeti, but it lapsed under the usual editorial pressures. Two new titles are currently in preparation - Bob Skinner's long awaited *Toad in the Hole*, a richly annotated selection of sources on the entombed toad phenomenon (see advertisement on inside front cover); and, representing the OP essay category, Michael Goss's *The Folklore and Sociology of 'Mystery Assailants'*.

'ALIEN' ARTIFACT MYSTERY

Inhabitants of the Russian town of Ukhta all know of the local legend that in ancient times "a piece of the sun" fell to earth in the area. A von-Danikenesque proof is usually offered to skeptics, in the form of hexagonal-shaped depressions found in rocks 760 yards below the surface, which are popularly explained as evidence of the landing of an alien spacecraft. Presumably these are down a mine (we are not given any further information).The ill-informed implication seems to be that the depth at which the marked rock was found indicates its antiquity, though no evidence of the geological upheaval needed to bury what was once on the surface is offered.

Investigating the claims, the Paleontology Institute of the Soviet Academy of Sciences quickly discerned that the markings were not the result of natural processes. They called in a team of criminologists - [for their forensic skills, or because they suspected a hoax?] - who announced that the marks were definitely not, as was claimed, impressions made by alien landing gear. They had been made by the heads of bolts of fairly modern design. "The digits 8 and 4 had been pressed on the imprints", said Tass.

That was the end of the mystery as far as the authorities were concerned. Only a **minor** query left: how do impressions from modern bolt heads come to be in rock over 2000 feet underground? AP. Albuquerque (NM) *Journal* 23 April; Houston (TX) *Chronicle* 27 April; *Soviet Weekly* 5 May 1984.

Science Frontiers

Compiled & Annotated by William R.Corliss.

Fungus Manufactures Phony Blueberry Flowers

Mummy-berry disease is a fungus that preys on blueberries. It propagates itself by turning blueberry leaves into whitish, bell-like structures resembling true blueberry flowers. Bees deceived by this ruse land on the fake blossoms, pause for a moment to sip a sugary fluid (fortuitously) exuding from lesions on the leaves, accidently pick up some fugus spores, and then fly off to true blueberry blossoms. The transferred spores infect other blueberry plants, causing them to produce white mummy-berries rather than blueberries. When spring comes round, the fungus-filled mummy-berries release the fungus to the leaves, and the cycle continues. ("A Fungus That Courts with Phony Flowers," *Science* 85, 6:10, September 1985.)

The explanations usually served up for such remarkable adaptations are: (1) It is the product of chance and natural selection; and (2) The Creator made things this way. Are there not other possibilities? Perhaps the fungus somehow stole the blueprints for the flower from the blueberry's genome, ie its genetic endowment. After all, viruses are always subverting cell machinery.

Geomagnetic Activity and Paranormal Experiences

"*Summary* – 25 well-documented (and published by Stevenson in 1970) cases of intense paranormal ('telepathic') experiences concerning death or illness of friends of family were analyzed according to the global geomagnetic activity (the AA index) at the times of their occurrence. The characteristics of these cases were representative of the general literature and occurred between the years 1878 and 1967. All 25 experiences were reported to have occurred on days when the geomagnetic activity was less than the means for those months. Repeated measured analysis of variance for the daily aa indices for the 7 days before to the 7 days after the experience confirmed the observation that they occurred on days that displayed much less geomagnetic activity than the days before or afterwards.

These results are commensurate with the hypothesis that extremely low fields, generated within the earth-ionospheric cavity but disrupted by the geomagnetic disturbances, may influence some human behavior." (Persinger, Michael A.: "Geophysical Variables and Behavior: XXX. Intense Paranormal Experiences Occur During Days of Quiet, Global, Geomagnetic Activity", *Perceptual and Motor Skills*, 61:320, 1985.)

Glitch in the Evolution of Funnel-Web Spider Venom?

The Australian funnel-web spider has a venom that appears to be effective only against humans, monkeys, baby rats, and fruit flies. None of these animals is normally on the spider's menu; those prey that are seem unaffected by the venom. Did the evolution of the poison miss its intended targets or did the spider's usual prey evolve resistance? It is also interesting that mature rats are immune to the venom, although neonatal rats are not. ("Did You Know?" *Ex Nihilo*, 7:16, no.3, 1985.) Facts taken from *The Australian Doctor,* January 20, 1984.

A Possible Crack in the Wall of the Temple of Relativity

"Stefan Marinov is a remarkable iconoclast who is convinced that Einstein's special theory of relativity is mistaken." Marinov apparently has been expelled from Russia because of his scientific and political opinions. So infuriated is he by the reluctance of mainstream scientific journals, such as *Nature*, to print his anti-relativity papers that he has threatened to immolate himself outside the British embassy in Vienna. Happily, he didn't strike the match, because it may be that he has something. Marinov claims that he has demonstrated experimentally that the velocity of light is not the same in all directions in all reference frames, as Einstein insisted. He says he can even detect the motion of the earth through absolute space and time, contrary to most Michelson-Morley-type experiments. Based upon some recent theoretical analysis, the journal *Nature* has bent a bit and now calls for repetitions of Marinov's experiments. (Maddox, John. "Stefan Marinov Wins Some Friends", *Nature*, 316 209 1985.)

Recently three books highly critical of relativity have been published: (1) Turner, Dean, and Hazelett, Richard eds: *The Einstein Myth and the Ives Papers*; (2) Santilla Ruggero Maria: *Il Grande Grido. Ethical Probe on Einstein's Followers in the USA*; (3) Dingle, Herbert: *Science at the Crossroads*.

The Night of the Polar Dinosaur

Somewhere west of Deadhorse, a small town on Prudhoe Bay in Northern Alaska, paleontologists have found the bones of at least three species of dinosaurs. But wait, the latitude there is 70° north today and, according to magnetic measurements of the rocks, it was about the same when the dinosaurs met their demise. At these high latitudes the dinosaurs either had to contend with two months of darkness each year or they had to migrate many hundreds of miles over the rough Alaskan landscape.

The visions of dinosaurs groping for tons of vegetable food in the polar night is about as incongruous as imagining them trekking down to the Lower 48! Scientists are now maintaining that these dinosaurs did prosper on the shore of the Arctic Ocean, even in the dark, because the climate was more equable or uniform. They are, however, surprised by the lack of mineral deposition in the dinosaur bones, which look rather "modern". (Anderson, Ian: "Alaskan Dinosaurs Confound Catastophe Theorists", *New Scientist*, p 18, August 22, 1985.)

The apparent survival of dinosaurs during two months of darkness is being used as an argument against asteroidal catastrophism, which it is claimed wiped out the dinosaurs with a long-lived dust cloud that blocked the sun.

Mysterious Spate of Sky Flashes

Bill Katz and a small group of Canadian amateur astronomers have accumulated a total of 14 bright flashes in Aries in just a year or so. "Point" meteors (meteors seen head-on) usually appear as flashes like this, but to see 14 in the same region of the sky in such a short span of time is truly remarkable. (Katz, Bill; "Chasing the Ogre," *Astronomy*, April 1985.)

Restless Gold

Thanks to the development of high-resolution electron microscopes and video recorders, we can now watch the bizarre behavior of tiny solid particles, which, it turns out, are not so solid after all. Ultrafine particles of gold about 18 Angstrom units across, containing only about 500 atoms, are not static aggregations. The shapes of the particles are always changing. The gold atoms move cooperatively to shift kalaidoscope-like into various crystal structures. They have, in fact, been dubbed 'quasi-solids'. A large gold particle may even ingest small gold particles. The phenomena have no explanations as yet. ("Japanese Gold in Atomic Motion", *Nature*, 315:628, 1985.)

The Australian Pyramids

"Standing in the bushland some distance from the town of Gympie in southern Queensland, is a crudely-built, 40-metre tall terraced stone pyramidal structure which, I believe, will one day help to alter the history of Australia – to prove that, 3000 years ago, joint Egyptian and Phoenician mineral-seeking expeditions established mining colonies here." Thus runs the lead paragraph of this article in a popular Australian publication. This pyramid boasts 18 recognizable terraces. The bottom 14 terraces are built from rather small stones; but the top four consist of slabs weighing up to 2 tons. Trees as old as 600 years poke up through the stones, attesting to a pre-European origin. Another much larger pyramid inhabits dense scrubland near Sydney.

The claim that these admittedly crude structures are Egyptian is based upon the discovery of artifacts in the area with Egyptian and Phoenician characteristics, ie a stone idol resembling a squatting ape, an onyx scarab beetle and cave paintings with Egyptian symbols. Aboriginal legends also tell of 'culture heroes' arriving at Gympie in large ships shaped like birds. (Gilroy, Rex: "Pyramids of Australia", *Australian Post*, August 30, 1984, p.9. Cr. A. Jones.)

And just what do the professional archaeologists say about all this?

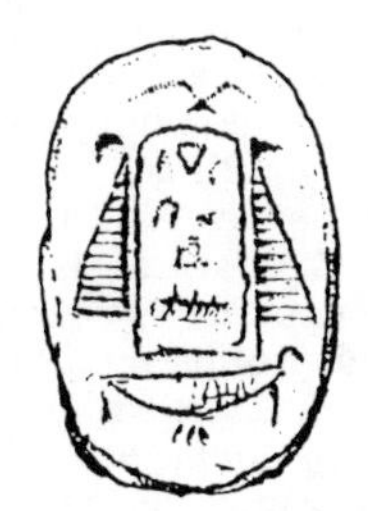

Underside of a stone scarab dug up in an Australian cane field. (From Ancient Man.)

Peace and Sunspots

Abstract . "Periods of international peace were found to occur in nearly regular cycles of 11 years by Edward Dewey in 1957 by analyzing the earlier data of Raymond Wheeler. In this paper the phase relationship between sunspot cycles and international battles was investigated. It was found that peaceful periods ended 7 out of 11 times within two years prior to sunspot peaks. The probability of this occurring by chance is less than .008.

Geomagnetic storms are postulated as the triggering event since, (1) geomagnetic storms are known to occur with greater frequency and intensity near sunspot peak, and (2) geomagnetic storms have been found by other researchers to be associated with increased frequency of accidents, illness, psychiatric hospital admissions, and crimes." (Payne, Buryl; "Cycles of Peace, Sunspots, and Geomagnetic Activity," *Cycles*, 35:101, 1984.)

Bone Bed Discovered In Florida

A new bone bed has been discovered south of Tampa. Palaeontologists say it is one of the richest fossil deposits ever found in the United States. It has yielded the bones of more than 70 species of animals, birds, and aquatic creatures. About 80% of the bones belong to plains animals, such as camels, horses, mammoths, etc. Bears, wolves, large cats, and a bird with an estimated 30-foot wingspan are also represented. Mixed in with all the land animals are sharks' teeth, turtle shells, and the bones of fresh & saltwater fish. The bones are all smashed and jumbled together, as if by some catastrophe. The big question is how bones from such different ecological nitches – plains, forests, ocean – came together in the same place. (Armstrong, Carol: "Florida Fossils Puzzle the Experts", *Creation Research Society Quarterly*, 21:198 , 1985.)

Science Frontiers ***is extracted from William Corliss' bimonthly collection of digests from current literature, which is sent free to regular customers of his publications. For more details write to*** **The Sourcebook Project, Box 107, Glen Arm, MD 21057, USA.**

Reviews

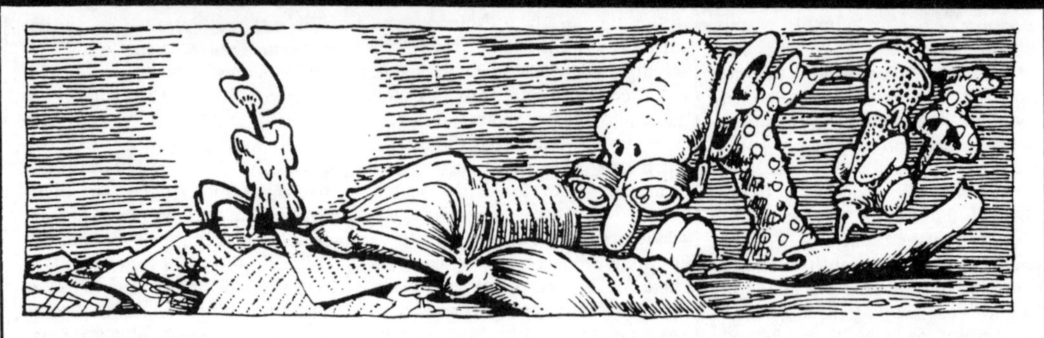

THE LOCH NESS MYSTERY SOLVED

by Ronald Binns (with R.J. Bell)
Open Books Publishing Ltd, Shepton Mallet, Somerset; 1983, £7.95, hb, pp228+x, index, illus, bib.

After 50 years, controversy continues over the claimed existence of the Loch Ness monster(s). The title of this book notwithstanding, it does not solve the mystery; and the suggested solution is nothing new: mirages, misinterpretations of inanimate objects, misperceptions of birds, otters, deer. Further, this solution is asserted but not coherently argued; the claimed evidence of others is not critically analyzed but rather attacked by misrepresensation and innuendo. The book is a sorry example of the genre that seeks to debunk claims of unusual phenomena but itself commits the sins of which the investigators and proponents of anomalies are accused.

The currently available evidence does not establish beyond doubt that large animals live in Loch Ness; there is ample room for criticism of the data. But there do exist some rather hard facts that the serious critic should address; Dinsdale's film, attested in so many important particulars by the expert analysts of The Royal Air Force and by computer-enhancement; sonar echoes from large, apparently moving objects under the water – detected over the last 15 years with several different types of apparatus by many independent investigators; underwater photographs obtained in 1972 and in 1975 by the Academy of Applied Science. Binns, however, offers little to shake this evidence; he takes the low road of ridiculing the less firm data and snidely denigrating the efforts of pioneerig investigators.

Some of the many errors in this book do not much matter since they do not bear directly on the argument (for example the field of view through binoculars (p120) cannot be calculated if only the magnification is known). Other errors are more germane to the discussion : for instance, the Macnab photo does not (p101) portray a hump at least 55 feet long: the tower is 64 feet high and covers 45mm in the photo as published by Binns, and the larger hump is 24mm long, ie about 34 feet. It is significant that all the errors I detected would tend to support the case against the monster: *randomly* made errors would point sometimes in one direction and sometimes in the other. So it is not easy to avoid the suspicion that Binns misrepresented deliberately, and that suspicion finds further support in statements that are not blatant factual errors yet sufficiently misleading as to have the same effect: for instance, that the case for Nessie rests overwhelmingly (p165) on eyewitnesses without any substantive supporting evidence (p173), or that it should be easy to find bones in the loch (p35). Binns writes that nothing in the report by the Royal Air Force, on Dinsdale's film, contradicts that a motorboat was filmed (p122) or supports the belief that he filmed a large unknown animal (p 109): yet he quotes (p109) the report which says, "probably an animate object", and he also demolishes in another place (p117) Maurice Burton's suggestion that Dinsdale's hump was a boat. When Binns writes (p118) that the RAF report contradicts Dinsdale, and says that he was "grossly inaccurate", he completely misrepresents that report, which explicitly acknowledges agreement with Dinsdale on the assessment of speed and distance (to within 10%) and disagrees only on Dinsdale's suggestion that the angular nature of the hump be compared with that in the Stuart photograph. Again, Binns is either dead wrong or very sneaky when he says that Mrs Whyte never lived "at Loch Ness" (p64): she lived for some 2 decades, beginning in 1937, a few miles from the loch (Constance Whyte, *More*

Than A Legend, Hamish Hamilton, 1957, pxviii).

In sum: let the reader be warned that every word selected by Binns is likely to carry a loaded value. When he says, as he often does, "significantly", then look for the innuendo that follows. And note the useage also of "solemnly" (eg p8), "boasted" (eg p11), "but" and "none other than" (p26), "Stalker's *Scotsman*" and "Campbell's *Courier*" and "the quality press" (p27), "amateur" and, in quotes, "'investigation'" (p24), "lurked" (p95) . . . the examples are truly legion.

Arguing deviously and tendentiously in these ways is deplorable enough, but Binns goes further and attacks almost every individual mentioned in the book in viciously personal ways; rather indiscriminately he maligns the quick and the dead, those who believe Nessies are real and those who do not. Sir Edward Mountain's watchers are directly accused (pp37-8) of faking photos; Philip Gosse's memory is maligned (pp204-5); a book by Compton MacKenzie is called "surprisingly" astute (p209); Rupert Gould is denigrated incessantly pp26, 32, 33, 42), as "the great sea-serpent scholar himself" and "Falstaffian eccentric" who "died in obscurity in 1948, as forgotten as his cherished monster". Witchell is insulted on pp59 and 87; the RAF photographic experts on p123; the computer-enhancement experts on p124; and Mackal on p137. Part of Binns repertoire is to ascribe thoughts and emotions to produce the desired effect on the reader; Binns tells us that Dinsdale, on various occasions, was "half-expecting", "tossing restlessly in his sleep", "brooding about the enigma", "increasingly obsessed", "in a state of nervous excitement", "oppressed", "deeply excited" or "shaking with excitement" or "overwhelmed with excitement", "on the brink of nervous exhaustion", and so on and on. Binns never reveals how he got this very detailed knowledge, to the extent that he can attest (p115) that Dinsdale was, on a second occasion, "in an identical condition" of psychological tension and excitement. Psychologists will no doubt be interested to know that such situations can be reproduced so precisely.

Psychologists could also venture reasons why Binns indulges in rumor-mongering and insinuation; but the substantive point is that such tactics are called upon to compensate for the inability to explain away on objective grounds the strong indications that Nessies are real animals. In this, the book is typical of the extremist debunkers, who sabotage their own endeavours: see, for example, the blundering critics of Velikovsky (Henry H. Bauer, *Beyond Velikovsky: The History of a Public Controversy*, University of Illinois Press, 1984).

Binns uses rhetorical devices to create misleading impressions. Inevitably, however, there come times when the truth cannot be entirely evaded, and self-contradictions appear: contrasting Nessies with flying saucers (pviii), Binns cites the "geographical remoteness" of UFOs but also that they are universally seen, a double self-contradiction and blatant error at the same time. The funniest self-contradiction, perhaps, is when Binns describes Sir Edward Mountain as "relaxed at nearby Beaufort Castle, chewing his nails". The oddest self-contradiction is the book's inability to decide whether it has one author or two. The dust-jacket and blurbs mention only Binns, and Plate 3 is "by the author". But the title page says "Ronald Binns with R.J. Bell", and the text refers to the "authors" (pp144, 168). In the Acknowledgements, "We. . .thank" a number of people including "R.J. Bell (Plates 15[f], 17, 18). . . All other photographs by the author"!

So this is in many ways a sloppy and reprehensible book. But it does have some good points, for example the comprehensive coverage of the literature, including items in newspapers. In passing and almost surreptitiously, the book also strengthens the case for Nessie by pointing out the absurdities of the Scotch-pine theory (p182) and the Burton vegetable mats (p45). Against Nessie, some valid points are raised. Campbell's inconsistency about one of his sightings does present a puzzle (but it was Gould in 1934, not Binns in 1983, who first pointed that out). It is true that several authors have not been scrupulously careful to verify historical references. It is also true that the road built in the 1930s was not "new", but a widening and straightening of an earlier one, and some authors did not make that clear. That Dinsdale and Burton had known one another was not evident from Burton's book, and those facts do bear noting when one tries to assess Burton's attitude. But those are very minor virtues indeed as against the sourness and deviousness of the book as a whole. "Monster hunters can never quite bring themselves to admit what their jumbled motives are" (p213); I wonder, can Binns and Bell?

Henry H. Bauer

FOOTNOTE: *A longer version of this review was. published in* Zetetic Scholar. *Binn's book has also been published in the USA, by Prometheus (February 1985); a paperback edition (Star Books, W.H. Allen & Co., 1984) contains a 2½ page "Postscript" with comments about activities during 1983.]*

ANCIENT MYSTERIES OF BRITAIN

by Janet & Colin Bord.
Grafton Books, London; 1986, hb £14.95, pp288, index, bib, colour plates, photos, maps.

The authors' *Mysterious Britain* (1972) was devoured by devotees of the (then) exciting new post-hippy thirst for our ancient past by giving them a guide to its mysterious relics in terms they could relate to. Since then the complex field of Earth Mysteries has flowered several subdisciplines of its own, but the need for an informed guide to the ruins is as strong as before. *Ancient Mysteries* reflects that need, but it is not a revision of their earlier book; rather it builds upon it, adding more or new information on those sites it duplicates, and is more like their *Guide to Ancient Sites in Britain* (1979) in layout.

The book is divided into twenty chapters, each dealing with a type of site or monument or folklore theme. Among the latter are sites related to King Arthur, giants and devils, dragons, and seasonable festivals. The two last chapters deal with leys, and some fortean locations (ghosts, UFO encounters, alien big cats, and monsters) though the few items mentioned will hardly whet the appetite of forteans. The book is well illustrated throughout, with photographs, mostly from the Bords' own collection; and the inclusion of eight pages of colour photos is a vote of confidence in both the authors and the book by the publishers. An excellent reference for schools and libraries.

RJMR

ANCIENT ASTRONAUTS, COSMIC COLLISIONS.

by William H. Stiebing Jr.
Prometheus Books, Buffalo, NY & London: 1984, £16.95 hb/£8.45 pb, pp216, index, bib, refs, illus.

Dubbed "the intellectual equivalent of a cold shower" by the *New Scientist*, this excellent addition to the literature of debunking deserves a warm welcome.

Stiebing, an associate professor of history, feels that academic aloofness from 'pseudoscience' hinders rather than helps the rationalist cause by leaving the field free for Von Daniken & Co. "The silence of scholars tends to make the claims of the theorists more believable", he writes.

In just over 200 pages the author brings scientific research out of the closet, dealing with the Flood legends and arkeology, Atlantis, Velikovsky, ancient astronauts, pyramidology and pre-Columbian discoveries of America in the space of about 30 pages each. The treatment of these subjects is admirably concise, with enough detail given, and chapter and verse cited, to point out the most damaging flaws in the popular theories. On the whole, Stiebing is more solidly referenced than predecessors such as Ronald Storey, and his book is nicely rounded off with an examination of the popularity of theorising of the 'ancient astronaut' variety. This the professor attributes to the "communications gap between scholars and the public."

The main criticism which may be levelled is that the book appears to have sprung from Stiebing's laudable desire to inform the public of his academic colleagues' work, rather than from any real interest or expertise in the fields concerned. His work therefore rests on a long series of references to academic secondary sources, and however impeccable most of these may be it is impossible for the reader to allow for errors, prejudice, or now-outdated thinking on the part of these earlier writers. This sort of copying is precisely the sort of thing that von D and his ilk are so often and so correctly criticised for, and it's a shame (if unsurprising) that Stiebing doesn't present much original thinking. As a work of synthesis, though, *Ancient Astronauts. . .* is of great value, providing the researcher with a startling point and – with a bibliography listing a couple of hundred books and articles – the means to work back into the literature. Best of all, the book teaches doubt.

Mike Dash

EVOLUTION AS A RELIGION: Strange Hopes and Stranger Fears

by Mary Midgley.
Methuen & Co, London; 1985; £4.95 pb, pp162, index, notes.

"Facts are not gathered in a vacuum, but to fill gaps in a world picture which already exists", writes Mary Midgley promisingly as she sets about excavating the rift that widened between Darwin's originally restrained ideas, and Herbert Spencer's notion (via Lamarck) of "Evolution" as a process that will turn us into "Super-intelligent Omega

Man". And she demonstrates, with thrilling zest, how this ludicrous and vainglorious Specerisan view, though disclaimed by modern scientists, still haunts their language and shapes their assumptions.

She finds scientific bigotry proceeding from "the dogmatic idea that science can simply be treated as the only important activity, having won the race with all other aims in a walkover. . . The really startling thing about this idea is its unthinkingness." The failure of their training, among other factors, to enable scientists properly to evaluate their own needs as imaginative, or moral beings – this unthinkingness in fact – leads them wildly to claim the authority of science for disconnected fantasies about the future of the human race.

Mrs Midgley doubts that it is possible for any human endeavour, least of all science, to proceed without a subjective world picture. Indeed the cult of objective reality is not only doomed, it creates a dangerous vacuum. "It is alarming to see how the human imagination, when denied its proper exercise, does not just decay quietly, but produces monsters."

The proper practice of science calls for an approach which takes account of this and is directed to the world as a whole; an approach "'about which there is something solemn, serious, and tender'". This in fact is William James's definition of religious orientation, which Midgley quotes to illustrate the idea that true scientific inquiry can be "one of the varieties of religious experience". Thus the good scientist seeks not to "raid the assets" of religion, but to share its search for meaning.

Having made a case for our right to assess the universe through our perceptions and institutions as individuals, Mary Midgley shakes up the bag and reassembles the rights and duties the various aspects of our social humanity place on us, in a different pecking order from the one which science would have us believe is absolute, and which 'evolution' would have us believe is inevitable.

As a scholarly elucidation of what science and religion should share, where they should diverge, and as an antidote to both scepticism and awe, I cannot recommend this exacting, exciting book highly enough.

Merrily Harpur

THE SASQUATCH
and Other Unkown Hominids

Edited by Vladimir Markotic. *(Western Publishers: Box 30193 – Stn B, Calgary, Alberta, Canada; 1984; price unknown, pb, pp335, refs, bib, photos.)*

This useful collection of 21 papers, some of them read at the 1978 Vancouver Conference but all previously unpublished, is Volume I of 'The Research on Unknown Hominoids'. Authors include Carleton Coon, Grover Krantz, Dmitri Bayanov, Marie-Jeanne Koffmann, John Green, Loren Coleman, Igor Bourtsev, René Dahinden, Gordon Strasenburgh and Charles Reed, and the book is divided into seven chapters: The Monsters in General, The Believers and the Skeptics, Reports, The Biological and Psychological Aspects of Sasquatch, The Patterson-Gimlin Film, Europe of Old, The Problems of Origin. Coverage is not limited to the North American continent, but extends also to the Soviet Union, China and Australia. Particularly noteworthy are Loren Coleman's paper on wild apes in North America, suggesting that many reports away from the north-west may be of some unknown ape-like creature, unrelated to the giant Sasquatch; Grover Krantz's succinct summary of the present knowledge of Sasquatches, and also his assessment of what they might be; the analyses of the Patterson-Gimlin film which conclude that the creature Patterson filmed was a genuine Sasquatch and not a man in a monkey-suit; and the extensive bibliographies. Most of the papers will be of great value and interest to students of Bigfoot/Sasquatch, as they are largely written by sensible, unbiased researchers. The book is serious in tone, and leaves the impression that at last the overwhelming evidence for the existence of relic hominoids around the world is being treated seriously by men of intelligence.

Janet Bord

Also Received

- **VISIONS*APPARITIONS *ALIEN VISITORS** by Hilary Evans *(Thorsons/ Aquarian Press 1986; pp £6.99, pp320, index, bib, plates).* A welcome paperback edition of Hilary's groundbreaking comparative survey of visionary encounters with ghosts, 'aliens', astral doubles, fairies, demons, non-human entities, apparitions, saints, and of course, the Virgin Mary. Essential reading for ufologists, folklorists and forteans.
- **WILHELM REICH** by David Broadella *(RKP/ Arkana, 1985; pp £5.95, pp400, index, bib).* A clear and comprehensive account of Reich's work, the arguments of his critics, and the research that continues Reich's work since his death. Includes an account of Reich's trial, by M R Sharaf.
- **SCIENCE OF MYTHOLOGY** by C G Jung and C Kerenyi *(RKP/Ark, 1985; pb £3.95, pp200, index, refs).*

Two essays by the mythologist Kerenyi, on the 'primordial child' and 'Kore', are reinterpreted and analysed psychologically by Jung; then Kerenyi added a further prolog and epilog.

● **THE COMPLEAT ANGLER** edited by Bryan Loughrey *(Penguin Books, 1985; pb £2.50, pp150, notes).* A new edition of Izaak Walton's 1653 classic, extolling the moral superiority of those "that love quietnesse, and vertue, and Angling." It falls within our pale because he refers to the antiquity of frog and fish rains.

● **DARWINIAN EVOLUTION** by Anthony Flew *(Granada/Paladin, 1984; pb £2.50, pp149, index, bib).* Another review of the evolution of Darwinian theory and its influence, with an orthodox overview of the 'creationist' challenge and the implications, "real and imagined", of the new field of 'sociobiology'. A compact and handy reference.

● **ALGENY** by Jeremy Rifkin *(Penguin Books, 1984; pb £2.95, pp298, index, bib, notes).* Yet another critique of Darwinism, but this book looks forward not back. It is a clear exposition on the implications of state-of-the-art bioengineering upon the course of human evolution. Rifkin conjures startling visions of the forces today's science is setting in motion, with almost unimaginable consequences for the future of all lifeforms on this planet, and maybe the universe. Eg: current technology can create 'biochips' (ie organic molecules capable of functioning as computer chips, but much faster) by engineering *E.coli* bacteria.

● **A CRIMINAL HISTORY OF MANKIND** by Colin Wilson *(Granada/Panther, 1985; pb £3.95, index, bib).* Wilson at his best, on the psychology of murders, contrasting collective acts with the intensely personal, the 'senseless' with the ritualistic killing, and the politics of violence with the sexuality of aggression. At the risk of glorifying acts of destruction, Wilson notes the almost mystical self-awareness of some murderers during their ghastly crimes.

● **PSYCHOLOGICAL COMMENTARIES ON THE TEACHINGS OF GURDJIEFF & OUSPENSKY** by Maurice Nicoll *(RKP/Shamballa, 1984; pb £12.95 each).* Volumes 4 & 5.

● **THE TRAVELLER'S GUIDE TO THE ASTRAL PLANE** by Steve Richards *(Thorsons/Aquarian Press 1983; pb £3.95, pp110, index, refs).* A competent review of the beliefs and experiences of those who spontaneously or by practice have found themselves temporarily 'outside the body'. Expecting yet another trashy rehash I was pleasantly surprised at the condensation of knowledge in this relatively thin book.

● **MYSTERIES ON THE HIGH SEAS** by Philip MacDougall *(David & Charles, 1984; hb £7.95, pp192, index, bib, plates).* "Carefully verified" cases of vanishing ships or ships found drifting and crewless. Hard facts, not credulous speculation.

● **A DICTIONARY OF HINDUISM** by Margaret and James Stutley *(RKP, 1985; pb £9.95, pp372, bib).* A valuable reference to mythology, folklore, and related subjects for the period 1500 BC – 1500 AD, with a huge bibliography. Large format paperback.

● **THE ILLUSTRATED DICTIONARY OF HINDU ICONOGRAPHY** by Margaret Stutley *(RKP, 1985; hb £25.00, pp175, bib, illus).* Ideal companion to above work; the style of entries are similar, but in this there are occasional line drawings.

● **EARTH ASCENDING** by Jose Arguelles *(Shamballa, 1984; pb $12.95, pp156, bib, colour plates, illus).* A magical intuitive exploration of the imagery suggested by the I Ching, Mayan calendars, DNA, the Cabbalistic Tree of Knowledge, Sunspot cycles, David Bohm's holonomic physics, and other mystical and geomantic systems. Attempts an expression of a holistic philosophy for the future.

● **THE SHOEMAKER** by Flora Rheta Schreiber *(Penguin Books, 1985; pb £2.50, pp432, index, appendix).* Gripping analysis of the psychotic killer-poet Joseph Kallinger, by the author of the bestselling study of a multiple-personality, *Sybil.*

Booklets

★ **SPOOKLIGHTS: A BRITISH SURVEY** by David Clarke & Granville Oldroyd. Corpse candles, Jack o' lanterns, Will o'the wisps, and perhaps more anciently, ignis fatuus; the spook light is reflected in many dialect phrases from all parts of Britain. There is a list of them in this excellent survey by Clarke and Oldroyd. It is a subject at the heart of the fortean canon: Fort included stories of mystery lights, and even the doings of strangely luminous birds (a subject which David Clarke has explored in a forthcoming article in *FT*). The authors have worked hard to unearth and collate accounts from many sources, which makes this collection unique and valuable. It includes discussion of the lights in various contexts: folklore, ghost-lore, marsh gas and other theories, the 'earthlights' hypothesis, the 1905 religious revival, ball lightning and ball-like tiny UFOs. Essential for fortean libraries. *(From David Clarke: 6 Old*

Retford Rd, Handsworth, Sheffield, South Yorks, S13 9QZ. 1985, pp44, notes & refs, illus, price £1.50.)

★ **THE FAIRIES REVENGE** by Anthony Roberts, in fine fiery flow, deploring the slide of our crass 'civilization', which alienates everything that our ancestors, who were closer to this earth and other worlds, once respected and revered. First in a series called 'Apocalyptic Archives'. *(Zodiac House, Gondolin, Westhay, Somerset; 1985, pp18, bib, price unknown.)*

★ **THE DRAGON OF CHRISTCHURCH** by Jeremy Harte. Being a translation from original Latin sources of the account by Hermann of Laon and others of the church at Laon, in France, on a fund-raising tour of England, who encountered a mysterious aerial phenomenon (a flame-breathing five-headed dragon!) at Christchurch in 1113; plus a few other 'wonders' they encountered on their journeys. Includes an appendix on medieval records of aerial dragons and 'firedrakes'. Thorough, densely packed with referenced information, and very interesting. This is how it should be. First occasional paper from the South-Western Antiquarian Society. *(c/o Jeremy Harte: 35a West St, Abbotsbury, Nr Weymouth, Dorset. 1985, pp20, price unknown.)*

★ **LOST LYONESSE** – A delightful little reprint of a 1902 essay on this legendary sunken land off Land's End, Cornwall, by Beckles Wilson, with an introduction by John Michell. *(Published in the 'Pocket Pals' series, by AdCo Associates: 2 Blenheim Cres, London W11 1NN. 1986, pp27, illus, price+p&p £1.50.)*

★ **DADDY WITCH AND OLD MOTHER RED CAP** by Nigel Pennick. An excellent little paper, being an attempt to identify the origin of the appellation 'red cap' applied to witches, reviewing the lives of some East Anglian witches of the Victorian era against the background of the Industrial Revolution and the incursion of mechanised farm equipment into rural life. *(Cornerstone Press: 142 Pheasant Rise, Bar Hill, Cambridge CB3 8SD. 1985, pp12, refs, price 55p + postage.)*

★ **HOLLOW EARTH APOCALYPSE: ASMIMOV'S WARNING** by Floria Benton. Rightly or wrongly, Benton has construed scattered remarks about engineering hollow 'mini-planets' as ships or colonies, made by Asimov, in his writing and interviews, as evidence that he believes in the Hollow Earth idea, and is warning us, as openly as he dares, about the coming consequences (polar axis shifting, and polar hole opening). The lords of this world want to keep this knowledge from us, she says, elevating Asimov to the role of modern saviour. I wonder what he thinks about it all? *(From the author at: 4 Dennis Dr, Park Place, Wilmington, DE 19808, USA. 1985, pp100, bib, illus, price unknown.)*

★ **SOME HAIRY MONSTERS** by Paul Lester. The author's ruminations upon Yeti, Bigfoot and Loys' Ape, King Kong and the yahoo, fragments, we are told, of a larger, unpublished, work. *(From the author at: Flat 4, 34 Summerfield Cres, Edgbaston, Birmingham B16 0ER. 1986, pp20, price 50p + postage.)*

★ **THE TRIAL OF THE BIDEFORD WITCHES** by Frank J Gent. The hunt for, trial and execution of witches in this Devon town between 1658 and 1682, with all the social, political, religious and historical background you could want. Peter Christie tells me he has only 10 copies left, at 95p + 25p postage. *(Originally published by the author in 1982, pp42. Apply to Peter Christie: 30 Lime Grove, Bideford, Devon.)*

★ **THE SECRET ROSE GARDEN OF. . .SHABISTARI**, trans. Florence Lederer. The first offering from our old fortean pal David Fideler's Phanes Press, which aims to reprint long unavailable Neoplatonist, Gnostic and other works of spiritual alchemy and mysticism. Shabistari was a Sufi poet, but these poems, written in 1311, speak directly to the hearts of all. *(Phanes Press, Box 6114, Grand Rapids, MI 49506, USA. 1985, pp92, price $5.95.)*

★ **STONEHENGE - ITS DRUIDS, CUSTODIANS, FESTIVALS AND FUTURE.** 1986 edition, enlarged, updated. Written by John Michell. *(from AdCo: 2 Blenheim Crescent, London W11 1NN. pp33, illus, price £2, incl. postage.)*

★ **EARTH MYSTERIES** by Brian Larkman & Philip Heselton. The first 'pocket' guide to the gamut of EM: including leys, markers, mazes, terrestrial zodiacs, dowsing, sacred geometry, stone markings, psychometry, archeaeology, the Dragon Project, folklore, earth energy, archaeo-astronomy, intuitive and mystical aspects, with glossary, further reading, and contacts. *(Published by the Northern Earth Mysteries Group: 170 Victoria Ave, Hull HU5 3DY. 1985, pp36, illus, price £1.)*

★ **THE KNIGHTS OF DANBURY** by Andrew Collins. Andy's further investigations into the origins of the mysterious knights of St Clere, taking in the folklore, mysteries and legends surrounding the Essex village of Danbury, makes a handsomely produced booklet. *(Earthquest Books: 19 St David's Way, Wickford, Essex SS11 8EX. 1985, pp86, index, bib, illus, price £1.95.)*

Classified Exchanges

FT welcomes an exchange of publications with those of mutual interest. This listing is free to regular publications, and represents exchange publications received since the last listing. **Symbols used** (when present): # = issue whole number. **v:n** = volume & number. **Pay** = to whom cheques should be made out if different from the title. All rates are inland or surface unless indicated: **O** = overseas rate. **E** = European rate. Many offer airmail rates, so inquire. **NFC** = no foreign cheques, remit in currency of country of origin. **Please mention FT when writing**.

FORTEAN

■ **ASSAP NEWS** - Newsletter of the Association for the Scientific Study of Anomalous Phenomena. 6/yr. Free to members. Enquiries to: Caroline Wise, ASSAP Membership Secretary, 56 Telemann Sq, Kidbrook, London SE3.

■ **CLYPEUS** - Fortean journal in Italian from the group Clypeus. Enquiries to: Clypeus: Box 604, I-10100 Torino, Italy.

■ **INFO JOURNAL** - One of the handful of essential journals for Forteans. $10/yr. International Fortean Organization: Box 367, Arlington, VA 22210, USA.

■ **JOURNAL OF METEOROLOGY** - Frequently has items of Fortean meteorology. 12/yr. Has a variety of sub rates from £15.50. J.Met: 54 Frome Rd, Bradford-on-Avon, Wilts BA15 1LD.

■ **JOURNAL OF VAMPIROLOGY** - Editor John L. Vellutini, who writes most of the material, is developing a fine exposition, covering every aspect of historical, criminal, mythological, pathological and psychopathological vampirism. 5/yr. $10. NFC. JOV: Box 881631, San Francisco, CA 94188, USA.

■ **FOLKLORE FRONTIERS** - First of the new title from Paul Screeton. Mapping new frontiers of urban belief tales. No.1: on Scargill and the Pit Strike, drugs, spiders in the yuccas, and phantom hitch-hikers. Plus reviews. 4 issues for £3. O: $8 (surf), $12 (air). NFC. Pay: Paul Screeton: 5 Egton Drive, Seaton Carew, Hartlepool, Cleveland TS25 2AT.

■ **KADATH** - A journal about forgotten civilizations, and their ruins & relics, in French. Write to: **Kadath23, 6 Boulevard St-Michel, B-1150 Bruxelles, Belgium.**

■ **PURSUIT** - The journal of the Society for the Investigation of the Unexplained, and essential reading for informed Forteans. 4/yr. Memb:$12. O.rates on application. SITU: Box 265, Little Silver, NJ 07739, USA.

■ **VISION** - A broad-based fortean magazine in Danish by veterans Klaus Aarsleff & Jakob Friis. Very glossy production with thick paper and full colour. 6/yr. Kr.33.00. **Vision**, Norrebrogade 34, 2200 Kobenhagen N, Denmark.

CRYPTOZOOLOGY

■ **BILK** - A newsletter on water monsters generally, with the emphasis on Europe, from Ulrich Magin. Yes, he's aware of the English usage of the word; Magin uses it as an acronym, standing for Behemoth (freshwater monsters), Isis (mermaids), Leviathan (sea serpents), and Kraken (giant cephalopods). 6/yr. E:£3. US:$5. Pay: Ulrich Magin: Stuhlbruderhofstr. 4, 6704 Mutterstadt, West Germany.

■ **CHAMP CHANNELS** - News of the Lake Champlain monster and related information; edited by its energetic investigator, Joseph Zarzynski. 4/yr. $8. O:$9. NFC. Lake Champlain Phenomena Investigation: Box 2134, Wilton, NY 12866, USA.

■ **CREATURE CHRONICLES** - Fortean news from Ohio. ?/yr. Inquiries to Ron Schaffner: Box 335, Loveland, OH 45140, USA.

■ **NESSLETTER** - The latest news of sightings, expeditions and controversies about Nessie and her cousins from the Ness Information Service. 12/yr. £2.50. O:$9. NIS: Rip Hepple: Huntshieldford, St Johns Chapel, Bishop Aukland, Co Durham DL13 1RQ.

PSI

■ **JOURNAL OF THE SOCIETY FOR PSYCHICAL RESEARCH** - 3/yr. Membership: £13/$34. SPR: 1 Adam & Eve Mews, London W8 6UG.

UFO

■ **APRO BULLETIN** - Essential reading for current US investigations from the venerable Aerial Phenomena Research Organization. 12/yr. Memb:$15. O:$18. APRO: 3610 E.Kleindale Rd, Tucson, AZ 85712, USA.

■ **BUFORA BULLETIN** - Magazine of the British UFO Research Association; lately more informative and better produced. 4/yr. Memb: £12.50. BUFORA Membership Sec: Pam Kennedy, 30 Vermont Rd, London SE19 3SR.

■ **FLYING SAUCER REVIEW** - Still essential reading for ufologists after 30 years on the front line! 6/yr. £7.50. O:$15. NFC. Pay: FSR Publications Ltd: Snodland, Kent ME6 5HJ.

■ **MAGONIA** - Essential for informed ufologists and forteans. 4/yr. £2. US:$5. O:£2.50. Pay: John Rimmer: ★ **new address:** John Dee Cottage, 5 James Terrace, Mortlake Churchyard, London SW14 8HB.

■ **NORTHERN UFO NEWS** - News & investigations from the north of England, including the thoughts of Jenny Randles. 6/yr. £4.50. NUFON: 8 Whitethroat Walk, Birchwood, Warrington, Cheshire WA3 6PQ.

■ **UFO NEWSCLIPPING SERVICE** - Monthly collections of clippings from all over the world, with several pages of Forteana too. 12/yr. Apply for rates. UFONS: Route 1, Box 200, Plumerville, AK 72127, USA.

■ **UFO NEWS FLASH** - Italian news and sightings in English. ?/yr. Details from: Massimo Greco: Box 29, I-25121 Brescia, Italy.

■ **UFO RESEARCH AUSTRALIA NEWSLETTER** - Essential for keeping informed on Australian research and cases. 6/yr. A$15. O:A$18(surf)/A$30(air). NFC. UFORAN: Box 229, Prospect, SA 5082, Australia.

EARTH MYSTERIES

■ **EARTHQUEST NEWS** - Editor Andy Collins investigates energetically fortean, psychic and earth-mystery phenomena in Essex (mainly). Essential reading. 4/yr. £3. E:£4. O:$8. Earthquest: 19 St Davids Way, Wickford, Essex SS11 8EX.

■ **THE LEY HUNTER** - Still the flagship of earth mysteries and ley research. 3 issues & separately edited supplement/yr. £4. E:£6. O:$20(air)$15(surf). TLH: Box 13, Welshpool, Powys, Wales.

■ **PRACTICAL GEOMANCY** - The past, present and future of geomantic practice. 3/yr. Single issue price £1. **Practical Geomancy**: 142 Pheasant Rise, Bar Hill, Cambridge CB3 8SD.

■ **QUICKSILVER MESSENGER** - 3/yr. £5. $16. NFC. ★ **Temporary new address:** Chris Ashton, c/o EEP, Jln Kapten Tendean 18, Jakarta-Selatan, Indonesia.

■ **STONEHENGE VIEWPOINT** - Each issue is filled with informative and imaginative explorations of every aspect of megalithic culture. 6/yr. £5. US:$8. Can:$10. SV: 2821 De La Vina St, Santa Barbara, CA 93105, USA. UK Agency: c/o 3rd Floor, 35 Gt Russell St, London WC1.

■ **TOUCHSTONE** - Newsletter for Surrey Earth Mysteries, edited by Jimmy Goddard. Enquiries to: Touchstone: 25 Albert Rd, Addlestone, Weybridge, Surrey.

OTHERS

■ **BLACK CHIP** - A journal of computing for anarchists. 4/yr. £2. Pay: Richard Alexander, 55 Dupont Rd, London SW20 8EH.

■ **THE GATE** - "covers a wide range of paranormal occurrences". 4/yr. $1/per copy. Pay: Beth Robbins: Box 43518, Richmond Heights, OH 44143, USA.

■ **KEEP THE TORCH LIT** - Occult/strange phenomena interface. Repros of newsclips, some fortean. Write: Anthony Egan: 612 East 14 St, 17 F, New York, NY 10009, USA.

■ **SHAVERTRON** - "The only source of post-Deluge Shaverania." And Hollow Earth related subjects. 3/yr. $9. O:$11 (surf), $13 (air). Pay: Richard Toronto: Box 248, Vallejo, CA 94590, USA.

■ **WHOLE EARTH REVIEW** - Continuation of the **CoEvolution Quarterly** and the **Whole Earth Software Catalog**. A broad-based wised-up New Age review of tools and ideas for the Computer Age. Essential to keep up with the times and techniques. 6/yr. $18. O:$22 (surf), $34 (air). WER: Box 27956, San Diego, CA 92128, USA.

Small independent magazines are labours of love and need your support.

Letters

Continued from p3.

not unknown, but were seen in Scotland in the autumn of 1938. Mary Falconer, walking to Loch Garget Beag, near Achlyness, Sutherland, noticed a number of grazing ponies. She approached one of them, which was white, but hesitated when she noticed it seemed bigger than a 'normal' pony. Suddenly she realised it was a 'water-horse'. The whole herd of 13 animals "galloped to the edge of the water, and plunging into the loch, sank below the surface in front of her eyes." [R.M. Roberton, *Selected Highland Folk Tales* (David and Charles, 1977) p142.]

If Mary Falconer's animals were the same as the Icelandic ones, they must have migrated north, and so there is a colony of kelpies in Iceland now. And they aren't the only ones who have moved, for the fairies seen near Akureyri, mentioned in the same issue, are surely the same ones seen in the year 1938 in Ireland. On the last day in August, according to *The Times* (6 Sept 1938), John Mulligan encountered two fairies near Ballinggarry, West Limerick. The day before, a boy named Keely had seen one at the same place. They were two feet high, had hard, hairy, earless human-like faces, and were dressed in red.

All of which begs the question: do fortean phenomena move on when their current location gets too crowded?

Ulrich Magin
Mutterstadt, W. Germany

THE BABY MASTERMIND

What a puzzling story PHANTOM FRIENDS [FT43,pp14] is! On the face of it, we are presented with evidence of supernatural communication between Anthony McQuone, aged 1, and the invisible spirit of an ancient Roman called Adam. A second reading reveals the following discrepancies:

1) Anthony said of Mrs Thatcher "she is bonum" thus revealing a grasp of Latin as profound as his political judgement. The word is *bona* in this context, with the feminine ending.

2) According to his father, Anthony "accurately names the varieties of trees and gives their Latin names". Were these names actually Latin or were they the binomial nomenclature used in science (inaccurately known as "Latin names" to laymen)? As Mr McQuone verified the terms in an encyclopaedia rather than a Latin dictionary, we must assume the latter.

3) Adam (hardly a typical Roman name, actually Hebrew, it was also popular with certain sects of early Christians) is described by Anthony as having black hair, brown eyes, a Van Dyke beard, a white toga and caliga (sic). Now, although we associate modern Italians (descendants of Goths and other barbarians) with a swarthy appearance, ancient Romans were actually fair-haired, blue or grey-eyed and clean-shaven. In fact the only instance of a Roman with a pointed beard which comes to mind is the emperor Julian the Apostate, who was ridiculed for aping Greek fashions.

4) Lastly those caligae (correct form of the plural) which are glossed by Anthony as "sandals" were actually army boots and only a military commander would be likely to wear them with a toga.

Given the dubious nature of Anthony's erudition and Adam's preposterous appearance, I was driven to suspect that either Mr McQuone invented the whole thing or that the story was wildly exaggerated by the reporter (or both). A more charitable possibility (proposed to me by Bob Rickard) is that young Anthony really is tapping into a cosmic database but is receiving a distorted or

Continued ☛

☛ *Continued*

contaminated signal. Yet again we find that a fortean story generates more and more questions the deeper one delves.

Mike Crowley
Harrow, Middlesex

[*Editor's note: Anthony McQuone's father Tony, 53, has died after a fall in a Surrey Psychiatric hospital.* Sun, *28 Mar 1985.*]

Coming Soon

NEXT ISSUE is likely to contain an assortment of items on trees, and eggs; suitably ominous events (suicides, quakes, auroras, etc) coinciding with Halley's comet; and coverage of the inquest on Jaqueline Fitzsimons, an alleged SHC victim.

FT48 will have a long article by Bob Rickard on levitation and teleportation accounts in the 15th and 16th centuries; a discussion by John Nicholson of the 'scientific' attitude of the day; with supplementary material on Joseph Glanvil.

Truss Fund

Our usual grateful thanks for their donations go to: David Bernard, Ron Bishop, John Deegan, Dr Franziska Dokter, M.Ferrier, Ron Gauntlett, Robyn Gurney, Ray Nelke, Ralph Noyes, Paul Thomas, and to Mike Dash for his standing order.

Remember – your donations really do help us in very practical ways to improve our service to you – so give in to that generous streak and bung some folding stuff our way!

Help!

Hilary Evans has announced the formation of a **ball-of-light international data exchange,** which makes for a clever acronym: **BOLIDE.** The purpose is to facilitate the exchange of data between researchers interested in both exploring the phenomenon as an interface between a variety of phenomenal categories, and in working towards a solution or solutions. To deter the time-wasters there is an initial subscription of £10/$15/120F. This is to reimburse Hilary for the costs of photocopies and mailing a newsletter. Enquiries to: *Hilary Evans: BOLIDE Coordinator, 1 Tranquil Vale, London SE3 0BU.*

INFORMATION, please on helicopters in relation to UFOs: phantom 'copters, 'copters changing into UFOs, and vice versa, and 'copter "mythology". Write to: Dennis Stillings, c/o Archaeus Project, 629 12th Avenue SE, Minneapolis, MN 55414 USA.

Tony McMunn, a Fire Officer at the Fire Service College in Gloucestershire, who appeared in the *Newsnight* documentary on SHC (see p8, this issue), has asked if 882FT readers could help his research into the subject by answering two questions: 1) is SHC fact or fiction? 2) Why does the human body burn in such a manner and with startling consequences, yet leave the surrounding area virtually untouched?

Write to: **ADO A.J.McMunn, Fire Service College, Moreton-in-the-Marsh, Glos GL56 0RH.**

Small Ads

Back Issues

- **FT31** – The Chinese Wildman; Gateways to Mystery; The Touch of Death; UFO muggers; mystery big cats; ball lightning; synchronous names; little people; fake doctors; Forteana from China; comix.
- **FT32** – The Mississauga Blob; Old Ives' Tales; Gateways (pt 2); occult murder; mystery big cats; fairy tales come true; Forteana from India and China; child sacrifice; mystery panthers in USA and Australia; comix.
- **FT33** – The Enfield Poltergeist; mythology of UFO abductions; Gateways (pt 3); mass hysteria at Nottingham; simulacra; coffin stories; Jeoff Watson's Nessie pix; UFOs; Forteana from China; giant snakes; comix.
- **FT34** – Congo dinosaur hunt; lake monster names; phantom hitch-hikers; interview with Dr Jean Bolen on synchronicity; the Welsh 'puma'; mystery big cats; beached whales; animal saboteurs; nature follows art; ice falls; inept crimes; Trashkashic records; odd Irish doings; giant squids; comix.
- **FT35** – The Myth of Darwinism; an SHC from 1744; The Runamo Runes; Forteana from Malaysia and China; spontaneous combustions; antiquities; strange trees; magic fuels; frog and stone falls; mystery big cats; bizarre bacteria; TV science; occult murder; Fortean travel in USA.
- **FT36** – Anomalistics; Photos of Jesus; Runamo Runes; Gent's Mag extracts; hermits and wildmen; strange tales; toads in holes; bleeding statues and visions; the Buddha's UFO; DIY surgery; coin, ice and sand falls; ASSAP and CSAR; jellyfish in the sky; Forteana from China; USA monitor lizards; Nessie; comix.
- **FT37** – Australia's Lizard Monsters; energy from space; encounters with Greek gods; interview with Dr Rupert Sheldrake on a New Science of Life; a female prophet; Irish oddities; mystery USA kangaroos; UFO hallucinations; falls of crabs, frogs, peas, fish; visions, stigmatics and fasting; plants in odd places; mystery UK bear scares; talking polts; reflections; homing rings; locked-up by friends and relatives.
- **FT38** – Psychometry of cattle mutilations; Isotope myth; synchronicity of clowns and 22; Sieveking's Selection; two BVM visions; talking polts; recent discoveries of old and new species; objects penetrating brains; double image; strange fires; Rasta folklore; comix, columns, letters.
- **FT39** – Robert Anton Wilson on Synchronicity in Joyce's *Finnegans Wake;* SHC Survivors inc Jack Angel; The ET Law; Entombed Toads; Gentlemans Magazine Extracts Pt 2; Mystery Cats; Chinese Hair Clipping Panics; Homing Wallets, Snippers & Snatchers Etc; Death Tableaux; Ice Falls; Updates on Material in Previous Issues; + Columns, Letters, Comix.
- **FT40** – More *Living Wonders* (Rat Kings, Hibernating birds, Winged cats, Falls of wheat & tadpoles, Dinosaur survival, Animal loyalty, Long returns, Avian abductions & more); Chronology of the Exmoor Beast; Fortean Follow-ups; *Gent's Mag* extracts pt. 3; Name synchronicity; Chessie; Chinese hair-clipping panics; End Times Bulletin; Ball & Bead lightning; Snakes & Bugs in tummies; Unconscious births; Japweed; the mystery of the Wiltshire cornfield holes; Ice falls; Vatican-Masonic connection; Creatures from the Black Lagoon; comix; letters; in a thick 72 page issue.
- **FT41** – Our 10th anniversary Special Issue. 76 pages of articles by the Bords, Peter Christie, Jerome Clark, Loren Coleman, Peter Costello, Hilary Evans, David Fideler, Bernard Heuvelmans, Michael Hoffman, John Keel, John Michell, Steve Moore, Nigel Pennick, Michael Persinger, Bob Rickard, Leslie Shepard, Doc Shiels, Ron Westrum, & Mr. X; and art by Hunt Emerson and Pokkettz.
- **FT 42** – Another jumbo 76 page issue, to include our *Strange Days* section, a news round-up of the whole spectrum of strangeness. Plus Doc Shiels' giant squid hypothesis for lake monsters, an interview with Dr Michael Persinger, author of *Space-Time Transients and Unusual Events*, and a new regular feature, gleaned from William Corliss' excellent bimonthly *Science Frontiers*. And the Exmoor Beast, the fire nanny case, world sightings of the Blessed Virgin, more bleeding statues and coffin humour, mermaid controversy.
- **FT 43** – Janet Bord summarises the downfall of the Cottingley fairy photographs, Wilford Anderson casts strong doubt on the identity of Christopher Columbus, and John Michell examines the York Minster fire mystery. Plus human horns, modern folklore, strange trees, drunken animals and Forteana from France, Iceland and the Philippines – and Science Frontiers, comix by Hunt Emerson and Pokkettz, and lots of recent enigmas in Strange Days.
- **FT 44** – Study of Thomas Short, 18th cent. portent chronicler, by Roger Musson, Steve Moore on Chinese falls, Dick Gwynn on lycanthropy and ergotism, Doc Shiels and Leslie Shepard on fairies, Hilary Evans and Nigel Watson on UFO hypotheses: plus spontaneous combustion, Oregon earth divot mystery and lake monster, weird tales from Africa, British alien big cat survey, teleporting astrologer, wolf boy and much else.

WILDMAN. Specially translated articles on the Chinese wildman, edited by Steve Moore. FT Occasional Paper No.1. UK £1.00. Overseas surface $2.50.

PUZZLING QUESTIONS – Some Observations on the History of Prodigies.
A gripping little book on society's reaction to, and use of, prodigies, including Fortean phenomena, in the last 2,000 years. By John Nicholson, one of England's few remaining pamphleteers. 52 pages. UK: £1.80; overseas surface: $3.00 (or equivalent).

BACK ISSUES £1.50 / US$3.00 each.
SUBSCRIPTIONS 4 issues £6 / US$12.
8 issues £12 / US$24.

FORTEAN TIMES, 96 MANSFIELD ROAD, LONDON NW3 2HX.

Headlines

SUNDAY PEOPLE, December 30, 1984 19

POODLE EATS CAR!

Death prompts coach to quit

Sleazy space scientist is sicko child molester

Chimpanzee's 'Cheers' for Cherries

ELEPHANT'S VIOLENT DISLIKE OF ONION

Man who broke into mosque 'not from this planet'

A Wolverhampton man who broke into a local mosque and was found writing in his own blood on the wall told police he did not come from this planet, a court heard today.

3 million filthy bugs attack!

FAMILY FLEES COCKROACHES!

A frightened family fled in horror from the nightmare of life in a home infested by 3 million filthy cockroaches!

"Those nasty insects have nearly driven us crazy. They crawl over your face and in your mouth at night. We found eight of 'em on the baby one night, one inside his left ear," said the desperate father, who asked not to be identified.

The disgusted dad of six has lived in the rotten roach nest with his wife and kids for two terrifying years

WEEKLY WORLD NEWS 50¢

Kidnapped heiress tells of her days and nights as a terrorist slave!

Oh my God, it's alive!

ANCIENT EGYPTIAN MUMMY STALKS VILLAGERS

Terror-stricken tomb robbers flee spirit of avenging princess

Rats invade Pawtucket

Primitive man is dead says an expert

Fox fury in Fife

Alcoholic rats may aid humans

NAKED RAPIST KILLED SHEEP WITH TEETH

Breathing May Have Caused Patient's Coma

Seductive eccentricity takes over from the jumbo sausage

SQUIRREL RUNS UP JOGGER'S PANTS SEARCHING FOR NUTS!

There's a corpse on the phone..

HOW I HAD MY MIND READ BY THE ABOMINABLE SNOW-WOMAN OF THE PAMIR MOUNTAINS

The Daily Telegraph, Friday, May 4, 1979

Woman's off-centre navel costs plastic surgeon £400,000

By IAN BALL in New York

SHROPSHIRE STAR FRIDAY, MAY 30, 1981

Student ate his landlord's finger—claim

TWO-HEADED SHEEP IN LAB SHOCK

FT improvement helps S. Pearson (?)

Missing girl's body examined

The Daily Telegraph, Thursday, September 16, 1982

Postcard warns pub

FLAT BATTERY SILENCES A-WAR ALERT

Scientists Seek to Develop Cannabis Contraceptive

P.R.A. de G.S. 1986

PHANTOMS COLLIDE

By Our Staff Correspondent in Bonn

Monkey to plead case

Accused man 'devoured his own trousers'

CORONER

... those blood have burst in ... nd my discov- ... e the woman by her boy- ... imes coroners ... etective work ... differ-

'Dead bodies are my meat and potatoes'

HUNTER SHOT BY KANGAROO

And a duck won its revenge by setting a swarm of wasps loose on a shooting party

Falling fish blamed on feuding pelicans

Sheep dip not so severe as predicted

SEE, SPEAK AND HEAR NO EVIL IN COURT

By Our New York Staff

A New York court is being posed special problems by a deaf and dumb juror who may be sitting in a case in which the physically - handicapped defendant does not speak English and the interpreter is blind.

Alec Naimen, 27, is being allowed as an experiment, to report for jury selection even though the court proceedings have to be relayed to him by a sign language expert.

Hector Guzman, charged with selling drugs, speaks only Spanish. His interpreter in the New York State Supreme Court will sit in court with his guide-dog.

17 FEB 1984

ALICE WAS TORMENTED BY MANHOLES

Her husband's collecting mania sent their marriage down the drain

Man in Black dies at 73

ALIENS RETURN TO NIGERIA

Man buried four days lived on toothpaste

Friday, February 22, 1984 19

'DONALD DUCK' DIES AT 80

Crocodile jailed for eating dog

F I N I S.